HTML & XHTML

The Definitive Guide

Other resources from O'Reilly

SIXTH EDITION

HTML & XHTML
The Definitive Guide

Chuck Musciano and Bill Kennedy

O'REILLY®

Beijing · Cambridge · Farnham · Köln · Paris · Sebastopol · Taipei · Tokyo

HTML & XHTML: The Definitive Guide, Sixth Edition
by Chuck Musciano and Bill Kennedy

Copyright © 2007, 2002, 2000, 1998, 1997, 1996 O'Reilly Media, Inc. All rights reserved.
Printed in the United States of America.

Published by O'Reilly Media, Inc., 1005 Gravenstein Highway North, Sebastopol, CA 95472.

O'Reilly books may be purchased for educational, business, or sales promotional use. Online editions are also available for most titles (*safari.oreilly.com*). For more information, contact our corporate/institutional sales department: (800) 998-9938 or *corporate@oreilly.com*.

Editor: Tatiana Apandi
Production Editor: Colleen Gorman
Copyeditor: Audrey Doyle
Proofreader: Colleen Gorman

Indexer: Johnna VanHoose Dinse
Cover Designer: Edie Freedman
Interior Designer: Melanie Wang
Illustrators: Robert Romano and Jessamyn Read

Printing History:

April 1996:	First Edition.
May 1997:	Second Edition.
August 1998:	Third Edition.
August 2000:	Fourth Edition.
August 2002:	Fifth Edition.
October 2006:	Sixth Edition.

RepKover™ This book uses RepKover,™ a durable and flexible lay-flat binding.

ISBN-10: 0-596-52732-2
ISBN-13: 978-0-596-52732-7
[M]

This book is dedicated to our wives and children,
Cindy, Courtney, and Cole, and Jeanne, Eva, and Ethan.
Without their love and patience, we never would have
had the time or strength to write.

Table of Contents

Preface

Learning Hypertext Markup Language (HTML) and Extensible Hypertext Markup Language (XHTML) is like learning any new language, computer or human. Most students first immerse themselves in examples. Studying others is a natural way to learn, making learning easy and fun. Our advice to anyone wanting to learn HTML and XHTML is to get out there on the Web with a suitable browser and see for yourself what looks good, what's effective, and what works for you. Examine others' documents and ponder the possibilities. Mimicry is how many of the current webmasters have learned the language.

Imitation can take you only so far, though. Examples can be both good and bad. Learning by example helps you talk the talk, but not walk the walk. To become truly conversant, you must learn how to use the language appropriately in many different situations. You could learn all that by example, if you live long enough.

Computer-based languages are more explicit than human languages, though the markup languages are much more forgiving than the programming ones. Nonetheless, you typically have to get the computer language syntax correct or it won't work. There are "standards," too. Committees of academics and industry experts define the proper syntax and usage of a computer language like HTML. The problem is that the browser technologies that you and your audience use to display your documents don't always keep up with the standards. Some can't, like the limited viewers used in the burgeoning mobile-device market. And then there are those that make up their own parts to the language; standards be damned.

Standards change, besides. HTML is undergoing a conversion into XHTML, making it an application of the Extensible Markup Language (XML). HTML and XHTML are so similar that we often refer to them as a single language, but there are key differences, which we discuss later in this Preface.

To be safe, the way to become fluent in HTML and XHTML is through a comprehensive, up-to-date language reference that covers the language syntax, semantics, and variations in detail to help you distinguish between good and bad usage.

There's one more step leading to fluency in a language. To become a true master of the language, you need to develop your own style. That means knowing not only what is appropriate, but also what is effective. Layout matters. So does the order of presentation within a document, between documents, and between document collections.

Our goal in writing this book is to help you become fluent in HTML and XHTML, fully versed in their syntax, semantics, and elements of style. We take the natural-learning approach, using examples (good ones, of course). We cover in detail every element of the currently accepted standard versions of the languages (HTML 4.01 and XHTML 1.0) as well as all of the current extensions supported by the popular browsers, explaining how each element works and how it interacts with all of the other elements.

And, with all due respect to Strunk and White, throughout the book we give you suggestions for style and composition to help you decide how best to use HTML and XHTML to accomplish a variety of tasks, from simple online documentation to complex marketing and sales presentations. We show you what works and what doesn't, what makes sense to those who view your pages, and what might be confusing.

In short, this book is a definitive guide to creating documents using HTML and XHTML, starting with basic syntax and semantics and finishing with broad style guidelines to help you create beautiful, informative, accessible documents that you'll be proud to deliver to your readers.

Our Audience

We wrote this book for anyone interested in learning and using the language of the Web, from the most casual user to the full-time design professional. We don't expect you to have any experience in HTML or XHTML before picking up this book. In fact, we don't even expect that you've ever browsed the Web, although we'd be very, very surprised if you haven't. Being connected to the Internet is not strictly necessary to use this book, but if you're not connected, this book becomes like a travel guide for the homebound.

The only things we ask you to have are a computer, an editor that can create simple text files, and copies of the latest web browsers. We used the latest Internet Explorer, Mozilla Firefox, Netscape Navigator, and Opera Software ASA's Opera for the examples in this book. Because HTML and XHTML documents are stored in a universally accepted format—plain text—and because the languages are completely independent of any specific computer, we won't even make an assumption about the kind of computer you're using. However, browsers do vary by platform and operating system, which means that your HTML or XHTML documents can look quite different depending on the computer and browser version. So we explain where we can how the various browsers use certain language features, paying particular attention to how they are different.

If you are new to HTML, the Web, or hypertext documentation in general, you should start by reading Chapter 1. In it, we describe how all these technologies come together to create web sites of interrelated documents.

If you are already familiar with the Web, but not with HTML or XHTML specifically, start by reading Chapter 2. This chapter is a brief overview of the most important features of the language and serves as a roadmap to how we approach the language in the remainder of the book.

Subsequent chapters deal with specific language features in a roughly top-down approach to HTML and XHTML. Read them in order for a complete tour through the language, or jump around to find the exact feature you're interested in.

Text Conventions

Throughout the book, we use a `constant-width` typeface to highlight any literal element of the HTML/XHTML standards, tags, and attributes. We always use lowercase letters for tags.* We use *italic* for filenames and to indicate new concepts when they are defined. Elements you need to supply when creating your own documents, such as tag attributes and user-defined strings, appear in *`constant-width italic`* in the code.

We discuss elements of the language throughout the book, but you'll find each one covered in depth (some might say in nauseating detail) in a shorthand, quick-reference definition box that looks like the one that follows (for the `<title>` element). The first line of the box contains the element name, followed by a brief description of its function. Next, we list the various attributes, if any, of the element: those things that you may or must specify as part of the element.

<title>

Function	Defines the document title
Attribute	`dirlang`
End tag	`</title>`; never omitted
Contains	*plain_text*
Used in	*head_content*

---

* HTML is case-insensitive with regard to tag and attribute names, but XHTML is case-sensitive. And some HTML items, such as source filenames, are case-sensitive, so be careful.

The icon identifies tags and attributes that aren't in the HTML 4.01 or XHTML 1.0 standards, and those that are handled very differently between the various popular browsers.

The description also includes the HTML ending tag, if any, for the element, along with a general indication of whether the end tag may be safely omitted in general use in HTML. For the few tags that require end tags in XHTML, but do not have them in HTML, the language lets you indicate that by placing a forward slash (/) before the tag's closing bracket, as in <br />. In these cases, the tag may also contain attributes, indicated with an intervening ellipsis, such as <br ... />.

The "Contains" header names the rule in the HTML grammar that defines the elements to be placed within this tag. Similarly, the "Used in" header lists those rules that allow this tag as part of their content. We define these rules in Appendix A.

Finally, HTML and XHTML are fairly intertwined languages. You will occasionally use elements in different ways depending on context, and many elements share identical attributes. Wherever possible, we place a cross-reference in the text that leads you to a related discussion elsewhere in the book. These cross-references, like the one at the end of this paragraph, serve as a crude paper model of hypertext documentation, one that would be replaced with a true hypertext link should this book be delivered in an electronic format. [The Syntax of a Tag, 3.3.1]

We encourage you to follow these cross-references whenever possible. Often, we cover an attribute briefly and expect you to jump to the cross-reference for a more detailed discussion. In other cases, following the link takes you to alternative uses of the element under discussion or to style and usage suggestions that relate to the current element.

Versions and Semantics

The latest HTML standard is version 4.01, but most updates and changes to the language standard were made in version 4.0. Therefore, throughout the book, we often refer to the HTML standard as HTML 4, encompassing versions 4.0 and later. We explicitly state the "dot" version number only when it is relevant.

The XHTML standard is currently in its first iteration, 1.0. The World Wide Web Consortium (W3C) has released a Working Draft of a second version (XHTML 2.0), but the standard is yet established. For the most part, XHTML 1.0 is identical to HTML 4.01; we detail their differences in Chapter 16. Throughout the book, we specifically note cases where XHTML handles a feature or element differently than the original language, HTML.

The HTML and XHTML standards make very clear the distinction between "element types" of a document and the markup "tags" that delimit those elements. For example, the standard refers to the paragraph element type, which is not the same as the <p> tag. The paragraph element consists of the accepted element-type name within the starting tag (<p>), intervening content, and the ending paragraph tag (</p>). The <p> tag is the starting tag for the paragraph element, and its contents, known as attributes, ultimately affect the paragraph element type's contents.

Although these are important distinctions, we're pragmatists. It is the markup tag that authors apply in their documents and that affects any intervening content. Accordingly, throughout the book, we relax the distinction between element types and tags, often talking about tags and all related contents and not necessarily using the term *element-type* when it would be technically appropriate to make the distinction. Forgive us the transgression, but we do so for the sake of clarity.

HTML Versus XHTML

It's not Latin, but HTML has reached old age in standard version 4.01. The W3C has no plans to develop another version and has officially said so. Rather, HTML is being subsumed and modularized as an Extensible Markup Language (XML). Its new name is XHTML, Extensible Hypertext Markup Language.

The emergence of XHTML is just another chapter in the often tumultuous history of HTML and the Web, where confusion for authors is the norm, not the exception. At its nadir, the elders of the W3C responsible for accepted and acceptable uses of the language—standards—lost control of the language in the browser "wars" between Netscape and Microsoft. The abortive HTML+ standard never got off the ground, and HTML 3.0 became so bogged down in debate that the W3C simply shelved the entire draft. HTML 3.0 never happened, despite what some opportunistic marketers claimed in their literature. Instead, by late 1996, the browser manufacturers convinced the W3C to release HTML standard version 3.2, which for all intents and purposes simply standardized most of Netscape's HTML extensions.

Netscape's dominance as the leading browser, and as a leader in web technologies, faded dramatically toward the end of the millennium. By then, Microsoft had effectively bundled Internet Explorer into the Windows operating system, not only as an installed application, but also as a dominant feature of the GUI desktop. In addition, Internet Explorer introduced several features (albeit nonstandard at the time) that appealed principally to the growing Internet business and marketing community.

Fortunately for those of us who appreciate and strongly support standards, the W3C took back its primacy role with HTML 4.0, which stands today as HTML version 4.01, released in December 1999. Absorbing many of the Netscape and Internet Explorer innovations, the standard is clearer and cleaner than any previous ones, establishes solid implementation models for consistency across browsers and platforms, provides strong support and incentives for the companion Cascading Style Sheets (CSS) standard for HTML-based displays, and makes provisions for alternative (nonvisual) user agents, as well as for more universal language supports.

Cleaner and clearer aside, the W3C realized that HTML could never keep up with the demands of the web community for more ways to distribute, process, and display documents. HTML offers only a limited set of document-creation primitives and is hopelessly incapable of handling nontraditional content like chemical formulae, musical notation, and mathematical expressions. Nor can it well support alternative display media, such as handheld computers and intelligent cellular phones.

To address these demands, the W3C developed the XML standard. XML provides a way to create new, standards-based markup languages that don't take an act of the W3C to implement. XML-compliant languages deliver information that can be parsed, processed, displayed, sliced, and diced by the many different communication technologies that have emerged since the Web sparked the digital communication revolution a decade ago. XHTML is HTML reformulated to adhere to the XML standard. It is the foundation language for the future of the Web.

Why not just drop HTML for XHTML? For many reasons. First and foremost, XHTML has not exactly taken the Web by storm. There's just too much current investment in HTML-based documentation and expertise for that to happen anytime soon. Besides, XHTML is HTML 4.01 reformulated as an application of XML. Know HTML 4 and you're all ready for the future.*

Deprecated Features

One of the unpopular things standards bearers have to do is make choices between popular and proper. The authors of the HTML and XHTML standards exercise that responsibility by "deprecating" those features of the language that interfere in the grand scheme of things.

For instance, the <center> tag tells the browser to display the enclosed text centered in the display window. But the CSS standard provides ways to center text, too. The W3C chooses to support the CSS way and discourages the use of <center> by deprecating the tag. The plan is, in some later standard version, to stop using <center> and other deprecated elements and attributes of the language.

Throughout the book, we specially note and continuously remind you when an HTML tag or other component is deprecated in the current standards. Should you stop using them now? Yes and no.

Yes, because there is a preferred and perhaps better way to accomplish the same thing. By exercising that alternative, you ensure that your documents will survive for many years to come on the Web. And, yes, because the tools you may use to prepare HTML/XHTML documents probably adhere to the preferred standard. You may not have a choice, unless you disable your tools. In any event, unless you hand-compose

---

* We plumb the depths of XML and XHTML in Chapters 15 and 16.

all your documents, you'll need to know how the preferred way works so that you can identify the code and modify it.

However compelling the reasons for not using deprecated elements and attributes are, they still are part of the standards. They remain well supported by most browsers and aren't expected to disappear anytime soon. In fact, since there is no plan to change the HTML standard, the "deprecated" stamp is very misleading.

So, no, you don't have to worry about deprecated HTML features. There is no reason to panic, certainly. We do, however, encourage you to make a move toward the standards soon.

A Definitive Guide

The paradox in all this is that even the HTML 4.01 standard is not the definitive resource. There are many more features of HTML in popular use and supported by the popular browsers than are included in the latest language standard. And there are many parts of the standards that are ignored. We promise you, things can get downright confusing.

We've managed to sort things out for you, though, so you don't have to sweat over what works and doesn't work with what browser. This book, therefore, is the definitive guide to HTML and XHTML. We give details for all the elements of the HTML 4.01 and XHTML 1.0 standards, plus the variety of interesting and useful extensions to the language. We also include detailed discussions of the CSS standard, since it is so intricately related to web page development.

In addition, there are a few things that are closely related but not directly part of HTML. For example, we touch, but do not handle, JavaScript, Common Gateway Interface (CGI), and Java programming. They all work closely with HTML documents and run with or alongside browsers, but they are not part of the language itself, so we don't delve into them. Besides, they are comprehensive topics that deserve their own books, such as *JavaScript: The Definitive Guide*, by David Flanagan; *CGI Programming with Perl*, by Scott Guelich, Shishir Gundavaram, and Gunther Birzneiks; *Cascading Style Sheets: The Definitive Guide*, by Eric Meyer; and *Learning Java*, by Pat Niemeyer and Jonathan Knudsen (all published by O'Reilly).

This is your definitive guide to HTML and XHTML as they are and should be used, including every extension we could find. Some extensions aren't documented anywhere, even in the plethora of online guides. But, if we've missed anything, certainly let us know and we'll put it in the next edition.

Using Code Examples

This book is here to help you get your job done. In general, you may use the code in this book in your programs and documentation. You do not need to contact us for permission unless you're reproducing a significant portion of the code. For example, writing a program that uses several chunks of code from this book does not require permission. Selling or distributing a CD-ROM of examples from O'Reilly books *does* require permission. Answering a question by citing this book and quoting example code does not require permission. Incorporating a significant amount of example code from this book into your product's documentation *does* require permission.

We appreciate, but do not require, attribution. An attribution usually includes the title, author, publisher, and ISBN. For example: "*HTML & XHTML: The Definitive Guide*, Sixth Edition, by Chuck Musciano and Bill Kennedy. Copyright 2007 O'Reilly Media, Inc., 978-0-596-52732-7."

Safari® Enabled

 When you see a Safari® Enabled icon on the cover of your favorite technology book, that means the book is available online through the O'Reilly Network Safari Bookshelf.

Safari offers a solution that's better than e-books. It's a virtual library that lets you easily search thousands of top tech books, cut and paste code samples, download chapters, and find quick answers when you need the most accurate, current information. Try it for free at *http://safari.oreilly.com*.

Comments and Questions

Please address comments and questions concerning this book to the publisher:

O'Reilly Media, Inc.
1005 Gravenstein Highway North
Sebastopol, CA 95472
800-998-9938 (in the United States or Canada)
707-829-0515 (international/local)
707-829-0104 (fax)

There is a web page for this book, which lists any errata, examples, or additional information. You can access this page at:

http://www.oreilly.com/catalog/html6

To comment or ask technical questions about this book, send email to:

bookquestions@oreilly.com

For more information about books, conferences, Resource Centers, and the O'Reilly Network, see the O'Reilly web site at:

http://www.oreilly.com

Acknowledgments

We did not compose, and certainly could not have composed, this or any other edition of the book without generous contributions from many people. Our wives, Jeanne and Cindy, and our children, Eva, Ethan, Courtney, and Cole (they happened *before* we started writing), formed the front lines of support. And there are numerous neighbors, friends, and colleagues who helped by sharing ideas, testing browsers, and letting us use their equipment to explore HTML. You know who you are, and we thank you all.

In addition, we thank our technical reviewers, Chat Clussman, Patrick Krekelberg, Sam Marshall, and Shlomi Fish, for carefully scrutinizing our work. We took most of your keen suggestions. We especially thank our O'Reilly editors, especially Mike Loukides and Tatiana Apandi, for their patience in keeping us two mavericks corralled. And special thanks to Tatiana for bringing this sixth edition to fruition.

CHAPTER 1

HTML, XHTML, and the World Wide Web

Though it began as a military experiment and spent its adolescence as a sandbox for academics and eccentrics, in less than a decade just before the new millennium, the worldwide network of computer networks (a.k.a. the *Internet*) matured into a highly diversified, financially important community of computer users and information vendors. From the boardroom to your living room, you can bump into Internet users of nearly any and all nationalities, of any and all persuasions, from serious to frivolous individuals, from businesses to nonprofit organizations, and from born-again Christian evangelists to pornographers.

In many ways, the *Web*—the open community of hypertext-enabled document servers and readers on the Internet—is responsible for the meteoric rise in the network's popularity. You, too, can become a valued member by contributing: writing HTML and XHTML documents and then making them available to web surfers worldwide.

Let's climb up the Internet family tree to gain some deeper insight into its magnificence, not only as an exercise of curiosity, but also to help us better understand just who and what we are dealing with when we go online.

1.1 The Internet

Although popular media accounts are often confused and confusing, the concept of the Internet really is rather simple: it's a worldwide collection of computer networks—a network of networks—sharing digital information via a common set of networking and software protocols.

Networks are not new to computers. What makes the Internet unique is its world-wide collection of digital telecommunication links that share a common set of computer-network technologies, protocols, and applications. Whether you run Microsoft Windows XP, Linux, Mac OS, or even the now ancient Windows 3.1, when connected to the Internet, all computers speak the same networking language and use functionally identical programs, so you can exchange information—even multimedia pictures and sound—with someone next door or across the planet.

The common and now quite familiar programs people use to communicate and distribute their work over the Internet have also found their way into private and semi-private networks. These so-called *intranets* and *extranets* use the same software, applications, and networking protocols as the Internet. But unlike the Internet, intranets are private networks, with access restricted to members of the institution. Likewise, extranets restrict access but use the Internet to provide services to members.

The Internet, on the other hand, seemingly has no restrictions. Anyone with a computer and the right networking software and connection can "get on the Net" and begin exchanging words, sounds, and pictures with others around the world, day or night: no membership required. And that's precisely what is confusing about the Internet.

Like an oriental bazaar, the Internet is not well organized, there are few content guides, and it can take a lot of time and technical expertise to tap its full potential. That's because....

1.1.1 In the Beginning

The Internet began in the late 1960s as an experiment in the design of robust computer networks. The goal was to construct a network of computers that could withstand the loss of several machines without compromising the ability of the remaining ones to communicate. Funding came from the U.S. Department of Defense, which had a vested interest in building information networks that could withstand nuclear attack.

The resulting network was a marvelous technical success, but it was limited in size and scope. For the most part, only defense contractors and academic institutions could gain access to what was then known as the ARPAnet (Advanced Research Projects Agency Network of the Department of Defense).

With the advent of high-speed modems for digital communication over common phone lines, some individuals and organizations not directly tied to the main digital pipelines began connecting to and taking advantage of the network's advanced and global communications. Nonetheless, it wasn't until around 1993 that the Internet really took off.

Several crucial events led to the meteoric rise in popularity of the Internet. First, in the early 1990s, businesses and individuals eager to take advantage of the ease and power of global digital communications finally pressured the largest computer networks on the mostly U.S. government-funded Internet to open their systems for nearly unrestricted traffic. (The network wasn't designed to route information based on content, meaning that commercial messages went through university computers that at the time forbade such activity.)

True to their academic traditions of free exchange and sharing, many of the original Internet members continued to make substantial portions of their electronic collections of documents and software available to the newcomers—free for the taking! Global communications, a wealth of free software and information: who could resist?

Well, frankly, the Internet was a tough row to hoe back then. Getting connected and using the various software tools, if they were even available for their computers, presented an insurmountable technology barrier for most people. And most available information was plain-vanilla text about academic subjects, not the neatly packaged fare that attracts users to services such as America Online. The Internet was just too disorganized, and, outside of the government and academia, few people had the knowledge or interest to learn how to use the arcane software or the time to spend rummaging through documents looking for ones of interest.

1.1.2 HTML and the Web

It took another spark to light the Internet rocket. At about the same time the Internet opened up for business, some physicists at CERN, the European Particle Physics Laboratory, released an authoring language and distribution system they developed for creating and sharing multimedia-enabled, integrated electronic documents over the Internet. And so was born *Hypertext Markup Language* (HTML), browser software, and the Web. No longer did authors have to distribute their work as fragmented collections of pictures, sounds, and text. HTML unified those elements. Moreover, the Web's systems enabled *hypertext linking*, whereby documents automatically reference other documents located anywhere around the world: less rummaging, more productive time online.

Lift-off happened when some bright students and faculty at the National Center for Supercomputing Applications (NCSA) at the University of Illinois, Urbana-Champaign wrote a web browser called Mosaic. Although designed primarily for viewing HTML documents, the software also had built-in tools to access the much more prolific resources on the Internet, such as FTP archives of software and Gopher-organized collections of documents.

With versions based on easy-to-use GUIs familiar to most computer owners, Mosaic became an instant success. It, like most Internet software, was available on the Net for free. Millions of users snatched up copies and began surfing the Internet for "cool web pages."

1.1.3 Golden Threads

Since those early days, the Web has spawned an entirely new medium for worldwide information exchange and commerce. For instance, when the marketeers caught on to the fact that they could cheaply produce and deliver eye-catching, wow-and-whiz-bang commercials and product catalogs to those millions of web surfers around the world, there was no stopping the stampede of blue suede shoes. Even the key developers of Mosaic and related web server technologies sensed potential riches. They left NCSA and made their fortunes with Netscape Communications by producing commercial web browsers and server software. That was until the sleeping giant, Microsoft, awoke. But that's another story....

Business users and marketing opportunities have helped invigorate the Internet and fuel its phenomenal growth. Internet-based commerce has become Very Big Business, exceeding $150 billion annually by 2005. Traditional bricks-and-mortar businesses have either opened web-based commercial sites or face extinction.

For some, particularly we Internet old-timers, business and marketing have also trashed the medium. In many ways, the Web has become a vast strip mall and an annoying advertising medium. Believe it or not, once upon a time, Internet users actually followed commonly held (but not formally codified) rules of *netiquette* that prohibited such things as spam email.

Nonetheless, the power of HTML and network distribution of information goes well beyond marketing and monetary rewards: serious informational pursuits also benefit. Publications complete with images and other media such as executable software can get to their intended audiences in the blink of an eye, instead of the months traditionally required for printing and mail delivery. Education takes a great leap forward when students gain access to the great libraries of the world. And at times of leisure, the interactive capabilities of HTML links can reinvigorate our otherwise television-numbed minds.

1.2 Talking the Internet Talk

Every computer connected to the Internet (even a beat-up old Apple II) has a unique address: a number whose format is defined by the *Internet Protocol* (IP), the standard that defines how messages are passed from one machine to another on the Net. An *IP address* is made up of four numbers, each less than 256, joined together by periods, such as 192.12.248.73 and 131.58.97.254.

While computers deal only with numbers, people prefer names. For this reason, most computers also have names bestowed upon them. By current estimates, there are hundreds of millions, if not billions, of devices on the Net, so it would be very difficult to come up with that many unique names, let alone keep track of them all. Instead, the Internet is a network of networks, and is divided into groups known as *domains*, which are further divided into one or more *subdomains*. So, while you might choose a very common name for your computer, it becomes unique when you append, like surnames, all of the machine's domain names as a period-separated suffix, creating a *fully qualified* domain name.

This naming stuff is easier than it sounds. For example, the fully qualified domain name *www.oreilly.com* translates to a machine named "www" that's part of the domain known as "oreilly," which, in turn, is part of the commercial (com) branch of the Internet. Other branches of the Internet include educational institutions (edu), nonprofit organizations (org), the U.S. government (gov), and Internet service providers (net). Computers and networks outside the United States may have two-letter abbreviations at the end of their names: for example, "ca" for Canada, "jp" for Japan, and "uk" for the United Kingdom.

Special computers, known as *nameservers*, keep tables of machine names and associated IP addresses and translate one into the other for us and for our machines. Domain names must be registered and paid for through any one of the now many for-profit registrars.* Once a unique domain name is registered, its owner makes it and its address available to other domain nameservers around the world.

1.2.1 Clients, Servers, and Browsers

The Internet connects two kinds of computers: *servers*, which serve up documents, and *clients*, which retrieve and display documents for us humans. Things that happen on the server machine are said to be on the *server side*, and activities on the client machine occur on the *client side*.

To access and display HTML documents, we run programs called *browsers* on our client computers. These browser clients talk to special *web servers* over the Internet to access, retrieve, and display electronic documents.

A variety of browsers are available today. Internet Explorer comes with Microsoft's operating system software, for example, while most other browsers are free for download on the Web. And most browsers run on client devices that have high-resolution, high-color graphical viewing screens. In fact, today's browsers share common HTML-rendering software under the hood, so to speak, and differ only by extraneous, albeit some very useful features. For instance, when you install Netscape Navigator version 8, you decide whether to use the NCSA Mosaic rendering software, portions of which also are under Microsoft's Internet Explorer, or Mozilla's software, which comes under the hood of another popular browser, Firefox.

---

* At one time, a single nonprofit organization known as InterNIC handled that function. Now ICANN.org coordinates U.S. government-related nameservers, but other organizations or individuals must work through a for-profit company to register their unique domain names.

This is very different from around the turn of the century, when Internet Explorer savagely competed with Netscape Navigator through unique extensions to the HTML language. Internet Explorer won. Many of its extensions even became HTML standards, and others such as Netscape's layout extensions disappeared and so got relegated to appendices in this book.

1.2.2 The Flow of Information

All web activity begins on the client side, when a user starts his browser. The browser begins by loading a *home page* document, either from local storage or from a server over some network, such as the Internet, a corporate intranet, or a town extranet. When starting up on the network, the client browser first consults a domain name system (DNS) server to translate the home page server's name, such as *www.oreilly.com*, into an IP address, before sending a request to that server over the Internet. This request (and the server's reply) is formatted according to the dictates of the *Hypertext Transfer Protocol* (HTTP) standard.

A server spends most of its time listening to the network, waiting for document requests with the server's unique address stamped on them. Upon receipt of a request, the server verifies that the requesting browser is allowed to retrieve documents from the server and, if so, checks for the requested document. If it finds the document, the server sends it to the browser. The server usually logs the request, typically including the client computer's IP address, the document requested, and the time. The server might also issue special attachments known as *cookies* that contain additional information about the requesting browser and its owner.

Back on the browser, the document arrives. If it's a plain-vanilla text file, most browsers display it in a common, plain-vanilla way. Document directories, too, are treated like plain documents, which most graphical browsers display as folder icons that the user may select, thereby requesting to view the contents of the subdirectory.

Browsers can retrieve many different types of files from a server. Unless assisted by a *helper* program or specially enabled by *plug-in* software or *applets*, which display an image or video file or play an audio file, the browser usually stores the file directly on a local disk for later use.

For the most part, however, the browser retrieves a special document that appears to be a plain text file but that contains both text and special markup codes called *tags*. The browser processes these HTML or XHTML documents, formatting the text based on the tags and downloading special accessory files, such as images.

The user reads the document, selects a hyperlink to another document, and the entire process starts over.

1.2.3 Beneath the Web

We should point out again that browsers and HTTP servers need not be part of the Web to function. In fact, you never need to be connected to the Internet or to any network, for that matter, to write HTML/XHTML documents and operate a browser. You can load and display locally stored documents and accessory files directly on your browser. Many organizations take advantage of this capability by distributing catalogs and product manuals, for instance, on a much less expensive, but much more interactively useful, CD-ROM, rather than via traditional print on paper. Many graphical-user applications even document their features through HTML/XHTML-based Help menus.

Isolating web documents is good for the author, too, since it gives you the opportunity to finish, in the editorial sense of the word, a document collection for later distribution. Diligent authors work locally to write and proof their documents before releasing them for general distribution, thereby sparing readers the agonies of broken image files and bogus hyperlinks.*

Organizations, too, can be connected to the Internet but also maintain private web sites and document collections for distribution to clients on their local networks, or intranets. In fact, private web sites are fast becoming the technology of choice for the paperless offices we've heard so much about during these last few years. With HTML and XHTML document collections, businesses can maintain personnel databases complete with employee photographs and online handbooks, collections of blueprints, parts, assembly manuals, and so on—all readily and easily accessed electronically by authorized users and displayed on a local computer.

1.2.4 Standards Organizations

Like many popular technologies, HTML started out as an informal specification used by only a few people. As more and more authors began to use the language, it became obvious that more formal means were needed to define and manage—i.e., to standardize—the language's features, making it easier for everyone to create and share documents.

1.2.4.1 The World Wide Web Consortium

The World Wide Web Consortium (W3C) was formed with the charter to define the standards for HTML and, later, XHTML. Members are responsible for drafting, circulating for review, and modifying the standard based on cross-Internet feedback to best meet the needs of many.

---

* Vigorous testing of HTML documents once they are made available on the Web is, of course, also highly recommended and necessary to rid them of various linking bugs.

Beyond HTML and XHTML, the W3C has the broader responsibility of standardizing any technology related to the Web; they manage the HTTP, Cascading Style Sheet (CSS), and Extensible Markup Language (XML) standards, as well as related standards for document addressing on the Web. They also solicit draft standards for extensions to existing web technologies.

If you want to track HTML, XML, XHTML, CSS, and other exciting web development and related technologies, contact the W3C at *http://www.w3.org*.

Also, several Internet newsgroups are devoted to the Web, each a part of the *comp.infosystems.www* hierarchy. These include *comp.infosystems.www.authoring.html* and *comp.infosystems.www.authoring.images*.

1.2.4.2 The Internet Engineering Task Force

Even broader in reach than W3C, the Internet Engineering Task Force (IETF) is responsible for defining and managing every aspect of Internet technology. The Web is just one small area under the purview of the IETF.

The IETF defines all of the technology of the Internet via official documents known as Requests for Comments, or RFCs. Individually numbered for easy reference, each RFC addresses a specific Internet technology—everything from the syntax of domain names and the allocation of IP addresses to the format of electronic mail messages.

To learn more about the IETF and follow the progress of various RFCs as they are circulated for review and revision, visit the IETF home page, *http://www.ietf.org*.

1.3 HTML and XHTML: What They Are

HTML and XHTML define the syntax and placement of special, embedded directions that aren't displayed by the browser but advise it how to display the contents of the document, including text, images, and other support media. The languages also make a document interactive through special hypertext links, which connect your document with other documents—on either your computer or someone else's—as well as with other Internet resources.

You've certainly heard of HTML and, perhaps, XHTML, but did you know that they are just two of many other markup languages? Indeed, HTML is the black sheep in the family of document markup languages. HTML was based on SGML, the Standard Generalized Markup Language. The powers that be created SGML with the intent that it would be the one and only markup metalanguage from which all other document markup elements would be created. Everything from hieroglyphics to HTML can be defined using SGML, negating any need for any other markup language.

The problem with SGML is that it is so broad and all-encompassing that mere mortals cannot use it. Using SGML effectively requires very expensive and complex tools that are completely beyond the scope of regular people who just want to bang out an

HTML document in their spare time. As a result, HTML adheres to some, but not all, SGML standards,* eliminating many of the more esoteric features so that it is readily useable and used.

Besides the fact that SGML is unwieldy and not well suited to describing the very popular HTML in a useful way, there was also a growing need to define other HTML-like markup languages to handle different network documents. Accordingly, the W3C defined XML. Like SGML, XML is a separate formal markup metalanguage that uses select features of SGML to define markup languages. It eliminates many features of SGML that aren't applicable to languages like HTML and simplifies other SGML elements in order to make them easier to use and understand.

However, HTML version 4.01 is not XML compliant. Hence, the W3C offers XHTML, a reformulation of HTML that is compliant with XML. XHTML attempts to support every last nit and feature of HTML 4.01 using the more rigid rules of XML. It generally succeeds, but it has enough differences to make life difficult for the standards-conscious HTML author.

1.4 HTML and XHTML: What They Aren't

Despite all their new, multimedia-enabling page-layout features, and the hot technologies that give life to HTML/XHTML documents over the Internet, it is also important to understand the languages' limitations. They are not word processing tools, desktop publishing solutions, or even programming languages. Their fundamental purpose is to define the structure of documents and document families so that they may be delivered quickly and easily to a user over a network for rendering on a variety of display devices; jacks-of-all-trades but masters of none, so to speak.

1.4.1 Content Versus Appearance

HTML and its progeny, XHTML, provide many different ways to let you define the appearance of your documents, but their focus is on structure, not appearance. Of course, appearance is important, since it can have either detrimental or beneficial effects on how users access and use the information in your documents. And that is why the companion CSS standard is important.

Nonetheless, we believe that content is paramount; appearance is secondary, particularly since it is less predictable, given the variety of browser graphics and text-formatting capabilities. In fact, HTML and XHTML contain many ways for structuring your document content without regard to the final appearance: section headers, structured lists, paragraphs, rules, titles, and embedded images are defined by the

---

* The HTML Document Type Definition (DTD) in Appendix D uses a subset of SGML to define the HTML 4.01 standard.

standard languages without regard for how these elements might be rendered by a browser. Consider, for example, a browser for the blind, wherein graphics on the page come with audio descriptions and alternative rules for navigation. The HTML/ XHTML standards define such a thing: content over visual presentation.

If you treat HTML or XHTML as a document-formatting tool, you will be sorely disappointed. There is simply not enough capability built into the languages to allow you to create the kinds of documents you might whip up with tools such as FrameMaker and Word. Attempts to subvert the supplied structuring elements to achieve specific formatting tricks seldom work across all browsers. In short, don't waste your time trying to force HTML and XHTML to do things they were never designed to do.

Instead, use HTML and XHTML in the manner for which they were designed: indicating the structure of a document so that the browser can then render its content appropriately. HTML and XHTML are rife with tags that let you indicate the semantics of your document content, something that is missing from or often badly implemented in word processors and page-layout programs. Create your documents using these tags and you'll be happier, your documents will look and work better, and your readers will benefit immensely.

1.5 Standards and Extensions

The basic syntax and semantics of HTML are defined in the HTML standard, now in its final version, 4.01. HTML matured quickly, in barely a decade. At one time, a new version would appear before you had a chance to finish reading an earlier edition of this book. Today, HTML has stopped evolving. As far as the W3C is concerned, XHTML has taken over. Now the wait is for browser manufacturers to implement the standards.

The XHTML standard currently is version 1.0. Fortunately, XHTML version 1.0 is, for the most part, a reconstitution of HTML version 4.01. There are some differences, which we explore in Chapter 16. The popular browsers continue to support HTML documents, so there is no cause to stampede to XHTML. Do, however, start walking in that direction: a newer XHTML version, 2.0, is under consideration at the W3C, and browser developers are slowly but surely dropping nonstandard HTML features from their products.

Obviously, browser developers rely upon standards and accepted conventions to have their software properly format and display common HTML and XHTML documents. Authors use the standards to make sure they are writing effective, correct documents that get displayed properly by the browsers.

However, standards are not always explicit; manufacturers have some leeway in how their browsers might display an element. And to complicate matters, commercial forces have pushed developers to add into their browsers nonstandard extensions meant to improve the language.

Confused? Don't be: in this book, we explore in detail the syntax, semantics, and idioms of the HTML version 4.01 and XHTML version 1.0 languages, along with the many important extensions that are supported in the latest versions of the most popular browsers.

1.5.1 Nonstandard Extensions

It doesn't take an advanced degree in The Obvious to know that distinction draws attention; so, too, with browsers. Extra whiz-bang features can give the edge in the otherwise standardized browser market. That can be a nightmare for authors. A lot of people want you to use the latest and greatest gimmick or even useful HTML/XHTML extension. But it's not part of the standard, and not all browsers support it. In fact, on occasion, the popular browsers support different ways of doing the same thing.

1.5.2 Extensions: Pro and Con

Every software vendor adheres largely to the technological standards. It's embarrassing to be incompatible, and your competitors will take every opportunity to remind buyers of your product's failure to comply, no matter how arcane or useless that standard might be. At the same time, vendors seek to make their products different from and better than the competition's offerings. Netscape's and Internet Explorer's extensions to standard HTML are perfect examples of these market pressures.

Many document authors feel safe using these extended browsers' nonstandard extensions because of their combined and commanding share of users. For better or worse, extensions to HTML in prominent browsers become part of the street version of the language, much like English slang creeping into the vocabulary of most Frenchmen, despite the best efforts of the Académie Française.

Fortunately, with HTML version 4.0, the W3C standards caught up with the browser manufacturers. In fact, the tables turned somewhat. The many extensions to HTML that originally appeared as extensions in Netscape Navigator and Microsoft Internet Explorer are now part of the HTML 4 and XHTML 1 standards, and there are other parts of the new standard which are not yet features of the popular browsers.

1.5.3 Avoiding Extensions

In general, we urge you to resist using extensions unless you have a compelling and overriding reason to do so. By using them, particularly in key portions of your documents, you run the risk of losing a substantial portion of your potential readership. To be fair, most browsers eschew extensions, so the point is moot now.

We admit that it is disingenuous of us to decry the use of extensions while presenting complete descriptions of their use. In keeping with the general philosophy of the Internet, we'll err on the side of handing out rope and guns to all interested parties while hoping you have enough smarts to keep from hanging yourself or shooting yourself in the foot.

Our advice still holds, though: use an extension only where it is necessary or very advantageous, and do so with the understanding that you are disenfranchising a portion of your audience. To that end, you might even consider providing separate, standards-based versions of your documents to accommodate users of other browsers.

1.5.4 Extensions Through Modules

XHTML version 1.1 provides a mechanism for extending the language in a standard way: XML modules. In fact, XHTML 1.1 is composed of modules itself.

XHTML modules divide the HTML language into discrete document types, each defining features and functions that are parts of the language. There are separate modules for XHTML forms, text, scripting, tables, and so on—all the nondeprecated elements of XHTML 1.0.

The advantage of modules is extensibility. In addition to using the markup features from the XHTML modules normally included in the standard, the new language lets you easily blend other XML modules into your documents, extending their features and capabilities in a standard way. For instance, the W3C has defined a MathML module that provides explicit markup elements for mathematical equations that you could use in your next XHTML-based math thesis.

Modules, let alone the XHTML version 1.1 language, are experimental and are not well supported by the popular browsers. Accordingly, we don't recommend that you use XHTML modules just yet. For now, the subject is beyond the scope of this book. Consult the W3C web site for more details.

1.6 Tools for the Web Designer

While you can use the barest of barebones text editors to create HTML and XHTML documents, most authors have a toolbox of software utilities that is a bit more elaborate than a simple text editor. At the barest minimum, you also need a browser, so you can test and refine your work. Beyond the essentials are some specialized software tools for developing and preparing HTML documents and accessory multimedia files.

1.6.1 Essentials

At the very least, you'll need a text editor, a browser to check your work, and, ideally, a connection to the Internet.

1.6.1.1 Text processor or WYSIWYG editor?

Some authors use the word processing capabilities of their specialized HTML/XHTML editing software. Some use a WYSIWYG-like (what-you-see-is-what-you-get, kind of) composition tool such as those that come with the latest versions of the popular word processors. Others, such as ourselves, prefer to compose their work on a common text editor and later insert the markup tags and their attributes. Still others include markup as they compose.

We think the stepwise approach—compose, then mark up—is the better way. We find that once we've defined and written the document's content, it's much easier to make a second pass to judiciously and effectively add the HTML/XHTML tags to format the text. Otherwise, the markup can obscure the content. Note, too, that unless specially trained (if they can be), spellcheckers and thesauruses typically choke on markup tags and their various parameters. You can spend what seems to be a lifetime clicking the Ignore button on all those otherwise valid markup tags when syntax- or spellchecking a document.

When and how you embed markup tags into your document dictates the tools you need. We recommend that you use a good word processor, which comes with more and better writing tools than simple text editors or the browser-based markup-language editors. You'll find, for instance, that an outliner, spellchecker, and thesaurus will best help you craft the document's flow and content, disregarding for the moment its look. The latest word processors encode your documents with HTML, too, but don't expect miracles. Except for boilerplate documents, you will probably need to nurse those automated HTML documents to full health. (Not to mention put them on a diet when you see how long the generated HTML is.) And it'll be a while before you'll see XHTML-specific markup tools in the popular word processors.

Another word of caution about automated composition tools: they typically change or insert content (e.g., replacing relative hyperlinks with full ones) and arrange your document in ways that will annoy you. Annoying, in particular, because they rarely give you the opportunity to do things your own way.

Become fluent in native HTML/XHTML. Be prepared to reverse some of the things a composition tool will do to your documents. And make sure you can wrest your document away from the tool so that you can make it do your bidding.

1.6.1.2 Browser software

Obviously, you should view your newly composed documents and test their functionality before you release them for use by others. For serious authors, particularly those looking to push their documents beyond the HTML/XHTML standards, we recommend that you have several browsers, perhaps with versions running on different computers, just to be sure one's delightful display isn't another's nightmare.

The currently popular—and therefore, most important—browsers are Microsoft Internet Explorer, Mozilla Firefox, Safari (for Apple), Opera, and Netscape Navigator, though the last is rapidly disappearing from the Web landscape. Most versions run on the variety of popular computing platforms, such as the various Microsoft OSes, Linux, Mac OS, and so forth. Different browser versions often vary in the elements of HTML and XHTML that they support. We make every effort to point out those differences throughout this book. Nevertheless, it helps to download not only the latest versions from their web sites, but also previous browser versions in order to better test your work for compatibility. This is particularly important given that several millions of the estimated more than one billion Web users worldwide still operate the ancient Internet Explorer version 5!

1.6.2 An Extended Toolkit

If you're serious about creating documents, you'll soon find that all sorts of nifty tools are available to make life easier. The list of freeware, shareware, and commercial products grows daily, so it's not very useful to provide a list here. This is, in fact, another good reason to frequent the various newsgroups and web sites that keep updated lists of HTML and XHTML resources on the Web. If you are really dedicated to writing in HTML and XHTML, you will visit those sites, and you will visit them regularly to keep abreast of the language, tools, and trends.

CHAPTER 2

Quick Start

We didn't spend hours studiously poring over some reference book before we wrote our first HTML document. You probably shouldn't, either. HTML is simple to read and understand, and it's simple to write. And once you've written an HTML document, you've nearly completed your first XHTML one, too. So let's get started without first learning a lot of arcane rules.

To help you get that quick, satisfying start, we've included this chapter as a brief summary of the many elements of HTML and its progeny, XHTML. Of course, we've left out a lot of details and some tricks that you should know. Read the upcoming chapters to get the essentials for becoming fluent in HTML and XHTML.

Even if you are familiar with the languages, we recommend that you work your way through this chapter before tackling the rest of the book. It not only gives you a working grasp of basic HTML/XHTML and their jargon, but you'll also be more productive later, flush with the confidence that comes from creating attractive documents in such a short time.

2.1 Writing Tools

Use any text editor to create an HTML or XHTML document, as long as it can save your work on a disk in text file format. That's because even though web documents include elaborate text layout and pictures, they're all just plain old text documents themselves. A fancier WYSIWYG editor or a translator for your favorite word processor is fine, too—although it may not support all the language features we discuss in this book. You'll probably end up touching up the source text they produce, in any case, and don't expect layout results like what you'd get with a page-layout application.

While it's not needed to compose documents, you should have at least one version of a popular browser installed on your computer to view your work. That's because, unless you use a special editor, the source document you compose won't look anything like what gets displayed by a browser, even though it's the same document. Make sure what your readers actually see is what you intended by viewing the document yourself with a browser. Besides, the popular ones are free over the Internet. We currently recommend Microsoft Internet Explorer, Mozilla Firefox, Apple Safari, Netscape Navigator, and Opera Software ASA.

Also note that you don't need a connection to the Internet or the Web to write and view your HTML or XHTML documents. You can compose and view your documents stored on a hard drive or floppy disk that's attached to your computer. You can even navigate among your local documents with the HTML/XHTML's hyperlinking capabilities without ever being connected to the Internet, or any other network, for that matter. In fact, we recommend that you work locally to develop and thoroughly test your documents before you share them with others.

We strongly recommend, however, that you *do* get a connection to the Internet if you are serious about composing your own documents. You can download and view others' interesting web pages and see how they accomplished some interesting feature—good or bad. Learning by example is fun, too. (Reusing others' work, on the other hand, is often questionable, if not downright illegal.) An Internet connection is essential if you include in your work hyperlinks to other documents on the Internet.

2.2 A First HTML Document

It seems every programming language book ever written starts off with a simple example on how to display the message, "Hello, World!" Well, you won't see a "Hello, World!" example in this book. After all, this is a style guide for the new millennium. Instead, ours sends greetings to the World Wide Web:

```
<html>
<head>
<title>My first HTML document</title>
</head>
<body>
<h2>My first HTML document</h2>
Hello, <i>World Wide Web!</i>
  <!-- No "Hello, World" for us -->
<p>
    Greetings from<br>
<a href="http://www.ora.com">O'Reilly</a>
<p>
Composed with care by:
<cite>(insert your name here)</cite>
<br>&copy;2000 and beyond
</body>
</html>
```

Go ahead: type in the example HTML source on a fresh word processing page and save it on your local disk as *myfirst.html*. Make sure you select to save it in plain text format; word processor-specific file formats like Microsoft Word's *.doc* files save hidden characters that can confuse the browser software and disrupt your HTML document's display.

After saving *myfirst.html* (or *myfirst.htm*, if you are using archaic DOS- or Windows 3.11-based file-naming conventions) onto disk, start up your browser and locate and open the file from the program's File menu. Your screen should look like Figure 2-1. Though look-and-feel elements such as menus and toolbars differ between browsers, the window's contents should be quite similar.

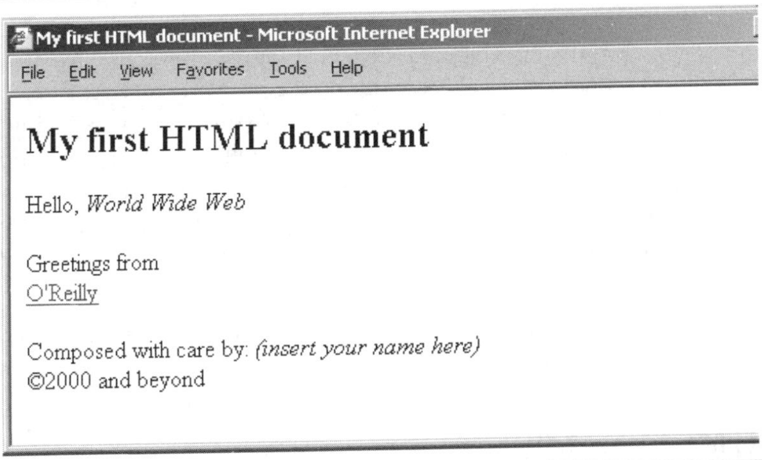

Figure 2-1. A very simple HTML document

2.3 Embedded Tags

You probably noticed right away, perhaps in surprise, that the browser displays less than half of the example source text. Closer inspection of the source reveals that what's missing is everything that's bracketed inside a pair of less-than (<) and greater-than (>) characters. [The Syntax of a Tag, 3.3.1]

HTML and XHTML are embedded languages: you insert their directions, or *tags*, into the same document that you and your readers load into a browser to view. The browser uses the information inside those tags to decide how to display or otherwise treat the subsequent contents of your document.

For instance, the <i> tag that follows the word *Hello* in the simple example tells the browser to display the following text in italics.* [Physical Style Tags, 4.5]

---

* Italicized text is a very simple example and one that most browsers, except the text-only variety (e.g., Lynx), can handle. In general, the browser tries to do as it is told, but as we demonstrate in upcoming chapters, browsers vary from computer to computer and from user to user, as do the fonts that are available and selected by the user for viewing HTML documents. Assume that not all are capable of or willing to display your HTML document exactly as it appears on your screen.

The first word in a tag is its formal name, which usually is fairly descriptive of its function, too. Any additional words in a tag are special *attributes*, sometimes with an associated value after an equals sign (=), which further define or modify the tag's actions.

2.3.1 Start and End Tags

Most tags define and affect a discrete region of your document. The region begins where the tag and its attributes first appear in the source document (a.k.a. the *start tag*) and continues until a corresponding *end tag*. An end tag is the tag's name preceded by a forward slash (/). For example, the end tag that matches the "start italicizing" <i> tag is </i>.

End tags never include attributes. In HTML, most tags, but not all, have an end tag. And, to make life a bit easier for HTML authors, the browser software often infers an end tag from surrounding and obvious context, so you needn't explicitly include some end tags in your source HTML document. (We tell you which are optional and which are never omitted when we describe each tag in later chapters.) Our simple example is missing an end tag that is so commonly inferred and hence not included in the source that some veteran HTML authors don't even know that it exists. Which one?

The XHTML standard is much more rigid, insisting that all tags have corresponding end tags. [End Tags, 16.3.2] [Handling Empty Elements, 16.3.3]

2.4 HTML Skeleton

Notice, too, that our simple example HTML document starts and ends with <html> and </html> tags. These tags tell the browser that the entire document is composed in HTML.* The HTML and XHTML standards require an <html> tag for compliant documents, but most browsers can detect and properly display HTML encoding in a text document that's missing this outermost structural tag. [<html>, 3.6.1]

Like our example, except for special frameset documents, all HTML and XHTML documents have two main structures: a *head* and a *body*, each bounded in the source by respectively named start and end tags. You put information about the document in the head and the contents you want displayed in the browser's window inside the body. Except in rare cases, you'll spend most of your time working on your document's body content. [<head>, 3.7.1] [<body>, 3.8.1]

There are several different document header tags that you can use to define how a particular document fits into a document collection and into the larger scheme of the Web. Some nonstandard header tags even animate your document.

---

* XHTML documents also begin with the <html> tag, but they contain additional information to differentiate them from common HTML documents. See Chapter 16 for details.

For most documents, however, the important header element is the title. Standards require that every HTML and XHTML document have a title, even though the currently popular browsers don't enforce that rule. Choose a meaningful title, one that instantly tells the reader what the document is about. Enclose yours, as we do for the title of our example, between the <title> and </title> tags in your document's header. The popular browsers typically display the title at the top of the document's window. [<title>, 3.7.2]

2.5 The Flesh on an HTML or XHTML Document

Except for the <html>, <head>, <body>, and <title> tags, the HTML and XHTML standards have few other required structural elements. You're free to include pretty much anything else in the contents of your document. (The web surfers among you know that authors have taken full advantage of that freedom, too.) Perhaps surprisingly, though, there are only three main types of HTML/XHTML content: tags (which we described previously), comments, and text.

2.5.1 Comments

A raw document with all its embedded tags can quickly become nearly unreadable, like computer-programming source code. We strongly recommend that you use comments to guide your composing eye.

Although it's part of your document, nothing in a comment, which goes between the special starting tag <!-- and ending tag --> comment delimiters, gets included in the browser display of your document. You see a comment in the source, as in our simple HTML example, but you don't see it on the display, as evidenced by our comment's absence in Figure 2-1. Anyone can download the source text of your documents and read the comments, though, so be careful what you write.

2.5.2 Text

If it isn't a tag or a comment, it's text. The bulk of content in most of your HTML/XHTML documents—the part readers see on their browser displays—is text. Special tags give the text structure, such as headings, lists, and tables. Others advise the browser how the content should be formatted and displayed.

2.5.3 Multimedia

What about images and other multimedia elements we see and hear as part of our web browser displays? Aren't they part of the HTML document? No. The data that comprises digital images, movies, sounds, and other multimedia elements that may be included in the browser display is in files separate from the main HTML/XHTML document. You include references to those multimedia elements via special tags. The browser uses those references to load and integrate other types of documents with your text.

We didn't include any special multimedia references in the previous example simply because they are separate, nontext documents that you can't just type into a text processor. We do, however, talk about and give examples of how to integrate images and other multimedia in your documents later in this chapter, as well as in extensive detail in subsequent chapters.

2.6 Text

Text-related HTML/XHTML markup tags comprise the richest set of all in the standard languages. That's because the original language—HTML—emerged as a way to enrich the structure and organization of text.

HTML came out of academia. What was and still is important to those early developers was the capability of their mostly academic, text-oriented documents to be scanned and read without sacrificing their capability to distribute documents over the Internet to a wide diversity of computer display platforms. (Unicode text is the only universal format on the global Internet.) Multimedia integration is something of an appendage to HTML and XHTML, albeit an important one.

Also, page layout is secondary to structure. We humans visually scan and decide textual relationships and structure based on how it looks; machines can only read encoded markings. Because documents have encoded tags that relate meaning, they lend themselves very well to computer-automated searches and to the recompilation of content—features very important to researchers. It's not so much *how* something is said as *what* is being said.

Accordingly, neither HTML nor XHTML is a page-layout language. In fact, given the diversity of user-customizable browsers, as well as the diversity of computer platforms for retrieval and display of electronic documents, all these markup languages strive to accomplish is to *advise*, not dictate, how the document might look when rendered by the browser. You cannot force the browser to display your document in any certain way. You'll hurt your brain if you insist otherwise.

2.6.1 Appearance of Text

For instance, you cannot predict what font and what absolute size—8- or 40-point Helvetica, Geneva, Subway, or whatever—will be used for a particular user's text display. OK, so the latest browsers now support standard Cascading Style Sheets (CSS) and other desktop publishing-like features that let you control the layout and appearance of your documents. But users may change their browser's display characteristics and override your carefully laid plans at will, quite a few of the older browsers out there don't support these new layout features, and some browsers are text-only with no nice fonts at all. What to do? Concentrate on content. Cool pages are a flash in the pan. Deep content will bring people back for more and more.

Nonetheless, style does matter for readability, and it is good to include it where you can, as long as it doesn't interfere with content presentation. You can attach common style attributes to your text with *physical* style tags, like the italic <i> tag in our simple example. More important and truer to the language's original purpose, HTML and XHTML have *content-based* style tags that attach *meaning* to various text passages. And you can alter text display characteristics, such as font style, size, color, and so on, with CSS.

Today's graphical browsers recognize the physical and content-related text style tags and change the appearance of their related text passages to visually convey meaning or structure. You can't predict exactly what that change will look like.

The HTML 4 standard (and even more so, the XHTML 1.0 standard) stresses that future browsers will not be so visually bound. Text contents may be heard or even felt, for example, not read by viewers. Context clues surely are better in those cases than physical styles.

2.6.1.1 Content-based text styles

Content-based style tags indicate to the browser that a portion of your HTML/XHTML text has a specific usage or meaning. The <cite> tag in our simple example, for instance, means the enclosed text is some sort of citation—the document's author, in this case. Browsers commonly, although not universally, display the citation text in italic, not as regular text. [Content-Based Style Tags, 4.4]

While it may or may not be obvious to the current reader that the text is a citation, someday someone might create a computer program that searches a vast collection of documents for embedded <cite> tags and compiles a special list of citations from the enclosed text. Similar software agents already scour the Internet for embedded information to compile listings, such as the infamous Google database of web sites.

The most common content-based style used today is that of emphasis, indicated with the <em> tag. And if you're feeling really emphatic, you might use the <strong> content style. Other content-based styles include <code>, for snippets of programming code; <kbd>, to denote text entered by the user via a keyboard; <samp>, to mark sample text; <dfn>, for definitions; and <var>, to delimit variable names within programming code samples. All of these tags have corresponding end tags.

2.6.1.2 Physical styles

Even the barest of barebones text processors conform to a few traditional text styles, such as italic and bold characters. While not word processing tools in the traditional sense, HTML and XHTML provide tags that explicitly tell the browser to display (if it can) a character, word, or phrase in a particular physical style.

Although you should use related content-based tags, for the reasons we argued earlier, sometimes form is more important than function. Use the `<i>` tag to italicize text without imposing any specific meaning, the `<b>` tag to display text in boldface, or the `<tt>` tag so that the browser, if it can, displays the text in a teletype-style monospaced typeface. [Physical Style Tags, 4.5]

It's easy to fall into the trap of using physical styles when you should really be using a content-based style instead. Discipline yourself now to use the content-based styles because, as we argued earlier, they convey meaning as well as style, thereby making your documents easier to automate and manage.

2.6.1.3 Special text characters

Not all text characters available to you for display by a browser can be typed from the keyboard. And some characters have special meanings, such as the brackets around tags, which if not somehow differentiated when used for plain text—the less-than sign (<) in a math equation, for example—will confuse the browser and trash your document. HTML and XHTML give you a way to include any of the many different characters that comprise the Unicode character set anywhere in your text through a special encoding of its *character entity*.

Like the copyright symbol in our simple example, a character entity starts with an ampersand (&), followed by its name, and terminated with a semicolon (;). Alternatively, you may also use the character's position number in the Unicode table of characters, preceded by the pound or sharp sign (#), in lieu of its name in the character-entity sequence. When rendering the document, the browser displays the proper character, if it exists in the user's font. [Character Entities, 3.5.2]

For obvious reasons, the most commonly used character entities are the greater-than (>), less-than (<), and ampersand (&) characters. Check Appendix F to find out what symbol the character entity ¦ represents. You'll be pleasantly surprised!

2.6.2 Text Structures

It's not obvious in our simple example, but the common carriage returns we use to separate paragraphs in our source document have no meaning in HTML or XHTML, except in special circumstances. You could have typed the document onto a single line in your text editor, and it would still appear the same in Figure 2-1.*

---

* We use a computer programming-like style of indentation so that our source HTML/XHTML documents are more readable. It's not obligatory, nor are there any formal style guidelines for source HTML/XHTML document text formats. We do, however, highly recommend that you adopt a consistent style so that you and others can easily follow your source documents.

You'd soon discover, too, if you hadn't read it here first, that except in special cases, browsers typically ignore leading and trailing spaces, and sometimes more than a few in between. (If you look closely at the source example, the line "Greetings from" looks like it should be indented by leading spaces, but it isn't in Figure 2-1.)

2.6.2.1 Divisions, paragraphs, and line breaks

A browser takes the text in the body of your document and "flows" it onto the computer screen, disregarding any common carriage-return or line-feed characters in the source. The browser fills as much of each line of the display window as possible, beginning flush against the left margin, before stopping after the rightmost word and moving on to the next line. Resize the browser window, and the text reflows to fill the new space, indicating HTML's inherent flexibility.

Of course, readers would rebel if your text just ran on and on, so HTML and XHTML provide both explicit and implicit ways to control the basic structure of your document. The most rudimentary and common ways are with the division (<div>), paragraph (<p>), and line-break (<br>) tags. All break the text flow, which consequently restarts on a new line. The differences are that the <div> and <p> tags define an elemental region of the document and text, respectively, the contents of which you may specially align within the browser window, apply text styles to, and alter with other block-related features.

Without special alignment attributes, the <div> and <br> tags simply break a line of text and place subsequent characters on the next line. The <p> tag adds more vertical space after the line break than either the <div> or <br> tag. [<div>, 4.1.1] [<p>, 4.1.2] [
, 4.6.1]

By the way, the HTML standard includes end tags for the paragraph and division tags, but not for the line-break tag.* Few authors ever include the paragraph end tag in their documents; the browser usually can figure out where one paragraph ends and another begins.† Give yourself a star if you knew that </p> even exists.

2.6.2.2 Headings

Besides breaking your text into divisions and paragraphs, you can also organize your documents into sections with headings. Just as they do on this and other pages in this printed book, headings not only divide and entitle discrete passages of text, but they also convey meaning visually. And headings readily lend themselves to machine-automated processing of your documents.

---

* With XHTML,
's start and end are between the same brackets: <br />. Browsers tend to be very forgiving and often ignore extraneous things, such as the forward slash in this case, so it's perfectly OK to get into the habit of adding that end mark.

† The paragraph end tag is being used more commonly now that the popular browsers support the paragraph-alignment attribute.

There are six heading tags, <h1> through <h6>, with corresponding end tags. Typically, the browser displays their contents in, respectively, very large to very small font sizes, and usually in boldface. The text inside the <h4> tag typically is the same size as the regular text. [Heading Tags, 4.2.1]

The heading tags also break the current text flow, standing alone on lines and separated from surrounding text, even though there aren't any explicit paragraph or line-break tags before or after a heading.

2.6.2.3 Horizontal rules

Besides headings, HTML and XHTML provide horizontal rule lines that help delineate and separate the sections of your document.

When the browser encounters an <hr> tag in your document, it breaks the flow of text and draws a line across the display window on a new line. The flow of text resumes immediately below the rule.* [<hr>, 5.1.1]

2.6.2.4 Preformatted text

Occasionally, you'll want the browser to display a block of text as is: for example, with indented lines and vertically aligned letters or numbers that don't change even though the browser window might get resized. The <pre> tag rises to those occasions. All text up to the closing </pre> end tag appears in the browser window exactly as you type it, including carriage returns, line feeds, and leading, trailing, and intervening spaces. Although very useful for tables and forms, <pre> text looks pretty dull; the popular browsers render the block in a monospace typeface. [<pre>, 4.6.5]

2.7 Hyperlinks

While text may be the meat and bones of an HTML or XHTML document, the heart is hypertext. Hypertext gives users the ability to retrieve and display a different document in their own or someone else's collection simply by a click of the keyboard or mouse on an associated word or phrase (*hyperlink*) in the document. Use these interactive hyperlinks to help readers easily navigate and find information in your own or others' collections of otherwise separate documents in a variety of formats, including multimedia, HTML, XHTML, other XML, and plain text. Hyperlinks literally bring the wealth of knowledge on the whole Internet to the tip of the mouse pointer.

To include a hyperlink to some other document in your own collection or on a server in Timbuktu, all you need to know is the document's unique address and how to drop an *anchor* into your document.

---

* Similar to <br>, with XHTML, the formal horizontal rule end tag is <hr />.

2.7.1 URLs

While it is hard to believe, given the billions of them out there, every document and resource on the Internet has a unique address, known as its *uniform resource locator* (URL; commonly pronounced "you-are-ell"). A URL consists of the document's name preceded by the hierarchy of directory names in which the file is stored (*pathname*), the Internet *domain name* of the server that hosts the file, and the software and manner by which the browser and the document's host server communicate to exchange the document (*protocol*):

> *protocol://server_domain_name/pathname*

Here are some sample URLs:

- *http://www.kumquat.com/docs/catalog/price_list.html*
- *price_list.html*
- *../figs/my_photo.png*
- *ftp://ftp.netcom.com/pub*

The first example is an *absolute* or complete URL. It includes every part of the URL format: protocol, server, and pathname of the document. While absolute URLs leave nothing to the imagination, they can lead to big headaches when you move documents to another directory or server. Fortunately, browsers also let you use *relative* URLs and automatically fill in any missing portions with respective parts from the current document's *base* URL. The second example is the simplest relative URL of all; with it, the browser assumes that the *price_list.html* document is located on the same server, in the same directory as the current document, and uses the same network protocol (*http*). Similarly, example three is a relative URL which looks up and into the */figs* directory for a picture file.

Although appearances may deceive, the last FTP example URL actually is absolute; it points directly at the contents of the */pub* directory. Moreover, the *ftp* protocol specification in the example accesses different software on the server than the *http* protocol in the other examples.

2.7.2 Anchors

The anchor (`<a>`) tag is the HTML/XHTML feature for defining both the source and the destination of a hyperlink.* You'll most often see and use the `<a>` tag with its `href` attribute to define a source hyperlink. The value of the `href` attribute is the URL of the destination.

---

* The nomenclature here is a bit unfortunate: the "anchor" tag should mark just a destination, not the jumping-off point of a hyperlink, too. You "drop anchor"; you don't jump off one. We won't even mention the atrociously confusing terminology the W3C uses for the various parts of a hyperlink, except to say that someone got things all "bass-ackward."

The contents of the source <a> tag—the words and/or images between it and its </a> end tag—is the portion of the document that is specially activated in the browser display and that users select to take a hyperlink. These anchor contents usually look different from the surrounding content (text in a different color or underlined, images with specially colored borders, or other effects), and the mouse-pointer icon changes when passed over them. The <a> tag contents, therefore, should be text or an image (icons are great) that explicitly or intuitively tells users where the hyperlink will take them. [<a>, 6.3.1]

For instance, the browser will specially display and change the mouse pointer when it passes over the "Kumquat Archive" text in the following example:

```
For more information on kumquats, visit our
<a href="http://www.kumquat.com/archive.html">
Kumquat Archive</a>
```

If the user clicks the mouse button on that text, the browser automatically retrieves from the server *www.kumquat.com* a web (*http:*) page named *archive.html*, then displays it for the user.

2.7.3 Hyperlink Names and Navigation

Pointing to another document in some collection somewhere on the other side of the world is not only cool, but it also supports your own web documents. Yet the hyperlink's chief duty is to help users navigate your collection in their search for valuable information. Hence, the concept of the home page and supporting documents has arisen.

None of your documents should run on and on. First, there's a serious performance issue: the value of your work suffers, no matter how rich it is, if the document takes forever to download and if, once it is retrieved, users must endlessly scroll up and down through the display to find a particular section.

Rather, design your work as a collection of several compact and succinct pages, like chapters in a book, each focused on a particular topic for quick selection and browsing by the user. Then use hyperlinks to organize that collection.

For instance, use your home page—the leading document of the collection—as a master index full of brief descriptions and respective hyperlinks to the rest of your collection.

You can also use either the name variant of the <a> tag or the id attribute of nearly all tags to specially identify sections of your document. Tag ids and name anchors serve as internal hyperlink targets in your documents to help users easily navigate within the same document or jump to a particular section within another document. Refer to that id'd section in a hyperlink by appending a pound sign (#) and the section name as the suffix to the URL.

For instance, to reference a specific topic in an archive, such as "Kumquat Stew Recipes" in our example Kumquat Archive, first mark the section title with an id:

```
...preceding content...
<h3 id="Stews">Kumquat Stew Recipes</h3>
```

in the same or another document, then prepare a source hyperlink that points directly to those recipes by including the section's id value as a suffix to the document's URL, separated by a pound sign:

```
For more information on kumquats, visit our
<a href="http://www.kumquat.com/archive.html">
  Kumquat Archive</a>,
and perhaps try one or two of our
<a href="http://www.kumquat.com/archive.html#Stews">
  Kumquat Stew Recipes</a>.
```

If selected by the user, the latter hyperlink causes the browser to download the *archive.html* document and start the display at our "Stews" section.

2.7.4 Anchors Beyond

Hyperlinks are not limited to other HTML and XHTML documents. Anchors let you point to nearly any type of document available over the Internet, including other Internet services.

However, "let" and "enable" are two different things. Browsers can manage the various Internet services, such as FTP and Gopher, so that users can download non-HTML documents. They don't yet fully or gracefully handle multimedia.

Today, there are few standards for the many types and formats of multimedia. Computer systems connected to the Web vary wildly in their capabilities to display those sound and video formats. Except for some graphics images, standard HTML/XHTML gives you no specific provision for display of multimedia documents except the ability to reference one in an anchor. The browser, which retrieves the multimedia document, must activate a special *helper* application, download and execute an associated *applet*, or have a *plug-in* accessory installed to decode and display it for the user right within the document's display.

Although HTML and most web browsers currently avoid the confusion by sidestepping it, that doesn't mean you can't or shouldn't exploit multimedia in your documents: just be aware of the limitations.

2.8 Images Are Special

Image files are multimedia elements that you can reference with anchors in your document for separate download and display by the browser. But, unlike other multimedia, standard HTML and XHTML have an explicit provision for image display "inline" with the text, and images can serve as intricate maps of hyperlinks. That's because there is some consensus in the industry concerning image file formats—specifically, GIF, PNG, and JPEG—and the graphical browsers have built-in decoders that integrate those image types into your document.[*]

---

[*] Some browsers support other multimedia besides GIF and JPEG graphics for inline display. Internet Explorer, for instance, supports a tag that plays background audio. In addition, the HTML 4 and XHTML standards provide a way to display other types of multimedia inline with document text through a general tag.

2.8.1 Inline Images

The HTML/XHTML tag for inline images is <img>; its required src attribute is the image file that you want to display in the document. [<img>, 5.2.6]

The browser separately loads images and places them into the text flow as though the image were some special, albeit sometimes very large, character. Normally, that means the browser aligns the bottom of the image to the bottom of the current line of text. You can change that with the special CSS align property, whose value you set to put the image at the top, middle, or bottom of adjacent text. Examine Figures 2-2 through 2-4 for the image alignment you prefer. Of course, wide images may take up the whole line and hence break the text flow. You can also place an image by itself, by including preceding and following division, paragraph, or line-break tags.

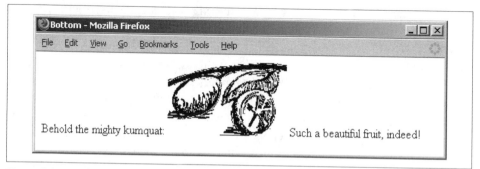

Figure 2-2. An inline image aligned with the bottom of the text (default)

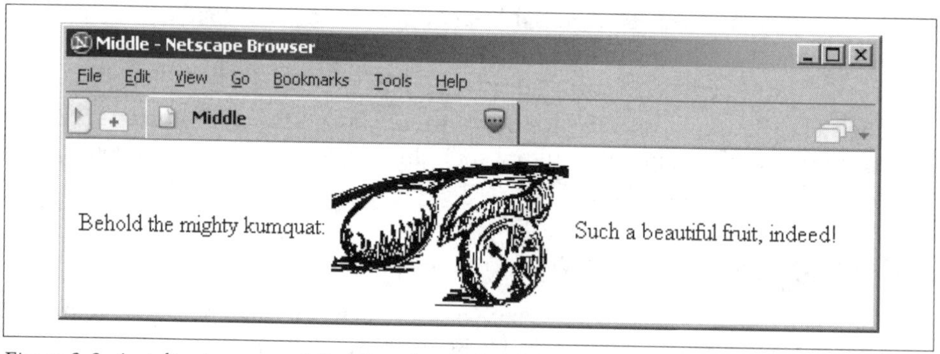

Figure 2-3. An inline image specially aligned with the middle of the text

Experienced HTML authors use images not only as supporting illustrations, but also as quite small inline characters or glyphs, added to aid browsing readers' eyes and to highlight sections of the documents. Veteran HTML authors* commonly add custom list bullets or more distinctive section dividers than the conventional horizontal

---

* XHTML is too new to call anyone a *veteran* or *experienced* XHTML author.

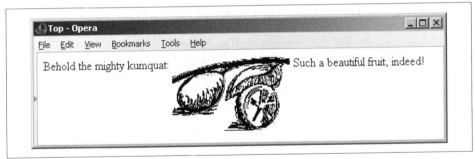

Figure 2-4. An inline image specially aligned with the top of the text

rules. Images, too, may be included in a hyperlink so that users may select an inline thumbnail sketch to download a full-screen image. The possibilities with inline images are endless.

We also should mention the alt attribute. Give it some text value that explains the image display for those who have disabled image display, or for browsers that may be able to read to the disabled user.

2.8.2 Image Maps

Image maps are images within an anchor with a special attribute: they may contain more than one hyperlink.

One way to enable an image map is by adding the ismap attribute to an <img> tag placed inside an anchor tag (<a>). When the user clicks somewhere in the image, the graphical browser sends the relative X,Y coordinates of the mouse position to the server that is also designated in the anchor. A special server program then translates the image coordinates into some special action, such as downloading another document. [Server-side considerations, 6.5.1.1]

A good example of the use of an image map might be to locate a hotel while traveling. For example, when the user clicks on a map of the region he intends to visit, your image map's server program might return the names, addresses, and phone numbers of local accommodations.

While they are very powerful and visually appealing, these so-called *server-side* image maps mean that authors must have some access to the map's coordinate-processing program on the server. Many authors don't even have access to the server, let alone a program on the server. A better solution is to take advantage of *client-side* image maps.

Instead of depending on a web server, the usemap attribute for the <img> tag, with the <map> and <area> tags, allows authors to embed the information the browser needs to process an image map in the same document as the image. Because of their reduced network bandwidth and server independence, the client-side image maps are popular among document authors and system administrators. [Client-Side Image Maps, 6.5.2]

2.9 Lists, Searchable Documents, and Forms

Thought we'd exhausted text elements? Headers, paragraphs, and line breaks are just the rudimentary text-organizational elements of a document. The languages also provide several advanced text-based structures, including three types of lists, "searchable" documents, and forms. Searchable documents and forms go beyond text formatting, too; they are a way to interact with your readers. Forms let users enter text and click checkboxes and radio buttons to select particular items and then send that information back to the server. A special server application then processes the form's information and responds accordingly; for example, filling a product order or collecting data for a user survey.[*]

The syntax for these special features and their various attributes can get rather complicated; they're not quick-start grist. We'll mention them here, but we urge you to read on for details in later chapters.

2.9.1 Unordered, Ordered, and Definition Lists

The three types of lists match those we are most familiar with: unordered, ordered, and definition lists. An unordered list—one in which the order of items is not important, such as a laundry or grocery list—gets bounded by <ul> and </ul> tags. Each item in the list, usually a word or short phrase, is marked by the <li> (list-item) tag and, particularly with XHTML, the </li> end tag. When rendered, the list item typically appears indented from the left margin, preceded by a bullet symbol. [<ul>, 7.1.1] [<li>, 7.3]

Ordered lists, bounded by the <ol> and </ol> tags, are identical in format to unordered ones, including the <li> tag (and </li> end tag with XHTML) for marking list items. However, the order of items is important—as in equipment assembly steps, for instance. The browser accordingly displays each item in the list preceded by an ascending number. [<ol>, 7.2.1]

Definition lists are slightly more complicated than unordered and ordered lists. Within a definition list's enclosing <dl> and </dl> tags, each list item has two parts, each with a special tag: a short name or title, contained within a <dt> tag, followed by its corresponding value or definition, denoted by the <dd> tag (XHTML includes respective end tags). When the tags are rendered, the browser usually puts the item name on a separate line (although not indented), and the definition, which may include several paragraphs, indented below it. [<dl>, 7.5.1]

The various types of lists may contain nearly any type of content normally allowed in the body of the document. So you can organize your collection of digitized family

---

[*] The server-side programming required for processing forms is beyond the scope of this book. We give some basic guidelines in the appropriate chapters, but please consult the server documentation and your server administrator for details.

photographs into an ordered list, for example, or put them into a definition list complete with text annotations. The markup language standards even let you put lists inside of lists (nesting), opening up a wealth of interesting combinations.

2.9.2 Searchable Documents and Forms

The original type of user interaction provided by early versions of HTML still available today, though deprecated in the standards, is an <isindex>-based *searchable* document. The browser provides some way for the user to type one or more words into a text input box and to pass those keywords to a related processing application on the server.[*] Obviously, searchable documents are very, very limited—one per document and only one user-input element. Fortunately, HTML and XHTML provide better, more extensive support for collecting user input through *forms*. [<isindex>, 6.6.1] [<form>, 9.2]

You can create one or more special form sections in your document, bounded with the <form> and </form> tags. Inside the form, you may put predefined as well as customized text-input boxes allowing for both single and multiline input. You may also insert checkboxes and radio buttons for single- and multiple-choice selections and special buttons that work to reset the form or send its contents to the server. Users fill out the form at their leisure, perhaps after reading the rest of the document, and click a special send button that makes the browser send the form's data to the server. A special server-side program you provide then processes the form and responds accordingly, perhaps by requesting more information from the user, modifying subsequent documents the server sends to the user, and so on. [<form>, 9.2]

Forms provide everything you might expect of an automated form, including input area labels, integrated contents for instructions, default input values, and so on—except automatic input verification, such as to check for the correct number of digits in a zip code or phone number, for instance; your server-side program or client-side JavaScripts need to perform that function.

2.10 Tables

For a language that emerged from academia—a world steeped in data—it's not surprising to find that HTML (and now its progeny, XHTML) supports a set of tags for data tables that not only align your numbers, but can specially format your text, too.

Eight tags enable tables; including the <table> tag itself and a <caption> tag for including a description of the table. Special tag attributes let you change the look and dimensions of the table. You create a table row by row, putting between the table

---

[*] Few authors have used the tag, apparently. The <isindex> tag has been "deprecated" in HTML version 4.0—sent out to pasture, so to speak, but not yet laid to rest.

row (`<tr>`) tag and its end tag (`</tr>`) either table header (`<th>`) or table data (`<td>`) tags and their respective contents for each cell in the table (end tags, too, with XHTML). Headers and data may contain nearly any regular content, including text, images, forms, and even another table. As a result, you can also use tables for advanced text formatting, such as for multicolumn text and sidebar headers (see Figure 2-5). For more information, see Chapter 10.

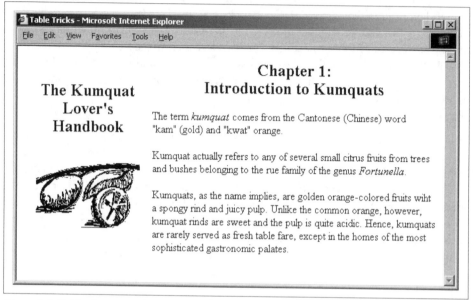

Figure 2-5. Tables let you perform page layout tricks, too

2.11 Frames

Anyone who has had more than one application window open on her graphical desktop at a time can immediately appreciate the benefits of frames. Frames let you divide the browser window into multiple display areas, each containing a different document.

Figure 2-6 is an example of a frame display. It shows how the document window may be divided into independent windows separated by rule lines and scroll bars. What is not immediately apparent in the example, though, is that each frame displays an independent document, and not necessarily HTML or XHTML ones, either. A frame may contain any valid content that the browser is capable of displaying, including multimedia. If the frame's contents include a hypertext link that the user selects, the new document's contents, even another frame document, may replace that same frame, another frame's content, or the entire browser window.

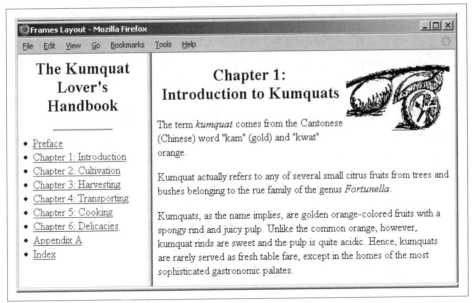

Figure 2-6. Frames divide the browser's window into two or more independent document displays

Frames are defined in a special document, in which you replace the <body> tag with one or more <frameset> tags that tell the browser how to divide its main window into discrete frames. Special <frame> tags go inside the <frameset> tag and point to the documents that go inside the frames. [<frameset>, 11.3.1]

The individual documents referenced and displayed in the frame document window act independently, to a degree; the frame document controls the entire window. You can, however, direct one frame's document to load new content into another frame. In Figure 2-6, for example, selecting a Chapter hyperlink in the Table of Contents frame has the browser load and display that chapter's contents in the frame on the right. That way, the table of contents is always available to the user as he browses the collection. For more information on frames, see Chapter 11.

2.12 Stylesheets and JavaScript

Browsers also have support for two powerful innovations to HTML: stylesheets and JavaScript. Like their desktop publishing cousins, stylesheets let you control how your web pages look—text font styles and sizes, colors, backgrounds, alignments, and so on. More important, stylesheets give you a way to impose display characteristics uniformly over the entire document and over an entire collection of documents.

JavaScript is a programming language with functions and commands that let you control how the browser behaves for the user. Now, this is not a JavaScript programming book, but we do cover the language in fair detail in later chapters to show you how to embed JavaScript programs into your documents and achieve some very powerful and fun effects.

The W3C—the putative standards organization—prefers that you use the CSS model for HTML/XHTML document design. All modern GUI browsers support CSS and JavaScript. The ancient Netscape 4 alone also supports a JavaScript Style Sheet (JSS) model, which we describe in Chapter 12, but we do not recommend that you use it. Let's rephrase that—don't waste your time on JSS. CSS is the universally approved, universally supported way to control how your documents *might* (not *will*) usually be displayed on users' browsers.

To illustrate CSS, here's a way to make all the top-level (h1) header text in your HTML document appear in the color red:

```
<html>
<head>
<title>CSS Example</title>
<!-- Hide CSS properties within comments so old browsers
don't choke on or display the unfamiliar contents. -->
  <style type="text/css">
    <!--
    h1 {color: red}
    -->
  </style>
</head>
<body>
<h1>I'll be red if your browser supports CSS</h1>
Something in between.
<h1>I should be red, too!</h1>
</body>
</html>
```

Of course, you can't see red in this black-and-white book, so we won't show the result in a figure. Believe us, or prove it to yourself by typing in and loading the example in your browser: the <h1>-enclosed text appears red on a color screen.

JavaScript is an object-based language. It views your document and the browser that displays your documents as a collection of parts ("objects") that have certain properties that you may change or compute. This is some very powerful stuff, but not something that most authors will want to handle. Rather, most of us probably will snatch the quick and easy, yet powerful JavaScript programs that proliferate across the Web and embed them in our own documents. We will tell you how in Chapter 12.

2.13 Forging Ahead

Clearly, this chapter represents the tip of the iceberg. If you've read this far, hopefully your appetite has been whetted for more. By now you've got a basic understanding of the scope and features of HTML and XHTML; proceed through subsequent chapters to expand your knowledge and learn more about each feature.

Anatomy of an HTML Document

Most HTML and XHTML documents are very simple, and writing one shouldn't intimidate even the most timid of computer users. First, although you might use a fancy WYSIWYG editor to help you compose it, a document is ultimately stored, distributed, and read by a browser as a simple text file.* That's why even the poorest user with a barebones text editor can compose the most elaborate of web pages. (Accomplished webmasters often elicit the admiration of "newbies" by composing astonishingly cool pages using the crudest text editor on a cheap laptop computer and performing in odd places, such as on a bus or in the bathroom.) Authors should, however, keep several of the popular browsers on hand, including recent versions of each, and alternate among them to view new documents under construction. Remember, browsers differ in how they display a page, not all browsers implement all of the language standards, and some have their own special extensions.

3.1 Appearances Can Deceive

Documents never look alike when displayed by a text editor and when displayed by a browser. Take a look at any source document on the Web. At the very least, return characters, tabs, and leading spaces, although important for readability of the source text document, are ignored for the most part when displayed by an HTML/XHTML

---

* Informally, both the text and the markup tags are ASCII characters. Technically, unless you specify otherwise, text and tags are made up of 8-bit characters as defined in the standard ISO-8859-1 Latin character set. The HTML/XHTML standards support alternative character encodings, including Arabic and Cyrillic. See Appendix F for details.

browser. There also is a lot of extra text in a source document, mostly from the display tags and interactivity markers and their parameters that affect portions of the document but don't appear in the display.

Accordingly, new authors are confronted with having to develop not only a presentation style for their web pages, but also a different style for their source text. The source document's layout should highlight the programming-like markup aspects of HTML and XHTML, not their display aspects. And it should be readable not only by you, the author, but by others as well.

Experienced document writers typically adopt a programming-like style, albeit very relaxed, for their source text. We do the same throughout this book, and that style will become apparent as you compare our source examples with the actual display of the document by a browser.

Our formatting style is simple, but it serves to create readable, easily maintained documents:

- Except for the structural tags such as <html>, <head>, <frameset>, and <body>, we place elements that structure the content of a document on a separate line and indented to show its nesting level within the document. Structural elements include lists, forms, tables, and similar tags.
- Elements that control the appearance or style of text get inserted in the current line of text. These include basic font style tags such as <b> (bold text) and document linkages such as <a> (hypertext anchor).
- Avoid, where possible, breaking a URL onto two lines.
- Add extra newline characters to set apart special sections of the source document—for instance, around paragraphs or tables.

The task of maintaining the indentation of your source file ranges from trivial to onerous. Some text editors, such as Emacs, manage the indentation automatically; others, such as common word processors, couldn't care less about indentation and leave the task completely up to you. If your editor makes your life difficult, you might consider striking a compromise, perhaps by indenting the tags to show structure, but leaving the actual text without indentation to make modifications easier.

No matter what compromises or stands you make on source-code style, it's important that you adopt one. You'll be very glad you did when you go back to that document you wrote three months ago searching for that really cool trick you did with... now, where was that?

3.2 Structure of an HTML Document

HTML and XHTML documents consist of text, which defines the content of the document, and tags, which define the structure and appearance of the document.

The structure of an HTML document is simple, consisting of an outer <html> tag enclosing the document:*

```
<html>
<head>
<title>Barebones HTML Document</title>
</head>
<body>
This illustrates, in a very <i>simp</i>le way,
the basic structure of an HTML document.
</body>
</html>
```

Most documents have a *head* and a *body*, delimited by the <head> and <body> tags. The head is where you give your document a title and where you indicate other parameters the browser may use when displaying the document. The body is where you put the actual contents of the document. This includes the text for display and document-control markers (tags) that advise the browser how to display the text. Tags also reference special-effects files, including graphics and sound, and indicate the hotspots (hyperlinks and anchors) that link your document to other documents.

3.3 Tags and Attributes

For the most part, tags—the markup elements of HTML and XHTML—are simple to understand and use, since they are made up of common words, abbreviations, and notations. For instance, the <i> and </i> tags respectively tell the browser to start and stop italicizing the text characters that come between them. Accordingly, the syllable "simp" in our barebones example in Figure 3-1 should appear italicized when displayed by the browser.

Figure 3-1. Compare this browser display with its Barebones source HTML shown earlier

The HTML and XHTML standards and their various extensions define how and where you place tags within a document. Let's take a closer look at that syntactic sugar that holds together all documents.

---

* The structure of an XHTML document is slightly more complicated, as we detail in Chapter 16.

3.3.1 The Syntax of a Tag

Every tag consists of a tag *name*, sometimes followed by an optional list of tag *attributes*, all placed between opening and closing brackets (< and >). The simplest tag is nothing more than a name appropriately enclosed in brackets, such as <head> and <i>. More complicated tags contain one or more attributes, which specify or modify the behavior of the tag.

According to the HTML standard, tag and attribute names are not case-sensitive. There's no difference in effect between <head>, <Head>, <HEAD>, and even <HeaD>; all of them are equivalent. With XHTML, case *is* important: all current standard tag and attribute names are in lowercase; always <head>, never <HEAD>.

For both HTML and XHTML, the values that you assign to a particular attribute may be case-sensitive, depending on your browser and server. In particular, file location and name references—or URLs—are case-sensitive. [Referencing Documents: The URL, 6.2]

Tag attributes, if any, belong after the tag name, each separated by one or more tab, space, or return characters. Their order of appearance is not important.

A tag attribute's value, if any, follows an equals sign (=) after the attribute name. You may include spaces around the equals sign so that width=6, width = 6, width =6, and width= 6 all mean the same. For readability, however, we prefer not to include spaces. That way, it's easier to pick out an attribute/value pair from a crowd of pairs in a lengthy tag.

With HTML, if an attribute's value is a single word or number (no spaces), you may simply add it after the equals sign. You should enclose all other values in single or double quotation marks, especially those values that contain several words separated by spaces. With XHTML, all attribute values must be enclosed in quotes. The length of the value is limited to 1,024 characters.

Most browsers are tolerant of how tags are punctuated and broken across lines. Nonetheless, avoid breaking tags across lines in your source document whenever possible. This rule promotes readability and reduces potential errors in your HTML documents.

3.3.2 Sample Tags

Here are some tags with attributes:

```
<a href="http://www.oreilly.com/catalog.html">
<ul compact>
<ul compact="compact">
<input type=text name=filename size=24 maxlength=80>
<link title="Table of Contents">
```

The first example is the `<a>` tag for a hyperlink to our publisher's web-based catalog of products. It has a single attribute, `href`, followed by the catalog's address in cyberspace—its URL.

The second example shows an HTML tag that formats text into an unordered list of items. Its single attribute—`compact`, which limits the space between list items—does not require a value.

The third example demonstrates how the second example must be written in XHTML. Notice the `compact` attribute now has a value, albeit a redundant one, and that its value is enclosed in double quotes.

The fourth example shows an HTML tag with multiple attributes, each with a value that does not require enclosing quotation marks. Of course, with XHTML, each attribute value must be enclosed in double quotes.

The last example shows proper use of enclosing quotation marks when the attribute value is more than one word long.

What is not immediately evident in these examples is that while HTML attribute names are not case-sensitive (`href` works the same as `HREF` and `HreF` in HTML), most attribute values are case-sensitive. The value `filename` for the `name` attribute in the `<input>` tag example is not the same as the value `Filename`, for instance.

3.3.3 Starting and Ending Tags

We alluded earlier to the fact that most tags have a beginning and an end and affect the portion of content between them. That enclosed segment may be large or small, from a single text character, syllable, or word—such as the italicized "simp" syllable in our barebones example—to the `<html>` tag that bounds the entire document. The starting component of any tag is the tag name and its attributes, if any. The corresponding ending tag is the tag name alone, preceded by a slash (/). Ending tags have no attributes.

3.3.4 Proper and Improper Nesting

You can put tags inside the affected segment of another tag (nested) for multiple tag effects on a single segment of the document. For example, a portion of the following text is both bold and included as part of an anchor defined by the `<a>` tag:

```
<body>
This is some text in the body, with a
<a href="another_doc.html">link, a portion of which
is <b>set in bold.</b></a>
</body>
```

According to the HTML and XHTML standards, you must end nested tags by starting with the most recent one and working your way back out—first in, last out. For instance, in this example, we end the bold tag (</b>) before ending the link tag (</a>) because we started in the reverse order: <a> tag first, then <b> tag. It's a good idea to follow that standard, even though most browsers don't absolutely insist you do so. You may get away with violating this nesting rule for one browser, and sometimes even with all current browsers. But eventually a new browser version won't allow the violation, and you'll be hard-pressed to straighten out your source HTML document. Also, be aware that the XHTML standard explicitly forbids improper nesting.

3.3.5 Tags Without Ends

According to the HTML standard, a few tags do not have ending tags. In fact, the standard forbids use of an end tag for these special ones, although most browsers are lenient and ignore the errant end tag. For example, the <br> tag causes a line break; it has no effect otherwise on the subsequent portion of the document and, hence, does not need an ending tag.

The HTML tags that do not have corresponding end tags are:

<area>	<base>	<basefont>
 	<col>	<frame>
<hr>	<img>	<input>
<isindex>	<link>	<meta>
<param>		

XHTML always requires end tags. [Handling Empty Elements, 16.3.3]

3.3.6 Omitting Tags

You often see documents in which the author seemingly has forgotten to include an ending tag, in apparent violation of the HTML and certainly the XHTML standards. Sometimes even the <body> tag is missing. But your browser doesn't complain, and the document displays just fine. What gives? The HTML standard lets you omit certain tags or their endings for clarity and ease of preparation. The HTML standard writers didn't intend the language to be tedious.

For example, the <p> tag that defines the start of a paragraph has a corresponding end tag, </p>, but the end tag rarely is used. In fact, many HTML authors don't even know it exists. [<p>, 4.1.2]

The HTML standard lets you omit a starting tag or ending tag whenever it can be unambiguously inferred by the surrounding context. Many browsers make good guesses when confronted with missing tags, leading the document author to assume that a valid omission was made.

We recommend that you almost always add the ending tag. It'll make life easier for yourself as you transition to XHTML as well as for the browser and anyone who might need to modify your document in the future.

3.3.7 Ignored or Redundant Tags

HTML browsers sometimes ignore tags. This usually happens with redundant tags whose effects merely cancel or substitute for themselves. The best example is a series of <p> tags, one after the other, with no intervening content. Unlike a text-processing tool, most browsers start to a new line only once. The extra <p> tags are redundant and the browser usually ignores them.

In addition, most HTML browsers ignore any tag that they don't understand or that the document author specified incorrectly. Browsers habitually forge ahead and make some sense of a document, no matter how badly formed and error ridden it may be. This isn't just a tactic to overcome errors; it's also an important strategy for extensibility. Imagine how much harder it would be to add new features to the language if the existing base of browsers choked on them.

The thing to watch out for with nonstandard tags that aren't supported by most browsers is their enclosed contents, if any. Browsers that recognize the new tag may process those contents differently than those that don't support the new tag. For example, older browsers, some of which are still in use by many people today, don't support styles. Dutifully, they ignore the <style> tag, but then go on to render its contents on the user's screen, effectively defeating the tag's purpose in addition to ruining the document's appearance. [Document-Level Stylesheets, 8.1.2]

3.4 Well-Formed Documents and XHTML

XHTML is HTML's prissy cousin. What would pass most beauty contests as a very proper and complete HTML document, done according to the book and including end-paragraph tags, might well be rejected by the XML judges as a malformed file.

To conform with XML, XHTML insists that documents be "well formed." Among other things, that means that every tag must have an ending tag—even the ones like <br> and <hr> for which the HTML standard forbids the use of an end tag. With XHTML, the ending is placed inside the start tag: <br />, for example. [Handling Empty Elements, 16.3.3]

It also means that tag and attribute names are case-sensitive and, according to the current XHTML standard, must be in lowercase. Hence, only <head> is acceptable, and it is *not* the same as <HEAD> or <HeAd>, as it is with the HTML standard. [Case Sensitivity, 16.3.4]

Well-formed XHTML documents, like HTML standard ones, must also conform to proper nesting. No argument there. [Correctly Nested Elements, 16.3.1]

In their defense, the XML standard and its offspring, XHTML, emphasize extensibility. That way, <p> can mean the beginning of a paragraph in HTML, whereas another variant of the language may define the contents of the <P> tag to be election-poll results that display quite differently—perhaps in tabular form, with red, white, and blue stripes and accompanying patriotic music.

We will discuss this further in Chapters 15 and 16, in which we detail the XML and XHTML standards (and the Forces of Conformity).

3.5 Document Content

Nearly everything else you put into your HTML or XHTML document that isn't a tag is, by definition, content, and the majority of that is text. Like tags, document content is encoded using a specific character set—by default, the ISO-8859-1 Latin character set. This character set is a superset of conventional ASCII, adding the necessary characters to support the Western European languages. If your keyboard does not allow you to directly enter the characters you need, you can use character entities to insert the desired characters.

3.5.1 Advice Versus Control

Perhaps the hardest rule to remember when marking up an HTML or XHTML document is that all the tags you insert regarding text display and formatting are only advice for the browser: they do not explicitly control how the browser will display the document. In fact, the browser can choose to ignore all of your tags and do what it pleases with the document content. What's worse, the user (of all people!) has control over the text-display characteristics of her own browser.

Get used to this lack of control. The best way to use markup to control the appearance of your documents is to concentrate on the content of the document, not on its final appearance. If you find yourself worrying excessively about spacing, alignment, text breaks, and character positioning, you'll surely end up with ulcers. You will have gone beyond the intent of HTML. If you focus on delivering information to users in an attractive manner, using the tags to advise the browser as to how best to display that information, you are using HTML or XHTML effectively, and your documents will render well on a wide range of browsers.

3.5.2 Character Entities

Besides common text, HTML and XHTML give you a way to display special text characters that you normally might not be able to include in your source document or that have other purposes. A good example is the less-than or opening bracket symbol (<). In HTML, it normally signifies the start of a tag, so if you insert it simply as part of your text, the browser will get confused and probably misinterpret your document.

For both HTML and XHTML, the ampersand character (&) instructs the browser to use a special character, formally known as a *character entity*. For example, the command < inserts that pesky less-than symbol into the rendered text and the browser does not confuse it to mean the start of a tag. Similarly, > inserts the greater-than symbol, and & inserts an ampersand. There can be no spaces between the ampersand, the entity name, and the required, trailing semicolon. (Semicolons aren't special characters; you don't need to use an ampersand sequence to display a semicolon normally.) [Handling Special Characters, 16.3.7]

You also may replace the entity name after the ampersand with a pound symbol (#) and a decimal value corresponding to the entity's position in the character set. Hence, the sequence < does the same thing as < and represents the less-than symbol. In fact, you could substitute all the normal content characters within an HTML document with ampersand special characters, such as A for the capital letter A or a for its lowercase version, but that would be silly. You can find a complete listing of all characters and their names and numerical equivalents in Appendix F.

Keep in mind that not all special characters can be rendered by all browsers. Some browsers just ignore many of the special characters; with others, the characters aren't available in the character sets on a specific platform. Be sure to test your documents on a range of browsers before electing to use some of the more obscure character entities.

3.5.3 Comments

Comments are another type of textual content that appears in the source HTML document but is not rendered by the user's browser. Comments fall between the special <!-- and --> markup elements. Browsers ignore the text between the comment character sequences. Here are some sample comments:

```
<!-- This is a comment -->
<!-- This is a
multiple-line comment
that ends on this line -->
```

There must be a space after the initial <!-- and preceding the final -->, but otherwise you can put nearly anything inside the comment. The biggest exception to this rule is that the HTML standard doesn't let you nest comments.[*]

Internet Explorer also lets you place comments within a special, nonstandard <comment> tag. Everything between the <comment> and </comment> tags is ignored by

---

[*] Early versions of Netscape did let you nest comments, but no longer. The practice is tricky, so just say no.

Internet Explorer. All other browsers display the comment to the user. Obviously, because of this undesirable behavior, we do not recommend using the `<comment>` tag. Instead, always use the `<!--` and `-->` sequences to delimit comments.

Besides the obvious use of comments for source documentation, many web servers use comments to take advantage of features specific to the document server software. These servers scan the document for specific character sequences within conventional HTML/XHTML comments and then perform some action based upon the commands embedded in the comments. The action might be as simple as including text from another file (known as a *server-side include*) or as complex as executing other commands on the server to generate the document contents dynamically.

3.6 HTML/XHTML Document Elements

Every HTML document should conform to the HTML SGML DTD, the formal Document Type Definition that defines the HTML standard. The DTD defines the tags and syntax that are used to create an HTML document. You can inform the browser which DTD your document complies with by placing a special Standard Generalized Markup Language (SGML) command in the first line of the document:

```
<!DOCTYPE HTML PUBLIC "-//W3C//DTD HTML 4.01//EN">
```

This cryptic message indicates that your document is intended to be compliant with the HTML 4.01 final DTD defined by the World Wide Web Consortium (W3C). Other versions of the DTD define more restricted versions of the HTML standard, and not all browsers support all versions of the HTML DTD. In fact, specifying any other `<!DOCTYPE>` may cause the browser to misinterpret your document when displaying it for the user. It's also unclear what `<!DOCTYPE>` to use if you include nonstandard, albeit popular extensions in the HTML document—even for the deprecated HTML 3.0 standard, for which a DTD was never released.

HTML developers are increasingly including an appropriate SGML DOCTYPE command as a prefix in their HTML documents. Because of the confusion of versions and standards, if you do choose to include a DOCTYPE in your HTML document, choose the appropriate one to ensure that your document is rendered correctly.

For XHTML authors, we do strongly recommend that you include the proper DOCTYPE statement in your XHTML documents, in conformance with XML standards. Read Chapters 15 and 16 for more about DTDs and the XML and XHTML standards.

3.6.1 The `<html>` Tag

As we saw earlier, the `<html>` and `</html>` tags serve to delimit the beginning and end of a document. Since the typical browser can easily infer from the enclosed source that it is an HTML or XHTML document, you don't really need to include the tag in your source HTML document.

<html>

Function	Delimits a complete HTML or XHTML document
Attributes	dir ⏵, lang, version
End tag	</html>; may be omitted in HTML
Contains	*head_tag, body_tag, frames*

That said, it's considered good form to include this tag so that other tools, particularly more mundane text-processing ones, can recognize your document as an HTML document. At the very least, the presence of the beginning and end <html> tags ensures that the beginning or the end of the document has not inadvertently been deleted. Besides, XHTML requires the <html> and </html> tags.

Between <html> and </html> are the document's head and body. Within the head, you'll find tags that identify the document and define its place within a document collection. Within the body is the actual document content, defined by tags that determine the layout and appearance of the document text. As you might expect, the document head is contained within <head> and </head> tags and the body is within <body> and </body> tags, all of which we define in more detail later in this chapter.*

By far, the most common form of the <html> tag is simply:

```
<html>
document head and body content
</html>
```

3.6.1.1 The dir attribute

The dir attribute specifies in which direction the browser should render text within the containing element. When used within the <html> tag, it determines how text will be presented within the entire document. When used within another tag, it controls the text's direction for just the content of that tag.

By default, the value of this tag is ltr, indicating that text is presented to the user left to right. Use the other value, rtl, to display text right to left, for languages like Arabic and Hebrew. Of course, the results depend on your content and the browser's support of HTML 4 or XHTML. Netscape and Internet Explorer versions 4 and earlier ignore the dir attribute. The HTML 4-compliant Internet Explorer versions 5 and 6 simply right-justify (dir=rtl) the text, although if you look closely at Figure 3-2, you'll notice that the browser moves the punctuation (the period) to the other side of the sentence.

---

* For the special HTML/XHTML frame document, a <frameset> tag replaces the <body> tag; more about this in Chapter 11.

Netscape 6 right-justified everything, including the ending period, but versions 7 and 8 did not (yet another sign that the browser wars are over):

```
<html dir=rtl>
<head>
<title>Display Directions</title>
</head>
<body>
This is how IE 6 renders right-to-left directed text.
</body>
</html>
```

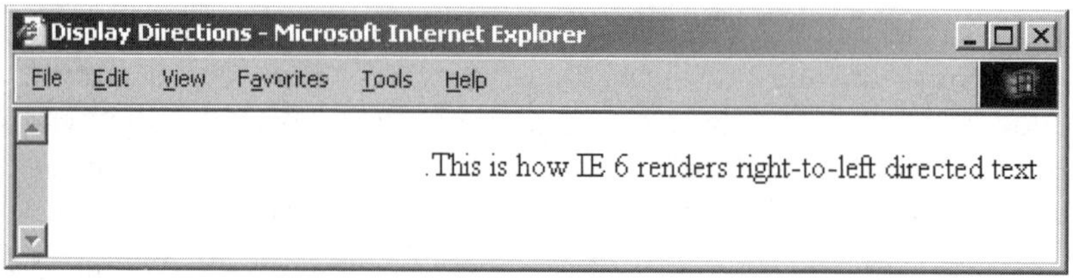

Figure 3-2. All current browsers just right-justify text with the dir attribute, and get the punctuation wrong, to boot

3.6.1.2 The lang attribute

When included within the <html> tag, the lang attribute specifies the language you've generally used within the document. When used within other tags, the lang attribute specifies the language you used within that tag's content. Ideally, browsers eventually will use lang to better render the text for the user.

Set the value of the lang attribute to an ISO-639 standard two-character language code. You may also indicate a dialect by following the International Organization for Standardization (ISO) language code with a dash and a subcode name. For example, "en" is the ISO language code for English; "en-US" is the complete code for U.S. English. Other common language codes include "fr" (French), "de" (German), "it" (Italian), "nl" (Dutch), "el" (Greek), "es" (Spanish), "pt" (Portuguese), "ar" (Arabic), "he" (Hebrew), "ru" (Russian), "zh" (Chinese), "ja" (Japanese), and "hi" (Hindi).

3.6.1.3 The version attribute

Use the version attribute to define the HTML standard version that you followed when composing the document. Its value, for HTML version 4.01, should read exactly:

```
version="-//W3C//DTD HTML 4.01//EN"
```

In general, version information within the <html> tag is more trouble than it is worth, and this attribute has been deprecated in HTML 4. Serious authors should instead use an SGML <!DOCTYPE> tag at the beginning of their documents, like this:

```
<!DOCTYPE HTML PUBLIC "-//W3C/DTD HTML 4.01//EN"
    "http://www.w3c.org/TR/html4/strict.dtd">
```

3.7 The Document Header

The document header describes the various properties of the document, including its title, position within the Web, and relationship with other documents. Most of the data contained within the document header is never actually rendered as content visible to the user.

3.7.1 The <head> Tag

The <head> tag serves to encapsulate other header tags. Place it at the beginning of your document, just after the <html> tag and before the <body> or <frameset> tag. Both the <head> tag and its corresponding end </head> tag can be unambiguously inferred by the browser and so can be safely omitted from an HTML, but not from an XHTML, document. We encourage you to include them in all your documents, since they promote readability and support document automation.

<table>
<tr><td colspan="2" align="center"><head></td></tr>
<tr><td>Function</td><td>Defines the document header</td></tr>
<tr><td>Attributes</td><td>dir, lang, profile</td></tr>
<tr><td>End tag</td><td></head>; rarely omitted in HTML</td></tr>
<tr><td>Contains</td><td>head_content</td></tr>
<tr><td>Used in</td><td>html_tag</td></tr>
</table>

The <head> tag may contain a number of other tags that help define and manage the document's content. These include, in any order of appearance: <base>, <isindex>, <link>, <meta>, <nextid>, <object>, <script>, <style>, and <title>.

3.7.1.1 The dir and lang attributes

As we discussed in the sections about the <html> tag attributes, dir and lang help extend HTML and XHTML to an international audience. [The dir attribute, 3.6.1.1] [The lang attribute, 3.6.1.2]

3.7.1.2 The profile attribute

Often, the header of a document contains a number of `<meta>` tags used to convey additional information about the document to the browser. In the future, authors may use predefined profiles of standard document metadata to better describe their documents. The `profile` attribute supplies the URL of the profile associated with the current document.

The format of a profile and how a browser might use it are not yet defined; this attribute is primarily a placeholder for future development.

3.7.2 The <title> Tag

The `<title>` tag does exactly what you might expect: the words you place inside its beginning and end tags define the title for your document. (This stuff is pretty much self-explanatory and easier than you might think at first glance.) The browser uses the title in some special manner, and it is most often placed in the browser window's title bar or on a status line. Usually, too, the title becomes the default name for a link to the document if the document is added to a link collection or to a user's favorites or bookmarks list.

<title>	
Function	Defines the document title
Attributes	`dir`, `lang`
End tag	`</title>`; never omitted
Contains	*plain_text*
Used in	*head_content*

The `<title>` tag is the only thing required within a document's head. Because the `<head>` tag itself and even the `<html>` tag can safely be omitted, the `<title>` tag could be the first line within a valid HTML document. Beyond that, most browsers will even supply a generic title for documents lacking a `<title>` tag, such as the document's filename, so you don't even have to supply a title. That goes a bit too far even for our down-and-dirty tastes, though. No respectable author should serve up a document missing the `<title>` tag and a title.

When you do include a `<title>`, don't forget to close it with the `</title>` end tag. Otherwise, your title's text ends up displayed in the body of your document, even though it may precede the `<body>` tag.

Browsers do not specially format title text, and they ignore anything other than text inside the title beginning and end tags. For instance, they will ignore any images or links to other documents.

Here's an even barer barebones example of a valid HTML document, to highlight the header and title tags; watch what happens when Netscape displays it in Figure 3-3:

```
<html>
<head>
<title>HTML and XHTML: The Definitive Guide</title>
</head>
</html>
```

Figure 3-3. What's in a <title>?

3.7.2.1 What's in a title?

Selecting the right title is crucial to defining a document and ensuring that it can be effectively used on the Web.

Keep in mind that users can access each document in your collection in nearly any order and independently of one another. Each document's title should therefore define the document both within the context of your other documents and on its own merits.

Titles that include references to document sequencing are usually inappropriate. Simple titles, like "Chapter 2" and "Part VI," do little to help a user understand what the document might contain. More descriptive titles, such as "Chapter 2: Advanced Square Dancing" and "Part VI: Churchill's Youth and Adulthood," convey both a sense of place within a larger set of documents and specific content that invites the reader to read on.

Self-referential titles also aren't very useful. A title such as "Home Page" is completely content-free, as are titles like "Feedback Page" and "Popular Links." You want a title to convey a sense of content and purpose so that users can decide, based upon the title alone, whether to visit that page. "The Kumquat Lover's Home Page" is descriptive and likely to draw in lovers of the bitter fruit, as are "Kumquat Lover's Feedback Page" and "Popular Links Frequented by Kumquat Lovers."

People spend a great deal of time creating documents for the Web, often only to squander that effort with an uninviting, ineffective title. As special software that automatically collects links for users becomes more prevalent on the Web, the only descriptive phrases associated with your pages when they are inserted into some vast link database will be the titles you choose for them. We can't emphasize this enough: take care to select descriptive, useful, context-independent titles for each of your documents.

3.7.2.2 The dir and lang attributes

The dir and lang attributes help extend HTML and XHTML to an international audience. [The dir attribute, 3.6.1.1] [The lang attribute, 3.6.1.2]

3.7.3 Related Header Tags

Other tags you may include within the <head> tag deal with specific aspects of document creation, management, linking, automation, or layout. That's why we only mention them here and describe them in greater detail in other, more appropriate sections and chapters of this book. Briefly, the special header tags are:

<base> *and* <link>
> Define the current document's base location and relationship to other documents. [<base>, 6.7.1] [<link>, 6.7.2]

<isindex>
> Deprecated in HTML 4, the <isindex> tag at one time could be used to create automatic document indexing forms, allowing users to search databases of information using the current document as a querying tool. [<isindex>, 6.6.1]

<nextid>
> Not supported in HTML 4 or XHTML, the <nextid> tag tried to make creation of unique labels easier when using document automation tools. [<nextid>, 6.8.2]

<meta>
> Provides additional document data not supplied by any of the other <head> tags. [<meta>, 6.8.1]

<object>
> Defines methods by which the browser can render nonstandard objects. [<object>, 12.2.1]

<script>
> Defines one or more scripts that elements within the document can invoke. [<script>, 12.3.1]

<style>
> Lets you create Cascading Style Sheet (CSS) properties to control body-content display characteristics for the entire document. [<style>, 8.1.2]

3.8 The Document Body

The document body is the meat of the matter. It's where you put the contents of your document. The beginning <body> and end </body> tags delimit the document body.

3.8.1 The <body> Tag

Within HTML 4 and XHTML, the <body> tag has a number of attributes that control the color and background of your document. Various browsers have extended the tag to give even greater control over your document's appearance.

<body>

Function	Defines the document body
Attributes	alink, background, bgcolor, bgproperties, class, dir, id, lang, leftmargin, link, onBlur, onClick, onDblClick, onFocus, onKeyDown, onKeyPress, onKeyUp, onLoad, onMouseDown, onMouseMove, onMouseOut, onMouseOver, onMouseUp, onUnload, style, text, title, topmargin, vlink
End tag	</body>; may be omitted in HTML
Contains	body_content
Used in	html_tag

Anything between the beginning <body> and end </body> tags is called *body content*. The simplest document might have only a sequence of text paragraphs within the <body> tag. More complex documents might include heavily formatted text, graphical figures, tables, and a variety of special effects.

Because the browser can infer the position of the <body> and </body> tags, they can safely be omitted from an HTML, but not an XHTML, document. Like the <html> and <head> tags, we recommend that you include both the <body> and </body> tags in your HTML documents, too, to make them more easily readable and maintainable.

The various attributes for the <body> tag can be loosely grouped into three sets: those that give you some control over the document's appearance, those that associate programmable functions with the document itself, and those that label and identify the body for later reference. We address the appearance attributes (alink, background, bgcolor, bgproperties, leftmargin, link, text, topmargin, and vlink) in Chapter 5; the class and style attributes for CSS in Chapter 8; JavaScript stylesheets and the programmatic attributes (the "on-event" ones) in Chapter 12; the language attributes (dir and lang) earlier in this chapter; and the identification attributes (id and title) in Chapter 4. [The dir attribute, 3.6.1.1] [The lang attribute, 3.6.1.2] [The id attribute, 4.1.1.4] [The title attribute, 4.1.1.5]

3.8.2 Frames

The HTML and XHTML standards define a special type of document in which you replace the <body> tag with one or more <frameset> tags. This so-called *frame* document divides the display window into one or more independent windows, each displaying a different document. We thoroughly describe this innovation in Chapter 11.

3.9 Editorial Markup

HTML 4.0 introduced two tags that can help groups of authors collaborate in the development of documents and maintain some semblance of editorial and version control. The insert (<ins>) and delete (<del>) tags respectively let you either designate portions of your document's body as new or added content or designate old stuff that should be replaced. And with special attributes, you can indicate when you made the change (datetime) and a reference to a document that may explain the change (cite).

3.9.1 The <ins> and <del> Tags

The <ins> and <del> tags let authors set off portions of body content that they intend to add to or delete from the current versions of their documents. HTML 4/XHTML-compliant browsers display the contents of the <ins> and <del> tags in some special way so that readers can quickly scan the document for the changes.

<ins> and <del>

Function	Define inserted and deleted document content (see Figure 3-4)
Attributes	cite, class, datetime, dir, id, lang, onClick, onDblClick, onKeyDown, onKeyPress, onKeyUp, onMouseDown, onMouseMove, onMouseOut, onMouseOver, onMouseUp, style, title
End tag	</ins> and </del>; never omitted
Contains	body_content
Used in	body_content

Netscape 4 and earlier versions ignore the tags, as did Internet Explorer 4 and its earlier versions. All current popular browsers now support the tags.

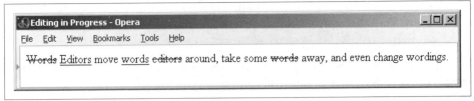

Figure 3-4. The <ins> and <del> tags in action

3.9.1.1 The cite attribute

The cite attribute lets you document the reasons for the insertion or deletion. Its value must be a URL that points to some other document that explains the inserted/deleted text. How a browser treats cite is a question for the future.

3.9.1.2 The datetime attribute

Although the reason for the change is important, knowing when a change was made is often more important. The datetime attribute for the <ins> and <del> tags takes a single value: a specially encoded date and timestamp. The rigorous format for the datetime value is YYYY-MM-DDThh:mm:ssTZD. The components are:

- YYYY is the year, such as 1998 or 2010.
- MM is the month; 01 for January through 12 for December.
- DD is the day; 01 through 31.
- T is a required character designating the beginning of the time segment of the stamp.
- hh is the hour in 24-hour format; 00 (midnight) through 23 (11 p.m.). (Add a following colon if you include the minutes.)
- mm are the minutes on the hour; 00 through 59. (Add a following colon if you include the seconds.)
- ss are the seconds; 00 through 59.
- TZD is the time-zone designator. It can be one of three values: Z, indicating Greenwich Mean Time,* or the hours, minutes, and seconds before (-) or after (+) Coordinated Universal Time (UTC), where time is relative to the time in Greenwich, England.

---

* Greenwich Mean Time is also know as "Zulu," thus the value of "Z."

For example:

```
2007-02-22T14:26Z
```

decodes to February 22, 2007 at 2:26 p.m. Greenwich Mean Time. To specify Eastern Standard Time, the code for the same time and date is:

```
2003-02-22T09:26-05:00
```

Notice that the local time zone may change depending on where the document gets edited, whereas the universal time will stay the same.

3.9.1.3 The class, dir, event, id, lang, style, title, and events attributes

There are several nearly universal attributes for the many HTML and XHTML tags. These attributes give you a common way to identify (title) and label (id) a tag's contents for later reference or automated treatment, to change the contents' display characteristics (class, style), and to reference the language used (lang) and related direction the text should flow (dir). There are also input events that may happen in and around the tagged contents that you may react to via an on-event attribute and some programming. [The dir attribute, 3.6.1.1] [The lang attribute, 3.6.1.2] [The id attribute, 4.1.1.4] [The id attribute, 4.1.1.4] [Inline Styles: The style Attribute, 8.1.1] [Style Classes, 8.3] [JavaScript Event Handlers, 12.3.3]

3.9.2 Using Editorial Markup

The uses of <ins> and <del> are obvious to anyone who has used a "boilerplate" document or form or has collaborated with others in the preparation of a document.

For example, law firms typically have a collection of online legal documents that are specially completed for each client. Law clerks usually do the "fill in," and the final document gets reviewed by a lawyer. To highlight those changes in the document so that they are readily evident to the reviewer, you might use the <ins> tag to indicate added text and the <del> tag to mark the text that was replaced. Optionally, use the cite and datetime attributes to indicate why and when the changes were made.

For example, the clerk might fill in a boilerplate document with the law firm's and representative's names, indicating the time and source for the change:

```
The party of the first part, as represented by
<ins datetime=2002-06-22T08:30Z
     cite="http://www.mull+dull.com/tom_muller.html">
Thomas Muller of Muller and Duller
</ins>
<del>[insert representation here]</del>
```

The editorial markup tags could also be used by editing tools to denote how documents were modified as authors make changes over a period of time. With the correct use of the `cite` and `datetime` attributes, it would be possible to recreate a version of a document from a specific point in time.

3.10 The <bdo> Tag

As we mentioned earlier, the authors of the HTML 4 standard made a concerted effort to include standard ways that web agents (browsers) are supposed to treat and display the many different human languages and dialects. Accordingly, the HTML 4 standard and its progeny, XHTML, contain the universal `dir` and `lang` attributes that let you explicitly advise the browser that the whole document or specific tagged segments within it are in a particular language. These language-related attributes, then, may affect some display characteristics; for example, the `dir` attribute tells the browser to write the words across the display from either left to right (`dir=ltr`), as for most Western languages, or right to left (`dir=rtl`), as for many Asian languages. [The dir attribute, 3.6.1.1] [The lang attribute, 3.6.1.2]

The various Unicode and ISO standards for language encoding and display may conflict with your best intentions. In particular, the contents of some other documents, such as a Multipurpose Internet Mail Extension (MIME)-encoded file, may already be properly formatted, and your document may misadvise the browser to undo that encoding. Hence, the HTML 4 and XHTML standards have the `<bdo>` tag. With it, you override any current and inherited `dir` specifications. And with the tag's required `dir` attribute, you definitively specify the direction in which the tag's contents should be displayed.

For example, Figure 3-5 shows how Internet Explorer handles the following HTML fragment containing a `<bdo>` redirection:

```
<bdo dir=rtl>This would be readable if in Chinese, perhaps.</bdo>
Back to the Western way of reading and writing.
```

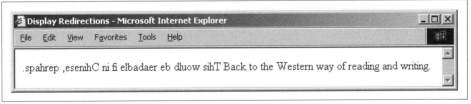

Figure 3-5. Tricks with <bdo> redirected text flow

Admittedly, the effects of the `<bdo>` tag are a bit esoteric, and the opportunities to use it currently are rare.

`<bdo>`

Function	Overrides bidirectional algorithms for content display
Attributes	class, dir, id, lang, style, title
End tag	`</bdo>`; never omitted
Contains	*text*
Used in	*body_content*

CHAPTER 4

Text Basics

Any successful presentation, even a thoughtful tome, should have its text organized into an attractive, effective document. Organizing text into attractive and effective documents is HTML and XHTML's forte. The languages give you a number of tools that help you mold your text and get your message across. They also help structure your document so that your target audience has easy access to your words.

Always keep in mind while designing your documents (here we go again!) that the markup tags, particularly with regard to text, only advise—they do not dictate—how a browser will ultimately render the document. Rendering varies from browser to browser. Don't get too entangled with trying to get just the right look and layout. Your attempts may and probably will be thwarted by the browser.

4.1 Divisions and Paragraphs

Like most text processors, a browser wraps the words it finds to fit the horizontal width of its viewing window. Widen the browser's window, and words automatically flow upward to fill the wider lines. Squeeze the window, and words wrap downward.

Unlike most text processors, however, HTML and XHTML use explicit division (`<div>`), paragraph (`<p>`), and line-break (`<br>`) tags to control the alignment and flow of text. Return characters, although quite useful for readability of the source document, typically are ignored by the browser—authors must use the `<br>` tag to explicitly force a common text line break. The `<p>` tag, while also causing a line break, carries with it meaning and effects beyond a simple return.

The `<div>` tag is a little different. When originally codified in the HTML 3.2 standard, `<div>` was meant to be a simple organizational tool—to divide the document into discrete sections. That somewhat obtuse meaning meant few authors used it. But recent innovations (alignment, styles, and the `id` attribute for document referencing and automation) now let you more distinctly label and thereby define individual sections of your documents, as well as control the alignment and appearance of those sections. These features breathe real life and meaning into the `<div>` tag.

By associating an `id` and a `class` name with the various sections of your document, each delimited by a `<div id=name class=name>` tag and attributes (you can do the same with other tags, like `<p>`, too), you not only label those divisions for later reference by a hyperlink and for automated processing and management (collecting all the bibliography divisions, for instance), but you may also define different, distinct display styles for those portions of your document. For instance, you might define one divisional class for your document's abstract (`<div class=abstract>`, for example), another for the body, a third for the conclusion, and a fourth divisional class for the bibliography (`<div class=biblio>`, for example).

Each class, then, might be given a different display definition in a document-level or externally related stylesheet: for example, the abstract indented and in an italic typeface (such as `div.abstract {left-margin: +0.5in; font-style: italic}`); the body in a left-justified roman typeface; the conclusion similar to the abstract; and the bibliography automatically numbered and formatted appropriately.

We provide a detailed description of stylesheets, classes, and their applications in Chapter 8.

4.1.1 The <div> Tag

As defined in the HTML 4.01 and XHTML 1.0 and 1.1 standards, a `<div>` tag divides your document into separate, distinct sections. It may be used strictly as an organizational tool, without any sort of formatting associated with it, but it becomes more effective if you add the `id` and `class` attributes to label the divisions. The `<div>` tag also may be combined with the `align` attribute to control the alignment of whole sections of your document's content in the display and with the many programmatic "on event" attributes for user interaction.

4.1.1.1 The align attribute

The `align` attribute for `<div>` positions the enclosed content to the `left` (default), `center`, or `right` of the display. In addition, you can specify `justify` to align both the left and the right margins of the text. The `<div>` tag may be nested, and the alignment of the nested `<div>` tag takes precedence over the containing `<div>` tag. Further, other nested alignment tags, such as `<center>`, aligned paragraphs (see `<p>` in section 4.1.2), or specially aligned table rows and cells override the effects of `<div>`. Like the `align` attribute for other tags, it is deprecated in the HTML and XHTML standards in deference to stylesheet-based layout controls.

\<div>

Function	Defines a block of text
Attributes	`align`, `class`, `dir`, `id`, `lang`, `nowrap` 🔲, `onClick`, `onDblClick`, `onKeyDown`, `onKeyPress`, `onKeyUp`, `onMouseDown`, `onMouseMove`, `onMouseOut`, `onMouseOver`, `onMouseUp`, `style`, `title`
End tag	`</div>`; usually omitted in HTML
Contains	*body_content*
Used in	*block*

4.1.1.2 The nowrap attribute

Supported by Internet Explorer and Opera, but not Firefox or Netscape Navigator, the `nowrap` attribute suppresses automatic word wrapping of the text within the division. Line breaks will occur only where you have placed carriage returns in your source document.

While the `nowrap` attribute probably doesn't make much sense for large sections of text that would otherwise be flowed together on the page, it can make things a bit easier when creating blocks of text with many explicit line breaks: poetry, for example, or addresses. You don't have to insert all those explicit `<br>` tags in a text flow within a `<div nowrap>` tag. On the other hand, a large number of users with browsers that ignore the `nowrap` attribute will see your text flow merrily along. If you are targeting only Internet Explorer or Opera with your documents, consider using `nowrap` where needed, but otherwise, we can't recommend this attribute for general use.

4.1.1.3 The dir and lang attributes

The `dir` attribute lets you advise the browser in which direction the text should be displayed, and the `lang` attribute lets you specify the language used within the division. [The dir attribute, 3.6.1.1] [The lang attribute, 3.6.1.2]

4.1.1.4 The id attribute

Use the `id` attribute to label the document division for later reference by a hyperlink, stylesheet, applet, or other automated process. In general, an acceptable `id` value is any quote-enclosed string that uniquely identifies the division and that later can be used to reference that document section unambiguously. Specifically, the value must begin with a letter, and can contain letters, numbers, hyphens, colons, underscores, and periods, but not spaces. Although we're introducing it within the context of the `<div>` tag, this attribute can be used with almost any tag.

When used as an element label, the value of the id attribute can be added to a URL to address the labeled element uniquely within the document. You can label both large portions of content (via a tag like <div>) and small snippets of text (using a tag like <i> or <span>). For example, you might label the abstract of a technical report using <div id="abstract">. A URL could jump right to that abstract by referencing report.html#abstract. When used in this manner, the value of the id attribute must be unique with respect to all other id attributes within the document and all the names defined by any <a> tags with the name attribute. [Linking Within a Document, 6.3.3]

When used as a stylesheet selector, the value of the id attribute is the name of a style rule that can be associated with the current tag. This provides a second set of definable style rules, similar to the various style classes you may create. A tag can use both the class and the id attributes to apply two different rules to a single tag. In this case, the name associated with the id attribute must be unique with respect to all other style IDs within the current document. You can find a more complete description of style classes and IDs in Chapter 8.

4.1.1.5 The title attribute

Use the optional title attribute and quote-enclosed string value to associate a descriptive phrase with the division. Like the id attribute, the title attribute can be used with almost any tag and behaves similarly for all tags.

There is no standards-defined usage for the value of the title attribute, but current browsers display the title when the mouse pauses over that element—in this case, anywhere in the <div>-defined text area. For example, use the title attribute to provide helpful tips within your document.

4.1.1.6 The class and style attributes

Use the style attribute with the <div> tag to create an inline style for the content enclosed by the tag. The class attribute lets you apply the style of a predefined class of the <div> tag to the contents of this division. The value of the class attribute is the name of a style defined in some document-level or externally defined stylesheet. In addition, class-identified divisions lend themselves well to computer processing of your documents; for example, extracting all divisions with the class name "biblio," for the automated assembly of a master bibliography. [Inline Styles: The style Attribute, 8.1.1] [Style Classes, 8.3]

4.1.1.7 Event attributes

Many user-related events may happen in and around a division, such as when a user clicks or double-clicks the mouse within its display space. The browser recognizes these events if it conforms to the current HTML or XHTML standard (all the popular ones do). With the respective on attribute and value, you may react to those events by displaying a user dialog box or activating some multimedia event. [JavaScript Event Handlers, 12.3.3]

4.1.2 The <p> Tag

The <p> tag signals the start of a paragraph. That's not well known even by some vet-eran webmasters, because it runs counterintuitive to what we've come to expect from experience. Most word processors we're familiar with use just one special character, typically the return character, to signal the *end* of a paragraph, not the beginning. By contrast, in HTML and XHTML, each paragraph should start with the paragraph tag <p> and end with the corresponding </p> end tag. Moreover, while a series of newline or return characters in a text processor-displayed document, created when the author hits the Enter key repeatedly, creates an empty paragraph for each one, browsers typi-cally ignore all but the first paragraph tag, as well as newline characters.

In practice, with HTML you can ignore the starting <p> tag at the beginning of the first paragraph and the </p> tags at the end of each paragraph: they can be implied from other tags that occur in the document and hence safely omitted.* For example:

```
<body>
This is the first paragraph, at the very beginning of the body of
this document.
<p>
The tag above signals the start of this second paragraph. When rendered
by a browser, it will begin slightly below the end of the first paragraph,
with a bit of extra whitespace between the two paragraphs.
<p>
This is the last paragraph in the example.
</body>
```

Notice that we haven't included the paragraph start tag (<p>) for the first paragraph or any end paragraph tags; they can be unambiguously inferred by the HTML browser and are therefore unnecessary.

<p>	
Function	Defines a paragraph of text
Attributes	align, class, dir, id, lang, onDblClick, onKeyDown, onKeyPress, onKeyUp, onMouseDown, onMouseMove, onMouseOut, onMouseOver, onMouseUp, style, title
End tag	</p>; often omitted in HTML
Contains	*text*
Used in	*block*

* XHTML, on the other hand, requires explicit starting and ending tags.

In general, you'll find that human document authors tend to omit postulated tags whenever possible, and automatic document generators tend to insert them. That may be because the software designers didn't want to run the risk of having their products chided by competitors as not adhering to the HTML standard, even though we're splitting letter-of-the-law hairs here. Go ahead and be defiant: omit that first paragraph's <p> tag and don't give a second thought to paragraph-ending </p> tags—provided, of course, that your document's structure and clarity are not compromised (that is, as long as you are aware that XHTML frowns severely on such laxity, too).

4.1.2.1 Paragraph rendering

When encountering a new paragraph (<p>) tag, the browser typically inserts one blank line plus some extra vertical space into the display before starting the new paragraph. The browser then collects all the words and, if present, inline images into the new paragraph, ignoring leading and trailing spaces (not spaces between words, of course) and return characters in the source text. The browser software then flows the resulting sequence of words and images into a paragraph that fits within the margins of its display window, automatically generating line breaks as needed to wrap the text within the window. For example, compare how a browser arranges the text into lines and paragraphs (Figure 4-1) to how the preceding example is printed on the page. The browser may also automatically hyphenate long words, and the paragraph may be full-justified to stretch the line of words out toward both margins.

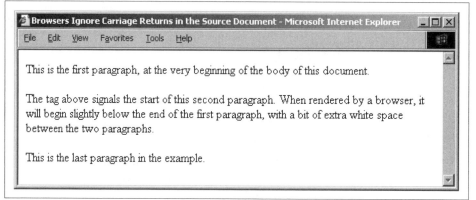

Figure 4-1. Browsers ignore common return characters in the source HTML/XHTML document

The net result is that you do not have to worry about line length, word wrap, and line breaks when composing your documents. The browser will take any arbitrary sequence of words and images and display a nicely formatted paragraph.

If you want to control line length and breaks explicitly, consider using a preformatted text block with the <pre> tag. If you need to force a line break, use the <br> tag. [<pre>, 4.6.5] [
, 4.6.1]

4.1.2.2 The align attribute

Most browsers automatically left-justify a new paragraph. To change this behavior, HTML 4 and XHTML give you the align attribute for the `<p>` tag and provide four kinds of content justification: left, right, center, and justify.

Figure 4-2 shows the effect of various alignments as rendered from the following source:

```
<p align=right>
Right over here!
<br>
This is too.
<p align=left>
Slide back left.
<p align=center>
Smack in the middle.
</p>
Left is the default.
```

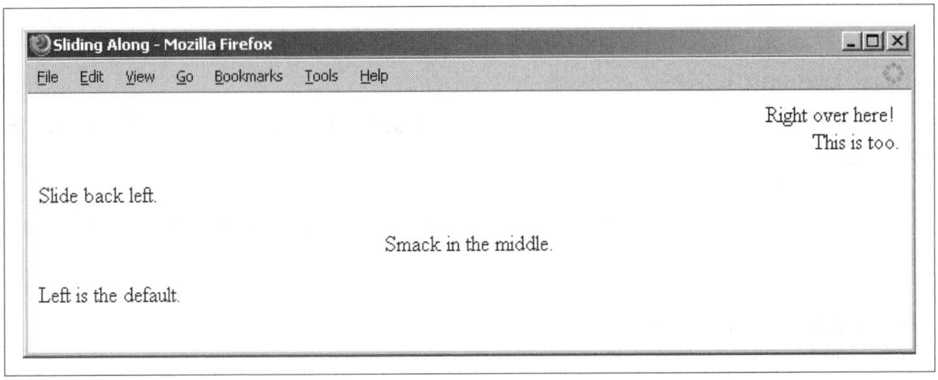

Figure 4-2. Effect of the align attribute on paragraph justification

Notice in the HTML example that the paragraph alignment remains in effect until the browser encounters another `<p>` tag or an ending `</p>` tag. We deliberately left out a final `<p>` tag in the example to illustrate the effects of the `</p>` end tag on paragraph justification. Other body elements—including forms, headers, tables, and most other body content-related tags—may also disrupt the current paragraph alignment and cause subsequent paragraphs to revert to the default left alignment.

Note that the align attribute is deprecated in HTML 4 and XHTML, in deference to stylesheet-based alignments.

4.1.2.3 The dir and lang attributes

The dir attribute lets you advise the browser in which direction the text within the paragraph should be displayed, and the lang attribute lets you specify the language used within that paragraph. The dir and lang attributes are supported by the popular browsers, even though there are no behaviors defined for any specific language. [The dir attribute, 3.6.1.1] [The lang attribute, 3.6.1.2]

4.1.2.4 The class, id, style, and title attributes

Use the id attribute to create a label for the paragraph that can later be used to unambiguously reference that paragraph in a hyperlink target, for automated searches, as a stylesheet selector, and with a host of other applications. [The id attribute, 4.1.1.4]

Use the optional title attribute and quote-enclosed string value to provide a descriptive phrase for the paragraph. [The title attribute, 4.1.1.5]

Use the style attribute with the <p> tag to create an inline style for the paragraph's contents. The class attribute lets you label the paragraph with a name that refers to a predefined class of the <p> tag previously declared in some document-level or externally defined stylesheet. Class-identified paragraphs lend themselves well to computer processing of your documents—for example, extracting all paragraphs whose class name is "citation," for automated assembly of a master list of citations. [Inline Styles: The style Attribute, 8.1.1] [Style Classes, 8.3]

4.1.2.5 Event attributes

As with divisions, a browser recognizes many user-initiated events, such as when a user clicks or double-clicks within a tag's display space, if the browser conforms to the current HTML or XHTML standard. With the respective on attribute and value, you may react to those events by displaying a user dialog box or activating some multimedia event. [JavaScript Event Handlers, 12.3.3]

4.1.2.6 Allowed paragraph content

A paragraph may contain any element allowed in a text flow, including conventional words and punctuation, links (<a>), images (<img>), line breaks (<br>), font changes (<b>, <i>, <tt>, <u>, <strike>, <big>, <small>, <sup>, <sub>, and <font>), and content-based style changes (<acronym>, <cite>, <code>, <dfn>, <em>, <kbd>, <samp>, <strong>, and <var>). If any other element occurs within the paragraph, it implies that the paragraph has ended, and the browser assumes that the closing </p> tag was not specified.

4.1.2.7 Allowed paragraph usage

You may specify a paragraph only within a *block*, along with other paragraphs, lists, forms, and preformatted text. In general, this means that paragraphs can appear where a flow of text is appropriate, such as in the body of a document, in an element in a list, and so on. Technically, paragraphs cannot appear within a header, anchor, or other element whose content is strictly text-only. In practice, most browsers ignore this restriction and format the paragraph as a part of the containing element.

4.2 Headings

Users have a hard enough time reading what's displayed on a screen. A long flow of text, unbroken by title, subtitles, and other headers, crosses the eyes and numbs the mind, not to mention the fact that it makes it nearly impossible to scan the text for a specific topic.

You should always break a flow of text into several smaller sections within one or more headings (like this book). There are six levels of HTML/XHTML headings that you can use to structure a text flow into a more readable, more manageable document. And, as we discuss in Chapters 5 and 8, there are a variety of graphical and text-style tricks that help divide your document and make its contents more accessible as well as more readable.

4.2.1 Heading Tags

The six heading tags—written as <h1>, <h2>, <h3>, <h4>, <h5>, and <h6>—indicate the highest (<h1>) to lowest (<h6>) precedence a heading may have in the document.

<h1>, <h2>, <h3>, <h4>, <h5>, <h6>

Function	Define one of six levels of headers
Attributes	align, class, dir, id, lang, onClick, onDblClick, onKeyDown, onKeyPress, onKeyUp, onMouseDown, onMouseMove, onMouseOut, onMouseOver, onMouseUp, style, title
End tag	</h1>, </h2>, </h3>, </h4>, </h5>, </h6>; never omitted
Contains	*text*
Used in	*body_content*

The text enclosed within a heading typically is rendered by the browser uniquely, depending upon the display technology available to it. The browser may choose to center, format in boldface, enlarge, italicize, underline, or change the color of headings to make each stand out within the document. And in order to thwart the most tedious writers, often users themselves can alter how a browser renders the different headings.

Fortunately, in practice most browsers use a diminishing character point size for the sequence of headers so that <h1> text is quite large and <h6> text is quite minuscule (see Figure 4-3, for example).

By tradition, authors have come to use <h1> headers for document titles, <h2> headers for section titles, and so on, often matching the way many of us were taught to outline our work with heads, subheads, and sub-subheads.

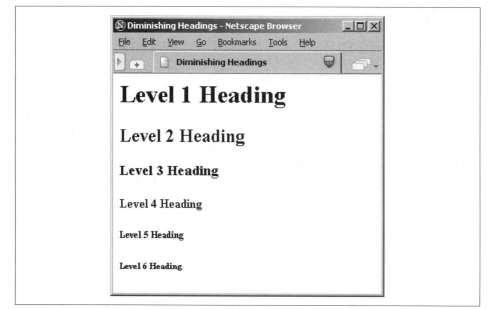

Figure 4-3. Browsers typically use diminishing text sizes for rendering headings

Finally, don't forget to include the appropriate heading end tags in your document. The browser won't insert them automatically for you, and omitting the ending tag for a heading can have disastrous consequences for your document.

4.2.1.1 The align attribute

The default heading alignment for most browsers is left. As with the <div> and <p> tags, the align attribute can change the alignment to left, center, right, or justify. Figure 4-4 shows these alternative alignments as rendered from the following source:

```
<h1 align=right>Right over here!</h1>
<h2 align=left>Slide back left.</h2>
<h3 align=center>Smack in the middle.</h3>
```

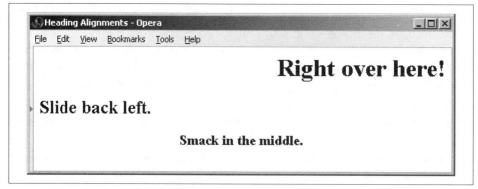

Figure 4-4. The heading's align attribute in action

The justify value for align is not yet supported by any browser, and don't hold your breath. The align attribute is deprecated in HTML 4 and XHTML, in deference to stylesheet-based controls.

4.2.1.2 The dir and lang attributes

The dir attribute lets you advise the browser in which direction the text within that paragraph should be displayed, and lang lets you specify the language used within the heading. [The dir attribute, 3.6.1.1] [The lang attribute, 3.6.1.2]

4.2.1.3 The class, id, style, and title attributes

Use the id attribute to create a label for the heading that can later be used to unambiguously reference that heading in a hyperlink target, for automated searches, as a stylesheet selector, and with a host of other applications. [The id attribute, 4.1.1.4]

Use the optional title attribute and quote-enclosed string value to provide a descriptive phrase for the heading. [The title attribute, 4.1.1.5]

Use the style attribute with the heading tags to create an inline style for the headings' contents. The class attribute lets you label the heading with a name that refers to a predefined class declared in some document-level or externally defined stylesheet. [Inline Styles: The style Attribute, 8.1.1] [Style Classes, 8.3]

4.2.1.4 Event attributes

Each user-initiated event that may happen in and around a heading is recognized by the browser if it conforms to the HTML or XHTML standard. With the respective on attribute and value, you may react to that event by displaying a user dialog box or activating some multimedia event. [JavaScript Event Handlers, 12.3.3]

4.2.2 Appropriate Use of Headings

It's often good form to repeat your document's title in the first heading tag because the title you specify in the <head> of your document doesn't appear in the user's main display window. The following HTML segment is a good example of repeating the document's title in the header and in the body of the document:

```
<html>
<head>
<title>Kumquat Farming in North America</title>
</head>
<body>
<h3>Kumquat Farming in North America</h3>
<p>
Perhaps one of the most enticing of all fruits is the...
```

Typically, the browser places the <title> text along the top of the main display. It may also place the title elsewhere in the document window and use it to create bookmarks or favorites entries, all of which vaguely are somewhere on the user's desktop. The level-three title heading in this example, on the other hand, will always appear at the very beginning of the document display. It serves as a visible title to the document, regardless of how the browser handles the `<title>` tag's contents. And, unlike the `<title>` text, the heading title gets printed at the beginning of the first page should the user elect to print the document, because it is part of the main text.[<title>, 3.7.2]

In our example, we chose to use a level-three heading (`<h3>`) whose rendered font typically is just a bit larger than the regular document text. Levels one and two are larger still and often are a bit overbearing. Choose a level of heading that you find useful and attractive and use that level consistently throughout your documents. Too big and it overwhelms the display window; too small and it's easily missed visually.

Once you have established the top-level heading for your document, use additional headings at the same or lower levels throughout to add structure and "scanability" to the document. If you use a level-three heading for the document title, for example, break your document into subsections using level-four headings. If you have the urge to subdivide your text further, consider using a level-two heading for the title, level three for the section dividers, and level four for the subsections.

4.2.3 Using Headings for Smaller Text

For most graphical browsers, the fonts used to display `<h1>`, `<h2>`, and `<h3>` headers are larger, `<h4>` is the same, and `<h5>` and `<h6>` are smaller than the regular text size. Authors typically use the latter two sizes for boilerplate text, such as a disclaimer or a copyright notice. Though style rules ought to be used instead, some authors use headers for their smaller text to format tables of contents or home pages that display a site's contents. Experiment with `<h5>` and `<h6>` to get the effect you want. Figure 4-5 shows how a typical browser renders the copyright reference in the following sample XHTML segment:

```
resulting in years of successful kumquat production
throughout North America.
</p>
<h6>This document copyright 2007 by the Kumquat Growers of
America. All rights reserved.</h6>
</body>
</html>
```

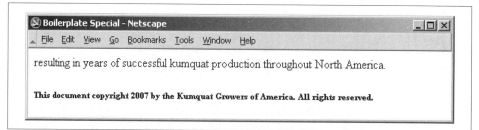

Figure 4-5. HTML/XHTML authors typically use heading level six for boilerplate text

4.2.4 Allowed Heading Content

A heading may contain any element allowed in text, including conventional text, hyperlinks (<a>), images (<img>), line breaks (<br>), font embellishments (<b>, <i>, <tt>, <u>, <strike>, <big>, <small>, <sup>, <sub>, and <font>), and content-based styles (<acronym>, <cite>, <code>, <dfn>, <em>, <kbd>, <samp>, <strong>, and <var>). In practice, however, font or style changes may not take effect within a heading because the heading itself prescribes a font change within the browser.

At one time early on, there was widespread abuse of the heading tags as a way to change the font of entire sections of a document. Technically, paragraphs, lists, and other block elements are not allowed within a heading and may be mistaken by the browser to indicate the implied end of the heading. In practice, most browsers apply the style of the heading to all contained paragraphs. We discourage this practice because it is not only a violation of HTML and XHTML standards, but also is usually ugly to look at. Imagine if your local paper printed all the copy in headline type!

Large sections of heading text defeat the purpose of the tag. If you really want to change the font or type sizes in your document, use the standard cascading style definitions. See Chapter 8 for details.

We strongly recommend that you carefully test your pages with more than one browser and at several different resolutions. As you might expect, your <h6> text may be readable at 640×480 resolution, but may disappear on a 1280×1024 display.

4.2.5 Allowed Heading Usage

Formally, the HTML and XHTML standards allow headings only within body content. In practice, most browsers recognize headings almost anywhere, formatting the rendered text to fit within the current element. In all cases, the occurrence of a heading signifies the end of any preceding paragraph or other text element, so you can't use the heading tags to change font sizes in the same line. Rather, use cascading style definitions to achieve those acute display effects. [Inline Styles: The style Attribute, 8.1.1]

4.2.6 Adding Images to Headings

It is possible to insert one or more images within your headings, from small bullets or icons to full-size logos. Combining a consistent set of headings with corresponding icons across a family of documents is not only visually attractive but also an effective way of aiding users' perusal of your document collection. [<img>, 5.2.6]

Adding an image to a heading is easy. For example, the following text puts an "information" icon inside the "For More Information" heading, as you can see in Figure 4-6:

```
<h2>
<img src="info.gif">
For More Information</h2>
```

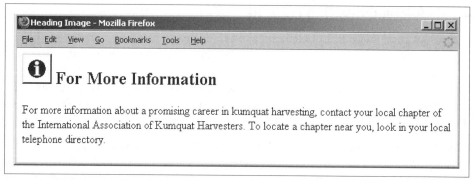

Figure 4-6. An image within a heading

In general, images within headings look best at the beginning of the heading, aligned with the bottom or middle of the heading text.

4.3 Changing Text Appearance and Meaning

A number of tags change the appearance of and associate hidden meaning with text. In general, these tags can be grouped into two flavors: content-based styles and physical styles.

In addition, the World Wide Web Consortium (W3C) standard for Cascading Style Sheets (CSS) is now well supported by the popular browsers, providing another, more comprehensive way for authors to control the look and layout of their document text. We describe the tag-based text styles in this chapter. See Chapter 8 for details about CSS.

4.3.1 Content-Based Styles

Content-based style tags inform the browser that the enclosed text has a specific meaning, context, or usage. The browser then formats the text in a manner consistent with that meaning, context, or usage. Note the distinction here. Content-based style tags confer meaning, not formatting. Accordingly, they are important for automated processes; machines don't care what the document looks like—at least for now.

Because font style is specified via semantic clues, the browser can choose a display style that is appropriate for the user. Because such styles vary by locale, using content-based styles helps ensure that your documents will have meaning to a broader range of readers. This is particularly important when a browser is targeted at blind or handicapped readers whose display options are radically different from conventional text or are extremely limited in some way.

The current HTML and XHTML standards do not define a format for each content-based style; they only specify that they must be rendered in a manner different from the regular text in a document. The standards don't even insist that the content-based styles be rendered differently from one another. In practice, you'll find that many of these tags have fairly obvious relationships with conventional print, having similar meanings and rendered styles, and are rendered in the same style and fonts by most browsers.

4.3.2 Physical Styles

We use the word *intent* a lot when we talk about content-based style tags. That's because the meaning conveyed by the tag is more important than the way a browser displays the text. In some cases, however, you might want the text to appear explicitly in some special way—italic or bold, for example—perhaps for legal or copyright reasons. In those cases, use a physical style for the text.

While the tendency with other text-processing systems is to control style and appearance explicitly, with HTML or XHTML you should avoid physical tags except on rare occasions. Provide the browser with as much contextual information as possible. Use the content-based styles. Even though current browsers may do nothing more than display their text in italic or bold, future browsers and various document-generation tools may use the content-based styles in any number of creative ways.

4.4 Content-Based Style Tags

It takes discipline to use HTML/XHTML content-based style tags because it is easier to simply think of how your text should look, not necessarily what it may also mean. Once you get started using content-based styles, your documents will be more consistent and better lend themselves to automated searching and content compilation.

<table>
<tr><td colspan="2" align="center">**Content-Based Style Tags**</td></tr>
<tr><td>**Function**</td><td>Alter the appearance of text based upon the meaning, context, or usage of the text</td></tr>
<tr><td>**Attributes**</td><td>`class`, `dir`, `id`, `lang`, `onClick`, `onDblClick`, `onKeyDown`, `onKeyPress`, `onKeyUp`, `onMouseDown`, `onMouseMove`, `onMouseOut`, `onMouseOver`, `onMouseUp`, `style`, `title`</td></tr>
<tr><td>**End tags**</td><td>Never omitted</td></tr>
<tr><td>**Contains**</td><td>*text*</td></tr>
<tr><td>**Used in**</td><td>*text*</td></tr>
</table>

4.4.1 The <abbr> Tag

First introduced in HTML 4.0, the <abbr> tag indicates that the enclosed text is an abbreviated form of a longer word or phrase. The browser might use this information to change the way it renders the enclosed text or substitute alternative text. Notice that we said *might*—not all of the popular browsers currently do anything to the text enclosed by the <abbr> tag, and we can't predict how other browsers will implement the tag in the future.

4.4.2 The <acronym> Tag

The <acronym> tag indicates that the enclosed text is an acronym, an abbreviation usually formed from the first letter of each word in a name or phrase, such as HTML and IBM. Like <abbr>, not all browsers change the display of the <acronym> content-based style tag's enclosed text.

4.4.3 The <cite> Tag

The <cite> tag usually indicates that the enclosed text is a bibliographic citation, such as a book or magazine title. By convention, the citation text is rendered in italics. See Figure 4-7 for how Internet Explorer renders this source text:

```
While kumquats are not mentioned in Melville's
<cite>Moby Dick</cite>, it is nonetheless apparent
that the mighty cetacean represents the bitter
"kumquat-ness" within every man. Indeed, when Ahab
spears the beast, its flesh is tough, much like the noble fruit.
```

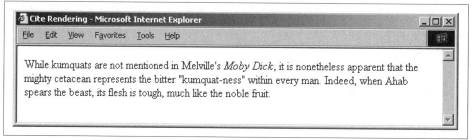

Figure 4-7. Internet Explorer renders <cite> in italics

Use the <cite> tag to set apart any reference to another document, especially those in traditional media, such as books, magazines, journal articles, and the like. If an online version of the referenced work exists, you also should enclose the citation within the <a> tag in order to make it a hyperlink to that online version.

The <cite> tag also has a hidden feature: it enables you or someone else to automatically extract a bibliography from your documents. It is easy to envision a browser that compiles tables of citations automatically, displaying them as footnotes or as a separate document entirely. The semantics of the <cite> tag go far beyond changing the appearance of the enclosed text; they enable the browser to present the content to the user in a variety of useful ways.

4.4.4 The <code> Tag

Software code warriors have become accustomed to a special style of text presentation for their source programs. The <code> tag is for them. It renders the enclosed text in a monospaced, teletype-style font such as Courier, familiar to most programmers and readers of O'Reilly books such as this one.

This following bit of en<code>ed text is rendered in a monospaced font style by Firefox, as shown in Figure 4-8 (though the effect is not dramatic, admittedly):

```
The array reference <code>a[i]</code> is identical to
the pointer reference <code>*(a+i)</code>.
```

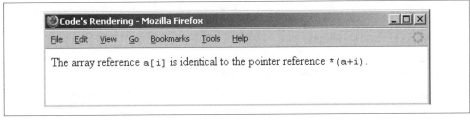

Figure 4-8. Use <code> to present computer-speak

You should use the <code> tag for text that represents computer source code or other machine-readable content. While the <code> tag usually just makes text appear in a monospaced font, the implication is that it is source code, and future browsers may add other display effects.*

For example, a programmer's browser might look for <code> segments and perform some additional text formatting, such as special indentation of loops and conditional clauses. If the only effect you desire is a monospaced font, use the <tt> tag. If you want to display the programming code in rigidly formatted monospaced text, use the <pre> tag. [The <tt> Tag, 4.5.10] [<pre>, 4.6.5]

4.4.5 The <dfn> Tag

Use <dfn> to tag defining instances of special terms or phrases. The popular browsers typically display <dfn> text in italics. In the future, <dfn> might assist in creating a document index or glossary.

---

* None of the popular browsers format <code> segments as a text processor might. Rather, use the <pre> tag in conjunction with <code> to achieve programming code-like display effects.

For example, use the `<dfn>` tag to introduce a new phrase to the reader:

```
When analyzing annual crop yields, <dfn>rind spectroscopy</dfn> may prove useful. By
comparing the relative levels of saturated hydrocarbons in fruit from adjacent trees,
rind spectroscopy has been shown to be 87% effective in predicting an outbreak of
trunk dropsy in trees under four years old.
```

Notice that we delimit only the first occurrence of "rind spectroscopy" with a `<dfn>` tag in the example. Good style tells us not to clutter the text with highlighted text. As with the many other, content-related and physical style tags, the fewer the better.* As a general style, especially in technical documentation, set off new terms when they are first introduced to help your readers better understand the topic at hand, but resist tagging the terms thereafter.

4.4.6 The `<em>` Tag

The `<em>` tag tells the client browser to present the enclosed text with emphasis. For nearly all browsers, this means the text is rendered in italic. For example, the popular browsers will emphasize by italicizing the words *always* and *never* in the following HTML/XHTML source:

```
Kumquat growers must <em>always</em> refer to kumquats
as "the noble fruit," <em>never</em> as just a "fruit."
```

Adding emphasis to your text is tricky business. Too little, and the emphatic phrases may be lost. Too much, and you lose the urgency. Like any seasoning, emphasis is best used sparingly.

Although invariably displayed in italic, the `<em>` tag has broader implications as well, and someday browsers may render emphasized text with a different special effect. The `<i>` tag explicitly italicizes text; use it if all you want is italic. Alternatively, you can include text display-altering cascading style definitions in your document. [The `<i>` Tag, 4.5.4]

Besides for emphasis, also consider using `<em>` when presenting new terms or as a fixed style when referring to a specific type of term or concept. For instance, one of O'Reilly's book styles is to specially format file and device names. You might use the `<em>` tag to differentiate those terms from simple italics used for emphasis.

4.4.7 The `<kbd>` Tag

Speaking of special styles for technical concepts, there is the `<kbd>` tag. As you probably already suspect, it is used to indicate text that is typed on a keyboard. Its enclosed text typically is rendered by the browser in a monospaced font.

---

* If you need convincing that less is better when applying the content-based and physical style tags, try reading a college textbook in which someone has highlighted what he considered important words and phrases with a yellow marker.

The <kbd> tag is most often used in computer-related documentation and manuals, such as in this example:

```
Type <kbd>quit</kbd> to exit the utility, or type
<kbd>menu</kbd> to return to the main menu.
```

4.4.8 The <samp> Tag

The <samp> tag indicates a sequence of literal characters that should have no other interpretation by the user. This tag is most often used when a sequence of characters is taken out of its normal context. For example, the following source:

```
The <samp>ae</samp> character sequence may be converted
to the &aelig; ligature if desired.
```

is rendered by Netscape, for instance, as shown in Figure 4-9.

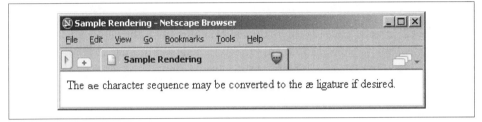

Figure 4-9. Setting off sample text using the <samp> tag

The special HTML reference for the ae ligature entity is æ and is converted to its appropriate æ ligature character by most browsers. For more information, see Appendix F.

The <samp> tag is not used very often. You should use it in those few cases where special emphasis needs to be placed on small character sequences taken out of their normal context.

4.4.9 The <strong> Tag

Like the <em> tag, the <strong> tag is for emphasizing text, except with more gusto. Browsers typically display the <strong> tag differently than the <em> tag, usually by making the text bold (versus italic) so that users can distinguish between the two. For example, in the following text, the emphasized "never" appears in italic by Opera, and the <strong> "forbidden" is rendered in bold characters (see Figure 4-10):

```
One should <em>never</em> make a disparaging remark about the
noble fruit. In particular, mentioning kumquats in conjunction
with vulgar phrases is expressly <strong>forbidden</strong> by
the Association bylaws.
```

If common sense tells us that the <em> tag should be used sparingly, the <strong> tag should appear in documents even more infrequently. <em> text is like shouting.

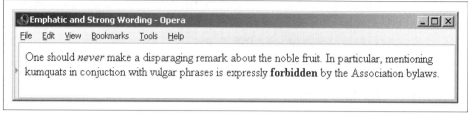

Figure 4-10. Strong and emphasized text are rendered differently

<strong> text is nothing short of a scream. Like a well-chosen epithet voiced by an otherwise taciturn person, restraint in the use of <strong> makes its use that much more noticeable and effective.

4.4.10 The <var> Tag

The <var> tag, another computer-documentation trick, indicates a variable name or a user-supplied value. The tag is often used in conjunction with the <code> and <pre> tags for displaying particular elements of computer-programming code samples and the like. Browsers typically render <var>-tagged text in italics, as shown in Figure 4-11, which displays the following example:

```
The user should type
<pre>
  cp <var>source-file</var>  <var>dest-file</var>
</pre>
replacing the <var>source-file</var> with the name of
the source file, and <var>dest-file</var> with the name
of the destination file.
```

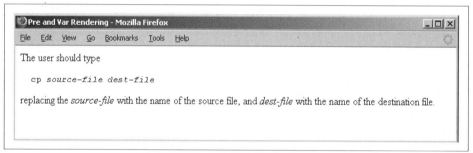

Figure 4-11. The <var> tag typically appears in preformatted (<pre>) computer code

Like the other computer-programming and documentation-related tags, the <var> tag not only makes it easy for users to understand and browse your documentation, but automated systems might someday use the appropriately tagged text to extract information and useful parameters mentioned in your documents. Once again, the more semantic information you provide to your browser, the better it can present that information to the user.

4.4.11 The class, style, id, and title Attributes

Although each content-based tag has a default display style, you can override that style by defining a new look for each tag. You can apply this new look to the content-based tags using either the style or the class attribute. [Inline Styles: The style Attribute, 8.1.1] [Style Classes, 8.3]

You also may assign a unique identifier (id) to the content-based style tag, as well as a less rigorous title, using the respective attributes and their accompanying quote-enclosed string values. [The id attribute, 4.1.1.4] [The title attribute, 4.1.1.5]

4.4.12 The dir and lang Attributes

The dir attribute advises the browser in which direction the text within the content-based style tag should be displayed, and lang lets you specify the language used within the tag. [The dir attribute, 3.6.1.1] [The lang attribute, 3.6.1.2]

4.4.13 Event Attributes

Things happen in and around a content-based tag's content, and, with the respective on attribute and value you may react to that event by displaying a user dialog or activating some multimedia event. [JavaScript Event Handlers, 12.3.3]

4.4.14 Summary of Content-Based Tags

The various graphical browsers render text inside content-based tags in similar fashion; text-only browsers such as Lynx have consistent styles for the tags. Table 4-1 summarizes these browsers' display styles for the native tags. However, stylesheet definitions may override these native display styles.

Table 4-1. Content-based tags

Tag	Netscape Navigator	Internet Explorer	Mozilla Firefox	Opera	Lynx
<abbr>	N/A	N/A	N/A	N/A	N/A
<acronym>	N/A	N/A	N/A	N/A	N/A
<cite>	*italic*	*italic*	*italic*	*italic*	monospace
<code>	monospace	monospace	monospace	monospace	monospace
<dfn>	*italic*	*italic*	*italic*	*italic*	N/A
<em>	*italic*	*italic*	*italic*	*italic*	monospace
<kbd>	monospace	monospace	monospace	monospace	monospace
<samp>	monospace	monospace	monospace	monospace	monospace
<strong>	**bold**	**bold**	**bold**	**bold**	monospace
<var>	*italic*	*italic*	*italic*	*italic*	monospace

4.4.15 Allowed Content

Any content-based style tag may contain any item allowed in text, including conventional text, anchors, images, and line breaks. In addition, other content-based and physical style tags can be embedded within the content.

4.4.16 Allowed Usage

Any content-based style tag may be used anywhere an item allowed in text is used. In practice, this means you can use the <em>, <code>, and other similar tags anywhere in your document except inside <title>, <listing>, and <xmp> tagged segments. You can use text style tags in headings, too, but their effects may be overridden by the effects of the heading tags themselves.

4.4.17 Combining Content-Based Styles

It may have occurred to you to combine two or more of the various content-based styles to create interesting and perhaps even useful hybrids. Thus, an emphatic citation might be achieved with:

```
<cite><em>Moby Dick</em></cite>
```

In practice, Dr. Frankenstein, the browser usually ignores the monster—as you can test by typing and viewing the example yourself, "Moby Dick" gets the citation without emphasis.

The HTML and XHTML standards do not require the browser to support every possible combination of content-based styles and do not define how the browser should handle such combinations. Someday maybe; for now, it's best to choose one tag.

4.5 Physical Style Tags

The current HTML and XHTML standards currently provide nine physical styles: bold, italic, monospaced, underlined, strikethrough, larger, smaller, superscripted, and subscripted text. Much to our relief, Internet Explorer has stopped supporting a tenth physical style, "blinking" text. We wish the others would "get it." All physical style tags require ending tags.

As we discuss physical tags in detail, keep in mind that they convey an acute styling for the immediate text. For more comprehensive, document-wide control of text display, use stylesheets (see Chapter 8).

4.5.1 The <b> Tag

The <b> tag is the physical equivalent of the <strong> content-based style tag, but without the latter's extended meaning. The <b> tag explicitly boldfaces a character or segment of text that is enclosed between it and its corresponding end tag (</b>). If a boldface font is not available, the browser may use some other representation, such as reverse video or underlining.

<table>
<tr><td colspan="2" align="center">**Physical Style Tags**</td></tr>
<tr><td>**Function**</td><td>Specify physical styles for text</td></tr>
<tr><td>**Attributes**</td><td>class, dir, id, lang, onClick, onDblClick, onKeyDown, onKeyPress, onKeyUp, onMouseDown, onMouseMove, onMouseOut, onMouseOver, onMouseUp, style, title</td></tr>
<tr><td>**End tags**</td><td>Never omitted</td></tr>
<tr><td>**Contains**</td><td>*text*</td></tr>
<tr><td>**Used in**</td><td>*text*</td></tr>
</table>

4.5.2 The <big> Tag

The <big> tag makes it easy to increase the size of text. It couldn't be simpler: the browser renders the text between the <big> tag and its matching </big> ending tag one font size larger than the surrounding text. If that text is already at the largest size, <big> has no effect. [<font>, 4.10.3]

Even better, you can nest <big> tags to enlarge the text. Each <big> tag makes the text one size larger, up to a limit of size seven, as defined by the font model.

4.5.3 The <blink> Tag (Obsolete Extension)

Text contained between the <blink> tag and its end tag, </blink>, does just that: it blinks on and off. Firefox, for example, simply and reiteratively reverses the background and foreground colors for the <blink>-enclosed text. Neither the HTML nor the XHTML standard includes <blink>. Originally, it was supported as an extension only by Netscape Navigator versions before version 6; then it was dropped in version 6, and was reinstated in versions 7 and later. Opera and Firefox support it, too—only Internet Explorer eschews it. You should, too.

We cannot effectively reproduce the animated effect in these static pages, but it is easy to imagine and best left to the imagination, too. Blinking text has two primary effects: it gets your readers' attention and then promptly annoys them to no end. Forget about blinking text.

4.5.4 The <i> Tag

The <i> tag is like the <em> content-based style tag. It and its necessary end tag (</i>) tell the browser to render the enclosed text in an italic or oblique typeface. If the typeface is not available to the browser, highlighting, reverse video, or underlining might be used.

4.5.5 The <s> Tag (Deprecated)

The <s> tag is an abbreviated form of the <strike> tag supported by all current browsers even though it is deprecated in HTML 4 and XHTML. In other words, the "s" stands for shy: don't use it; <s> will go away, eventually.

4.5.6 The <small> Tag

The <small> tag works just like its <big> counterpart (see [The <big> Tag, 4.5.2]), except it decreases the size of text instead of increasing it. If the enclosed text is already at the smallest size supported by the font model, <small> has no effect.

As you can with <big>, you can nest <small> tags to sequentially shrink text. Each <small> tag makes the text one size smaller than the containing <small> tag, to a limit of size 1.

4.5.7 The <strike> Tag (Deprecated)

The popular browsers put a line through ("strike through") text that appears inside the <strike> tag and its </strike> end tag. Presumably, it is an editing markup that tells the reader to ignore the text passage, reminiscent of the days before typewriter correction tape. You'll rarely, if ever, see the tag in use today: it is deprecated in HTML 4 and XHTML, just one step away from complete elimination from the standard.

4.5.8 The <sub> Tag

The text contained between the _{tag and its} end tag gets displayed half a character's height lower, but in the same font and size as the current text flow. Both <sub> and its <sup> counterpart are useful for math equations and in scientific notation, as well as with chemical formulæ.

4.5.9 The <sup> Tag

The ^{tag and its} end tag superscript the enclosed text; it gets displayed half a character's height higher, but in the same font and size as the current text flow. This tag is useful for adding footnotes to your documents, along with exponential values in equations. When you use it in combination with the <a> tag, you can create nice, hyperlinked footnotes:

```
The larval quat
weevil<a href="footnotes.html#note74"><sup><small>74</small></sup></a> is a
```

This example assumes that *footnotes.html* contains all your footnotes, appropriately delimited as named document fragments.

4.5.10 The <tt> Tag

Like the <code> and <kbd> tags, the <tt> tag and its necessary </tt> end tag direct the browser to display the enclosed text in a monospaced typeface. For those browsers

---

that already use a monospaced typeface, this tag may make no discernible change in the presentation of the text.

4.5.11 The <u> Tag (Deprecated)

This tag tells the browser to underline the text contained between the <u> and the corresponding </u> tag. The underlining technique is simplistic, drawing the line under spaces and punctuation as well as the text. This tag is deprecated in HTML 4 and XHTML, but the popular browsers support it.

The same display effects for the <u> tag are better achieved by using stylesheets, covered in Chapter 8.

4.5.12 The dir and lang Attributes

The dir attribute lets you advise the browser in which direction the text within the physical tag should be displayed, and lang lets you specify the language used within the tag. [The dir attribute, 3.6.1.1] [The lang attribute, 3.6.1.2]

4.5.13 The class, style, id, and title Attributes

Although each physical tag has a defined style, you can override that style by defining your own look for each tag. You can apply this new look to the physical tags using either the style or the class attribute. [Inline Styles: The style Attribute, 8.1.1] [Style Classes, 8.3]

You also may assign a unique ID to the physical style tag, as well as a less rigorous title, using the respective attribute and accompanying quote-enclosed string value. [The id attribute, 4.1.1.4] [The title attribute, 4.1.1.5]

4.5.14 Event Attributes

As with content-based style tags, user-initiated mouse and keyboard events can happen in and around a physical style tag's contents. The browser recognizes many of these events if it conforms to current standards, and with the respective on attribute and value, you may react to the event by displaying a user dialog box or activating some multimedia event. [JavaScript Event Handlers, 12.3.3]

4.5.15 Summary of Physical Style Tags

The various graphical browsers render text inside the physical style tags in a similar fashion. Table 4-2 summarizes these browsers' display styles for these tags. Stylesheet definitions may override these native display styles.

Table 4-2. Physical style tags

Tag	Meaning	Display style
<b>	Bold contents	**Bold**
<big>	Increased font size	Bigger text
<blink> (obsolete)	Alternating fore- and background colors	Blinking text
<i>	Italic contents	*Italic*
<small>	Decreased font size	Smaller text
<s>, <strike> (deprecated)	Strikethrough text	Strike
<sub>	Subscripted text	sub$_{script}$
<sup>	Superscripted text	super^{script}
<tt>	Teletypewriter style	monospaced
<u> (deprecated)	Underlined contents	Underlined

The following HTML source example illustrates some of the various physical tags as rendered by Firefox (see Figure 4-12):

```
Explicitly <b>boldfaced</b>, <i>italicized</i>, or
<tt>teletype-style</tt> text should be used
<big><big>sparingly</big></big>.
Otherwise, drink <strike>lots</strike> 1x10<sup>6</sup>
drops of H<sub><small><small>2</small></small></sub>O.
```

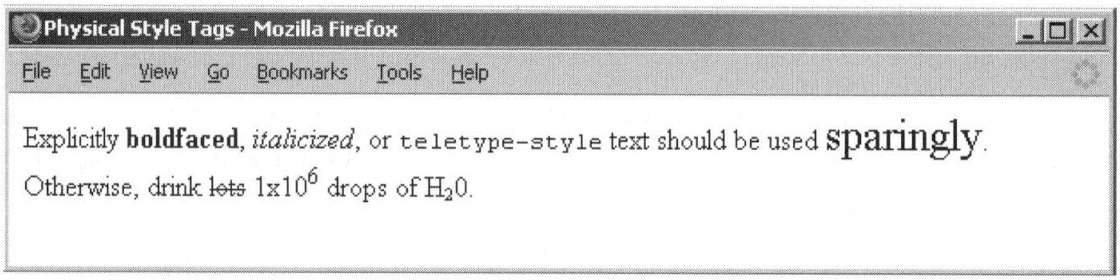

Figure 4-12. Use physical text tags with caution

4.5.16 Allowed Content

Any physical style tag may contain any item allowed in text, including conventional text, anchors, images, and line breaks. You can also combine physical style tags with other content-based tags.

4.5.17 Allowed Usage

You can use any physical style tag anywhere you can use an item allowed in text. In general, this means anywhere within a document, except in the <title>, <listing>, and <xmp> tags. You can use a physical style tag in a heading, but the browser will probably override and ignore its effect in lieu of the heading tag.

4.5.18 Combining Physical Styles

You will probably have better luck combining physical tags than you might have combining content-based tags to achieve multiple effects. For instance, all the popular browsers render the following in bold and italic typeface:

```
<b><i>Thar she blows!</i></b>
```

Other browsers may elect to ignore such nesting. The standards require the browser to "do its best" to support every possible combination of styles, but do not define how the browser should handle such combinations. Although most browsers make a good attempt at doing so, do not assume all combinations will be available to you.

4.6 Precise Spacing and Layout

CSS notwithstanding, the original concept of HTML is for specifying document content without indicating format; to delineate the structure and semantics of a document, not how that document is to be presented to the user. Normally, you should leave word wrapping, character and line spacing, and other presentation details up to the browser. That way, the document's content—its rich information, not its good looks—is what matters. When looks matter more, such as for commercial presentations, look to stylesheets for layout control (see Chapter 8).

4.6.1 The
 Tag

The <br> tag interrupts the normal line filling and word wrapping of paragraphs within an HTML or XHTML document. It has no ending tag with HTML;[*] it simply marks the point in the flow where a new line should begin. Most browsers simply stop adding words and images to the current line, move down and over to the left margin, and resume filling and wrapping.

<table>
<tr><td colspan="2" align="center">
</td></tr>
<tr><td>Function</td><td>Inserts a line break into a text flow</td></tr>
<tr><td>Attributes</td><td>class, clear, id, style, title</td></tr>
<tr><td>End tag</td><td>None in HTML; </br> or <br ... /> in XHTML</td></tr>
<tr><td>Contains</td><td>Nothing</td></tr>
<tr><td>Used in</td><td>text</td></tr>
</table>

---

[*] With XHTML, put the end inside the start tag: <br />. See Chapter 16 for details.

This effect is handy when formatting conventional text with fixed line breaks, such as addresses, song lyrics, and poetry. Notice, for example, the lyrical breaks when the following source is rendered by a GUI browser:

```
<h3>
Heartbreak Hotel</h3>
<p>
Ever since my baby left me<br>
I've found a new place to dwell.<br>
It's down at the end of lonely street<br>
Called <cite>Heartbreak Hotel</cite>.
</p>
```

The results are shown in Figure 4-13.

Figure 4-13. Give lyrics their breaks (<br>)

Also notice how the <br> tag simply causes text to start a new line, and the browser, when encountering the <p> tag, typically inserts some vertical space between adjacent paragraphs. [<p>, 4.1.2]

4.6.1.1 The clear attribute

Normally, the <br> tag tells the browser to stop the current flow of text immediately and resume at the left margin of the next line or against the right border of a left-justified inline graphic or table. Sometimes you'd rather the current text flow resume below any tables or images currently blocking the left or right margin.

HTML 4 and XHTML provide that capability with the clear attribute for the <br> tag. It can have one of three values—left, right, or all—each related to one or both of the margins. When the specified margin or margins are clear of images, the browser resumes the text flow.

Figure 4-14 illustrates the effects of the clear attribute when the browser renders the following HTML fragment:

```
<img src="kumquat.gif" align=left>
This text should wrap around the image, flowing between the
```

```
image and the right margin of the document.
<br clear=left>
This text will flow as well, but will be below the image,
extending across the full width of the page. There will be
whitespace above this text and to the right of the image.
```

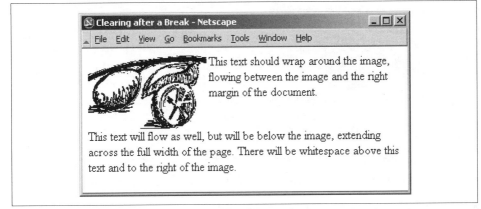

Figure 4-14. Clearing images before resuming text flow after the <br> tag

Inline images are just that—normally in line with text, but usually only a single line of text. Additional lines of text flow below the image, unless that image is specially aligned by right or left attribute values for the <img> tag (similarly for <table>). Hence, the clear attribute for the <br> tag works only in combination with left- or right-aligned images or tables. [<img>, 5.2.6] [The align attribute (deprecated), 10.2.1.1]

The following XHTML code fragment illustrates how to use the <br> tag and its clear attribute as well as the <img> tag's alignment attributes to place captions directly above, centered on the right, and below an image that is aligned against the left margin of the browser window:

```
Paragraph tags separate leading and following
text flow from the captions.
<p>
I'm the caption on top of the image.
<br />
<img src="kumquat.gif" align="absmiddle">
This one's centered on the right.
<br clear="left" />
This caption should be directly below the image.
</p>
<p />
```

Figure 4-15 illustrates the results of this example code.

You might also include a <br clear=all> tag just after an <img> tag or table that is at the very end of a section of your document. That way, you ensure that the subsequent section's text doesn't flow up and against that image and confuse the reader. [<img>, 5.2.6]

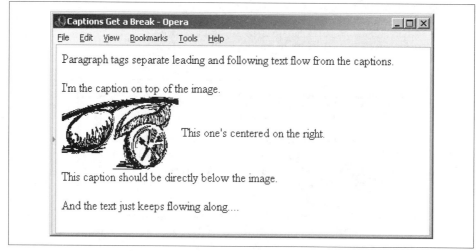

Figure 4-15. Captions placed on top, center-right, and below an image

4.6.1.2 The class, id, style, and title attributes

You can associate additional display rules for the <br> tag using stylesheets. You can apply the rules to the <br> tag using either the style or the class attribute. [Inline Styles: The style Attribute, 8.1.1] [Style Classes, 8.3]

You also may assign a unique ID to the <br> tag, as well as a less rigorous title, using the respective attribute and accompanying quote-enclosed string value. [The id attribute, 4.1.1.4] [The title attribute, 4.1.1.5]

4.6.2 The <nobr> Tag (Extension)

Occasionally, you may want a phrase to appear unbroken on a single line in the user's browser window, even if that means the text extends beyond the visible region of the window. Computer commands are good examples. Typically, you type in a computer command—even a multiword one—on a single line. Because you cannot predict exactly how many words will fit inside an individual's browser window, the sequence of computer-command words may end up broken into two or more lines of text. Command syntax is confusing enough; it doesn't need the extra cross-eyed effect of being wrapped onto two lines.

With standard HTML and XHTML, the way to make sure text phrases stay intact across the browser display is to enclose those segments in a <pre> tag and format it by hand. That's acceptable and nearly universal for all browsers. However, <pre> alters the display font from the regular text, and manual line breaks inside the <pre> tag are not always rendered correctly. [<pre>, 4.6.5]

Function	Creates a region of nonbreaking text
Attributes	None
End tag	`</nobr>`; always used
Contains	*text*
Used in	*block*

The current browsers offer the `<nobr>` tag alternative to `<pre>`, which keeps enclosed text intact on a single line while retaining normal text style.* `<nobr>` makes the browser treat the tag's contents as though they are a single, unbroken word. The tag contents retain the current font style, and you can change to another style within the tag.

Here's the `<nobr>` tag in action with our computer-command example:

```
When prompted by the computer, enter
<nobr>
<tt>find . -name \*.html -exec rm \{\}\;</tt>.
</nobr>
<br>
<nobr>After a few moments, the load on your server will begin
to diminish and will eventually drop to zero.</nobr>
```

Notice in the example source and its display (Figure 4-16) that we've included the special `<tt>` tag inside the first `<nobr>` tag, thereby rendering the contents in monospaced font. If the `<nobr>`-tagged text cannot fit on a partially filled line of text, the extended browser precedes it with a line break, as shown in the figure. The second `<nobr>` segment in the example demonstrates that the text may extend beyond the right window boundary if the segment is too long to fit on a single line. For some reason, Netscape, but not the other popular browsers, fails to provide a horizontal scroll bar so that users can read the extended text, though. [The <tt> Tag, 4.5.10]

The `<nobr>` tag does not suspend the browser's normal line-filling process; it still collects and inserts images and—believe it or not—asserts forced line breaks caused by the `<br>` and `<p>` tags, for example. The `<nobr>` tag's only action is to suppress an automatic line break when the current line reaches the right margin.

In addition, you might think this tag is needed only to suppress line breaks for phrases, not for a sequence of characters without spaces that can exceed the browser window's display boundaries. Today's browsers do not hyphenate words automatically, but

---

* Be aware that `<nobr>` and its colleague `<wbr>` are extensions to the language and not part of the HTML standard.

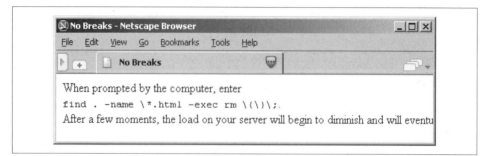

Figure 4-16. The <nobr> extension suppresses text wrapping; for reasons unknown, Netscape doesn't enable a scroll bar so that you can read the extended text

someday soon they probably will. It makes sense to protect any break-sensitive sequences of characters with the <nobr> tag.

4.6.3 The <wbr> Tag (Extension)

The <wbr> tag is the height of text-layout finesse, offered as an extension by Internet Explorer, but not any others. Used with the <nobr> tag, <wbr> advises Internet Explorer when it may insert a line break in an otherwise nonbreakable sequence of text. Unlike the <br> tag, which always causes a line break, even within an <nobr>-tagged segment, the <wbr> tag works only when placed inside an <nobr>-tagged content segment and causes a line break only if the current line has already extended beyond the browser's display window margins.

<wbr> [!]

Function	Defines a potential line-break point if needed
Attributes	None
End tag	None in HTML; </wbr> or <wbr ... /> in XHTML
Contains	Nothing
Used in	*text*

Now, <wbr> may seem incredibly esoteric to you, but scowl not. There may come a time when you want to make sure portions of your document appear on a single line, but you don't want to overrun the browser window margins so far that readers will have to camp on the horizontal scroll bar just to read your fine prose. By inserting the <wbr> tag at appropriate points in the nonbreaking sequence, you let the browser gently break the text into more manageable lines:

```
<nobr>
This is a very long sequence of text that is
forced to be on a single line, even if doing so causes
<wbr>
the browser to extend the document window beyond the
size of the viewing pane and the poor user must scroll right
<wbr>
to read the entire line.
</nobr>
```

You'll notice in our Internet Explorer-rendered version (Figure 4-17) that both <wbr> tags take effect. By increasing the horizontal window size or reducing the font size, you may fit the entire segment before the first <wbr> tag within the browser window. In that case, only the second <wbr> would have an effect; all the text leading up to it would extend beyond the window's margins.

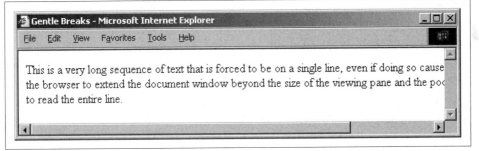

Figure 4-17. Gentle line breaks with Internet Explorer's <wbr>extension tag

4.6.4 Better Line-Breaking Rules

Unlike some browsers, and to their credit, the popular browsers do not consider tags to be line-break opportunities. Consider the unfortunate consequences to your document's display if, while rendering the following example segment, the browser puts the comma adjacent to the "du" or the period adjacent to the "df" on a separate line.

```
Make sure you type <tt>du</tt>, not <tt>df</tt>.
```

4.6.5 The <pre> Tag

The HTML/XHTML standards' <pre> tag and its required end tag (</pre>) define a segment inside which the browser renders text in exactly the character and line spacing written in the source document. Normal word wrapping and paragraph filling are disabled, and extraneous leading and trailing spaces are honored. Browsers display all text between the <pre> and </pre> tags in a monospaced font.

Authors most often use the <pre> formatting tag when the integrity of columns and rows of characters must be retained; for instance, in tables of numbers that must line up correctly. Another application for <pre> is to set aside a blank segment—a series

	<pre>
Function	Renders a block of text without any formatting
Attributes	class, dir, id, lang, onClick, onDblClick, onKeyDown, onKeyPress, onKeyUp, onMouseDown, onMouseMove, onMouseOut, onMouseOver, onMouseUp, style, title, width
End tag	</pre>; never omitted
Contains	*pre_content*
Used in	*block*

of blank lines—in the document display, perhaps to clearly separate one content section from another or to temporarily hide a portion of the document when it first loads and is rendered by the user's browser.

Tab characters have their desired effect within the <pre> block, with tab stops defined at every eighth character position. We discourage their use, however, because tabs aren't consistently implemented among the various browsers. Use spaces to ensure correct horizontal positioning of text within <pre>-formatted text segments.

A common use of the <pre> tag is to present computer source code, as in the following example:

```
<p>
The processing program is:
<pre>
main(int argc, char **argv)

{
    FILE *f;
    int i;

    if (argc != 2)
      fprintf(stderr, "usage: %s &lt;file&gt;\n",
          argv[0]);
    <a href="http:process.c">process</a>(argv[1]);
    exit(0);
}
</pre>
```

Figure 4-18 shows the result.

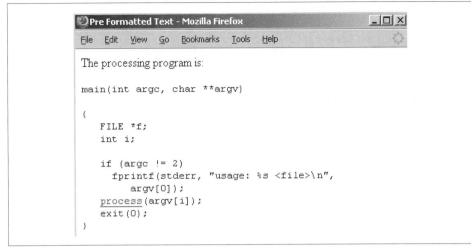

Figure 4-18. Use the <pre> tag to preserve the integrity of columns and rows

4.6.5.1 Allowable content

The text within a <pre> segment may contain physical and content-based style changes, along with anchors, images, and horizontal rules. When possible, the browser should honor style changes, within the constraint of using a monospaced font for the entire <pre> block. Tags that cause a paragraph break (heading, <p>, and <address> tags, for example) must not be used within the <pre> block. Some browsers will interpret paragraph-ending tags as simple line breaks, but this behavior is not consistent across all browsers.

Style markup and other tags are allowed in a <pre> block, so you must use entity equivalents for the literal characters: < for <, > for >, and & for &.

You place tags into the <pre> block as you would in any other portion of the HTML/XHTML document. For instance, study the reference to the "process" function in the previous example. It contains a hyperlink (using the <a> tag) to its source file, *process.c*.

4.6.5.2 The width attribute

The <pre> tag has an optional attribute, width, which determines the number of characters to fit on a single line within the <pre> block. The browser may use this value to select a font or font size that fits the specified number of characters on each line in the <pre> block. It does not mean that the browser will wrap and fill text to the specified width. Rather, lines longer than the specified width simply extend beyond the visible region of the browser's window.

The width attribute is only advice for the user's browser; it may or may not be able to adjust the view font to the specified width.

4.6.5.3 The dir and lang attributes

The dir attribute lets you advise the browser in which direction the text within the <pre> segment should be displayed, and lang lets you specify the language used within that tag. [The dir attribute, 3.6.1.1] [The lang attribute, 3.6.1.2]

4.6.5.4 The class, id, style, and title attributes

Although the browsers usually display <pre> content in a defined style, you can override that style and add special effects, such as a background picture, by defining your own style for the tag. You can apply this new look to the <pre> tags using either the style or the class attribute. [Inline Styles: The style Attribute, 8.1.1] [Style Classes, 8.3]

You also may assign a unique ID to the <pre> tag, as well as a less rigorous title, using the respective attribute and accompanying quote-enclosed string value. [The id attribute, 4.1.1.4] [The title attribute, 4.1.1.5]

4.6.5.5 Event attributes

As with most other tagged segments of content, user-related events can happen in and around <pre> content, such as when a user clicks or double-clicks within its display space. Current browsers recognize many of these events. With the respective on attribute and value, you may react to those events by displaying a user dialog box or activating some multimedia event. [JavaScript Event Handlers, 12.3.3]

4.6.6 The <center> Tag (Deprecated)

The <center> tag is another one with obvious effects: its contents, including text, graphics, tables, and so on, are centered horizontally inside the browser's window. For text, this means that each line gets centered after the text flow is filled and wrapped. The <center> alignment remains in effect until it is canceled with its </center> end tag.

<center> 📄

Function	Centers a section of text
Attributes	align, class, dir, id, lang, onClick, onDblClick, onKeyDown, onKeyPress, onKeyUp, onMouseDown, onMouseMove, onMouseOut, onMouseOver, onMouseUp, style, title
End tag	</center>; never omitted
Contains	body_content
Used in	block

Line by line is a common, albeit primitive, way to center text, and it should be used judiciously; browsers do not attempt to balance a centered paragraph or other block-related elements, such as elements in a list, so keep your centered text short and sweet. Titles make good centering candidates; a centered list usually is difficult to follow. HTML authors commonly use <center> to center a table or image in the display window, too. There is no explicit center alignment option for inline images or tables, but there are ways to achieve the effect using stylesheets.

Because users will have varying window widths, display resolutions, and so on, you may also want to employ the <nobr> and <wbr> extension tags (see sections 4.6.2 and 4.6.3) to keep your centered text intact and looking good. For example:

```
<center>
<nobr>
Copyright 2000 by QuatCo Enterprises.<wbr>
All rights reserved.
</nobr>
</center>
```

The <nobr> tags in the sample source help ensure that the text remains on a single line, and the <wbr> tag controls where the line may be broken if it exceeds the browser's display-window width.

Centering is useful for creating distinctive section headers, although you may achieve the same effect with an explicit align=center attribute in the respective heading tag. You might also center text using align=center in conjunction with the <div> or <p> tag. In general, the <center> tag can be replaced by an equivalent <div align=center> or similar tag, and its use is discouraged.

Indeed, like <font> and other HTML 3.2 standard tags that have fallen into disfavor in the wake of stylesheets, the <center> tag is deprecated in the HTML 4 and XHTML standards, to be replaced by its CSS equivalent. Nonetheless, its use in HTML documents is fairly common, and the popular browsers are sure to support it for many revisions to come. Still, be aware of its eventual demise.

4.6.6.1 The dir and lang attributes

The dir attribute lets you advise the browser in which direction the text within the <center> segment should be displayed, and lang lets you specify the language used within the tag. [The dir attribute, 3.6.1.1] [The lang attribute, 3.6.1.2]

4.6.6.2 The class, id, style, and title attributes

Use the style attribute to specify an inline style for the <center> tag, or use the class attribute to apply a predefined style class to the tag. [Inline Styles: The style Attribute, 8.1.1] [Style Classes, 8.3]

You may assign a unique ID to the <center> tag, as well as a title, using the respective attribute and accompanying quote-enclosed string value. [The id attribute, 4.1.1.4] [The title attribute, 4.1.1.5]

4.6.6.3 Event attributes

As with most other tagged segments of content, user-related events can happen in and around the <center> tag, such as when a user clicks or double-clicks within its display space. The current browsers recognize many of these events. With the respective on attribute and value, you may react to those events by displaying a user dialog box or activating some multimedia event. [JavaScript Event Handlers, 12.3.3]

4.6.7 The <listing> Tag (Obsolete)

The <listing> tag is an obsolete tag, explicitly removed from the HTML 4 standard, meaning that you shouldn't use it. We include it here for historical reasons because some browsers support it, and it has the same effect on text formatting as the <pre> tag with a specified width of 132 characters.

<listing>

Function	Renders a block of text without any formatting
Attributes	class, style
End tag	</listing>; never omitted
Contains	*literal_text*
Used in	*block*

The only difference between <pre> and <listing> is that no other markup is allowed within the <listing> tag, so you don't have to replace the literal <, >, and & characters with their entity equivalents in a <listing> block, as you must inside a <pre> block.

Because the <listing> tag is the same as a <pre width=132> tag, and because it might not be supported in later versions of the popular browsers, we recommend that you stay away from using <listing>.

4.6.8 The <xmp> Tag (Obsolete)

Like the <listing> tag, the <xmp> tag is obsolete and you should not use it, even though the popular browsers support it. We include it here mostly for historical reasons.

<table>
<tr><td colspan="2" align="center">**<xmp>** 🗋</td></tr>
<tr><td>**Function**</td><td>Renders a block of text without any formatting</td></tr>
<tr><td>**Attributes**</td><td>class, style</td></tr>
<tr><td>**End tag**</td><td></xmp>; never omitted</td></tr>
<tr><td>**Contains**</td><td>*literal_text*</td></tr>
<tr><td>**Used in**</td><td>*block*</td></tr>
</table>

The <xmp> tag formats text just like the <pre> tag with a specified width of 80 characters. However, unlike the <pre> tag, you don't have to replace the literal <, >, and & characters with their entity equivalents within an <xmp> block. The name <xmp> is short for "example"; the language's designers intended that the tag be used to format examples of text originally displayed on 80-column-wide displays. Because the 80-column display has mostly gone the way of green screens and teletypes and the effect of an <xmp> tag is basically the same as <pre width=80>, don't use <xmp>; it may disappear in subsequent versions of HTML.

4.6.9 The <plaintext> Tag (Obsolete)

Throw the <plaintext> tag out of your bag of HTML tricks; it's obsolete, like <listing> and <xmp>, and is included here for historical reasons. Authors once used <plaintext> to tell the browser to treat the rest of the document's text as written, with no markup. There was no ending tag for <plaintext> (of course, no markup!), but there was an end to <plaintext>. Forget about it.

<table>
<tr><td colspan="2" align="center">**<plaintext>**</td></tr>
<tr><td>**Function**</td><td>Renders a block of text without any formatting</td></tr>
<tr><td>**Attributes**</td><td>None</td></tr>
<tr><td>**End tag**</td><td>None</td></tr>
<tr><td>**Contains**</td><td>*literal_text*</td></tr>
<tr><td>**Used in**</td><td>*block*</td></tr>
</table>

4.7 Block Quotes

A common element in conventional documents is the block quote, a lengthy copy of text from another document. Traditionally, short quotes are set off with quotation marks, and block quotes are made entirely of separate paragraphs within the main document, typically with special indentation and sometimes italicized—features that you may change through style or class definitions (see Chapter 8).

4.7.1 The <blockquote> Tag

All of the text within the <blockquote> and </blockquote> tags is set off from the regular document text, usually with indented left and right margins and sometimes in italicized typeface. Actual rendering varies from browser to browser, of course.

<blockquote>

Function	Defines a block quotation
Attributes	cite, class, dir, id, lang, onClick, onDblClick, onKeyDown, onKeyPress, onKeyUp, onMouseDown, onMouseMove, onMouseOut, onMouseOver, onMouseUp, style, title
End tag	</blockquote>; never omitted
Contains	*body_content*
Used in	*block*

The HTML and XHTML standards allow any and all markup within the <blockquote>, although some physical and content-based styles may conflict with the font the browser uses for the block quote. Experimentation will reveal those warts.

The <blockquote> tag is often used to set off long quotations from other sources. For example, popular browsers display the following as an indented block of text:

```
We acted incorrectly in arbitrarily changing the Kumquat
Festival date. Quoting from the Kumquat Growers' Bylaws:
<blockquote>
  The date of the Kumquat Festival may only be changed by
  a two-thirds vote of the General Membership, provided
  that a <strong>60 percent quorum</strong> of the Membership
  is present.
</blockquote>
(Emphasis mine) Since such a quorum was not present, the
vote is invalid.
```

Figure 4-19 displays the results.

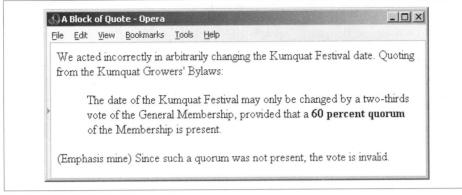

We acted incorrectly in arbitrarily changing the Kumquat Festival date. Quoting from the Kumquat Growers' Bylaws:

> The date of the Kumquat Festival may only be changed by a two-thirds vote of the General Membership, provided that a **60 percent quorum** of the Membership is present.

(Emphasis mine) Since such a quorum was not present, the vote is invalid.

Figure 4-19. Block quotes get their own space

4.7.1.1 The cite attribute

The cite attribute lets you indicate the source of a quote. The attribute's value should be a quote-enclosed URL that points to the online document and, if possible, the exact location in the document where the quote came from.

For instance, you could cite the specific section in the Kumquat Growers' Bylaws in our example. Presumably, someday the browser may actually let you click and view that specific citation via its embedded URL. Today, you must embed an explicit hyperlink to the document; see Chapter 6:

```
<blockquote cite="http://www.kumquat.com/growers/bylaws#s23.4">
```

4.7.1.2 The dir and lang attributes

The dir attribute lets you advise the browser in which direction the text within the <blockquote> segment should be displayed, and lang lets you specify the language used within that tag. [The dir attribute, 3.6.1.1] [The lang attribute, 3.6.1.2]

4.7.1.3 The class, id, style, and title attributes

Use the style attribute to specify an inline style for the <blockquote> tag, or use the class attribute to apply a predefined style class to the tag. [Inline Styles: The style Attribute, 8.1.1] [Style Classes, 8.3]

You may assign a unique ID to the <blockquote> tag, as well as a title, using the respective attribute and accompanying quote-enclosed string value. [The id attribute, 4.1.1.4] [The title attribute, 4.1.1.5]

4.7.1.4 Event attributes

As with most other tagged segments of content, user-related events can happen in and around the <blockquote> tag, such as when a user clicks or double-clicks within its display space. The current browsers recognize many of these events. With the respective on attribute and value, you may react to those events by displaying a user dialog box or activating some multimedia event. [JavaScript Event Handlers, 12.3.3]

4.7.2 The <q> Tag

Introduced in HTML 4.0, the <q> tag is virtually identical to its <blockquote> counterpart. The difference is in their display and application. You use <q> for short quotes that may be inline with surrounding plain text. The HTML and XHTML standards dictate that the <q>-enclosed text begin and end with double quotes. All the popular browsers except Internet Explorer support <q> and place double quotes at each end of the enclosed text. The result is that you'll get two sets of quotation marks if you include your own quotes to satisfy Internet Explorer. Nonetheless, we recommend that you use the <q> tag, not only because we like standards, but because we see beyond their display effects to applications in document handling, information extraction, and so forth.

Use the <blockquote> tag, on the other hand, for longer segments that the browser will set off—usually as an indented block—from the surrounding content, such as that shown in Figure 4-20.

<q> 🗎

Function	Defines a short quotation
Attributes	cite, class, dir, id, lang, onClick, onDblClick, onKeyDown, onKeyPress, onKeyUp, onMouseDown, onMouseMove, onMouseOut, onMouseOver, onMouseUp, style, title
End tag	</q>; never omitted
Contains	*body_content*
Used in	*text*

4.7.2.1 The cite attribute

The cite attribute works with the <q> tag just like it does for the <blockquote> tag: it lets you indicate the source of a quote. The attribute's value should be a quote-enclosed URL that points to the online document and, if possible, the exact location in the document where the quote came from.

4.7.2.2 The dir and lang attributes

The dir attribute lets you advise the browser in which direction the text within the <q> segment should be displayed, and lang lets you specify the language used within that tag. [The dir attribute, 3.6.1.1] [The lang attribute, 3.6.1.2]

4.7.2.3 The class, id, style, and title attributes

Use the style attribute to specify an inline style for the <q> tag, or use the class attribute to apply a predefined style class to the tag. [Inline Styles: The style Attribute, 8.1.1] [Style Classes, 8.3]

You may assign a unique ID to the <q> tag, as well as a title, using the respective attribute and accompanying quote-enclosed string value. [The id attribute, 4.1.1.4] [The title attribute, 4.1.1.5]

4.7.2.4 Event attributes

As with most other tagged segments of content, user-related events can happen in and around the <q> tag, such as when a user clicks or double-clicks within its display space. The current browsers recognize many of these events. With the respective on attribute and value, you may react to those events by displaying a user dialog box or activating some multimedia event. [JavaScript Event Handlers, 12.3.3]

4.8 Addresses

Addresses are common elements in text documents, so there is a special tag that sets addresses apart from the rest of a document's text. While this may seem a bit extravagant—addresses have few formatting peculiarities that would require a special tag—it is yet another example of content, not format, being the primary focus of HTML and XHTML markup.

By defining text that constitutes an address, the author lets the browser format that text in a different manner and process that text in ways helpful to users. It also makes the content readily accessible to automated readers and extractors. For instance, an online directory might include addresses the browser collects into a separate document or table, or automated tools might extract addresses from a collection of documents to build a separate database of addresses.

4.8.1 The <address> Tag

The <address> tag and its required end tag (</address>) tell a browser that the enclosed text is a contact address, typically snail mail or email. The address may include other contact information, too. The browser may format the text in a different manner from the rest of the document text or use the address in some special way. You also have control over the display properties through the style and class attributes for the tag (see Chapter 8).

The text within the <address> tag may contain any element normally found in the body of a document, excluding another <address> tag. Style changes are allowed, but they may conflict with the style the browser chose to render the <address> element.

\<address\>

Function	Defines an address
Attributes	class, dir, id, lang, onClick, onDblClick, onKeyDown, onKeyPress, onKeyUp, onMouseDown, onMouseMove, onMouseOut, onMouseOver, onMouseUp, style, title
End tag	\</address\>; never omitted
Contains	*body_content*
Used in	*address_content*

We think that most, if not all, documents should have their authors' addresses included somewhere convenient to the user, usually at the end. At the very least, the address should be the author or webmaster's email address, along with a link to their home page. Street addresses and phone numbers are optional; personal ones usually are not included, for privacy reasons.

For example, the address for the webmaster responsible for a collection of commercial web documents often appears in source documents as follows, including the special mailto: URL protocol that lets users activate the browser's email tool:

```
<address>
  <a href="mailto:webmaster@oreilly.com">Webmaster</a><br>
  O'Reilly<br>
  Cambridge, Massachusetts<br>
</address>
```

Figure 4-20 displays the results, which are identical for all the popular browsers in that, by default, the body of the address gets displayed in italics.

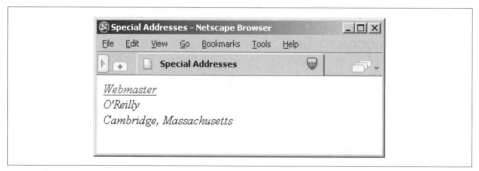

Figure 4-20. The \<address\> tag in action

Whether it is short and sweet or long and complete, make sure every document you create has an address attached to it. If something is worth creating and putting on

---

the Web, it is worth comment and query by your readership. Anonymous documents carry little credibility on the Web.

4.8.1.1 The dir and lang attributes

The `dir` attribute lets you advise the browser in which direction the text within the `<address>` segment should be displayed, and `lang` lets you specify the language used within that tag. [The dir attribute, 3.6.1.1] [The lang attribute, 3.6.1.2]

4.8.1.2 The class, id, style, and title attributes

Use the `style` attribute to specify an inline style for the `<address>` tag, or use the `class` attribute to apply a predefined style class to the tag. [Inline Styles: The style Attribute, 8.1.1] [Style Classes, 8.3]

You may assign a unique ID to the `<address>` tag, as well as a title, using the respective attribute and accompanying quote-enclosed string value. [The id attribute, 4.1.1.4] [The title attribute, 4.1.1.5]

4.8.1.3 Event attributes

As with most other tagged segments of content, user-related events can happen in and around the `<address>` tag, such as when a user clicks or double-clicks within its display space. The current browsers recognize many of these events. With the respective on attribute and value, you may react to those events by displaying a user dialog box or activating some multimedia event. [JavaScript Event Handlers, 12.3.3]

4.9 Special Character Encoding

For the most part, characters within documents that are not part of a tag are rendered as is by the browser. However, some characters have special meaning and are not directly rendered, and other characters can't be typed into the source document from a conventional keyboard. Special characters need either a special name or a numeric character encoding for inclusion in a document.

4.9.1 Special Characters

As has become obvious in the discussion and examples leading up to this section, three characters in source documents have very special meaning: the less-than sign (<), the greater-than sign (>), and the ampersand (&). These characters delimit tags and special character references. They'll confuse a browser if left dangling alone or with improper tag syntax, so you have to go out of your way to include their actual, literal characters in your documents.*

---

* The only exception is that these characters may appear literally within the `<listing>` and `<xmp>` tags, but this is a moot point because the tags are obsolete.

Similarly, you have to use special encoding to include double quotation mark characters within a quoted string, or when you want to include a special character that doesn't appear on your keyboard but is part of the ISO Latin-1 character set that most browsers implement and support.

4.9.2 Inserting Special Characters

To include a special character in your document, enclose either its standard entity name or a pound sign (#) and its numeric position in the Latin-1 standard character set* inside a leading ampersand and an ending semicolon, without any spaces in between. Whew. That's a long explanation for what is really a simple thing to do, as the following examples illustrate. The first example shows how to include a greater-than sign in a snippet of code by using the character's entity name. The second demonstrates how to include a greater-than sign in your text by referencing its Latin-1 numeric value:

```
if a &gt; b, then t = 0
if a &#62; b, then t = 0
```

Both examples cause the text to be rendered as follows:

```
if a > b, then t = 0
```

The complete set of character entity values and names appears in Appendix F. You could write an entire document using character encodings, but that would be silly.

4.10 HTML's Obsolete Expanded Font Handling

In earlier versions of this book, we rejoiced that HTML version 3.2 had introduced a font-handling model for richer, more versatile text displays. When HTML 4 deprecated these special font-handling tags, we nonetheless included them in the same prominent position within this chapter because they were still part of the HTML 3.2 standard and were still very popular with HTML authors, besides being well supported by all the popular browsers. We could not do the same for this edition of the book.

Like many deprecated HTML tags and attributes, the expanded font-handling tags of HTML 3.2 were here yesterday and are gone today. Internet Explorer, the world's most popular browser, displays all of them; other browsers display some, but not other font-related tags. Accordingly, we include the Extended Font Model tags in this chapter, but at the end of this chapter and with all the implicit red flags waving hard.

---

* The popular ASCII character set is a subset of the more comprehensive Latin-1 character set. Composed by the well-respected International Organization for Standardization (ISO), the Latin-1 set is a list of all letters, numbers, punctuation marks, and so on, commonly used by Western-language writers, organized by number and encoded with special names. Appendix F contains the complete Latin-1 character set and encoding.

The W3C wants authors to use CSS, not acute tags and attributes, for explicit control of the font styles, colors, and sizes of the text characters. That's why these extended font tags and related attributes have fallen into disfavor. It's now time for you to eschew the extended font tags, too.

4.10.1 The Extended Font Size Model

Instead of absolute point values, the Extended Font Model of HTML 3.2 uses a relative means for sizing fonts. Sizes range from 1, the smallest, to 7, the largest; the default (base) font size is 3.

It is almost impossible to state reliably the actual font sizes used for the various virtual sizes. Most browsers let the user change the physical font size, and the default sizes vary from browser to browser. It may be helpful to know, however, that each virtual size is successively 20 percent larger or smaller than the default font size, 3. Thus, font size 4 is 20 percent larger, font size 5 is 40 percent larger, and so on, and font size 2 is 20 percent smaller and font size 1 is 40 percent smaller than font size 3.

4.10.2 The <basefont> Tag (Deprecated)

The <basefont> tag lets you define the basic size for the font that the browser will use to render normal document text. We don't recommend that you use it, as it has been deprecated in the HTML 4 and XHTML standards and is no longer supported by most browsers, except Internet Explorer.

<basefont> 🗋

Function	Defines the base font size for relative font-size changes
Attributes	color, face, id, name, size
End tag	</basefont>; often omitted in HTML
Contains	Nothing
Used in	*block, head_content*

The <basefont> tag recognizes the size attribute, whose value determines the document's base font size. You may specify it as an absolute value, from 1 to 7, or as a relative value (by placing a plus or minus sign before the value). In the latter case, the base font size is increased or decreased by that relative amount. The default base font size is 3.

Internet Explorer supports two additional attributes for the <basefont> tag: color and name. HTML 4 also defines the face attribute as a synonym for the name attribute.

These attributes control the color and typeface used for the text in a document and are used just like the analogous color and face attributes for the <font> tag, described in the next section.

HTML 4 also defines the id attribute for the <basefont> tag, allowing you to label the tag uniquely for later access to its contents. [The id attribute, 4.1.1.4]

Authors typically include the <basefont> tag in the head of an HTML document, if at all, to set the base font size for the entire document. Nonetheless, the tag may appear nearly anywhere in the document, and it may appear several times throughout the document, each with a new size attribute. With each occurrence, the <basefont> tag's effects are immediate and hold for all subsequent text.

In an egregious deviation from the HTML and Standard Generalized Markup Language (SGML) standards, Internet Explorer does *not* interpret the ending </basefont> tag as terminating the effects of the most recent <basefont> tag. Instead, the </basefont> end tag resets the base font size to the default value of 3, which is the same as writing <basefont size=3>.

The following example source and Figure 4-21 illustrate how Internet Explorer responds to the <basefont> tag and </basefont> end tag:

```
Unless the base font size was reset above,
Inernet Explorer renders this part in font size 3.
<basefont size=7>
This text should be rather large (size 7).
<basefont size=6> Oh,
<basefont size=4> no!
<basefont size=2> I'm
<basefont size=1> shrinking!
</basefont><br>
Ahhhh, back to normal.
```

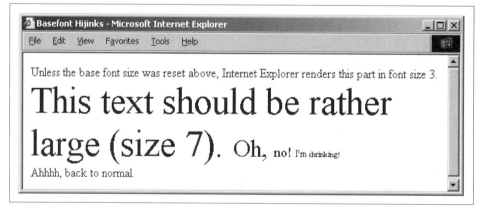

Figure 4-21. Playing with <basefont>

We recommend against using </basefont>; use <basefont size=3> instead.

4.10.3 The <font> Tag (Deprecated)

The <font> tag lets you change the size, style, and color of text. We don't recommend that you use it, because it has been deprecated in the HTML 4 and XHTML standards, even though all the popular browsers still support it. But should you decide to ignore our advice, use it like any other physical or content-based style tag for changing the appearance of a short segment of text.

Function	Sets the font size for text
Attributes	class, color, dir, face, id, lang, size, style, title
End tag	</font>; never omitted
Contains	*text*
Used in	*text*

<font> 🗋

To control the color of text for the entire document, see the attributes for the <body> tag, described. [Additions and Extensions to the <body> Tag, 5.3.1]

4.10.3.1 The size attribute

The value of the size attribute must be one of the virtual font sizes (1–7) described earlier, defined as an absolute size for the enclosed text or preceded by a plus or minus sign (+ or –) to define a relative font size that the browser adds to or subtracts from the base font size (see section 4.10.2). The browsers automatically round the size to 1 or 7 if the calculated value exceeds either boundary.

In general, use absolute size values when you want the rendered text to be an extreme size, either very large or very small, or when you want an entire paragraph of text to be a specific size.

For example, using the largest font for the first character of a paragraph makes for a crude form of illuminated manuscript (see Figure 4-22):

```
<p>
<font size=7>C</font>all me Ishmael.
```

Also, use an absolute font when inserting a delightfully unreadable bit of "fine" print—boilerplate or legalese—at the bottom of your document (see Figure 4-23):

```
<p>
<font size=1>
All rights reserved. Unauthorized redistribution of this document is
prohibited. Opinions expressed herein are those of the authors, not the
Internet Service Provider.
```

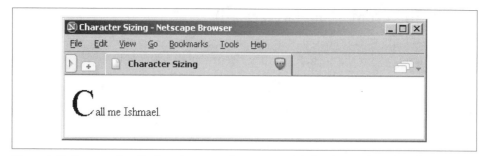

Figure 4-22. Exaggerating the first character of a sentence with the size attribute for <font>

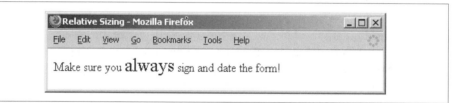

Figure 4-23. Use the tiniest font for boilerplate text

Except for the extremes, use relative font sizes to render text in a size different from the surrounding text, to emphasize a word or phrase. For an exaggerated example, see Figure 4-24:

```
<p>
Make sure you <font size=+2>always</font> sign and date the form!
```

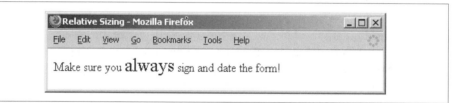

Figure 4-24. Use relative sizes for most text embellishments

If your relative size change results in a size greater than 7, the browser uses font size 7. Similarly, font sizes less than 1 are rendered with font size 1.

Note that specifying size=+1 or size=-1 is identical in effect to using the <big> and <small> tags, respectively. However, nested relative changes to the font size are not cumulative, as they are for the alternative tags. Each <font> tag is relative to the base font size, not the current font size. For example (see Figure 4-25):

```
<p>
The ghost moaned, "oo<font size=+1>oo<font size=+2>oo<font
size=+3>oo</font>oo</font>oo</font>oo."
```

Contrast this with the <big> and <small> tags, which increase or decrease the font size one level for each nesting of the tags. [The <big> Tag, 4.5.2]

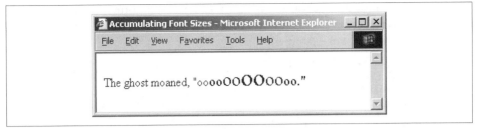

Figure 4-25. Relative font sizes accumulate

4.10.3.2 The color attribute

Still supported by the popular browsers, the color attribute for the <font> tag sets the color of the enclosed text. The value of the attribute may be expressed in either of two ways: as the red, green, and blue (RGB) components of the desired color, or as a standard color name. Enclosing quotes are recommended but not required.

The RGB color value, denoted by a preceding pound sign, is a six-digit hexadecimal number. The first two digits are the red component, from 00 (no red) to FF (bright red). Similarly, the next two digits are the green component and the last two digits are the blue component. Black is the absence of color, #000000; white is all colors, #FFFFFF.

For example, to create basic yellow text, you might use:

```
Here comes the <font color="#FFFF00">sun</font>!
```

Alternatively, you can set the enclosed font color using any one of the many standard color names. See Appendix G for a list of common ones. For instance, you could have made the previous sample text yellow with the following source:

```
Here comes the <font color=yellow>sun</font>!
```

4.10.3.3 The face attribute

In earlier versions, Internet Explorer and Netscape Navigator let you change the font style in a text passage with the face attribute for the <font> tag.* While this is still supported in most browsers, we strongly recommend that you manage your font faces using appropriate styles. Interpretation of the face attribute varies among browsers and missing glyphs within a font can cause unexpected behavior with the displayed text.

The quote-enclosed value of face is one or more display font names separated with commas. The font face displayed by the browser depends on which fonts are available on the individual user's system. The browser parses the list of font names, one

---

* For the HTML purist, the once-powerful user who had ultimate control over the browser, this is egregious indeed. Form over function; look over content—what's next? Embedded video commercials you can't stop?

after the other, until it matches one with a font name supported by the user's system. If none matches, the text display defaults to the font style the user set in the browser's preferences. For example:

```
This text is in the default font. But,
<font face="Braggadocio, Machine, Zapf Dingbats">
heaven only knows</font>
what font face is this one?
```

If the browser user has the Braggadocio, Machine, or none of the listed font typefaces installed in her system, she will be able to read the "heaven only knows" message in the respective or default font style. Otherwise, the message may be garbled, because the Zapf Dingbats font contains symbols, not letters. Of course, the alternative is true, too; you may intend that the message be a symbol-encoded secret.

4.10.3.4 The dir and lang attributes

The dir attribute lets you advise the browser in which direction the text within the tag should be displayed, and lang lets you specify the language used for the tag's contents. [The dir attribute, 3.6.1.1] [The lang attribute, 3.6.1.2]

4.10.3.5 The class, id, style, and title attributes

You can associate additional display rules for the <font> tag using stylesheets. You can apply the rules to the <font> tag using either the style or class attribute. [Inline Styles: The style Attribute, 8.1.1] [Style Classes, 8.3]

You also can assign a unique ID to the <font> tag, as well as a less rigorous title, using the respective attribute and accompanying quote-enclosed string value. [The id attribute, 4.1.1.4] [The title attribute, 4.1.1.5]

Rules, Images, and Multimedia

While the body of most documents is text, an appropriate seasoning of horizontal rules, images, and other multimedia elements makes for a much more inviting and attractive document. These features are not simply gratuitous geegaws that make your documents look pretty, mind you. Multimedia elements bring HTML and XHTML documents alive, providing a dimension of valuable information often unavailable in other media, such as print. In this chapter, we describe in detail how you can insert special multimedia elements into your documents, when their use is appropriate, and how to avoid overdoing it.

You also might want to jump ahead and skim Chapter 12, where we describe some catchall tags (the HTML 4 and XHTML standard <object> and the popular browsers' <embed>) that let you insert all kinds of content and datafile types, including multimedia, into your documents.

5.1 Horizontal Rules

Horizontal rules give you a way to separate sections of your document visually. That way, you give readers a clean, consistent, visual indication that one portion of your document has ended and another portion has begun. Horizontal rules effectively set off small sections of text, delimit document headers and footers, and provide extra visual punch to headings within your document.

5.1.1 The <hr> Tag

The <hr> tag tells the browser to insert a horizontal rule across the display window. With HTML, it has no end tag. For XHTML, include the end-tag slash (/) symbol as the last character in the tag itself after any attributes (<hr .../>), or include an end tag immediately following (<hr></hr>).

Like the <br> tag, <hr> forces a simple line break. Unlike <br>, <hr> causes the paragraph alignment to revert to the default (left justified). The browser places the rule immediately below the current line, and content flow resumes below the rule. [
, 4.6.1]

<hr>

Function	Breaks text flow and inserts a horizontal rule
Attributes	align, class, color 🖋, dir, id, lang, noshade, onClick, onDblClick, onKeyDown, onKeyPress, onKeyUp, onMouseDown, onMouseMove, onMouseOut, onMouseOver, onMouseUp, size, style, title, width
End tag	None in HTML; </hr> or <hr ... /> in XHTML
Contains	Nothing
Used in	*body_content*

The browser decides how to render a horizontal rule. Typically, the rule extends across the entire document. Graphical browsers also may render it with a chiseled or embossed effect; character-based browsers most likely use dashes or underscores to create the rule.

There is no additional space above or below a horizontal rule. If you want to set it off from the surrounding text, you must explicitly place the rule in a new paragraph, followed by another paragraph containing the subsequent text. For example, note the spacing around the horizontal rules in the following HTML source and in Figure 5-1:

```
This text is directly above the rule.
<hr>
And this text is immediately below.
<p>
Whereas this text will have space before the rule.
<p>
<hr>
<p>
And this text has space after the rule.
```

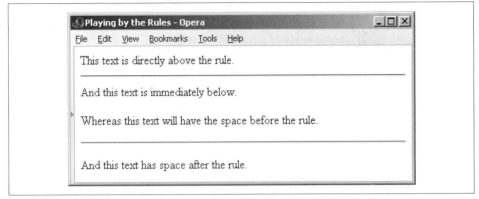

Figure 5-1. Paragraph tags give your text extra elbowroom

A paragraph tag following the rule tag is necessary if you want the content beneath the rule line aligned in any style other than the default left.

5.1.1.1 The size attribute

Normally, browsers render horizontal rules 2 to 3 pixels* thick with a chiseled, 3D appearance, making the rule look incised into the page. You may thicken the rules with the size attribute. The required value is the thickness, in pixels. You can see the effects of this attribute in Figure 5-2, as constructed from the following source:

```
<p>
This is conventional document text,
followed by the standard 2-pixel tall rule line.
<hr>
The next three rule lines are 12, 36, and 72 pixels
tall, respectively.
<hr size=12>
<hr size=36>
<hr size=72>
```

The size attribute is deprecated in HTML 4 and XHTML because you can achieve its effects with appropriate use of stylesheets.

5.1.1.2 The noshade attribute

You may not want a 3D rule line, preferring a flat, 2D rule. Just add the noshade attribute to the <hr> tag to eliminate the 3D effect. No value is required with HTML. Use noshade="noshade" with XHTML.

---

* A pixel is one of the many tiny dots that make up the display on your computer. While display sizes vary, a good rule of thumb is that one pixel equals one point on a 75-dot-per-inch display monitor. A point is a unit of measure used in printing and is roughly equal to 1/72 of an inch (there are 72.27 points in an inch, to be exact). Typical typefaces used by various browsers are usually 12 points tall, yielding up to six lines of text per inch.

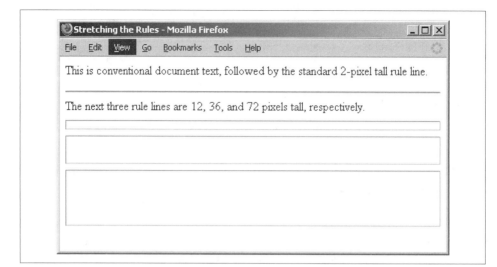

Figure 5-2. The popular browsers let you vary the horizontal rule size

Note the difference in appearance of a "normal" 3D rule versus the noshade 2D one in Figure 5-3. (We've also exaggerated the rule's thickness for obvious effect, as evident in the source HTML fragment.)

```
<hr size=32>
<p>
<hr size=32 noshade>
```

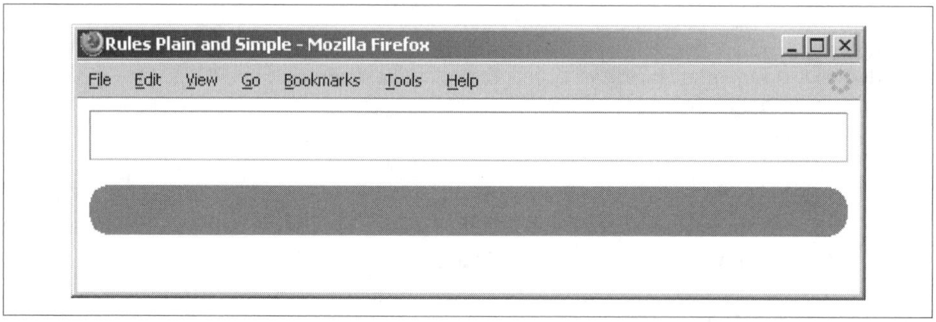

Interestingly, Internet Explorer's noshade rule has blunt ends instead of the rounded ones the other browsers render, like that in Figure 5-3. Nevertheless, the noshade attribute is deprecated in HTML 4 and XHTML because you can achieve its effects with appropriate use of stylesheets.

Figure 5-3. Normal 3D rule versus the noshade 2D option

5.1.1.3 The width attribute

The default rule is drawn across the full width of the view window. You can shorten or lengthen rules with the `width` attribute, creating rule lines that either are an absolute number of pixels wide or extend across a certain percentage of the current text flow. Most browsers automatically center partial-width rules; see the `align` attribute (see section 4.1.1.1) to left- or right-justify horizontal rules.

Here are some examples of width-specified horizontal rules (see Figure 5-4):

```
The following rules are 40 and 320 pixels wide no matter
the actual width of the browser window:
<hr width=40>
<hr width=320>
Whereas these next two rules will always extend across
10 and 75 percent of the window, regardless of its width:
<hr width="10%">
<hr width="75%">
```

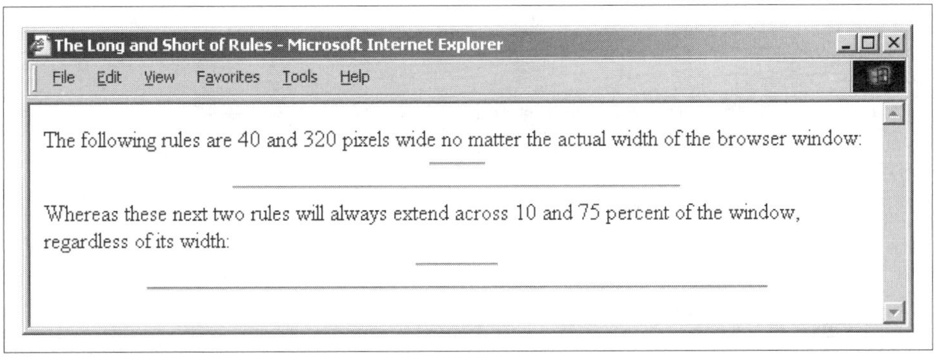

Figure 5-4. The long and short of absolute and relative rule widths

Notice, too, that the relative (percentage) value for the `width` attribute is enclosed in quotation marks; the absolute (integer) pixel value is not. In fact, the quotation marks aren't absolutely necessary with standard HTML (though they are required for XHTML). Further, because the percent symbol normally means that an encoded character follows it, failure to enclose the percentage for the width value in quotation marks may confuse some browsers and trash a portion of your rendered document.

In general, it isn't a good idea to specify the width of a rule as an exact number of pixels. Browser windows vary greatly in their width, and what might be a small rule on one browser might be annoyingly large on another. For this reason, we recommend specifying rule width as a percentage of the window width. That way, when the width of the browser window changes the rules retain their same relative size.

The `width` attribute is deprecated in HTML 4 and XHTML because you can achieve its effects with appropriate use of stylesheets.

5.1.1.4 The align attribute

The `align` attribute for a horizontal rule can have one of three values: `left`, `center`, or `right`. For those rules whose width is less than that of the current text flow, the rule will be positioned accordingly, relative to the window margins. The default alignment is `center`.

A varied rule alignment makes for nice section dividers. For example, the following source alternates a 35-percent-wide rule from right to center to the left margin (see Figure 5-5):

```
<hr width="35%" align=right>
<h3>Fruit Packing Advice</h3>
...
<hr width="35%" align=center>
<h3>Shipping Kumquats</h3>
...
<hr width="35%" align=left>
<h3>Juice Processing</h3>
...
```

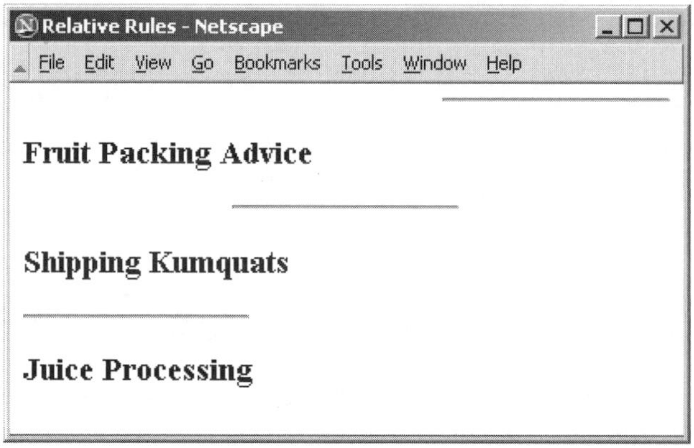

Figure 5-5. Varying horizontal rule alignment makes for subtle section dividers

The `align` attribute is deprecated in HTML 4 and XHTML because you can achieve its effects with appropriate use of stylesheets.

5.1.1.5 The color attribute

Supported by Internet Explorer and Netscape Navigator versions 7 and 8, but not other popular browsers such as Opera, the `color` attribute lets you set the color of the rule line. The value of this attribute is either the name of a color or a hexadecimal triplet that defines a specific color. For a complete list of color names and values, see Appendix G.

By default, a rule is set to the same color as the document background, with the chiseled edges slightly darker and lighter than the background color. You lose the 3D effect when you specify another color, either in a stylesheet or with the color attribute.

5.1.1.6 Combining rule attributes

You may combine the various rule attributes; their order isn't important. To create big rectangles, for example, combine the size and width attributes (see Figure 5-6):

```
<hr size=32 width="50%" align=center>
```

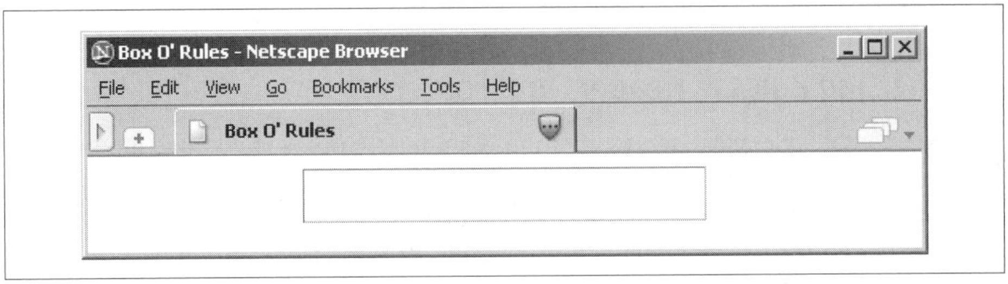

Figure 5-6. Combining rule attributes for special effects

In fact, some combinations of rule attributes are necessary—align and width, for example. Align alone appears to do nothing because the default rule width stretches all the way across the display window.

5.1.1.7 The class, dir, event, id, lang, style, and title attributes

There are several nearly universal attributes for the many content tags. These attributes give you a common way to identify (title) and label (id) a tag's contents for later reference or automated treatment, to change the contents' display characteristics (class, style), to reference the language (lang) used, and to specify the direction in which the text should flow (dir). Of course, how language and the direction of text affect a horizontal rule is unclear. Nonetheless, they are standard attributes for the tag. [The dir attribute, 3.6.1.1] [The lang attribute, 3.6.1.2] [The id attribute, 4.1.1.4] [The title attribute, 4.1.1.5] [Inline Styles: The style Attribute, 8.1.1] [Style Classes, 8.3]

In addition, there are all the user events that may happen in and around the horizontal rule that the browser senses and that you may react to via an on-event attribute and some programming. [JavaScript Event Handlers, 12.3.3]

5.1.2 Using Rules to Divide Your Document

Horizontal rules provide a handy visual navigation device for your readers. To use <hr> effectively as a section divider, first determine how many levels of headings your document has and how long you expect each section of the document to be. Then decide which of your headings warrants being set apart by a rule.

A horizontal rule can also delimit the front matter of a document, separating the table of contents from the document body, for example. Also use a horizontal rule to separate the document body from a trailing index, bibliography, or list of figures.

Experienced authors also use horizontal rules to mark the beginning and end of a form. This is especially handy for long forms that make users scroll up and down the page to view all the fields. By consistently marking the beginning and end of a form with a rule, you help users stay within the form, better ensuring that they won't inadvertently miss a portion when filling out its contents.

5.1.3 Using Rules in Headers and Footers

A fundamental style approach to creating document families is to have a consistent look and feel, including a standard header and footer for each document. Typically, the header contains navigational tools that help users easily jump to internal sections as well as related documents in the family, and the footer contains author and document information as well as feedback mechanisms, such as an email link to the webmaster.

To ensure that these headers and footers don't infringe on the main document contents, consider using rules directly below the header and above the footer. For example (see also Figure 5-7):

```
<body>
Kumquat Growers Handbook - Growing Season Guidelines
<hr>
<h1 align=center>Growing Season Guidelines</h1>
Growing season for the noble fruit varies throughout
North America, as shown in the following map:
<p>
<img src="pics/growing-season.gif">
<p>
<hr>
<i>Provided as a public service by the
<a href="feedback.html">Kumquat Lovers of America</a></i>
```

By consistently setting apart your headers and footers using rules, you help users locate and focus upon the main body of your document.

5.2 Inserting Images in Your Documents

One of the most compelling features of HTML and XHTML is their ability to include images with your document text, either as intrinsic components of the document (inline images), as separate documents specially selected for download via hyperlinks, or as background to your document or elements within the document. When

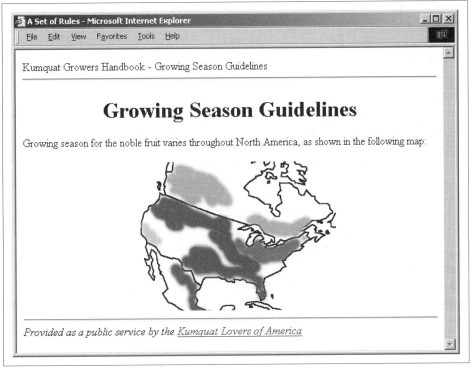

Figure 5-7. Clearly delineate headers and footers with horizontal rules

judiciously added to the body content, images—static and animated icons, pictures, illustrations, drawings, and so on—can make your documents more attractive, inviting, and professional looking, as well as informative and easy to browse. You may also specially enable an image so that it becomes a visual map of hyperlinks. When used to excess, however, images make your document cluttered, confusing, and inaccessible, and they unnecessarily lengthen the time it takes for users to download and view your pages.

5.2.1 Understanding Image Formats

Neither HTML nor XHTML prescribes an official format for images. However, the popular browsers specifically accommodate certain image formats: GIF, PNG, and JPEG, in particular (see the following sections for explanations). Most other multimedia formats require special accessory applications that each browser owner must obtain, install, and successfully operate to view the special files. So it's not too surprising that GIF, PNG, and JPEG are the de facto image standards on the Web.

Both image formats were already in widespread use before the Web came into being, so there's lots of supporting software out there to help you prepare your graphics for either format. However, each has its own advantages and drawbacks, including features that some browsers exploit for special display effects.

5.2.1.1 GIF

The Graphics Interchange Format (GIF) was first developed for image transfer among users of the CompuServe online service. The format has several features that make it popular for use in HTML and XHTML documents. Its encoding is cross-platform so that with appropriate GIF-decoding software (included with most browsers), the graphics you create and make into a GIF file on a Macintosh, for example, can be loaded into a Windows-based PC, decoded, and viewed without a lot of fuss. The second main feature is that GIF uses special compression technology that can significantly reduce the size of the image file for faster transfer over a network. GIF compression is "lossless," too; none of an image's original data is altered or deleted, so the uncompressed and decoded image exactly matches its original. Also, GIF images can be easily animated.

Even though GIF image files invariably have the *.gif* (or *.GIF*) filename suffix, there actually are two GIF versions: the original GIF87 and an expanded GIF89a, which supports several new features—including transparent backgrounds, interlaced storage, and animation—that are popular with web authors (see section 5.2.1.2). The currently popular browsers support both GIF versions, which use the same encoding scheme that maps 8-bit pixel values to a color table, for a maximum of 256 colors per image. Most GIF images have even fewer colors; there are special tools to simplify the colors in more elaborate graphics. By simplifying the GIF images, you create a smaller color map and enhance pixel redundancy for better file compression and, consequently, faster downloading.

However, because of the limited number of colors, a GIF-encoded image is not always appropriate, particularly for photorealistic pictures (see the discussion in section 5.2.1.3). GIFs make excellent icons, reduced-color images, and drawings.

Because most graphical browsers explicitly support the GIF format, it is currently the most widely accepted image-encoding format on the Web. It is acceptable for both inline images and externally linked ones. When in doubt as to which image format to use, choose GIF.* It will work in almost any situation.

5.2.1.2 Interlacing, transparency, and animation

You can make GIF images perform three special tricks: interlacing, transparency, and animation. With interlacing, a GIF image seemingly materializes on the display, instead of progressively flowing onto it from top to bottom. Normally, a GIF-encoded image is a sequence of pixel data in order, row by row, from the top to the

---

* We cannot resist the temptation to point out that choosy authors choose GIF.

---

bottom of the image. While the common GIF image renders onscreen like pulling down a window shade, interlaced GIFs open like a Venetian blind. That's because interlacing sequences every fourth row of the image. Users get to see a full image—top to bottom, albeit fuzzy—in a quarter of the time it takes to download and display the remainder of the image. The resulting quarter-done image usually is clear enough so that users with slow network connections can evaluate whether to take the time to download the remainder of the image file.

Not all graphical browsers, although able to display an interlaced GIF, are actually able to display the materializing effects of interlacing. With those that do, users still can defeat the effect by choosing to delay image display until after download and decoding. Older browsers, on the other hand, always download and decode images before display and don't support the effect at all.

Another popular effect available with GIF images—GIF89a-formatted images, that is—is the ability to make a portion of them transparent so that what's underneath (usually, the browser window's background) shows through. The transparent GIF image has one color in its color map designated as the background color. The browser simply ignores any pixel in the image that uses that background color, thereby letting the display window's background show through. By carefully cropping its dimensions and by using a solid, contiguous background color, you can make a transparent image seamlessly meld into or float above a page's surrounding content.

Transparent GIF images are great for any graphic that you want to meld into the document and not stand out as a rectangular block. Transparent GIF logos are very popular, as are transparent icons and dingbats—any graphic that should appear to have an arbitrary, natural shape. You may also insert a transparent image inline with conventional text to act as a special character glyph within conventional text.

The downside to transparency is that the GIF image will look lousy if you don't remove its border when it is included in a hyperlink anchor (<a>) tag or is otherwise specially framed. And content flow happens around the image's rectangular dimensions, not adjacent to its apparent shape. That can lead to unnecessarily isolated images or odd-looking sections in your web pages.

The third unique trick available with GIF89a-formatted images is the ability to do simple frame-by-frame animation. Using special GIF-animation software utilities, you may prepare a single GIF89a file that contains a series of GIF images. The browser displays each image in the file, one after the other, something like the page-flipping animation booklets we had and perhaps drew as kids. Special control segments between each image in the GIF file let you set the number of times the browser runs through the complete sequence (looping), how long to pause between each image, whether the image space gets wiped to background before the browser displays the next image, and so on. By combining these control features with those normally available for GIF images, including individual color tables, transparency, and interlacing, you can create some very appealing and elaborate animations.*

Simple GIF animation is powerful for one other important reason: you don't need to specially program your HTML documents to achieve animation. But there is one major downside that limits their use for anything other than small, icon-size, or thin bands of space in the browser window: GIF animation files get large fast, even if you are careful not to repeat static portions of the image in successive animation cells. And if you have several animations in one document, download delays may—and usually will—annoy the user. If any feature deserves close scrutiny for excess, it's GIF animation.

Any and all GIF tricks—interlacing, transparency, and animation—don't just happen; you need special software to prepare the GIF file. Many image tools now save your creations or acquired images in GIF format, and most now let you enable transparency and make interlaced GIF files. There also are a slew of shareware and freeware programs specialized for these tasks, as well as for creating GIF animations. Look into your favorite Internet software archives for GIF graphics and conversion tools, and see Chapter 17 for details on creating transparent images.

5.2.1.3 JPEG

The Joint Photographic Experts Group (JPEG) is a standards body that developed what is now known as the JPEG image-encoding format. Like GIFs, JPEG images are platform independent and specially compressed for high-speed transfer via digital communication technologies. Unlike GIF, JPEG supports tens of thousands of colors for more detailed, photorealistic digital images. And JPEG uses special algorithms that yield much higher data-compression ratios. It is not uncommon, for example, for a 200 KB GIF image to be reduced to a 30 KB JPEG image. To achieve that amazing compression, JPEG does lose some image data. However, you can adjust the degree of "lossiness" with special JPEG tools so that although the uncompressed image may not exactly match the original, it will be close enough that most people cannot tell the difference.

Although JPEG is an excellent choice for photographs, it's not a particularly good choice for illustrations. The algorithms used for compressing and uncompressing the image leave noticeable artifacts when dealing with large areas of one color. Therefore, if you're trying to display a drawing, the GIF format may be preferable.

The JPEG format, usually designated by the *.jpg* (or *.JPG*) filename suffix, is nearly universally understood by today's graphical browsers. On rare occasions, you'll come across an older browser that cannot directly display JPEG images.

---

* Songline Studios has published an entire book dedicated to GIF animation: *GIF Animation Studio*, by Richard Koman.

5.2.1.4 PNG

The Portable Network Graphics (PNG) technology originated to replace GIF, but not because GIF wasn't up to the job. Indeed, GIF was and probably still is the most widely implemented graphics format on the Internet. Instead, many Internet users got enraged when in 1993, after GIF had attained its popularity and widespread use, Unisys decided to enforce its patent and collect royalties on GIF's essential compression technology. That action ran against the widespread philosophy of free exchange and use enjoyed by the mostly academic community of Internet users, and prompted an informal Internet working group led by Thomas Boutell to develop the PNG alternative.

PNG's advantages over GIF and JPEG, besides providing a litigation-free alternative format, include a broader selection of color formats (24-bit true-color RGB, a grayscale and GIF-like 8-bit palette) and better lossless compression. PNG's unique and attractive features include alpha channels which let you specify many more than GIF's one layer of transparency (more than 65,000, actually) and can simulate 3D imagery, gamma correction which controls cross-platform image brightness for more vivid graphics, and two-dimensional interlacing which provides for a finer progressively developing image.

PNG does not support animation. Though you may hesitate to use PNG on that basis alone, we encourage you to try it out anyway, especially for high-color and high-quality images.

5.2.2 When to Use Images

Most pictures are worth a thousand words. But don't forget that no one pays attention to a blabbermouth. First and foremost, think of your document images as visual tools, not as gratuitous trappings. They should support your text content and help readers navigate your documents. Use images to clarify, illustrate, or exemplify the contents. Content-supporting photographs, charts, graphs, maps, and drawings are all natural and appropriate candidates. Product photographs are essential components in online catalogs and shopping guides, for example. And link-enabled icons and dingbats, including animated images, can be effective visual guides to internal and external resources. If an image doesn't do any of these valuable services for your document, throw it out already!

One of the most important considerations when adding images to a document is the additional delay they add to the retrieval time for a document over the network, particularly for modem connections. While a common text document might run, at most, 10,000 or 15,000 bytes, images can easily extend to hundreds of thousands of bytes each. And the total retrieval time for a document is not only equal to the sum of all its component parts, but also to compounded networking overhead delays.

Depending on the speed of the connection (*bandwidth*, usually expressed as bits or bytes per second) as well as network congestion that can delay connections, a single document containing one 100 KB image may take less than a second through a cable modem connection in the wee hours of the morning, when most everyone else is asleep, to well over *10 minutes* with a cell phone at noon. You get the picture?

With that said, of course, pictures and other multimedia are driving Internet providers to come up with faster, better, more robust ways to deliver web content. Modem connections are quickly going the way of the horse and carriage, replaced by technologies like high-speed cable modems and the Asymmetric Digital Subscriber Line (ADSL).

Still, as the price lowers, use goes up, so there is the issue of congestion. And don't forget cell phone browsers and our Third World neighbors, where connections are spotty and slow. Besides, if you are competing for access to an overburdened server, it doesn't matter how fast your connection may be.

5.2.3 When to Use Text

Text hasn't gone out of style. For some users, it is the only accessible portion of your document. We argue that, in most circumstances, your documents should be usable by readers who cannot view images, or have disabled automatic download in their browsers to improve their connections. While the urge to add images to all of your documents may be strong, sometimes pure text documents make more sense.

Documents being converted to the Web from other formats rarely have embedded images. Reference materials and other serious content often are completely usable in a text-only form.

You should create text-only documents when access speed is critical. If you know that many users will be vying for your pages, you should accommodate them by avoiding the use of images within your documents. In some extreme cases, you might provide a home (leading) page that lets readers decide between duplicate collections of your work: one containing the images and another stripped of them. (The popular browsers include special picture icons as placeholders for yet-to-be-downloaded images, which can trash and muddle your document's layout into an unreadable mess.)

Text is most appropriate—supporting images only, without frills and nonessential graphics—if your documents are to be readily searchable by any of the many web indexing services. These search engines almost always ignore images. If you provide the major content of your pages with images, very little information about your documents will find its way into the online web directories.

5.2.4 Speeding Image Downloads

There are several ways to reduce the overhead and delays inherent with images, besides being very choosy about which to include in your documents:

Keep it simple

A full-screen, 24-bit color graphic, even when reduced in size by digital compression with one of the standard formats, such as GIF, PNG, or JPEG, is still going to be a network-bandwidth hog. First decide between image integrity and size. Then acquire and use the proper image-management tool that optimizes your image for the application, particularly for special effects like GIF animation or PNG's 3D effects. Simplify your drawings. Stay away from panoramic photographs. Avoid large, empty backgrounds in your images, as well as gratuitous borders and other space-consuming elements. Also avoid *dithering* (blending two colors among adjacent pixels to achieve a third color); this technique can significantly reduce the compressibility of your images. Strive for large areas of uniform colors, which compress readily.

Reuse images

This is particularly true for icons and GIF animations. Most browsers cache incoming document components in local storage for the very purpose of quick, network-connectionless retrieval of data. For smaller GIF animation files, try to prepare each successive image to update only portions that change in the animation, instead of redrawing the entire image (this speeds up the animation, too).

Divide large documents into smaller segments

This is a general rule that includes images. Many small document segments, organized through hyperlinks and effective tables of contents, tend to be better accepted by users than a few large documents. In general, people would rather "flip" several pages than dawdle, waiting for a large one to download. (It's related to the TV channel-surfing syndrome.) One accepted rule of thumb is to keep your documents smaller than 50 KB each, so even the slowest connections won't overly frustrate your readers.

Isolate necessarily large graphics

Provide a special link to large images, perhaps one that includes a thumbnail of the graphic, thereby letting readers decide whether and when they want to spend the time downloading the full image. Because the downloaded image isn't mixed with other document components like inline images, it's also much easier for the reader to identify and save the image on her system's local storage for later study. (For details on noninline image downloads, see section 5.6.2.)

Specify image dimensions

Finally, another way to improve performance is by including the image's rectangular height and width information in its tag. By supplying those dimensions, you eliminate the extra steps the extended browsers must take to download, examine, and calculate an image's space in the document, allowing them to render the page more quickly. There is a downside to this approach, however, that we explore in section 5.2.6.12.

5.2.5 JPEG, PNG, or GIF?

You may choose to use only one type of image format in your HTML documents if your sources for images or your software tool set prefer one over the other format. All are nearly universally supported by today's browsers, so there shouldn't be any user-viewing problems.

Nevertheless, we recommend that you acquire the facilities to create and convert to at least the three formats we describe in this chapter to take advantage of their unique capabilities. For instance, use GIF's animation and PNG's transparency feature for icons and dingbats. Alternatively, use JPEG's deep compression, albeit at a loss of some integrity, for large and colorful images for faster downloading.

5.2.6 The <img> Tag

The <img> tag lets you reference and insert a graphic image into the current text flow of your document. There is no implied line or paragraph break before or after the <img> tag, so images can be truly "in line" with text and other content.

<img>

Function	Inserts an image into a document
Attributes	align, alt, border, class, controls ⬚, dir, dynsrc ⬚, height, hspace, id, ismap, lang, longdesc ⬚, loop ⬚, lowsrc ⬚, name ⬚, onAbort, onClick, onDblClick, onError, onKeyDown, onKeyPress, onKeyUp, onLoad, onMouseDown, onMouseMove, onMouseOut, onMouseOver, onMouseUp, src, start ⬚, style, title, usemap, vspace, width
End tag	None in HTML; </img> or <img ... /> in XHTML
Contains	Nothing
Used in	*text*

The format of the image itself is not defined by the HTML or XHTML standard, although the popular graphical browsers support most common formats like GIF, PNG, and JPEG images. The standards don't specify or restrict the size or dimensions of the image, either. Images may have any number of colors as allowed by their format, but how those colors are rendered is highly browser dependent.

Image presentation in general is very browser specific. Images may be ignored by nongraphical browsers. Browsers operating in a constrained environment may modify the image size or complexity. And users, particularly those with slow network connections, may choose to defer image loading altogether. Accordingly, you should make sure your documents make sense and are useful even if the images are completely removed.

The HTML version of the <img> tag has no end tag. With XHTML, either use </img> immediately following the <img> tag and its attributes, or make the last character in the tag the end-tag slash mark: <img src="kumquat.gif" />, for example.

5.2.6.1 The src attribute

The src attribute for the <img> tag is required (unless you use dynsrc with Internet Explorer-based movies; see section 5.2.7.1). Its value is the image file's URL, either absolute or relative to the document referencing the image. To unclutter their document storage, authors typically collect image files into a separate folder, which they often name something like "pics" or "images." [Referencing Documents: The URL, 6.2]

For example, this HTML fragment places an image of a famous kumquat packing plant into the narrative text (see Figure 5-8):

```
Here we are, on day 17 of the tour, in the kumquat packing plant:
<p>
<img src="pics/packing_plant.gif">
<p>
What an exciting moment, to see the boxes of fruit piled high to
```

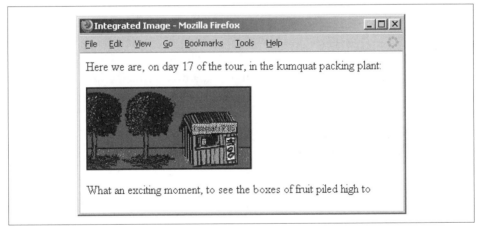

Figure 5-8. Image integrated with text

In the example, the paragraph (<p>) tags surrounding the <img> tag cause the browser to render the image by itself, with some vertical space after the preceding text and before the trailing text. Text may also abut the image, as we describe in section 4.1.1.1.

5.2.6.2 The lowsrc attribute

To the benefit of users, particularly those with slow network connections, early versions of Netscape provided the lowsrc companion to the src attribute in the <img> tag as a way to speed up document rendering. The lowsrc attribute's value, like src, is the URL of an image file. Netscape before version 6 would load and display the lowsrc image when it first encountered the <img> tag. Then, when the document had been completely loaded and the user could read it, Netscape would retrieve the image specified by the src attribute.

No other browser besides Netscape versions 4 and earlier supports lowsrc. Netscape version 6 simply uses the dimensions of the lowsrc image to temporarily allocate display space for the image as it renders the document. The earlier versions of Netscape also used the lowsrc dimensions to resize the final image, which you could exploit for some special effects. This no longer works. Instead, we recommend that you eschew the Netscape extension and explicitly allocate image space with the height and width attributes described later in this chapter.

5.2.6.3 The alt and longdesc attributes

The alt attribute specifies alternative text the browser may show if image display is not possible or is disabled by the user. Especially favored by visually impaired users, the popular browsers also let us choose to display alt text along with the image. So although it's an option, it's one we highly recommend you exercise for most images in your document. This way, if the image is not available, the user still has some indication of what's missing. And for users with certain disabilities, alt often is the only way they can appreciate your images.

In addition, Internet Explorer displays the alternative description in a text box when users pass the mouse over the image. Accordingly, you might embed short, parenthetical information that pops up when users pass over a small, inline icon, such as that shown in Figure 5-9.

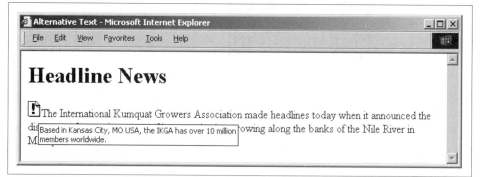

Figure 5-9. Internet Explorer displays alt text in a temporary pop-up window

The value for the `alt` attribute is a text string of up to 1,024 characters, including spaces and punctuation. The string must be enclosed in quotation marks. The `alt` text may contain entity references to special characters, but it may not contain any other sort of markup; in particular, style tags aren't allowed.

Graphical browsers don't normally display the `alt` attribute if the image is available and the user has enabled picture downloading. Otherwise, they insert the `alt` attribute's text as a label next to an image-placeholder icon. Well-chosen `alt` labels thereby additionally support those users with graphical browsers who have disabled automatic image download because of a slow connection to the Web.

Nongraphical, text-only browsers such as the ancient Lynx put the `alt` text directly into the content flow, just like any other text element. So, when used effectively, the alt tag sometimes can transparently substitute for missing images. (Your text-only browser users will appreciate not being constantly reminded of their second-class web citizenship.) For example, consider using an asterisk as the `alt` attribute alternative to a special bullet icon:

```
<h3><img src="pics/fancy_bullet.gif" alt="*">Introduction</h3>
```

A graphical browser displays the bullet image; in a nongraphical browser, the `alt` asterisk takes the place of the missing bullet. Similarly, use `alt` text to replace special image bullets for list items. For example, the following code:

```
<ul>
  <li> Kumquat recipes <img src="pics/new.gif" alt="(New!)">
  <li> Annual harvest dates
</ul>
```

displays the *new.gif* image with graphical browsers and the text "(New!)" with text-only browsers. The alt attribute uses even more complex text (see Figure 5-10):

```
Here we are, on day 17 of the tour, in the kumquat
packing plant:
<p>
<img src="pics/packing_plant.gif"
  alt="[Image of our tour group outside the main packing plant]">
<p>
What an exciting moment, to see the boxes of fruit moving
```

According to the HTML 4.01 specification, the `alt` attribute is required for all `<img>` tags. To be truly compliant, include empty `alt` attributes (`alt=""`) with all your images.

The `longdesc` attribute is similar to the `alt` attribute but allows for longer descriptions. The value of `longdesc` is the URL of a document containing a description of the image. If you have a description longer than 1,024 characters, use the `longdesc` attribute to link to it. Neither HTML 4 nor XHTML specifies what the content of the description must be, and no browsers currently implement `longdesc`; all bets are off when deciding how to create those long descriptions.

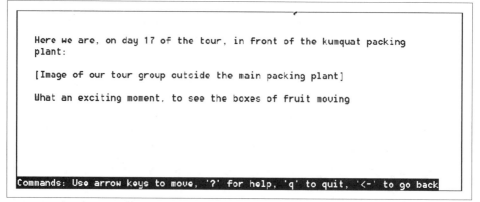

```
Here we are, on day 17 of the tour, in front of the kumquat packing
plant:

[Image of our tour group outside the main packing plant]

What an exciting moment, to see the boxes of fruit moving




Commands: Use arrow keys to move, '?' for help, 'q' to quit, '<-' to go back
```

Figure 5-10. Text-only browsers such as Lynx display an image's alt attribute text

5.2.6.4 The align attribute

The standards don't define a default alignment for images with respect to other text and images in the same line of text: you can't always predict how the text and images will look.* HTML images normally appear in line with a single line of text. Common print media such as magazines wrap text around images, with several lines next to and abutting the image, not just a single line.

Fortunately, document designers also can exert some control over the alignment of images with the surrounding text through the align attribute for the <img> tag. The HTML and XHTML standards specify five image-alignment attribute values: left, right, top, middle, and bottom. The left and right values flow any subsequent text to the left or right of the image, which is moved to the corresponding margin (Figure 5-11). The remaining three align the image vertically with respect to the surrounding text.

All of the popular browsers, including Opera, Firefox, Netscape, and Internet Explorer, agree that align=bottom is the default vertical alignment, and similarly position images at the top of the uppermost character in the line of text, also shown in Figure 5-11.

The browsers disagree, however, on where to place an align=middle image with regard to text. As shown in Figure 5-11, Netscape and Opera place it in the apparent middle of the text. Internet Explorer and Firefox, on the other hand, place the image at the middle of the tallest element, not necessarily the tallest text (Figure 5-12).

---

* Most of the popular graphical browsers insert an image so that its base aligns with the baseline of the text—the same alignment specified by the attribute value of bottom. But document designers should assume that alignment varies among browsers and should always include the desired type of image alignment.

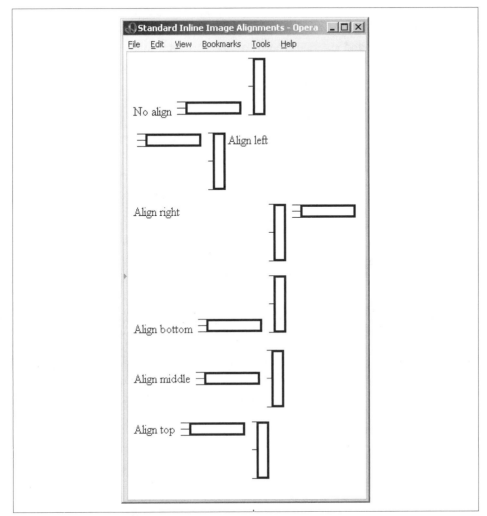

Figure 5-11. Standard inline image alignments

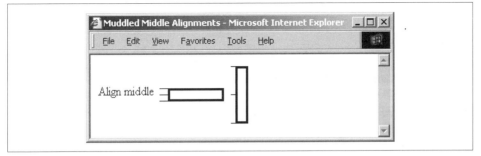

Figure 5-12. Internet Explorer and Firefox align the middle of images to the middle of the tallest element, not to the middle of the text

The browsers also support, to varying degrees, five vertical image alignment extensions—texttop, center, absmiddle, baseline, and absbottom (if you are confused as to exactly what each alignment value means, please raise your hand):

texttop

> The align=texttop attribute and value tell the browser to align the top of the image with the top of the tallest *text* item in the current line, as opposed to the top option, which aligns the top of the image with the top of the tallest item, image or text, in the current line. If the line contains no other images that extend above the top of the text, texttop and top have the same effect. Opera does not support texttop, whereas the other popular browsers treat it identically as described.

center

> Originally introduced by Internet Explorer, the center image alignment value gets treated by Internet Explorer, Netscape, and Firefox exactly the same as they individually treat middle, which, as you may recall, differs among the browsers. Opera, on the other hand, ignores align=center altogether.

absmiddle

> If you set the align attribute of the <img> tag to absmiddle, the browser will fit the absolute middle of the image to the absolute middle of the current line. This is different from the common middle and center options, which align the middle of the image with the baseline of the current line of text (the bottom of the characters). Though Netscape and Opera do not distinguish absmiddle from middle alignments, Firefox and Internet Explorer use it to differentially align images from their middle values—in other words, Firefox and Internet Explorer's absmiddle alignment is the same as Netscape's middle.

bottom *and* baseline *(default)*

> The bottom and baseline image-alignment values have the same effect as if you didn't include any alignment attribute at all: the browsers align the bottom of the image in the same horizontal plane as the baseline of the text. This is not to be confused with absbottom, which takes into account letter *descenders*. (Did we see a hand up in the audience?)

absbottom

> The align=absbottom attribute-value pair tells the browser to align the bottom of the image with the true bottom of the current line of text. The true bottom is the lowest point in the text, taking into account descenders, even if there are no characters with descenders in the line. A descender is the tail on a "y," for example; the baseline of the text is the bottom of the "v" in the "y" character. Opera, the standard bearer, ignores absbottom, whereas the other popular browsers treat it as advertised (Figure 5-13).

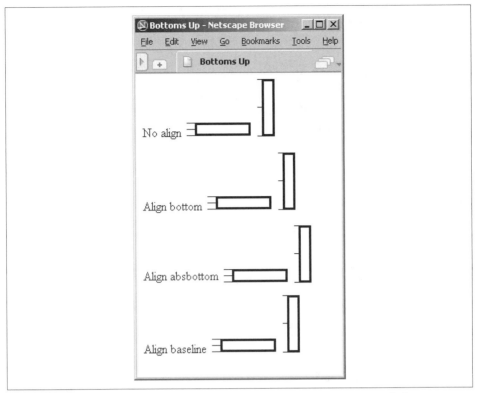

Figure 5-13. Browsers take into account text descenders when aligning images with the
align=absbottom attribute

Use the top or middle alignment value for best integration of icons, dingbats, or other special inline effects with the text content. Otherwise, align=bottom (the default) usually gives the best appearance. When aligning one or more images on a single line, select the alignment that gives the best overall appearance to your document.

5.2.6.5 Wrapping text around images

The left and right image-alignment values tell the browser to place an image against the left or right margin, respectively, of the current text flow. The browser then renders subsequent document content in the remaining portion of the flow adjacent to the image. The net result is that the document content following the image gets wrapped around the image:

```
<img src="pics/kumquat.gif" align=left>
The kumquat is the smallest of the citrus fruits, similar in appearance to a
tiny orange. The similarity ends with its appearance, however. While oranges
are generally
sweet, kumquats are extremely bitter. Theirs is an acquired taste, to be sure.
```

Figure 5-14 shows text flow around a left-aligned image.

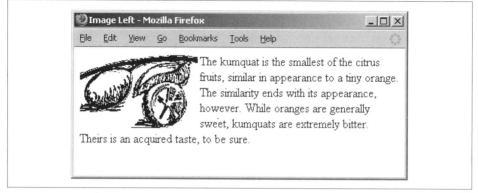

Figure 5-14. Text flow around a left-aligned image

You can place images against both margins simultaneously (Figure 5-15), and the text will run down the middle of the page between them:

```
<img src="pics/kumquat.gif" align=left>
<img src="pics/tree.gif" align=right>
The kumquat is the smallest of the citrus fruits, similar in appearance to a
tiny orange. The similarity ends with its appearance, however. While oranges
are generally sweet, kumquats are extremely bitter. Theirs is an acquired taste,
to be sure.
```

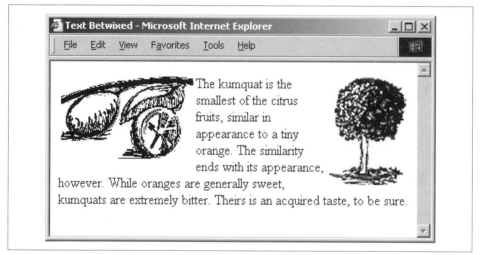

Figure 5-15. Running text between left- and right-aligned images

While text is flowing around an image, the left (or right) margin of the page is temporarily redefined to be adjacent to the image as opposed to the edge of the page. Subsequent images with the same alignment will stack up against each other. The following source fragment achieves that staggered image effect:

```
<img src="pics/marcia.gif" align=left>
Marcia!
<br>
<img src="pics/jan.gif" align=left>
Jan!
<br>
<img src="pics/cindy.gif" align=left>
Cindy!
```

The results of this example are shown in Figure 5-16.

Figure 5-16. Three very lovely girls from a very old sitcom

When the text flows beyond the bottom of the image, the margin returns to its former position, typically at the edge of the browser window.

5.2.6.6 Centering an image

Have you noticed that you can't horizontally center an image in the browser window with the align attribute? The middle and absmiddle values center the image vertically with the current line, but the image is horizontally justified depending on what content comes before it in the current flow and the dimensions of the browser window.

You can horizontally center an inline image in the browser window, but only if it's isolated from surrounding content, such as by paragraph, division, or line-break tags. Then, either use the <center> tag or use the align=center attribute or center-justified style in the paragraph or division tag to center the image. For example:

```
Kumquats are tasty treats
<br>
<center>
<img src="pics/kumquat.gif">
</center>
that everyone should strive to eat!
```

Use the paragraph tag with its `align=center` attribute if you want some extra space above and below the centered image:

```
Kumquats are tasty treats
<p align=center>
<img src="pics/kumquat.gif">
</p>
that everyone should strive to eat!
```

5.2.6.7 Align and <center> are deprecated

The HTML 4 and XHTML standards have deprecated the `align` attribute for all tags, including `<img>`, in deference to stylesheets. They've deprecated `<center>`, too. Nonetheless, the attribute and tag are very popular among HTML authors and remain well supported by the popular browsers. So, while we do expect that someday both `align` and `<center>` will disappear, it won't be anytime soon. Just don't say we didn't warn you.

What if you don't want to use `align` or `<center>`? Some authors and many of the WYSIWYG editors use HTML/XHTML tables to align content. That's one way, albeit involved (see Chapter 10). The World Wide Web Consortium (W3C) wants you to use styles. For example, use the `margin-left` style to indent the image from the left side of the display. You can read lots more about Cascading Style Sheets (CSS) in Chapter 8.

5.2.6.8 The border attribute

Browsers normally render images that also are hyperlinks (i.e., images included in an `<a>` tag) with a 2-pixel-wide colored border, indicating to the reader that he can select the image to visit the associated document. Use the `border` attribute and a pixel-width thickness value to remove (`border=0`) or widen that image border. Be aware that this attribute, too, is deprecated in HTML 4 and XHTML, in deference to stylesheets, but continues to be well supported by the popular browsers.

Figure 5-17 shows you the thick and thin of image borders, as rendered by Internet Explorer from the following XHTML source:

```
<a href="test.html">
 <img src="pics/kumquat.gif" border="1" />
</a>
<a href="test.html">
  <img src="pics/kumquat.gif" border="2" />
</a>
<a href="test.html">
  <img src="pics/kumquat.gif" border="4" />
</a>
<a href="test.html">
  <img src="pics/kumquat.gif" border="8" />
</a>
```

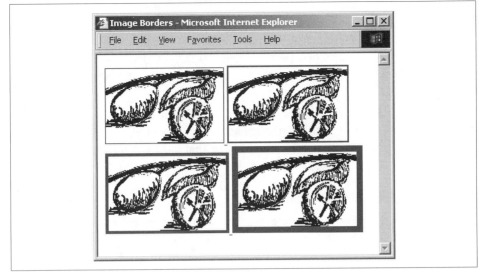

Figure 5-17. The thick and thin of image borders

5.2.6.9 Removing the image border

You can eliminate the border around an image hyperlink altogether with the border=0 attribute within the <img> tag. For some images, particularly image maps, the absence of a border can improve the appearance of your pages. Images that are clearly link buttons to other pages may also look best without borders.

Be careful, though, that by removing the border, you don't diminish your page's usability. No border means you've removed a common visual indicator of a link, making it more difficult for your readers to find the links on the page. Browsers will change the mouse cursor as the reader passes it over an image that is a hyperlink, but you should not assume they will, nor should you make readers test your borderless images to find hidden links.

We strongly recommend that with borderless images you use some additional way to let your readers know to click the images. Even including simple text instructions will go a long way toward making your pages more accessible to readers.

5.2.6.10 The height and width attributes

Ever watch the display of a page's contents shift around erratically while the document is loading? That happens because the browser readjusts the page layout to accommodate each loaded image. The browser determines the size of an image—and, hence, the rectangular space to reserve for it in the display window—by retrieving the image file and extracting its embedded height and width specifications. The browser then adjusts the page's display layout to insert that picture in the display.* This is not the most efficient way to render a document because the browser must sequentially examine each image file and calculate its screen space before rendering adjacent and subsequent document content. That can significantly increase the amount of time it takes to render the document and can disrupt reading by the user.

A more efficient way for authors to specify an image's dimensions is with the `height` and `width` <img> attributes. That way, the browser can reserve space before actually downloading an image, speeding document rendering and eliminating the content shifting. Both attributes require an integer value that indicates the image size in pixels; the order in which they appear in the <img> tag is not important.

5.2.6.11 Resizing and flood-filling images

A hidden feature of the `height` and `width` attributes is that you don't need to specify the actual image dimensions; the attribute values can be larger or smaller than the actual size of the image. The browser automatically scales the image to fit the predefined space. This gives you a down-and-dirty way of creating thumbnail versions of large images and a way to enlarge very small pictures. Be careful, though: the browser still must download the entire file, no matter what its final rendered size is, and you will distort an image if you don't retain its original height versus width proportions.

Another trick with `height` and `width` provides an easy way to flood-fill areas of your page and can also improve document performance. Suppose you want to insert a colored bar across your document.† Instead of creating an image to fill the full dimensions, create one that is just 1 pixel high and wide and set it to the desired color. Then use the `height` and `width` attributes to scale it to the larger size:

```
<img src="pics/one-pixel.gif" width=640 height=20>
```

The smaller image downloads much faster than a full-scale one, and the `width` and `height` attributes have Firefox, for example, create the desired bright-red colored bar after the tiny image arrives at the browser (Figure 5-18).

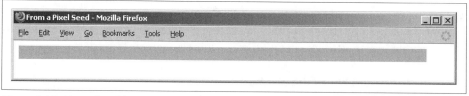

Figure 5-18. This colored horizontal bar was made from a 1-pixel image

---

* Another reminder that images are separate files, which are loaded individually and in addition to the source document.

† This is one way to create colored horizontal rules, since Netscape doesn't support the `color` attribute for the <hr> tag.

One last trick with the width attribute is to use a percentage value rather than an absolute pixel value. This causes the browser to scale the image to a percentage of the document window width. Thus, to create a colored bar 20 pixels high and the width of the window, you could use:

```
<img src="pics/one-pixel.gif" width="100%" height=20>
```

As the document window changes size, the image will change size as well.

If you provide a percentage width and omit the height, the browser will retain the image's aspect ratio as it grows and shrinks. This means that the height will always be in the correct proportion to the width, and the image will display without distortion.

5.2.6.12 Problems with height and width

Although the height and width attributes for the <img> tag can improve performance and let you perform neat tricks, there is a knotty downside to using them. The browser sets aside the specified rectangle of space to the prescribed dimensions in the display window, even if the user has turned off automatic download of images. What the user often is left with is a page full of semi-empty frames with meaningless picture-placeholder icons inside. The page looks terribly unfinished and is mostly useless. Without accompanying dimensions, on the other hand, the browser simply inserts a placeholder icon inline with the surrounding text, so at least there's something there to read in the display.

We don't have a solution for this dilemma, other than to insist that you use the alt attribute with some descriptive text so that users at least know what they are missing. We do recommend that you include these size attributes because we encourage any practice that improves display performance.

5.2.6.13 The hspace and vspace attributes

Graphical browsers usually don't give you much space between an image and the text around it. And unless you create a transparent image border that expands the space between them, the typical 2-pixel buffer between an image and adjacent text is just too close for most designers' comfort. Add the image into a hyperlink, and the special colored border will negate any transparent buffer space you labored to create, as well as drawing even more attention to how close the adjacent text butts up against the image.

The hspace and vspace attributes can give your images breathing room. With hspace, you specify the number of pixels of extra space to leave between the image and text on the left and right sides of the image; the vspace value is the number of pixels on the top and bottom:

```
<img src="pics/kumquat.gif" align=left>
The kumquat is the smallest of the citrus fruits, similar
in appearance to a tiny orange. The similarity ends with its
appearance, however. While oranges are generally sweet,
```

```
kumquats are extremely bitter. Theirs is an acquired taste,
to be sure. Most folks, at first taste, wonder how you could
ever eat another, let alone enjoy it!
<p>
<img src="pics/kumquat.gif" align=left hspace=10 vspace=10>
The kumquat is the smallest of the citrus fruits, similar
in appearance to a tiny orange. The similarity ends with its
appearance, however. While oranges are generally sweet,
kumquats are extremely bitter. Theirs is an acquired taste,
to be sure. Most folks, at first taste, wonder how you could
ever eat another, let alone enjoy it!
```

Figure 5-19 shows the difference between two wrapped images.

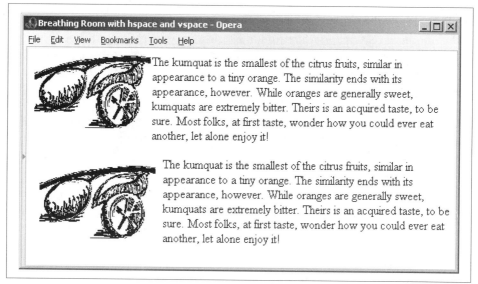

Figure 5-19. Improve image/text interfaces with vspace and hspace

We're sure you'll agree that the additional space around the image makes the text easier to read and the overall page more attractive.

5.2.6.14 The ismap and usemap attributes

The ismap and usemap attributes for the <img> tag tell the browser that the image is a special mouse-selectable visual map of one or more hyperlinks, commonly known as an *image map*. You can specify the ismap style of image maps only within an <a> tag hyperlink. [<a>, 6.3.1]

For example (notice the redundant attribute and value, as well as the trailing end-tag slash mark in the <img> tag, which are telltale signs of XHTML):

```
<a href="/cgi-bin/images/map2">
  <img src="pics/map2.gif" ismap="ismap" />
</a>
```

The browser automatically sends the coordinates of the mouse relative to the upper-left corner of the image to the server when the user clicks somewhere on the ismap image. Special server software (the */cgi-bin/images/map2* program, in the example) may then use those coordinates to determine a response.

The ismap attribute is a *server-side* mechanism because it relies on the server for processing user input. The usemap attribute provides a *client-side* image-map mechanism that effectively eliminates server-side processing of the mouse coordinates and its incumbent network delays and problems. Using special <map> and <area> tags, HTML authors provide a map of coordinates for the hyperlink-sensitive regions in the usemap image, along with related hyperlink URLs. The value of the usemap attribute is a URL that points to that special <map> section. The browser on the user's client computer translates the coordinates of a click of the mouse on the image into some action, including loading and displaying another document. [<map>, 6.5.3] [<area>, 6.5.4]

For example, the following source specially encodes the 100×100-pixel *map2.gif* image into four segments, each of which, if clicked by the user, links to a different document. Notice that we've included, validly, the ismap image-map processing capability in the example <img> tag so that users of other, usemap-incapable browsers have access to the alternative, server-side mechanism to process the image map:

```
<a href="/cgi-bin/images/map2">
  <img src="pics/map2.gif" ismap usemap="#map2">
</a>
...
<map name="map2">
  <area coords=0,0,49,49" href="link1.html">
  <area coords="50,0,99,49" href="link2.html">
  <area coords="0,50,49,99" href="link3.html">
  <area coords="50,50,99,99" href="link4.html">
</map>
```

Geographical maps make excellent ismap and usemap examples: browsing a nation-wide company's pages, for instance, the users might click on their hometowns on a map to get the addresses and phone numbers for nearby retail outlets. The advantage of usemap client-side image-map processing is that it does not require a server or special server software and so, unlike the ismap mechanism, can be used in nonweb (networkless) environments, such as local files and CD-ROMs.

Please read our more complete discussion of anchors and links, including image maps within links, in section 6.5.

5.2.6.15 The class, dir, event, id, lang, style, and title attributes

Several nearly universal attributes give you a common way to identify (title) and label (id) the image tag's contents for later reference or automated treatment, to change the contents' display characteristics (class, style), to reference the language (lang) used, and to specify the direction in which the text should flow (dir). And, of course, there are all the user events that may happen in and around the tagged contents that the browser senses and that you may react to via an on-event attribute and some programming. [Inline Styles: The style Attribute, 8.1.1] [Style Classes, 8.3]

Of these many HTML 4 and XHTML attributes, id is the most important. It lets you label the image for later access by a program or browser operation (see Chapter 12). [The id attribute, 4.1.1.4]

The remaining attributes have questionable meaning in context with <img>. Granted, a few stylesheet options are available that may influence an image's display, and it's good to include a title (although alt is better). However, it's hard to imagine the influence that language (lang) or its presentation direction (dir) might have on an image. [The dir attribute, 3.6.1.1] [The lang attribute, 3.6.1.2]

5.2.6.16 The name, onAbort, onError, onLoad, and other event attributes

There are four <img> attributes originally supported by Netscape and now by all the popular browsers that enable you to use JavaScript to manipulate images. The first is the name attribute.* Now redundant with the id attribute, name lets you label the image so that a JavaScript applet can reference it. For example:

```
<img src="pics/kumquat.gif" name="kumquat">
```

lets you later refer to that picture of a kumquat as simply "kumquat" in a JavaScript applet, perhaps to erase or otherwise modify it. You cannot individually manipulate an image with JavaScript if it is not named or doesn't have an associated id.

The other three attributes let you provide some special JavaScript event handlers. The value of each attribute is a chunk of JavaScript code, enclosed in quotation marks; it may consist of one or more JavaScript expressions, separated by semicolons.

The popular browsers invoke the onAbort event handler if the user stops loading an image, usually by clicking the browser's Stop button. You might, for instance, use an onAbort message to warn users if they stop loading some essential image, such as an image map (see section 6.5):

```
<img src="pics/kumquat.gif" usemap="#map1"
onAbort="window.alert('Caution: This image contains important hyperlinks.
Please load the entire image.')">
```

The onError attribute is invoked if some error occurs during the loading of the image, but not for a missing image or one that the user chose to stop loading. Presumably, the applet could attempt to recover from the error or load a different image in its place.

---

* HTML version 4.01 and XHTML have adopted the name attribute, too.

The currently popular browsers execute the JavaScript code associated with the `<img>` tag's onLoad attribute right after the browser successfully loads and displays the image.

See section 12.3.3 for more information about JavaScript and event handlers.

5.2.6.17 Combining <img> attributes

You may combine any of the various standard and extension attributes for images where and when they make sense. The order for inclusion of multiple attributes in the `<img>` tag is not important, either. Just be careful not to use redundant attributes, or you won't be able to predict the outcome.

5.2.7 Video Extensions

Internet Explorer supports special video-related `<img>` attribute extensions that let you embed movies into your HTML documents: controls, dynsrc, loop, and start. These are not HTML 4 and are unlikely to become XHTML standard attributes. In fact, users have to specifically enable them with Internet Explorer's "Play video in web pages" Advanced Internet Options.

Equivalent behavior is available with all the popular browsers via an extension program known as a *plug-in*. Plug-ins place an additional burden on the user in that each user must find and install the appropriate plug-in software before being able to view the inline video. The Internet Explorer `<img>` tag extensions, on the other hand, made video display an intrinsic part of the browser. [Embedded Content, 12.2]

5.2.7.1 The dynsrc attribute

Use the dynsrc attribute extension in the `<img>` tag to reference an AVI, MPG or MPEG, MOV, WMV, or any popular movie format for inline display by Internet Explorer. Its required value is the URL of the movie file, enclosed in quotation marks. For example, this text displays the tag and attribute for an AVI movie file titled *intro.avi*:

```
<img dynsrc="movies/intro.avi">
```

Internet Explorer sets aside a video viewport in the HTML display window and plays the movie, with audio if it's included in the clip and if your computer is able to play audio. Internet Explorer treats dynsrc movies similar to inline images: in line with current body content and according to the dimension of the video frame. And, like common images, the dynsrc-referenced movie file gets displayed immediately after download from the server. You may change those defaults and add some user controls with other attributes, as described later.

Because all other browsers currently ignore the special Internet Explorer attributes for movies, they may become confused by an `<img>` tag that does not contain the otherwise required `src` attribute and an image URL. We recommend that you include the `src` attribute and a valid image file URL in all `<img>` tags, including those that reference a movie for Internet Explorer users. The other browsers display the still image in place of the movie; Internet Explorer does the reverse and plays the movie, but does not display the image. Note that the order of attributes does not matter. For example:

```
<img dynsrc="movies/intro.avi" src="pics/mvstill.gif">
```

Internet Explorer loads and plays the AVI movie *intro.avi*; other graphical browsers will load and display the *mvstill.gif* image instead.

5.2.7.2 The controls attribute

Normally, Internet Explorer plays a movie inside a framed viewport once, without any visible user controls. Although no longer supported in Internet Explorer version 5 or later, with older versions of the browser the `controls` attribute (no value) enabled users to restart, stop, and continue the movie by clicking inside that viewport with the mouse. If the movie clip includes a soundtrack, the earlier Internet Explorer provided an audio volume control as well. For example:

```
<img dynsrc="movies/intro.avi" controls src="pics/mvstill.gif">
```

5.2.7.3 The loop attribute

Internet Explorer normally plays a movie clip from beginning to end once, after download. The `loop` attribute for the movie `<img>` tag lets you have the clip play repeatedly for an integer number of times set by the attribute's value, or forever if the value is `infinite`. The user may still cut the loop short by clicking the browser's Stop button or by moving on to another document.

The following *intro.avi* movie clip will play from beginning to end, then restart at the beginning and play through to the end nine more times:

```
<img dynsrc="movies/intro.avi" loop=10 src="pics/mvstill.gif">
```

Whereas the following movie will play over and over again, incessantly:

```
<img dynsrc="movies/intro.avi" loop=infinite src="pics/mvstill.gif">
```

Looping movies aren't necessarily meant to annoy. Some special-effects animations, for instance, are a sequence of repeated frames or segments. Instead of stringing the redundant segments into one long movie, which extends its download time, simply loop the single, compact segment.

5.2.7.4 The start attribute

Normally, an Internet Explorer movie clip starts playing as soon as it's downloaded. You can modify that behavior with the start attribute in the movie's `<img>` tag. By setting its value to mouseover, you delay playback until the user passes the mouse pointer over the movie viewport. The other valid start attribute value, fileopen, is the default: start playback just after download. It is included because both values may be combined in the start attribute, to cause the movie to play back automatically once, after download, and then whenever the user passes the mouse over its viewport. When combining the start attribute values, add a value-separating comma, with no intervening spaces, or else enclose them in quotes.

For example, our by-now-infamous *intro.avi* movie will play once when its host HTML document is loaded by the Internet Explorer user and again whenever he passes the mouse over the movie's viewport:

```
<img dynsrc="movies/intro.avi" start="fileopen,mouseover" src="pics/mvstill.gif">
```

5.2.7.5 Combining movie <img> attributes

Treat Internet Explorer inline movies as you would any image, mixing and matching the various movie-specific as well as the standard and extended <img> tag attributes and values supported by the browser. For example, you might align the movie (or its image alternative, if displayed by another browser) to the right of the browser window:

```
<img dynsrc="movies/intro.avi" src="pics/mvstill.gif" align=right>
```

Combining attributes to achieve a special effect is good. We also recommend that you combine attributes to give control to the user, when appropriate.

As we stated earlier in section 5.2.7.4, by combining attributes, you can also delay playback until the user passes the mouse over its viewport. Magically, the movie comes alive and plays continuously:

```
<img dynsrc="movies/magic.avi" start=mouseover loop=infinite src="pics/magic.gif">
```

5.3 Document Colors and Background Images

The HTML 4 and XHTML standards provide a number of attributes for the <body> tag that let you define text, link, and document background colors, in addition to defining an image to be used as the document background. All the popular browsers additionally extend these attributes to include document margins and better background image control. And, of course, the latest stylesheet technologies integrated into the current browsers let you manipulate all of these various display parameters.

5.3.1 Additions and Extensions to the <body> Tag

The attributes that control the document background, text color, and document margins are used with the <body> tag. [<body>, 3.8.1]

5.3.1.1 The bgcolor attribute

One standard, although deprecated, way you can change the default background color in the browser window to another hue is with the bgcolor attribute for the <body> tag. Like the color attribute for the <font> tag, the required value of the bgcolor attribute may be expressed in either of two ways: as the red, green, and blue (RGB) components of the desired color, or as a standard color name. Appendix G provides a complete discussion of RGB color encoding along with a table of acceptable color names you can use with the bgcolor attribute.

Setting the background color is easy. To get a pure red background using RGB encoding, try:

```
<body bgcolor="#FF0000">
```

For a subtler background, try:

```
<body bgcolor="peach">
```

5.3.1.2 The background attribute

If a splash of color isn't enough, you may also place an image into the background of a document with the background attribute in the <body> tag.

The required value of the background attribute is the URL of an image. The browser automatically repeats (tiles) the image both horizontally and vertically to fill the entire window.

You normally should choose a small, somewhat dim image to create an interesting but unobtrusive background pattern. Besides, a small, simple image traverses the network much faster than an intricate, full-screen image.

Figures 5-20 and 5-21 show you how the extended browsers render a single wood panel as an individual picture and then tile it to create a paneled wall when included as a document's background:

```
<body>
<img src="pics/wood_panel.gif">
```

versus:

```
<body background="pics/wood_panel.gif">
```

Figure 5-20. A single wood panel...

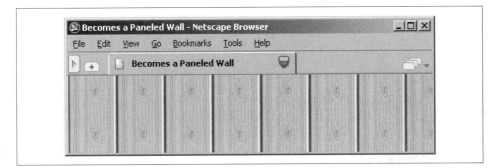

Figure 5-21. ...becomes many as the <body> background

Background images of various dimensions and sizes create interesting vertical and horizontal effects on the page. For instance, a tall, skinny image might set off your document heading:

```
<body background="pics/vertical_fountain.gif">
<h3>Kumquat Lore</h3>
For centuries, many myths and legends have arisen around the kumquat.
...
```

If *vertical_fountain.gif* is a narrow, tall image whose color grows lighter toward its base and whose length exceeds the length of the document body, the resulting document might look like the one shown in Figure 5-22.

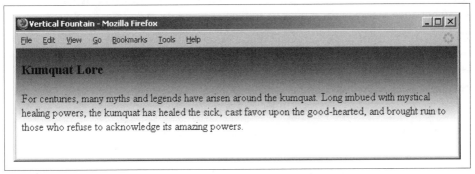

Figure 5-22. A tall and skinny background

You can achieve a similar effect horizontally with an image that is much wider than it is long (see Figure 5-23).

The background attribute is deprecated in HTML 4 and XHTML because you can achieve similar effects using stylesheets.

5.3.1.3 The bgproperties attribute

The popular browsers no longer support the bgproperties attribute extension for the <body> tag. It worked only in conjunction with the background attribute extension and

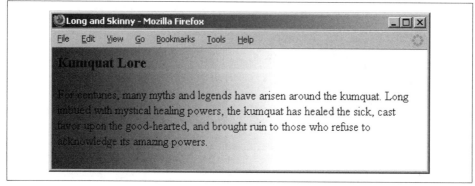

Figure 5-23. A long and skinny background

had a single value, fixed. Its effect was to freeze the background image to the browser window, so it did not scroll with the other window contents. Hence, the example *H2Omark.gif* background image might serve as a watermark for the document:

```
<body background="pics/H2Omark.gif" bgproperties="fixed">
```

5.3.1.4 The text attribute

Once you alter a document's background color or add a background image, you also might need to adjust the text color to ensure that users can read the text. The HTML 4/XHTML text standard attribute for the <body> tag does just that: it sets the color of all nonanchor text in the entire document.

Give the text attribute a color value in the same format as you use to specify a background color (see bgcolor in the earlier section, 5.3.1.1)—an RGB triplet or color name, as described in Appendix G. For example, to produce a document with blue text on a pale yellow background, use:

```
<body bgcolor="#777700" text="blue">
```

Of course, it's best to select a text color that contrasts well with your background color or image.

The text attribute is deprecated in HTML 4 and XHTML because you can achieve similar effects using stylesheets.

5.3.1.5 The link, vlink, and alink attributes

The link, vlink, and alink attributes of the <body> tag control the color of hypertext (text inside the <a> tag) in your documents. All three accept values that specify a color as an RGB triplet or color name, just like the text and bgcolor attributes.

The link attribute determines the color of all hyperlinks the user has not yet followed. The vlink attribute sets the color of all links the user has followed at one time or another. The alink attribute defines a color for active link text—i.e., a link that is currently selected by the user and is under the mouse cursor with the mouse button depressed.

Like text color, you should be careful to select link colors that can be read against the document background. Moreover, the link colors should be different from the regular text as well as from each other.

These attributes are deprecated in HTML 4 and XHTML because you can achieve similar effects using stylesheets.

5.3.1.6 The leftmargin attribute

Once peculiar to Internet Explorer but now supported by all the popular browsers, the leftmargin attribute extension for the <body> tag lets you indent the left margin relative to the left edge of the browser's window, much like a margin on a sheet of paper. Antiquated browsers ignore this attribute, and just left-justify the body content to the left edge of the document window.

The value of the leftmargin attribute is the integer number of pixels for that left-margin indent; a value of 10 is the default. The margin is filled with the background color or image.

For example, Internet Explorer renders the following text justified against a margin 50 pixels away from the left edge of the browser window (see Figure 5-24):

```
<body leftmargin=50>
Modern browsers lets you indent the<br>
&lt;--left margin<br>
away from the left edge of the window.
</body>
```

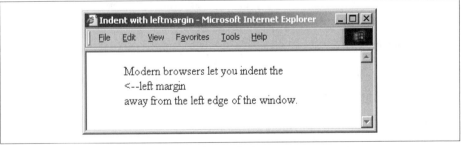

Figure 5-24. The leftmargin attribute for indenting body content

5.3.1.7 The topmargin attribute

Like leftmargin, the topmargin attribute extension used to be exclusive to Internet Explorer, but now all the popular browsers support it well. You may include it in the <body> tag to set a margin of space at the top of the document. The margin space is filled with the document's background color or image.

Body content begins flowing below the integer number of pixels you specify as the value for topmargin; a value of 0 is the default.

For example, Opera renders the following text at least 50 pixels down from the top edge of the browser window (see Figure 5-25):

```
<body topmargin=50>
^^^^^^^^^^^^^^^^^^^^^^^^^^^^^^^^^^^^^^^^^^^^^^^^^
Modern browsers give your documents
a little extra headroom with topmargin.
</body>
```

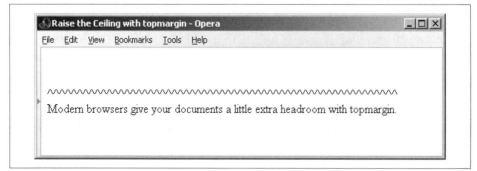

Figure 5-25. The topmargin attribute for lowering body content

5.3.1.8 The style and class attributes

You also can set all the various style-related <body> features, and then some, with CSS. But although you may include the style attribute with the <body> tag to create an inline style for the entire document body, we recommend that you set those styles at the document level (using the <style> tag inside the document head) or via a collection-level (imported) stylesheet.

Use the class attribute and name value to apply the appropriate style of a predefined class of the <body> tag to the contents. (Because there can be only one body per document, what is the point of setting a class name otherwise?) We cover the use of style and class definitions in Chapter 8.

5.3.1.9 Mixing and matching body attributes

Although background and bgcolor attributes can appear in the same <body> tag, a background image will effectively hide the selected background color unless the image contains substantial portions of transparent areas, as we described earlier in this chapter. But even if the image does hide the background color, go ahead and include the bgcolor attribute and some appropriate color value. Users can turn off image downloading, which includes background images, so otherwise they may find your page left naked and unappealing. Moreover, without a bgcolor attribute or a downloaded (for whatever reason) background image, the browsers merrily ignore your text and link color attributes, too, reverting instead to their own default values or the ones the user has chosen.

5.3.2 Extending a Warning

Much like early users of the Macintosh felt compelled to create documents using ransom-note typography ("I've got 40 fonts on this thing, and I'm going to use them all!"), many authors cannot avoid adding some sort of textured background to every document they create ("I've got 13 wood grains and 22 kinds of marbling, and I'm going to use them all!").

In reality, texture-mapped backgrounds, except for the very clever ones, add no information to your documents. The value of your document ultimately lies in its text and imagery, not the cheesy blue swirly pattern in the background. No matter how cool it looks, your readers are not benefiting and you could be losing readability.

We advise you not to use the color extensions except for comparatively frivolous endeavors or unless the extension really adds to the document's value, such as for business advertising and marketing pages.

5.3.2.1 Problems with background images

Here are some of the things that can go wrong with background images:

- The time to load the document is increased by the amount of time needed to load the image. Until the background image is completely downloaded, no further document rendering is possible.

- The background image takes up room in the browser's local cache, displacing other images that might actually contain useful information. This makes other documents, which might not even have backgrounds, take longer to load.

- The colors in the image may not be available on the user's display, forcing the browser to dither the image. This replaces large areas of a single color with repeating patterns of several other closer, but not cleaner, colors and can make the text more difficult to read.

- Because the browser must actually display an image in the background, as opposed to filling an area with a single color, scrolling through the document can take much longer.

- Even if it's clear onscreen, text printed on top of an image invariably is more difficult, if not impossible, to read.

- Fonts vary widely among machines; the ones you use with your browser that work fine with a background pattern often end up jagged and difficult to read on another machine.

5.3.2.2 Problems with background, text, and link colors

You also will encounter a slew of problems if you play with background colors, including the following:

- The color you choose, while just lovely in your eyes, may look terrible to the user. Why annoy them by changing what users most likely have already set as their own default background colors?

- While you may be a member of the "light text on a dark background" school of document design, many people also favor the "dark text on a light background" style that has been consistently popular for more than 3,000 years. Instead of bucking the trend, assume that users have already set their browsers to a comfortable color scheme.

- Some users are colorblind. What may be a nifty-looking combination of colors to you may be completely unreadable to others. One combination in particular to avoid is green for unvisited links and red for visited links. Millions of men are afflicted with red/green colorblindness.

- Your brilliant hue may not be available on the user's display, and the browser may be forced to choose one that's close instead. Some colors for the text and the background might be the same color on limited-color displays!

- For the same reason just listed, active, unvisited, and visited links may wind up as the same color on limited-color displays.

- By changing text colors, particularly those for visited and unvisited links, you may completely confuse users. By changing those colors, you effectively force them to experiment with your page, clicking a few links here and there to learn your color scheme.

- Most page designers have no formal training in cognitive psychology, fine arts, graphic arts, or industrial design, yet feel fully capable of selecting appropriate colors for their documents. If you must fiddle with the colors, ask a professional to pick them for you.

5.3.2.3 And then again

There is no denying the fact that these extensions result in some very stunning HTML and XHTML documents. And they are fun to explore and play with. So, instead of leaving this section on a sour note of caution, we encourage you to go ahead and play—just play carefully.

5.4 Background Audio

One other form of inline multimedia is generally available to web surfers—audio. Most browsers treat audio multimedia as separate documents, downloaded and displayed by special helper applications, applets, or plug-ins. Internet Explorer and

Opera, on the other hand, contain built-in sound decoders and support a special tag (<bgsound>) that lets you integrate with your document an audio file that plays in the background as a soundtrack for your page. [Applets and Objects, 12.1] [Embedded Content, 12.2]

We applaud the developers of Internet Explorer and Opera for providing a mechanism that more cleanly integrates audio into HTML and XHTML documents. The possibilities with audio are very enticing, but at the same time, we caution authors that special tags and attributes for audio don't work with other browsers, and whether this is the method that the majority of browsers will eventually support is not at all assured.

5.4.1 The <bgsound> Tag

Use the <bgsound> tag to play a soundtrack in the background. This tag is for Internet Explorer and Opera documents only. Other browsers ignore the tag. It downloads and plays an audio file when the user first downloads and displays the host document. The background sound file also will replay whenever the user refreshes the browser display.

<bgsound>

Function	Plays a soundtrack in the document's background
Attributes	loop, src
End tag	None in HTML
Contains	Nothing
Used in	*body_content*

5.4.1.1 The src attribute

The src attribute is required for the <bgsound> tag. Its value references the URL for the related sound file. For example, when Internet Explorer or Opera users first download a document containing the tag:

```
<bgsound src="audio/welcome.wav">
```

they will hear the *welcome.wav* audio file—perhaps an inviting message—play once through their computers' sound systems.

Currently, <bgsound> can handle several different sound format files, including *.wav*, the native format for PCs; *.au*, the native format for most Unix workstations; and MIDI, a universal music-encoding scheme (see also Table 5-1).

Table 5-1. Common multimedia formats and respective filename extensions

Format	Type	Extension	Platform of origin
Graphics Interchange Format	Image	*gif*	Any
Joint Photographic Experts Group	Image	*jpg, jpeg, jpe*	Any
X Bit Map	Image	*xbm*	Unix
Tagged Image File Format	Image	*tif, tiff*	Any
PICT	Image	*pic, pict*	Apple
Rasterfile	Image	*ras*	Sun
Portable Network Graphics	Image	*png*	Any
Moving Pictures Expert Group	Movie	*mpg, mpeg*	Any
Audio Video Interleave	Movie	*avi*	Microsoft
QuickTime	Movie	*qt, mov*	Apple
Windows Media Video	Movie	*wmv*	Microsoft
Shockwave	Movie	*dvr*	Macromedia
Real Video	Movie	*ra, rm, ram*	Real Networks
DivX	Movie	*div, divx, tix, mp4*	DivX
AU	Audio	*au, snd*	Sun
Waveform Audio	Audio	*wav*	Microsoft
Audio Interchange File Format	Audio	*aif, aiff*	Apple
Musical Instrument Digital Interface	Audio	*midi, mid*	Any
PostScript	Document	*ps, eps, ai*	Any
Acrobat	Document	*pdf*	Any

5.4.1.2 The loop attribute

As with inline movies, the `loop` attribute for the browser's `<bgsound>` tag lets you replay a background soundtrack a certain number of times (or indefinitely), at least until the user moves on to another page or quits the browser.

The value of the `loop` attribute is the integer number of times to replay the audio file, or `infinite`, which makes the soundtrack repeat endlessly.

For example:

```
<bgsound src="audio/tadum.wav" loop=10>
```

repeats the ta-dum soundtrack 10 times, whereas:

```
<bgsound src="audio/noise.wav" loop=infinite>
```

continuously plays the noise soundtrack.

5.4.2 Alternative Audio Support

There are other ways to include audio in your documents, using more general mechanisms that support other embedded media as well. The most common alternative to the `<bgsound>` tag is the `<embed>` tag, originally implemented by Netscape and supplanted by the `<object>` tag in the HTML 4 and XHTML standards. Take a look in Chapter 12 for details.

Ultimately, you should handle all background audio, including spoken (aural) document content, using the various audio extensions defined in a CSS standard. While we cover the speech synthesis-related extensions in Chapter 8, they are not yet supported by any browser. When such support becomes widely available, all of these early audio extensions will go the way of the `<blink>` and `<isindex>` tags, early specialized tags deprecated in favor of more generalized and powerful features.

5.5 Animated Text

In what appears to be an effort to woo advertisers, Internet Explorer added a form of animated text to HTML that all the popular browsers now support. The animation is simple—text scrolling horizontally across the display—but effective for moving banners and other elements that readily and easily animate an otherwise static document. On the other hand, like the `<blink>` tag, animated text can easily become intrusive and abusive for the reader. Use with caution, please, if at all.

5.5.1 The <marquee> Tag

The `<marquee>` tag defines the text that scrolls across the user's display. The `<marquee>` tag is not a standard tag. For this reason alone, we do not recommend that you use this extension.

<marquee> 📄

Function	Creates a scrolling text marquee
Attributes	align, behavior, bgcolor, class, controls, direction, height, hspace, loop, scrollamount, scrolldelay, style, vspace, width
End tag	`</marquee>`; never omitted
Contains	*plain_text*
Used in	*body_content*

The text between the `<marquee>` tag and its required `</marquee>` end tag scrolls horizontally across the display. The various tag attributes control the size of the display area, its appearance, its alignment with the surrounding text, and the scrolling speed.

The `<marquee>` tag and attributes are ignored by some browsers, but its contents are not. They are displayed as static text, sans any alignment or special treatment afforded by the `<marquee>` tag attributes.

5.5.1.1 The align attribute

The popular browsers place `<marquee>` text into the surrounding body content just as if it were an embedded image. As a result, you can align the marquee within the surrounding text.

The `align` attribute accepts a value of `top`, `middle`, or `bottom`, meaning that the specified point of the marquee will be aligned with the corresponding point in the surrounding text. Thus:

```
<marquee align=top>
```

aligns the top of the marquee area with the top of the surrounding text. Also see the `height`, `width`, `hspace`, and `vspace` attributes (later in this chapter), which control the dimensions of the marquee.

5.5.1.2 The behavior, direction, and loop attributes

Together, these three attributes control the style, direction, and duration of the scrolling in your marquee.

The `behavior` attribute accepts three values:

scroll (*default*)
> This value causes the marquee to act like the grand marquee in Times Square: the marquee area is initially empty; the text then scrolls in from one side (controlled by the `direction` attribute), continues across until it reaches the other side of the marquee, and then scrolls off until the marquee is once again empty.

slide
> This value causes the marquee to start empty. Text then scrolls in from one side (controlled by the `direction` attribute), stops when it reaches the other side, and remains onscreen.

alternate
> This value causes the marquee to start with the text fully visible at one end of the marquee area. The text then scrolls until it reaches the other end, whereupon it reverses direction and scrolls back to its starting point.

If you do not specify a marquee behavior, the default behavior is `scroll`.

The `direction` attribute sets the direction for marquee text scrolling. Acceptable values are either `left` (the default) or `right`. Note that the starting end for the scrolling is opposite to the direction: left means that the text starts at the right of the marquee and scrolls to the left. Remember also that rightward-scrolling text is counter-intuitive to anyone who reads left to right.

The loop attribute determines how many times the marquee text scrolls. If an integer value is provided, the scrolling action is repeated that many times. If the value is infinite, the scrolling repeats until the user moves on to another document within the browser.

Putting some of these attributes together:

```
<marquee align=center loop=infinite>
  Kumquats aren't filling
  ..........        Taste great, too!
</marquee>
```

The example message starts at the right side of the display window (default), scrolls leftward all the way across and off the display, and then starts over again until the user moves on to another page. Notice the intervening periods and spaces for the "trailer"; you can't append one marquee to another.

Also, the slide style of scrolling looks jerky when repeated and should be scrolled only once. Other scrolling behaviors work well with repeated scrolling.

5.5.1.3 The bgcolor attribute

The bgcolor attribute lets you change the background color of the marquee area. It accepts either an RGB color value or one of the standard color names. See Appendix G for a full discussion of both color-specification methods.

To create a marquee area whose color is yellow, you would write:

```
<marquee bgcolor=yellow>
```

5.5.1.4 The height and width attributes

The height and width attributes determine the size of the marquee area. If not specified, the marquee area extends all the way across the display and will be just high enough to enclose the marquee text.

Both attributes accept either a numeric value, indicating an absolute size in pixels, or a percentage, indicating the size as a percentage of the browser window height and width.

For example, to create a marquee that is 50 pixels tall and occupies one-third of the display window width, use:

```
<marquee height=50 width="33%">
```

While it is generally a good idea to ensure that the height attribute is large enough to contain the enclosed text, it is not uncommon to specify a width that is smaller than the enclosed text. In this case, the text scrolls the smaller marquee area, resulting in a kind of "viewport" marquee familiar to most people.

5.5.1.5 The hspace and vspace attributes

The hspace and vspace attributes let you create some space between the marquee and the surrounding text. This usually makes the marquee stand out from the text around it.

Both attributes require an integer value specifying the space needed in pixels. The hspace attribute creates space to the left and right of the marquee; the vspace attribute creates space above and below the marquee. To create 10 pixels of space all the way around your marquee, for example, use:

```
<marquee vspace=10 hspace=10>
```

5.5.1.6 The scrollamount and scrolldelay attributes

These attributes control the speed and smoothness of the scrolling marquee.

The scrollamount attribute value is the number of pixels needed to move text each successive movement during the scrolling process. Lower values mean smoother but slower scrolling; higher numbers create faster, jerkier text motion.

The scrolldelay attribute lets you set the number of milliseconds to wait between successive movements during the scrolling process. The smaller this value, the faster the scrolling.

You can use a low scrolldelay to mitigate the slowness of a small, smooth scrollamount. For example:

```
<marquee scrollamount=1 scrolldelay=1>
```

scrolls the text one pixel for each movement but does so as fast as possible. In this case, the scrolling speed is limited by the capabilities of the user's computer.

5.6 Other Multimedia Content

The Web is completely open-minded about the types of content that can be exchanged by servers and browsers. In this section, we look at a different way to reference images, along with audio, video, and other document formats.

5.6.1 Embedded Versus Referenced Content

Images currently enjoy a special status among the various media that can be included within an HTML or XHTML document and displayed inline with other content by all but a few browsers. Sometimes, however, as we discussed earlier in this chapter, you may also reference images externally—particularly large ones in which details are important but not immediately necessary to the document content. Other multimedia elements, including digital audio and video, can be referenced as separate documents external to the current one.

You normally use the anchor tag (<a>) to link external multimedia elements to the current document. Just like other link elements selected by the user, the browser downloads the multimedia object and presents it to the user, possibly with the assistance of an external application or plug-in. Referenced content is always a two-step process: present the document that links to the desired multimedia object, then present the object if the user selects the link. [<a>, 6.3.1]

In the case of images, you can choose how to present images to the user: inline and immediately available via the <img> tag, or referenced and subsequently available via the <a> tag. If your images are small and critical to the current document, you should provide them inline. If they are large or are only a secondary element of the current document, make them available as referenced content via the <a> tag.

If you choose to provide images via the <a> tag, it is sometimes a courtesy to your readers to indicate the size of the referenced image in the referencing document and perhaps provide a thumbnail sketch. Users can then determine whether it is worth their time and expense to retrieve it.

5.6.2 Referencing Audio, Video, and Images

You reference any external document, regardless of type or format, via a conventional anchor (<a>) link:

```
The <a href="sounds/anthem.au">Kumquat Grower's Anthem</a> is a rousing tribute to
the thousands of 'quat growers around the world.
```

Just like any referenced document, the server delivers the desired multimedia object to the browser when the user selects the link. If the browser finds that the document is not HTML or XHTML, but rather some other format, it automatically invokes an appropriate rendering tool to display or otherwise convey the contents of the object to the user.

You can configure your browser with special helper applications that handle different document formats in different ways. Audio files, for example, might be passed to an audio-processing tool, and video files are given to a video-playing tool. If a browser has not been configured to handle a particular document format, the browser will inform you and offer to simply save the document to disk. You can later use an appropriate viewing tool to examine the document.

Browsers identify and specially handle multimedia files from one of two different hints: either from the file's Multipurpose Internet Mail Extension (MIME) type, provided by the server, or from a special suffix in the file's name. The browser prefers MIME because of its richer description of the file and its contents, but it will infer the file's contents (type and format) from the file suffix: *.gif* or *.jpg*, for GIF or JPEG encoded images, for example, or *.au* for a special sound file.

Because not all browsers look for a MIME type or are necessarily correctly configured with helper applications by their users, you should always use the correct file suffix in the names of multimedia objects. Refer to Table 5-1 for more information.

5.6.3 Appropriate Linking Styles

Creating effective links to external multimedia documents is critical. The user needs some indication of what the object is and perhaps the kind of application the linked object needs to execute. Moreover, most multimedia objects are quite large, so common courtesy tells us to provide users with some indication of the time and expense involved in downloading them.

In lieu of, or in addition to, the anchor and surrounding text, a small thumbnail of a large image, or a familiar icon that indicates the referenced object's format, is useful.

5.6.4 Embedding Other Document Types

The Web can deliver nearly any type of electronic document, not just graphics, sound, and video files. To display them, however, the client browser needs a helper application installed and referenced. Recent browsers also support plug-in accessory software and, as described in Chapter 12, may extend the browser for some special function, including inline display of multimedia objects.

For example, consider a company whose extensive product documentation was prepared and stored in some popular layout application such as Adobe Acrobat, FrameMaker, QuarkXPress, or PageMaker. The Web offers an excellent way for distributing that documentation over a worldwide network, but converting to HTML or XHTML would be too costly at this time.

The solution is to prepare a few HTML or XHTML documents that catalog and link the alternative files and invoke the appropriate display applet. Or, make sure that the users' browsers have the plug-in software or are configured to invoke the appropriate helper application. Adobe's Acrobat Reader is a very popular plug-in, for example. If the document is in Acrobat (*.pdf*) format and if a link to an Acrobat document is chosen, the tool is started and accordingly displays the document, often right in the browser's window.

CHAPTER 6

Links and Webs

Up to this point, we've dealt with HTML and XHTML documents as standalone entities, concentrating on the language elements you use for structure and to format your work. The true power of these markup languages, however, lies in their ability to join collections of documents together into a full library of information and to link your library of documents with other collections around the world. Just as readers have considerable control over how the document looks onscreen, with hyperlinks they also have control over the order of presentation as they navigate through your information. It's the "HT" in HTML and XHTML—hypertext—and it's the twist that spins the Web.

6.1 Hypertext Basics

A fundamental feature of hypertext is that you can hyperlink documents; you can point to another place inside the current document, inside another document in the local collection, or inside a document anywhere on the Internet. The documents become an intricately woven web of information. (Get the name analogy now?) The target document usually is somehow related to and enriches the source; the linking element in the source should convey that relationship to the reader.

You can use hyperlinks for all kinds of effects. You can use them inside tables of contents and lists of topics. With a click of the mouse on their browser screen or a press of a key on their keyboard, readers select and automatically jump to a topic of interest in the same document or to another document located in an entirely different collection somewhere around the world.

Hyperlinks also point readers to more information about a mentioned topic. "For more information, see Kumquats on Parade," for example. Authors use hyperlinks to reduce repetitive information. For instance, we recommend you sign your name to each document. Instead of including full contact information in each document, you can use a hyperlink to connect your name to a single document that contains your address, phone number, and so forth.

A hyperlink, or *anchor* in standard parlance, is marked by the <a> tag and comes in two flavors. As we describe in detail later, one type of anchor creates a hotspot in the document that, when activated and selected (usually with a mouse) by the user, causes the browser to link. It automatically loads and displays another portion of the same or another document or triggers some Internet service-related action, such as sending email or downloading a special file. The other type of anchor creates a label, a place in a document that can be referenced as a hyperlink.[*]

Also, some mouse-related events are associated with hyperlinks, which, through JavaScript, let you incorporate some exciting effects.

6.2 Referencing Documents: The URL

Every document on the Web has a unique address. (Imagine the chaos if they didn't.) The document's address is known as its *uniform resource locator* (URL).[†]

Several HTML/XHTML tags include a URL attribute value, including hyperlinks, inline images, and forms. All use the same URL syntax to specify the location of a web resource, regardless of the type or content of that resource. That's why it's known as a *uniform* resource locator.

Because they can be used to represent almost any resource on the Internet, URLs come in a variety of flavors. All URLs, however, have the same top-level syntax:

    scheme:scheme_specific_part

The *scheme* describes the kind of object the URL references; the *scheme_specific_part* is, well, the part that is peculiar to the specific scheme. The important thing to note is that the *scheme* is always separated from the *scheme_specific_part* by a colon, with no intervening spaces.

---

[*] Both types of anchors use the same tag; perhaps that's why they have the same name. We find it's easier if you differentiate them and think of the type that provides the hotspot and address of a hyperlink as the "link" and the type that marks the target portion of a document as the "anchor."

[†] "URL" usually is pronounced "you are ell," not "earl."

6.2.1 Writing a URL

Write URLs using the displayable characters in the US-ASCII character set. For example, surely you have heard what has become annoyingly common on the radio for an announced business web site: "h, t, t, p, colon, slash, slash, w, w, w, dot, blah-blah, dot, com." That's a simple URL, written:

```
http://www.blah-blah.com
```

If you need to use a character in a URL that is not part of this character set, you must encode the character using a special notation. The encoding notation replaces the desired character with three characters: a percent sign and two hexadecimal digits whose values correspond to the position of the character in the ASCII character set.

This is easier than it sounds. One of the most common special characters is the space (owners of older Macintoshes, take special notice), whose position in the character set is 20 hexadecimal.* You can't type a space in a URL (well, you can, but it won't work). Rather, replace spaces in the URL with %20:

```
http://www.kumquat.com/new%20pricing.html
```

This URL actually retrieves a document named *new pricing.html* from the *www.kumquat.com* server.

6.2.1.1 Handling reserved and unsafe characters

In addition to the nonprinting characters, you'll need to encode *reserved* and *unsafe* characters in your URLs as well.

Reserved characters are those that have a specific meaning within the URL itself. For example, the slash character separates elements of a pathname within a URL. If you need to include in a URL a slash that is not intended to be an element separator, you'll need to encode it as %2F:

```
http://www.calculator.com/compute?3%2f4
```

This URL actually references the resource named compute on the *www.calculator.com* server and passes the string 3/4 to it, as delineated by the question mark (?). Presumably, the resource is a server-side program that performs some arithmetic function on the passed value and returns a result.

Unsafe characters are those that have no special meaning within the URL but may have a special meaning in the context in which the URL is written. For example, double quotes ("") delimit URL attribute values in tags. If you were to include a double quotation mark directly in a URL, you would probably confuse the browser. Instead, you should encode the double quotation mark as %22 to avoid any possible conflict.

---

* Hexadecimal numbering is based on 16 characters: 0 through 9 followed by A through F, which in decimal are equivalent to values 0 through 15. Also, letter case for these extended values is not significant; "a" (10 decimal) is the same as "A," for example.

Table 6-1 shows other reserved and unsafe characters that should always be encoded.

Table 6-1. Reserved and unsafe characters and their URL encodings

Character	Description	Usage	Encoding
;	Semicolon	Reserved	%3B
/	Slash	Reserved	%2F
?	Question mark	Reserved	%3F
:	Colon	Reserved	%3A
@	At sign	Reserved	%40
=	Equals sign	Reserved	%3D
&	Ampersand	Reserved	%26
<	Less-than sign	Unsafe	%3C
>	Greater-than sign	Unsafe	%3E
"	Double quotation mark	Unsafe	%22
#	Hash symbol	Unsafe	%23
%	Percent	Unsafe	%25
{	Left curly brace	Unsafe	%7B
}	Right curly brace	Unsafe	%7D
		Vertical bar	Unsafe	%7C
\	Backslash	Unsafe	%5C
^	Caret	Unsafe	%5E
~	Tilde	Unsafe	%7E
[	Left square bracket	Unsafe	%5B
]	Right square bracket	Unsafe	%5D
`	Back single quotation mark	Unsafe	%60

In general, you should always encode a character if there is some doubt as to whether it can be placed as is in a URL. As a rule of thumb, any character other than a letter, number, or any of the symbolic characters like $-_.+!*'( ) should be encoded.

It is never an error to encode a character, unless that character has a specific meaning in the URL. For example, encoding the slashes in an HTTP URL causes them to be used as regular characters, not as pathname delimiters, breaking the URL. Similarly, encoding an ampersand when it is used as a parameter separator in a URL will defeat the intended purpose. Instead, write these ampersands using & to keep their intended function intact.

6.2.2 Absolute and Relative URLs

You may address a URL in one of two ways: *absolute* or *relative*. An absolute URL is the complete address of a resource and has everything your system needs to find a document and its server on the Web. At the very least, an absolute URL contains the scheme and all required elements of the *scheme_specific_part* of the URL. It may also contain any of the optional portions of the *scheme_specific_part*.

With a relative URL, you provide an abbreviated document address that, when automatically combined with a base address by the system, becomes a complete address for the document. Within the relative URL, any component of the URL may be omitted. The browser automatically fills in the missing pieces of the relative URL using corresponding elements of a base URL. This base URL is usually the URL of the document containing the relative URL, but it may be another document specified with the <base> tag, as we will discuss later in this chapter. [<base>, 6.7.1]

6.2.2.1 Relative schemes and servers

A common form of a relative URL is missing the scheme and server name. Because many related documents are on the same server, it makes sense to omit the scheme and server name from the relative URL. For instance, assume the base document was last retrieved from the server *www.kumquat.com*. This relative URL:

```
another-doc.html
```

is equivalent to the absolute URL:

```
http://www.kumquat.com/another-doc.html
```

Table 6-2 shows how the base and relative URLs in this example are combined to form an absolute URL.

Table 6-2. Forming an absolute URL

	Protocol	Server	Directory	File
Base URL	http	*www.kumquat.com*	/	
Relative URL	↓	↓	↓	*another-doc.html*
↓	↓	↓	↓	↓
Absolute URL	http	*www.kumquat.com*	/	*another-doc.html*

6.2.2.2 Relative document directories

Another common form of a relative URL omits the leading slash and one or more directory names from the beginning of the document pathname. The directory of the base URL is automatically assumed to replace these missing components. It's the most common abbreviation, because most authors place their collections of documents and subdirectories of support resources in the same directory path as the home page. For example, you might have a *special* subdirectory containing FTP files referenced in your document. Let's say that the absolute URL for that document is:

```
http://www.kumquat.com/planting/guide.html
```

A relative URL for the file *README.txt* in the *special* subdirectory looks like this:

```
ftp:special/README.txt
```

You'll actually be retrieving:

```
ftp://www.kumquat.com/planting/special/README.txt
```

Visually, the operation looks like that in Table 6-3.

Table 6-3. Forming an absolute FTP URL

	Protocol	Server	Directory	File
Base URL	http	*www.kumquat.com*	*/planting*	*guide.html*
Relative URL	ftp	↓	*special*	*README.txt*
↓	↓	↓	↓	↓
Absolute URL	ftp	*www.kumquat.com*	*/planting/special*	*README.txt*

6.2.2.3 Using relative URLs

Relative URLs are more than just a typing convenience. Because they are relative to the current server and directory, you can move an entire set of documents to another directory or even another server and never have to change a single relative link. Imagine the difficulties if you had to go into every source document and change the URL for every link every time you moved it. You'd loathe using hyperlinks! Use relative URLs wherever possible.

6.2.3 The http URL

The http URL is by far the most common. It is used to access documents from a web server, and it has two formats:

```
http://server:port/path#fragment
http://server:port/path?search
```

Some of the parts are optional. In fact, the most common form of the http URL is simply:

```
http://server/path
```

which designates the unique server and the directory path and name of a document.

6.2.3.1 The http server

The *server* is the unique Internet name or IP numerical address of the computer system that stores the web resource. We suspect you'll mostly use more easily remembered

Internet names for the servers in your URLs.[*] The name consists of several parts, including the server's actual name and the successive names of its network domain, each part separated by a period. Typical Internet names look like *www.oreilly.com* or *hoohoo.ncsa.uiuc.edu*.[†]

It has become something of a convention that webmasters name their servers *www* for quick and easy identification on the Web. For instance, O'Reilly Media's web server's name is *www*, which, along with the publisher's domain name, becomes the very easily remembered web site, *www.oreilly.com*. Similarly, MobileRobots' web server is named *www.mobilerobots.com*. Being a nonprofit organization, the World Wide Web Consortium's main server has a different domain suffix: *www.w3c.org*. The naming convention has very obvious benefits, which you, too, should take advantage of if you are called upon to create a web server for your organization.

You may also specify the address of a server using its numerical IP address. The address is a sequence of four numbers, 0 to 255, separated by periods. Valid IP addresses look like 137.237.1.87 or 192.249.1.33.

It'd be a dull diversion to tell you now what the numbers mean or how to derive an IP address from a domain name, particularly because you'll rarely, if ever, use one in a URL. Rather, this is a good place to hyperlink: pick up any good Internet networking treatise for rigorous detail on IP addressing, such as Ed Krol's *The Whole Internet User's Guide and Catalog* (O'Reilly).

6.2.3.2 The http port

The *port* is the number of the communication port by which the client browser connects to the server. It's a networking thing—servers perform many functions besides serving up web documents and resources to client browsers: electronic mail, FTP document fetches, filesystem sharing, and so on. Although all that network activity may come into the server on a single wire, it's typically divided into software-managed "ports" for service-specific communications—something analogous to boxes at your local post office.

The default URL port for web servers is 80. Special secure web servers—Secure HTTP (SHTTP) or Secure Sockets Layer (SSL)—run on port 443. Most web servers today use

---

[*] Each Internet-connected computer has a unique address—a numeric (Internet Protocol, or IP) address, of course, because computers deal only in numbers. Humans prefer names, so the Internet folks provide us with a collection of special servers and software (the domain name system, or DNS) that automatically resolve Internet names into IP addresses.

[†] The three-letter suffix of the domain name identifies the type of organization or business that operates that portion of the Internet. For instance, "com" is a commercial enterprise, "edu" is an academic institution, and "gov" identifies a government-based domain. Outside the United States, a less-descriptive suffix is often assigned—typically a two-letter abbreviation of the country name, such as "jp" for Japan and "de" for Deutschland. Many organizations around the world now use the generic three-letter suffixes in place of the more conventional two-letter national suffixes.

port 80; you need to include a port number along with an immediately preceding colon in your URL if the target server does *not* use port 80 for web communication.

When the Web was in its infancy, pioneer webmasters ran their Wild Wild Web connections on all sorts of port numbers. For technical and security reasons, system-administrator privileges are required to install a server on port 80. Lacking such privileges, these webmasters chose other, more easily accessible, port numbers.

Now that web servers have become acceptable and are under the care and feeding of responsible administrators, documents being served on some port other than 80 or 443 should make you wonder whether that server is really on the up and up. Most likely, the maverick server is being run by a clever user unbeknownst to the server's bona fide system administrators.

6.2.3.3 The http path

The document *path* is the Unix-style hierarchical location of the file in the server's storage system. The pathname consists of one or more names separated by slashes. All but the last name represent directories leading down to the document. The last name is usually that of the document itself, though the web server will typically default to a file called *index.html*.

It has become a convention that for easy identification, HTML document names end with the suffix *.html* (otherwise, they're plain ASCII text files, remember?). Although recent versions of Windows allow longer suffixes, old-time developers often stick to the three-letter *.htm* name suffix for HTML documents.

Although the server name in a URL is not case-sensitive, the document pathname may be. Because most web servers are run on Linux-based systems, and Linux filenames are case-sensitive, those document pathnames will be case-sensitive, too. Web servers running on Windows machines are not case-sensitive, so those document pathnames are not. Because it is impossible to know the operating system of the server you are accessing, always assume that the server has case-sensitive pathnames and take care to get the case correct when typing your URLs.

Certain conventions regarding the document pathname have arisen. If the last element of the document path is a directory, not a single document, the server usually will send back either a listing of the directory contents or the HTML index document in that directory. You should end the document name for a directory with a trailing slash character, but in practice, most servers will honor the request even if this character is omitted.

If the directory name is just a slash alone, or nothing at all, the server decides what to serve to your browser—typically, a so-called *home page* in the root directory stored as a file named *index.html*. Every well-designed web server should have an attractive, well-designed home page; it's a shorthand way for users to access your web collection because they don't need to remember the document's actual filename, just your server's name. That's why, for example, you can type *http://www.oreilly.com* into Netscape's Open dialog box and get O'Reilly's home page.

Another twist: if the first component of the document path starts with the tilde character (~), it means that the rest of the pathname begins from the personal directory in the home directory of the specified user on the server machine. For instance, the URL *http://www.kumquat.com/~chuck* would retrieve the top-level page from Chuck's document collection.

Different servers have different ways of locating documents within a user's home directory. Many search for the documents in a directory named *public_html*. Unix-based servers are fond of the name *index.html* for home pages. When all else fails, servers tend to cough up a directory listing or the default HTML document in the home page directory.

6.2.3.4 The http document fragment

The *fragment* is an identifier that points to a specific section of a document. In URL specifications, it follows the server and pathname and is separated by the pound sign (#). A fragment identifier indicates to the browser that it should begin displaying the target document at the indicated fragment name. As we describe in more detail later in this chapter, you insert fragment names into a document either with the universal id tag attribute or with the name attribute for the <a> tag. In the following example, the browser loads the file named *kumquat_locations.html* from the *www.kumquat.com* server, and then displays the document starting at the section of the page named Northeast:

```
http://www.kumquat.com/kumquat_locations.html#Northeast
```

Like a pathname, a fragment name may be any sequence of characters, as long as you are careful with spaces and other symbolic characters.

The fragment name and the preceding hash symbol are optional; omit them when referencing a document without defined fragments.

Formally, the fragment element applies only to HTML and XHTML documents. If the target of the URL is some other document type, the browser may misinterpret the fragment name.

Fragments are useful for long documents. By identifying key sections of your document with a fragment name, you make it easy for readers to link directly to that portion of the document, avoiding the tedium of scrolling or searching through the document to get to the section that interests them.

As a rule of thumb, we recommend that every section header in your documents be accompanied by an equivalent fragment name. By consistently following this rule, you'll make it possible for readers to jump to any section in any of your documents. Fragments also make it easier to build tables of contents for your document families.

6.2.3.5 The http search parameter

The *search* component of the http URL, along with its preceding question mark, is optional. It indicates that the path is a searchable or executable resource on the server. The content of the search component is passed to the server as parameters that control the search or execution function.

The actual encoding of parameters in the search component depends upon the server and the resource being referenced. We cover the parameters for searchable resources later in this chapter, when we discuss searchable documents. We discuss parameters for executable resources in Chapter 9.

Although our initial presentation of http URLs indicated that a URL may have either a fragment identifier or a search component, some browsers let you use both in a single URL. If you so desire, you can follow the search parameter with a fragment identifier, telling the browser to begin displaying the results of the search at the indicated fragment. Netscape, for example, supports this usage.

We don't recommend this kind of URL, though. First and foremost, it doesn't work on all browsers. Just as important, using a fragment implies that you are sure that the results of the search will have a fragment of that name defined within the document. For large document collections, this is hardly likely. You are better off omitting the fragment, showing the search results from the beginning of the document, and avoiding potential confusion among your readers.

6.2.3.6 Sample http URLs

Here are some sample http URLs:

```
http://www.oreilly.com/catalog.html
http://www.oreilly.com
http://www.kumquat.com:8080
http://www.kumquat.com/planting/guide.html#soil_prep
http://www.kumquat.com/find_a_quat?state=Florida
```

The first example is an explicit reference to a bona fide HTML document named *catalog.html* that is stored in the root directory of the *www.oreilly.com* server. The second references the top-level home page on that same server. That home page may or may not be *catalog.html.* Sample three also assumes that there is a home page in the root directory of the *www.kumquat.com* server and that the web connection is to the nonstandard port 8080.

The fourth example is the URL for retrieving the web document named *guide.html* from the *planting* directory on the *www.kumquat.com* server. Once retrieved, the browser should display the document beginning at the fragment named *soil_ prep.*

The last example invokes an executable resource named *find_a_quat* with the parameter named state set to the value Florida. Presumably, this resource generates an HTML or XHTML response, presumably a new document about kumquats in Florida that is subsequently displayed by the browser.

6.2.4 The file URL

The file URL is perhaps the second most common one used, but it is not readily recognized by web users and particularly web authors. It points to a file stored on a computer without indicating the protocol used to retrieve the file. As such, it has limited use in a networked environment. That's a good thing. The file URL lets you load and display a locally stored document and is particularly useful for referencing personal HTML/XHTML document collections, such as those "under construction" and not yet ready for general distribution, or document collections on CD-ROM. The file URL has the following format:

```
file://server/path
```

6.2.4.1 The file server

The file *server* can be, like the http one, an Internet domain name or IP address of the computer containing the file to be retrieved. Unlike http, however, which requires Transmission Control Protocol/Internet Protocol (TCP/IP) networking, the file server may also be the unqualified but unique name of a computer on a personal network, or a storage device on the same computer, such as a CD-ROM, or mapped from another networked computer. No assumptions are made as to how the browser might contact the machine to obtain the file; presumably the browser can make some connection, perhaps via a Network File System or FTP, to obtain the file.

If you omit the server name by including an extra slash (/) in the URL, or if you use the special name *localhost*, the browser retrieves the file from the machine on which the browser is running. In this case, the browser simply accesses the file using the normal facilities of the local operating system. In fact, this is the most common usage of the file URL. By creating document families on a diskette or CD-ROM and referencing your hyperlinks using the *file:///* URL, you create a distributable, standalone document collection that does not require a network connection to use.

6.2.4.2 The file path

This is the path of the file to be retrieved on the desired server. The syntax of the path may differ based on the operating system of the server; be sure to encode any potentially dangerous characters in the path.

6.2.4.3 Sample file URLs

The file URL is easy:

```
file://localhost/home/chuck/document.html
file:///home/chuck/document.html
file://marketing.kumquat.com/monthly_sales.html
file://D:/monthly_sales.html
```

The first URL retrieves *home/chuck/document.html* from the user's local machine off the current storage device, typically *C:* on a Windows PC. The second is identical to the first, except we've omitted the *localhost* reference to the server; the server name defaults to the local drive.

The third example uses some protocol to retrieve *monthly_sales.html* from the *marketing.kumquat.com* server, and the fourth example uses the local PC's operating system to retrieve the same file from the *D:* drive or device.

6.2.5 The mailto URL

The mailto URL is very common in HTML/XHTML documents. It has the browser send an electronic mail message to a named recipient. It has the format:

    mailto:*address*

The *address* is any valid email address, usually of the form:

    user@server

Thus, a typical mailto URL might look like:

    mailto:chuckandbill@kumquats.com

You may include multiple recipients in the mailto URL, separated by commas. For example, this URL addresses the message to all three recipients:

    mailto:chuck@kumquats.com,bill@kumquats.com,booktech@ora.com

There should be no spaces before or after the commas in the URL.

6.2.5.1 Defining mail header fields

The popular browsers open an email helper or plug-in application when the user selects a mailto URL. It may be the default email program for their system, or a common application such as Outlook Express with Internet Explorer or Netscape's built-in Communicator. With some browsers, users can designate their own email programs for handling mailto URLs by altering a specification in their browsers' Options or Preferences.

Like http search parameters that you attach at the end of the URL, separated by question marks (?), you include email-related parameters with the mailto URL in the HTML document. Typically, additional parameters may include the message's header fields, such as the subject, cc (carbon copy), and bcc (blind carbon copy) recipients. How these additional fields are handled depends on the email program.

A few examples are in order:

    mailto:chuckandbill@kumquats.com?subject=Loved your book!
    mailto:chuck@kumquats.com?cc=booktech@oreilly.com
    mailto:bill@kumquats.com?bcc=archive@myserver.com

As you can probably guess, the first URL sets the subject of the message. Note that some email programs allow spaces in the parameter value and others do not. Annoyingly, you can't replace spaces with their hexadecimal equivalent, %20, because many email programs won't make the proper substitution. It's best to use spaces because the email programs that don't honor the spaces simply truncate the parameter to the first word.

The second URL places the address *booktech@oreilly.com* in the cc field of the message. Similarly, the last example sets the bcc field. You may also set several fields in one URL by separating the field definitions with ampersands. For example, this URL sets the subject and cc addresses:

```
mailto:chuckandbill@kumquats.com?subject=Loved your book!&cc=booktech@oreilly.
com&bcc=archive@myserver.com
```

Not all email programs accept or recognize the bcc and cc extensions in the mailto URL—some either ignore them or append them to a preceding subject. Thus, when forming a mailto URL, it's best to order the extra fields as subject first, followed by cc and bcc. And don't depend on the cc and bcc recipients being included in the email.

6.2.6 The ftp URL

The ftp URL is used to retrieve documents from a File Transfer Protocol (FTP) server.* It has the format:

```
ftp://user:password@server:port/path;type=typecode
```

6.2.6.1 The ftp user and password

FTP is an authenticated service, meaning that you usually must have a valid username and password in order to retrieve documents from a server. However, most FTP servers also support restricted, nonauthenticated access known as *anonymous FTP*. In this mode, anyone can supply the username "anonymous" or "guest" and be granted access to a limited portion of the server's documents. Most FTP servers also assume (but may not grant) anonymous access if the username and password are omitted.

If you are using an authenticated ftp URL to access a site that requires a username and password, include the user and password components in the URL, along with the colon (:) and at sign (@). If you keep the user component and at sign but omit the password and the preceding colon, most browsers prompt you for a password after connecting to the FTP server. This is the recommended way of accessing authenticated resources on an FTP server because it prevents others from seeing your password.

---

* FTP is an ancient Internet protocol that dates back to the Dark Ages, around 1975. It was designed as a simple way to move files among machines and is popular and useful to this day. Many HTML/XHTML authors use FTP to place files on their web servers.

We recommend you *never* place an ftp URL with a username and password in any HTML/XHTML document. The reasoning is simple: anyone can retrieve the simple text document, extract the username and password from the URL, log into the FTP server, and tamper with its documents.

6.2.6.2 The ftp server and port

The ftp *server* and *port* operate by the same rules as the server and port in an http URL. The server must be a valid Internet domain name or IP address, and the optional port specifies the port on which the server is listening for requests. If omitted, the default port number is 21.

6.2.6.3 The ftp path and typecode

The *path* component of an ftp URL represents a series of directories, separated by slashes, leading to the file to be retrieved. By default, the file is retrieved as a binary file; you can change this by adding the *typecode* (and the preceding *;type=*) to the URL.

If the typecode is set to *d*, the path is assumed to be a directory. The browser requests a listing of the directory contents from the server and displays this listing to the user. If the typecode is any other letter, it is used as a parameter to the FTP type command before retrieving the file referenced by the path. While some FTP servers may implement other codes, most servers accept *i* to initiate a binary transfer and *a* to treat the file as a stream of ASCII text.

6.2.6.4 Sample ftp URLs

Here are some sample ftp URLs:

```
ftp://www.kumquat.com/sales/pricing
ftp://bob@bobs-box.com/results;type=d
ftp://bob:secret@bobs-box.com/listing;type=a
```

The first example retrieves the file named *pricing* from the *sales* directory on the anonymous FTP server at *www.kumquat.com*. The second logs into the FTP server on *bobs-box.com* as user *bob*, prompting for a password before retrieving the contents of the directory named *results* and displaying them to the user. The last example logs into *bobs-box.com* as *bob* with the password *secret* and retrieves the file named *listing*, treating its contents as ASCII characters.

6.2.7 The javascript URL

The javascript URL actually is a pseudoprotocol, not usually included in discussions of URLs. With advanced browsers such as Netscape, Opera, Firefox, and Internet Explorer, the javascript URL can be associated with a hyperlink and used to execute JavaScript commands when the user selects the link. While these URLs will work, we don't recommend using them. Instead, authors should use the `onclick` attribute to associate JavaScript commands with elements in their documents.

6.2.7.1 The javascript URL arguments

Following the javascript pseudoprotocol is one or more semicolon-separated Java-Script expressions and methods, including references to multi-expression JavaScript functions that you embed within the `<script>` tag in your documents (see Chapter 12 for details). For example:

```
javascript:window.alert('Hello, world!')
javascript:doFlash('red', 'blue'); window.alert('Do not press me!')
```

are valid URLs you may include as the value for a link reference (see section 6.3.1.2). The first example contains a single JavaScript method that activates an alert dialog with the simple message "Hello, world!", if the user allows JavaScript to run with their browser.

The second javascript URL example contains two arguments: the first calls a Java-Script function, `doFlash`, which presumably you have located elsewhere in the document within the `<script>` tag and which perhaps flashes the background color of the document window between red and blue. The second expression is the same alert method as in the first example, with a slightly different message.

The javascript URL may appear in a hyperlink sans arguments, too. In that case, the browser may open, if enabled, a special JavaScript editor wherein the user types in and tests various expressions and methods.

6.2.8 The news URL

Although rarely used anymore, the news URL accesses either a single message or an entire newsgroup within the Usenet news system. It has two forms:

```
news:newsgroup
news:message_id
```

An unfortunate limitation in news URLs is that they don't allow you to specify a news server. Rather, users specify news servers in their browser preferences. At one time, not long ago, Internet newsgroups were nearly universally distributed; all news servers carried all the same newsgroups and their respective articles, so one news server was as good as any. Today, the sheer bulk of disk space needed to store the daily volume of newsgroup activity is often prohibitive for any single news server, and there's also local censorship of newsgroups. Hence, you cannot expect that all newsgroups, and certainly not all articles for a particular newsgroup, will be available on the user's news server.

Many users' browsers may not be correctly configured to read news. We recommend that you avoid placing news URLs in your documents except in rare cases.

6.2.8.1 Accessing entire newsgroups

Several thousand newsgroups are devoted to nearly every conceivable topic under the sun, and beyond. Each group has a unique name, composed of hierarchical elements separated by periods. For example, the World Wide Web announcements newsgroup is:

```
comp.infosys.www.announce
```

To access this group, use the URL:

```
news:comp.infosys.www.announce
```

6.2.8.2 Accessing single messages

Every message on a news server has a unique message identifier (ID) associated with it. This ID has the form:

unique_string@server

The *unique_string* is a sequence of ASCII characters; the server is usually the name of the machine from which the message originated. The *unique_string* must be unique among all the messages that originated from the server. A sample URL to access a single message might be:

```
news:12A7789B@news.kumquat.com
```

In general, message IDs are cryptic sequences of characters not readily understood by humans. Moreover, the life span of a message on a server is usually measured in days, after which the message is deleted and the message ID is no longer valid. The bottom line: single-message news URLs are difficult to create, become invalid quickly, and generally are not used.

6.2.9 The nntp URL

The nntp URL goes beyond the news URL to provide a complete mechanism for accessing articles in the Usenet news system. It has the form:

```
nntp://server:port/newsgroup/article
```

6.2.9.1 The nntp server and port

The nntp *server* and *port* are defined similarly to the http server and port, described earlier. The server must be the Internet domain name or IP address of an nntp server; the port is the port on which that server is listening for requests.

If the port and its preceding colon are omitted, the default port of 119 is used.

6.2.9.2 The nntp newsgroup and article

The *newsgroup* is the name of the group from which an article is to be retrieved, as just defined in section 6.2.8 The *article* is the numeric ID of the desired article within that newsgroup. Although the article number is easier to determine than a message ID, it falls prey to the same limitations of single-message references using the news URL, just described in section 6.2.8. Specifically, articles do not last long on most nntp servers, and nntp URLs quickly become invalid as a result.

6.2.9.3 Sample nntp URLs

A sample nntp URL might be:

```
nntp://news.kumquat.com/alt.fan.kumquats/417
```

This URL retrieves article 417 from the *alt.fan.kumquats* newsgroup on *news. kumquat.com*. Keep in mind that the article will be served only to machines that are allowed to retrieve articles from this server. In general, most nntp servers restrict access to those machines on the same local area network.

6.2.10 The telnet URL

The telnet URL opens an interactive session with a desired server, allowing the user to log in and use the machine. Often, the connection to the machine automatically starts a specific service for the user; in other cases, the user must know the commands to type to use the system. The telnet URL has the form:

```
telnet://user:password@server:port/
```

6.2.10.1 The Telnet user and password

Specify the Telnet user and password are defined exactly like the user and password components of the ftp URL, described previously. In particular, the same caveats apply regarding protecting your password and never placing it within a URL.

Just like the ftp URL, if you omit the password from the URL, the browser should prompt you for a password just before contacting the Telnet server.

If you omit both the user and the password, the Telnet occurs without supplying a username. For some servers, Telnet automatically connects to a default service when no username is supplied. For others, the browser may prompt for a username and password when making the connection to the Telnet server.

6.2.10.2 The Telnet server and port

The Telnet server and port are defined similarly to the http server and port, described earlier. The server must be the Internet domain name or IP address of a Telnet server; the port is the port on which that server is listening for requests. If the port and its preceding colon are omitted, the default port of 23 is used.

6.2.11 The gopher URL

Gopher is a web-like document-retrieval system that achieved some popularity on the Internet just before the Web took off, making gopher obsolete. Some gopher servers still exist, though, and the gopher URL lets you access gopher documents.

The gopher URL has the form:

```
gopher://server:port/path
```

6.2.11.1 The gopher server and port

The gopher server and port are defined similarly to the http server and port, described previously. The server must be the Internet domain name or IP address of a gopher server; the port is the port on which that server is listening for requests.

If the port and its preceding colon are omitted, the default port of 70 is used.

6.2.11.2 The gopher path

The gopher path can take one of three forms:

```
type/selectortype/selector%09searchtype/selector%09search%09gopherplus
```

The *type* is a single character value denoting the type of the gopher resource. If the entire path is omitted from the gopher URL, the type defaults to 1.

The *selector* corresponds to the path of a resource on the gopher server. It may be omitted, in which case the top-level index of the gopher server is retrieved.

If the gopher resource is actually a gopher search engine, the *search* component provides the string for which to search. The search string must be preceded by an encoded horizontal tab (%09).

If the gopher server supports gopher+ resources, the *gopherplus* component supplies the necessary information to locate that resource. The exact content of this component varies based upon the resources on the gopher server. This component is preceded by an encoded horizontal tab (%09). If you want to include the *gopherplus* component but omit the *search* component, you must still supply both encoded tabs within the URL.

6.3 Creating Hyperlinks

Use the HTML/XHTML <a> tag to create links to other documents and to name anchors for fragment indentifiers within documents.

6.3.1 The <a> Tag

You will use the <a> tag most commonly with its href attribute to create a hypertext link, or *hyperlink*, to another place in the same document or to another document. In these cases, the current document is the source of the link; the value of the href attribute, a URL, is the target.[*]

---

[*] You may run across the terms *head* and *tail*, which reference the target and source of a hyperlink. This naming scheme assumes that the referenced document (the head) has many tails that are embedded in many referencing documents throughout the Web. We find this naming convention confusing and stick to the concept of source and target documents throughout this book.

The other way you can use the <a> tag is with the name attribute, to mark a hyperlink target, or fragment identifier, in a document. This method, although part of the HTML 4 and XHTML standards, is slowly succumbing to the id attribute, which lets you mark nearly any element, including paragraphs, divisions, forms, and so on, as a hyperlink target.

<a>	
Function	Defines anchors within a text flow
Attributes	accesskey, charset, class, coords, dir, href, hreflang, id, lang, name, onBlur, onClick, onDblClick, onFocus, onKeyDown, onKeyPress, onKeyUp, onMouseDown, onMouseMove, onMouseOut, onMouseOver, onMouseUp, rel, rev, shape, style, tabindex, target, title, type
End tag	</a>; never omitted
Contains	a_content
Used in	text

The standards let you use both the name and href attributes within a single <a> tag, defining a link to another document and a fragment identifier within the current document. We recommend against this because it overloads a single tag with multiple functions and some browsers may not be able to handle it. Instead, use two <a> tags when such a need arises. Your source will be easier to understand and modify and will work better across a wider range of browsers.

6.3.1.1 Allowed content

Between the <a> tag and its required end tag, you may put only regular text, inline elements, line breaks, and images. The browser renders all of these elements normally, but with the addition of some special effects to indicate that they are hyperlinks to other documents. For instance, the popular graphical browsers typically underline and color the text and draw a colored border around images that are enclosed by <a> tags.

6.3.1.2 The href attribute

Use the href attribute to specify the URL of the target of a hyperlink. Its value is any valid document URL, absolute or relative, including a fragment identifier or a JavaScript code fragment. If the user selects the contents of the <a> tag, the browser will attempt to retrieve and display the document indicated by the URL specified by the href attribute or execute the list of JavaScript expressions, methods, and functions. [Referencing Documents: The URL, 6.2]

A simple <a> tag that references another document might be:

```
The <a href="http:growing_season.html">growing
season</a> for kumquats in the Northeast.
```

which appears in the browser display shown in Figure 6-1.

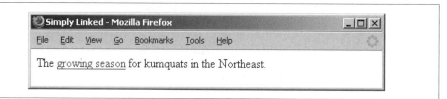

Figure 6-1. Hyperlink to another HTML document

Notice that the browser specially renders the phrase "growing season", letting the user know that it is a link to another document. Users usually have the option to set their own text color for the link and have the color change when a link is taken; blue initially and then red after it has been selected at least once, for instance. More complex anchors might include images:

```
<ul>
  <li><a href="pruning_tips.html">
       <img src="pics/new.gif" align=center>
       New pruning tips!</a>
  <p>
  <li><a href="xhistory.html">
       <img src="pics/new2.gif" align=center>
       Kumquats throughout history</a>
</ul>
```

Most graphical browsers such as Internet Explorer, but not Opera for some reason, place a special border around images that are part of an anchor, as shown in Figure 6-2. Remove that hyperlink border with the border=0 attribute and value within the <img> tag for the image. [The border attribute, 5.2.6.8]

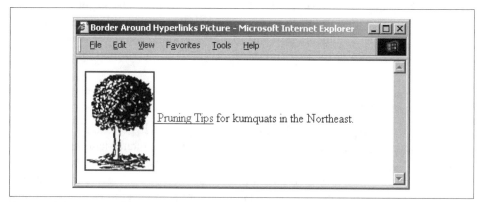

Figure 6-2. Internet Explorer puts a special border around an image that is inside an anchor

6.3.1.3 The name and id attributes

Use the name and id attributes with the <a> tag to create a fragment identifier within a document. Once created, the fragment identifier becomes a potential target of a link.

Prior to HTML 4.0, the only way to create a fragment identifier was to use the name attribute with the <a> tag. With the advent of the id attribute in HTML 4.0, and its ability to be used with almost any tag, any HTML or XHTML element can be a fragment identifier. The <a> tag retains the name attribute for historic purposes and honors the id attribute as well. These attributes can be used interchangeably, with id being the more "modern" version of the name attribute. Both name and id can be specified in conjunction with the href attribute, allowing a single <a> to be both a hyperlink and a fragment identifier.

An easy way to think of a fragment identifier is as the HTML analog of the goto statement label common in many programming languages. The name attribute within the <a> tag or the id attribute within the <a> or other tags places a label within a document. When that label is used in a link to that document, it is the equivalent of telling the browser to goto that label.

The value of the id or name attribute is a character string, enclosed in quotation marks. The string must begin with a letter, followed by letters, numbers, hyphens, underscores, colons, and periods. The value must be a unique label, not reused in any other name or id attribute in the same document, although it can be reused in different documents.

Here are some name and id examples:

```
<h2><a name="Pruning">Pruning Your Kumquat Tree</a></h2>
<h2 id="Pruning">Pruning Your Kumquat Tree</h2>
```

Notice that we set the anchor in a section header of a presumably large document. It's a practice we encourage you to follow for all major sections of your work for easier reference and future smart processing, such as automated extraction of topics.

The following link, when taken by the user:

```
<a href="growing_guide.html#Pruning">
```

jumps directly to the section of the document we named in the previous examples.

Browsers don't display the contents of the anchor <a> tag with the name or id attribute in any special way. Technically, you do not have to put any document content within the <a> tag with the name attribute because it simply marks a location in the document. In practice, though, some browsers ignore the tag unless some document content—a word or phrase, even an image—is between the <a> and </a> tags. For this reason, it's probably a good idea to have at least one displayable element in the body of any <a> tag.

6.3.1.4 The event attributes

A number of event handlers are built into modern browsers. These handlers watch for certain conditions and user actions, such as a click of the mouse or when an image finishes loading into the browser window. With client-side JavaScript, you may include selected event handlers as attributes of certain tags and execute one or more JavaScript commands and functions when the event occurs.

With the anchor (<a>) tag, you may associate JavaScript code with a number of mouse- and keyboard-related events. The value of the event handler is—enclosed in quotation marks—one or a sequence of semicolon-separated JavaScript expressions, methods, and function references that the browser executes when the event occurs. [JavaScript Event Handlers, 12.3.3]

A popular, albeit simple, use of the onMouseOver event with a hyperlink is to print an expanded description of the tag's destination in the JavaScript-aware browser's status box (Figure 6-3). Normally, the browser displays the frequently cryptic destination URL there whenever the user passes the mouse pointer over an <a> tag's contents:

```
<a href="http://www.ora.com/kumquats/homecooking/recipes.html#quat5"
onMouseOver="status='A yummy recipe for kumquat soup.'; return true;">
<img src="pics/bowl.gif" border=0>
</a>
```

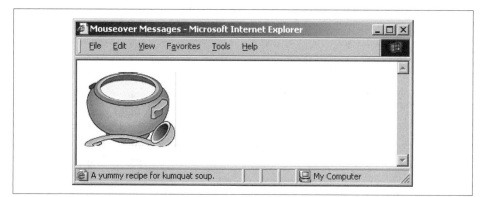

Figure 6-3. Use JavaScript to display a message in the browser's status box

We argue that the contents of the tag itself should explain the link, but sometimes window space is tight and an expanded explanation is helpful, such as when the link is in a table of contents.

See Chapter 12 for more about JavaScript.

6.3.1.5 The rel and rev attributes

The optional rel and rev attributes for the <a> tag express a formal relationship and direction between source and target documents. The rel attribute specifies the

---

relationship from the source document to the target, and the rev attribute specifies the relationship from the target to the source. Both attributes can be placed in a single <a> tag, and the browser may use them to specially alter the appearance of the anchor content or to automatically construct document navigation menus. Other tools also may use these attributes to build special link collections, tables of contents, and indexes.

The value of either the rel or rev attribute is a space-separated list of relationships. The actual relationship names and their meanings are up to you: they are not formally addressed by the HTML or XHTML standards. For example, a document that is part of a sequence of documents might include its relationship in a link:

```
<a href="part-14.html" rel=next rev=prev>
```

The relationship from the source to the target is that of moving to the next document; the reverse relationship is that of moving to the previous document.

These document relationships are also used in the <link> tag in the document <head>. The <link> tag establishes the relationship without actually creating a link to the target document; the <a> tag creates the link and imbues it with the relationship attributes. [<link>, 6.7.2]

Commonly used document relationships include:

next
> Links to the next document in a collection

prev
> Links to the previous document in a collection

head
> Links to the top-level document in a collection

toc
> Links to a collection's table of contents

parent
> Links to the document above the source

child
> Links to the document below the source

index
> Links to the index for this document

glossary
> Links to the glossary for this document

Few browsers take advantage of these attributes to modify the link appearance. However, these attributes are a great way to document links you create, and we recommend that you take the time to insert them whenever possible.

6.3.1.6 The style and class attributes

Use the style and class attributes for the `<a>` tag to control the display style for the content enclosed by the tag and to format the content according to a predefined class of the `<a>` tag. [Inline Styles: The style Attribute, 8.1.1] [Style Classes, 8.3]

6.3.1.7 The lang and dir attributes

Like almost all other tags, the `<a>` tag accepts the lang and dir attributes, denoting the language used for the content within the `<a>` tag and the direction in which that language is rendered. [The dir attribute, 3.6.1.1] [The lang attribute, 3.6.1.2]

6.3.1.8 The target attribute

The target attribute lets you specify where to display the contents of a selected hyperlink. Commonly used in conjunction with frames or multiple browser windows, the value of this attribute is the name of the frame or window in which the referenced document should be loaded. If the named frame or window exists, the document is loaded in that frame or window. If not, a new window is created and given the specified name, and the document is loaded in that new window. For more information, including a list of special target names, see section 11.7.

6.3.1.9 The title attribute

The title attribute lets you specify a title for the document to which you are linking. The value of the attribute is any string, enclosed in quotation marks. The browser might use it when displaying the link, perhaps flashing the title when the mouse passes over the link. The browser might also use the title attribute when adding this link to a user's bookmarks or favorites.

The title attribute is especially useful for referencing an otherwise unlabeled resource, such as an image or a non-HTML document. For example, the browser might include the following title on this otherwise wordless image display page:

```
<a href="pics/kumquat.gif"
    title="A photograph of the Noble Fruit">
```

Ideally, the value specified should match the title of the referenced document, but it's not required.

6.3.1.10 The charset, hreflang, and type attributes

According to the HTML 4 and XHTML standards, the charset attribute specifies the character encoding used in the document that is the destination of the link. The value of this attribute must be the name of a standard character set: "euc-jp," for example. The default value is "ISO-8859-1."

The `hreflang` attribute may be specified only when the `href` attribute is used. Like the `lang` attribute, its value is an International Organization for Standardization (ISO) standard two-character language code. Unlike the `lang` attribute, the `hreflang` attribute does not address the language used by the contents of the tag. Instead, it specifies the language used in the document referenced by the `href` attribute. [The lang attribute, 3.6.1.2]

The `type` attribute specifies the content type of the resource referenced by the `<a>` tag. Its value is any Multipurpose Internet Mail Extension (MIME) encoding type. For example, you might inform the browser that you are linking to a plain ASCII document with:

```
<a href="readme.txt" type="text/plain">
```

The browser might use this information when displaying the referenced document, or might even present the link differently based upon the content type.

6.3.1.11 The coords and shape attributes

Two more attributes are defined in the HTML and XHTML standards for the `<a>` tag but are not supported by the currently popular browsers. Like the attributes of the same names for the `<area>` tag, the `coords` and `shape` attributes define a region of influence for the `<a>` tag. You should use these attributes with the `<a>` tag only when that tag is part of the content of a `<map>` tag, as described later in this chapter. [<map>, 6.5.3] [The coords attribute, 6.5.4.2] [The shape attribute, 6.5.4.7]

6.3.1.12 The accesskey and tabindex attributes

Traditionally, users of graphical browsers select and execute a hyperlink by pointing and clicking the mouse device on the region of the browser display defined by the anchor. What is less well known is that you may choose a hyperlink, among other objects in the browser window, by pressing the Tab key and then activate that link by pressing the Enter key. With the `tabindex` attribute, you may reorder the sequence in which the browser steps through to each object when the user presses the Tab key. The value of this attribute is an integer greater than 0. The browser starts with the object whose `tabindex=1` and moves through the other objects in increasing `tabindex` order.

With the `accesskey` attribute, you may select an alternative "hot key" that, when pressed, activates the specific link. The value of this attribute is a single character that is pressed in conjunction with an Alt or "meta" key, depending on the browser and computing platform. Ideally, this character should appear in the content of the `<a>` tag; if so, the browser may choose to display the character differently to indicate that it is a hot key.

See an expanded description for both of these attributes in Chapter 9.

6.3.2 Linking to Other Documents

Say you make a hyperlink to another document with the `<a>` tag and its `href` attribute, which defines the URL of the target document. The contents of the `<a>` tag are presented to the user in some distinctive manner to indicate the link is available.

When creating a link to another document, you should consider adding the `title`, `rel`, and `rev` attributes to the `<a>` tag. They help document the link you are creating and allow the browser to embellish the display anchor contents.

6.3.3 Linking Within a Document

Creating a link within the same document or to a specific fragment of another document is a two-step process. The first step is to make the target fragment; the second is to create the link to the fragment.

Use the `<a>` tag with its `name` attribute to identify a fragment. Here's a sample fragment identifier:

```
<h3><a name="Section_7">Section 7</a></h3>
```

Alternatively, use the `id` attribute and embed the hyperlink target directly in a defining tag, such as a header:*

```
<h3 id="Section_7">Section 7</h3>
```

A hyperlink to the fragment is an `<a>` tag with the `href` attribute, in which the attribute's value—the target URL—ends with the fragment's name, preceded by the pound sign (#). A reference to the previous example's fragment identifier, then, might look like this:

```
See <a href="index.html#Section_7">Section 7</a>
for further details.
```

By far, the most common use of fragment identifiers is in creating a table of contents for a lengthy document. Begin by dividing your document into several logical sections, using appropriate headers and consistent formatting. At the start of each section, add a fragment identifier for that section, typically as part of the section title. Finally, make a list of links to those fragment identifiers at the beginning of your document.

Our sample document extolling the life and wonders of the mighty kumquat, for example, is quite long and involved, including many sections and subsections of interest. It is a document to be read and read again. In order to make it easy for kumquat lovers everywhere to find their section of interest quickly, we've included fragment identifiers for each major section and placed an ordered list of links—a hotlinked table of contents, as it were—at the beginning of each Kumquat Lover's document, a sample of which follows, along with sample fragment identifiers that appear

---

* We prefer the `id` way, although not all browsers support it, yet.

in the same document. The ellipses symbol (...) means that there are intervening segments of content, of course:

```
...
<h3>Table of Contents</h3>
<ol>
  <li><a href="#soil_prep">Soil Preparation</a>
  <li><a href="#dig_hole">Digging the Hole</a>
  <li><a href="#planting">Planting the Tree</a>
</ol>
...
<h3 id=soil_prep>Soil Preparation</h3>
...
<h3 id=dig_hole>Digging the Hole</h3>
...
<h3 id=planting>Planting the Tree</h3>
...
```

The kumquat lover can thereby click the desired link in the table of contents and jump directly to the section of interest, without lots of tedious scrolling.

Notice also that this example uses relative URLs—a good idea if you ever intend to move or rename the document without breaking all the hyperlinks.

6.4 Creating Effective Links

A document becomes hypertext when you toss in a few links in the same way that water becomes soup when you throw in a few vegetables. Technically, you've met the goal, but the outcome may not be very tasty.

Inserting anchors into your documents is something of an art, requiring good writing skills, HTML/XHTML prowess, and an architectural sense of your documents and their relationships to others on the Web. Effective links flow seamlessly into a document, quietly supplying additional browsing opportunities to the reader without disturbing the current document. Poorly designed links scream out, interrupt the flow of the source document, and generally annoy the reader.

While there are as many linking styles as there are authors, here are a few of the more popular ways to link your documents. All do two things: they give the reader quick access to related information, and they tell the reader how the link is related to the current contents.

6.4.1 Lists of Links

Perhaps the most common way to present hyperlinks is in ordered or unordered lists in the style of a table of contents or list of resources.

Two schools of style exist. One puts the entire list item into the source anchor; the other abbreviates the item and puts a shorthand phrase in the source anchor. In the former, make sure you keep the anchor content short and sweet; in the latter, use a direct writing style that makes it easy to embed the link.

If your list of links becomes overly long, consider organizing it into several sublists grouped by topic. Readers can then scan the topics (set off, perhaps, as <h3> headers) for the appropriate list and then scan that list for the desired document.

The alternative list style is much more descriptive, but also wordier, so you have to be careful that it doesn't end up cluttered:

```
<p>
Kumquat-related documents include:
<ul>
  <li>A concise guide to <a href="kumquat_farming.html">
      profitable kumquat farming</a>,
      including a variety of business plans, lists of fruit
      packing companies, and farming supply companies.
  <li>101 different ways to <a href="kumquat_uses">
      use a kumquat</a>, including stewed kumquats and kumquat pie!
  <li>The kumquat is a hardy tree, but even the greenest of
      thumbs can use a few <a href="news:alt.kumquat_growers">
      growing tips</a> to increase
      their yield.
  <li>The business of kumquats is an expanding one, as
      shown by this 10 year overview of the
      <a href="http://www.oreilly.com/kumquat_report/">
      kumquat industry</a>.
</ul>
```

It sometimes gets hard to read a source HTML document, and it will become even more tedious with XHTML. Imagine the clutter if we'd used anchors with fragment identifiers for each subtopic in the list-item explanations. Nonetheless, it looks pristine and easily navigable when displayed by a browser such as Opera, as shown in Figure 6-4.

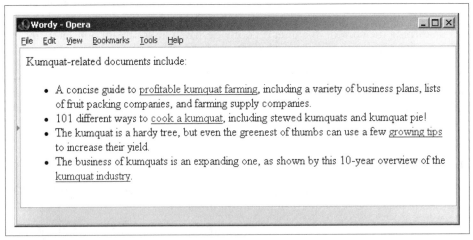

Figure 6-4. Wordy but effectively descriptive link list

This more descriptive style of presenting a link list tries hard to draw readers into the linked document by giving a fuller taste of what they can expect to find. Because each list element is longer and requires more scanning by the reader, you should use this style sparingly and dramatically limit the number of links.

Use the brief list style when presenting large numbers of links to a well-informed audience. The second, more descriptive style is better suited to a smaller number of links for which your readership is less well-versed in the topic at hand.

6.4.2 Inline References

If you aren't collecting links into lists, you're probably sprinkling them throughout your document. So-called *inline links* are more in keeping with the true spirit of hypertext because they enable readers to mark their current place in the document, visit the related topic in more depth or find a better explanation, and then come back to the original and continue reading. That's very personalized information processing.

The biggest mistake novice authors make, however, is to overload their documents with links and treat them as though they are panic buttons demanding to be pressed. You may have seen this style of linking; HTML pages with the word *here* all over the place, like the panic-ridden example in Figure 6-5 (we can't bring ourselves to show you the source for this travesty).

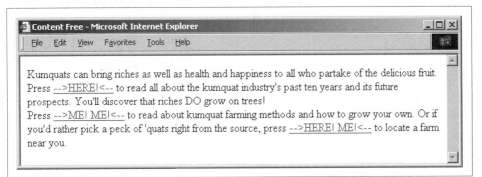

Figure 6-5. Links should not wave and yell, like first-graders, "Here! Me! Me!"

As links, phrases such as "click here" and "also available" are content-free and annoying. They make the person who is scanning the page for an important link read all the surrounding text to actually find the reference.

The better, more refined style for an inline link is to make every one contain a noun or noun/verb phrase relating to the topic at hand. Compare how kumquat farming and industry news references are treated in Figure 6-6 to the "Here! Me! Me!" example in Figure 6-5.

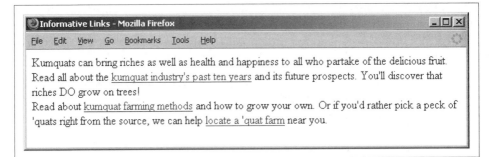

Figure 6-6. Kinder, gentler inline links work best

A quick scan of Figure 6-6 immediately yields useful links to "kumquat farming methods" and "kumquat industry's past ten years." There is no need to read the surrounding text to understand where the link will take you. Indeed, the immediately surrounding content in our example, as for most inline links, serves only as syntactic sugar in support of the embedded links.

Embedding links into the general discourse of a document takes more effort than creating link lists. You have to actually understand the content of the current document as well as the target documents, be able to express that relationship in just a few words, and then intelligently incorporate that link at some key place in the source document. Hopefully this key place is where you might expect the user to be ready to interrupt her reading and ask a question or request more information. To make matters even more difficult, particularly for the traditional tech writer, this form of author-reader conversation is most effective when presented in active voice (he, she, or it does something to an object versus the object having something done to it). The effort expended is worthwhile, resulting in more informative, easily read documents. Remember, you'll write the document once, but it will be read thousands, if not millions, of times. Please your readers, please.

6.4.3 Linking Dos and Don'ts

Here are some hints for creating links:

Keep the link content as concise as possible
> Long links or huge inline graphic icons for links are visually disruptive and potentially confusing.

Never place two links immediately adjacent to one another
> Most browsers make it difficult to tell where one link stops and the next link starts. Separate them with regular text or line breaks.

Be consistent
> If you are using inline references, make all of your links inline references. If you choose to use lists of links, stick to either the short or the long form; try not to mix styles in a single document.

Try reading your document with all the nonanchor text removed

If some links suddenly make no sense, rewrite them so that they stand on their own. (Many people scan documents looking only for links; the surrounding text becomes little more than a gray background to the more visually compelling links.)

6.4.4   Using Images and Links

It has become fashionable to use images and icons instead of words for link contents. For instance, instead of the word *next*, you might use an icon of a little pointing hand. A link to the home page is not complete without a picture of a little house. Links to searching tools must now contain a picture of a magnifying glass, a question mark, or binoculars. And all those flashing, GIF-animated little advertisements!

Resist falling prey to the "Mount Everest syndrome" of inserting images simply because you can. Again, it's a matter of context. If you or your document's readers can't tell at a glance what relationship a link has with the current document, you've failed. Use cute images for links sparingly, consistently, and only in ways that help readers scan your document for important information and leads. Also, be ever mindful that your pages may be read by someone from nearly anywhere on Earth (perhaps beyond, even) and that images do not translate consistently across cultural boundaries. (Ever hear what the "OK" hand sign common in the United States means to a Japanese person?)

Creating consistent iconography for a collection of pages is a daunting task that you really should perform with the assistance of someone formally schooled in visual design. Trust us, the kind of mind that produces nifty code and writes XHTML well is rarely suited to creating beautiful, compelling imagery. Find a good visual designer; your pages and readers will benefit immeasurably.

6.5   Mouse-Sensitive Images

Normally, an image placed within an anchor simply becomes part of the anchor content. The browser may alter the image in some special way (usually with a special border) to alert the reader that it is a hyperlink, but users click the image in the same way they click a textual hyperlink.

The HTML and XHTML standards provide a feature that lets you embed many different links inside the same image. Clicking different areas of the image causes the browser to link to different target documents. Such mouse-sensitive images, known as *image maps*, open up a variety of creative linking styles.

There are two ways to create image maps, known as *server-side* and *client-side* image maps. The former, enabled by the ismap attribute for the <img> tag, requires access to a server and related image-map processing applications. The latter is created with the usemap attribute for the <img> tag, along with corresponding <map> and <area> tags.

Translation of the mouse position in the image to a link to another document happens on the user's machine, so client-side image maps don't require a special server connection and can even be implemented in non-Web environments, such as on a local hard drive or in a CD-ROM-based document collection. Any HTML/XHTML can implement a client-side (usemap) image map. [<map>, 6.5.3] [<area>, 6.5.4] [<img>, 5.2.6]

6.5.1 Server-Side Image Maps

You add an image to an anchor simply by placing an <img> tag within the body of the <a> tag. Make that embedded image into a mouse-sensitive one by adding the ismap attribute to the <img> tag. This special <img> attribute tells the browser that the image is a special map containing more than one link. (The ismap attribute is ignored by the browser if the <img> tag is not within an <a> tag.)

When the user clicks someplace within the image, the browser passes the coordinates of the mouse pointer along with the URL specified in the <a> tag to the document server. The server uses the mouse-pointer coordinates to determine which document to deliver back to the browser.

When ismap is used, the href attribute of the containing <a> tag must contain the URL of a server application or, for some HTTP servers, a related map file that contains the coordinate and linking information. If the URL is simply that of a conventional document, errors may result, and the desired document probably will not be retrieved.

The coordinates of the mouse position are screen pixels counted from the upper-left corner of the image, beginning with (0,0). The browser adds the mouse coordinates, preceded by a question mark, to the end of the URL.

For example, if a user clicks 43 pixels over and 15 pixels down from the upper-left corner of the image displayed from the following link:

```
<a href="/cgi-bin/imagemap/toolbar.map">
<img ismap src="pics/toolbar.gif">
</a>
```

the browser sends the following search parameters to the HTTP server:

```
/cgi-bin/imagemap/toolbar.map?43,15
```

In the example, *toolbar.map* is a special image-map file located inside the *cgi-bin/ imagemap* directory and containing coordinates and links. A special image-map process uses that file to match the passed coordinates (43,15 in our example) and return the selected hyperlink document.

6.5.1.1 Server-side considerations

With mouse-sensitive, ismap-enabled image maps, the browser is required to pass along only the URL and mouse coordinates to the server. The server converts the coordinates into a specific document. The conversion process differs among servers and is not defined by the HTML or XHTML standard.

You need to consult with your web server administrators and perhaps even read your server's documentation to determine how to create and program a server-side image map. Most servers come with some software utility, typically located in a *cgi-bin/imagemap* directory, to handle image maps. And most of these use a text file containing the image-map regions and related hyperlinks that is referenced by your image-map URL to process the image-map query.

Here's an example image-map file describing the sensitive regions in our example image:

```
# Imagemap file=toolbar.map

default                 dflt.html
circ 100,30,50          link1.html
rect 180,120,290,500    link2.html
poly 80,80,90,72,160,90 link3.html
```

Each sensitive region of the image map is described by a geometric shape and defining coordinates in pixels, such as the circle with its center point and radius, the rectangle's upper-left and lower-right edge coordinates, and the loci of a polygon. All coordinates are relative to the upper-left corner of the image (0,0). Each shape has a related URL.

An image-map processing application typically tests each shape in the order in which it appears in the image file and returns the document specified by the corresponding URL to the browser if the user's mouse X,Y coordinates fall within the boundaries of that shape. That means it's OK to overlap shapes; just be aware which takes precedence. Also, the entire image need not be covered with sensitive regions: if the passed coordinates don't fall within a specified shape, the default document gets sent back to the browser.

This is just one example of how an image map may be processed and the accessory files required for that process. Please huddle with your webmaster and server manuals to discover how to implement a server-side image map for your own documents and system.

6.5.2 Client-Side Image Maps

The obvious downside to server-side image maps is that they require a server. That means you need access to the required HTTP server or its */cgi-bin* directory, either of which is rarely available to anyone other than owners or system administrators. And server-side image maps limit portability because not all image-map processing applications are the same.

Server-side image maps also mean delays for the user while browsing because the browser must get the server's attention to process the image coordinates. This is true even if there's no action to take, such as when the user clicks on a section of the image that isn't hyperlinked and doesn't lead anywhere.

Client-side image maps suffer from none of these difficulties. Enabled by the usemap attribute for the <img> tag and defined by special <map> and <area> extension tags, client-side image maps let authors include in their documents coordinates and links that describe the sensitive regions of an image. The browser on the client computer translates the coordinates of the mouse position within the image into an action, such as loading and displaying another document. And special JavaScript-enabled attributes provide a wealth of special effects for client-side image maps. [JavaScript Event Handlers, 12.3.3]

To create a client-side image map, include the usemap attribute as part of the <img> tag.* Its value is the URL of a <map> segment in an HTML document that contains the map coordinates and related link URLs. The document in the URL identifies the HTML or XHTML document containing the map; the fragment identifier in the URL identifies the map itself. Most often, the map is in the same document as the image, and the URL can be reduced to the fragment identifier: a pound sign (#) followed by the map name.

For example, the following source fragment tells the browser that the *map.gif* image is a client-side image map and that its mouse-sensitive coordinates and related link URLs are found in the map fragment of the current document:

```
<img src="pics/map.gif" usemap="#map">
```

6.5.3 The <map> Tag

For client-side image maps to work, you must provide a set of coordinates and URLs that define the mouse-sensitive regions of a client-side image map and the hyperlink to take for each region that the user may click or otherwise select.† Include those coordinates and links as values of attributes in conventional <a> tags or special <area> tags; the collection of <area> specifications or <a> tags is enclosed within the <map> tag and its end tag, </map>. The <map> segment may appear anywhere in the body of the document.

<table>
<tr><td colspan="2" align="center">**<map>**</td></tr>
<tr><td>**Function**</td><td>Encloses client-side image-map (usemap) specifications</td></tr>
<tr><td>**Attributes**</td><td>class, dir, id, lang, name, onClick, onDblClick, onKeyDown, onKeyPress, onKeyUp, onMouseDown, onMouseMove, onMouseOut, onMouseOver, onMouseUp, style, title</td></tr>
<tr><td>**End tag**</td><td></map>; never omitted</td></tr>
<tr><td>**Contains**</td><td>*map_content*</td></tr>
<tr><td>**Used in**</td><td>*body_content*</td></tr>
</table>

---

* Alternatively, according to the HTML 4 standard, you may reference a client-side image map by including the usemap attribute with the <object> and form <input> tags. See Chapter 12 for details.

† The Tab key also steps through the hyperlinks in a document, including client-side image maps. Select a chosen hyperlink with the Enter key.

More specifically, the <map> tag may contain either a sequence of <area> tags or conventional HTML/XHTML content including <a> tags. You cannot mix and match <area> tags with conventional content. Browsers may display conventional content within the <map> tag; <area> tag contents will not. If you are concerned about compatibility with older browsers, use only <map> tags containing <area> tags.

If you do place <a> tags within a <map> tag, they must include the shape and coords attributes that define a region within the objects that reference the <map> tag.

6.5.3.1 The name attribute

The value of the name attribute in the <map> tag is the name used by the usemap attribute in an <img> or <object> tag to locate the image-map specification. The name must be unique and not used by another <map> in the document, but more than one image map may reference the same <map> specifications. [The ismap and usemap attributes, 5.2.6.14]

6.5.3.2 The class, id, style, and title attributes

The stylesheet display-related style and class attributes for the <map> tag are useful only when the <map> tag contains conventional content, in which case they apply to the content of the tag. [Inline Styles: The style Attribute, 8.1.1] [Style Classes, 8.3]

The id and title attributes, on the other hand, are straightforward. They are standard ways to respectively label the tag for later reference by a hyperlink or program or to title the section for later review. [The id attribute, 4.1.1.4] [The title attribute, 4.1.1.5]

6.5.3.3 The event attributes

The various event attributes allow you to assign JavaScript handlers to events that may occur within the confines of the map. [JavaScript Event Handlers, 12.3.3]

6.5.4 The <area> Tag

The guts of a client-side image map are the <area> tags within the map segment. These <area> tags define each mouse-sensitive region and the action the browser should take if the user selects it in an associated client-side image map.

The region defined by an <area> tag acts just like any other hyperlink: when the user moves the mouse pointer over the region of the image, the pointer icon changes, typically into a hand, and the browser may display the URL of the related hyperlink in the status box at the bottom of the browser window.* Regions of the client-side image map not defined in at least one <area> tag are not mouse sensitive.

---

* That is, unless you activate a JavaScript event handler that writes the contents of the status box. See the onMouse event handlers in section 6.3.1.4.

`<area>`

Function	Defines coordinates and links for a region on a client-side image map
Attributes	accesskey, alt, class, coords, dir, href, id, lang, nohref, notab, onBlur, onClick, onDblClick, onFocus, onKeyDown, onKeyPress, onKeyUp, onMouseDown, onMouseMove, onMouseOut, onMouseUp, shape, style, tabindex, taborder 🄽, target 🄽, title, type
End tag	None in HTML; `</area>` or `<area ... />` in XHTML
Contains	Nothing
Used in	*map_content*

6.5.4.1 The alt attribute

Like its cousin for the `<img>` tag, the `alt` attribute for the `<area>` tag attaches a text label to the image, except in this case the label is associated with a particular area of the image. The popular browsers display this label to the user when the mouse passes over the area, and nongraphical browsers may use it to present the client-side image map as a list of links identified by the `alt` labels.

6.5.4.2 The coords attribute

The required `coords` attribute of the `<area>` tag defines coordinates of a mouse-sensitive region in a client-side image map. The number of coordinates and their meanings depend upon the region's shape as determined by the `shape` attribute, discussed later in this chapter. You may define hyperlink regions as rectangles, circles, and polygons within a client-side image map.

The appropriate values for each shape include:

circle *or* circ
> `coords="x,y,r "`, where *x* and *y* define the position of the center of the circle (0,0 is the upper-left corner of the image) and *r* is its radius in pixels.

polygon *or* poly
> `coords="x1,y1,x2,y2,x3,y3,..."`, where each pair of X,Y coordinates defines a vertex of the polygon, with 0,0 being the upper-left corner of the image. At least three pairs of coordinates are required to define a triangle; higher-order polygons require a larger number of vertices. The polygon is automatically closed, so it is not necessary to repeat the first coordinate at the end of the list to close the region.

rectangle *or* rect

coords="*x1,y1,x2,y2*", where the first coordinate pair is one corner of the rectangle and the other pair is the corner diagonally opposite, with 0,0 being the upper-left corner of the image. Note that a rectangle is just a shortened way of specifying a polygon with four vertices.

For example, the following XHTML fragment defines a single mouse-sensitive region in the lower-right quarter of a 100×100-pixel image and another circular region smack in the middle:

```
<map name="map1">
  <area shape="rect" coords="75,75,99,99" nohref="nohref" />
  <area shape="circ" coords="50,50,25" nohref="nohref" />
</map>
```

If the coordinates in one <area> tag overlap with another region, the first <area> tag takes precedence. The browsers ignore coordinates that extend beyond the boundaries of the image.

6.5.4.3 The href attribute

Like the href attribute for the anchor (<a>) tag, the href attribute for the <area> tag defines the URL of the desired link if its region in the associated image map is clicked. The value of the href attribute is any valid URL, relative or absolute, including JavaScript code.

For example, the browser will load and display the *link4.html* document if the user clicks in the lower-right quarter of a 100×100-pixel image, as defined by the first image-map <area> tag in the following HTML example:

```
<map name="map">
  <area coords="75,75,99,99" href="link4.html">
  <area coords="0,0,25,25" href="javascript:window.alert('Oooh, tickles!');" >
</map>
```

The second <area> tag in the example uses a javascript URL, which, when the user clicks in the upper-left quadrant of the image map, executes a JavaScript alert method that displays the silly message in a dialog box.

6.5.4.4 The nohref attribute

The nohref attribute for the <area> tag defines a mouse-sensitive region in a client-side image map for which no action is taken, even though the user may select it. You must include either an href or a nohref attribute for each <area> tag.

6.5.4.5 The notab, taborder, and tabindex attributes

As an alternative to the mouse, a user may choose a document "hotspot," such as a hyperlink embedded in an image map, by pressing the Tab key. Once the user chooses the hotspot, he activates the hyperlink by pressing the Enter key. By default, the browser steps to each hotspot in the order in which they appear in the document. You can now change that default order with what was originally introduced by Internet Explorer with the taborder attribute and is now standardized as the tabindex attribute. The value of the attribute is an integer indicating the position of this area in the overall tab sequence for the document.

Supported by Internet Explorer only and not part of the HTML 4 and XHTML standards, notab areas get passed over as the user presses the Tab key to move the cursor around the document. Otherwise, this area will be part of the tabbing sequence. The attribute is useful, of course, in combination with the nohref attribute.

Internet Explorer version 4 supported the notab and taborder attributes. Versions 5 and later support tabindex, too, so use the standard rather than the extension attributes.

6.5.4.6 The event attributes

The same mouse-related JavaScript event handlers that work for the anchor (<a>) tag also work with client-side image-map hyperlinks. The value of the event handler is— enclosed in quotation marks—one or a sequence of semicolon-separated JavaScript expressions, methods, and function references that the browser executes when the event occurs. [JavaScript Event Handlers, 12.3.3]

For example, a popular, albeit simple, use of the onMouseOver event is to print a more descriptive explanation in the browser's status box whenever the user passes the mouse pointer over a region of the image map:

```
<area href="http://www.oreilly.com/kumquats/homecooking/recipes.html#quat5"
    onMouseOver="self.status='A recipe for kumquat soup.';return true">
```

We should point out that the current versions of the popular browsers automatically display the alt attribute's string value, ostensibly accomplishing the same task. So we recommend that you include the alt attribute and value in lieu of hacking Java-Script. And, in context with a text-based hyperlink, we argue that the contents of the tag itself should explain the link. But images can be deceptive, so we urge you to take advantage of both the alt attribute and event handlers to provide text descriptions with your image maps.

6.5.4.7 The shape attribute

Use the shape attribute to define the shape of an image map's mouse-sensitive region: a circle (circ or circle), polygon (poly or polygon), or rectangle (rect or rectangle).

The value of the shape attribute affects how the browser interprets the value of the coords attribute. If you don't include a shape attribute, the value default is assumed. According to the standard, default means that the area covers the entire image. In practice, the browsers default to a rectangular area and expect to find four coords values. If you don't specify a shape and don't include four coordinates with the tag, the browsers ignore the area altogether.

In fact, only the most recent versions of the popular browsers recognize the shape value default to provide a catchall area for clicks that fall outside all the other defined hotspots. Because areas are in a "first-come, first-served" order in the <map> tag, you should place the default area last. Otherwise, it covers up any and all areas that follow in your image map.

The browsers are lax in their implementation of the shape names. Netscape 4, for example, doesn't recognize "rectangle" but does recognize "rect" for a rectangular shape. For this reason, we recommend that you use the abbreviated names.

6.5.4.8 The target attribute

The target attribute gives you a way to control where the contents of the selected hyperlink in the image map get displayed. The attribute is commonly used in conjunction with frames or multiple browser windows, and its the value is the name of the frame or window in which the referenced document should be loaded. If the named frame or window exists, the document is loaded in that frame or window. If not, a new window is created and given the specified name, and the document is loaded in that new window. For more information, including a list of special target names, see section 11.7.

6.5.4.9 The title attribute

The title attribute lets you specify a title for the document to which the image map's area links. The value of the attribute is any string, enclosed in quotes. The browser might use the title when displaying the link, perhaps flashing the title when the mouse passes over the area. The browser might also use the title attribute when adding this link to a user's bookmarks or favorites.

The title attribute is especially useful for referencing an otherwise unlabeled resource, such as an image or a non-HTML document. Ideally, the value specified should match the title of the referenced document, but this isn't required.

6.5.4.10 The class, dir, id, lang, and style attributes

The class and style attributes allow you to supply display properties and class names to control the appearance of the area, although their value seems limited for this tag. The id attribute allows you to create a name for the area that might be referenced by a hyperlink. [The id attribute, 4.1.1.4] [Inline Styles: The style Attribute, 8.1.1] [Style Classes, 8.3]

The lang and dir attributes define the language used for this area and the direction in which text is rendered. Again, their use is not apparent with this tag. [The dir attribute, 3.6.1.1] [The lang attribute, 3.6.1.2]

6.5.5 A Client-Side Image-Map Example

The following example HTML fragment draws together the various components of a client-side image map discussed earlier in this section. It includes the <img> tag with the image reference and a usemap attribute with a name that points to a <map> that defines four mouse-sensitive regions (three plus a default) and related links:

```
<body>
...
<img src="pics/map.gif" usemap="#map1" border=0>
...
<map name="map1">
  <area shape=rect coords="0,20,40,100"
      href="k_juice.html"
      onMouseOver="self.status='How to prepare kumquat juice.'
      ;return true">
  <area shape=rect coords="50,50,80,100"
      href="k_soup.html"
      onMouseOver="self.status='A recipe for hearty kumquat soup.'
      ;return true">
  <area shape=rect coords="90,50,140,100"
      href="k_fruit.html"
      onMouseOver="self.status='Care and handling of the native kumquat.'
      ;return true">
  <area shape=default
      href="javascript:window.alert('Choose the cup or one of the bowls.')"
      onMouseOver="self.status='Select the cup or a bowl for more information.'
      ;return true">
</map>
```

See Figure 6-7 for the results.

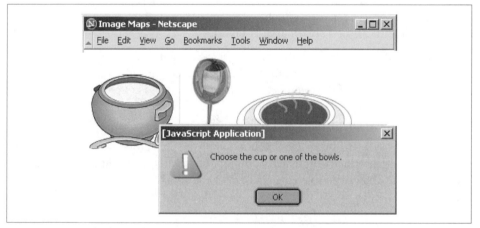

Figure 6-7. A simple client-side image map with JavaScript-enabled mouse events

6.5.6 Handling Other Browsers

Unlike its server-side ismap counterpart, the client-side image-map tag with attributes
(<img usemap>) doesn't need to be included in an <a> tag. But it may be so that you
can gracefully handle browsers that are unable to process client-side image maps.

For example, the ancient Mosaic and early versions of Netscape simply load a document named *main.html* if the user clicks the *map.gif* image referenced in the following
source fragment. More recent browsers, on the other hand, divide the image into
mouse-sensitive regions, as defined in the associated <map>, and link to a particular name
anchor within the same *main.html* document if the user selects the image-map region:

```
<a href="main.html">
  <img src="pics/map.gif" ismap usemap="#map1">
</a>
...
<map name="map1">
  <area coords="0,0,49,49" href="main.html#link1">
  <area coords="50,0,99,49" href="main.html#link2">
  <area coords="0,50,49,99" href="main.html#link3">
  <area coords="50,50,99,99" href="main.html#link4">
</map>
```

To make an image map backward compatible with all image-map-capable browsers,
you may also include client-side and server-side processing for the same image map.
Capable browsers will honor the faster client-side processing; all other browsers will
ignore the usemap attribute in the <img> tag and rely upon the referenced server process to handle user selections in the traditional way. For example:

```
<a href="/cgi-bin/images/map.proc">
  <img src="pics/map2.gif" usemap="#map2" ismap>
</a>
...
<map name="map2">
  <area coords="0,0,49,49" href="link1.html">
  <area coords="50,0,99,49" href="link2.html">
  <area coords="0,50,49,99" href="link3.html">
  <area coords="50,50,99,99" href="link4.html">
</map>
```

6.5.7 Effective Use of Mouse-Sensitive Images

Some of the most visually compelling pages on the Web have mouse- and hot-key-sen-
sitive images: maps with regions that (when clicked or selected with the Tab and Enter
keys) lead, for example, to more information about a country or town or result in more
detail about the location and who to contact at a regional branch of a business. We've
seen an image of a fashion model whose various clothing parts lead to their respective
catalog entries, complete with detailed descriptions and prices for ordering.

The visual nature of these "hyperactive" pictures, coupled with the need for an effective
interface, means that you should strongly consider having an artist, a user-interface

designer, and even a human-factors expert evaluate your imagery. At the very least, engage in a bit of user testing to make sure people know what region of the image to select to move to the desired document. Make sure the sensitive areas of the image indicate this to the user using a consistent visual mechanism. Consider using borders, drop shadows, or color changes to indicate those areas that the user can select.

Finally, always remember that the decision to use mouse-sensitive images is an explicit decision to exclude text-based and image-restricted browsers from your pages. This includes browsers connecting to the Internet via slow modem connections. For these people, downloading your beautiful images is simply too expensive. To keep from disenfranchising a growing population, make sure any page that has a mouse-sensitive image has a text-only equivalent easily accessible from a link on the image-enabled version. Some thoughtful webmasters even provide separate pages for users preferring full graphics versus mostly text.

6.6 Creating Searchable Documents

Another extensible form of an HTML link that does not use the <a> tag is one that causes the server to search a database for a document that contains a user-specified keyword or words. An HTML document that contains such a link is known as a *searchable* document.

6.6.1 The <isindex> Tag (Deprecated)

Before it was deprecated in both the HTML 4 and XHTML standards, authors used to use the <isindex> tag to pass keywords along with a search engine's URL to the server. The server then matched the keywords against a database of terms to select the next document for display. Today's authors mostly use forms to pass information to the server and supporting programs. See Chapter 9 for details.

<isindex>

Function	Indicates that a document can be searched
Attributes	action 🔗, class, dir, id, lang, prompt, style, title
End tag	None in HTML; </isindex> or <isindex ... /> in XHTML
Contains	Nothing
Used in	*head_content*

When a browser encounters the <isindex> tag, it adds a standard search interface to the document (rendered by Internet Explorer in Figure 6-8):

```
<html>
<head>
<title>Kumquat Advice Database</title>
<base href="cgi-bin/quat-query">
<isindex>
</head>
<body>
<h3>Kumquat Advice Database</h3>
<p>
Search this database to learn more about kumquats!
</body>
</html>
```

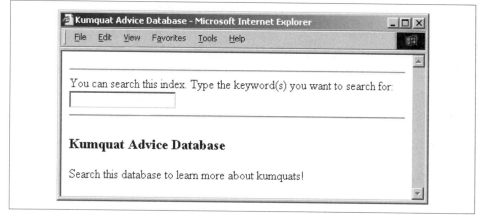

Figure 6-8. A searchable document

The user types a list of space-separated keywords into the field provided. When the user presses the Enter key, the browser automatically appends the query list to the end of a URL and passes the information to the server for further processing.

While the HTML and XHTML standards allow the deprecated <isindex> tag to be placed only in the document header, most browsers let the tag appear anywhere in the document and insert the search field in the content flow where the <isindex> tag appears. This convenient extension lets you add instructions and other useful elements before presenting the user with the actual search field.

6.6.1.1 The prompt attribute

The browser provides a leading prompt just above or to the left of the user-entry field. Internet Explorer's default prompt has even changed over the years. Version 5, for example, used "This is a searchable index. Enter search keywords:". Figure 6-8 shows the new one with version 6's prompt. That default prompt is not the best for all occasions, so it is possible to change it with the prompt attribute.

When added to the <isindex> tag, the value of the prompt attribute is the string of text that precedes the keyword entry field the browser places in the document.

For example, compare Figure 6-8 with Figure 6-9, in which we added the following prompt to the previous source example:

```
<isindex prompt="To learn more about kumquats, enter a keyword:">
```

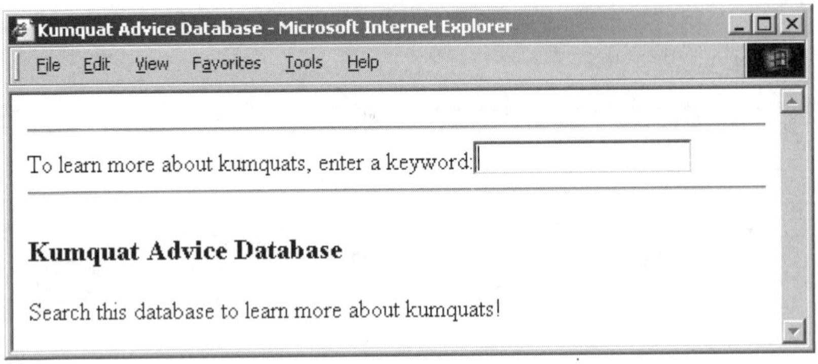

Figure 6-9. The prompt attribute creates custom prompts in searchable documents

Older browsers ignore the prompt attribute, but there is little reason not to include a better prompt string for your more up-to-date readership.

6.6.1.2 The query URL

Besides the <isindex> tag in the header of a searchable document, the other important element of this special tag is the query URL. By default, it is the URL of the source document itself—not good if your document can't handle the query. Rather, most authors use the <base> attribute to point to a different URL for the search. [<base>, 6.7.1]

The browser appends a question mark to the query URL, followed by the specified search parameters. Nonprintable characters are appropriately encoded; multiple parameters are separated by plus signs (+).

In the previous example, if a user typed "insect control" in the search field, the browser would retrieve the URL:

```
cgi-bin/quat-query?insect+control
```

6.6.1.3 The action attribute

For Internet Explorer only, you can specify the query URL for the index with the action attribute. The effect is exactly as though you had used the href attribute with the <base> tag: the browser links to the specified URL with the search parameters appended to the URL.

While the action attribute provides the desirable feature of divorcing the document's base URL from the search index URL, it will cause your searches to fail if the user is not using Internet Explorer. For this reason, we do not recommend that you use the action attribute to specify the query URL for the search.

6.6.1.4 The class, dir, id, lang, style, and title attributes

The class and style attributes allow you to supply display properties and class names to control the appearance of the tag, although their value seems limited for <isindex>. The id and title attributes allow you to create a name and title for the tag; the name might be referenced by a hyperlink. [The id attribute, 4.1.1.4] [Inline Styles: The style Attribute, 8.1.1] [Style Classes, 8.3]

The dir and lang attributes define the language used for this tag and the direction in which text is rendered. Again, their use is not apparent with <isindex>. [The dir attribute, 3.6.1.1] [The lang attribute, 3.6.1.2]

6.6.1.5 Server dependencies

Like image maps, searchable documents require support from the server to make things work. How the server interprets the query URL and its parameters is not defined by the HTML or XHTML standards.

You should consult your server's documentation to determine how you can receive and use the search parameters to locate the desired document. Typically, the server breaks the parameters out of the query URL and passes them to a program designated by the URL.

6.7 Relationships

Very few documents stand alone. Instead, a document is usually part of a collection of documents, each connected by one or several of the hypertext strands we describe in this chapter. One document may be a part of several collections, linking to some documents and being linked to by others. Readers move among the document families as they follow the links that interest them.

When you link two documents, you establish an explicit relationship between them. Conscientious authors use the rel attribute of the <a> tag to indicate the nature of the link. In addition, two other tags may be used within a document to further clarify the location of a document within a document family and its relationship to the other documents in that family. These tags, <base> and <link>, are placed within the body of the <head> tag. [<head>, 3.7.1]

6.7.1 The <base> Header Element

As we previously explained, URLs within a document can be either absolute (with every element of the URL explicitly provided by the author) or relative (with certain elements of the URL omitted and supplied by the browser). Normally, the browser fills in the blanks of a relative URL by drawing the missing pieces from the URL of the current document. You can change that with the <base> tag.

<base>	
Function	Defines the base URL for other anchors in the document
Attributes	href, target
End tag	None in HTML; </base> or <base ... /> in XHTML
Contains	Nothing
Used in	*head_content*

The <base> tag should appear only in the document header, not in its body contents. The browser thereafter uses the specified base URL, not the current document's URL, to resolve all relative URLs, including those found in <a>, <img>, <link>, and <form> tags. It also defines the URL that will be used to resolve queries in searchable documents containing the <isindex> tag. [Referencing Documents: The URL, 6.2]

6.7.1.1 The href attribute

The href attribute must have a valid URL as its value, which the browser then uses to define the absolute URL against which relative URLs are based within the document.

For example, the <base> tag in this XHTML document head:

```
<head>
<base href="http://www.kumquat.com/" />
</head>
...
```

tells the browser that any relative URLs within this document are relative to the top-level document directory on *www.kumquat.com*, regardless of the address and directory of the machine from which the user retrieved the current document.

Contrary to what you may expect, you can make the base URL relative, not absolute. The browser should (but doesn't always) form an absolute base URL out of this relative URL by filling in the missing pieces with the URL of the document itself. This property can be used to good advantage. For instance, in this next HTML example:

```
<head>
<base href="/info/">
</head>
...
```

the browser makes the <base> URL into one relative to the server's /info directory, which probably is not the same directory of the current document. Imagine if you had to readdress every link in your document with that common directory. Not only does the <base> tag help you shorten those URLs in your document that have a common root, but it also lets you constrain the directory from which relative references are retrieved without binding the document to a specific server.

6.7.1.2 The target attribute

When working with documents inside frames, the target attribute with the <a> tag ensures that a referenced URL gets loaded into the correct frame. Similarly, the target attribute for the <base> tag lets you establish the default name of one of the frames or windows in which the browser is to display redirected hyperlinked documents. [An Overview of Frames, 11.1]

If you have no other default target for your hyperlinks within your frames, you may want to consider using <base target=_top>. This ensures that links that are not specifically targeted to a frame or window will load in the top-level browser window. This eliminates the embarrassing and common error of having references to pages on other sites appear within a frame on your pages, instead of within their own pages. A minor bit of HTML, to be sure, but it makes life much easier for your readers.

6.7.1.3 Using <base>

The most important reason for using <base> is to ensure that any relative URLs within the document will resolve into correct document addresses, even if the documents themselves are moved or renamed. This is particularly important when creating a document collection. By placing the correct <base> tag in each document, you can move the entire collection between directories and even servers without breaking all of the links within the documents. You also need to use the <base> tag for a searchable document (<isindex>) if you want user queries posed to a URL different from that of the host document.

A document that contains both the <isindex> tag and other relative URLs may have problems if the relative URLs are not relative to the desired index-processing URL. Because this is usually the case, don't use relative URLs in searchable documents that use the <base> tag to specify the query URL for the document.

6.7.2 The <link> Header Element

Use the <link> tag to define the relationship between the current document and another in a web collection.

The <link> tag belongs in the <head> content and nowhere else. Use the attributes of the <link> tag like those of the <a> tag, but their effects serve only to document the relationship between documents. The <link> tag has no content, and only XHTML supports the closing </link> tag.

<link>

Function	Defines a relationship between this document and another document
Attributes	charset, class, dir, href, hreflang, id, lang, media, onClick, onDblClick, onKeyDown, onKeyPress, onKeyUp, onMouseDown, onMouseMove, onMouseOut, onMouseOver, onMouseUp, rel, rev, style, target, title, type
End tag	None in HTML; </link> or <link ... /> in XHTML
Contains	Nothing
Used in	*head_content*

6.7.2.1 The href attribute

As with its other tag applications, the href attribute specifies the URL of the target <link> tag. It is a required attribute, and its value is any valid document URL. The specified document is assumed to have a relationship to the current document.

6.7.2.2 The rel and rev attributes

The rel and rev attributes express the relationship between the source and target documents. The rel attribute specifies the relationship from the source document to the target; the rev attribute specifies the relationship from the target document to the source document. Both attributes can be included in a single <link> tag.

The value of either attribute is a space-separated list of relationships. The actual relationship names are not specified by the HTML standard, although some have come into common usage. For example, a document that is part of a sequence of documents might use:

```
<link href="part-14.html" rel=next rev=prev>
```

when referencing the next document in the series. The relationship from the source to the target is that of moving to the next document; the reverse relationship is that of moving to the previous document.

6.7.2.3 The title attribute

The title attribute lets you specify the title of the document to which you are linking. This attribute is useful when referencing a resource that does not have a title, such as an image or a non-HTML document. In this case, the browser might use the <link> title when displaying the referenced document. For example:

```
<link href="pics/kumquat.gif"
    title="A photograph of the Noble Fruit">
```

tells the browser to use the indicated title when displaying the referenced image.

The value of the attribute is an arbitrary character string, enclosed in quotation marks.

6.7.2.4 The type attribute

The type attribute provides the MIME content type of the linked document. Supported by all the popular browsers, the HTML 4 and XHTML standard type attribute can be used with any linked document. It is often used to define the type of a linked stylesheet. In this context, the value of the type attribute is usually text/css. For example:

```
<link href="styles/classic.css" rel=stylesheet type="text/css">
```

creates a link to an external stylesheet within the <head> of a document. See Chapter 8 for details.

6.7.2.5 How browsers might use <link>

Although the standards do not require browsers to do anything with the information provided by the <link> tag, it's not hard to envision how this information might be used to enhance the presentation of a document.

As a simple example, suppose you consistently provide <link> tags for each of your documents that define next, prev, and parent links. A browser could use this information to place at the top or bottom of each document a standard toolbar containing buttons that would jump to the appropriate related document. By relegating the task of providing simple navigational links to the browser, you are free to concentrate on the more important content of your document.

As a more complex example, suppose that a browser expects to find a <link> tag defining a glossary for the current document and that this glossary document is itself a searchable document. Whenever a reader clicked on a word or phrase in the document, the browser could automatically search the glossary for the definition of the selected phrase, presenting the result in a small pop-up window.

As the Web evolves, expect to see more and more uses of the <link> tag to define document relationships explicitly.

6.7.2.6 Other <link> attributes

The HTML 4 and XHTML standards also include the ubiquitous collection of attributes related to stylesheets and user events, and language for the <link> tag. You can refer to the corresponding section describing these attributes for the <a> tag for a complete description of their usage. [<a>, 6.3.1]

Because you put the <link> tag in the <head> section, whose contents are not displayed, it may seem that these attributes are useless. It is entirely possible that some future browser may find some way to display the <link> information to the user, possibly as a navigation bar or a set of hot-list selections. In those cases, the display and rendering information would prove useful. Currently, no browser provides these capabilities.

6.8 Supporting Document Automation

Two additional header tags have the primary functions of supporting document automation and interacting with the web server itself and with document-generation tools.

6.8.1 The <meta> Header Element

Given the rich set of header tags for defining a document and its relationship with others that go unused by most authors, you'd think we'd all be satisfied. But no, there's always someone with special needs. These authors want to be able to give even more information about their precious documents—information that browsers, readers of the source, or document-indexing tools might use. The <meta> tag is for those of you who need to go beyond the beyond.

<meta>

Function	Supplies additional information about a document
Attributes	charset 🔒, content, dir, http_equiv, lang, name, scheme
End tag	None in HTML; </meta> or <meta ... /> in XHTML
Contains	Nothing
Used in	*head_content*

The <meta> tag belongs in the document header and has no content. Instead, attributes of the tag define name/value pairs that associate the document. In certain cases, the web server serving the document uses these values to further define the document content type to the browser.

6.8.1.1 The name attribute

The name attribute supplies the name of the name/value pair defined by the <meta> tag. Neither the HTML nor the XHTML standard specifies any predefined <meta> names. In general, you are free to use any name that makes sense to you and other readers of your source document.

One commonly used name is keywords, which defines a set of keywords for the document. When encountered by any of the popular search engines on the Web, these keywords may be used to categorize the document. If you want your documents to be indexed by a search engine, consider putting this kind of tag in the <head> of each document:

```
<meta name="keywords" content="kumquats, cooking, peeling, eating">
```

If the name attribute is not provided, the name of the name/value pair is taken from the http-equiv attribute.

6.8.1.2 The content attribute

The content attribute provides the value of the name/value pair. It can be any valid string (enclosed in quotes if it contains spaces). It should always be specified in conjunction with either a name or an http-equiv attribute.

As an example, you might place the author's name in a document with:

```
<meta name="Authors" content="Chuck Musciano & Bill Kennedy">
```

6.8.1.3 The http-equiv attribute

The http-equiv attribute supplies a name for the name/value pair and instructs the server to include the name/value pair in the MIME document header that is passed to the browser before sending the actual document.

When a server sends a document to a browser, it first sends a number of name/value pairs. While some servers might send a number of these pairs, all servers send at least one:

```
content-type: text/html
```

This tells the browser to expect to receive an HTML document.

When you use the <meta> tag with the http-equiv attribute, the server will add your name/value pairs to the content header it sends to the browser. For example, adding:

```
<meta http-equiv="charset" content="iso-8859-1">
<meta http-equiv="expires" content="31 Dec 99">
```

causes the header sent to the browser to contain:

```
content-type: text/html
charset: iso-8859-1
expires: 31 Dec 99
```

Of course, adding these additional header fields makes sense only if your browser accepts the fields and uses them in some appropriate manner.

6.8.1.4 The charset attribute

Internet Explorer versions 5 and earlier provided explicit support for a charset attribute in the <meta> tag. Set the value of the attribute to the name of the character set to be used for the document. This is not the recommended way to define a document's character set. Rather, we recommend always using the http-equiv and content attributes to define the character set.

6.8.1.5 The scheme attribute

This attribute specifies the scheme to be used to interpret the property's value. This scheme should be defined within the profile specified by the profile attribute of the <head> tag. [<head>, 3.7.1]

6.8.2 The <nextid> Header Element (Archaic)

This tag is not defined in the HTML 4 and XHTML standards and should not be used. We describe it here for historical reasons.

<nextid>

Function	Defines the next valid document entity identifier
Attributes	n
End tag	None
Contains	Nothing
Used in	*head_content*

The idea behind the <nextid> tag is to provide some way of automatically indexing fragment identifiers.

6.8.2.1 The n attribute

The n attribute specifies the name of the next generated fragment identifier. It is typically an alphabetic string followed by a two-digit number. A typical <nextid> tag might look like this:

```
<html>
<head>
<nextid n=DOC54>
</head>
...
```

An automatic document generator might use the nextid information to successively name fragment identifiers DOC54, DOC55, and so forth, within this document.

CHAPTER 7

Formatted Lists

Making information more accessible is the single most important quality of HTML and its progeny, XHTML. The languages' excellent collection of text style and formatting tools help you organize your information into documents readers can quickly understand, scan, and extract, possibly with automated browser agents.

Beyond embellishing your text with specialized text tags, HTML and XHTML provide a rich set of tools that help you organize content into formatted lists. There's nothing magical or mysterious about lists. In fact, the beauty of lists is their simplicity. They're based on common list paradigms we encounter every day, such as unordered grocery lists, ordered instruction lists, and dictionary-like definition lists. All are familiar, comfortable ways of organizing content. All provide powerful means for quickly understanding, scanning, and extracting pertinent information from your web documents.

7.1 Unordered Lists

Like a laundry or shopping list, an *unordered list* is a collection of related items that have no special order or sequence. The most common unordered list you'll find on the Web is a collection of hyperlinks to other documents. Some common topic, such as "Related Kumquat Lovers' Sites," allies the items in an unordered list, but they have no order among themselves.

7.1.1 The <ul> Tag

The <ul> tag signals to the browser that the following content, between it and the </ul> end tag, is an unordered list of items. Inside, a leading <li> tag identifies each item in the unordered list. Otherwise, nearly anything HTML/XHTML-wise goes, including other lists, text, and multimedia elements.

<ul>

Function   Defines an unordered list

Attributes   class, compact 🛈, dir, id, lang, onClick, onDblClick, onKeyDown, onKeyPress, onKeyUp, onMouseDown, onMouseMove, onMouseOut, onMouseOver, onMouseUp, style, title, type 🛈

End tag   </ul>; never omitted

Contains   *list_content*

Used in   *block*

Typically, the browser adds a leading bullet character and formats each unordered list item on a new line, indented somewhat from the left margin of the document. The actual rendering of unordered lists, although similar for the popular browsers (see Figure 7-1), is not dictated by the standards, so you shouldn't get bent out of shape trying to attain exact positioning of the elements.

Here is an example XHTML unordered list, as shown in Figure 7-1:

```
Popular Kumquat recipes:
<ul>
  <li>Pickled Kumquats</li>
  <li>'Quats and 'Kraut (a holiday favorite!)</li>
  <li>'Quatshakes</li>
</ul>
There are so many more to please every palate!
```

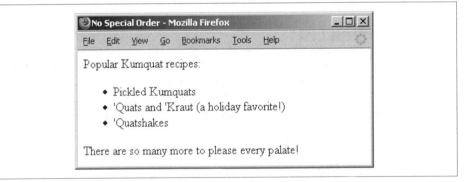

Figure 7-1. A simple unordered list

Tricky HTML authors sometimes use nested unordered lists, with and without <li>-tagged items, to take advantage of the automatic, successive indenting. You can produce some fairly slick text segments that way. Just don't depend on it for all browsers, including future ones. Rather, it's best to use the border property with a style definition in the paragraph (<p>) or division (<div>) tag to indent nonlist sections of your document (see Chapter 8).

7.1.1.1 The type attribute

The graphical browsers automatically bullet each <li>-tagged item in an unordered list. Netscape and Firefox use a diamond like that shown in Figure 7-1, whereas Internet Explorer and Opera use a solid circle, for example. Browsers that support HTML 3.2 and later versions, including 4.0 and 4.01, as well as XHTML 1.0, let you use the type attribute to specify which bullet symbol you'd rather have precede items in an unordered list. This attribute may have the value of disc, circle, or square. All the items within that list thereafter use the specified bullet symbol, unless an individual item overrides the list bullet type, as described later in this chapter.

With the advent of standard Cascading Style Sheets (CSS), the World Wide Web Consortium (W3C) has deprecated the type attribute in HTML 4 and in XHTML. Expect it to disappear.

7.1.1.2 Compact unordered lists

If you like wide-open spaces, you'll hate the optional compact attribute for the <ul> tag. It tells the browser to squeeze the unordered list into an even smaller, more compact text block. Typically, the browser reduces the line spacing between list items; it also may reduce the indentation between list items, if it does anything at all with indentation (usually it doesn't).

Some browsers ignore the compact attribute, so you shouldn't depend on its formatting attributes. Also, the attribute is deprecated in the HTML 4 and XHTML standards, so it hasn't long to live.

7.1.1.3 The style and class attributes

The style and class attributes bring CSS-based display control to lists, providing far more comprehensive control than you would get through individual attributes like type. Combine the style attribute with the <ul> tag, for instance, to assign your own bullet icon image, instead of using the common circle, disc, or square. The class attribute lets you apply the style of a predefined class of the <ul> tag to the contents of the unordered list. The value of the class attribute is the name of a style defined in some document-level or externally defined stylesheet. For more information, see Chapter 8. [Inline Styles: The style Attribute, 8.1.1] [Style Classes, 8.3]

.

7.1.1.4 The lang and dir attributes

The lang attribute lets you specify the language used within a list, and dir lets you advise the browser in which direction the text should be displayed. The value of the lang attribute is any of the International Organization for Standardization (ISO) standard two-character language abbreviations, including an optional language modifier. For example, adding lang=en-UK tells the browser that the list is in English ("en") as spoken and written in the United Kingdom ("UK"). Presumably, the browser may make layout or typographic decisions based upon your language choice. [The lang attribute, 3.6.1.2]

The dir attribute tells the browser in which direction to display the list contents—from left to right (dir=ltr), like English and French, or from right to left (dir=rtl), as with Hebrew and Chinese. [The dir attribute, 3.6.1.1]

7.1.1.5 The id and title attributes

Use the id attribute to specially label the unordered list. An acceptable value is any quote-enclosed string that uniquely identifies the list and can later be used to unambiguously reference the list in a hyperlink target, for automated searches, as a stylesheet selector, and for a host of other applications. [The id attribute, 4.1.1.4]

You also can use the optional title attribute and quote-enclosed string value to identify the list. Unlike an id attribute, a title does not have to be unique. [The title attribute, 4.1.1.5]

7.1.1.6 The event attributes

The many user-related events that may happen in and around a list, such as when a user clicks or double-clicks within its display space, are recognized by current browsers. With the respective on attribute and value, you may react to those events by displaying a user dialog box or activating some multimedia event. [JavaScript Event Handlers, 12.3.3]

7.2 Ordered Lists

Use an ordered list when the sequence of the list items is important. A list of instructions is a good example, as are tables of contents and lists of document footnotes or endnotes.

7.2.1 The <ol> Tag

The typical browser formats the contents of an ordered list just like an unordered list, except that the items are numbered rather than bulleted. The numbering starts at one and is incremented by one for each successive ordered list element tagged with <li>. [<li>, 7.3]

<table>
<tr><td colspan="2" align="center"><ol></td></tr>
<tr><td>Function</td><td>Defines an ordered list</td></tr>
<tr><td>Attributes</td><td>class, compact, dir, id, lang, onClick, onDblClick, onKeyDown, onKeyPress, onKeyUp, onMouseDown, onMouseMove, onMouseOut, onMouseOver, onMouseUp, start, style, title, type</td></tr>
<tr><td>End tag</td><td></ol>; never omitted</td></tr>
<tr><td>Contains</td><td>list_content</td></tr>
<tr><td>Used in</td><td>block</td></tr>
</table>

HTML 3.2 introduced a number of features that provide a wide variety of ordered lists. You can change the start value of the list and select from five different numbering styles.

Here is a sample XHTML ordered list:

```
<h3>Pickled Kumquats</h3>
Here's an easy way to make a delicious batch of pickled 'quats:
<ol>
  <li>Rinse 50 pounds of fresh kumquats</li>
  <li>Bring eight gallons white vinegar to rolling boil</li>
  <li>Add kumquats gradually, keeping vinegar boiling</li>
  <li>Boil for one hour, or until kumquats are tender</li>
  <li>Place in sealed jars and enjoy!</li>
</ol>
```

Opera renders the example as shown in Figure 7-2.

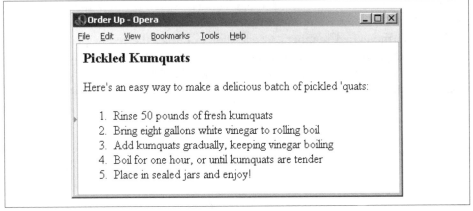

Figure 7-2. An ordered list

7.2.1.1 The start attribute

Normally, browsers automatically number ordered list items beginning with the Arabic numeral 1. The start attribute for the <ol> tag lets you change that beginning value. To start numbering a list at 5, for example:

```
<ol start=5>
    <li> This is item number 5.</li>
    <li> This is number 6!</li>
    <li> And so forth...</li>
</ol>
```

7.2.1.2 The type attribute

By default, browsers number ordered list items with a sequence of Arabic numerals. Besides being able to start the sequence at some number other than 1, you can use the type attribute with the <ol> tag to change the numbering style itself. The attribute may have a value of A for numbering with capital letters, a for numbering with lowercase letters, I for capital Roman numerals, i for lowercase Roman numerals, or 1 for common Arabic numerals. See Table 7-1.

Table 7-1. HTML type values for numbering ordered lists

Type value	Generated style	Sample sequence
A	Capital letters	A, B, C, D
a	Lowercase letters	a, b, c, d
I	Capital Roman numerals	I, II, III, IV
i	Lowercase Roman numerals	i, ii, iii, iv
1	Arabic numerals	1, 2, 3, 4

The start and type attributes work in tandem. The start attribute sets the starting value of the item counter (an integer) at the beginning of an ordered list. The type attribute sets the actual numbering style. For example, the following ordered list starts numbering items at 8, but because the style of numbering is set to i, the first number is the lowercase Roman numeral "viii." Subsequent items are numbered with the same style, and each value is incremented by 1, as shown in this HTML example, and rendered as shown in Figure 7-3:[*]

```
<ol start=8 type="i">
    <li> This is the Roman number 8.
    <li> The numerals increment by 1.
    <li> And so forth...
</ol>
```

---

[*] Notice that we don't include the </li> end tag in the HTML example but do in all the XHTML ones. Some end tags are optional with HTML but must be included in all XHTML documents.

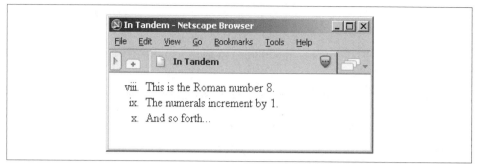

Figure 7-3. The start and type attributes work in tandem

The type and value of individual items in a list can be different from those of the list as a whole, described in section 7.3.1 later in this chapter. As mentioned earlier, the start and type attributes are deprecated in HTML 4 and XHTML. Consider using stylesheets instead.

7.2.1.3 Compact ordered lists

Like the <ul> tag, the <ol> tag has an optional compact attribute that is deprecated in the HTML 4 and XHTML standards. Unless you absolutely need to use it, don't.

7.2.1.4 The class, dir, id, lang, event, style, and title attributes

These attributes are applicable with ordered lists, too; their effects are identical to those for unordered lists. [The class and style attributes, 4.1.1.6] [The lang and dir attributes, 6.3.1.7] [The id and title attributes, 7.1.1.5] [The event attributes, 6.3.1.4]

7.3 The <li> Tag

It should be quite obvious to you by now that the <li> tag defines an item in a list. It's the universal tag for list items in ordered (<ol>) and unordered (<ul>) lists, as we discussed earlier, and for directories (<dir>) and menus (<menu>), which we discuss in detail later in this chapter.

Because the end of a list element can always be inferred by the surrounding document structure, most authors omit the ending </li> tags for their HTML list elements. That makes sense because it becomes easier to add, delete, and move elements around within a list. However, XHTML requires the end tag, so it's best to get used to including it in your documents.

Although universal in meaning, there are some differences and restrictions to the use of the <li> tag for each list type. In unordered and ordered lists, nearly anything can follow the <li> tag, including other lists and multiple paragraphs. Typically, if it handles indentation at all, the browser successively indents nested list items, and the content in those items is justified to the innermost indented margin.

<table>
<tr><td colspan="2" align="center">**<li>**</td></tr>
<tr><td>**Function**</td><td>Defines an item within an ordered, unordered, directory, or menu list</td></tr>
<tr><td>**Attributes**</td><td>class, dir, id, lang, onClick, onDblClick, onKeyDown, onKeyPress, onKeyUp, onMouseDown, onMouseMove, onMouseOut, onMouseOver, onMouseUp, style, title, type, value</td></tr>
<tr><td>**End tag**</td><td></li>; often omitted in HTML</td></tr>
<tr><td>**Contains**</td><td>*flow*</td></tr>
<tr><td>**Used in**</td><td>*list_content*</td></tr>
</table>

Directory and menu lists are another matter. They are lists of short items, like a single word or simple text blurb and nothing else. Consequently, <li> items within <dir> and <menu> tags may not contain other lists or other block elements, including paragraphs, preformatted blocks, or forms.

Clean documents, fully compliant with the HTML and XHTML standards, should not contain any text or other document item inside the unordered, ordered, directory, or menu lists that is not contained within an <li> tag. Most browsers tolerate violations to this rule, but you can't hold the browser responsible for compliant rendering of exceptional cases, either.

7.3.1 Changing the Style and Sequence of Individual List Items

Just as you can change the bullet or numbering style for all of the items in an unordered or ordered list, you can change the style for individual items within those lists. With ordered lists, you also can change the value of the item number. As you'll see, the combinations of changing style and numbering can lead to a variety of useful list structures, particularly when included with nested lists. Do note, however, that the standards have deprecated these attributes in deference to their CSS counterparts.

7.3.1.1 The type attribute

Acceptable values for the type attribute in the <li> tag are the same as the values for the appropriate list type: items within unordered lists may have their type set to circle, square, or disc, and items in an ordered list may have their type set to any of the values shown previously in Table 7-1.

Be careful. With earlier browsers, such as Netscape Navigator and Internet Explorer versions 4 and earlier, a change in the bullet or numbering type in one list item similarly affected subsequent items in the list. Not so for HTML 4–compliant browsers, including Netscape version 6, Internet Explorer versions 5 and later, Firefox, and Opera! The type attribute's effects are acute and limited to only the current <li> tag. Subsequent items revert to the default type; each must contain the specified type.

The type attribute changes the display style of the individual list item's leading number, and only that item, but not the value of the number, which persistently increments by one. Figure 7-4 shows the effect that changing the type for an individual item in an ordered list has on subsequent items, as rendered from the following XHTML source:

```
<ol>
  <li type=A>Changing the numbering type</li>
  <li type=I>Uppercase Roman numerals</li>
  <li type=i>Lowercase Roman numerals</li>
  <li type=1>Plain ol' numbers</li>
  <li type=a>Doesn't alter the order.</li>
  <li> &lt;-- But, although numbering continues sequentially,</li>
  <li> types don't persist. See? I should've been a "g"!</li>
</ol>
```

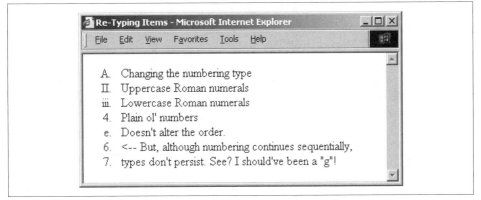

Figure 7-4. Changing the numbering style for each item in an ordered list

You can use the stylesheet-related style and class attributes to affect individual type changes in ordered and unordered lists that may or may not affect subsequent list items. See Chapter 8 for details (particularly section 8.4.8.5).

7.3.1.2 The value attribute

The value attribute changes the numbers of a specific list item and all of the list items that follow it. Because the ordered list is the only type with sequentially numbered items, the value attribute is valid only when used within an <li> tag inside an ordered list.

To change the current and subsequent numbers attached to each item in an ordered list, simply set the value attribute to an integer. The following source uses the value attribute to jump the numbering on items in an XHTML ordered list, and gets rendered by modern browsers as shown in Figure 7-5:

```
<ol>
  <li>Item number 1</li>
  <li>And the second</li>
  <li value=9> Jump to number 9</li>
  <li>And continue with 10...</li>
</ol>
```

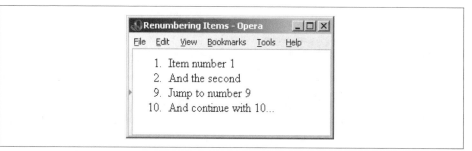

Figure 7-5. The value attribute lets you change individual item numbers in an ordered list

7.3.1.3 The style and class attributes

The style attribute for the `<li>` tag creates an inline style for the elements enclosed by the tag, overriding any other style rule in effect. The class attribute lets you format the content according to a predefined class of the `<li>` tag; its value is the name of that class. [Inline Styles: The style Attribute, 8.1.1] [Style Classes, 8.3]

7.3.1.4 The class, dir, id, lang, event, style, and title attributes

You can apply these attributes to individual list items; they have similar effects for ordered and unordered lists. [The class and style attributes, 4.1.1.6] [The lang and dir attributes, 6.3.1.7] [The id and title attributes, 7.1.1.5] [The event attributes, 6.3.1.4]

7.4 Nesting Lists

Except when placed inside directories or menus, lists nested inside other lists are fine. You can embed menu and directory lists within other lists. Indents for each nested list are cumulative, so do not nest lists too deeply; the list contents could quickly turn into a thin ribbon of text flush against the right edge of the browser document window.

7.4.1 Nested Unordered Lists

The items in each nested unordered list may be preceded by a different bullet character at the discretion of the browser. For example, Internet Explorer displays an alternating series of hollow, solid circular, and square bullets for the various nests in the following source fragment, as shown in Figure 7-6:

```
<ul>
  <li>Morning Kumquat Delicacies
    <ul>
      <li>Hot Dishes
        <ul>
          <li>Kumquat omelet</li>
          <li>Kumquat waffles
            <ul>
              <li>Country style</li>
              <li>Belgian</li>
            </ul>
          </li>
        </ul>
      </li>
      <li>Cold Dishes
        <ul>
          <li>Kumquats and cornflakes</li>
          <li>Pickled Kumquats</li>
          <li>Diced Kumquats</li>
        </ul>
      </li>
    </ul>
  </li>
</ul>
```

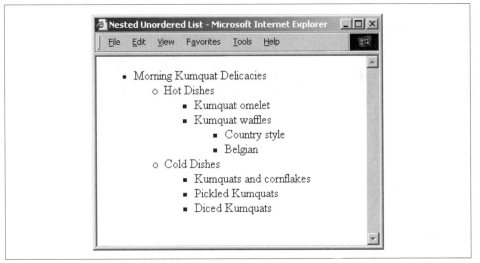

Figure 7-6. Bullets change for nested unordered list items

You can change the bullet style for each unordered list and even for individual list items, but the repertoire of bullets is limited, typically a simple solid disc for level-one items, an open circle for level two, and a solid square for subsequent levels.

7.4.2 Nested Ordered Lists

By default, browsers number the items in ordered lists beginning with the Arabic numeral 1, nested or not. It would be great if the standards numbered nested ordered lists in some rational, consecutive manner; e.g., the items in the second nest of the third main ordered list might be successively numbered "3.2.1," "3.2.2," "3.2.3," and so on.

With the type and value attributes, however, you do have a lot more latitude in how you create nested ordered lists. An excellent example is the traditional style for outlining, which uses the many different ways of numbering items offered by the type attribute (see Figure 7-7):

```
<ol type="A">
  <li>A History of Kumquats
    <ol type="1">
      <li>Early History
        <ol type="a">
          <li>The Fossil Record</li>
          <li>Kumquats: The Missing Link?</li>
        </ol>
      </li>
      <li>Mayan Use of Kumquats</li>
      <li>Kumquats in the New World</li>
    </ol>
  </li>
  <li>Future Use of Kumquats</li>
</ol>
```

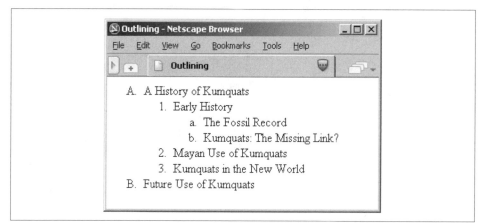

Figure 7-7. The type attribute lets you do traditional outlining with ordered lists

7.5 Definition Lists

HTML and XHTML also support a list style entirely different from the ordered and unordered lists we've discussed so far: definition lists. Like the entries you find in a dictionary or encyclopedia, complete with text, pictures, and other multimedia elements, the definition list is the ideal way to present a glossary, list of terms, or other name/value list.

7.5.1 The <dl> Tag

The definition list is enclosed by the <dl> and </dl> tags. Within the tags, each item in a definition list is composed of two parts: a term, followed by its definition or explanation. Instead of <li>, each item name in a <dl> list is marked with the <dt> tag, followed by the item's definition or explanation marked by the <dd> tag.

<table>
<tr><td colspan="2" align="center"><dl></td></tr>
<tr><td>Function</td><td>Defines a definition list</td></tr>
<tr><td>Attributes</td><td>class, compact, dir, id, lang, onClick, onDblClick, onKeyDown, onKeyPress, onKeyUp, onMouseDown, onMouseMove, onMouseOut, onMouseOver, onMouseUp, style, title, type</td></tr>
<tr><td>End tag</td><td></dl>; never omitted</td></tr>
<tr><td>Contains</td><td>dl_content</td></tr>
<tr><td>Used in</td><td>block</td></tr>
</table>

Unless you change the display attributes with stylesheet rules, browsers typically render the item or term name at the left margin and render the definition or explanation below it and indented. If the definition terms are very short (typically less than three characters), the browser may choose to place the first portion of the definition on the same line as the term. See how the following source XHTML definition list gets displayed in Figure 7-8:

```
<h3>Common Kumquat Parasites</h3>
<dl>
  <dt>Leaf mites</dt>
  <dd>The leaf mite will ravage the Kumquat tree, stripping it
      of any and all vegetation.</dd>
  <dt>Trunk dropsy</dt>
  <dd>This microscopic larvae of the common opossum
      chigger will consume the structural elements of the
      tree trunk, causing it to collapse inward.</dd>
</dl>
```

As with other list types, you can add more space between the definition list items by inserting paragraph <p> tags at the end of their content or by defining a spacious style for the respective tags.

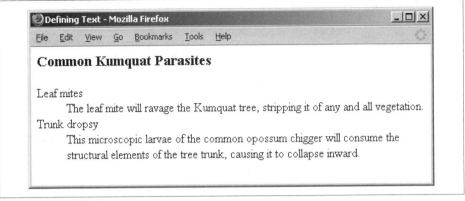

Figure 7-8. A definition list example

7.5.1.1 More compact definition lists

The `<dl>` tag supports the compact attribute, advising the browser to make the list presentation as small as possible. Few browsers, if any, honor this attribute, and it has been deprecated in HTML 4 and XHTML.

7.5.1.2 The class, dir, id, lang, style, title, and event attributes

The many other attributes for the `<dl>` tag should be quite familiar by now. The style and class attributes let you control the display style, the id and title tag attributes let you uniquely label its contents, the lang and dir attributes let you specify its native language and the direction in which the text will be rendered, and the many on-event attributes let you react to user-initiated mouse and keyboard actions on the contents. Not all are implemented by the currently popular browsers for this tag or for many others. [The dir attribute, 3.6.1.1] [The lang attribute, 3.6.1.2] [The id attribute, 4.1.1.4] [The title attribute, 4.1.1.5] [Inline Styles: The style Attribute, 8.1.1] [Style Classes, 8.3] [JavaScript Event Handlers, 12.3.3]

7.5.2 The <dt> Tag

The `<dt>` tag defines the term component of a definition list. It is valid only when used within a definition (`<dl>`) list preceding the term or item, before the `<dd>` tag and the term's definition or explanation.

Traditionally, the definition term that follows the `<dt>` tag is short and sweet—one or a few words. Technically, it can be any length. If the definition term is long, the browser may exercise the option of extending the item beyond the display window or wrapping it onto the next line, where the definition begins.

Because the end of the `<dt>` tag immediately precedes the start of the matching `<dd>` tag, it is unambiguous, so the `</dt>` end tag is not required in HTML documents.

<table>
<tr><td colspan="2" align="center"><dt></td></tr>
<tr><td>Function</td><td>Defines a definition list term</td></tr>
<tr><td>Attributes</td><td>class, dir, id, lang, onClick, onDblClick, onKeyDown, onKeyPress, onKeyUp, onMouseDown, onMouseMove, onMouseOut, onMouseOver, onMouseUp, style, title</td></tr>
<tr><td>End tag</td><td></dt>; may be omitted in HTML</td></tr>
<tr><td>Contains</td><td>text</td></tr>
<tr><td>Used in</td><td>dl_content</td></tr>
</table>

However, the XHTML standard insists that it be present, so get used to including it in your documents.

7.5.2.1 Formatting text with <dt>

In practice, browsers are either too lenient or too dumb to enforce the rules, so some tricky HTML authors misuse the <dt> tag to shift the left margin right and left, respectively, for fancy text displays. (Remember, tab characters and leading spaces usually don't work with regular text.) We don't condone violating the HTML, and certainly not the XHTML standard, and we caution you once again about tricked-up documents. Use stylesheets instead.

7.5.2.2 The class, dir, id, lang, style, title, and event attributes

The <dt> tag supports the standard HTML 4/XHTML tag attributes. The style and class attributes let you control the display style, the id and title tag attributes let you uniquely label its contents, the lang and dir attributes let you specify its native language and the direction in which the text will be rendered, and the many on-event attributes let you react to user-initiated mouse and keyboard actions on the contents. Not all are implemented by the currently popular browsers for this tag or for many others. [The dir attribute, 3.6.1.1] [The lang attribute, 3.6.1.2] [The id attribute, 4.1.1.4] [The title attribute, 4.1.1.5] [Inline Styles: The style Attribute, 8.1.1] [Style Classes, 8.3] [JavaScript Event Handlers, 12.3.3]

7.5.3 The <dd> Tag

The <dd> tag marks the start of the definition portion of an item in a definition list. According to the HTML and XHTML standards, <dd> belongs only inside a definition (<dl>) list, immediately following the <dt> tag and term and preceding the definition or explanation.

<table>
<tr><td colspan="2" align="center"><dd></td></tr>
<tr><td>Function</td><td>Defines a definition list term</td></tr>
<tr><td>Attributes</td><td>class, dir, id, lang, onClick, onDblClick, onKeyDown, onKeyPress, onKeyUp, onMouseDown, onMouseMove, onMouseOut, onMouseOver, onMouseUp, style, title</td></tr>
<tr><td>End tag</td><td></dd>; may be omitted in HTML</td></tr>
<tr><td>Contains</td><td>flow</td></tr>
<tr><td>Used in</td><td>dl_content</td></tr>
</table>

The content that follows the <dd> tag may be any HTML or XHTML construct, including other lists, block text, and multimedia elements. Although treating it otherwise identically as conventional content, browsers typically indent definition list (<dd>) definitions. Because the start of another term and definition (<dt>) or the required end tag of the definition (</dl>) unambiguously terminates the preceding definition, the </dd> end tag is not needed, and its absence makes your source text more readable. However, once again, XHTML insists that the end tag appear in your documents, so you may as well get used to adding </dd> to your documents.

7.5.3.1 The class, dir, id, lang, style, title, and event attributes

The <dt> tag supports the standard tag attributes. The style and class attributes let you control the display style, the id and title tag attributes let you uniquely label its contents, the lang and dir attributes let you specify its native language and the direction in which the text will be rendered, and the many on-event attributes let you react to user-initiated mouse and keyboard actions on the contents. Not all are implemented by the currently popular browsers for this tag or for many others. [The dir attribute, 3.6.1.1] [The lang attribute, 3.6.1.2] [The id attribute, 4.1.1.4] [The title attribute, 4.1.1.5] [Inline Styles: The style Attribute, 8.1.1] [Style Classes, 8.3] [JavaScript Event Handlers, 12.3.3]

7.6 Appropriate List Usage

In general, use unordered lists for:

- Link collections
- Short, nonsequenced groups of text
- Emphasizing the high points of a presentation

In general, use ordered lists for:

- Tables of contents
- Instruction sequences
- Sets of sequential sections of text
- Assigning numbers to short phrases that can be referenced elsewhere

In general, use definition lists for:

- Glossaries
- Custom bullets (make the item after the <dt> tag an icon-size bullet image)
- Any list of name/value pairs

7.7 Directory Lists

The directory list is a specialized form of unordered list. It has been deprecated in the HTML 4 and XHTML standards. We don't recommend that you use it at all. [<ul>, 7.1.1]

7.7.1 The <dir> Tag (Deprecated)

The designers of HTML originally dedicated the <dir> tag for displaying lists of files. As such, the browser, if it treats <dir> and <ul> differently at all (most don't), expects the various list elements to be quite short, possibly no longer than 20 or so characters. Some browsers display the elements in a multicolumn format and may not use a leading bullet.

<dir> 🔲

Function	Defines a directory list
Attributes	class, dir, id, lang, onClick, onDblClick, onKeyDown, onKeyPress, onKeyUp, onMouseDown, onMouseMove, onMouseOut, onMouseOver, onMouseUp, style, title
End tag	</dir>; never omitted
Contains	*list_content*
Used in	*block*

As with an unordered list, you define directory list items with the <li> tag. When used within a directory list, however, the <li> tag may not contain any block element, including paragraphs, other lists, preformatted text, or forms.

The following example puts the directory tag to its traditional task of presenting a list of filenames:

```
The distribution tape has the following files on it:
<dir>
   <li><code>README</code></li>
   <li><code>Makefile</code></li>
   <li><code>main.c</code></li>
   <li><code>config.h</code></li>
   <li><code>util.c</code></li>
</dir>
```

Notice that we used the <code> tag to ensure that the filenames would be rendered in an appropriate manner (see Figure 7-9).

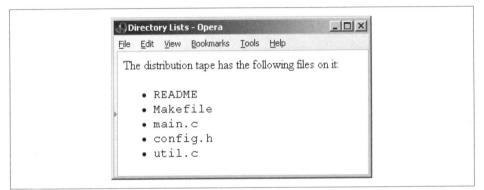

Figure 7-9. An example <dir> list

7.7.1.1 The <dir> attributes

The attributes for the <dir> tag are identical to those for <ul>, with the same effects.

7.8 Menu Lists

The menu list is yet another specialized form of the unordered list. Like <dir>, it is deprecated in the HTML 4 and XHTML standards, so we don't recommend using it. [<ul>, 7.1.1]

7.8.1 The <menu> Tag (Deprecated)

The <menu> tag displays a list of short choices to the reader, such as a menu of links to other documents. The browser may use a special (typically more compact) representation of items in a menu list compared with the general unordered list, or even use some sort of graphical pull-down menu to implement the menu list. If the list items are short enough, the browser may even display them in a multicolumn format and may not precede each list item with a bullet.

Like an unordered list, define the menu list items with the <li> tag. When used within a menu list, however, the <li> tag may not contain any block elements, including paragraphs, other lists, preformatted text, or forms.

Compare the following source text and display (Figure 7-10) with the directory (Figure 7-9) and unordered (Figure 7-1) list displays presented earlier in the chapter:

```
Some popular kumquat recipes include:
<menu>
  <li>Pickled Kumquats</li>
  <li>'Quats and 'Kraut (a holiday favorite!)</li>
  <li>'Quatshakes</li>
</menu>
There are many more to please every palate!
```

Figure 7-10. Sample <menu> list

<menu> 📄

Function	Defines a menu list
Attributes	class, dir, id, lang, onClick, onDblClick, onKeyDown, onKeyPress, onKeyUp, onMouseDown, onMouseMove, onMouseOut, onMouseOver, onMouseUp, style, title
End tag	</menu>; never omitted
Contains	*list_content*
Used in	*block*

CHAPTER 8

Cascading Style Sheets

Stylesheets are the way publishing professionals manage the overall "look" of their publications—backgrounds, fonts, colors, and so on—from a single page to huge collections of documents. Most desktop publishing software supports stylesheets, as do popular word processors, so using stylesheets for HTML documents is obvious.

For the most part, HTML focuses on content over style. Authors are encouraged to worry about providing high-quality information and leave it to the browser to worry about presentation. We strongly urge you to adopt this philosophy in your documents—don't mistake style for substance.

However, presentation is for the benefit of the reader, and even the original designers of HTML understand the interplay between style and readability—for example, through the physical style and header tags. Stylesheets extend that presentation with several additional effects, including colors, a wider selection of fonts, and even sounds so that users can better distinguish elements of your document. But most importantly, stylesheets let you control the presentation attributes for all the tags in a document—for a single document or a collection of many documents—from a single master.

In early 1996, the World Wide Web Consortium (W3C) put together a draft proposal defining Cascading Style Sheets (CSS) for HTML. This draft proposal quickly matured into a recommended standard. In mid-1998, the W3C extended the original specification to create CSS2, which includes presentation standards for a variety of media besides the familiar onscreen browser, along with several other enhancements.

The W3C continues to work on a minor version upgrade (version 2.1) and a draft of CSS3, but these are not imminent. Indeed, no current browser or web agent fully complies with the CSS2 standard. However, because we realize that eventual compliance with the W3C standard is likely, we'll cover all the components of the CSS2 standard in this chapter. As always, we'll denote clearly what is real, what is proposed, and what is actually supported.[*]

---

[*] In the fall of 2000, work began on CSS3. As CSS3 is still under construction and browsers have not yet even become fully compliant with CSS2, we focus on CSS2 throughout this chapter.

8.1 The Elements of Styles

At the simplest level, a style is nothing more than a rule the browser follows to render a particular HTML or XHTML tag's contents.[*] Each tag has a number of style properties associated with it, whose values define how that tag is rendered by the browser. A rule defines a specific value for one or more properties of a tag. For example, most tags can have a color property, the value of which defines the color in which the modern GUI browser should display the contents of the tag. Other properties include fonts, line spacing, margins, borders, sound volume, and voice, which we describe in detail later in this chapter.

There are three ways to attach a style to a tag: inline, on the document level, or through the use of an external stylesheet. You may use one or more stylesheets for your documents. The browser either merges the style definitions from each style or redefines the style characteristic for a tag's contents. Styles from these various sources are applied to your document, combining and defining style properties that cascade from external stylesheets through local document styles, and ending with inline styles. This cascade of properties and style rules gives rise to the standard's name: Cascading Style Sheets.

We cover the syntactic basics of the three stylesheet techniques here. We delve more deeply into the appropriate use of inline, document-level, and external stylesheets at the end of this chapter.

8.1.1 Inline Styles: The style Attribute

The *inline style* is the simplest way to attach a style to a tag—just include a style attribute with the tag along with a list of properties and their values. The browser uses those style properties and values to render the contents of that tag.

For instance, the following style tells the browser to display the level-1 header text, "I'm so bluuuuoooo!", not only in the <h1> tag style, but also colored blue and italicized:

```
<h1 style="color: blue; font-style: italic">I'm so bluuuuoooo!</h1>
```

Inline styles can be difficult to maintain, because they add more contents to their tags' definitions, making them harder to read. Also, because they have only a local effect, they must be sprinkled throughout your document. Use the inline style attribute sparingly and only in those rare circumstances when you cannot achieve the same effects otherwise.

---

[*] We explicitly avoided the term *display* here because it connotes visual presentation, whereas the CSS2 standard works hard to suggest many different ways of presenting the tagged contents of a document.

8.1.2 Document-Level Stylesheets

The real power of stylesheets becomes more evident when you place a list of presentation rules at the beginning of your HTML or XHTML document. Placed within the <head> and enclosed within their own <style> and </style> tags, *document-level stylesheets* affect all the same tags within that document, except for tags that contain overriding inline style attributes.*

<style>

Function	Defines a document-level stylesheet
Attributes	dir, lang, media, title, type
End tag	</style>; rarely omitted in HTML
Contains	*styles*
Used in	*head_content*

Everything between the <style> and </style> tags is considered part of the style rules that the browser is to apply when rendering the document. Actually, the contents of the <style> tag are not HTML or XHTML and are not bound by the normal rules for markup content. The <style> tag, in effect, lets you insert foreign content into your document that the browser uses to format your tags.

For example, a styles-conscious browser displays the contents of all <h1> tags as blue, italic text in an HTML document that has the following document-level stylesheet definition in its head:

```
<head>
<title>All True Blue</title>
<style type="text/css">
  <!--
  /* make all level-1 headers blue in italics */
  h1 {color: blue; font-style: italic}
  -->
</style>
</head>
<body>
<h1>I'm so bluuuuoooo!</h1>
...
<h1>I am ba-loooooo, tooooo!</h1>
```

---

* XHTML-based document-level stylesheets are specially enclosed in CDATA sections of your documents. See section 16.3.7 in Chapter 16 for details.

8.1.2.1 The type attribute

Other types of stylesheets are available for HTML/XHTML besides CSS. Like the JavaScript stylesheets we describe in Chapter 12, they are not well supported, if at all, by the popular browsers, so we don't spend a lot of time on them in this book. Nonetheless, the browser needs a way to distinguish which stylesheet you use in your document. Use the type attribute within the <style> tag for that. All cascading stylesheets are of the type text/css; JavaScript stylesheets use the type text/javascript. You may omit the type attribute and hope the browser figures out the kinds of styles you are using, but we suggest you always include the type attribute, so there is no opportunity for confusion. [JavaScript Stylesheets (Antiquated), 12.4]

8.1.2.2 The media attribute

HTML and XHTML documents can wind up in the strangest places these days, such as on cellular phones. To help the browser figure out the best way to render your documents, include the media attribute within the <style> tag. The value of this attribute is the document's intended medium, although it doesn't preclude rendering by other media. The default value is screen (computer display). Other values include tty (text only), tv (television), projection (theaters), handheld (PDAs and cell phones), print (ink on paper), braille (tactile devices), embossed (Braille printers), aural (audio; speech synthesis, for instance), and all (many different types of media).

If you want to explicitly list several types of media, instead of specifying all, use a quote-enclosed, comma-separated list of media types as the value of the media attribute. For example:

```
<style type="text/css" media="screen,print">
```

tells the browser that your document contains CSS both for printing and for computer displays.

Be careful specifying media, because the browser cannot apply the styles you define unless the document is being rendered on one of your specified media. Thus, the browser would not apply our example set of styles designed for media="screen,print" if the user is, for instance, connected to the Web with a handheld computer.

How do you create different style definitions for different media without creating multiple copies of your document? The CSS2 standard lets you define media-specific stylesheets through its extension to the @import at-rule and through the @media at-rule, which we describe in section 8.1.5 later in this chapter.

8.1.2.3 The dir, lang, and title attributes

As with any HTML/XHTML element, you can associate a descriptive title with the <!--
<DEFANGED_STYLE> tag and specify the language and text-rendering direction with the title, lang, and dir attributes. [The dir attribute, 3.6.1.1] [The lang attribute, 3.6.1.2] [The id attribute, 4.1.1.4]

8.1.3 Style-Free Browsers

Certainly you noticed that, in the preceding document-level stylesheet example, we enclosed the contents of the `<style>` tag inside an HTML comment (`<!--`) tag. Older, style-free browsers ignore the `<style>` tag, but then blithely go on to display its contents. Current browsers expect style rules to appear within an HTML comment and process them accordingly, whereas older browsers appropriately ignore the unrecognized `<style>` tag and go on to treat the comment tag and its intervening text normally. That works.

The order of the tags is very important. Here's the approach, which you may have noticed in our document-level style example:

```
<style>
<!--
  h1 {color: blue; font-style: italic}
-->
</style>
```

Use a `<style>` tag, followed by an HTML comment, then followed by the document-level style rule(s). Finally, in order, close the comment and the `</style>` tag.

XHTML documents require a slightly different approach. In those documents, we enclose document-level styles in a CDATA section rather than an HTML comment tag. See section 16.3.7 for details.

Also, as they do for other attributes they don't recognize, the style-free browsers ignore inline style attributes and their values, so there are no detrimental effects in that regard for your document displays.

8.1.4 External Stylesheets

You can also place style definitions into a separate document (a text file with the Multi-purpose Internet Mail Extension, or MIME, type of `text/css`) and import this *external stylesheet* into your document. Use the same stylesheet for other documents in your collection, too, even entire collections of documents, to achieve a consistent look and feel. Because an external stylesheet is a separate file and the browser loads it over the network, you can store it anywhere, reuse it often, and even use others' stylesheets.

For example, suppose we create a file named *gen_styles.css* containing the following style rule:

```
h1 {color: blue; font-style: italic}
```

For each and every one of the documents in our collections, we can tell the browser to read the contents of the *gen_styles.css* file, which in turn colors all the `<h1>` tag contents blue and renders the text in italic. Of course, that is true only if the user's machine is capable of these style tricks, she's using a styles-conscious browser, and the style isn't overridden by a document-level or inline style definition.

You can load external stylesheets into your document in two different ways: by linking them or by importing them.

8.1.4.1 Linked external stylesheets

One way to load an external stylesheet is to use the `<link>` tag within the `<head>` of your document:

```
<head>
<title>Style linked</title>
<link rel=stylesheet type="text/css"
      href="http://www.kumquats.com/styles/gen_styles.css"
      title="The blues">
</head>
<body>
<h1>I'm so bluuuuoooo!</h1>
...
<h1> I am ba-looooooo, tooooo!</h1>
```

Recall that the `<link>` tag creates a relationship between the current document and some other document on the Web. In this example, we tell the browser that the document named in the `href` attribute is a cascading stylesheet (`css`), as indicated by the type attribute. Referencing an external stylesheet in `<link>` requires that you include the `href` and `type` attributes. We also tell the browser explicitly, albeit optionally, that the file's relationship to our document is that it is a `stylesheet`, and we provide a `title` making it available for later reference by the browser. [The <link> Header Element, 6.7.2]

The stylesheet-specifying `<link>` tag and its required `href` and `type` attributes must appear in the `<head>` of a document. The URL of the stylesheet may be absolute or relative to the document's base URL.

8.1.4.2 Imported external stylesheets

The second technique for loading an external stylesheet imports the file with a special command (a.k.a. *at-rule*) within the `<style>` tag:

```
<head>
<title>Imported stylesheet</title>
<style type="text/css">
  <!--
    @import url(http://www.kumquats.com/styles/gen_styles.css);
    @import "http://www.kumquats.com/styles/spec_styles.css";
    body {background: url(backgrounds/marble.gif)}
  -->
</style>
</head>
```

The `@import` at-rule expects a single URL for the network path to the external stylesheet. As shown in this example, the URL may be either a string enclosed in double quotes and ending with a semicolon or the contents of the `url` keyword, enclosed in parentheses, with a trailing semicolon. The URL may be absolute or relative to the document's base URL.

The @import at-rule must appear *before* any conventional style rules, either in the <style> tag or in an external stylesheet. Otherwise, the standard insists that the browser ignore the errant @import. By first importing all the various stylesheets, then processing document-level style rules, the CSS2 standard cascades: the last one standing wins. [URL property values, 8.4.1.4]

The @import at-rule can appear in a document-level style definition or even in another external stylesheet, letting you create nested stylesheets.

8.1.5 Media-Specific Styles

Besides the media attribute for the <style> tag, the CSS2 standard has two other features that let you apply different stylesheets, depending on the agent or device that renders your document. This way, for instance, you can have one style or whole stylesheet take effect when your document gets rendered on a computer screen and another set of styles for when the contents get punched out on a Braille printer. And what about those cell phones that access the Web?

Like the media attribute for the <style> tag that affects the entire stylesheet, you can specify whether the user's document processor loads and uses an imported stylesheet. Do that by adding a media-type keyword or a series of comma-separated keywords to the end of the @import at-rule. For instance, the following example lets the user agent decide whether to import and use the speech-synthesis stylesheet or a common PC display and print stylesheet, if it is able to render the specified media types:

```
@import url(http://www.kumquats.com/styles/visual_styles.css) screen,print;
@import "http://www.kumquats.com/styles/speech_styles.css" aural;
```

The @import CSS2 media types are the same as those for the <style> tag's media attribute, including all, aural, braille, embossed, handheld, print, projection, screen, tty, and tv.

Another CSS2 way to select media is through the explicit @media at-rule, which lets you include media-specific rules within the same stylesheet, either at the document level or in an external stylesheet. At the document level, as with @import, the @media at-rule must appear within the contents of the <style> tag. The at-rules may not appear within another rule. Unlike @import, @media may appear subsequent to other style rules, and its style-rule contents override previous rules according to the cascading standard.

The contents of @media include one or more comma-separated media-type keywords followed by a curly brace ({})-enclosed set of style rules. For example:

```
body {background: white}
@media tv, projection     {
    body {background: yellow}
    }
```

The yellow attribute to the @media at-rule causes the body's background color to display yellow, rather than the default white set in the general style rule, when the document is rendered on a television or projection screen (as specified by the tv and projection attributes).

8.1.6 Linked Versus Imported Stylesheets

At first glance, it may appear that linked and imported stylesheets are equivalent, using different syntax for the same functionality. This is true if you use just one <link> tag in your document. However, special CSS2-standard rules come into play if you include two or more <link> tags within a single document.

With one <link> tag, the browser should load the styles in the referenced stylesheet and format the document accordingly, with any document-level and inline styles overriding the external definitions. With two or more <link> tags, the browser should present the user with a list of all the linked stylesheets. The user then selects one of the linked sheets, which the browser loads and uses to format the document; the other linked stylesheets get ignored.

On the other hand, the styles-conscious browser merges, as opposed to separating, multiple @imported stylesheets to form a single set of style rules for your document. The last imported stylesheet takes precedence if there are duplicate definitions among the stylesheets. Hence, if the external *gen_styles.css* stylesheet specification first tells the browser to make <h1> contents blue and italic, and then a later *spec_styles.css* tells the browser to make <h1> text red, the <h1> tag contents appear red and italic. And if we later define another color—say, yellow—for <h1> tags in a document-level style definition, the <h1> tags are all yellow and italic. Cascading effects. See?

In practice, the popular browsers treat linked stylesheets just like imported ones by cascading their effects. The browsers do not currently let you choose from among linked choices. Imported styles override linked external styles, just as the document-level and inline styles override external style definitions. To bring this all together, consider this example:

```
<html>
<head>
<link rel=stylesheet href=sheet1.css type=text/css>
<link rel=stylesheet href=sheet2.css type=text/css>
<style>
<!--
  @import url(sheet3.css);
  @import url(sheet4.css);
-->
</style>
</head>
```

Using the CSS2 model, the browser should prompt the user to choose *sheet1.css* or *sheet2.css*. It should then load the selected sheet, followed by *sheet3.css* and *sheet4.css*. Duplicate styles defined in *sheet3.css* or *sheet4.css*, and in any inline styles, override styles defined in the selected sheet. In practice, the popular browsers cascade the stylesheet rules as defined in the example order *sheet1* through *sheet4*.

8.1.7 Limitations of Current Browsers

All the popular browsers support the `<link>` tag to apply an external stylesheet to a document. None supports multiple, user-selectable `<link>` stylesheets, as proposed by the CSS2 standard. Instead, they treat the `<link>` stylesheets as they do `@import` or document-level styles, by cascading the rules.

Netscape version 6, but not earlier versions, Internet Explorer versions 5 and later, as well as all versions of Opera and Firefox, honor the `@import` and the `@media` at-rules, for both document-level and external sheets, allowing sheets to be nested.

Achieving media-specific styles through external stylesheets with earlier Netscape browsers is hopeless. Assume, therefore, that most people who have Netscape version 4 will render your documents on a common PC screen, so make `screen` the default. Then embed all other media-specific styles, such as those for print or Braille, within `@media` at-rules so that CSS-compliant agents properly select styles based on the rendering medium.

Another alternative is to create media-specific `<style>` tags within each document. Run, do not walk, away from that idea.

8.1.8 Style Comments

Comments are welcome inside the `<style>` tag and in external stylesheets, but treat them differently than HTML comments: stylesheets aren't HTML. Rather, enclose style comments between /* and */ markers, as we did in the example in section 8.1.2, earlier in this chapter. (Those of you who are familiar with the C programming language will recognize these comment markings.) Use this comment syntax for both document-level and external stylesheets. Comments cannot be nested.

We recommend documenting your styles whenever possible, especially in external stylesheets. Whenever the possibility exists that other authors may use your styles, comments make it much easier to understand your styles.

8.1.9 Style Precedence

You may import multiple external stylesheets and combine them with document-level and inline style effects in many different ways. Their effects cascade (hence the name, of course). You may specify the font type for our example `<h1>` tag, for instance, in an external style definition, whereas its color may come from a document-level stylesheet.

Stylesheet effects are not cumulative, however: of the many styles that may define different values for the same property—colors for the contents of our example tag, for instance—the one that takes precedence can be found by following these rules, listed here in order:

Sort by origin
> A style-defined "closer" to a tag takes precedence over a more "distant" style; an inline style takes precedence over a document-level style, which takes precedence over the effects of an external style.

If more than one applicable style exists, sort by class
> A property defined as a class of a tag (see section 8.3, later in this chapter) takes precedence over a property defined for the tag in general.

If multiple styles still exist, sort by specificity
> The properties for a more specific contextual style (see section 8.2.3, later in this chapter) take precedence over properties defined for a less specific context.

If multiple styles still exist, sort by order
> The property specified latest takes precedence.

The relationship between style properties and conventional tag attributes is almost impossible to predict. For instance, stylesheet-dictated background and foreground colors—whether defined externally, at the document level, or inline—override the various color attributes that may appear within a tag. But the align attribute of an inline image usually takes precedence over a style-dictated alignment.

Myriad style and tag presentation-attribute combinations exist. You need a crystal ball to predict which combination wins and which loses the precedence battle. The rules of redundancy and style-versus-attribute precedence are elucidated in the W3C CSS2 standard, but no clear pattern of precedence is implemented in the styles-conscious browsers. This is particularly unfortunate because there will be an extended period, perhaps several more years, in which users may or may not use styles-conscious browsers. Authors must implement both styles and nonstyle presentation controls to achieve the same effects.

Nonetheless, our recommendation is to run—as fast as you can—from one-shot, inline, localized kinds of presentation effects such as those afforded by the <font> tag and color attribute. They have served their temporary purpose; it's now time to bring consistency (without the pain!) back into your document presentation. Use styles.

8.2 Style Syntax

The syntax of a style—its "rule," as you may have gleaned from our previous examples—is very straightforward.

8.2.1 The Basics

A style rule is made up of at least two basic parts: a *selector*, which is the name of the HTML or XHTML markup element (tag name) that the style rule affects, followed by a curly brace ({})-enclosed, semicolon-separated list of one or more style property:value pairs:

```
selector {property1:value1; property2:value1; ...}
```

For instance, we might define the color property for the contents of all the level-1 header elements of our document to be the value green:

```
h1 {color: green}
```

In this example, h1 is the selector, which is also the name of the level-1 header element, color is the style property, and green is the value.

Most properties require at least one value, but may have two or more values. Comma-separated values typically indicate a series of options as accepted by the property, of which the first valid value applies to the property, whereas space-separated values each apply separately to the property. The last valid value may override a previous value:

```
selector {property3:value1 value2 value3}
selector {property4:value1, value2, value3}
```

For instance, the following display background will be black, not white or gray, even though you specify both white and black values in the rule:

```
body {background: white black}
```

Current styles-conscious browsers ignore letter case in any element of a style rule. Hence, H1 and h1 are the same selector, and COLOR, color, ColOR, and cOLor are equivalent properties. At one time, convention dictated that HTML authors write selector names in uppercase characters, such as H1, P, and STRONG. This convention is still common and is used in the W3C's own CSS2 document.

However, current standards dictate, particularly for XML-compliant documents, that element names be identical to their respective Document Type Definitions (DTDs). With XHTML, for instance, all element names are lowercase (e.g., h1, p, and strong), so their respective CSS2 selectors must be in lowercase. We abide by the latter convention.

Any valid element name (a tag name minus its enclosing < and > characters and attributes) can be a selector. You may include more than one tag name in the list of selectors, as we explain in the following sections.

8.2.2 Multiple Selectors

When separated by commas, all the elements named in the selector list are affected by the property values in the style rule. This makes life easy for authors. For instance:

```
h1, h2, h3, h4, h5, h6 {text-align: center}
```

does exactly the same thing as:

```
h1 {text-align: center}
h2 {text-align: center}
h3 {text-align: center}
```

```
h4 {text-align: center}
h5 {text-align: center}
h6 {text-align: center}
```

Both styles tell the browser to center the contents of header levels 1 through 6. For most authors, the first version is easier to type, understand, and modify. And it takes less time and fewer resources to transmit across a network, though the effect is trivial. Define styles in the manner that is most comfortable for you. You don't have to use multiple selectors.

8.2.3 Contextual Selectors

Normally, the styles-conscious browser applies document-level or imported styles to a tag's contents wherever they appear in your document, without regard to context. However, the CSS2 standard defines a way to have a style applied only when a tag occurs within a certain context within a document, such as when it is nested within other tags.

To create a contextual selector, list the tags in the order in which they should be nested in your document, outermost tag first. Then, when the browser encounters that nesting order, the style properties are applied to the last tag in the list.

For example, here's how you might use contextual styles to create a classic outline, complete with uppercase Roman numerals for the outer level, capital letters for the next level, Arabic numerals for the next, and lowercase letters for the innermost level:

```
ol li {list-style: upper-roman}
ol ol li {list-style: upper-alpha}
ol ol ol li {list-style: decimal}
ol ol ol ol li {list-style: lower-alpha}
```

According to the example stylesheet, when the styles-conscious browser encounters the <li> tag nested within one <ol> tag, it uses the upper-roman value for the list-style property of the <li> tag. When it sees an <li> tag nested within two <ol> tags, the browser uses the upper-alpha list style. Nest an <li> tag within three and four <ol> tags, and you'll see the decimal and lower-alpha list styles, respectively. Compare Figure 8-1, displayed from the preceding example, with using the <ol> tag's type attribute to achieve similar effects, as shown in Figure 7-7 in Chapter 7.

Similarly, you may impose a specific style on tags related only by context. For instance, this contextual style definition colors the emphasis (<em>) tag's contents red only when it appears inside a level-1 header tag (<h1>), not elsewhere in the document:

```
h1 em {color: red}
```

If there is potential ambiguity between two contextual styles, the more specific context prevails.

Like individual tags, you may have several contextual selectors mixed with individual selectors, separated by commas, sharing the same list of style declarations. For example:

```
h1 em, p strong, address {color: red}
```

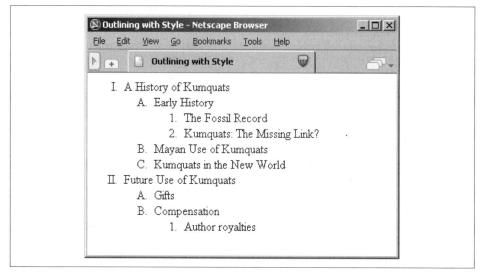

Figure 8-1. Nested ordered list styles

means you'll see red whenever the <em> tag appears within an <h1> tag, when the <strong> tag appears within a <p> tag, and for the contents of the <address> tag.

The nesting need not be exact to match the rule. For example, if you nest the <strong> tag within a <ul> tag within a <p> tag, you'll still match the rule for p strong that we defined earlier. If a particular nesting matches several style rules, the most specific rule is used. For example, if you defined two contextual selectors:

```
p strong {color: red}
p ul strong {color: blue}
```

and you use the sequence <p><ul><strong> in your document, the second, more specific rule applies, coloring the contents of the <strong> tag blue.

8.2.4 Universal, Child, and Adjacent Selectors

The CSS2 standard defines additional patterns for selectors besides commas and spaces, as illustrated in the following examples:

```
* {color: purple; font: ZapfDingBats}
ol > li {font-size: 200%; font-style: italic}
h1 + h2 {margin-top: +4mm}
```

In the first example, the universal asterisk selector applies the style to all elements of your document so that any text gets displayed in Zapf Dingbat characters.* The second example selects a particular child/parent relationship; in this case, items in an

---

* Assuming, of course, that the style is not overridden by a subsequent rule.

ordered list. The third example illustrates the adjacent selector type, which selects for one tag immediately following another in your document. In this case, the special selector adds vertical space to instances in which your document has a level-2 header immediately following a level-1 header.

8.2.5 Attribute Selectors

It is possible to attach a style to only those HTML/XHTML elements that have specific attributes. You do this by listing the desired attributes in square brackets ([ ]) next to the element name, before the style definition:

```
div[align] { font-style: italic }
div[align=left] {font-style: italic }
div[title~="bibliography"] { font-size: smaller }
div[lang|="en"] {color: green }
```

The first example is the simplest: it italicizes the subsequent text contents of only those <div> tags that contain the align attribute, regardless of the value assigned to the attribute. The second example is a bit pickier; it matches only <div> tags whose align attributes are set to left.

The third example matches any <div> tag whose title attribute contains the word *bibliography*, specifically delimited by one or more spaces. Partial word matches do not count; if you used div[title~="a"], you would match only <div> tags whose title attributes contained a single "a" delimited by spaces (or at the beginning or end of the title).

The final example matches any <div> tag whose lang attribute is set to a hyphen-separated list of words, beginning with "en." This example matches attributes such as lang=en, lang=en-us, and lang=en-uk.

You may combine the universal selector with attribute selectors to match any element with a specific attribute. For example:

```
*[class=comment] { display: none }
```

would hide all the elements in your document whose class attributes are set to comment.

Netscape, Firefox, Opera, and other modern browsers support attribute selectors; for unknown reasons, Internet Explorer does not.

8.2.6 Pseudoelements

Some elemental relationships in your documents you cannot explicitly tag. The drop-cap is a common print style, but how do you select the first letter in a paragraph? There are ways, but you have to identify each instance separately. There is no tag for the first line in a paragraph. And sometimes you might want the browser to automatically generate content, such as to add the prefix "Item #" and automatically number each item in an ordered list.

CSS2 introduces four new pseudoelements that let you define special relationships and styles for their display (:first-line, :first-letter, :before, and :after). Declare each as a colon-separated suffix of a standard markup element. For example:

```
p:first-line {font-size: 200%; font-style: italic}
```

means that the browser should display the first line of each paragraph italicized and twice as large as the rest of the text. Similarly:

```
p:first-letter {font-size: 200%; float: left}
```

tells the browser to make the first letter of a paragraph twice as large as the remaining text and to float the letter to the left, allowing the first two lines of the paragraph to float around the larger initial letter (see Figure 8-2).*

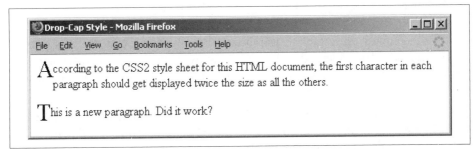

Figure 8-2. Use the first-letter pseudoelement to select the first letter of text within a tag's content

The :before and :after pseudoelements let you identify where in your document you insert generated content such as list numbers and special lead-in headers. Hence, these pseudoelements go hand in hand with the CSS2 content and counter properties. To whet your appetite, consider this example:

```
ul {counter-reset: item; list-style: none}
ul li:before {content: "Item #" counters(item, ".") " ";
             counter-increment: item}
...
<ul>
  <li> This is item number 1.</li>
  <ul>
    <li> This is sub-item number 1.1.</li>
  </ul>
  <li> This is item number 2.</li>
  <ul>
    <li> This is sub-item 2.1.</li>
    <li> This is sub-item 2.2.</li>
  ... and so on
```

---

* The properties you can specify for the :first-letter and :first-line pseudoelements are font, color, background, text-decoration, vertical-align, text-transform, line-height, and clear. And in addition, the :first-letter pseudoelement accepts the margin properties, padding properties, border properties, and float. The :first-line pseudoelement also accepts the word-spacing and letter-spacing properties.

All the popular browsers support the pseudoelements, generating effects such as that shown in Figure 8-2. However, Internet Explorer does not support the content property and Netscape doesn't support counters. So only the newcomers, Firefox and Opera, properly display the progressively numbered unordered list items, defined by the foregoing example and shown in Figure 8-3.

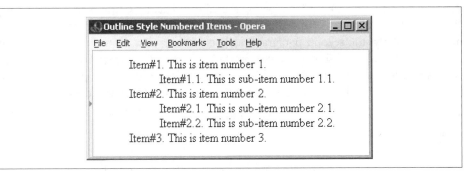

Figure 8-3. Style counters combine with pseudoelements to create outline-line numbering

8.3 Style Classes

CSS2 allows you to define several different styles for the same element by naming a class for each style at the document level or in an external stylesheet. Later in a document, you explicitly select which style to apply by including the styles-related `class` attribute with the related `name` value in the respective tag.

8.3.1 Regular Classes

For example, in a technical paper, you might want to define one paragraph style for the abstract, another for equations, and a third for centered quotations. Differentiate these paragraphs by defining each as a different style class:

```
<style type="text/css">
<!--
p.abstract {font-style: italic;
           margin-left: 0.5cm;
           margin-right: 0.5cm}
p.equation {font-family: Symbol;
           text-align: center}
h1, p.centered {text-align: center;
               margin-left: 0.5cm;
               margin-right: 0.5cm}
-->
</style>
```

Notice first in the example that defining a class is simply a matter of appending a period-separated class name as a suffix to the tag name as the selector in a style rule. Unlike the XHTML-compliant selector, which is the name of the standard tag and must be in lowercase, the class name can be any sequence of letters, numbers, and hyphens, but it must begin with a letter.* Careful, though: case does matter, so abstract is not the same as AbsTRact. Classes, like selectors, may be included with other selectors, separated by commas, as in the third example. The only restriction on classes is that they cannot be nested; for example, p.equation.centered is not valid.

Accordingly, the first rule in the example creates a class of paragraph styles named abstract whose text is italic and indented from the left and right margins by 0.5 centimeters. Similarly, the second paragraph style class, equation, instructs the browser to center the text and to use the Symbol typeface to display the text. The last style rule creates a style with centered text and 0.5-centimeter margins, applying this style to all level-1 headers as well as creating a class of the <p> tag named centered with that style.

To use a particular class of a tag, you add the class attribute to the tag, as in this example (Figure 8-4):

```
<p class=abstract>
This is the abstract paragraph.  See how the margins are indented?
</p>
<h3>The equation paragraph follows</h3>
<p class=equation>
a = b + 1
</p>
<p class=centered>
This paragraph's text should be centered.
</p>
```

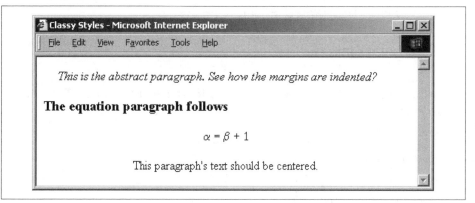

Figure 8-4. Use classes to distinguish different styles for the same tag

For each paragraph, the value of the class attribute is the name of the class to be used for that tag.

---

* Due to its support of JavaScript stylesheets, Netscape 4 cannot handle class names that happen to match JavaScript keywords. The class abstract, for instance, generates an error in Netscape 4.

8.3.2 Generic Classes

You also may define a class without associating it with a particular tag and apply that class selectively through your documents for a variety of tags. For example:

```
.italic {font-style: italic}
```

creates a generic class named `italic`. To use it, simply include its name with the `class` attribute. For instance, `<p class=italic>` and `<h1 class=italic>` create an italic paragraph and level-1 header, respectively.

Generic classes are quite handy and make it easy to apply a particular style to a broad range of tags. All the popular browsers support CSS2 generic classes.

8.3.3 ID Classes

Almost all HTML tags accept the `id` attribute, which assigns a unique identifier to an element within the document. Besides being the target of a URL or identified in an automated document-processing tool, the `id` attribute can also specify a style rule for the element.

To create a style class that the styles-conscious browser applies to only those portions of your document explicitly tagged with the `id` attribute, follow the same syntax as for style classes, except with a # character before the class name instead of a period. For example:

```
<style>
<!--
#yellow {color : yellow}
h1#blue {color : blue}
-->
</style>
```

Within your document, use that same `id` name to apply the style, such as `<h1 id=blue>` to create a blue heading. Or, as in the example, use `id=yellow` elsewhere in the document to turn a tag's contents yellow. You can mix and match both `class` and `id` attributes, giving you a limited ability to apply two independent style rules to a single element.

There is a dramatic drawback to using style classes this way: the HTML and XHTML standards dictate that the value of the `id` attribute be unique for each instance in which it's used within the document. Yet here, we have to use the same value to apply the style class more than once.

Even though current browsers let you get away with it, we strongly discourage creating and using the `id` kinds of style classes. Stick to the standard style class convention to create correct, robust documents.

8.3.4 Pseudoclasses

In addition to conventional style classes, the CSS2 standard defines pseudoclasses, which allow you to define the display style for certain tag *states*, such as changing the display style when a user selects a hyperlink. You create pseudoclasses as you do regular classes, but with two notable differences: they are attached to the tag name with a colon rather than a period, and they have predefined names, not arbitrary ones you may give them. There are seven pseudoclasses, three of which are explicitly associated with the <a> tag.

8.3.4.1 Hyperlink pseudoclasses

CSS2-compliant browsers distinguish three special states for the hyperlinks created by the <a> tag: not yet visited, currently being visited, and already visited. The browser may change the appearance of the tag's contents to indicate its state, such as with underlining or color. Through pseudoclasses, you may control how these states get displayed by defining styles for a:link (not visited), a:active (being visited), and a:visited.

The :link pseudoclass controls the appearance of links that are not selected by the user and have not yet been visited. The :active pseudoclass defines the appearance of links that are currently selected by the user and are being processed by the browser. The :visited pseudoclass defines those links that the user has already visited.

To completely define all three states of the <a> tag, you might write:

```
a:link {color: blue}
a:active {color: red; font-weight: bold}
a:visited {color: green}
```

In this example, the styles-conscious browser renders unvisited links in blue. When the user selects a link, the browser changes its color to red and makes it bold. Once visited, the link reverts to green.

8.3.4.2 Interaction pseudoclasses

The CSS2 standard defines two new pseudoclasses that, along with :active, relate to user actions and advise the interactive agent, such as a browser, how to display the affected element as the user interacts with the element. In other words, these two pseudoclasses—hover and focus—are dynamic.

For instance, when you drag the mouse over a hyperlink in your document, the browser may change the mouse-pointer icon. Hovering can be associated with a style that appears only while the mouse is over the element. For example, if you add the :hover pseudoclass to our example list of hyperlink style rules:

```
a:hover {color: yellow}
```

the text associated with unvisited links normally appears blue, but turns yellow when you point to it with the mouse, red after you click the link and while you are visiting it, and green after you're done visiting the hyperlink.

Similarly, the :focus pseudoclass lets you change the style for an element when it becomes the object of attention. An element may be under focus when you tab to it, click on it, or, depending on the browser, advance the cursor to it. Regardless of how the focus got to the element, the style rules associated with the focus pseudoclass are applied only while the element has the focus.

8.3.4.3 Nesting and language pseudoclasses

The CSS2 :first-child pseudoclass lets you specify how an element may be rendered when it is the first instance, or child, of the containing element. For instance, the following rule gets applied to a paragraph when it is the first element of a division; there can be no intervening elements (notice the special greater-than bracket syntax relating the first child with its parent element):

```
div > p:first-child  {font-style: italic}
```

Accordingly, the first paragraph in the following HTML fragment would be rendered in italics by a CSS2-compliant browser because it is the first child element of its division. Conversely, the second paragraph comes after a level-2 header, which is the first child of the second division. So, that second paragraph in the example gets rendered in plain text, because it is not the first child of its division (Figure 8-5):

```
<div>
  <p>
    I get to be in italics because my paragraph is the first child of the division.
  </p>
</div>
<div>
  <h2> New Division</h2>
  <p>
    I'm in plain text because my paragraph is a second child of the division.
```

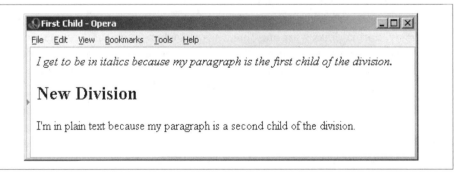

Figure 8-5. The first-child pseudoclass in action

Finally, the CSS2 standard defines a new pseudoclass that lets you select an element based on its language. For instance, you might include the lang=fr attribute in a <div> tag to instruct the browser that the division contains French language text. The browser may specially treat the text. Or, you may impose a specific style with the pseudoclass :lang. For example:

```
div:lang(it) {font-family: Roman}
```

says that text in divisions of a document that contain the Italian language should use the Roman font family. Appropriate, don't you think? Notice that you specify the language in parentheses immediately after the lang keyword. Use the same two-letter International Organization for Standardization (ISO) standard code for the pseudoclass :lang as you do for the lang attribute. [The lang attribute, 3.6.1.2]

8.3.4.4 Browser support of pseudoclasses

None of the popular browsers supports the :lang or :focus pseudoclass yet. All the current popular browsers support the :link, :active, :hover, and :visited pseudoclasses for the hyperlink tag (<a>), as well as :first-child. Even though you may use :active for other elements, none of the browsers yet supports applications beyond the <a> tag.

8.3.5 Mixing Classes

Mix pseudoclasses with regular classes by appending the pseudoclass name to the selector's class name. For example, here are some rules that define plain, normal, and fancy anchors:

```
a.plain:link, a.plain:active, a.plain:visited {color: blue}
a:link {color: blue}
a:visited {color: green}
a:active {color: red}
a.fancy:link {font-style: italic}
a.fancy:visited {font-style: normal}
a.fancy:active {font-weight: bold; font-size: 150%}
```

The plain version of <a> is always blue, no matter what the state of the link is. Accordingly, normal links start out blue, turn red when active, and convert to green when visited. The fancy link inherits the color scheme of the normal <a> tag, but italicizes the text for unvisited links, converts back to normal text after being visited, and actually grows 50 percent in size and becomes bold when active.

A word of warning about that last property of the fancy class: specifying a font-size change for a transient display property results in lots of browser redisplay activity when the user clicks the link. Given that some browsers run on slow machines, this may not be visually refreshing for your readers. Given also that implementing that sort of display change is something of a pain, it is unlikely that most browsers will support radical appearance changes in <a> tag pseudoclasses.

8.3.6 Class Inheritance

Classes inherit the style properties of their generic base tags. For instance, all the properties of the plain <p> tag apply to a specially defined paragraph class, except where the class overrides a particular property.

Classes cannot inherit from other classes, only from the unclassed versions of the tags they represent. In general, therefore, you should put as many common styles as possible into the rule for the basic version of a tag and create classes only for those properties that are unique to that class. This makes maintenance and sharing of your style classes easier, especially for large document collections.

8.4 Style Properties

At the heart of the CSS2 standard are the many properties that let you control how the styles-conscious browser presents your documents to the user. The standard collects these properties into six groups: fonts, colors and backgrounds, text, boxes and layout, lists, and tag classification. We'll stick with that taxonomy and preface the whole shebang with a discussion of property values and inheritance before diving into the properties themselves.

You'll find a summary of the style properties in Appendix C.

8.4.1 Property Values

Most properties set a value to some characteristic of your document for rendering by the browser—the size of the characters in a font or the color of level-2 headers, for example. As we discussed earlier, when describing the syntax of styles, you give value to a CSS2 property by following the property's keyword with a colon (:) and one or more space- or comma-separated numbers or value-related keywords. For example:

```
color:blue
font-family: Helvetica, Univers, sans-serif
```

color and font-family are the properties in these two style examples; blue and the various comma-separated font names are their values, respectively.

There are eight kinds of property values: keywords, length values, percentage values, URLs, colors, angles, time, and frequencies.

8.4.1.1 Keyword property values

A property may have a keyword value that expresses action or dimension. For instance, the effects of underline and line-through are obvious property values. And you express property dimensions with such keywords as small and xx-large. Some keywords are even relational: bolder, for instance, is an acceptable value for the font-weight property. Keyword values are not case sensitive: Underline, UNDERLINE, and underline are all acceptable keyword values.

8.4.1.2 Length property values

So-called length values (a term taken from the CSS2 standard) explicitly set the size of a property. They are numbers, some with decimals, too. Length values may have a leading + or – sign to indicate that the value is to be added to or subtracted from the current value of the property. Length values must be followed immediately by a two-letter unit abbreviation, with no intervening spaces.

There are three kinds of length-value units: relative, pixels, and absolute. Relative units specify a size that is relative to the size of some other property of the content. Currently, there are only two relative units: em, which is the width of the lowercase letter "m" in the current font; and x-height, abbreviated ex, which is the height of the letter "x" in the current font.

Pixels are the tiny dots of colored light that make up the onscreen text and images on a computer monitor or TV image. The pixels unit, abbreviated px, is equal to the minute size of 1 pixel, so you may express the size of some properties by how many pixels across or down they run.

Absolute property value units are more familiar to us all. They include inches (in), centimeters (cm), millimeters (mm), points (pt; 1/72 of an inch), and picas (pc; 12 points).

All of the following are valid length values, although the current styles-conscious browsers do not recognize all units:

```
1in
1.5cm
+0.25mm
-3pt
-2.5pc
+100em
-2.75ex
250px
```

8.4.1.3 Percentage property values

Similar to the relative length property value type, a percentage value describes a proportion relative to some other aspect of the content. It has an optional sign, meaning it may be added to or subtracted from the current value for that property, and optional decimal portion to its numeric value. Percentage values have the percent sign (%) suffix. For example:

```
line-height: 120%
```

computes the separation between lines to be 120 percent of the current line height (usually relative to the text font height). Note that this value is not dynamic: changes made to the font height after the rule has been processed by the browser do not affect the computed line height.

8.4.1.4 URL property values

Some properties also accept, if not expect, a URL value. The syntax for a CSS2 URL property value is different from that in HTML/XHTML:

```
url(service://server.com/pathname)
```

With CSS2 properties, the keyword url is required, as are the opening and closing parentheses. Do not leave any spaces between url and the opening parenthesis. The url value may contain either an absolute or a relative URL. However, the URL is relative to the stylesheet's URL, not necessarily the document's base URL. This means that if you use a url value in a document-level or inline style, the URL is relative to the HTML document containing the style document. Otherwise, the URL is relative to the @imported or <link>ed external stylesheet's URL.

8.4.1.5 Color property values

Color values specify colors in a property (surprised?). You can specify a color as a color name or a hexadecimal RGB triple, as for common HTML/XHTML attributes, or as a decimal RGB triple unique to style properties. Both color names and hexadecimal RGB triple notation are described in Appendix G.

With CSS2, too, you may assign just one hexadecimal digit instead of two to the red, green, and blue (RGB) components of a color. That digit is simply doubled to create a conventional six-digit triple. Thus, the color #78C is equivalent to #7788CC. In general, three-digit color values are handy only for simple colors.

The decimal RGB triple notation is unique:

```
rgb(red, green, blue)
```

The *red*, *green*, and *blue* intensity values are decimal integers in the range 0 to 255, or integer percentages. As with a url value, do not leave any spaces between rgb and the opening parenthesis.

For example, in decimal RGB convention, the color white is rgb(255, 255, 255) or rgb(100%, 100%, 100%), and a medium yellow is rgb(127, 127, 0) or rgb(50%, 50%, 0%).

8.4.1.6 Angle, time, and frequency property values

A few properties require a value that expresses an angle, such as the heading of a compass. These properties take a numeric value followed by the units deg (degrees), grad (gradations), or rad (radians). Similarly, express time values as numbers followed by either ms (milliseconds) or s (seconds) units.

Finally, frequency values are numbers followed by Hz (hertz) or kHz (1 kilohertz = 1000 Hz). Interestingly, there is no corresponding MHz or GHz units, because frequencies in CSS2 refer to audio, not TV, FM radio, Bluetooth wireless networking, or other electromagnetic waves.

8.4.2 Property Inheritance

In lieu of a specific rule for a particular element, properties and their values for tags within tags are inherited from the parent tag. Thus, setting a property for the <body> tag effectively applies that property to every tag in the body of your document, except for those that specifically override it. So, to make all the text in your document blue, you need only write:

```
body {color: blue}
```

instead of creating a rule for every tag you use in your document.

This inheritance extends to any level. If you later created a <div> tag with text styled by a different color, the styles-conscious browser would display all the text contents of that <div> tag and all its enclosed tags in that new color. When the <div> tag ends, the color reverts to that of the containing <body> tag.

In many of the following property descriptions, we refer to the tag containing the current tag as the *parent element* of that tag.

8.4.3 Font Properties

The loudest complaint that we hear about HTML and its progeny, XHTML, is that they lack font styles and characteristics that even the simplest of text editors implement. The various <font> attributes address part of the problem, but they are tedious to use, because each text font change requires a different <font> tag.

Stylesheets simplify all that, of course. The CSS2 standard provides seven font properties that modify the appearance of text contained within the affected tag: font-family, font-size, font-size-adjust, font-style, font-variant, font-stretch, and font-weight. In addition, there is a universal font property in which you can declare all the font values.

Please be aware that stylesheets cannot overcome limitations of the user's display/document-rendering system, and the browser cannot conjure effects if the fonts it uses do not provide the means.

8.4.3.1 The font-family property

The font-family property accepts a comma-separated list of font names. The browser uses the first font named in the list that also is installed and available for display on the client machine for text display.

Font-name values are for specific font styles, such as Helvetica and Courier, or for a generic font style, as defined by the CSS2 standard: serif, sans-serif, cursive, fantasy, and monospace. The browser defines which font it actually uses for each generic font. For instance, Courier is the most popular choice for a monospaced font.

Because fonts vary wildly among browsers, you should usually provide several choices when specifying a font style, ending with a suitable generic font. For example:

```
h1 {font-family: Helvetica, Univers, sans-serif}
```

causes the browser to look for and use Helvetica, and then Univers. If neither font is available for the client display, the browser uses the generic sans-serif typeface.

Enclose font names that contain spaces—New Century Schoolbook, for example—in quotation marks. For instance:

```
p {font-family: Times, "New Century Schoolbook", Palatino, serif}
```

With inline styles, that extra set of double quotation marks causes problems. The solution is to use single quotation marks in an inline style:

```
<p style="font-family: Times, 'New Century Schoolbook', Palatino, serif">
```

In practice, you don't have to use quotation marks, because font-name values are comma separated, so the browser normally ignores the spaces. Hence, both of the following are legal:

```
p {font-family: Times, New Century Schoolbook, Palatino, serif}
<p style="font-family: Times, New Century Schoolbook, Palatino, serif">
```

Nonetheless, we recommend that you use quotation marks. It's a good habit to get into, and it makes things that much less ambiguous.

8.4.3.2 The font-size property

The font-size property lets you prescribe absolute or relative length values, percentages, and keywords to define the font size. For example:

```
p {font-size: 12pt}
p {font-size: 120%}
p {font-size: +2pt}
p {font-size: medium}
p {font-size: larger}
```

The first rule is probably the most used, because it is the most familiar: it sets the font size for text enclosed in your document's paragraph(s) to a specific number of points (12 in this example). The second example rule sets the font size to be 20 percent larger than the parent element's font size. The third increases the font's normal size by 2 points.

The fourth example selects a predefined font size set by the browser, identified by the medium keyword. Valid absolute-size keywords are xx-small, x-small, small, medium, large, x-large, and xx-large; these usually correspond to the seven font sizes used with the size attribute of the <font> tag.

The last font-size rule selects the next size larger than the font associated with the parent element. Thus, if the size were normally medium, it would be changed to large. You can also specify smaller, with the expected results.

None of the current browsers handles incremented or decremented font sizes correctly. Rather, they ignore the decrement sign and size altogether, and misinterpret the incremented size value as an absolute size. For instance, in the middle example in this section, the font size would end up as 2 points, not 2 points larger than the normal size.

8.4.3.3 The font-stretch property

In addition to different sizes, font families sometimes contain condensed and expanded versions, in which the characters are squeezed or stretched, respectively. Use the font-stretch property to choose more compressed or stretched-out characters from your font.

Use the property value of normal to select the normal-size version of the font. The relative values wider and narrower select the next-wider or next-narrower variant of the font's characters, respectively, but not wider or narrower than the most ("ultra") expanded or contracted one in the family.

The remaining font-stretch property values choose specific variants from the font family. Starting from the most condensed and ending with the most expanded, the values are ultra-condensed, extra-condensed, condensed, semi-condensed, semi-expanded, expanded, extra-expanded, and ultra-expanded.

The font-stretch property, of course, assumes that your display fonts support stretchable fonts. Even so, the currently popular browsers ignore this property.

8.4.3.4 The font-size-adjust property

Without too many details, the legibility and display size of a font depend principally on its *aspect ratio*: the ratio of its rendered size to its x-height, which is a measure of the font's lowercase glyph height. Fonts with aspect ratios approaching 1.0 tend to be more legible at smaller sizes than fonts with aspect ratios approaching 0.

Also, because of aspect ratios, the actual display size of one font may appear smaller or larger than another font at the same size. So, when one font is not available for rendering, the substituted font may distort the presentation.

The font-size-adjust property lets you readjust the substituted font's aspect ratio so that it better fits the display. Use the property value of none to ignore the aspect ratio. Otherwise, include your desired aspect ratio (a decimal value less than one), typically the aspect ratio for your first-choice display font. The styles-conscious browser computes and displays the substituted font at a size adjusted to your specified aspect ratio:

    s = (n/a) * fs

where s is the new, computer font size for display of the substituted font, calculated as the font-size-adjust value n divided by the substituted font's aspect ratio a times the current font size fs.

For example, let's imagine that your first-choice font is Times New Roman, which has an aspect ratio of 0.45. If it's not available, the browser may then substitute

Comic Sans MS, which has an aspect ratio of 0.54. So that the substitution maintains nearly equivalent sizing for the font display—say, at an 18-px font size—with the `font-size-adjust` property set to 0.45, the CSS2-compliant browser would display or print the text with the substituted Comic Sans MS font at the smaller size of (0.45/0.54 × 18 px) = 15 px.

Unfortunately, we can't show you how the popular browsers would do this because they don't support it.

8.4.3.5 The font-style property

Use the `font-style` property to slant text. The default style is `normal` and may be changed to `italic` or `oblique`. For example:

```
h2 {font-style: italic}
```

makes all level-2 header text italic. Netscape 4 supported only the `italic` value for `font-style`; all current browsers support both values, although it is usually difficult to distinguish italic from oblique.

8.4.3.6 The font-variant property

Use the `font-variant` property to display text in small capitals. The default value for this property is `normal`, indicating the conventional version of the font. Otherwise, give the property the value `small-caps` to select a version of the font in which the lowercase letters have been replaced with small capital letters.

All the current browsers support this property. Internet Explorer versions 4 and 5 incorrectly displayed `small-caps` as all uppercase letters.

8.4.3.7 The font-weight property

The `font-weight` property controls the weight or boldness of the lettering. The default value of this property is `normal`. You may specify `bold` to obtain a bold version of a font or use the relative `bolder` and `lighter` values to obtain a version of the font that is bolder or lighter than the parent element's font.

To specify varying levels of lightness or boldness, set the value to a multiple of 100, between the values `100` (lightest) and `900` (boldest). The value `400` is equal to the `normal` version of the font, and `700` is the same as specifying `bold`.

The current browsers fully support this property.

8.4.3.8 The font property

More often than not, you'll find yourself specifying more than one font-related property at a time for a tag's text content display. A complete font specification can get somewhat unwieldy. For example:

```
p {font-family: Times, Garamond, serif;
   font-weight: bold;
   font-size: 12pt;
   line-height: 14pt}
```

To mitigate this troublesome and potentially unreadable collection, use the comprehensive font property and group all the attributes into one set of declarations:

```
p {font: bold 12pt/14pt Times, Garamond, serif}
```

The grouping and ordering of font attributes is important within the font property. The font style, weight, and variant attributes must be specified first, followed by the font size and the line height separated by a slash character, and ending with the list of font families. Of all the properties, the size and family are required; the others may be omitted.

Here are a few more example font style rules:

```
em {font: italic 14pt Times}
h1 {font: 24pt/48pt sans-serif}
code {font: 12pt Courier, monospace}
```

The first example tells the styles-conscious browser to emphasize <em> text using a 14-point italic Times face. The second rule has <h1> text displayed in the boldest 24-point sans-serif font available, with an extra 24 points of space between the lines of text. Finally, text within a <code> tag is set in 12-point Courier or the browser-defined monospaced font.

We leave it to your imagination to conjure up examples of the abuses you could foster with font styles. Perhaps a recent issue of *Wired* magazine, notorious for avant-garde fonts and other print-related abuses, would be helpful in that regard.

8.4.4 Font Selection and Synthesis

The original CSS standard, CSS1, had a simplistic font-matching algorithm: if your specified font does not exist in the local client's font collection, substitute a generic font. Of course, the results are often less than pleasing to the eye and can wreak havoc with the display. Moreover, there are often more suitable font substitutes than generic ones. The CSS2 standard significantly extends the CSS1 font-matching model and includes a new at-rule that lets authors define, download, and use new fonts in their documents.

8.4.4.1 CSS2 font-matching steps

The CSS2 font-matching algorithm has four steps. The first step is simply to use the specified font when it is found on the user's machine; this could be one of several font families specified in the stylesheet rule, parsed in their order of appearance.

The second step, taken when none of the fonts specified in the rule exists on the user's machine, has the browser attempt to find a close match among similar local fonts. For example, a request for Helvetica might wind up using Arial, a similar sans-serif font.

The third step in the CSS2 font-matching algorithm has the browser try to synthesize a font, taking a local font and changing it to match the specified one. For example, a request for 72-point Helvetica might be satisfied by taking the local 12-point Arial font and scaling it up to match the desired size.

Failing all three previous steps, the browser may take a fourth step and download the desired font, provided the author has supplied suitable external font definitions. These external font definitions are created with the @font-face at-rule, whose general syntax is:

```
@font-face {
    descriptor : value;
    ...
    descriptor : value
    }
```

Each @font-face at-rule defines a new font to the browser. Subsequent requests for fonts may be satisfied by these new fonts. The browser uses the various descriptor values to ensure that the font supplied matches the font requested.

8.4.4.2 Basic font descriptors

The basic font descriptors that you use in the @font-face at-rule correspond to the CSS2 font properties and accept the same values as those properties. Accordingly, use the font-family, font-style, font-variant, font-weight, font-stretch, and font-size descriptors and their associated values to define a new font to the browser. For example:

```
@font-face {
    font-family : "Kumquat Sans";
    font-style : normal, italic;
    src : url("http://www.kumquat.com/foundry/kumquat-sans")
    }
```

defines a font named Kumquat Sans that is available for download from *www. kumquat.com*. Within that downloadable font, both the normal and the italic versions of Kumquat Sans are available. Because we provide no other font descriptors, the browser assumes that all other font properties (weight, variant, etc.) can be satisfied within this font.

In general, omitting a font descriptor lets the browser match any value provided for that descriptor. By providing one or more values for a font descriptor, you are restricting the browser to match only those values in later font requests. Hence, you should be as specific as possible when defining a font this way, to better ensure that the browser makes good matches later. For example, if a font does not contain an italic version and you fail to tell the browser, it may use an incorrect font when attempting to fulfill a request for an italic style of that font.

8.4.4.3 The src descriptor

The src descriptor in the @font-face at-rule tells the browser where to retrieve the font. For downloadable fonts, the value of this descriptor is its document URL, expressed in CSS2 syntax with the `url` keyword. To reference locally installed fonts—ones stored on the user's machine—with `src`, use the keyword `local` rather than `url` and supply the local name of the font.

The `src` descriptor's value may also be a list of locations, separated by commas. In our previous example, we could have used:

```
src : url("http://www.kumquat.com/foundry/kumquat-sans"), local("Lucida Sans")
```

which asks the browser to download and use Kumquat Sans from *www.kumquat.com* and, if that fails, to look for a locally installed copy of Lucida Sans.

You can even provide hints to the browser. CSS2 is decidedly nonpartisan when it comes to the format of the font file. Recognizing that a number of different font formats exist, the standard lets you use any format you want, presuming that the browser can make sense of it. To provide a format hint, use the keyword `format` followed by one or more format names, such as:

```
src : url("http://www.kumquat.com/foundry/kumquat-sans") format("type-1"),
      local("Lucida Sans") format("truetype", "intellitype")
```

In this case, the external font is in Type 1 format, and the local flavors of Lucida Sans are available in both TrueType and Intellifont formats. Other recognized font formats include `truedoc-pfr`, `opentype`, `embedded-opentype`, `truetype`, `truetype-gx`, and `speedo`.

8.4.4.4 Advanced font descriptors

In addition to the standard font descriptors, CSS2 supports a number of more esoteric ones that further refine the defined font. Typical page designers do not have much need for these descriptors, but more discriminating typographers may find them useful.

The `unicode-range` descriptor accepts a comma-separated list of Unicode values, each beginning with `U+` followed by a hexadecimal value. You can specify ranges of values by adding a dash and another hexadecimal value; the question mark matches any value in that position.

The purpose of the `unicode-range` descriptor is to define exactly which character glyphs are defined in the font. If characters used in your document are not available, the browser does not download and use the font. For example, a value of `U+2A70` indicates that the font contains the glyph at that position in the font. Using `U+2A7?` represents characters in the range 2A70 to 2A7F, and `U+2A70-2A9F` defines a broader range. For the most part, this descriptor is used to restrict the use of special symbol fonts to just those symbols defined in the font.

The `units-per-em` descriptor accepts a single numeric value defining the size of the font's em area. This value is important if you specify the values of other descriptors using em units.

The `panose-1` descriptor accepts exactly 10 integer values, separated by spaces, corresponding to the Panose-1 characterization of this font. Defining the actual Panose-1 values is well beyond the scope of this book; interested authors should refer to appropriate documentation for the Panose-1 system for more information.

The `stemv` and `stemh` descriptors define the thickness, in ems, of the vertical and horizontal strokes of the font. Similarly, the `cap-height` and `x-height` descriptors define the height of the upper- and lowercase glyphs in the font. Finally, the `ascent` and `descent` descriptors define the font's maximum height and depth. If you use any of these descriptors, you must also specify the `units-per-em` descriptor.

The `slope` descriptor defines the slope of the vertical stroke of the font. This is important for matching italic and oblique versions of a font.

The `baseline`, `centerline`, `mathline`, and `topline` descriptors define the conventional baseline, center baseline, mathematical baseline, and top baseline of the font. All accept a numeric value expressed in ems. All require that you specify the `units-per-em` descriptor, too.

The `bbox` descriptor accepts exactly two coordinate (X, Y) pairs, specifying the lower-left and upper-right corners of the font's bounding box. The `bbox` descriptor is important if the browser chooses to synthesize a font based on this font. By specifying the size of the bounding box, you ensure that the synthesized font occupies the same space as the desired one.

The `widths` descriptor accepts a comma-separated list of Unicode ranges, followed by space-separated values which define the widths of the characters in the indicated range. If you supply one value for a range, all the characters in that range have the same width. Multiple values are assigned to successive characters in a range. Like the `bbox` descriptor, the `widths` descriptor is used to ensure good fidelity between a synthesized font and its requested counterpart.

Finally, the optional `definitions-src` descriptor provides the URL of a file that contains all of the descriptors for a font. This is handy if you need to define a font in great detail. Instead of including the lengthy descriptors in each document or stylesheet that uses the font, you define the descriptors once in a separate file and reference that file using the `definitions-src` descriptor.

8.4.5 Color and Background Properties

Every element in your document has a foreground and a background color. In some cases, the background is not one color, but a colorful image. The `color` and `background` style properties control these colors and images.

The children of an HTML/XHTML element normally inherit the foreground color of their parent. For instance, if you make `<body>` text red, the styles-conscious browser also displays header and paragraph text in red.

Background properties behave differently, however—they are not inherited. Instead, each element has a default background that is transparent, allowing the parent's background to show through. Thus, setting the background image of the <body> tag does not cause that image to be reloaded for every element within the body tag. Instead, the browser loads the image once and displays it behind the rest of the document, serving as the background for all elements that do not themselves have an explicit background color or image.

All the current popular browsers support the following background and color properties.

8.4.5.1 The background-color property

The background-color property controls the (you guessed it!) background color of an element. Set it to a color value or to the keyword transparent (the default value). The effects should be obvious.

While you may have become accustomed to setting the background color of an entire document through the special attributes for the <body> tag, you can apply the background-color style property to any element. For example, to set the background color of one item in a bulleted list, you could use:

```
<li style="background-color: blue">
```

Similarly, you could give all the table header cells in a document a snapshot negative effect with:

```
th {background-color: black; color: white}
```

If you really want your emphasized text to stand out, paint its background red:

```
em {background-color: red}
```

8.4.5.2 The background-image property

The background-image property puts an image behind the contents of an element. Its value is either a URL or the keyword none (the default value).

As with background colors, you can place a background image behind the entire document or behind selected elements of a document. With this style property, effects such as placing an image behind a table or selected text are now simple:

```
<table style="background-image: url(backgrounds/woodgrain.gif)">
li.marble {background-image: url(backgrounds/marble.gif)}
```

The first example uses an inline style to place a wood grain finish behind a table. The second defines a list-item class that places a marble background behind <li> tags that use the class=marble attribute. For example, this XHTML snippet:

```
<h2>Here's what's for dinner tonight:</h2>
<ul>
    <li class="marble">Liver with Onions</li>
    <li class="marble">Mashed Potatoes and Gravy</li>
    <li class="marble">Green Beans</li>
```

```
    <li class="marble">Choice of Milk, Tea, or Coffee</li>
</ul>
<h2>And for dessert:</h2>
<ul>
    <li>Creamed Quats in Milk (YUM! YUM!)</li>
</ul>
```

produces a result like that in Figure 8-6.

Figure 8-6. Placing a background image behind an element

If the image is larger than the containing element, it is clipped to the area occupied by the element. If the image is smaller, it is repeated to tile the area occupied by the element, as dictated by the value of the background-repeat attribute.

You control the starting position of the image within the element with the background-position property. The background-attachment property manages the scrolling behavior of the image.

While it may seem that a background color and a background image are mutually exclusive, you should usually define a background color even if you are using a background image. That way, if the image is unavailable—for example, when the user doesn't automatically download images—the browser displays the background color instead. In addition, if the background image has transparent areas, the background color is used to fill in those areas.

8.4.5.3 The background-attachment property

If you specify a background image for an element, use the background-attachment property to control how that image is attached to the browser's display window. With the default value scroll, the browser moves the background image with the element as the user scrolls through the document. A value of fixed prevents the image from moving.

8.4.5.4 The background-position property

By default, the styles-conscious browser begins rendering a background image starting in the upper-left corner of the allotted display area. With the background-
position property, you can offset the starting position of the background image by
an absolute (length) or relative (percentage or keyword) offset. The resulting, potentially "cropped," image fills the area from that offset starting point.

You may specify one or two values for the background-position property. If you use a
single value, it applies to both the vertical and horizontal positions. With two values, the first is the horizontal offset and the second is the vertical offset.

Length values (with their appropriate units; see section 8.4.1.2, earlier in this chapter)
indicate an absolute distance from the upper-left corner of the element behind which
you display the background image. Negative length values effectively crop the corresponding top and left sides of the image within the allotted viewport, just as an image
that is too big for the browser's window gets cropped on the bottom and right sides.

For example:

```
table {background-image: url(backgrounds/marble.gif);
       background-position: 10px 20px}
```

offsets the marble background 10 pixels to the right and 20 pixels down from the
upper-left corner of any <table> element in your document.

Percentage values are a bit trickier but somewhat easier to use. Measured from 0 per-
cent to 100 percent from left to right and top to bottom, the center of the element's
content display space is at 50%, 50%. Similarly, the position one-third of the way
across the area and two-thirds of the way down is at 33%, 66%. So, to offset the
background for our example dinner menu to the center of the element's content dis-
play space, we use:*

```
background-position: 50%
```

Why use a number when a single word will do? You can use the keywords left,
center, and right, as well as top, center, and bottom, for 0%, 50%, and 100%, respec-
tively. To center an image in the tag's content area, use:

```
background-position: center
```

You can mix and match length and percentage values,† too, so that:

```
background-position: 1cm 50%
```

places the image one centimeter to the right of the tag's left edge, centered vertically
in the tag's area.

---

* Interestingly, this property worked as advertised with Internet Explorer versions 4 and 5 but is broken in ver-
sion 6, as it is with other popular browsers: the offset works only if you set the background-repeat property.

† That is, if the browser supports the value units. So far, Internet Explorer and Netscape support only a meager
repertoire of length units—pixels and percents.

Note that with relative offsets, the image moves relative to the tag's contents when the user resizes the browser display window because the space allotted to the content also gets resized. By contrast, the image stays in the same place relative to the element's contents if you use absolute offset values.

Finally, one might also expect that the repeating background (by default; see the following section, 8.4.5.5) would tile down and to the right of the offset. Not so. Current browsers "wrap" the image around to fill the element's allotted display space. For example, look closely at Figure 8-7 and notice the tiling effects for an offset versus non-offset background image displayed from the following example style fragments:

```
<style type=css/text>
<!--
pre {background-image: url(backgrounds/vert.gif)}
pre.offset {background-image: url(backgrounds/vert.gif); background-position: -20px -
20px}
-->
</style>
...
The following background image is offset by -20 pixels left and up:
<pre class=offset>




</pre>
<p>
This background image is not offset:
<pre>




</pre>
```

8.4.5.5 The background-repeat property

Normally, the browser tiles a background image to fill the allotted space, repeating the image both horizontally and vertically. Use the background-repeat property to alter this repeat (default value) behavior. To have the image repeat horizontally but not vertically, use the value repeat-x. For only vertical repetition, use repeat-y. To suppress tiling altogether, use no-repeat.

A common use of this property is to place a watermark or logo in the background of a page without repeating the image over and over. For instance, this code places the watermark image in the background at the center of the page:

```
body {background-image: url(backgrounds/watermark.gif);
      background-position: center center;
      background-repeat: no-repeat
      }
```

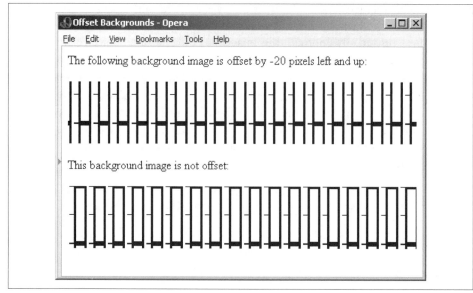

Figure 8-7. Background-offset with tiling

A popular trick is to create a vertical ribbon down the righthand side of the page:

```
body {background-image: url(backgrounds/ribbon.gif);
     background-position: top right;
     background-repeat: repeat-y
     }
```

8.4.5.6 The background property

Like the various font properties, the many background CSS2 properties can get cumbersome to write and hard to read later. So, like the font property, there is also a general background property.

The background property accepts values from any and all of the background-color, background-image, background-attachment, background-repeat, and background-position properties, in any order. If you do not specify values for some of the properties, those properties are explicitly set to their default values. Thus:

```
background: red
```

sets the background-color property to red and resets the other background properties to their default values. A more complex example:

```
background: url(backgrounds/marble.gif) blue repeat-y fixed center
```

sets all the background image and color properties at once, resulting in a marble image on top of a blue background (blue showing through any transparent areas). The image repeats vertically, starting from the center of the content display area, and does not scroll when the user scrolls the display. Notice that we include just a single position value (center), and the browser uses it for both the vertical and horizontal positions.

8.4.5.7 The color property

The color property sets the foreground color for a tag's contents—the color of the text lettering, for instance. Its value is either the name of a color, a hexadecimal RGB triple, or a decimal RGB triple, as outlined earlier in section 8.4.1.5. The following are all valid property declarations:

```
color: mauve
color: #ff7bd5
color: rgb(255, 125, 213)
color: rgb(100%, 49%, 84%)
```

Generally, you'll use the color property with text, but you may also modify nontextual content of a tag. For instance, the following example produces a green horizontal rule:

```
hr {color: green}
```

If you don't specify a color for an element, it inherits the color of its parent element.

8.4.6 Text Properties

Cascading stylesheets make a distinction between font properties, which control the size, style, and appearance of text, and text properties, which control how text is aligned and presented to the user.

8.4.6.1 The letter-spacing property

The letter-spacing property puts additional space between text letters as they are displayed by the browser. Set the property with either a length value or the default keyword normal, indicating that the browser should use normal letter spacing. For example:

```
blockquote {letter-spacing: 2px}
```

puts an additional two pixels between adjacent letters within the <blockquote> tag. Figure 8-8 illustrates what happens when you put five pixels between characters.

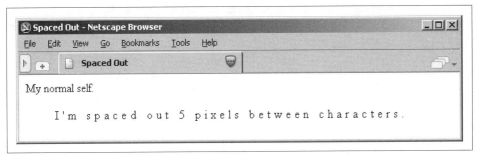

Figure 8-8. The letter-spacing property lets you stretch text

All the popular browsers support this property.

8.4.6.2 The line-height property

Use the line-height property to define the minimum spacing between lines of a tag's text content. Normally, browsers single-space text lines—the top of the next line is just a few points below the last line. By adding to that line height, you increase the amount of space between lines.

The line-height value can be an absolute or a relative length, a percentage, a scaling factor, or the keyword normal. For example:

```
p {line-height: 14pt}
p {line-height: 120%}
p {line-height: 2.0}
```

The first example sets the line height to exactly 14 points between baselines of adjacent lines of text. The second computes the line height to 120 percent of the font size. The last example uses a scaling factor to set the line height to twice as large as the font size, creating double-spaced text. The value normal, the default, is usually equal to a scaling factor of 1.0 to 1.2.

Keep in mind that absolute and percentage values for line-height compute the line height based on the value of the font-size property. Children of the element inherit the computed property value. Subsequent changes to font-size by either the parent or the child elements do not change the computed line height.

Scaling factors, on the other hand, defer the line-height computation until the browser actually displays the text. Hence, varying font sizes affect line height locally. In general, it is best to use a scaling factor for the line-height property so that the line height changes automatically as the font size changes.

Although it is usually considered separate from font properties, you may include this text-related line-height property's value as part of the shorthand notation of the font property. [The font property, 8.4.3.8]

8.4.6.3 The text-align property

Text justified with respect to the page margins is a rudimentary feature of nearly all text processors. The text-align property brings that capability to HTML for any block-level tag. (The W3C standards people prefer that you use CSS2 text-align styles rather than the explicit align attribute for block-level tags such as <div> and <p>.) Use one of four values: left, right, center, or justify. The default value is, of course, left.*

For example:

```
div {text-align: right}
```

tells the styles-conscious browser to align all the text inside <div> tags against the right margin. The justify value tells the browser to align the text to both the left and right margins, spreading the letters and words in the middle to fit.

---

* For left-to-right locales. In right-to-left locales, the default is right.

All the popular browsers currently support the left, right, and center alignments, but not justify.

8.4.6.4 The text-decoration property

The text-decoration property produces text embellishments, some of which are also available with the original physical style tags. Its value is one or more of the keywords underline, overline, line-through, and blink. The value none is the default, which tells the styles-conscious browser to present text normally.

The text-decoration property is handy for defining different link appearances:

```
a:visited, a:link, a:active {text-decoration: underline overline}
```

This puts lines above and below the links in your document.

This text property is not inherited, and nontextual elements are not affected by the text-decoration property.

Interestingly, all the popular browsers support the text-decoration property, but only Internet Explorer has the good taste not to support its blink value.

8.4.6.5 The text-indent property

Although less common today, it is still standard practice to indent the first line of a paragraph of text.* And some text blocks, such as definitions, typically "out-dent" the first line, creating what is called a *hanging indent*.

The CSS2 text-indent property lets you apply these features to any block tag and thereby control the amount of indentation of the first line of the block. Use length and percentage values: negative values create the hanging indent, and percentage values compute the indentation as a percentage of the parent element's width. The default value is 0.

To indent all the paragraphs in your document, for example, you could use:

```
p {text-indent: 3em}
```

The length unit em scales the indent as the font of the paragraph changes in size on different browsers.

Hanging indents are a bit trickier, because you have to watch out for the element borders. Negative indentation does not shift the left margin of the text; it simply shifts the first line of the element left, possibly into the margin, border, or padding of the parent element. For this reason, hanging indents work as expected only if you also shift the left margin of the element to the right by an amount equal to or greater than the size of the hanging indent. For example:

```
p.wrong {text-indent: -3em}
p.hang {text-indent: -3em; margin-left: 3em}
p.large {text-indent: -3em; margin-left: 6em}
```

---

* But not, obviously, in this book.

creates three paragraph styles. The first creates a hanging indent that extends into the left margin, the second creates a conventional hanging indent, and the third creates a paragraph whose body is indented more than the hanging indent. Figure 8-9 shows all three styles in use.

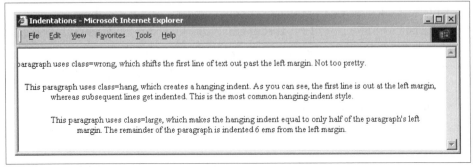

Figure 8-9. The effects of text-indent and margin-left on a paragraph

All the popular browsers support the text-indent property.

8.4.6.6 The text-shadow property

The text-shadow property lets you give your text a three-dimensional appearance through the time-honored use of shadowing. Values for the property include a required offset and optional blur radius and color. The property may include more than one set of values, separated with commas, to achieve a stack of shadows, with each subsequent set of values layered on top of the previous one but always beneath the original text.

The property's required offset is composed of two length values: the first specifies the horizontal offset, and the second specifies the vertical offset. Positive values place the shadow to the right and below the respective length distance from the text. Negative values move the shadow left and up, respectively.

The optional blur radius is also a length value that specifies the boundaries for blurring, an effect that depends on the rendering agent. The other shadow value is color. This, of course, may be an RGB triple or color name, as for other properties, and specifies the shadow color. If you don't specify this value, text-shadow uses the color value of the color property. For example:

```
h1 {text-shadow; 10px 10px 2px yellow}
p:first-letter {text-shadow: -5px -5px purple, 10px 10px orange}
```

The first text-shadow example puts a 2-pixel blurred-yellow shadow behind, 10 pixels below, and 10 pixels to the right of level-1 headers in your document. The second example puts two shadows behind the first letter of each paragraph. The purple shadow sits 5 pixels above and 5 pixels to the left of that first letter. The other shadow, like in the first example (although orange in this case), goes 10 pixels to the right and 10 pixels below the first letter of each paragraph.

Unfortunately, we can't show you any of these effects, because none of the popular browsers supports this property.

8.4.6.7 The text-transform property

The text-transform property lets you automatically convert portions or all of your document's text into uppercase or lowercase lettering. Acceptable values are capitalize, uppercase, lowercase, and none.

capitalize renders the first letter of each word in the text into uppercase, even if the source document's text is in lowercase. The uppercase and lowercase values respectively render all the text in the corresponding case. none, of course, cancels any transformations. For example:

```
h1 {text-transform: uppercase}
```

formats all the letters in level-1 headers, presumably titles, in uppercase text, whereas:

```
h2 {text-transform: capitalize}
```

makes sure that each word in level-2 headers begins with a capital letter, a convention that might be appropriate for section heads, for instance.

Note that while uppercase and lowercase affect the entire text, capitalize affects only the first letter of each word in the text. Consequently, transforming the word "htMl" with capitalize generates "HtMl."

All the popular browsers support the text-transform property.

8.4.6.8 The vertical-align property

The vertical-align property controls the relative position of an element with respect to the line containing the element. Valid values for this property include:

baseline
: Align the baseline of the element with the baseline of the containing element.

middle
: Align the middle of the element with the middle (usually the x-height) of the containing element.

sub
: Subscript the element.

super
: Superscript the element.

text-top
: Align the top of the element with the top of the font of the parent element.

text-bottom
: Align the bottom of the element with the bottom of the font of the parent element.

top
: Align the top of the element with the top of the tallest element in the current line.

bottom
: Align the bottom of the element with the bottom of the lowest element in the current line.

In addition, a percentage value indicates a position relative to the current baseline so that a position of 50% puts the element halfway up the line height above the baseline. A position value of -100% puts the element an entire line height below the baseline of the current line.

All the popular browsers agree on where to place images relative to a line of text for baseline (default and the same as no vertical-align specification), middle (but not center), super (but not sub), text-top, text-bottom, top (same as text-top; but not bottom), and for both plus and minus percentage offset values. Figure 8-10 shows you how Internet Explorer treats the various vertical-align values.

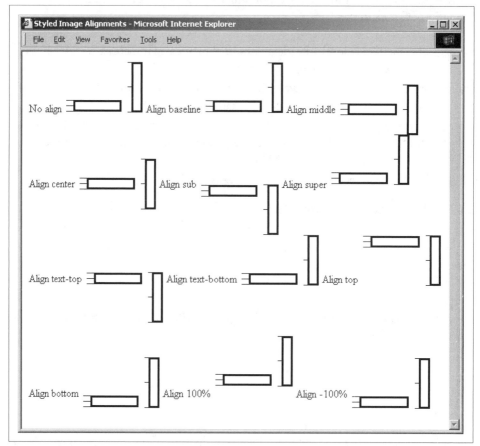

Figure 8-10. Internet Explorer's treatment of the vertical alignment property values

For the differences, Firefox treats center like Internet Explorer and different from middle (Figure 8-10), whereas Netscape treats center identical to middle, but Opera doesn't recognize the value at all. With sub, it's Netscape's turn to agree with Firefox and place the bottom of the subscripted image at the bottom of the character descender, whereas Opera places the bottom of the image perceptively below the baseline, but unlike Internet Explorer, not so low as to be just above the next line of text.

With the bottom value, it's Opera's turn to agree—with Internet Explorer, aligning the bottom of the image with the bottom of the line just above the next line of text, whereas Firefox and Netscape place the bottom of the image at the bottom of the character descender. Clear as mud? Perhaps Figures 8-11 through 8-13 will help you to visualize the differences when also compared with Figure 8-10.

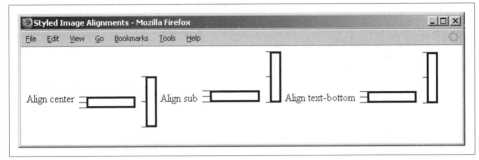

Figure 8-11. Firefox's rendering of selected vertical-align values

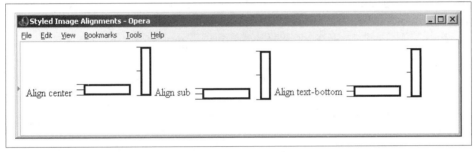

Figure 8-12. Opera's rendering of selected vertical-align values

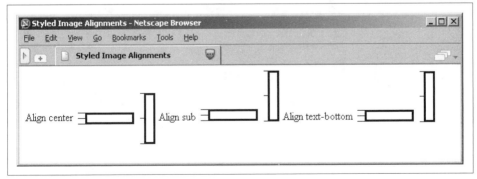

Figure 8-13. Netscape's rendering of selected vertical-align values

8.4.6.9 The word-spacing property

Use the word-spacing property to add space between words within a tag. You can specify a length value, or use the keyword normal to revert to normal word spacing. For example:

    h3 {word-spacing: 25px}

places an additional 25 pixels of space between words in the <h3> tag.

All the currently popular browsers support the word-spacing property.

8.4.7 Box Properties

The CSS2 model assumes that HTML and XHTML elements always fit within rectangular boxes. Using the properties defined in this section, you can control the size, appearance, and position of the boxes containing the elements in your documents.

8.4.7.1 The CSS2 formatting model

Each element in a document fits into a rectangular space or box. The CSS2 authors call this box the *core content area* and surround it with three more boxes: the padding, the border, and the margin. Figure 8-14 shows these boxes and defines some useful terminology.

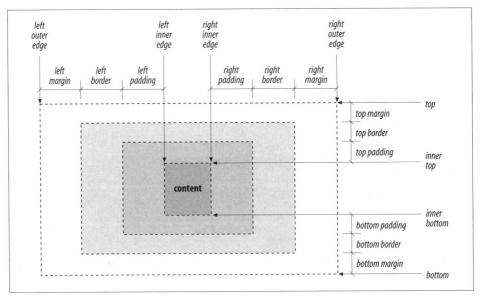

Figure 8-14. The CSS2 formatting model and terminology

The top, bottom, left-outer, and right-outer edges bound the content area of an element and all of its padding, border, and margin spaces. The inner-top, inner-bottom, left-inner, and right-inner edges define the sides of the core content area. The extra space around the element is the area between the inner and outer edges, including the padding, border, and margin. A browser may omit any and all of these extra spaces for any element, and for many, the inner and outer edges are the same.

When elements are vertically adjacent, the bottom margin of the upper elements and the top margin of the lower elements overlap so that the total space between the elements is the greater of the adjacent margins. For example, if one paragraph has a bottom margin of 1 inch, and the next paragraph has a top margin of 0.5 inches, the greater of the two margins, 1 inch, is placed between the two paragraphs. This practice is known as *margin collapsing* and generally results in better document appearance.

Horizontally adjacent elements do not have overlapping margins. Instead, the CSS2 model adds together adjacent horizontal margins. For example, if a paragraph has a left margin of 1 inch and is adjacent to an element with a right margin of 0.5 inches, the total space between the two is 1.5 inches. This rule also applies to nested elements so that a paragraph within a division has a left margin equal to the sum of the division's left margin and the paragraph's left margin.

As shown in Figure 8-14, the total width of an element is equal to the sum of seven items: the left and right margins, the left and right borders, the left and right padding, and the element's content itself. The sum of these seven items must equal the width of the containing element. Of these seven items, only three (the element's width and its left and right margins) can be given the value auto, indicating that the browser can compute a value for that property. When this becomes necessary, the browser follows these rules:

- If none of these properties is set to auto and the total width is less than the width of the parent element, the margin-right property is set to auto and made large enough to make the total width equal to the width of the parent element.
- If exactly one property is set to auto, that property is made large enough to make the total width equal to the width of the parent element.
- If width, margin-left, and margin-right are set to auto, the CSS2-compliant browser sets both margin-left and margin-right to 0 and sets width large enough to make the total equal to the width of the parent element.
- If both the left and right margins are set to auto, they are always set to equal values, centering the element within its parent.

There are special rules for floating elements. A floating element (such as an image with align=left specified) does not have its margins collapsed with the margins of containing or preceding elements, unless the floating element has negative margins. Figure 8-15 shows how the following bit of HTML might be rendered:

```
<body>
<p>
<img align=left src="pics/img.gif">
Some sample text...
</body>
```

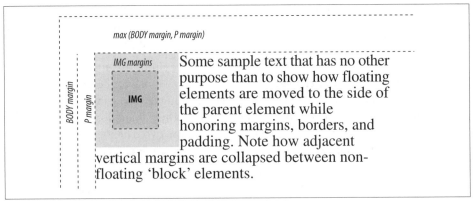

Figure 8-15. Handling the margins of floating elements

The browser moves the image, including its margins, as far as possible to the left and toward the top of the paragraph without overlapping the left and top margins of the paragraph or the document body. The left margins of the paragraph and the containing body are added, and their top margins are collapsed.

8.4.7.2 The border properties

The border surrounding an element has a color, a thickness, and a style. You can use various properties to control these three aspects of the border on each of the four sides of an element. Shorthand properties make it easy to define the same color, thickness, and style for the entire border, if desired. Border properties are not inherited; you must explicitly set them for each element that has a border.

8.4.7.3 The border-color property

Use the border-color property to set the border color. If this property is not specified, the browser draws the border using the value of the element's color property.

The border-color property accepts from one to four color values. The number of values determines how they are applied to the borders (summarized in Table 8-1). If you include just one property value, all four sides of the border are set to the specified color. Two values set the top and bottom borders to the first value and the left and right borders to the second value. With three values, the first is the top border, the second sets the right and left borders, and the third color value is for the bottom border. Four values specify colors for the top, right, bottom, and left borders, in that order.

Table 8-1. Order of effects for multiple border, margin, and padding property values

Number of values	Affected border(s), margin(s), or padding
1	All items have the same value.
2	The first value sets *top* and *bottom*; the second value sets *left* and *right*.
3	The first value sets *top*; the second sets both *left* and *right*; the third value sets *bottom*.
4	The first value sets *top*; the second sets *right*; the third sets *bottom*; the fourth value sets *left*.

8.4.7.4 The border-width property

The `border-width` property lets you change the width of the border. Like the border-color property, it accepts from one to four values that are applied to the various borders in a similar manner (refer to Table 8-1).

Besides a specific length value, you may also specify the width of a border as one of the keywords `thin`, `medium`, or `thick`. The default value, if the width is not explicitly set, is `medium`. Some typical border widths are:

```
border: 1px
border: thin thick medium
border: thick 2mm
```

The first example sets all four borders to exactly 1 pixel. The second makes the top border `thin`, the right and left borders `thick`, and the bottom border `medium`. The last example makes the top and bottom borders `thick` and the right and left borders 2 millimeters wide.

If you are uncomfortable defining all four borders with one property, you can use the individual `border-top-width`, `border-bottom-width`, `border-left-width`, and `border-right-width` properties to define the thickness of each border. Each property accepts just one value; the default is `medium`.

All the currently popular browsers support this property.

8.4.7.5 The border-style property

According to the CSS2 model, you may apply a number of embellishments to your HTML element borders.

The `border-style` property values include `none` (default), `dotted`, `dashed`, `solid`, `double`, `groove`, `ridge`, `inset`, and `outset`. The border-style-conscious browser applies one to four values for the property to each border, in the same order as for the border colors and widths, as described in Table 8-1.

The browser draws `dotted`, `dashed`, `solid`, and `double` borders as flat lines on top of the tag's background. The `groove`, `ridge`, `inset`, and `outset` values create three-dimensional borders: the `groove` is an incised line, the `ridge` is an embossed line, the `inset` border makes the entire tag area appear set into the document, and the `outset` border makes the entire tag area appear raised above the document. The effect of the three-dimensional nature of these last four styles on the tag's background image is undefined and left up to the browser. Netscape supports three-dimensional effects.

All the currently popular browsers support the border styles. An example is shown in Figure 8-16.

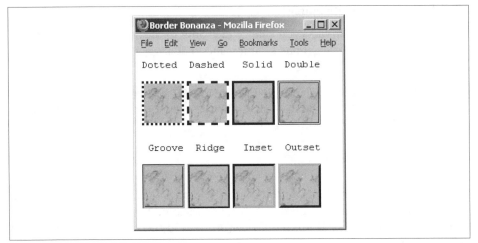

Figure 8-16. The border-style property nicely frames images

8.4.7.6 Borders in shorthand

Specifying a complex border can get tedious, so the CSS2 standard provides five shorthand properties that accept any or all of the width, color, and style values for one or all of the border edges. The border-top, border-bottom, border-left, and border-right properties affect their respective borders' sides; the comprehensive border property controls all four sides of the border simultaneously. For example:

```
border-top: thick solid blue
border-left: 1ex inset
border-bottom: blue dashed
border: red double 2px
```

The first property makes the top border a thick, solid, blue line. The second sets the left border to use an inset effect that is as thick as the x-height of the element's font, while leaving the color the same as the element's color. The third property creates a blue dashed line at the bottom of the element, using the default medium thickness. Finally, the last property makes all four borders a red double line, 2 pixels thick.

That last property raises two issues. First, you cannot supply multiple values to the border property to selectively affect certain borders, as you can with the individual border-color, border-width, and border-style properties. The border property always affects all four borders around an element.

Second, a bit of reflection should reveal that it is not possible to create a double-line border just 2 pixels thick. In cases like this, the browser is free to adjust the thickness to render the border properly.

While we usually think of borders surrounding block elements such as images, tables, and text flows, you also can apply borders to inline tags. This lets you put a box around a word or phrase within a text flow. The implementation of borders on inline tags that span multiple lines is undefined and left to the browser.

All of the currently popular browsers support the border styles.

8.4.7.7 The clear property

Like its cousin attribute for the <br> tag, the clear property tells the browser whether to place a tag's contents adjacent to a "floating" element or on the first line below it. Text flows around floating elements such as images and tables with an align=left or align=right attribute or any HTML/XHTML element with its float property set to anything but none. [
, 4.6.1] [The float property, 8.4.7.9]

The value of the clear property can be none, left, right, or both. A value of none, the default, means that the browser acts normally and places the tag's contents adjacent to floating elements on either side, if there is room to do so. The value left prevents contents from being placed adjacent to a floating element on its left; right prevents placement on the right side of a floating element; and both prevents the tag's contents from appearing adjacent to any floating element.

The effect of this style is the same as preceding the tag with a <br> tag with its clear attribute set. Hence:

```
h1 {clear: left}
```

has the same effect as preceding every <h1> tag with <br clear=left>.

8.4.7.8 The clip property

Normally, the content of an element is completely visible within the display space of the element. The clip property defines a viewing window within an element's display space, letting you hide unwanted elements and focus attention on some area or aspect of the content.

The default value of the clip property is auto, meaning that the viewing window matches the box of the element. Instead, you may specify a shape that creates a distinct viewing window into the element's display area. Currently, the only shape supported by CSS2* is a rectangle, denoted by the rect keyword. For example:

```
p {overflow : hidden;
    clip : rect(15px, -10px, 5px, 10px) }
```

The four values define the top, right, bottom, and left edges of the clipping rectangle. Each value is an offset relative to the box edges defined for the element. So, in this example, the top of the clipping area is 15 pixels below the top of the element's box, the right edge is 10 pixels to the right of the box, the bottom is 5 pixels above the bottom of the box, and the left edge is 10 pixels to the right of the left side of the box.

---

* Presumably, future versions of the standard will expand to include other shapes.

Note that the clip property takes effect only when the overflow property of an element is set to some value other than visible. When overflow is set to visible, no clipping occurs and the clip property is ignored.

The popular browsers don't yet support the clip property.

8.4.7.9 The float property

The float property designates a tag's display space as a floating element and causes text to flow around it in a specified manner. It is generally analogous to the align attribute for images and tables, but you can apply it to any element, including text. [The align attribute (deprecated), 10.2.1.1]

The float property accepts one of three values: left, right, or none (the default). Using none disables the float property. The others work like their align attribute-value counterparts, telling the browser to place the content to either side of the flow and allow other content to be rendered next to it.

Accordingly, the browser places a tag's contents (including its margins, padding, and borders) specified with float: left against the left margin of the current text flow, and subsequent content flows to its right, down and below the tag's contents. The float: right pair puts the tag contents against the right edge of the flow and flows other content on its left, down and below the tag's contents.

Although the float property is most commonly used with tables and images, it is perfectly acceptable to apply it to a text element. For example, the following creates a "run-in" header, with the text flowing around the header text, as shown in Figure 8-17:

```
h2 {float: left;
text-align: center;
margin-right: 10px }
```

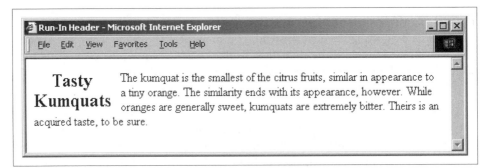

Figure 8-17. Use the float property with text blocks to create run-in headers

All the popular browsers support this property.

8.4.7.10 The height property

As you might suspect, the height property controls the height of the associated tag's display region. You'll find it most often used with images and tables, but you can use it to control the height of other document elements as well.

The value of the height property is either a length value or the keyword auto (the default). Using auto implies that the affected tag has an initial height that should be used when displaying the tag. Otherwise, the height of the tag is set to the desired height. If an absolute value is used, the height is set to that length value. For example:

```
img {height: 100px}
```

tells the browser to display the image referenced by the <img> tag scaled so that it is 100 pixels tall. If you use a relative value, the base size to which it is relative is browser and tag dependent.

When scaling elements to a specific height, you can preserve the aspect ratio of the object by also setting the width property of the tag to auto. Thus:

```
img {height: 100px; width: auto}
```

ensures that the images are always 100 pixels tall, with an appropriately scaled width. [The width property, 8.4.7.16]

If you want to constrain the height of an element to a range rather than a specific value, use the min-height and max-height properties. These properties accept values like the height property and establish a range for the height of the element. The browser then adjusts the height of the element to fall within the desired range.

All of the popular browsers fully support the height property, but none of the browsers yet supports the min-height and max-height properties.

8.4.7.11 The margin properties

Like the border properties, the various margin properties let you control the margin space around an element, just outside of its border (see Figure 8-14). Margins are always transparent, allowing the background color or image of the containing element to show through. As a result, you can specify only the size of a margin; it has no color or rendered style.

The margin-left, margin-right, margin-top, and margin-bottom properties all accept a length or percentage value indicating the amount of space to reserve around the element. In addition, the keyword auto tells the styles-conscious browser to revert to the margins it normally would place around an element. Percentage values are computed as a percentage of the containing element's width. The default margin, if not specified, is 0.

These are all valid margin settings:

```
body {margin-left: 1in; margin-top: 0.5in; margin-right: 1in}
p {margin-left: -0.5cm}
img {margin-left: 10%}
```

The first example creates 1-inch margins down the right and left edges of the entire document and a 0.5-inch margin across the top of the document. The second example shifts the left edge of the <p> tag 0.5 centimeters left, into the left margin. The last example creates a margin to the left of the <img> tag equal to 10 percent of the parent element's width.

As you can the shorthand border property, you can use the shorthand margin property to define all four margins, using from one to four values, which affect the margins in the order described in Table 8-1. Using this notation, our <body> margins in the previous example could also have been specified as:

```
body {margin: 0.5in 1in}
```

The margin-left and margin-right properties interact with the width property to determine the total width of an element, as described earlier in section 8.4.7.1.

All the popular browsers support the margin properties and values.

8.4.7.12 The padding properties

Like the margin properties, the various padding properties let you control the padding space around an element, between the element's content area and its border (see Figure 8-14, earlier in the chapter).

Padding always is rendered using the background color or image of the element. As a result, you can specify only the size of the padding; it has no color or rendered style.

The padding-left, padding-right, padding-top, and padding-bottom properties all accept a length or percentage value indicating the amount of space the styles-conscious browser should reserve around the element. Percentage values are computed as a percentage of the containing element's width. Padding can never be negative. The default padding is 0.

These are valid padding settings:

```
p {padding-left: 0.5cm}
img {padding-left: 10%}
```

The first example creates 0.5 centimeters of padding between the contents of the <p> tag and its left border. The second example creates padding to the left of the <img> tag equal to 10 percent of the parent element's width.

Like the shorthand margin and border properties, you can use the shorthand padding property to define all four padding amounts, using from one to four values to affect the padding sides as described in Table 8-1. Internet Explorer does not support the padding property, but all the other popular browsers do.

8.4.7.13 The overflow property

The overflow property tells the browser how to handle content that overflows the display area of an element. The default value of this property, visible, tells the browser to render all content, making it visible even if it falls outside of the element's display area.

Erring on the side of caution, you most often want the browser to display all of your document's contents. But in rare cases, elements may overlap, creating an ugly display. To prevent such mishaps, set the overflow property to either hidden, scroll, or auto.

The hidden value forces the browser to hide all content that overflows its allotted space, making it invisible to the user. The value scroll creates scroll bars for the element, which viewers may use to see the hidden content. However, scroll bars are added to the element even if the content does not overflow.

Adding permanent scroll bars ensures that the scroll bars do not come and go as the content of the element changes in size in a dynamic document. The downside to this is the clutter and distractions that scroll bars create. Avoid all this with the auto value for the overflow property. When on auto, scroll bars appear only when they are needed. If the element's content changes so that it is not clipped, the scroll bars are removed from the element.

None of the currently popular browsers supports the overflow property.

8.4.7.14 The position properties

Without intervention, the browser flows document elements together, positioned sequentially through the display. You can change this standard behavior with the CSS2 position property, in conjunction with the top, bottom, left, and right properties.

If the position property is set to static, conventional HTML/XHTML layout and positioning rules apply, with the left and top edges of the element's box determined by the browser. To shift an element with respect to its containing flow, set the position property to relative. In this case, the top, bottom, left, and right properties are used to compute the box position relative to its normal position in the flow. Subsequent elements are not affected by this position change and are placed in the flow as though this element had not been shifted.

Setting the position property to absolute removes the element from the containing flow, allowing subsequent elements to move up accordingly. The position of the element is then computed relative to the containing block, using the top, bottom, left, and right properties. This type of positioning allows an element to be placed in a fixed position with respect to its containing element but to move as that containing element moves.

Finally, setting the position property to fixed positions an element with respect to the window or page in which it is displayed. Like absolute positioning, the element is removed from the containing flow, with other elements shifting accordingly. The top, bottom, left, and right properties are used to set the element's position with respect to the containing window or page. Note that for continuous media (such as a scrolling browser display), the element is displayed once at the desired position. For printed media, the element is printed on each page at the desired position. You might used `fixed` positioning to place headers and footers at the top and bottom of the browser window or at the top and bottom of each printed page.

The `top`, `bottom`, `left`, and `right` properties each accept a length or percentage value. When the `position` attribute is set to `relative`, the percentage is based on the size of the element's box. When `position` is set to `absolute` or `fixed`, the percentage is based on the size of the containing element's box. When length values are used, they specify offsets from the corresponding edge of the element's containing box. For example, to position an element such that its bottom is 1 centimeter above the bottom of the browser window (or each printed page), you would set the `position` property to `fixed` and the `bottom` property to `1cm`.

8.4.7.15 The visibility property

The `visibility` property determines whether the contents of an element are visible in the display. The space set aside for the element is still created and affects the layout of the document, but the content of the element may be made invisible within that space.

The default value for this property, `visible`, causes the element's content to be displayed. Setting this property to `hidden` makes the content invisible without removing the element's display box, altering the layout of the document. Note that you can remove an element's content and display box from the document by setting the `display` property to `none`.

This property is often used in dynamic documents, where changing its value for an element removes its content from the display without reformatting the document.

When this property is used in conjunction with table rows, row groups, columns, and column groups, you may also specify the value `collapse`. Used in this context, the `collapse` value removes the associated row(s) or column(s) from the table without otherwise reformatting or redrawing the table. Within dynamic documents, this lets you remove elements from a table without reformatting the entire table. Used outside of a table, the `collapse` value has the same effect as the `hidden` value.

8.4.7.16 The width property

The `width` property is the companion to the `height` property and controls the width of an associated tag. Specifically, it defines the width of the element's content area, as shown in Figure 8-8. You'll see it most often used with images and tables, but you could conceivably use it to control the width of other elements as well.

The value for the `width` property is either a length or percentage value, or the keyword `auto`. The value `auto` is the default and implies that the affected tag has an initial width that should be used when displaying the tag. If a length value is used, the width is set to that value; percentage values compute the width to be a percentage of the width of the containing element. For example:

```
img {width: 100px}
```

displays the image referenced by the <img> tag scaled to 100 pixels wide.

When scaling elements to a specific width, the aspect ratio of the object is preserved if the height property of the tag is set to auto. Thus:

```
img {width: 100px; height: auto}
```

makes all the images 100 pixels wide and scales their heights appropriately. [The height property, 8.4.7.10]

If you want to constrain the width of an element to a range rather than a specific value, use the min-width and max-width properties. These properties accept values like the width property and establish a range for the width of the element. The browser then adjusts the width of the element to fall within the desired range.

The width property interacts with the margin-left and margin-right properties to determine the total width of an element, as described earlier in section 8.4.7.1.

8.4.7.17 The z-index property

In addition to the x and y positions of an element within the browser window or on the printed page, each element has a vertical, or z, position. Elements with higher z positions are "closer" to the viewer and obscure elements underneath them.

Z positions are not absolute throughout a document. Instead, z positions are relative to the containing element. For example, two <div> elements within a document might be positioned to lie on top of one another. The first <div> might have a z position of 1, and the second might have a z position of 2. The entire contents of the second <div> are displayed over (or in front of) the first <div>. If elements within the first <div> have z positions of 3 or 4, they are still displayed within their containing <div>s and do not "jump out" in front of the second <div>.

You control the z position of an element with the z-index property. The value of the z-index property is a positive integer that sets the z position of the element with respect to its containing element. With the z-index property, you can dynamically alter the z position of an element to make it visible, or position a text element in front of an image to label items of interest.

8.4.8 List Properties

The CSS2 standard also lets you control the appearance of list elements—specifically, ordered and unordered lists. Browsers format list items just like any other block item, except that the block has some sort of marker preceding the contents. For unordered lists, the marker is a bullet of some sort; for numbered lists, the marker is a numeric or alphabetic character or symbol. The CSS2 list properties let you control the appearance and position of the marker associated with a list item.

8.4.8.1 The list-style-image property

The `list-style-image` property defines the image that the browser uses to mark a list item. The value of this property is the URL of an image file or the keyword none. The default value is none.

The image is the preferred list marker. If it is available, the browser displays it in place of any other defined marker. If the image is unavailable, or if the user has disabled image loading, the browser uses the marker defined by the `list-style-type` property (see section 8.4.8.3, later in this chapter).

HTML/XHTML authors use the `list-style-image` property to define custom bullets for their unordered lists. While you conceivably could use any image as a bullet, we recommend that you keep your marker GIF or JPEG images small, to ensure attractively rendered lists.

For example, by placing the desired bullet image in the file *mybullet.gif* on your server, you could use that image:

```
li {list-style-image: url(pics/mybullet.gif); list-style-type: square}
```

In this case, the browser uses the image if it is able to successfully download *mybullet.gif*. Otherwise, the browser uses a conventional square bullet.

All the popular browsers support the `list-style-image` property, as shown in Figure 8-18.

8.4.8.2 The list-style-position property

There are two ways to position the marker associated with a list item: inside the block associated with the item or outside the block. Accordingly, the `list-style-position` property accepts one of two values: inside or outside.

The default value is outside, meaning that the item marker hangs to the left of the item, like this:

- This is a bulleted list
  with an "outside" marker

The value inside causes the marker to be drawn with the list item flowing around it, much like a floating image:

- This is a bulleted list
with an "inside" marker

Notice that the second line of text is not indented but instead lines up with the left edge of the marker.

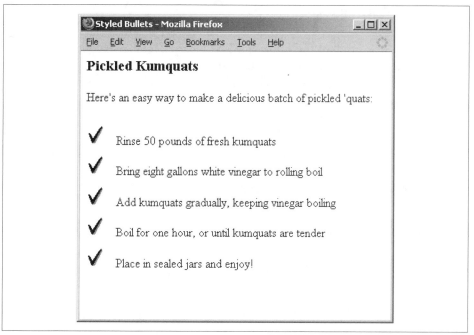

Figure 8-18. The list-style-image property lets you use your own bullets

The current versions of the popular browsers fully support the list-style-position property.

8.4.8.3 The list-style-type property

The list-style-type property serves double duty in a sense, determining how a styles-conscious browser renders both ordered and unordered list items. The property has the same effect as the type attribute on a list item. [The type attribute, 6.7.2.4]

When applied to items within an unordered list, the list-style-type property uses one of four values—disc, circle, square, or none—and marks the unordered list items with a corresponding dingbat. The default value of a level-1 list item is disc, although browsers change that default depending on the nesting level of the list.

When applied to items within an ordered list, the list-style-type property uses one of six values—decimal, lower-roman, upper-roman, lower-alpha, upper-alpha, or none—corresponding to the item numbers expressed as decimal values, lowercase Roman numerals, uppercase Roman numerals, lowercase letters, uppercase letters, or with no style, respectively. Most browsers use decimal numbering as the default.

The popular browsers support list-style-type as well as the list-style property described in the next section.

8.4.8.4 The list-style property

The list-style property is the shorthand version for all the other list-style properties. It accepts any or all of the values allowed for the list-style-type, list-style-position, and list-style-image properties, in any order and with values appropriate for the type of list they are to affect. These are valid list-style properties:

```
li {list-style: disc}
li {list-style: lower-roman inside}
li {list-style: url(http://www.kumquat.com/images/tiny-quat.gif) square}
```

The first example creates list items that use a disc as the bullet image. The second causes numbered list items to use lowercase Roman numerals, drawn inside the list item's block. In the last example, the styles-conscious browser uses a square as the bullet image if the referenced image is unavailable.

8.4.8.5 Using list properties effectively

Although you can apply list properties to any element, they affect only the appearance of elements whose display property is set to list-item. Normally, the only tag with this property is the <li> tag.

However, this shouldn't deter you from using these properties elsewhere, particularly with the <ul> and <ol> tags. Because these properties are inherited by elements whose parents have them set, modifying a list property for the <ul> and <ol> tags subsequently modifies it for all the <li> tags contained within that list. This makes it much easier to define lists with a particular appearance.

For example, suppose you want to create a list style that uses lowercase Roman numerals. One way is to define a class of the <li> tag with the appropriate list-style-type defined:

```
li.roman {list-style-type: lower-roman}
```

Within your list, you'll need to specify each list element using that class:

```
<ol>
  <li class=roman>Item one
  <li class=roman>Item two
  <li class=roman>And so forth
</ol>
```

Having to repeat the class name is tedious and error-prone. A better solution is to define a class of the <ol> tag:

```
ol.roman {list-style-type: lower-roman}
```

Any <li> tag within the list inherits the property and uses lowercase Roman numerals:

```
<ol class=roman>
  <li>Item one
  <li>Item two
  <li>And so forth
</ol>
```

This is much easier to understand and manage. If you want to change the numbering style later, you need only change the <ol> tag properties, instead of finding and changing each instance of the <li> tag in the list.

You can use these properties in a much more global sense, too. Setting a list property on the <body> tag changes the appearance of all lists in the document; setting it on a <div> tag changes all the lists within that division.

8.4.9 Table Properties

For the most part, HTML/XHTML browsers render table content using the same properties that control the rendering of conventional document content. However, a few special circumstances occur only within tables. To give authors greater control over these items, CSS2 has added a few table-specific properties. The popular browsers do not yet support any of them.

8.4.9.1 The border-collapse, border-spacing, and empty-cells properties

There are two divergent views regarding cell borders within tables. The first view holds that each cell is an independent entity with unique borders. The second view holds that adjacent cells share the border side and that changing a border in one cell should affect the neighboring cell.

To give the most control to authors, CSS2 provides the border-collapse property, which lets you choose the model that suits your style. By default, the value of this property is collapse, meaning adjacent cells share their border style. Alternatively, you can set the border-collapse property to separate, which enlarges the table so that borders are rendered separately and distinctly around each cell.

If you choose the separate model, you can also use the border-spacing property to set the spacing between adjacent borders. The default border spacing is 0, meaning that adjacent cell borders touch each other, although some browsers may use a different default. By increasing this value, you cause the browser to insert additional space between borders, allowing the background color or image of the table to show through. If you specify just one value for border-spacing, it sets the spacing for both horizontal and vertical borders. If you provide two values, the first sets the horizontal spacing and the second determines the vertical spacing.

Within the separate model, you can also control how borders are drawn around empty cells. By default, borders are drawn around every cell in a table, even if it has no content. You can change this by switching the empty-cells property from its default value of show to the value hide. When this property is set, empty cells simply show the table background. If a whole row of cells is empty, the browser removes the row from the table entirely.

8.4.9.2 The caption-side property

Use the caption-side property only with the <caption> element. It accepts values of top (default), bottom, left, or right, and tells the browser where to place the caption adjacent to its associated table. The caption-side property provides a more consistent method of placing the caption than the browser-dependent and standards-deprecated align attribute of the <caption> tag.

All of the popular browsers, except Internet Explorer, support caption-side.

8.4.9.3 The speak-header property

An audio-capable browser might offer a number of ways for users to navigate by hearing the contents of a table. A simplistic approach would have the browser read the table contents in order, from top to bottom and right to left. A more sophisticated audio browser organizes the table contents according to their respective headers and reads the information in a more comprehensible manner. To avoid confusion in any case, the browser must provide some way to tell the user which cell it is reading.

The speak-header property provides two ways for a browser to identify a cell or collection of cells in the table. If once (the default) is specified, the browser reads the contents of a header cell only once before proceeding to read the contents of each associated data cell. This way, a user moving across a row of cells would hear the row header and column header of the first cell in the row, but would hear the changing column headers only as she moved to subsequent cells in the row.

If you set the speak-header property to always, the browser prefaces the reading of each cell's contents with a reading of its associated header. This may prove more useful with complex tables or where the header values make it easier to understand the table contents—especially when a table contains only numbers.

Note that headers are spoken only when the browser knows which header cells are associated with which data cells. Conscientious authors always use the header attribute with their table cells, to specify the header cells related to each data cell in their tables.

8.4.9.4 The table-layout property

Table layout is a tough task for any browser. To create an attractive table, the browser must find the widest cell in each column, adjust that column to accommodate the width, and then adjust the overall table to accommodate all of its columns. For large tables, document rendering can be noticeably slowed as the browser makes several passes over the table, trying to get things just right.

To help in this process, use the table-layout property. If you set the property to fixed, the browser determines column widths based on the widths of cells in the first row of the table. If you explicitly set the column widths, setting the table's table-layout property to fixed makes the table-rendering process even faster, enhancing the readers' experience as they view your document.

By default, the table-layout property is set to auto, which forces the browser to use the more time-consuming, multiple-pass layout algorithm, even if you specify the widths of your columns in the table. If your table content is variable and you cannot explicitly set the widths, leave the table-layout property set to auto. If you can fix your column widths and your table content is amenable, set table-layout to fixed.

8.4.10 Classification Properties

Classification properties are the most fundamental of the CSS2 style properties. They do not directly control how a styles-conscious browser renders HTML or XHTML elements. Instead, they tell the browser how to classify and handle various tags and their contents as they are encountered.

For the most part, you should not set these properties on an element unless you are trying to achieve a specific effect.

8.4.10.1 The display property

Every element in an HTML or XHTML document can be classified, for display purposes, as a block item, an inline item, or a list item. Block elements, like headings, paragraphs, tables, and lists, are formatted as separate blocks of text, separate from their previous and following block items. Inline items, like the physical and content-based style tags and hyperlink anchors, are rendered within the current line of text within a containing block. List items, specifically <li>-tagged content, are rendered like block items, with a preceding bullet or number known as a *marker*.

The display property lets you change an element's display type to block, inline, list-item, or none. The first three values change the element's classification accordingly; the value none turns off the element, preventing it and its children from being displayed in the document.

Conceivably, you could wreak all sorts of havoc by switching element classifications, forcing paragraphs to be displayed as list items and converting hyperlinks to block elements. In practice, this is just puerile monkey business, and we don't recommend that you change element classifications without a very good reason to do so.

All the popular browsers support this property, but Internet Explorer supports only the block and none values.

8.4.10.2 The white-space property

The white-space property defines how the styles-conscious browser treats whitespace (tabs, spaces, and carriage returns) within a block tag. The keyword value normal—the default—collapses whitespace so that one or more spaces, tabs, and carriage returns are treated as a single space between words. The value pre emulates the <pre> tag, in that the browser retains and displays all spaces, tabs, and carriage returns. Finally, the nowrap value tells the browser to ignore carriage returns and not insert automatic line breaks; all line breaking must be done with explicit `<br>` tags.

Like the `display` property, the `white-space` property is rarely used for good purposes. Don't change how elements handle whitespace without a compelling reason for doing so.

Internet Explorer only supports the `nowrap` value, and the other popular browsers support both `pre` and `nowrap` values for the `white-space` property.

8.4.11 Generated Content Properties

The idea of generated content is not new to HTML. Even the earliest browsers automatically appended appropriate bullets or numbers to enhance the readability of your unordered and ordered list items. Such features are hardly enough, though, and authors have wished for better content-generation tools in HTML. CSS2 finally comes through, giving authors the ability to create arbitrary content, numbered lists, and all sorts of element-based content.

The foundation of the CSS2 generated-content model is the `content` and `quotes` properties, along with the `:before` and `:after` pseudoelements. You use the former to define the content you need, and use the latter to position that content with respect to the elements in your document.

8.4.11.1 The :before and :after pseudoelements

We introduced you to pseudoelements earlier in this chapter, and you even saw some in action (refer to Figures 8-2 and 8-3). The `:before` and `:after` pseudoelements operate similarly. Append either to a style-element selector to select and specify the content and properties of generated content in your document. In general, any content created within these pseudoelements inherits the display attributes of the parent element, such that fonts, sizes, and colors applied to an element are also applied to its generated content. For example:

```
p.note { color : blue }
p.note:before { content : "Note: " }
```

This style example inserts the word *Note:* before every `<p class=note>` element. The inserted text is rendered in blue, like the rest of the paragraph. Replacing it with this style would color the inserted text red, and the remainder of the note would be blue:

```
p.note:before {content : "Note: "; color : red}
```

Any generated content, before or after an element, is included in the box of an element and affects its formatting, flow, size, and layout.

8.4.11.2 The content property

The content property accepts a wide variety of values, ranging from simple strings to automatic counter references. You can include any number of these values, separated by spaces, in a single content property. The browser concatenates the values to form a single value that it then inserts into the document.

The simplest of content values is a quote-enclosed string. You may not include HTML or XHTML markup in the string. Rather, use escape sequences to generate special text (e.g., \A, which generates a line break).

CSS2 escape sequences are like HTML/XHTML character entities. Whereas character entities begin with the ampersand (&), followed by the name or decimal value of a character (# suffix for the latter), you create the same characters for CSS2 string-content property values by preceding the hexadecimal equivalent of the character with a backslash (\). The escape sequence \A is the same as the character entity &#010, which, if you consult Appendix F, you'll find is the line-feed character.

The content property also accepts URL values. Expressed in styles, not HTML-like fashion, the URL may point to any object acceptable to the browser, including text, images, and sound files. For example, to place a decorative symbol next to each equation in a document, you might use:

```
p.equation:before { content : url("http://www.kumquat.com/decorative-symbol.jpg") }
```

Keep in mind that the object shouldn't contain HTML/XHTML markup because the browser inserts its contents verbatim into the document.

The content property also supports automatic generation of contextually correct, locale-specific quotation marks. You insert them using the open-quote and close-quote keywords. These keywords insert the appropriate quotation mark and increment or decrement, respectively, the browser's nested quotation counter. You can control the appearance of the quotation marks using the quotes property, described shortly. You may also use the no-open-quote and no-close-quote keywords, which increment or decrement the nesting depth without inserting a quotation mark.

A clever feature of the content property is its ability to have the browser render the value of any attribute of its associated element. The attr value has a single parameter, corresponding to the name of an attribute. If that attribute is defined for the element, its value is inserted into the document. To display the URL of an image after the image, for instance, you might write:

```
img:after { content : "("attr(src) ") " }
```

If the attribute is not defined for the element, no content gets inserted, although the other values for the content property (like the parentheses we included in the earlier example) would still be inserted.

One of the most powerful features of the content property is its ability to create numbered lists. We cover this in detail in the upcoming section, 8.4.11.4.

All the popular browsers support the :before and :after pseudoelements, but Internet Explorer does not support the content property.

8.4.11.3 Specifying quotation marks

While you insert quotation marks using the open-quote and close-quote values with the content property, you control the actual characters used for quotation marks with the quotes property.

The value of this property is one or more pairs of strings. The first pair defines the open and close quotation marks for the outermost level of quotations in your document. The next pair specifies the next level, and so forth. If the quotation level exceeds the supplied pairs of characters, the browser starts over with the outermost pair. Note that while most languages use single characters as quotation marks, you can specify strings of any length to be used as quotation marks.

You may also want to specify alternative quotation marks based on the language used. You can use the :lang pseudoelement to associate different quotes properties with different languages. For example:

```
q:lang(en) { quotes : `"' `"' "`" "'" }
q:lang(no) { quotes : "&#171;" "&#187;" "<" ">" }
```

ensures that English and Norwegian documents use their respective quotation marks.

8.4.11.4 Creating counters

You can create simple numbered lists easily in HTML and XHTML with the <ol> element. More complex numbered lists, especially nested numbered lists, are impossible with the markup languages, though. Instead, CSS2 provides the notion of a counter whose value can be set and changed as the browser renders your document. Insert the value of the counter using special functions recognized by the content property, and alter the appearance and format of the counter with other CSS2 properties.

Every CSS2 counter has a name. To create a counter, simply mention its name in the counter-reset or counter-increment properties associated with any element. If an instance of that named counter does not already exist in the current document nesting level, the CSS2-conscious browser automatically creates it. Thereafter, set or reset the value of the counter as needed. For example, suppose we want to use <h1> elements as chapter headings, with <h2> elements as section headings. Both chapters and sections are numbered, with section headings being reset with each new chapter. You can achieve this with:

```
h1:before { counter-increment : chapter; counter-reset : section }
h2:before { counter-increment : section }
```

When the CSS2-conscious browser encounters the first <h1> element in the document, it creates both the chapter and section counters and resets their values to 0. At the same time, and for every encounter thereafter, the CSS2-conscious browser enacts the `counter-increment` property to set the chapter counter to 1, representing Chapter 1, then 2, and so on. As <h2> elements are encountered within a chapter, the `section` counter gets incremented according to the h2 style rule, numbering each section in order. Notice, too, that the `section` counter gets reset by the h1 rule so that the section counter restarts for each chapter.[*]

Both the `counter-reset` and `counter-increment` properties accept lists of counter names, letting you reset or increment groups of counters in one property. You can also supply a numeric value after a counter name so that with `counter-reset`, the counter gets initialized to that specified value, and `counter-increment` adds the value to the current counter value. Negative numbers are allowed, too, so that you may count down, if desired.

For example, if we want our document to begin with Chapter 7 and we want section numbers to increase by 2, we might rewrite the previous example as follows:

```
body { counter-reset : chapter 6 }
h1:before { counter-increment : chapter; counter-reset : section }
h2:before { counter-increment : section 2 }
```

Notice how we created the `chapter` counter in the earliest possible element in our document, using a value one less than the desired first value. When the browser encounters the first <h1> element, it creates, sets to 6, and then increments the chapter counter.

The scope of a counter name is the nesting level in which it is defined; it is not necessarily document-wide. If you use the same counter name in a child element, the browser creates a new instance of the counter at that level. In our example, all the <h1> and <h2> elements exist at the same nesting level, so one instance of the `chapter` and `section` counters serves that whole level. If you nested a <div> tag in that element, which in turn contained <h1> and <h2> elements, new instances of both counters would be created at that new level.

This nesting behavior is critical for nested numbered lists to work. If you associate a counter with the <li> element and then nest several ordered lists, each list level has its own instance of the counter, with separate number sequences at each level.

8.4.11.5 Using counters in your documents

Creating counters is of little use if you don't display their values in your documents. The display is not automatic. To show a counter, use the special `counter( )` and `counters( )` values in the content property.

---

[*] Note here that the browser doesn't display counters unless you explicitly tell it to. See "Using counters in your documents."

The counter( ) value requires the name of a counter inside its parentheses, with an optional format specification. The browser then displays the value of the specified counter within the generated content in the format desired. The format can be any list format accepted by the list-style-type property, as described earlier in section 8.4.8.3.

For example, to actually display the numbers of our numbered chapters and sections, we expand our style rules for the <h1> and <h2> elements:

```
h1:before { counter-increment : chapter;
    counter-reset : section;
    content : "Chapter " counter(chapter) ": " }
h2:before { counter-increment : section;
    content : "Section " counter(section) ": "}
```

Then, when the CSS2-conscious browser encounters this in the document:

```
<h1>Kumquat Growers</h1>
```

it renders it as shown in Figure 8-19. To number our chapters using Roman numerals, we would change the properties to:

```
h1:before { counter-increment : chapter;
    counter-reset : section;
    content : "Chapter " counter(chapter, upper-roman) ": " }
h2:before { counter-increment : section;
    content : "Section " counter(section, lower-roman) ": "}
```

The counter( ) value is the value of the counter at the current nesting level. To access all the values of the same-named counter at all nesting levels, use the plural counters( ) value instead. Include the counter name in the parentheses and a separator string. The browser puts the separator string between each list of values for the counter in the display. You may also supply a format type to switch from the default decimal numbering.

The counters( ) value is most useful when creating nested numbered lists. Consider these properties:

```
ol { counter-reset: item }
li:before { counter-increment: item ;
    content: counters(item, ".") }
```

If you nest several <ol> elements in your document, each <li> includes all the nested values, separated by periods. This should create the familiar numbering pattern[*] of 1, 1.1, 1.1.1, and so on, as the nesting increases, as we demonstrated much earlier in this chapter (refer to Figure 8-3).

Again, only the newcomers Firefox and Opera properly display styles-generated counters and content.

---

[*] Surely you've noticed it in this book!

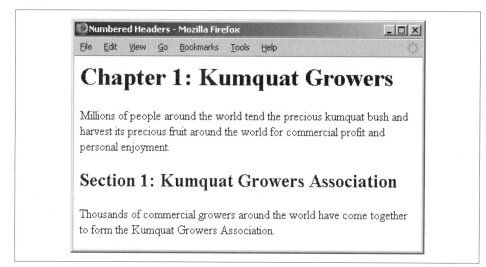

Figure 8-19. Use CSS2 counters to automatically number chapters and sections

8.4.11.6 Creating markers

According to the CSS2 standard, the browser should place styles-generated content before or after the conventional HTML/XHTML content of the affected element, and it should therefore become part of the element's flow. This is not acceptable for numbered lists, where the number should be displayed separate from the content of each numbered item. To do this, add the display property to your generated content, with the special value of marker. To make our nested numbered list example completely correct, for instance, we use the rules:

```
ul { counter-reset: item }
li:before { display : marker;
   counter-increment: item ;
   content: counters(item, ".") }
```

This way, the generated counter number gets rendered to the left of the element's actual content. In a similar fashion, you can place markers after an element. For example, use the following properties to create numbered equations within chapters (the <blockquote> element delineates the equation):

```
h1:before { counter-increment : chapter;
   counter-reset : equation }
blockquote:after { counter-increment : equation;
   display : marker;
   content : "("counter(chapter, upper-roman) "-" counter(equation) ")" }
```

When rendering a marker, the browser determines where to place the marker content in relation to the element's actual content. You modify this behavior with the marker-offset property. It accepts a numerical (length) value equal to the distance between the edge of the marker and the edge of the associated element. For example, to ensure that our equation numbers get shifted 0.5 inches away from the related equation, we could use:

```
h1:before { counter-increment : chapter;
    counter-reset : equation }
blockquote:after { counter-increment : equation;
    display : marker;
    content : "("counter(chapter, upper-roman) "-" counter(equation) ")";
    marker-offset : 0.5in }
```

8.4.12 Audio Properties

From its humble beginnings, HTML has been a visual medium for computer display devices. Although increasing attention has been paid to other media as the standard evolved, CSS2 is the first real effort to comprehensively address using HTML/XHTML documents for nonvisual media.

For example, CSS2 forecasts that someday some browsers will be able to speak the textual content of a document, using some sort of text-to-speech technology. Such a browser would be of enormous help for the visually impaired and would also allow web browsing via the phone and other devices where a visual display is not readily available or usable. Imagine the excitement of driving down the road while your favorite web pages are read to you!*

CSS2 attempts to standardize these alternative renderings by defining a number of properties that control the aural experience of a web listener. None of them is currently supported in any popular browser, but we envision a time in the near future when you may be able to take advantage of some or all of these properties.

8.4.12.1 The volume property

The most basic aural property is volume. It accepts numeric length or percentage values along with a few keywords corresponding to preset volume levels.

Numeric values range from 0 to 100, with 0 corresponding·to the minimum audible level and 100 being the maximum comfortable level. Note that 0 is not the same as silent, as the minimum audible level in an environment with loud background noise (like a factory floor) may be quite high.

Percentage values compute an element's volume as a percentage of the containing element's volume. Computed values less than 0 are set to 0; values greater than 100 are set to 100. Thus, to make an element twice as loud as its parent element, set the volume property to 200%. If the volume of the parent element is 75, the child element's volume gets set to the limit of 100.

---

* Conversely, imagine the annoyance of someone having web pages read to them while you try to enjoy a quiet meal or watch a movie. We are constantly reminded that every advance in technology has a dark side.

You also may specify a keyword value for the volume property. Here, silent actually turns the sound off. The x-soft value corresponds to a value of 0; soft is the same as the numeric volume of 25; medium is 50, loud is 75, and x-loud corresponds to 100.

8.4.12.2 Speaking properties

Three properties control whether and how text is converted to speech. The first is speak, which turns speech on and off. By default, the value of speak is normal, meaning that text is converted to speech using standard, locale-specific rules for pronunciation, grammar, and inflection. If you set speak to none, speech is turned off. You might use this feature to suppress speaking of secondary content or content that does not readily translate to audio, such as a table.

Finally, you can set the speak property to spell-out, which spells out each word. This is useful for acronyms and abbreviations. For example, using:

```
acronym { speak : spell-out }
```

ensures that acronyms such as URL get translated aurally as "you-are-ell" and not as "earl."

By default, the speak-punctuation property is set to none, causing punctuation to be expressed as pauses and inflection in the generated speech. If you give this property the code value, punctuation is spoken literally. This might be useful for aurally reproducing programming code fragments or literal transcriptions of some content.*

The speak-numeral property defaults to the value continuous, meaning that numerals are pronounced as a single number. Accordingly, the number "1234" would be reproduced as "one thousand two hundred thirty-four." When set to digits, the numbers are pronounced digit by digit, such as "one, two, three, four."

8.4.12.3 Voice characteristics

To create a richer listening experience, CSS2 defines a number of properties that alter the spoken content. This lets you use different voices for different content, speed up the speech, and change the pitch and stress levels in the speech.

The speech-rate property accepts a numeric length value that defines the number of words spoken per minute. The default value is locale dependent because different cultures have different notions of a "normal" rate of speech. Instead of a specific value, you may use any of the keywords x-slow, slow, medium, fast, and x-fast, corresponding to 80, 120, 180, 300, and 500 words per minute, respectively. The faster keyword sets the rate to 40 words per minute faster than the containing element, and slower sets the rate to 40 words per minute slower than the containing element.

---

* Regrettably, there is no victor-borge mode for this property. Perhaps CSS3 will address this egregious oversight.

The voice-family property is the aural analog of the font-family property. A voice family defines a style and type of speech. Such definitions are browser and platform specific, much like fonts. It is assumed that browsers will define generic voice families, such as "male," "female," and "child," and may also offer specific voice families like "television announcer" or "book author." The value of the voice-family property is a comma-separated list of these voice family names; the browser goes down the list until it finds a voice family that it can use to speak the element's text.

The pitch property controls the average pitch, with units in hertz (hz), of the spoken content. The basic pitch of a voice is defined by the voice family. Altering the pitch lets you create a variation of the basic voice, much like changing the point size of a font. For example, with a change in pitch, the "book author" might be made to sound like a chipmunk.*

You can set the pitch property to a numeric value such as 120hz or 210hz (the average pitches of typical male and female voices) or to one of the keywords x-low, low, medium, high, or x-high. Unlike other speech property keywords, these do not correspond to specific pitch frequencies but instead depend on the base pitch of the voice family. The only requirement is that these keywords correspond to increasingly lower or higher pitches.

While the pitch property sets the average pitch, the pitch-range property defines how far the pitch can change as the browser reproduces text aurally. The value of this property is a numeric value ranging from 0 to 100, with a default value of 50. Setting the pitch-range to 0 produces a flat, monotonic voice; values over 50 produce increasingly animated and excited-sounding voices.

The stress property controls the amount of inflection that is placed on elements in the spoken text. Various languages have differing rules for stressing syllables and adding inflection based on grammar and pronunciation rules. The stress property accepts a value in the range of 0 to 100, with the default value of 50 corresponding to "normal" stress. Using a value of 0 eliminates inflection in the spoken content. Values over 50 increasingly exaggerate the inflection of certain spoken elements.

The richness property controls the quality or fullness of the voice. A richer voice tends to fill a room and carries farther than a less rich, or smoother, voice. Like pitch and stress, the richness property accepts a numeric value in the range of 0 to 100, with a default value of 50. Values approaching 0 make the voice softer. Values over 50 make the voice fuller and more booming.

---

* Assuming, of course, that she doesn't already sound like a chipmunk.

8.4.12.4 Pause properties

Like whitespace in a printed document, insert pauses in spoken content to offset and thereby draw attention to content as well as to create a better-paced, more understandable spoken presentation.

The pause-before and pause-after properties generate pauses just before or just after an element's spoken content. These properties accept either an absolute time value (using the s or ms unit) or a percentage value. With a percentage value, the pause is relative to the length of time required to speak a single word. For example, if the speech rate is 120 words per minute, one word, on average, is spoken every 0.5 seconds. A pause of 100 percent, therefore, would be 0.5 seconds long; a 20 percent pause would be 0.1 seconds long, and so on.

The pause property sets both the pause-before and pause-after properties at once. Use one value for pause to set both properties; the first of two values sets pause-before, and the second sets the pause-after property value.

8.4.12.5 Cue properties

Cue properties let you insert audible cues before or after an element. For example, you might precede each chapter in a book with a musical cue, or denote the end of quoted text with an audible tone.

The cue-before and cue-after properties take as their value the URL of a sound file, which the browser loads and plays before or after the styled document element, respectively. Technically, the sound can be of any duration, but the presumption is that audible cues are short and nonintrusive, enhancing the audio experience instead of overwhelming it.

Use the cue property to set both the cue-before and cue-after properties at once. If you provide one URL value, it sets both cue sounds; with two values, the first sets the cue-before sound and the second sets the cue-after sound.

8.4.12.6 Audio mixing

To create a more pleasant listening experience, you may want to play background music during a spoken passage. The play-during property meets this need. Its values are the URL of the sound file and several keywords that control playback.

The repeat keyword repeats the background audio until the spoken content is complete. If you don't use this keyword, the background sound plays once, even if it is shorter than the spoken content. A background sound that is longer than the spoken content ends when the content ends.

The mix keyword tells the CSS2-conscious browser to meld the background sound with any other background sounds that may be playing as defined by some parent element.

If you don't use this keyword, child-element background sounds replace parent-element background sounds, which resume when the current element has finished.

In lieu of a URL representing the background sound, you can use the value none. This lets you silence all background sounds, such as one or more playing from parent elements, while the current element is being spoken.

8.4.12.7 Spatial positioning

While a rendered document exists on a two-dimensional page, spoken content can be placed anywhere in the three-dimensional space surrounding the listener. The CSS2 standard defines the azimuth and elevation properties so that you can place spoken content from elements in different places around the listener. azimuth relates to where and elevation tells how far above or below the sound appears to the listener.

The azimuth property accepts either an angle value or keywords indicating a position around the listener. The position directly in front of the listener is defined to be 0 degrees. The listener's right is at 90 degrees, and directly behind is 180 degrees. The listener's left is at 270 degrees or, equivalently, –90 degrees.

Position keywords include a base position, possibly modified by the behind keyword. These keywords correspond to the angular positions listed in Table 8-2.

Table 8-2. Angular equivalents for azimuth keywords

Keyword	Angular position	Angular position when used with behind
left-side	270	270
far-left	300	240
left	320	220
center-left	340	200
center	0	180
center-right	20	160
right	40	140
far-right	60	120
right-side	90	90

The leftwards keyword subtracts 20 degrees from the parent element's azimuth. Similarly, rightwards adds 20 degrees to the parent element's azimuth. Note that this process can continue until you work your way around the listener; these values add or subtract 20 degrees no matter what the azimuth of the parent is.

The elevation property accepts an angular value ranging from –90 degrees to 90 degrees, corresponding to from directly below the listener to directly above the listener. Zero degrees is considered to be level with the listener's ears. You can also use the below, level, and above keywords for –90, 0, and 90 degrees, respectively.

Use the `higher` keyword to increase the elevation by 10 degrees over the parent element's `elevation`; `lower` changes the elevation of the sound to 10 degrees below the parent element's `elevation`.

8.4.13 Paged Media

Printing has never been HTML's strong suit. In fact, the HTML and XHTML standards have intentionally ignored printing because printing assumes page layout, and HTML and XHTML are not layout tools.

Authors use cascading stylesheets to format and lay out their HTML/XHTML document contents, so it is not surprising that the CSS2 standard introduces some basic pagination control features that let authors help the browser figure out how to best print their documents. These features fall into two groups: those that define a particular page layout and those that control the pagination of a document.

8.4.13.1 Defining pages

As an extension to the box model, CSS2 defines a *page box*, a box of finite dimensions in which content is rendered. The page box does not necessarily correspond to a physical sheet of paper; the user agent maps one or more page boxes to sheets of paper during the printing process. Many small page boxes may fit on a single sheet; large page boxes may be scaled to fit on a sheet or may be broken across several sheets at the discretion of the browser.

During the printing process, content flows into the page box, is paginated appropriately, and is transferred to a target sheet on a hard-copy output device. The dimensions of the page box may differ from the browser's display window, so the flow and rendering of a printed document may be completely different from its onscreen representation. As always, obtaining a specific rendered appearance for your documents is generally impossible. However, you can use the CSS2 pagination features to help the browser print your document in an attractive, useful manner.

You define a page box using the special `@page` at-rule. Immediately following the `@page` keyword is an optional name for the page, followed by a list of properties separated by semicolons and enclosed in curly braces. These properties define the size, margins, and appearance of the page box.

Use the `size` property to specify the size of the page box. The value of this property is either one or two length values, or one of the special keywords `portrait`, `landscape`, or `auto`. If you provide a single length value, it creates a square, setting both the width and the height of the page to that value. Two length values set the width and the height of the page, respectively. The `portrait` keyword specifies the locally accepted page size that is taller than it is wide (typically 8×11), and `landscape` uses a locally accepted page size that is wider than it is tall (typically 11×8 inches). Finally, auto creates a page box that is the same size as the target sheet of paper on which the document is printed.

In general, you should use the special page size keywords to ensure that your document prints well in the local environment. Using:

```
@page normal { size : 8.5in 11in }
```

works fine in the U.S. but may fail in European locales. Instead, use:

```
@page normal { size : portrait }
```

which should select an 8.5"×11" page in the U.S. and an A4 sheet in Europe.[*]

Use the margin, margin-top, margin-bottom, margin-left, and margin-right properties within the @page at-rule to set margins for your page. Keep in mind that the browser may define margins for rendering the page box within the target sheet, so your margins are in addition to those margins. The default margins for the page box are not defined and are browser dependent.

Finally, the marks property is used within the @page at-rule to create crop and registration marks outside the page box on the target sheet. By default, no marks are printed. You may use one or both of the crop and cross keywords to create crop marks and registration marks, respectively, on the target print page.

8.4.13.2 Left, right, and first pages

In many printing applications, authors want different page layouts for the first page of their document as well as differing formats for right and left pages in double-sided documents. CSS2 accommodates all of these cases using three pseudoclasses attached to the name of a page.

The :first pseudoclass applies the page format to the first page in a document. Page-layout attributes specified in the :first page override corresponding attributes in the general page layout. You can use the :first pseudoclass in conjunction with a named page layout; the appropriate first-page layout is applied if the first page of the document is rendered using the named page.

In a similar fashion, the :left and :right pseudoclasses define left and right page layouts for your document. Again, named pages can have left and right variations. The browser automatically applies appropriate left and right layouts to every page in the document, if such layouts exist.

You need not specify named pages to use any of these pseudoclasses. Indeed, most documents do not do so. For example, if you use these settings:

```
@page :first { margin-top : 3in }
@page :left { margin-left : 2in; margin-right : 1in }
@page :right { margin-left : 1in; margin-right : 2in }
```

---

[*] The word *normal* in the rule is the page name, of course.

without further intervention, the first page of your document will have a 3-inch top margin (and an appropriate right and left margin, depending on how your locale defines whether the first page of a document is on the right or the left). Subsequent pages will alternate between wide and narrow inner and outer margins.

8.4.13.3 Using named pages

Once you create a named page layout, you can use it in your document by adding the page property to a style that is later applied to an element in your document. If an element has a page layout that is different from that of the preceding or containing element, a page break is inserted into the document, and formatting resumes using the new page layout. When the scope of the element ends, the page layout reverts to the previous layout, with appropriate page breaks as needed.

For example, this style renders all the tables in your document on landscape pages:

```
@page { size : portrait }
@page rotated { size : landscape }
table { page : rotated }
```

While printing, if the browser encounters a <table> element in your document and the current page layout is the default portrait layout, it starts a new page and prints the table on a landscape page. If nontabular content follows the table, the browser inserts another page break, and the flow resumes on the default portrait-size page. Several tables in a row would be rendered on a single landscape sheet, if they all fit.

8.4.13.4 Controlling pagination

Unless you specify otherwise, page breaks occur only when the page format changes or when the content overflows the current page box. To otherwise force or suppress page breaks, use the page-break-before, page-break-after, and page-break-inside properties.

Both the page-break-before and page-break-after properties accept the auto, always, avoid, left, and right keywords. auto is the default; it lets the browser generate page breaks as needed. The keyword always forces a page break before or after the element, and avoid suppresses a page break immediately before or after the element. The left and right keywords force one or two page breaks so that the element is rendered on a lefthand or righthand page.

Using pagination properties is straightforward. Suppose your document has level-1 headers start new chapters, with sections denoted by level-2 headers. You'd like each chapter to start on a new, righthand page, but you don't want section headers to be split across a page break from the subsequent content. Accordingly, you might write your CSS2 print rule as follows:

```
h1 { page-break-before : right }
h2 { page-break-after : avoid }
```

Use only the auto and avoid values with the page-break-inside property. auto allows page breaks within the element (the default behavior), and avoid suppresses them. Even so, elements that are larger than the printed page get broken up; that is why the keyword is avoid and not prevent.

If you prefer that your tables not be broken across pages if possible, you would write the following rule:

```
table { page-break-inside : avoid }
```

8.4.13.5 Controlling widows and orphans

In typographic lingo, *orphans* are those lines of a paragraph stranded at the bottom of a page due to a page break, and *widows* are those lines remaining at the top of a page following a page break. Generally, printed pages do not look attractive with single lines of text stranded at the top or bottom. Most printers try to leave at least two or more lines of text at the top or bottom of each page.

If you want to take control of this behavior, you can apply the widows and orphans properties to an element. The value of each property is the minimum number of lines of text that can be left at the top or bottom of the page, respectively. The default is 2, meaning that the browser generates page breaks as needed to ensure that at least two lines of text from the element appear at the top or bottom of each page. You generally want to apply this property to all of the elements in your document, to ensure consistent pagination throughout.

8.5 Tagless Styles: The <span> Tag

Up to now, we have used cascading stylesheets to change the appearance of content within a designated tag. In some cases, however, you may want to alter the appearance of only a portion of a tag's contents—usually text. Designate these special segments with the <span> tag.

<span>	
Function	Delimits an arbitrary amount of text
Attributes	class, dir, id, lang, onClick, onDblClick, onKeyDown, onKeyPress, onKeyUp, onMouseDown, onMouseMove, onMouseOut, onMouseOver, onMouseUp, style, title
End tag	</span>; never omitted
Contains	*html_content*
Used in	*body_content*

The <span> tag simply delimits a portion of content (constrained by normal tag-nesting rules, of course). Browsers treat the <span> tag as another physical or content-based style tag—the only difference is that the default meaning of the <span> tag is to leave the text alone.

The <span> tag became part of HTML so that you could apply style, display, and event management to an arbitrary section of document content. Define a style for the <span> tag as you would any other HTML or XHTML tag:

```
span {color: purple}
span.bigger {font-size: larger}
```

and use it like any other HTML or XHTML tag:

```
Quat harvest projections are <span class=bigger>bigger than ever</span>!
```

Similarly, apply an inline style to the <span> tag to modify the appearance of its contents:

```
Quat harvest projections are <span style="font-size: larger">bigger than ever</span>!
```

Like any other physical or content-based style tag, <span> tags can be nested and may contain other tags.

The <span> tag also supports the many common tag attributes. The style and class attributes, of course, let you control the display style; the id and title tag attributes let you uniquely label its contents; the dir and lang attributes let you specify its native language; and the many on-event attributes let you react to user-initiated mouse and keyboard actions on the contents. Not all are implemented by the currently popular browsers for this tag or for many others. [The dir attribute, 3.6.1.1] [The lang attribute, 3.6.1.2] [The id attribute, 4.1.1.4] [The title attribute, 4.1.1.5] [Inline Styles: The style Attribute, 8.1.1] [Style Classes, 8.3] [JavaScript Event Handlers, 12.3.3]

8.6 Applying Styles to Documents

You should consider several issues before, during, and after you use styles in your web documents and document collections. The first, overarching issue is whether to use them at all. Frankly, few of the style effects are unique; you can achieve most of them, albeit less easily and with much less consistency, via the physical and content-based style tags (e.g., <i> and <em>) and the various tag attributes (e.g., color and background).

8.6.1 To Style or Not to Style

We think the CSS2 standard is a winner, not only over JavaScript-based standards but also for the convenience and effectiveness of all of your markup documents, including HTML, XHTML, and most other XML-compliant ones. Most browsers in use today support CSS1 and many of the features of CSS2. The benefits are clear. So, why wouldn't you use styles?

Although we strongly urge you to learn and use CSS2 stylesheets for your documents, we realize that creating stylesheets is an investment of time and energy that pays off only in the long run. Designing a stylesheet for a one- or two-page document is probably not time effective, particularly if you won't be reusing the stylesheet for any other documents. In general, however, we believe the choice is not *if* you should use CSS2 stylesheets, but *when*.

8.6.2 Which Type of Stylesheet, and When

Once you have decided to use cascading stylesheets (for pain or pleasure), the next question is which type of stylesheet—inline, document level, or external—you should apply, and when. Each has its pros and cons; each is best applied under certain circumstances.

8.6.2.1 The pros and cons of external styles

Because stylesheets provide consistency in the presentation of your documents, external stylesheets are the best and easiest way to manage styles for your entire document collection. Simply place the desired style rules in a stylesheet, and apply those styles to the desired documents. Because all of the documents are affected by a single stylesheet, conversion of the entire collection to a new style is as simple as changing a single rule in the corresponding external stylesheet.

Even in cases where documents may differ in style, it is often possible to collect a few basic style rules in a single sheet that can be shared among several otherwise different documents, including:

- Background color
- Background image
- Font sizes and faces
- Margins
- Text alignment

Another benefit of external stylesheets is that other web authors who want to copy your style can easily access that sheet and make their pages look like yours. Imitation being the sincerest form of flattery, you should not be troubled when someone elects to emulate the look and feel of your pages. More to the point, you can't stop them from linking to your stylesheets, so you might as well learn to like it. Like conventional HTML documents, it is not possible to encrypt or otherwise hide your stylesheets so that others cannot view and use them.

The biggest problem with external stylesheets is that they may increase the amount of time needed to access a given web page. Not only must the browser download the page itself, but it must also download the stylesheet before the page can be displayed to the user. While most stylesheets are relatively small, their existence can definitely be felt when accessing the Web over a slow connection.

Without appropriate discipline, external stylesheets can become large and unwieldy. When creating stylesheets, include only those styles that are common to the pages using the sheet. If a set of styles is needed for only one or two pages, you are better off isolating them in a separate sheet or adding them to those documents using document-level styles. Otherwise, you may find yourself expending an exorbitant amount of effort counteracting the effects of external styles in many individual documents.

8.6.2.2 The pros and cons of document-level styles

Document-level styles are most useful when creating custom documents. They let you override one or more rules in your externally defined style to create a slightly different document.

You might also want to use document-level styles to experiment with new style rules before moving them to your stylesheets. By adding and changing rules using document-level styles, you eliminate the risk of adding a broken style to your stylesheets, breaking the appearance of all the documents that use that sheet.

The biggest problem with document styles is that you may succumb to using them in lieu of creating a formal, external stylesheet to manage your document collection. It is easy to simply add rules to each document, cutting and pasting as you create new documents. Unfortunately, managing a collection of documents with document-level styles is tedious and error-prone. Even a simple change can result in hours of editing and potential mistakes.

As a rule of thumb, any style rule that impacts three or more documents should be moved to a stylesheet and applied to those documents using the <link> tag or @import at-rule. Adhering to this rule as you create your document families pays off in the long run when it is time to change your styles.

8.6.2.3 The pros and cons of inline styles

At the end of the cascade, inline styles override the more general styles. Get into the habit now of using inline styles rarely and just for that purpose. You cannot reuse inline styles, making style management difficult. Moreover, such changes are spread throughout your documents, making finding and altering inline styles error-prone. (That's why we might eschew tag- and attribute-based styles in the first place, no?)

Anytime you use an inline style, think long and hard about whether you might accomplish the same effect using a style class definition. For instance, you are better off defining:

```
<style type="text/css">
<!--
  p.centered {text-align: center}
  em.blue {color: blue}
-->
</style>
```

and later using:

```
<p class=centered>
<em class=blue>
```

rather than:

```
<p style="text-align: center">
<em style="color: blue">
```

Your styles are easier to find and manage and can easily be reused throughout your documents.

CHAPTER 9

Forms

Forms, forms, forms, forms: we fill 'em out for nearly everything, from the moment we're born, 'til the moment we die. Pretty mundane, really. So what's to explain all the hoopla and excitement over HTML forms? Simply this: they make HTML and, of course, XHTML truly interactive.

When you think about it, interacting with a web page is basically a lot of button pushing: click here, click there, go here, go there—there's no real interactivity, and it's certainly not personalized. Programs such as applets, servlets, JSPs, and ASPs provide extensive user-interaction capability but can be difficult to write. Forms, on the other hand, are easily made in HTML/XHTML and make it possible to create documents that collect and process user input and to formulate personalized replies.

This powerful mechanism has far-reaching implications, particularly for electronic commerce. It finishes an online catalog by giving buyers a way to immediately order products and services. It gives nonprofit organizations a way to sign up new members. It lets market researchers collect user data. It gives you an automated way to interact with your readers.

Mull over the ways you might want to interact with your readers while we take a look at both the client- and server-side details of creating forms.

9.1 Form Fundamentals

Forms are composed of one or more text-input boxes, clickable buttons, multiple-choice checkboxes, and even pull-down menus and image maps, all placed inside the

<form> tag. You can have more than one form in a document, and within each one you also may put regular body content, including text and images. The text is particularly useful for providing form element labels, prompts, and instructions to the users on how to fill out the form. And, within the various form elements, you can use JavaScript event handlers for a variety of effects, such as testing and verifying form contents and calculating a running sum.

A user fills out the various fields in the form, then clicks a special Submit button (or, sometimes, presses the Enter key) to submit the form to a server. The browser packages up the user-supplied values and choices and sends them to a server or to an email address.* The server passes the information along to a supporting program or application that processes the information and creates a reply, usually in HTML. The reply simply may be a thank you, or it might prompt the user on how to fill out the form correctly or to supply missing fields. The server sends the reply to the browser client, which then presents it to the user. With emailed forms, the information is simply put into someone's mailbox; there is no notification of the form being sent.

The server-side, data-processing aspects of forms are not part of the HTML or XHTML standard; they are defined by the server's software. While a complete discussion of server-side forms programming is beyond the scope of this book, we'd be remiss if we did not include at least a simple example to get you started. To that purpose, we've included at the end of this chapter a few skeletal programs that illustrate some of the common styles of server-side forms programming.

A final caveat: as is its wont, the World Wide Web Consortium (W3C) has been working on an XML-based definition of forms. This new version of forms, known as XForms, is currently a "working document," subject to review and changes as needed. XForms differs from the conventional forms model in almost every way: the forms are defined differently, data is validated differently, and information is transmitted to the server differently. As you might imagine, XForms is not currently supported by any browser or server, although a preliminary version of XForms is available for testing as part of the Mozilla XForms Project. Given its lack of general support, dramatic differences from the current model, and the long odds that XForms will replace the millions of forms already in use, it would be premature to address it in any detail in this chapter. Instead, we'll cover the forms as defined in HTML and XHTML, and leave you with a warning that a new forms model may be coming at some point in the future.

---

* The popular browsers may also encrypt the information, securing it from credit card thieves, for example. However, the encryption facility must be supported on the server as well: consult the web server documentation for details.

9.2 The <form> Tag

Place a form anywhere inside the body of a document, with its elements enclosed by the <form> tag and its respective end tag (</form>). You can, and we recommend you often do, include regular body content inside a form to specially label user-input fields and to provide directions.

<form>

Function	Defines a form
Attributes	accept, action, charset, class, dir, enctype, id, lang, method, name, onClick, onDblClick, onKeyDown, onKeyPress, onKeyUp, onMouseDown, onMouseMove, onMouseOut, onMouseOver, onMouseUp, onReset, onSubmit, style, target, title
End tag	</form>; never omitted
Contains	*form_content*
Used in	*block*

Browsers flow the special form elements into the containing paragraphs as though they were small images embedded into the text. There aren't any special layout rules for form elements, so you need to use other elements, such as tables and stylesheets, to control the placement of elements within the text flow.

You must define at least two special form attributes, which provide the name of the form's processing server and the method by which the parameters are to be sent to the server. A third, optional attribute lets you change how the parameters get encoded for secure transmission over the network.

9.2.1 The action Attribute

The required action attribute for the <form> tag gives the URL of the application that is to receive and process the form's data. Most webmasters keep their forms-processing applications in a special directory on their web server, usually named *cgi-bin*, which stands for Common Gateway Interface-binaries.* Keeping these special forms-processing programs and applications in one directory makes it easier to manage and secure the server.

---

* The Common Gateway Interface (CGI) defines the protocol by which servers interact with programs that process form data.

A typical `<form>` tag with the action attribute looks like this:

```
<form action="http://www.kumquat.com/cgi-bin/update">
...
</form>
```

The example URL tells the browser to contact the web server named www in the kumquat.com domain and pass along the user's form values to the application named update located in the *cgi-bin* directory.

In general, if you see a URL that references a document in a directory named *cgi-bin*, you can be pretty sure that the document is actually an application that dynamically creates the desired page each time it's invoked.

9.2.2 The enctype Attribute

The browser specially encodes the form's data before passing that data to the server so that it does not become scrambled or corrupted during the transmission. It is up to the server to either decode the parameters or pass them, still encoded, to the application.

The standard encoding format is the Internet Media Type application/x-www-form-urlencoded. You can change that encoding with the optional enctype attribute in the `<form>` tag. The only optional encoding formats currently supported are multipart/form-data and text/plain.

The multipart/form-data alternative is required for those forms that contain file-selection fields for upload by the user. You should use the text/plain format in conjunction with a mailto URL in the action attribute for sending forms to an email address rather than a server. Unless your forms need file-selection fields or you must use a mailto URL in the action attribute, you probably should ignore this attribute and simply rely upon the browser and your processing server to use the default encoding type. [File-selection controls, 9.5.1.3]

9.2.2.1 The application/x-www-form-urlencoded encoding

The standard encoding—application/x-www-form-urlencoded—converts any spaces in the form values into a plus sign (+), nonalphanumeric characters into a percent sign (%) followed by two hexadecimal digits that are the ASCII code of the character, and the line breaks in multiline form data into %0D%0A.

The standard encoding also includes a name for each field in the form. (A *field* is a discrete element in the form, whose value can be nearly anything from a single number to several lines of text—the user's address, for example.) If there is more than one value in the field, the values are separated by ampersands.

For example, here's what the browser sends to the server after the user fills out a form with two input fields labeled name and address; the former field has just one line of text, and the latter field has several lines of input:

```
name=O'Reilly+Media&address=1005+Gravenstein+Highway+North%0D%0A
Sebastopol,%0D%0ACA+95472
```

We've broken the value into two lines here for clarity, but in reality, the browser sends the data in an unbroken string. The name field is O'Reilly Media, and the value of the address field, complete with embedded newline characters, is:

```
1005 Gravenstein Highway North
Sebastopol,
CA 95472
```

9.2.2.2 The multipart/form-data encoding

The multipart/form-data encoding encapsulates the fields in the form as several parts of a single Multipurpose Internet Mail Extension (MIME)-compatible compound document. Each field has its own section in the resulting file, set off by a standard delimiter. Within each section, one or more header lines define the name of the field, followed by one or more lines containing the value of the field. Because the value part of each section can contain binary data or otherwise unprintable characters, no character conversion or encoding occurs within the transmitted data.

This encoding format is by nature more verbose and longer than the application/x-www-form-urlencoded format. As such, you can use it only when the method attribute of the <form> tag is set to post, as described in section 9.2.4, later in this chapter. A simple example makes it easy to understand this format. Here's our previous example, when transmitted as multipart/form-data:

```
-----------------------------146931364513459
Content-Disposition: form-data; name="name"

O'Reilly Media
-----------------------------146931364513459
Content-Disposition: form-data; name="address"

1005 Gravenstein Highway North
Sebastopol,
CA 95472
-----------------------------146931364513459--
```

The first line of the transmission defines the delimiter that appears before each section of the document. It always consists of 30 dashes and a long random number that distinguishes it from other text that might appear in actual field values.

The next lines contain the header fields for the first section. There is always a Content-Disposition field indicating that the section contains form data and providing the name of the form element whose value is in this section. You may see other header fields; in particular, some file-selection fields include a Content-Type header field that indicates the type of data contained in the file being transmitted.

After the headers, there is a single blank line followed by the actual value of the field on one or more lines. The section concludes with a repeat of the delimiter line that started the transmission. Another section follows immediately, and the pattern repeats until all of the form parameters have been transmitted. The end of the transmission is indicated by an extra two dashes at the end of the last delimiter line.

As we pointed out earlier, use multipart/form-data encoding only when your form contains a file-selection field. Here's an example of how the transmission of a file-selection field might look:

```
----------------------------146931364513459
Content-Disposition: form-data; name="thefile"; filename="test"
Content-Type: text/plain

First line of the file
...
Last line of the file
----------------------------146931364513459--
```

The only notable difference is that the Content-Disposition field contains an extra element, filename, which defines the name of the file being transmitted. There might also be a Content-Type field to further describe the file's contents.

9.2.2.3 The text/plain encoding

Use this encoding only when you don't have access to a forms-processing server and need to send the form information by email (the form's action attribute must be a mailto URL). The conventional encodings are designed for computer consumption; text/plain is designed with people in mind.

In this encoding, each element in the form is placed on a single line, with the name and value separated by an equals sign. Returning to our name and address example, the form data would be returned as:

```
name=O'Reilly Media
address=1005 Gravenstein Highway North%0D%0ASebastopol,%0D%0ACA 95472
```

As you can see, the only characters still encoded in this form are the carriage-return and line-feed characters in multiline text-input areas. Otherwise, the result is easily readable and generally parsable by simple tools.

9.2.3 The accept-charset Attribute

The accept-charset attribute was introduced in the HTML 4.0 standard. It lets you specify a list of character sets that the server must support to properly interpret the form data. The value of this attribute is a quote-enclosed list of one or more International Organization for Standardization (ISO) character set names. The browser may choose to disregard the form or handle it differently if the acceptable character sets do not match the character set the user is using. The default value of this attribute is unknown, implying that the form's character set is the same as that of the document containing the form.

9.2.4 The method Attribute

This attribute for the <form> tag sets the method by which the browser sends the form's data to the server for processing. There are two ways: the POST method and the GET method. If method is not specified, GET is used.

With the POST method, the browser sends the data in two steps: the browser first contacts the forms-processing server specified in the action attribute and then, once contact is made, sends the data to the server in a separate transmission.

On the server side, POST-style applications are expected to read the parameters from a standard location once they begin execution. Once read, the parameters must be decoded before the application can use the form values. Your particular server defines exactly how your POST-style applications can expect to receive their parameters.

The GET method, on the other hand, contacts the forms-processing server and sends the form data in a single transmission step: the browser appends the data to the form's action URL, separated by the question mark character.

The common browsers transmit the form information by either method; some servers receive the form data by only one or the other method. You indicate which of the two methods—POST or GET—your forms-processing server handles with the method attribute in the <form> tag.

Here's the complete tag including the GET transmission method attribute for the previous form example:

```
<form method=GET
    action="http://www.kumquat.com/cgi-bin/update">
    ...
</form>
```

9.2.4.1 POST or GET?

Which one should you use if your forms-processing server supports both the POST and GET methods? Here are some rules of thumb:

- For best form-transmission performance, send small forms with a few short fields via the GET method.

- Because some server operating systems limit the number and length of command-line arguments that can be passed to an application at once, use the POST method to send forms that have many fields or that have long text fields.

- If you are inexperienced in writing server-side forms-processing applications, choose GET. The extra steps involved in reading and decoding POST-style transmitted parameters, while not too difficult, may be more than you are willing to tackle.

- If security is an issue, choose POST. GET places the form parameters directly in the application URL, where they easily can be captured by network sniffers or extracted from a server logfile. If the parameters contain sensitive information like credit card numbers, you may be compromising your users without their knowledge. While POST applications are not without their security holes, they can at least take advantage of encryption when transmitting the parameters as a separate transaction with the server.

- If you want to invoke the server-side application outside the realm of a form, including passing it parameters, use GET, because it lets you include form-like parameters as part of a URL. POST-style applications, on the other hand, expect an extra transmission from the browser after the URL—something you can't do as part of a conventional <a> tag.

9.2.4.2 Passing parameters explicitly

The foregoing bit of advice warrants some explanation. Suppose you had a simple form with two elements named x and y. The browser encodes them like this:

```
x=27&y=33
```

If method=GET, the browser also includes the server-side's processing application's URL as a prefix, like this:

```
http://www.kumquat.com/cgi-bin/update?x=27&y=33
```

There is nothing to keep you from creating a conventional <a> tag that invokes the form with any parameter value you desire, like so:

```
<a href="http://www.kumquat.com/cgi-bin/update?x=19&y=104">
```

The only hitch is that the ampersand that separates the parameters is also the character-entity insertion character. When placed within the href attribute of the <a> tag, the ampersand causes the browser to replace the characters following it with a corresponding character entity.

To keep this from happening, you must replace the literal ampersand with its entity equivalent, either & or & (see Appendix F). With this substitution, our example of the alternative form reference to the server-side application looks like this:

```
<a href="http://www.kumquat.com/cgi-bin/update?x=19&amp;y=104">
```

Because of the potential confusion that arises from having to escape the ampersands in the URL, server implementers are encouraged to also accept the semicolon as a parameter separator. You might want to check the documentation to see whether your server honors this convention.

9.2.5 The target Attribute

It is possible to redirect the results of a form to another window or frame. Simply add the target attribute to your <form> tag and provide the name of the window or frame to receive the results.

Like the target attribute used in conjunction with the <a> tag, you can use a number of special names with the target attribute in the <form> tag to create a new window or to replace the contents of existing windows and frames. [The target Attribute for the <a> Tag, 11.7.1]

9.2.6 The id, name, and title Attributes

The id attribute lets you attach a unique string label to your form for reference by programs (applets) and hyperlinks. Before id was introduced in HTML 4.0, Netscape used the name attribute to achieve similar effects, although it cannot be used in a hyperlink. To be compatible with the broadest range of browsers, we recommend that for now you include both name and id with <form>, if needed. In the future, you should use only the id attribute for this purpose.

The title attribute defines a quote-enclosed string value to label the form. However, it titles only the form segment; its value cannot be used in an applet reference or hyperlink. [The id attribute, 4.1.1.4] [The title attribute, 4.1.1.5]

9.2.7 The class, style, lang, and dir Attributes

The style attribute creates an inline style for the elements enclosed by the form, overriding any other style rules in effect. The class attribute lets you format the content according to a predefined class of the <form> tag; its value is the name of that class. [Inline Styles: The style Attribute, 8.1.1] [Style Classes, 8.3]

The actual effects of style with <form> are hard to predict, however. In general, style properties affect the body content—text, in particular—that you may include as part of the form's contents, but <form> styles do affect the display characteristics of the form elements.

For instance, you may create a special font face and background color style for the form. The form's text labels, but not the text inside a text-input form element, appear in the specified font face and background color. Similarly, the text labels you put beside a set of radio buttons appear in the form-specified style, but the radio buttons themselves do not.

The lang attribute lets you specify the language used within the form, with its value being any of the ISO standard two-character language abbreviations, including an optional language modifier. For example, adding lang=en-UK tells the browser that the list is in English ("en") as spoken and written in the United Kingdom ("UK"). Presumably, the browser may make layout or typographic decisions based upon your language choice.

Similarly, the dir attribute tells the browser in which direction to display the list contents—from left to right (dir=ltr), like English and French, or from right to left (dir=rtl), as with Hebrew and Chinese.

The popular browsers support the dir and lang attributes, even though no behaviors are defined for any specific language. [The dir attribute, 3.6.1.1] [The lang attribute, 3.6.1.2]

9.2.8 The Event Attributes

As for most other elements in a document, the <form> tag honors the standard mouse and keyboard event-related attributes the compliant browser will recognize. We describe the majority of these attributes in detail in Chapter 12. [JavaScript Event Handlers, 12.3.3]

Forms have two special event-related attributes: onSubmit and onReset. The value of each event attribute is—enclosed in quotation marks—one or a sequence of semicolon-separated JavaScript expressions, methods, and function references. With onSubmit, the browser executes these commands before it actually submits the form's data to the server or sends it to an email address.

You may use the onSubmit event for a variety of effects. The most popular is for a client-side forms-verification program that scans the form data and prompts the user to complete one or more missing elements. Another popular and much simpler use is to inform users when a mailto URL form is being processed via email.

The onReset attribute is used just like the onSubmit attribute, except that the associated program code is executed only if the user presses a Reset button in the form.

9.3 A Simple Form Example

In a moment, we'll examine each of the many form controls in detail. Let's first take a quick look at a simple example, to see how forms are put together. This HTML form (shown in Figure 9-1) gathers basic demographic information about a user:

```
<form method=POST action="http://www.kumquat.com/demo">
  Name:
    <input type=text name=name size=32 maxlength=80>
  <p>
  Sex:
    <input type=radio name=sex value="M"> Male
    <input type=radio name=sex value="F"> Female
  <p>
  Annual Income:
    <select name=income size=1>
      <option>Under $25,000
      <option>$25,001 to $50,000
      <option>$50,001 and higher
    </select>
  <p>
  <input type=submit>
</form>
```

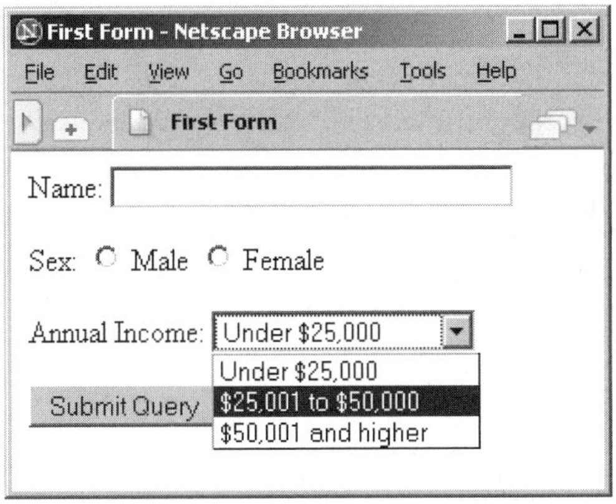

Figure 9-1. A simple form

The first line of the example starts the form and indicates we'll be using the POST method for data transmission. The form's user-input controls follow, each defined by an <input> tag and type attribute. There are three controls in the simple example, each contained within its own paragraph.

The first control is a conventional text-entry field, letting the user type up to 80 characters but displaying only 32 of them at a time. The next one is a multiple-choice option, which lets the user select only one of two radio buttons. This is followed by a pull-down menu for choosing one of three options. The final control is a simple submission button, which, when clicked by the user, sets the form's processing in motion.

9.4 Using Email to Collect Form Data

It is increasingly common to find authors who have no access to a web server other than to upload their documents. Consequently, they have no ability to create or manage CGI programs. In fact, some Internet service providers (ISPs), particularly those hosting space for hundreds or even thousands of sites, typically disable CGI services to limit their servers' processing load and as a security precaution.

If you are working with one of the many sites where you cannot get a form processed to save your life, all is not lost: you can use a mailto URL as the value of the form's action attribute. The latest browsers automatically email the various form parameters and values to the address supplied in the URL. The recipient of the mail can then process the form and take action accordingly.

By substituting the following for the <form> tag in our previous example:

```
<form method=POST action="mailto:chuckandbill@oreilly.com"
    enctype="text/plain"
    onSubmit="window.alert('This form is being sent by email, even
    though it may not appear that anything has happened...')">
```

the form data gets emailed to chuckandbill when submitted by the user, not other-wise processed by a server. Notice, too, that we have a simple JavaScript alert message that appears when the browser gets ready to send out the form data. The alert tells the user not to expect confirmation that the form data was sent (see Figure 9-2).

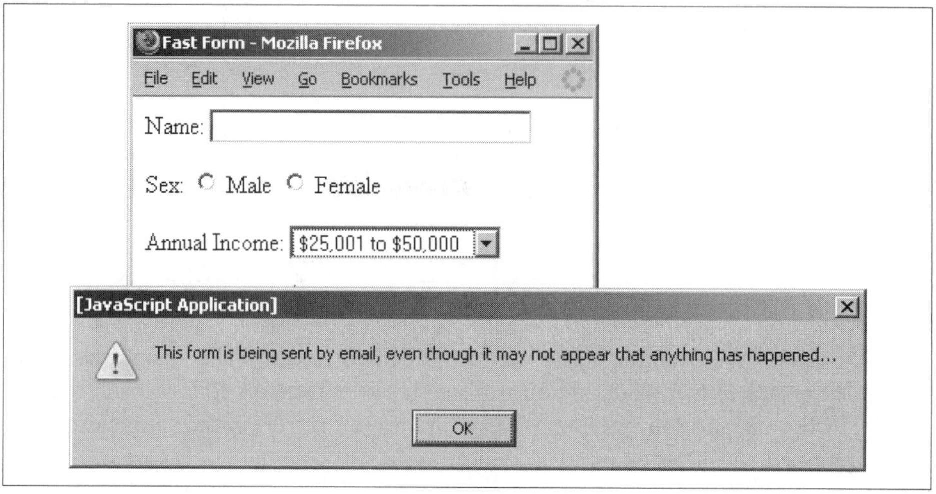

Figure 9-2. A warning about a mailto form submission

Also, unless disabled by the user or if you omit the method=POST attribute, the browser typically warns users that they are about to send unencrypted (text/plain) and thereby unsecured information over the network and gives them the option to cancel the submission. Otherwise, the form is sent via email without incident or notification.

The body of the resulting emailed form message looks something like this:

```
name=Bill Kennedy
sex=M
income=Under $25,000
```

9.4.1 Problems with Email Forms

If you choose to use either mailto or a form-to-email facility, there are several problems you may have to deal with:

- Your forms won't work on browsers that don't support a mailto URL as a form action. All of the currently popular browsers do support mailto forms.
- Some browsers, including some early versions (pre-version 5) of Internet Explorer, do not properly place the form data into the email message body and may even open an email dialog box, confusing the user.
- A mailto URL doesn't present users with a confirmation page to assure them that their forms have been processed. After executing the mailto form, the user is

left looking at the form, as though nothing had happened. (As we did in the preceding example, use JavaScript to overcome some of this dilemma with an onSubmit or onClick event handler.)

- Your data may arrive in a form that is difficult, if not impossible, to read, unless you use a readable enctype, such as text/plain.

- *Most importantly*, you lose whatever security protections the server may have provided with the form.

The last problem deserves additional explanation. Some web providers support secure web servers that attach an encryption key to your web page when sent to the user's browser. The popular browsers use that key to encrypt any data your document may send back to that same server, including the user's form data. Because only the client's browser and the server know the key, only that server is able to decipher the information coming back to it from the client browser, effectively securing the information from nefarious eavesdroppers and hackers.

However, if you use email to retrieve the form data, the server decrypts it before packaging the form information into the body of an email message and sending it to you. Email normally is highly susceptible to eavesdropping and other types of snooping. Its contents are very insecure.

So, please, if you use an email method to retrieve sensitive form data, such as credit cards and personal information, be aware of the potential consequences. And don't be fooled or fool your users with a "secure" server when insecure email comes out the back end.

In spite of all these problems, email forms present an attractive alternative to the web author constrained by a restricted server. Our advice: use CGI scripts if at all possible and fall back on mailto URLs if all else fails.

9.5 The <input> Tag

Use the <input> tag to define any one of a number of common form "controls," as they are called in the HTML and XHTML standards, including text fields, multiple-choice lists, clickable images, and submission buttons. Although there are many attributes for the <input> tag, only the name attribute is required for each element (but not for a submission or reset button; see the following explanation). And as we describe in detail later, each type of input control uses only a subset of the allowed attributes. Additional <input> attributes may be required based upon which type of form element you specify.

Table 9-1 summarizes the various form <input> types and attributes, required and optional.

<input>

Function	Creates an input element within a form
Attributes	accept, accesskey, align, alt, border ⚑, checked, class, dir, disabled, id, lang, maxlength, name, notab ⚑, onBlur, onChange, onClick, onDblClick, onFocus, onKeyDown, onKeyPress, onKeyUp, onMouseDown, onMouseMove, onMouseOut, onMouseOver, onMouseUp, onSelect, size, src, tabindex, taborder ⚑, title, type, usemap, value
End tag	None in HTML; </input> or <input ... /> in XHTML
Contains	Nothing
Used in	*form_content*

Table 9-1. Required and some common form element attributes

Attributes (× = required; ▲ = optional; *blank* = not supported)

Form tag or <input> type	accept	accesskey	align	alt	border	cols	checked	disabled	maxlength	multiple	name	notab	onBlur	onChange	onClick	onFocus	onSelect	readonly	rows	size	src	tabindex	taborder	usemap	value	wrap
button		▲						▲			×	▲	▲		▲	▲						▲	▲		×	
checkbox		▲					▲	▲			×	▲			▲			▲				▲	▲		×	
file	▲	▲							▲	▲	×	▲	▲	▲	▲	▲		▲		▲		▲	▲		▲	
hidden											×														×	
image	▲	▲	▲	▲				▲			▲	▲			▲						×	▲	▲	▲		
password		▲						▲	▲		×	▲	▲	▲	▲	▲	▲	▲		▲		▲	▲		×	
radio		▲					▲	▲			×	▲			▲		▲					▲	▲		×	
reset		▲						▲				▲			▲							▲	▲		▲	
submit		▲						▲			▲	▲			▲							▲	▲		▲	
text		▲						▲	▲		×	▲	▲	▲	▲	▲	▲	▲		▲		▲	▲		▲	
<button>		▲						▲			×		▲		▲	▲						▲			▲	
<select>								▲		▲	×		▲	▲	▲	▲				▲		▲				
<textarea>		▲			▲	▲		▲			×		▲	▲	▲	▲	▲	▲	▲			▲				▲

You select the type of control to include in the form with the <input> tag's type attribute, and you name the field (used during the form submission process to the server; see earlier description) with the name attribute. If you do not specify it, the type field defaults to a value of text. Although the value of the name attribute is technically an arbitrary string, we recommend that you use a name without embedded spaces or punctuation. If you stick to just letters and numbers (but no leading digits) and represent spaces with the underscore (_) character, you'll have fewer problems. For example, cost_in_dollars and overhead_percentage are good choices for element names; $cost and overhead % might cause problems.

In addition, notice that the name you give to a form control is directly associated with the data that the user inputs to that control and that gets passed to the forms-processing server. It is not the same as nor does it share the same namespace with the name attribute for a hyperlink fragment or a frame document.

9.5.1 Text Fields in Forms

The HTML and XHTML standards let you include four types of text-entry controls in your forms: a conventional text-entry field, a masked field for secure data entry, a field that names a file to be transmitted as part of your form data, and a special multiline text-entry <textarea> tag. The first three types are <input>-based controls; the fourth is a separate tag that we describe later in this chapter, in section 9.7.

9.5.1.1 Conventional text fields

The most common form input control is the text-entry field for usernames, addresses, and other unique data. A text-entry field appears in the browser window as an empty box on one line and accepts a single line of user input. Eventually, that line of text becomes the value of the control when the user submits the form to the server. To create a text-entry field inside a form in your document you set the type of the <input> form element to text. Include a name attribute as well; it's required.

What constitutes a line of text differs among the various browsers. Fortunately, HTML and XHTML give us a way, with the size and maxlength attributes, to dictate the width (in the number of characters) of the text-input display box, and how many total characters to accept from the user, respectively. The value for either attribute is an integer equal to the maximum number of characters you'll allow the user to see and type in the field. If maxlength exceeds size, the text scrolls back and forth within the text-entry box. If maxlength is smaller than size, there is extra blank space in the text-entry box to make up the difference between the two attributes.

The default value for size depends on the browser, but typically it is 80 characters; the default value for maxlength is unlimited. We recommend that you set them yourself. Adjust the size attribute so that the text-entry box does not extend beyond the right margin of a typical browser window (about 60 characters with a very short prompt). Set maxlength to a reasonable number of characters; for example, two for state abbreviations, 12 for phone numbers, and so on.

A text-entry field is usually blank until the user types something into it. You may, however, specify an initial default value for the field with the value attribute. The user may modify the default, of course. If the user presses a form's Reset button, the value of the field is reset to this default value. [Reset buttons, 9.5.4.2]

All of these are valid text-entry form controls:

```
<input type=text name=comments>
<input type=text name=zipcode size=10 maxlength=10>
<input type="text" name="address" size="30" maxlength="256" />
<input type="text" name="rate" size="3" maxlength="3" value="100" />
```

The first example is HTML and creates a text-entry field set to the browser's default width and maximum length. As we argued, this is not a good idea, because defaults may vary among browsers, and your form layout is sure to look bad with some of them. Rather, fix the width and maximum number of acceptable input characters as we do in the second example: it lets the user type in up to 10 characters inside an input box 10 characters wide. Its value is sent to the server with the name zipcode when the user submits the form.

The third example is XHTML and tells the browser to display a text-input box 30 characters wide into which the user may type up to 256 characters. The browser automatically scrolls text inside the input box to expose the extra characters.

The last text-input control is XHTML, too. It tells the browser to display a text box three characters wide, into which the user can type up to three characters. Its initial value is set to 100.

Notice that in the second and fourth examples it is implied that the user will enter certain kinds of data—a postal code or a numeric rate, respectively. Except for limiting *how many*, neither HTML nor XHTML provide a way for you to dictate *what* characters may be typed into a text-input field. For instance, in the last example field, the user may type "ABC," even though you intend the field's value to be a number less than 1,000. Your server-side application or applet must trap erroneous or mistaken input, check for incomplete forms, and send the appropriate error message to the user when things aren't right. That can be a tedious process, so we emphasize again: provide clear and precise instructions and prompts. Make sure your forms tell users what kinds of input you expect from them, thereby reducing the number of mistakes they may make when filling them out.

9.5.1.2 Masked text controls

Like the Lone Ranger and Zorro, the mask is on the good guys in a masked text field. It behaves just like a conventional text control in a form, except that the user-typed characters don't appear onscreen. Rather, the browser obscures the characters in masked text to keep such things as passwords and other sensitive codes away from prying eyes.

To create a masked text control, set the value of the type attribute to password. All other attributes and semantics of the conventional text control apply to the masked one. Hence, you must provide a name, and you may specify a size and maxlength for the field, as well as an initial value (we recommend it).

Don't be misled: a masked text control is not all that secure. The typed-in value is only obscured onscreen; the browser transmits it unencrypted when the form is submitted to the server, unless you are using a web server running Secure Sockets Layer (SSL) (https server, for example). So, while prying eyes may not see them onscreen, devious bad guys may steal the information electronically.

9.5.1.3 File-selection controls

As its name implies, the file-selection control lets a user select a file stored on the computer and send it to the server when she submits the form. Create a file-selection control in a form by setting the value of the type attribute to file. Like other text controls, the size and maxlength of a file-selection field should be set to appropriate values, with the browser creating a field 20 characters wide, if not otherwise directed.

The browser presents the file-selection form control to the user like other text fields, accompanied by a button labeled Browse to its right. Users either type the pathname of the file directly as text into the field or, with the Browse option, select the pathname of the file from a system-specific dialog box.

The Browse button opens a platform-specific file-selection dialog box that allows users to select a value for the field. In this case, the entire pathname of the selected file is placed into the field, even if the length of that pathname exceeds the control's specified maxlength.

Use the accept attribute to constrain the types of files that the browser lets the user browse, even though it does not constrain what they may type in as the pathname. accept's value is a comma-separated list of MIME encodings; users browse and select only files whose type matches one of those in the list. For example, to restrict the selection to images, you might add accept="image/*" to the file-selection <input> tag.

Unlike other form input controls, the file-selection field works correctly only with a specific form data encoding and transmission method. If you include one or more file-selection fields in your form, you must set the enctype attribute of the <form> tag to multipart/form-data and the <form> tag's method attribute to post. Otherwise, the file-selection field behaves like a regular text field, transmitting its value (that is, the file's pathname) to the server instead of the contents of the file itself.

All of this is easier than it may sound. For example, here is an HTML form that collects a person's name and favorite file:

```
<form enctype="multipart/form-data" method=post
    action="cgi-bin/save_file">
Your name: <input type=text size=20 name=the_name>
<p>
Your favorite file: <input type=file size=20 name=fav_file>
</form>
```

The data transmitted from the browser to the server for this example form has two parts. The first contains the value for the name field, and the second contains the name and contents of the specified file:

```
------------------------------6099238414674
Content-Disposition: form-data; name="the_name"

One line of text field contents
------------------------------6099238414674
Content-Disposition: form-data; name="fav_file"; filename="abc"

First line of file
...
Last line of file
------------------------------6099238414674--
```

The browsers don't check that the user has specified a valid file. If no file is specified, the filename portion of the Content-Disposition header is empty. If the file doesn't exist, its name appears in the filename subheader, but there is no Content-Type header or subsequent lines of file content. Valid files may contain nonprintable or binary data; there is no way to restrict user-selectable file types. In light of these potential problems, the forms-processing application on the server should be robust enough to handle missing files, erroneous files, extremely large files, and files with unusual or unexpected formats.

9.5.2 Checkboxes

The checkbox form control gives users a way to select or deselect an item quickly and easily in your form. Checkboxes also may be grouped to create a set of choices, any and all of which the user may select or deselect.

Create individual checkboxes by setting the type attribute for each <input> tag to checkbox. Include the required name and value attributes. Only the values of those items selected by the user appear in the submitted form. The optional checked attribute (no value) tells the browser to display a selected (checked) checkbox and include its value when submitting the form to the server unless the user deliberately deselects (unchecks) the box.

The value of the checked checkbox submitted to the server is the text string you specify in the required value attribute. For example, in XHTML:

```
<form>
  What pets do you own?
  <p>
    <input type="checkbox" name="pets" value="dog" /> Dog
  <br />
    <input type="checkbox" checked="checked" name="pets" value="cat" /> Cat
  <br />
    <input type="checkbox" name="pets" value="bird" /> Bird
```

```
  <br />
    <input type="checkbox" name="pets" value="fish" /> Fish
  </p>
</form>
```

creates a checkbox group as shown in Figure 9-3.

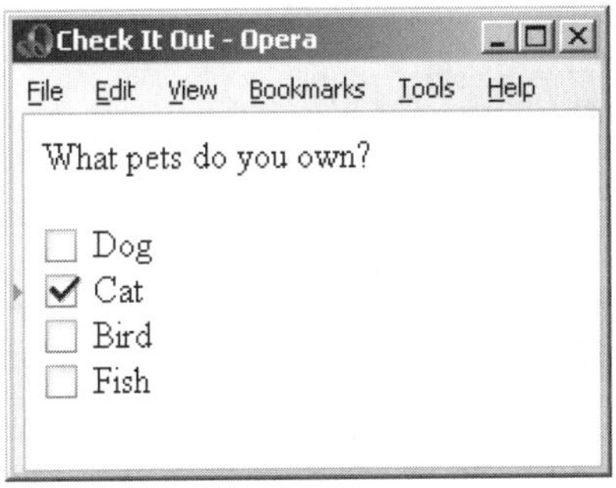

Figure 9-3. A checkbox group

Although part of the group, each checkbox control appears as a separate choice onscreen. Notice, too, with all due respect to dog, bird, and fish lovers, that we've preselected the Cat checkbox with the checked attribute in its tag. We've also provided text labels; the similar value attributes don't appear in the browser's window but are the values submitted with their associated name to the server if the user selects the checkbox. Also, you need to use paragraph or line-break tags to control the layout of your checkbox group, as you do for other form controls.

In the example, if the user selects Cat and Fish and submits the form, the values included in the parameter list sent to the server would be:

```
pets=cat
pets=fish
```

9.5.3 Radio Buttons

Radio button form controls are similar in behavior to checkboxes, except that the user can select only one in the group.* Create a radio button by setting the type attribute of the <input> tag to radio. As with checkbox controls, radio buttons each require a name and value attribute. Radio buttons with the same name are members of a group. One of them may be checked by including the checked attribute with that element. If you don't check one in the group, the browser does it automatically for you by checking the first element in the group.

---

* Some of us are old enough, while not yet senile, to recall when automobile radios had mechanical push buttons for selecting a station. Pushing in one button popped out the previously depressed one, implementing a mechanical one-of-many choice mechanism.

You should give each radio button element a different value so that the forms-processing server can sort them out after form submission.

Here's the previous example reworked in HTML so that you get to choose only one animal as a favorite pet (see Figure 9-4):

```
<form>
  Which type of animal is your favorite pet?
  <p>
    <input type=radio name=favorite value="dog"> Dog
    <input type=radio checked name=favorite value="cat"> Cat
    <input type=radio name=favorite value="bird"> Bird
    <input type=radio name=favorite value="fish"> Fish
</form>
```

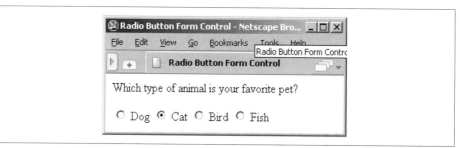

Figure 9-4. Radio buttons allow only one selection per group

As in the previous example with checkboxes, we've tipped our hat toward felines, making the Cat radio button the default choice. If the user selects an alternative—Bird, for instance—the browser automatically deselects Cat and selects Bird. When the user submits the form to the server, the browser includes only one value with the name "favorite" in the list of form parameters; favorite=bird, if that was the last choice.

One of the controls in a group of radio buttons always is selected, so it makes no sense to create a single radio button. Instead, use groups of two or more options, such as for On/Off and Yes/No types of form controls.

9.5.4 Action Buttons

Although the terminology is potentially confusing, there is another class of buttons for forms. Unlike the radio buttons and checkboxes described previously, these special types of form controls act immediately, their effects cannot be reversed, and they affect the entire contents of the form, not just the value of a single field. These "action" buttons (for lack of a better term) include submit, reset, regular, and image buttons. When the user selects them, both the submit and image buttons cause the browser to submit all of the form's parameters to the forms-processing server. A regular button does not submit the form but can be used to invoke an applet to manipulate or validate the form. The reset button acts locally to erase any user input and have the form revert to its original (default) contents.

In this section, we describe the action buttons that you may create with the standard form `<input>` element. In the next section, we describe in detail the newer `<button>` tag that achieves identical effects and allows you greater control over the presentation and display of your form buttons.

9.5.4.1 Submission buttons

The submit button (`<input type=submit>`) does what its name implies, setting in motion the form's submission to the server from the browser. You may have more than one submit button in a form. You may also include `name` and `value` attributes with the submit type of form `<input>` button.

With the simplest submit button (one without a `name` or `value` attribute), the browser displays a small rectangle or oval with the default label "Submit." Otherwise, the browser labels the button with the text you include with the tag's `value` attribute. If you provide a `name` attribute, the browser adds the `value` attribute for the submit button to the parameter list and sends it along to the server. That's good, because it gives you a way to identify which submit button in a form the user selected, letting you process any one of several different forms with a single forms-processing application.

All of the following are valid submission buttons:

```
<input type=submit>
<input type=submit value="Order Kumquats">
<input type="submit" value="Ship Overnight" name="ship_style" />
```

The first one is in HTML and is also the simplest: the browser displays a button, labeled "Submit," which activates the forms-processing sequence when the user clicks it. It does not add an element to the parameter list that the browser passes to the forms-processing server and application.

The second example HTML button has a `value` attribute that makes the displayed button's label "Order Kumquats" but, like the first example, does not include the button's value in the form's parameter list.

The last example, in XHTML, sets the button label and makes it part of the form's parameter list. When the user clicks this submission button, it adds the parameter `ship_style="Ship Overnight"` to the form's parameter list.

9.5.4.2 Reset buttons

The reset type of form `<input>` button is nearly self-explanatory: it lets the user reset—erase or set to some default value—all elements in the form. Unlike the other buttons, a reset button does not initiate form processing. Instead, the browser does the work of resetting the form elements. The server never knows (or cares, for that matter) whether or when the user selects a reset button.

By default, the browser displays a reset button with the label "Reset." You can change that by specifying a `value` attribute with your own button label.

Here are two sample reset buttons:

```
<input type=reset>
<input type="reset" value="Use Defaults" />
```

The first one, in HTML, creates a reset button that is by default labeled "Reset" by the browser. The second example, in XHTML, tells the browser to label the reset button with "Use Defaults." Both examples initiate the same response in the browser by resetting the form to its original contents.

9.5.4.3 Custom image buttons

The image type of form <input> element is a special submit button made out of a picture that, when selected by the user, tells the browser to submit the form to the server. Upon submission, the browser also includes the X,Y coordinates of the mouse pointer within the image in the form's parameter list, much like the mouse-sensitive image maps we discussed in Chapter 6.

Image buttons require an src attribute and, as its value, the URL of the image file. You can include a name attribute and a descriptive alt attribute for use by nongraphical browsers. Although it is deprecated in HTML 4, you also may use align to control alignment of the image within the current line of text. Use the border attribute to control the width, if any, of the frame that Netscape and Firefox put around the form image, much like the border attribute for the <img> tag. (Neither Internet Explorer nor Opera puts borders around form <input> images.)

Here are a couple of valid image buttons:

```
<input type="image" src="pics/map.gif" name="map" />
<input type=image src="pics/xmap.gif" align=top name=map>
```

The browser displays the designated image within the form's content flow. The second button's image is aligned with the top of the adjacent text, as specified by the align attribute. Netscape and Firefox add a border, as they do when an image is part of an anchor (<a>) tag, to signal that the image is a form button.

When the user clicks the image, the browser sends the horizontal offset, in pixels, of the mouse from the left edge of the image and the vertical offset from the top edge of the image to the server. These values are assigned the name of the image as specified with the name attribute, followed by .x and .y, respectively. Thus, if someone clicked the image specified in the first example, the browser would send parameters named map.x and map.y to the server.

Image buttons behave much like mouse-sensitive image maps (usemap), and like the programs or client-side <map> tags that process image maps, your forms processor may use the X,Y mouse-pointer parameters to choose a special course of action. You should use an image button when you need the additional form information to process the user's request. If an image map of links is all you need, use a mouse-sensitive image map. Mouse-sensitive images also have the added benefit of providing server-side support for automatic detection of shape selection within the image, letting you deal with the image as a selectable collection of shapes. Form buttons with images require you to write code that determines where the user clicked on the image and how the server can translate this position to an appropriate action.

Oddly, the HTML 4 and XHTML standards allow the use of the usemap attribute with an image button, but do not explain how such a use might conflict with normal server processing of the X,Y coordinates of the mouse position. We recommend not mixing the two, using mouse-sensitive images outside of forms and image buttons within forms.

9.5.4.4 Push buttons

Using the <input type=button> tag (or the <button> tag, described later in this chapter, in section 9.6), you create a button that the user may click, but that does not submit or reset the form. Use the value attribute to set the label on the button. The name attribute, if included in the tag, causes the supplied value to be passed to the forms-processing script.

You might wonder what value the button type provides: little or none, unless you supply one or more of the on-event attributes along with a snippet of JavaScript to be executed when the user interacts with the button. Thus empowered, these buttons provide a way for the user to initiate form content validation, update fields, manipulate the document, and perform all other kinds of client-side activity. [JavaScript Event Handlers, 12.3.3]

9.5.4.5 Multiple buttons in a single form

You can have several buttons of the same or different types in a single form. Even simple forms often have both reset and submit buttons, for example. To distinguish between them, make sure each has a different value attribute, which the browser uses for the button label. Depending on the way you program the forms-processing application, you might make the name of each button different, but it is usually easier to name all similarly acting buttons the same and let the button-handling subroutine sort them out by value. For instance (all in HTML):

```
<input type=submit name=edit value="Add">
<input type=submit name=edit value="Delete">
<input type=submit name=edit value="Change">
<input type=submit name=edit value="Cancel">
```

When the user selects one of these example buttons, a form parameter named edit gets sent to the server. The value of this parameter is one of the button names. The server-side application takes the value and behaves accordingly.

Because an image button doesn't have a value attribute, the only way to distinguish among several image buttons on a single form is to ensure that they all have different names.

9.5.5 Hidden Fields

The last type of form <input> control we describe in this chapter is hidden from view. No, we're not trying to conceal anything; it's a way to embed information into your forms that the browser or user cannot ignore or alter. The browser automatically includes the <input type=hidden> tag's required name and value attributes in the submitted form's parameter list. These attributes serve to label the form and can be invaluable when sorting out different forms or form versions from a collection of submitted and saved forms.

Another use for hidden fields is to manage user-server interactions. For instance, it helps the server to know that the current form has come from a person who made a similar request a few moments ago. Normally, the server does not retain this information, and each transaction between the server and client is completely independent from all other transactions.

For example, the first form the user submits might have asked for some basic information, such as the user's name and where she lives. Based on that initial contact, the server might create a second form asking more specific questions of the user. Because it is tedious for users to reenter the same basic information from the first form, you can program the server to put the originally submitted values back into the second form in hidden fields. When the second form comes back, all the important information from both forms is there, and the second form can be matched to the first one, if necessary.

Hidden fields also may direct the server toward some specific action. For example, you might embed the following hidden field:

```
<input type=hidden name=action value=change>
```

Then, if you have one server-side application that handles the processing of several forms, each form might contain a different action code to help that server application sort them out.

9.6 The <button> Tag

As we described earlier, you create an action button with standard HTML or XHTML by including its type value in the standard <input> tag. For instance, the <input type=submit> form control creates a button that, when selected by the user, tells the browser to send the form's contents to the processing server or to an email address (the mailto option). Display-wise, you don't have any direct control over what that submit button looks like, beyond changing the default label "Submit" to some other word or short phrase (e.g., "Hit me" or "Outta here!").

First introduced in the HTML 4.0 standard, the <button> tag acts the same as <input>, but it gives you more control over how the browser displays the element. In particular, all of the attributes you might use with the <input type=button> element are acceptable with the <button> tag.

<table>
<tr><td colspan="2" align="center">**<button>**</td></tr>
<tr><td>**Function**</td><td>Creates a button element within a form</td></tr>
<tr><td>**Attributes**</td><td>accesskey, class, dir, disabled, id, lang, name, notab 🛅 , onBlur, onClick, onDblClick, onFocus, onKeyDown, onKeyPress, onKeyUp, onMouseDown, onMouseMove, onMouseOut, onMouseOver, onMouseUp, style, tabindex, taborder 🛅 , title, type, value</td></tr>
<tr><td>**End tag**</td><td></button>; never omitted</td></tr>
<tr><td>**Contains**</td><td>*button_content*</td></tr>
<tr><td>**Used in**</td><td>*form_content*</td></tr>
</table>

9.6.1 The <button> Button

Neither the HTML 4 nor the XHTML standard is overly clear as to what display enhancements to a form the <button> element should provide, other than to suggest that the contents should be 3D and visually appear to react like a push button when the user selects it (i.e., go in and back out when pressed). All the popular browsers support <button>.

The <button> control provides for a greater variety and richer contents than its <input> analogs. Everything between the <button> and </button> tags becomes the content of the button, including any acceptable body content, such as text or multimedia. For instance, you could include an image and related text within a button, creating attractive labeled icons in your buttons. The only *verboten* element is an image map because its mouse- and keyboard-sensitive actions interfere with the form button.

9.6.2 The type Attribute

Use the type attribute for the <button> tag to define the button's action. You should set its value to submit, reset, or button. Like its <input> analog, a <button type=submit> form element, when selected by the user, tells the browser to package and send the contents of the form to the forms-processing server or email it to the mailto recipient. Using type=reset creates a conventional reset button, and using type=button creates a conventional push button.

For example, Figure 9-5 shows the following *exclaim.gif* icon inset on a 3D button that pushes in and pops back out when the user clicks it with the mouse. In doing so, the browser submits the form to the server:

```
<button type=submit>
Order <img src="icons/exclaim.gif" align=middle alt="Order Now"> Now!
</button>
```

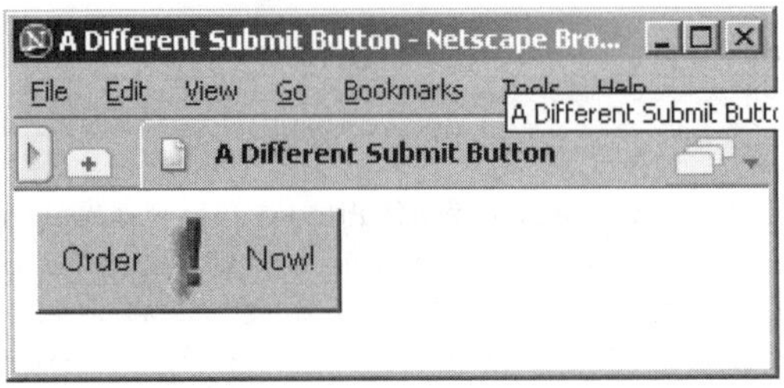

Figure 9-5. A form-submit <button>

Notice that you can exploit the rich set of <img> tag attributes, including align and alt, for this <button> style of form control.

Because the <button> tag is so similar to the <input type=button> element, why have it at all? The only reason is to provide far richer content for buttons. If your buttons are conventional text buttons, the <input> tag will suffice. If you want to create fancy, mixed-content buttons, you'll need to use the <button> tag.

9.7 Multiline Text Areas

The conventional and hidden-text types for forms restrict user input to a single line of characters. The <textarea> form tag sets users free.

9.7.1 The <textarea> Tag

As part of a form, the <textarea> tag creates a multiline text-entry area in the user's browser display. In it, the user may type a nearly unlimited number of lines of text. Upon submission of the form, the browser collects all the lines of text, each separated by %0D%0A (carriage return/line feed), and sends them to the server as the value of this form element, using the name specified by the required name attribute.

You may include plain text inside the <textarea> tag and its end tag (</textarea>). That default text must be plain text, with no tags or other special elements. The user may modify the contents and the browser uses that text as the default value if the user presses a reset button for the form. Hence, the text content is most often included for instructions and examples:

```
Tell us about yourself:
<textarea name=address cols=40 rows=4>
  Your Name Here
  1234 My Street
  Anytown, State Zipcode
</textarea>
```

<table>
<tr><td colspan="2" align="center">**<textarea>**</td></tr>
<tr><td>**Function**</td><td>Creates a multiline text-input area</td></tr>
<tr><td>**Attributes**</td><td>accesskey, class, cols, dir, disabled, id, lang, name, notab ⬛,
onBlur, onChange, onClick, onDblClick, onFocus, onKeyDown,
onKeyPress, onKeyUp, onMouseDown, onMouseMove, onMouseOut,
onMouseOver, onMouseUp, onSelect, readonly, rows, style, tabindex,
taborder ⬛, title, wrap</td></tr>
<tr><td>**End tag**</td><td></textarea>; never omitted</td></tr>
<tr><td>**Contains**</td><td>*plain_text*</td></tr>
<tr><td>**Used in**</td><td>*form_content*</td></tr>
</table>

9.7.1.1 The rows and cols attributes

A multiline text-input area stands alone onscreen: body content flows above and below, but not around it. You can control its dimensions, however, by defining the cols and rows attributes for the visible rectangular area set aside by the browser for multiline input. We suggest you set these attributes. The common browsers have a habit of setting aside the smallest, least readable region possible for <textarea> input, and the user can't resize it. Both attributes require integer values for the respective dimension's size in characters. The browser automatically scrolls text that exceeds either dimension.

9.7.1.2 The wrap attribute

Normally, the browser sends the text that you type into the text area to the server exactly as typed, with lines broken only where the user pressed the Enter key. Because this is often not the action the user desired, you can enable word wrapping within the text area. When the user types a line that is longer than the width of the text area, the browser automatically moves the extra text down to the next line, breaking the line at the nearest point between words in the line.

With the wrap attribute set to virtual, the text is wrapped within the text area for presentation to the user, but is transmitted to the server as though no wrapping had occurred except where the user pressed the Enter key.

With the wrap attribute set to physical, the text is wrapped within the text area and is transmitted to the server as though the user had actually typed it that way. This is the most useful way to use word wrap because the text is transmitted exactly as the user sees it in the text area.

To obtain the default action, set the wrap attribute to off.

As an example, consider the following 60 characters of text that are being typed into a 40-character-wide text area:

```
Word wrapping is a feature that makes life easier for users.
```

With wrap=off, the text area contains one line and the user must scroll to the right to see all of the text. One line of text is transmitted to the server.

With wrap=virtual, the text area contains two lines of text, broken after the word *makes*. Only one line of text is transmitted to the server: the entire line with no embedded newline characters.

With wrap=physical, the text area contains two lines of text, broken after the word *makes*. Two lines of text are sent to the server, separated by a newline character after the word *makes*.

9.8 Multiple-Choice Elements

Checkboxes and radio buttons give you powerful means for creating multiple-choice questions and answers, but they can lead to long forms that are tedious to write and put a fair amount of clutter onscreen. The <select> tag gives you two compact alternatives: pull-down menus and scrolling lists.

9.8.1 The <select> Tag

By placing a list of <option>-tagged items inside the <select> tag of a form, you magically create a pull-down menu of choices. Figure 9-2, earlier in this chapter, displays a <select> pull-down menu.

<select>

Function	Creates single- and multiple-choice menus
Attributes	class, dir, disabled, id, lang, multiple, name, notab ⃞, onBlur, onChange, onClick, onDblClick, onFocus, onKeyDown, onKeyPress, onKeyUp, onMouseDown, onMouseMove, onMouseOut, onMouseOver, onMouseUp, size, style, tabindex, taborder ⃞, title
End tag	</select>; never omitted
Contains	*select_content*
Used in	*form_content*

As with other form tags, the name attribute is required and used by the browser when submitting the <select> choices to the server. Unlike with radio buttons, no item is preselected, so if the user doesn't select one, the browser doesn't send any value to the server with the submitted form.

Otherwise, the browser submits the selected item with the name attribute value when submitting <select> form data to the server.

9.8.1.1 The multiple attribute

To allow more than one option selection at a time, add the multiple attribute to the <select> tag. This causes the <select> element to behave like an <input type=checkbox> element. When submitted, the browser collects the multiple selections, separated with commas, into a single parameter list, such as:

```
pets=dog,cat,mouse
```

If you don't include the multiple attribute, the user may select only one option at a time, just like in a group of radio buttons.

9.8.1.2 The size attribute

The size attribute determines how many options are visible to the user at a time. The value of size should be a positive integer. The default value is 1. When size=1 without multiple, the browser typically displays the <select> list as a pop-up menu. With size values greater than 1 or with multiple, the browser typically displays the <select> element's contents as a scrolling list.

In the following XHTML example, we've converted our previous checkbox example into a scrolling, multiple-choice menu. Notice that the size attribute tells the browser to display three options at a time:[*]

```
What pets do you have?
  <select name="pets" size="3" multiple="multiple">
    <option>Dog</option>
    <option>Cat</option>
    <option>Bird</option>
    <option>Fish</option>
  </select>
```

The result is shown in Figure 9-6.

9.8.2 The <option> Tag

Use the <option> tag to define each item within a <select> form control. The browser displays the <option> tag's contents as an element within the <select> tag's menu or scrolling list, so the contents must be plain text only, without any other sort of markup.

---

[*] Notice the </option> end tags. They are not usually included in standard HTML documents but must appear in XHTML.

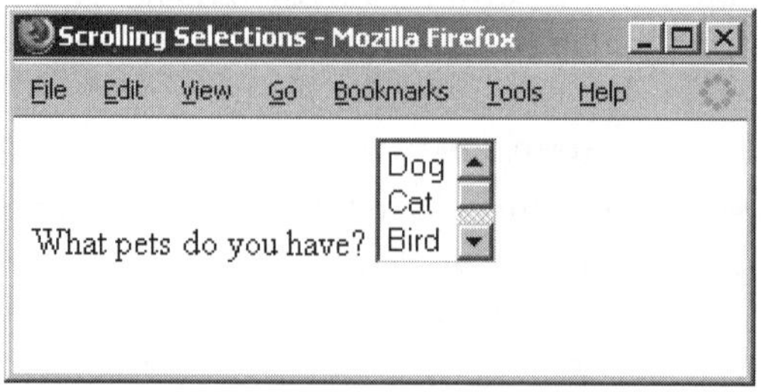

Figure 9-6. A <select> element, formatted with size=3

<option>

Function	Defines available options within a <select> menu
Attributes	class, dir, disabled, id, label, lang, onClick, onDblClick, onKeyDown, onKeyPress, onKeyUp, onMouseDown, onMouseMove, onMouseOut, onMouseOver, onMouseUp, selected, style, title, value
End tag	</option>; usually omitted in HTML
Contains	*plain_text*
Used in	*select_content*

9.8.2.1 The value attribute

Use the value attribute to set a value for each option the browser sends to the server if the user selects that option. If the value attribute has not been specified, the value of the option is set to the content of the <option> tag. As an example, consider these HTML options:

```
<option value=Dog>Dog
<option>Dog
```

Both have the same value. The first is explicitly set within the <option> tag; the second defaults to the content of the <option> tag itself: "Dog".

9.8.2.2 The selected attribute

By default, all options within a multiple-choice <select> tag are unselected and therefore not included in the parameters list when the client submits the form to the server. Include the selected attribute inside the <option> tag to preselect one or more options, which the user may then deselect.

The HTML version of the selected attribute has no value; the XHTML version has the value selected="selected". Single-choice <select> tags preselect the first option if no option is explicitly preselected.

9.8.2.3 The label attribute

Normally, the browser creates a label from the contents of the <option> tag when displaying it to the user. If the label attribute is supplied, its value is used as the label instead.

9.8.3 The <optgroup> Tag

Menus of choices in forms can be quite large, making them difficult to display and use. In these cases, it is helpful to group related choices, which can then be presented as a set of nested, cascading menus to the user. Introduced in HTML 4.0, the <optgroup> tag brings this capability to HTML and XHTML forms, albeit in a limited way.

You can use the <optgroup> tag only within a <select> tag, and it may contain only <option> tags. The browser creates submenus for each <optgroup> tag within the main <select> menu.

For example, with HTML you might use <optgroup> to present a form menu of states organized by region (Figure 9-7):

```
<select name=state>
    <optgroup label=Northeast>
        <option>Maine
        <option>New Hampshire
        ...
    </optgroup>
    <optgroup label=South>
        <option>Florida
        <option>Georgia
    </optgroup>
    ...
</select>
```

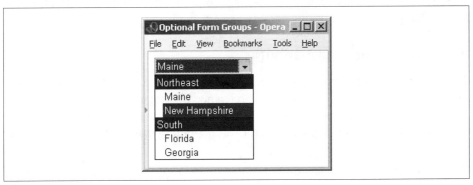

Figure 9-7. The <optgroup> tag helps organize form <select> menus

Like that shown for Opera in Figure 9-7, the other popular GUI browsers similarly indent the <optgroup> items within a scrolling menu, though the others italicize and make the group headers bold.

The biggest drawback to the <optgroup> tag is that it cannot be nested, limiting you to one level of submenus. Presumably, this restriction will be lifted in a future version of XHTML.

<table>
<tr><td colspan="2" align="center"><optgroup></td></tr>
<tr><td>Function</td><td>Groups related <option> elements within a <select> menu</td></tr>
<tr><td>Attributes</td><td>class, dir, disabled, id, label, lang, onClick, onDblClick, onKeyDown, onKeyPress, onKeyUp, onMouseDown, onMouseMove, onMouseOut, onMouseOver, onMouseUp, style, title</td></tr>
<tr><td>End tag</td><td></optgroup>; may be omitted in HTML</td></tr>
<tr><td>Contains</td><td>optgroup_content</td></tr>
<tr><td>Used in</td><td>select_content</td></tr>
</table>

9.8.3.1 The label attribute

Use the label attribute to define an <optgroup> submenu title to the user. You should keep the label short and to the point to ensure that the menu can be displayed easily on a large variety of displays.

9.9 General Form-Control Attributes

The many form-control tags contain common attributes that, like most other tags, generally serve to label, set up the display, extend the text language, and make the tag extensible programmatically.

9.9.1 The id and title Attributes

The id attribute, as for most other standard tags, lets you attach a unique string label to the form control and its contents for reference by programs (applets) and hyperlinks. This name is distinct from the name assigned to a control element with the name attribute. Names assigned with the id attribute are not passed to the server when the form is processed.

The title attribute is similar to id in that it uses a quote-enclosed string value to label the form control. However, it titles only the form segment; you cannot use its value in an applet reference or hyperlink. Browsers may use the title as pop-up help for the user or in nonvisual presentation of the form. [The id attribute, 4.1.1.4] [The title attribute, 4.1.1.5]

9.9.2 The event Attributes

Like most other elements, most of the form controls support a number of user mouse and keyboard event-related attributes that the HTML 4/XHTML-compliant browser recognizes and lets you specially process using JavaScript or a Java applet, for example. We describe the majority of these events in detail in Chapter 12.

9.9.3 The style, class, lang, and dir Attributes

The style attribute for the various form controls creates an inline style for the elements enclosed by the tag, overriding any other style rules in effect. The class attribute lets you format the content according to a predefined class of the <form> tag; its value is the name of that class. [Inline Styles: The style Attribute, 8.1.1] [Style Classes, 8.3]

The lang attribute specifies the language used within a control, accepting as its value any of the ISO standard two-character language abbreviations, including an optional language modifier. For example, adding lang=en-UK tells the browser that the list is in English ("en") as spoken and written in the United Kingdom ("UK"). Presumably, the browser may make layout or typographic decisions based upon your language choice. [The lang attribute, 3.6.1.2]

Similarly, the dir attribute tells the browser in which direction to display the control contents—either from left to right (dir=ltr), like English and French, or from right to left (dir=rtl), as with Hebrew and Chinese. [The dir attribute, 3.6.1.1]

The popular browsers support the dir and lang attributes, even though there are no behaviors defined for any specific language.

9.9.4 The tabindex, taborder ⚠, and notab ⚠ Attributes

By default, all elements (except hidden elements) are part of the form's tab order. As the user presses the Tab key, the browser shifts the input focus from element to element in the form. For most browsers, the tabbing order of the elements matches the order of the elements within the <form> tag. With the tabindex attribute, you can change the order and the position of those elements within the tab order.

To reposition an element within the tab order, set the value of the attribute to the element's desired position in the tab order, with the first element in the order being number one. If you really want to change a form's tab order, we suggest you include the tabindex attribute with every element in the form, with an appropriate value for each element. In this way, you'll be sure to place every element explicitly in the tab order, and there will be no surprises when the user tabs through the form.

The value of the tabindex attribute is a positive integer indicating the position of the tagged contents in the overall tab sequence for the document. The tabbing order begins with elements with explicit tabindex values, starting from the lowest to the highest numbers. Same-valued tags get tab-selected in the order in which they appear in the document. All other selectable tags, such as the various form controls and hyperlinks, are the last to get tabbed, in the order in which they appear in the document. To exclude an element from the tab order, set the value of tabindex to 0. The element is skipped when the user tabs around the form.

Internet Explorer introduced the concept of tab-order management with its proprietary taborder and notab attributes. The taborder attribute functions exactly like the tabindex attribute, and notab is equivalent to tabindex=0. Internet Explorer versions 5 and later now support the standard tabindex, as do the other popular browsers. Consequently, we strongly suggest that you use the tabindex attribute and not taborder.

9.9.5 The accesskey Attribute

Many user interfaces promote the idea of shortcut keys: short sequences of keystrokes that give you quick access to an element in the user interface. HTML 4 and XHTML provide support for this capability with the accesskey attribute. The value of the accesskey attribute is a single character that, when pressed in conjunction with some other special key, causes focus to shift immediately to the associated form element. This special key varies with each user interface: PC users press the Alt key, whereas Unix keyboard users typically press the Meta key.

For example, adding accesskey="T" to a <textarea> element would cause focus to shift to that text area when a Windows user pressed Alt-T. Note that the value of the accesskey attribute is a single character and is case sensitive (a capital "T" is not the same as its lowercase cousin, for instance).

All the popular browsers support the accesskey attribute. Be careful to test your hot-key options, however. For instance, while Alt-f works with Internet Explorer to jump-select the tag with the accesskey="f" attribute, in Netscape this key combination opens the File pull-down menu.

Also note that the accesskey option not only jumps to but also selects the associated form element. So, for instance, if you associate an accesskey with a radio button, by pressing the access-key combination, the user display not only shifts focus to that radio button but also selects it, as though the user had clicked the mouse on that element. The same goes for all action form elements: jump and select.

9.9.6 The disabled and readonly Attributes

The HTML 4 and XHTML standards let you define but otherwise disable a form control simply by inserting the disabled attribute within the tag. A disabled form control appears in the display but cannot be accessed via the Tab key or otherwise selected with the mouse. Its parameters are not passed to the server when the user submits the form.

Browsers can change the appearance of disabled elements and alter any labels associated with them. The popular browsers gray out disabled radio and submit buttons, as in the following HTML fragment (also shown in Figure 9-8):

```
<form>
  Name:
    <input type=text name=name size=32 maxlength=80 readonly>
  <p>
  Sex:
    <input type=radio name=sex value="M" disabled> Male
    <input type=radio name=sex value="F" accesskey="z"> Female
  <p>
  Income:
    <select name=income size=1 disabled>
      <option>Under $25,000
      <option>$25,001 to $50,000
      <option>$50,001 and higher
    </select>
  <p>
  <input type=submit disabled>
</form>
```

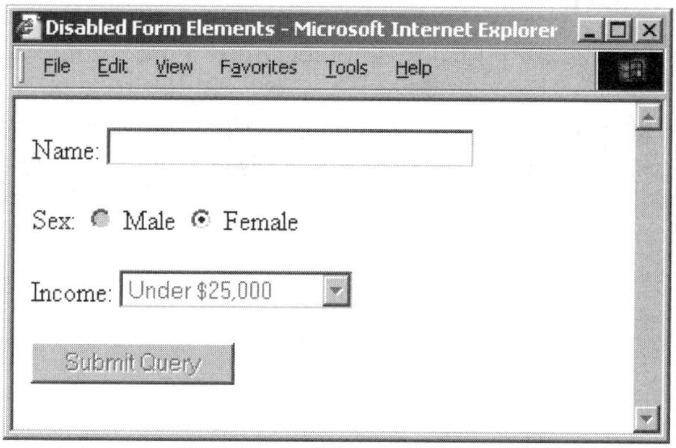

Figure 9-8. Disabled form controls turn gray

Similarly, the user may not alter a text-related <input> or <textarea> form control that you designate as readonly with the attribute. These elements are still part of the tab order and may be selected, and the value of the control gets sent to the server when the user submits the form. The user just can't alter the value. So, in a sense, a form control rendered readonly is the visible analog of the <input type=hidden> control.

What is the point of all these hidden and unchangeable form elements? Automation. By automatically generating enabled and disabled form elements, you can tailor the form to the user. For example, if the user indicates on one form that she is female, a subsequent form may contain that information in a hidden attribute, and certain elements in the form may be displayed for familiarity while certain elements are disabled to make the form easier to navigate.

9.10 Labeling and Grouping Form Elements

The common text and other content you may use to label and otherwise explain a form are static. Other than by their visual relationship to the form's input areas, these labels and instructions are unassociated with the form controls that they serve. Because of this, forms are not easily understood and navigable, particularly by people with impaired vision. Try it. Get a simple personal-information form onscreen, close your eyes, and find the place to enter your name.

The HTML 4.0 standard introduced three tags that make navigation of forms easier for users, particularly those with disabilities. They include a way to group and caption regions of the form and a way to individually label form controls. All are supposed to get special treatment by the browser, such as being rendered by a speech synthesizer as well as specially displayed, and can be easily accessed from the user keyboard—that is, when browsers become fully HTML 4/XHTML compliant.

9.10.1 The <label> Tag

Use the <label> tag to define relationships between a form control, such as a text-input field, and one or more text labels. According to the latest standards, the text in a label is to receive special treatment by the browser. Browsers may choose a special display style for the label (you can, too, with stylesheets). And when selected by the user, the browser automatically transfers focus to a label's associated form control.

<label>	
Function	Creates a label for a form element
Attributes	accesskey, class, dir, for, id, lang, onBlur, onClick, onDblClick, onFocus, onKeyDown, onKeyPress, onKeyUp, onMouseDown, onMouseMove, onMouseOut, onMouseOver, onMouseUp, style, title
End tag	</label>; never omitted
Contains	*label_contents*
Used in	*form_content*

9.10.1.1 Implicit and explicit associations

One or more labels get associated with a form control in one of two ways: implicitly, by including the form control as contents of the label tag, or explicitly, by naming the ID of the target form control in the <label> tag's for attribute.

For example, in XHTML:

```
<label for="SSN">Social Security Number:</label>
<input type="text" name="SocSecNum" id="SSN" />
<label>Date of birth: <input type="text" name="DofB" /></label>
```

The first label explicitly relates the text "Social Security Number:" with the form's Social Security number text-input control (SocSecNum), because its for attribute's value is identical to the control's id, SSN. The second label ("Date of birth:") does not require a for attribute, nor does its related control require an id attribute, because they are implicitly joined by placing the <input> tag within the <label> tag.

Be careful not to confuse the name and id attributes. The former creates a name for an element that the browser sends to the server-side forms processor; id creates a name that <label> tags and URLs can use. Note also that although a label may reference only a single form control, several labels may reference a single control. Thus, you can steer users to a particular form input region from several places in a document.

9.10.1.2 Other label attributes

Labels also share many of the general display, access, and event-related tag attributes described earlier in section 9.9. In addition to the standard HTML 4 and XHTML event attributes, labels also support the onfocus and onblur attributes.

9.10.2 Forming a Group

Beyond individual labels, you may group a set of form controls and label the group with the <fieldset> and <legend> tags. Again, the HTML 4 and XHTML standards attempt to make forms more readily accessible by users, particularly those with disabilities. Grouping form controls into explicit sections gives you the opportunity to specially display and otherwise manage the form contents.

9.10.2.1 The <fieldset> tag

The <fieldset> tag encapsulates a section of form contents, creating a group of related form fields. <fieldset> doesn't have any required or unique attributes.

When a group of form elements are placed within a <fieldset> tag, the browser may display them in a special manner. This might include a special border, 3D effects, or even creating a subform to handle the elements.

`<fieldset>`

Function	Groups related elements within a form
Attributes	class, dir, id, lang, onClick, onDblClick, onKeyDown, onKeyPress, onKeyUp, onMouseDown, onMouseMove, onMouseOut, onMouseOver, onMouseUp, style, title
End tag	`</fieldset>`; never omitted
Contains	*form_content*
Used in	*form_content*

9.10.2.2 The `<legend>` tag

Use the `<legend>` tag to create a label for a fieldset in a form. The tag may appear only inside a `<fieldset>`. As with `<label>`, the `<legend>` contents are to be specially treated by the HTML 4/XHTML-compliant browser, transferring focus to associated form elements when selected and serving to improve accessibility of users to a `<fieldset>`.

`<legend>`

Function	Creates a legend for a field set within a form
Attributes	accesskey, align, class, dir, id, lang, onClick, onDblClick, onKeyDown, onKeyPress, onKeyUp, onMouseDown, onMouseMove, onMouseOut, onMouseOver, onMouseUp, style, title
End tag	`</legend>`; may be omitted in HTML
Contains	*legend_content*
Used in	*form_content*

In addition to supporting many of the form element attributes described earlier in section 9.9, the `<legend>` tag accepts the accesskey attribute and the align attribute. The value of align may be top, bottom, left, or right, instructing the browser where the legend should be placed with respect to the field set.

Bringing all these tags together, here are a field set and legend containing a few form elements, individually labeled:

```
<fieldset>
    <legend>Personal information</legend>
```

```
        <label>Name:<input type="text" /></label>
        <label>Address:<input type="text" /></label>
        <label>Phone:<input type="text" /></label>
    </fieldset>
```

Notice in Figure 9-9 how Firefox neatly puts a frame around the field set and through the legend but doesn't otherwise format the field set's contents. Obviously, you'll need to do some format-tweaking yourself.

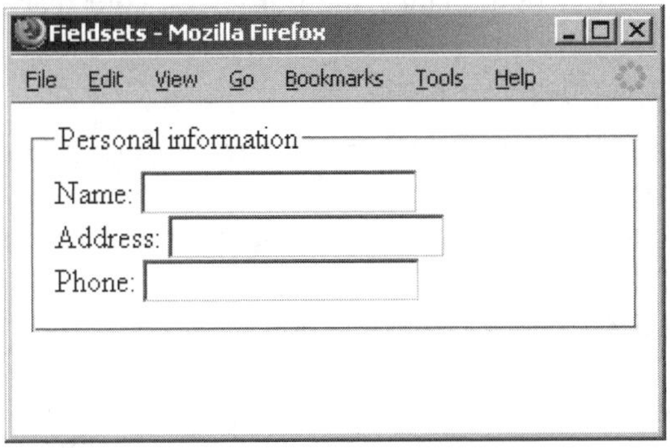

Figure 9-9. Browsers fully frame form fieldsets

9.11 Creating Effective Forms

Properly done, a form can provide an effective user interface for your readers. With some server-side programming tricks, you can use forms to personalize the documents that you present to readers and thereby significantly increase the value of your pages on the Web.

9.11.1 Browser Constraints

Unlike other GUIs, browser displays are static. They have little or no capability for real-time data validation, for example, or for updating the values in a form based upon user input, giving users no help or guidance.* Consequently, poorly designed web forms are difficult to fill out.

Make sure your forms assist users as much as possible. For example, adjust the size of text-input fields to give clues on acceptable input; five-character (or nine-character) zip codes, for instance. Use checkboxes, radio buttons, and selection lists whenever possible to narrow the list of choices the user must make.

---

* This is not entirely true. While neither HTML nor XHTML provides for data validation and user guidance, it is possible to attach to your form elements Java or JavaScript applets that do a very nice job of validating form data, updating form fields based upon user input, and guiding users through your forms.

Make sure you also adequately document your forms. Explain how to fill them out, supplying examples for each field. Provide appropriate hyperlinks to documentation that describes each field, if necessary.

When the form is submitted, make sure that the server-side application exhaustively validates the user's data. If an error is discovered, present the user with intelligent error messages and possible corrections. One of the most frustrating aspects of filling out forms is to have to start over from scratch whenever the server discovers an error. To alleviate this ugly redundancy and burden on your readers, consider spending extra time and resources on the server side that returns the user's completed form with the erroneous fields flagged for changes.

While these suggestions require significant effort on your part, they pay off many times over by making life easier for your users. Remember, you create the form just once, but it may be used thousands or even millions of times by users.

9.11.2 Handling Limited Displays

Although most PCs have been upgraded to provide resolution significantly better than the 600×480 that was common when we wrote the first edition of this book, many devices (WebTV, cell phones with built-in browsers, PDAs) dictate that form design should be conservative. The best compromise is to assume a document-viewing window roughly 75 readable characters wide and 30 to 50 lines tall.* You should design your forms (and all your documents) so that they are effective when viewed through a window of this size.

You should structure your form to scroll naturally into two or three logical sections. The user can fill out the first section, page down; fill out the second section, page down; and so forth.

You should also avoid wide input elements. It is difficult enough to deal with a scrolling text field or text area without having to scroll the document itself horizontally to see additional portions of the input element.

9.11.3 User-Interface Considerations

When you elect to create a form, you immediately assume another role: that of a user-interface designer. While a complete discussion of user-interface design is beyond the scope of this book, it helps to understand a few basic design rules to create effective, attractive forms.

---

* Some devices, such as cell phones, have tiny displays, as small as four lines. A better approach, though beyond the scope of this book, is to tailor your design to the device, using Extensible Stylesheet Transformations (XSLT).

Any user interface is perceived at several levels simultaneously. Forms are no different. At the lowest level, your brain recognizes shapes within the document, attempting to categorize the elements of the form. At a higher level, you are reading the text guides and prompts, trying to determine what input is required of you. At the highest level, you are seeking to accomplish a goal with the interface as your tool.

A good form accommodates all three of these perceptive needs. Input elements should be organized in logical groups so that your brain can process the form layout in chunks of related fields. Consistent, well-written prompts and supporting text assist and lead the user to enter the correct information. Text prompts also remind users of the task at hand and reinforce the form's goal.

9.11.4 Creating Forms That Flow

Users process forms in a predictable order, one element after another, seeking to find the next element as they finish the previous one. To accommodate this searching process, you should design your forms so that one field leads naturally to another and related fields are grouped together. Similarly, groups should lead naturally to one another and should be formatted in a consistent manner.

Simply stringing a number of fields together does not constitute an effective form. You must put yourself in the place of your users, who are using the form for the first time. Test your form on unsuspecting friends and colleagues before you release it to the general public. Is it easy to determine the purpose of the form? Where do you start filling things out? Can the user find a button to click to submit the form? Is there an opportunity to confirm decisions? Do readers understand what is expected of them for each field?

Your forms should lead the user naturally through the process of supplying the necessary data for the application. You wouldn't ask for a street address before asking for the user's name; other rules may dictate the ordering of other groups of input elements. To see whether your form really works, make sure you view it on several browsers and have several people fill it out and comment on its effectiveness.

9.11.5 Good Form, Old Chap

At first glance, the basic rule of HTML and XHTML—content, not style—seems in direct opposition to the basic rule of good interface design—precise, consistent layout. Even so, it is possible to use some elements to greatly improve the layout and readability of most forms.

Traditional page layout uses a grid of columns to align common elements within a page. The resulting implied vertical and horizontal "edges" of adjacent elements give a sense of order and organization to the page and make it easy for the eye to scan and follow.

HTML and XHTML make it hard, but you can accomplish the same sort of layout for your forms. For example, you can group related elements and separate groups with empty paragraphs or horizontal rules.

Vertical alignment is more difficult, but not impossible. In general, forms are easier to use if you arrange the input elements vertically and aligned to a common margin. One popular form layout keeps the left edge of the input elements aligned, with the element labels immediately to the left of the elements. This is done by using tables to place and align each form element and its label. Here is our previous HTML form example, with the labels placed in the first column and the corresponding elements in the second:

```
<form method=POST action="http://www.kumquat.com/demo">
  <table border=0>
    <tr valign=top>
      <td align=right>Name:</td>
      <td align=left><input type=text name=name size=32 maxlength=80>
      </td>
    </tr>
    <tr valign=top >
      <td align=right>Sex:</td>
      <td align=left>
        <input type=radio name=sex value="M"> Male <br>
        <input type=radio name=sex value="F"> Female
      </td>
    </tr>
    <tr valign=top >
      <td align=right>Income:</td>
      <td align=left>
        <select name=income size=1>
          <option>Under $25,000
          <option>$25,001 to $50,000
          <option>$50,001 and higher
        </select>
      </td>
    </tr>
    <tr valign=top>
      <td colspan=2 align=center>
        <input type=submit value="Submit Query">
      </td>
    </tr>
  </table>
</form>
```

Notice in the resulting rendered form, shown in Figure 9-10, that the table has placed each input element in its own row. The `align` attributes in the table cells force the labels to the right and the elements to the left, creating a vertical margin through the form. By spanning the cell in the last row, the submission button is centered with respect to the entire form. In general, using tables in this manner makes form layout much easier and more consistent throughout your documents. If you find this example at all difficult, see Chapter 10, which explains in detail all the glories of tables.

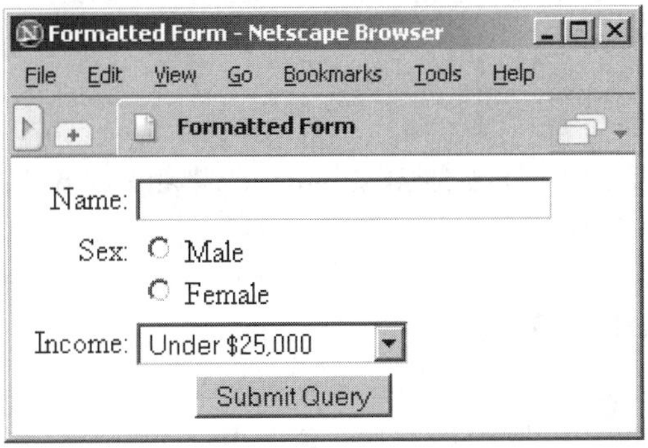

Figure 9-10. Use a consistent vertical margin to align form elements

You may find other consistent ways to lay out your forms. The key is to find a useful layout style that works well across most browsers and stick with it. Even though HTML and XHTML have limited tools to control layout and positioning, take advantage of what is available in order to make your forms more attractive and easier to use.

9.12 Forms Programming

If you create forms, sooner or later you'll need to create the server-side application that processes them. Don't panic. There is nothing magic about server-side programming, nor is it overly difficult. With a little practice and some perseverance, you'll be cranking out forms applications.

The most important advice we can give about forms programming is easy to remember: copy others' work. Writing a forms application from scratch is fairly hard; copying a functioning forms application and modifying it to support your form is far easier.

Fortunately, server vendors know this, and they usually supply sample forms applications with their server. Rummage about for a directory named *cgi-src*, and you should discover a number of useful examples you can easily copy and reuse.

We can't hope to replicate all the useful stuff that came with your server or provide a complete treatise on forms programming. What we can do is offer a simple example of GET and POST applications, giving you a feel for the work involved and hopefully getting you moving in the right direction.

Before we begin, keep in mind that not all servers invoke these applications in the same manner. Our examples cover the broad class of servers derived from the original National Center for Supercomputing Applications (NCSA) HTTP server. They also should work with the very popular and public-domain Apache server. In all cases, consult your server documentation for complete details. You will find even more detailed information in *CGI Programming with Perl*, by Scott Guelich, Gunther

Birznieks, and Shishir Gundavaram, and *Webmaster in a Nutshell*, by Stephen Spain-hour and Robert Eckstein, both published by O'Reilly.

One alternative to CGI programming is the Java servlet model, covered in *Java Servlet Programming*, by Jason Hunter with William Crawford (O'Reilly). Servlets can be used to process GET and POST form submissions, although they are actually more general objects. There are no examples of servlets in this book.

9.12.1 Returning Results

Before we begin, we need to discuss how server-side applications end. All server-side applications pass their results back to the server (and on to the user) by writing those results to the application's standard output as a MIME-encoded file. Hence, the first line of the application's output must be a MIME Content-Type descriptor. If your application returns an HTML document, the first line is:

```
Content-type: text/html
```

The second line must be completely empty. Your application can return other content types, too—just include the correct MIME type. A GIF image, for example, is preceded with:

```
Content-type: image/gif
```

Generic text that is not to be interpreted as HTML can be returned with:

```
Content-type: text/plain
```

This is often useful for returning the output of other commands that generate plain text rather than HTML.

9.12.2 Handling GET Forms

With the GET method, the browser passes form parameters as part of the URL that invokes the server-side forms application. A typical invocation of a GET-style application might use a URL like this:

```
http://www.kumquat.com/cgi-bin/dump_get?name=bob&phone=555-1212
```

When the *www.kumquat.com* server processes this URL, it invokes the application named *dump_get* that is stored in the directory named *cgi-bin*. Everything after the question mark is passed to the application as parameters.

Things diverge a bit at this point, due to the nature of the GET-style URL. While forms place name/value pairs in the URL, it is possible to invoke a GET-style application with only values in the URL. Thus, the following is a valid invocation as well, with parameters separated by plus signs (+):

```
http://www.kumquat.com/cgi-bin/dump_get?bob+555-1212
```

This is a common invocation when the browser references the application via a searchable document with the <isindex> tag. The parameters typed by the user into the document's text-entry field get passed to the server-side application as unnamed parameters separated by plus signs.

If you invoke your GET application with named parameters, your server passes those parameters to the application in one way; unnamed parameters are passed differently.

9.12.2.1 Using named parameters with GET applications

Named parameters are passed to GET applications by creating an environment variable named QUERY_STRING and setting its value to the entire portion of the URL following the question mark. Using our previous example, the value of QUERY_STRING would be set to:

```
name=bob&phone=555-1212
```

Your application must retrieve this variable and extract from it the parameter name/value pairs. Fortunately, most servers come with a set of utility routines that perform this task for you, so a simple C program that just dumps the parameters might look like this:

```
#include <stdio.h>
#include <stdlib.h>

#define MAX_ENTRIES 10000

typedef struct {char *name;
                char *val;
                } entry;

char *makeword(char *line, char stop);
char x2c(char *what);
void unescape_url(char *url);
void plustospace(char *str);

main(int argc, char *argv[])

{   entry entries[MAX_ENTRIES];
    int num_entries, i;
    char *query_string;

/* Get the value of the QUERY_STRING environment variable */
    query_string = getenv("QUERY_STRING");

/* Extract the parameters, building a table of entries */
    for (num_entries = 0; query_string[0]; num_entries++) {
        entries[num_entries].val = makeword(query_string, '&');

        plustospace(entries[num_entries].val);
        unescape_url(entries[num_entries].val);
```

```
        entries[num_entries].name =
            makeword(entries[num_entries].val, '=');
        }

    /* Spit out the HTML boilerplate */
        printf("Content-type: text/html\n");
        printf("\n");

        printf(<html>);
        printf(<head>);
        printf("<title>Named Parameter Echo</title>\n");
        printf("</head>");
        printf(<body>);
        printf("You entered the following parameters:\n");
        printf("<ul>\n");

    /* Echo the parameters back to the user */
        for(i = 0; i < num_entries; i++)
            printf("<li> %s = %s\n", entries[i].name,
                        entries[i].val);

    /* And close out with more boilerplate */
        printf("</ul>\n");
        printf("</body>\n");
        printf("</html>\n");
    }
```

The example program begins with a few declarations that define the utility routines that scan through a character string and extract the parameter names and values.[*] The body of the program obtains the value of the QUERY_STRING environment variable using the getenv( ) system call, uses the utility routines to extract the parameters from that value, and then generates a simple HTML document that echoes those values back to the user.

For real applications, you should insert your actual processing code after the parameter extraction and before the HTML generation. Of course, you'll also need to change the HTML generation to match your application's functionality.

9.12.2.2 Using unnamed parameters with GET applications

Unnamed parameters get passed to the application as command-line parameters. This makes writing the server-side application almost trivial. Here is a simple shell script that dumps the parameter values back to the user:

```
#!/bin/csh -f
#
# Dump unnamed GET parameters back to the user

echo "Content-type: text/html"
```

---

[*] These routines are usually supplied by the server vendor. They are not part of the standard C or Unix library.

```
echo
echo '<html>'
echo '<head>'
echo '<title>Unnamed Parameter Echo</title>'
echo '</head>'
echo '<body>'
echo 'You entered the following parameters:'
echo '<ul>'

foreach i ($*)
    echo '<li>' $i
end

echo '</ul>'
echo '</body>'

exit 0
```

Again, we follow the same general style: output a generic document header, including the MIME Content-Type, followed by the parameters and some closing boilerplate. To convert this to a real application, replace the foreach loop with commands that actually do something.

9.12.3 Handling POST Forms

Forms-processing applications that accept HTML/XHTML POST-style parameters expect to read encoded parameters from their standard input. Like GET-style applications with named parameters, they can take advantage of the server's utility routines to parse these parameters.

Here is a program that echoes the POST-style parameters back to the user:

```
#include <stdio.h>
#include <stdlib.h>

#define MAX_ENTRIES 10000

typedef struct {char *name;
                char *val;
                } entry;

char *makeword(char *line, char stop);
char *fmakeword(FILE *f, char stop, int *len);
char x2c(char *what);
void unescape_url(char *url);
void plustospace(char *str);

main(int argc, char *argv[])

{   entry entries[MAX_ENTRIES];
    int num_entries, i;
```

```
    /* Parse parameters from stdin, building a table of entries */
        for (num_entries = 0; !feof(stdin); num_entries++) {
            entries[num_entries].val = fmakeword(stdin, '&', &cl);
            plustospace(entries[num_entries].val);
            unescape_url(entries[num_entries].val);
            entries[num_entries].name =
                makeword(entries[num_entries].val, '=');
        }

    /* Spit out the HTML boilerplate */
        printf("Content-type: text/html\n");
        printf("\n");
        printf(<html>);
        printf(<head>);
        printf("<title>Named Parameter Echo</title>\n");
        printf("</head>");
        printf(<body>);
        printf("You entered the following parameters:\n");
        printf("<ul>\n");

    /* Echo the parameters back to the user */
        for(i = 0; i < num_entries; i++)
            printf("<li> %s = %s\n", entries[i].name,
                        entries[i].val);

    /* And close out with more boilerplate */
        printf("</ul>\n");
        printf("</body>\n");
        printf("</html>\n");
    }
```

Again, we follow the same general form. The program starts by declaring the various utility routines needed to parse the parameters, along with a data structure to hold the parameter list. The actual code begins by reading the parameter list from the standard input and building a list of parameter names and values in the array named entries. Once this is complete, a boilerplate document header is written to the standard output, followed by the parameters and some closing boilerplate.

Like the other examples, this program is handy for checking the parameters being passed to the server application early in the forms- and application-debugging process. You can also use it as a skeleton for other applications by inserting appropriate processing code after the parameter list is built up and altering the output section to send back the appropriate results.

Tables

Of all the extensions that found their way into HTML and XHTML, none is more welcome than tables. While tables are useful for the general display of tabular data, they also serve an important role in managing document layout. Creative use of tables, as we'll show in this chapter, can go a long way to enliven an otherwise dull document layout. And you can apply all the Cascading Style Sheet (CSS) styles to the various elements of a table to achieve a desktop-published look and feel.

10.1 The Standard Table Model

The standard model for tables is fairly straightforward: a table is a collection of numbers and words arranged in rows and columns of *cells*. Most cells contain the data values; others contain row and column headers that describe the data.

You define a table and include all of its elements between the `<table>` tag and its corresponding `</table>` end tag. Table elements, including data items, row and column headers, and captions, each have their own markup tags. Working from left to right and top to bottom, you define, in sequence, the header and data for each column cell across and down the table.

The latest standards also provide a rich collection of tag attributes, many of which once were popular extensions to HTML as supported by the popular browsers. They make your tables look good, by enabling special alignment of the table values and headers, borders, table rule lines, and automatic sizing of the data cells to accommodate their content, among other capabilities. The various popular browsers have slightly different sets of table attributes; we'll point out those variations as we go.

10.1.1 Table Contents

You can put nearly anything you might have within the body of an HTML or XHTML document inside a table cell, including images, forms, rules, headings, and even another table. The browser treats each cell as a window unto itself, flowing the cell's content to fill the space, but with some special formatting provisions and extensions.

10.1.2 An Example Table

Here's a quick example that should satisfy your itching curiosity to see what an HTML table looks like in a source document and when finally rendered, as shown in Figure 10-1. More importantly, it shows you the basic structure of a table, from which you can infer many of the elements, tag syntax and order, attributes, and so on, and to which you may refer as you read the following various detailed descriptions:

```
<table border cellspacing=0 cellpadding=5>
  <caption align=bottom>
    Kumquat versus a poked eye, by gender</caption>
  <tr>
    <td colspan=2 rowspan=2></td>
    <th colspan=2 align=center>Preference</th>
  </tr>
  <tr>
    <th>Eating Kumquats</th>
    <th>Poke In The Eye</th>
  </tr>
  <tr align=center>
    <th rowspan=2>Gender</th>
    <th>Male</th>
    <td>73%</td>
    <td>27%</td>
  </tr>
  <tr align=center>
    <th>Female</th>
    <td>16%</td>
    <td>84%</td>
  </tr>
</table>
```

10.1.3 Missing Features

At one time, standard HTML tables didn't have all the features of a full-fledged table-generation tool you might find in a popular word processor. Rather, the popular browsers, Internet Explorer and Netscape in particular, provided extensions to the language.

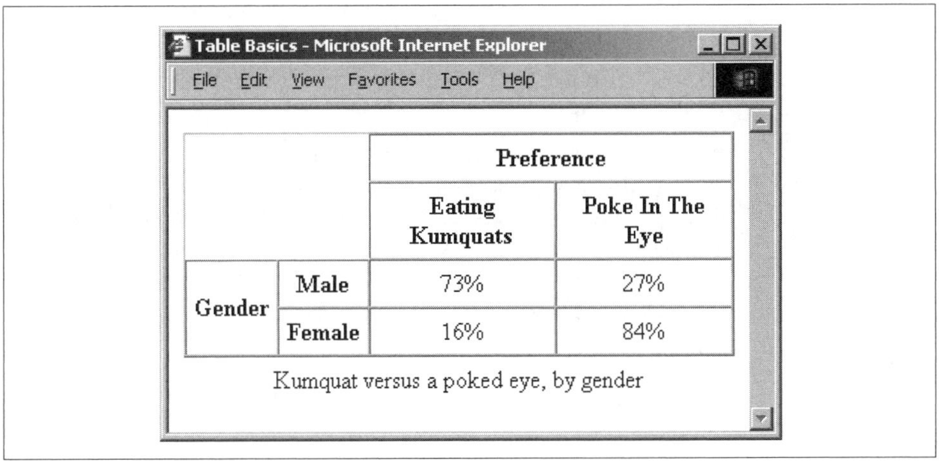

Figure 10-1. HTML table example

Missing were features that supported running headers and footers, particularly useful when printing a lengthy table. Another missing feature was control over table rules and divisions.

Today, the standards are ahead of the browsers in terms of table features; HTML 4 and XHTML standardize the many extensions and provide additional solutions.

10.2 Basic Table Tags

You can create a wide variety of tables with only five tags: the <table> tag, which encapsulates a table and its elements in the document's body content; the <tr> tag, which defines a table row; the <th> and <td> tags, which define the table's headers and data cells; and the <caption> tag, which defines a title or caption for the table. Beyond these core tags, you may also define and control whole sections of tables, including adding running headers and footers, with the <colgroup>, <col>, <tbody>, <thead>, and <tfoot> tags. Each tag has one or more required and optional attributes, some of which affect not only the tag itself but also related tags.

10.2.1 The <table> Tag

The <table> tag and its </table> end tag define and encapsulate a table within the body of your document. Unless you place them within the browser window by stylesheet, paragraph, division-level, or other alignment options, the browser stops the current text flow, breaks the line, inserts the table beginning on a new line, and then restarts the text flow on a new line below the table.

<table>

Function	Defines a table
Attributes	align, background, bgcolor, border, bordercolor 🔾, bordercolordark 🔾, bordercolorlight 🔾, cellpadding, cellspacing, class, cols, dir, frame, height, hspace, id, lang, nowrap, onClick, onDblClick, onKeyDown, onKeyPress, onKeyUp, onMouseDown, onMouseMove, onMouseOut, onMouseOver, onMouseUp, rules, style, summary, title, valign, vspace, width
End tag	</table>; never omitted
Contains	*table_content*
Used in	*block*

The only content allowed within the <table> is one or more <tr> tags, which define each row of table contents, along with the various table sectioning tags: <thead>, <tfoot>, <tbody>, <col>, and <colgroup>.

10.2.1.1 The align attribute (deprecated)

The HTML 4 and XHTML standards have deprecated this attribute in favor of the align property provided by CSS, yet it remains popular and is currently well supported by the popular browsers.

Like images, tables are rectangular objects that float in the browser display, aligned according to the current text flow. Normally, the browser left-justifies a table, abutting its left edge to the left margin of the display window. Or the table may be centered if under the influence of the <center> tag, a centered paragraph, or a centered division. Unlike images, however, tables are not inline objects. Text content normally flows above and below a table, not beside it. You can change that display behavior with the align attribute or a cascading style definition for the <table> tag.

The align attribute accepts a value of either left, right, or center, indicating that the table should be placed flush against the left or right margin of the text flow, with the text flowing around the table, or in the middle with text flowing above and below, respectively.

Note that the align attribute within the <table> tag is different from those used within a table's element tags, <tr>, <td>, and <th>. In those tags, the attribute controls text alignment within the table's cells, not alignment of the table within the containing body-text flow.

10.2.1.2 The bgcolor and background attributes

You can make the background of a table a different color than the document's background with the bgcolor attribute for the <table> tag. You must set the color value for the bgcolor attribute to either a red, blue, and green (RGB) color value or a standard color name. Appendix G provides both the syntax of color values and the acceptable color names.

The popular browsers give every cell in the table (but not the caption) this background color. You may also set individual row and cell colors by providing the bgcolor attribute or a style attribute for those rows or cells.

The background attribute, a nonstandard extension supported by all the popular browsers, supplies the URL of an image that is tiled to fill the background of the table. The image is clipped if the table is smaller than the image. By using this attribute with a borderless table, you can put text over an image contained within a document.

10.2.1.3 The border attribute

The optional border attribute for the <table> tag tells the browser to draw lines around the table and the rows and cells within it. The default is no borders at all. You may specify a value for border, but you don't have to with HTML. Alone, the attribute simply enables borders and a set of default characteristics. With XHTML, use border="border" to achieve the same default results. Otherwise, in HTML or with XHTML, supply an integer value for border equal to the pixel width of the 3D chiseled-edge lines that surround the outside of the table and make it appear to be embossed onto the page.

10.2.1.4 The frame and rules attributes

With Netscape 4, the border attribute was all or nothing, affecting the appearance and spacing both of the frame around the table and of the rule lines between data cells. Internet Explorer versions 4 and later and Netscape 6 and later versions, as well as the popular Firefox and Opera, let you individually modify the various line segments that make up the borders around the table (frame) and around the data cells (rules).

The standard frame attribute modifies border's effects for the lines that surround the table. The default value—what you get if you don't use frame at all—is box, which tells the browser to draw all four lines around the table. The value border does the same thing as box. The value void removes all four of the frame segments. The frame values above, below, lhs, and rhs draw the various border segments on the top, bottom, left, and right side, respectively, of the table. The value hsides draws borders on the top and bottom (horizontal) sides of the table; vsides draws borders on the left and right (vertical) sides of the table.

With standard tables now supported by the latest versions of all the popular browsers, you also may control the thickness of a table's internal cell borders via the rules attribute. The default behavior, represented by the value of all, is to draw borders around all cells. Specifying groups places thicker borders between row and column groups defined by the <thead>, <tbody>, <tfoot>, <col>, and <colgroup> tags. Using rows or cols places borders only between every row or column, respectively, and using none removes borders from every cell in the table.

10.2.1.5 The bordercolor, bordercolorlight, and bordercolordark attributes

The popular browsers normally draw a table border in three colors, using light and dark variations on the document's background color to achieve a 3D effect. Internet Explorer's nonstandard bordercolor attribute lets you set the color of the table borders and rules to something other than the background (if borders are enabled, of course). The bordercolor attribute's value can be either an RGB hexadecimal color value or a standard color name, both of which we describe fully in Appendix G.

Internet Explorer also lets you set the border edge colors individually with special extension attributes: the bordercolorlight and bordercolordark colors shade the lighter and darker edges of the border. The 3D beveled-border effect is tied to the relationship between these two colors. In general, the light color should be about 25 percent brighter than the border color, and the dark color should be about 25 percent darker. That is, if you use them at all: only your Internet Explorer users will see the effects.

10.2.1.6 The cellspacing attribute

The cellspacing attribute controls the amount of space placed between adjacent cells in a table and along the outer edges of cells along the edges of a table.

Browsers normally put two pixels of space between cells and along the outer edges of a table. If you include a border attribute in the <table> tag, the cell spacing between interior cells grows by two more pixels (for a total of four) to make space for the chiseled edge on the interior border. The outer edges of edge cells grow by the value of the border attribute.

By including the cellspacing attribute, you can widen or reduce the interior cell borders. For instance, to make the thinnest possible interior cell borders, include the border and cellspacing=0 attributes in the table's tag.

10.2.1.7 The cellpadding attribute

The cellpadding attribute controls the amount of space between the edge of a cell and its contents, which by default is 1 pixel. You may make all the cell contents in a table touch their respective cell borders by including cellpadding=0 in the table tag. You may also increase the cellpadding space by making its value greater than 1.

10.2.1.8 Combining the border, cellspacing, and cellpadding attributes

The interactions between the border, cellspacing, and cellpadding attributes of the <table> tag combine in ways that can be confusing. Figure 10-2 summarizes how the attributes create interior and exterior borders of various widths.

While all sorts of combinations of the border and cellspacing attributes are possible, these are the most common:

- border=1 and cellspacing=0 produces the narrowest possible interior and exterior borders: 2 pixels wide.
- border=n and cellspacing=0 makes the narrowest possible interior borders (2 pixels wide) with an external border that is $n + 1$ pixels wide.
- border=1 and cellspacing=n tables have equal-width exterior and interior borders, all with chiseled edges just 1 pixel wide. All borders will be $n + 2$ pixels wide.

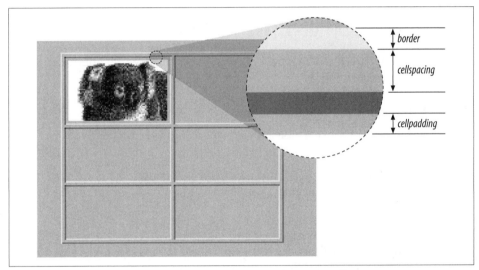

Figure 10-2. The border, cellspacing, and cellpadding attributes of a table

10.2.1.9 The cols attribute

To format a table, the browser must first read a table's entire content to determine the number and width of each column in the table. This can be a lengthy process for long tables, forcing users to wait to see your pages. The nonstandard cols attribute tells the browser, in advance, how many columns to expect in the table. The value of this attribute is an integer value defining the number of columns in the table.

The cols attribute only advises the browser. If you define a different number of columns, the browser is free to ignore the cols attribute in order to render the table correctly. In general, it is good form to include this attribute with your <table> tag, if only to help the browser do a faster job of formatting your tables.

10.2.1.10 The valign and nowrap attributes

The valign attribute sets the default vertical alignment of data in cells for the entire table. Acceptable values for the valign attribute in <table> are top, bottom, middle, and baseline; the default vertical position is the center of the cell.

Browsers treat each table cell as though it's a browser window unto itself, flowing contents inside the cell as they would common body contents (although they are subject to special table-cell alignment properties). Accordingly, the browsers automatically wrap text lines to fill the allotted table cell space. The nowrap attribute, when included in the <table> tag, stops that normal word wrapping in all rows in the table. With nowrap, the browser assembles the contents of the cell onto a single line, unless you insert a <br> or <p> tag, which then forces a break so that the contents continue on a new line inside the table cell.

With the <table> tag, only Opera supports valign. None of the browsers supports nowrap at that level. Instead, you can achieve similar effects by including a valign or nowrap attribute within the individual <tr>, <td>, and <th> tags, an approach that all the popular browsers support.

10.2.1.11 The width and height attributes

Browsers automatically make a table only as wide as needed to correctly display all of the cell contents. If necessary, you can make a table wider with the width attribute.

The value of the width attribute is either an integer number of pixels or a relative percentage of the screen width, including values greater than 100 percent. For example:

```
<table width=400>
```

tells the extended browser to make the table 400 pixels wide, including any borders and cell spacing that extend into the outer edge of the table. If the table is wider than 400 pixels, the browser ignores the attribute. Alternatively:

```
<table width="50%">
```

tells the browser to make the table half as wide as the display window. Again, this width includes any borders or cell spacing that extends into the outer edge of the table and has no effect if the table normally is more than half the user's current screen width.

Use relative widths for tables you want to resize automatically to the user's window; for instance, tables you always want to extend across the entire window (<table width="100%">). Use an absolute width value for carefully formatted tables whose contents become hard to read in wide display windows.

Also with the popular browsers, you can use the nonstandard height attribute to suggest a recommended height for the table. The browser makes the table no shorter than this height but may make the table taller if needed to contain the table's contents. This attribute is useful when trying to stretch tables to fit in a frame or some specific area of a document but is of little use otherwise, particularly because it is not a standard attribute.

10.2.1.12 The summary attribute

The summary attribute was introduced to HTML in the 4.0 standard. Its value is a quote-enclosed string that describes the purpose and summarizes the contents of the table. Its intended use, according to the standard, is to provide extended access to nonvisual browsers, particularly for users with disabilities.

10.2.1.13 The hspace and vspace attributes

As with images, give your table some extra space within the body of your document. Use the nonstandard hspace and vspace attributes in the <table> tag, each with a value equal to the number of pixels of space to offset the table from the left and right or top and bottom, respectively, of the enclosing text. Interestingly, all of the popular browsers, except for Internet Explorer, support these as <table> attributes, even though Internet Explorer supports them with the <img> tag.

10.2.2 Common Table Attributes

The HTML and XHTML standards, combined with the CSS standard, provide a number of attributes common not only to the <table> tag and the other table-creation tags, but to most other tags as well.

10.2.2.1 The id and title attributes

Use the id attribute with a quote-enclosed string value to uniquely label a <table> tag for later reference by a hyperlink or an applet. Use the title attribute with a string value to optionally title the table or any of its segments for general reference. A title's value need not be unique, and the browser may or may not use it. The popular browsers, for example, display the title attribute's text value whenever the user passes the mouse pointer over the element's contents. [The id attribute, 4.1.1.4] [The title attribute, 4.1.1.5]

10.2.2.2 The dir and lang attributes

Although its contents are predominantly in English, the Web is worldwide. The HTML 4 and XHTML standards take pains to extend the language to all cultures. We support that effort wholeheartedly. The dir and lang attributes are just small parts of that process.

The dir attribute advises the browser in which direction the text of the contents should flow—from left to right (dir=ltr), as for common Western languages like English and German, or right to left (dir=rtl), as for common Eastern languages like Hebrew and Chinese.

The lang attribute lets you explicitly indicate the language used in the table or even individual cell contents. Its value should be an International Organization for Standardization (ISO) standard two-letter primary code followed by an optional dialect subcode, with a hyphen (-) between the two.

All the latest versions of the popular browsers support the dir and lang attributes. [The dir attribute, 3.6.1.1] [The lang attribute, 3.6.1.2]

10.2.2.3 The class and style attributes

The CSS standard is the sanctioned way to define display attributes for HTML/ XHTML elements, and it is rapidly becoming the only way. Use the style attribute to define display characteristics for the table and its elements that take immediate effect and override the display styles that may be currently in effect for the whole document. Use the class attribute to reference a stylesheet that defines the unique display characteristics for the table and its elements.

We discuss the class and style attributes and the CSS standard in detail in Chapter 8. Their effects apply to all aspects of tables, and are well supported by the popular browsers. [Inline Styles: The style Attribute, 8.1.1] [Style Classes, 8.3]

10.2.2.4 The event attributes

Most of today's browsers have internal mechanisms that detect the various user-initiated mouse and keyboard events that can happen in and around your tables and their elements. For instance, the user might click the mouse pointer in one of the table cells or highlight the caption and then press the Enter key.

With the various event attributes, such as onClick and onKeyDown, you can react to these events by having the browser execute one or more JavaScript commands or applets that you reference as the value to the respective event attribute. See Chapter 12 for details.

10.2.3 The <tr> Tag

Make a new row in a table with the <tr> tag. Place within the <tr> tag one or more cells containing headers, defined with the <th> tag, or data, defined with the <td> tag (see section 10.2.4). The <tr> tag accepts a number of special attributes that control its behavior, along with the common table attributes described earlier in section 10.2.2 .

Every row in a table has the same number of cells as the longest row; the browser automatically creates empty cells to pad rows with fewer defined cells.

<table>
<tr>
<td colspan="2" align="center">**<tr>**</td>
</tr>
<tr>
<td>**Function**</td>
<td>Defines a row within a table</td>
</tr>
<tr>
<td>**Attributes**</td>
<td>align, background 🖹, bgcolor, bordercolor 🖹, bordercolordark 🖹, bordercolorlight 🖹, char, charoff, class, dir, id, lang, nowrap, onClick, onDblClick, onKeyDown, onKeyPress, onKeyUp, onMouseDown, onMouseMove, onMouseOut, onMouseOver, onMouseUp, style, title, valign</td>
</tr>
<tr>
<td>**End tag**</td>
<td></tr>; may be omitted in HTML</td>
</tr>
<tr>
<td>**Contains**</td>
<td>*tr_content*</td>
</tr>
<tr>
<td>**Used in**</td>
<td>*table_content*</td>
</tr>
</table>

10.2.3.1 The align and valign attributes

The align attribute for the <table> tag may be deprecated in the HTML and XHTML standards, but it is alive and kicking for <tr> and other table elements. The align attribute for the <tr> tag lets you change the default horizontal alignment of all the contents of the cells in a row. The attribute affects all the cells within the current row, but not subsequent rows.

An align attribute value of left, right, center, justify, or char causes the browser to align the contents of each cell in the row against the left or right edge, in the center of the cell, spread across the cell, or to a specified character in the cell, respectively.

Similarly, you can change the default vertical alignment for the contents of data cells contained within a table row with the valign attribute. Normally, browsers render cell contents centered vertically. By including the valign attribute in the <tr> tag with a value of top, bottom, center, middle, or baseline (Internet Explorer only), you tell the browser to place the table row's contents flush against the top or bottom of their cells, centered, or aligned to the baseline of the top line of text in other cells in the row, respectively (see Figure 10-3):

```
<table border="border">
  <tr>
    <th>Alignment</th>
    <th>Top</th>
    <th>Baseline</th>
    <th>Center</th>
    <th>Middle></th>
    <th>Bottom</th>
  </tr>
  <tr align="center">
    <th><h1>Baseline_  _<br />Another line</h1></th>
    <td valign="top">AAyy</td>
```

```
      <td valign="baseline">_AAyy_</td>
      <td valign="center">AAyy</td>
      <td valign="middle">AAyy</td>
      <td valign="bottom">AAyy</td>
    </tr>
  </table>
```

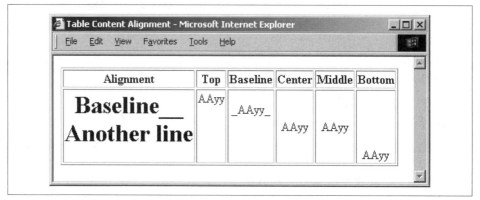

Figure 10-3. Effects of the valign attribute; only Internet Explorer (shown here) supports the baseline value for valign

You also can specify the horizontal and vertical alignments for individual cells within a row (see 10.2.3.1). Use the alignment attributes in the `<tr>` tag to specify the most common cell-content justifications for the row (if not the default), and use a different `align` or `valign` attribute for those individual cells that deviate from the common alignment.

Table 10-1 contains the horizontal (`align`) and vertical (`valign`) table cell-content attribute values and options. Values in parentheses are the defaults for the popular browsers.

Table 10-1. Table cell-content alignment attribute values and options

Attribute	Headers (<th>)	Data (<td>)
align	Left	(Left)
	(Center)	Center
	Right	Right
	Justify	Justify
	Char[a]	Char[a]
valign	Top	Top
	(Center)	(Center)
	(Middle)	(Middle)
	Bottom	Bottom
	Baseline	Baseline

[a] Value not yet supported.

10.2.3.2 The char and charoff attributes

Even simple word processors let you line up decimal points for numbers in a table. Until the advent of the HTML 4.0 standard, however, the language was deficient in this feature. Now you may include the char attribute to indicate which letter in each of the table row's cells should be the axis for that alignment. You need not include a value with char. If you don't, the default character is language based: it's a period in English, for example, and a comma in French. Include the char attribute and a single letter as its value to specify a different alignment character.

Use the charoff attribute and an integer value to specify the offset to the first occurrence of the alignment character on each line. If a line doesn't include the alignment character, it should be horizontally shifted to end at the alignment position.

The char and charoff attributes are defined in HTML 4 and XHTML but are not yet supported by any of the popular browsers.

10.2.3.3 The bgcolor and background attributes

Like its relative for the <table> tag, the bgcolor attribute for the <tr> tag sets the background color of the entire row. Its value is either an RGB color value or a standard color name. Appendix G provides both the syntax of color values and the acceptable color names.

Every cell in the row is given this background color. You can change individual cell colors by providing the bgcolor attribute for those cells.

The nonstandard background attribute with its image-file URL value places a graphic tiled into and behind the text of the entire table row. For example, this tag fills the table row with bricks:

```
<tr background="bricks.gif">
```

All the popular browsers support bgcolor and all support the background extension, except Internet Explorer.

10.2.3.4 The bordercolor, bordercolorlight, and bordercolordark attributes

Like their nonstandard brethren for the <table> tag, Internet Explorer only lets you use these attributes to set the color of the borders within the current row.

Their values override any values set by the corresponding attributes in the containing <table> tag. See the corresponding descriptions of these extensions in section 10.2.1.5, earlier in this chapter, for details. Color values can be either RGB color values or standard color names, both of which we describe fully in Appendix G.

10.2.3.5 The nowrap attribute

Browsers treat each table cell as though it were a browser window unto itself, flowing contents inside the cell as they would common body contents (although subject to special table cell-alignment properties). Accordingly, the browsers automatically wrap text lines to fill the allotted table cell space. The nowrap attribute, when included in a table row, stops that normal word wrapping in all cells in that row. With nowrap, the browser assembles the contents of the cell onto a single line, unless you insert a <br> or <p> tag, which forces a break so that the contents continue on a new line inside the table cell.

10.2.4 The <th> and <td> Tags

The <th> and <td> tags go inside the <tr> tags of a table to create the header and data cells, respectively, and to define the cell contents within the rows. The tags operate similarly; the only real differences are that the browsers render header text—meant to title or otherwise describe table data—in boldface font style and that the default alignment of their respective contents may be different than for data. Data typically gets left-justified by default; headers get centered (refer to Table 10-1).

<th> and <td>	
Function	Define table data and header cells
Attributes	abbr, align, background, bgcolor, bordercolor ⬛, bordercolordark ⬛, bordercolorlight ⬛, char, charoff, class, colspan, dir, headers, height, id, lang, nowrap, onClick, onDblClick, onKeyDown, onKeyPress, onKeyUp, onMouseDown, onMouseMove, onMouseOut, onMouseOver, onMouseUp, rowspan, scope, style, title, valign, width
End tag	</th> or </td>; may be omitted in HTML
Contains	*body_content*
Used in	*tr_content*

Like those available for the table row (<tr>) tag, the table cell tags support a rich set of style and content-alignment attributes that you may apply to a single data or header cell. These attributes override the default values for the current row. Special attributes control the number of columns or rows a cell may span in the table. The <th> and <td> tags also accept the common table attributes described earlier in section 10.2.2.

The contents of the <th> and <td> tags can be anything you might put in the body of a document, including text, images, forms, and so on—even another table. And, as described earlier, the browser automatically creates a table large enough, both vertically and horizontally, to display all the contents of any and all the cells.

If a particular row has fewer header or data items than other rows, the browser adds empty cells at the end to fill the row. If you need to make an empty cell before the end of a row—for instance, to indicate a missing data point—create a header or data cell with no content.

Empty cells look different from those containing data or headers if the table has borders: the empty cell does not appear embossed onto the window but instead is simply left blank. If you want to create an empty cell that has incised borders like all the other cells in your table, be sure to place a minimal amount of content in the cell: a single <br> tag, for instance.

10.2.4.1 The align and valign attributes

The align and valign attributes are identical to those of the same name for the table row tag (<tr>; see 10.2.3, earlier in this chapter), except that when used with a <th> or <td> tag, they control the horizontal or vertical alignment of content in just the current cell. Their value overrides any alignment established by the respective align or valign attribute of the <tr> tag but does not affect the alignment of subsequent cells. Refer to Table 10-1 for alignment details.

You may set the align attribute's value to left, right, or center, causing the browsers to align the cell contents against the left or right edge or in the center of the cell, respectively.

In earlier versions, Internet Explorer (version 5) also supported the align value justify so that the words spread out to fill the cell, as in a newspaper column. No longer.

The valign attribute may have a value of top (default), bottom, center, middle, or baseline, telling the browser to align the cell's contents to the top or bottom edge, in the center or middle of the cell, or (Internet Explorer only) to the baseline of the first line of text in other cells in the row.

10.2.4.2 The width attribute

Like its twin in the <table> tag that lets you widen a table, the width attribute for table cell tags lets you widen an individual cell and hence the entire column it occupies. You set the width to an integer number of pixels or a percentage indicating the cell's width as a fraction of the table as a whole.

For example:

```
<th width=400>
```

sets the current header cell's width, and hence the entire column of cells, to 400 pixels wide. Alternatively:

```
<td width="40%">
```

creates a data cell with a column occupying 40 percent of the entire table's width.

Because the popular browsers make all cells in a column the same width, you should place a width attribute in only one cell within a column, preferably the first instance of the cell in the first row, for source readability. If two or more cells in the same column happen to have width attributes, the widest one is honored. You can't make a column thinner than the minimum needed to display all of the cells in the column. Accordingly, if the browser determines that the column of cells needs to be at least 150 pixels wide to accommodate all the cells' contents, it ignores a width attribute in one of the column's cell tags that attempts to make the cell only 100 pixels wide.

10.2.4.3 The height attribute

The height attribute lets you specify a minimum height, in pixels, for the current cell. Because all cells in a row have the same height, you need to specify this attribute on only one cell in the row, preferably the first. If some other cell in the row needs to be taller to accommodate its contents, the browser ignores the height attribute, and all the cells in the row are set to the larger size.

By default, all the cells in a row are the height of the largest cell in the row that just accommodates its contents.

10.2.4.4 The colspan attribute

It's common to have a table header that describes several columns beneath it, like the headers we used in Figure 10-1. Use the colspan attribute in a table header or data tag to extend a table cell across two or more columns in its row. Set the value of the colspan attribute to an integer value equal to the number of columns you want the header or data cell to span. For example:

```
<td colspan="3">
```

tells the browser to make the cell occupy the same horizontal space as three cells in rows above or below it. The browser flows the contents of the cell to occupy the entire space.

What happens if there aren't enough extra cells on the right? The browser just extends the cell over as many columns as exist to the right; it doesn't add extra empty cells to each row to accommodate an overextended colspan value. You may defeat that limitation by adding the needed extra but contentless cells to a single row. (Give them a single <br> tag as their contents if you want an embossed border around them.)

10.2.4.5 The rowspan attribute

Just as the colspan attribute layers a table cell across several columns, the rowspan attribute stretches a cell down two or more rows in the table.

Include the rowspan attribute in the <th> or <td> tag of the uppermost row of the table where you want the cell to begin and set its value equal to the number of rows you want it to span. The cell then occupies the same space as the current row and an appropriate number of cells below that row. The browser flows the contents of the cell to occupy the entire extended space. For example:

```
<td rowspan="3">
```

creates a cell that occupies the current row plus the two rows below it.

Like the colspan attribute, the browser ignores overextended rowspan attributes and extends the current cell only down rows you've explicitly defined by other <tr> tags following the current row. The browsers do not add empty rows to a table to fill a rowspan below the last defined row in a table.

10.2.4.6 Combining the colspan and rowspan attributes

You may extend a single cell both across several columns and down several rows by including both the colspan and rowspan attributes in its table header or data tag. For example:

```
<th colspan="3" rowspan="4">
```

creates a header cell that, as you might expect, spans across three columns and down four rows, including the current cell and extending two more cells to the right and three more cells down. The browser flows the contents of the cell to occupy the entire space, aligned inside according to the current row's alignment specifications or to those you explicitly include in the same tag, as described earlier.

10.2.4.7 The nowrap attribute

Browsers treat each table cell as though it were a browser window unto itself, flowing contents inside the cell as they would common body contents (although subject to special table cell-alignment properties). Accordingly, the browsers automatically wrap text lines to fill the allotted table cell space. The nowrap attribute, when included in a table header or data tag, stops that normal word wrapping. With nowrap, the browser assembles the contents of the cell onto a single line, unless you insert a <br> or <p> tag, which forces a break so that the contents continue on a new line inside the table cell.

10.2.4.8 The bgcolor and background attributes

Yet again, you can change the background color—this time for an individual data cell. This attribute's value is either an RGB hexadecimal color value or a standard color name. Appendix G provides both the syntax of color values and the acceptable color names.

The background attribute supplies the URL of an image that is tiled to fill the background of the cell. The image is clipped if the cell is smaller than the image. Interestingly, Internet Explorer, like all the other popular browsers, supports background when applied to a single cell, but unlike the other popular browsers, does not support background for <table> or <tr>.

Neither background nor bgcolor overrides a related stylesheet property.

10.2.4.9 The bordercolor, bordercolorlight, and bordercolordark attributes

Internet Explorer lets you alter the colors that make up an individual cell's border—if table borders are turned on with the border attribute, of course. See the respective attributes' descriptions under the <table> tag in section 10.2.1.5, earlier in this chapter, for details.

The values for these three attributes override any values set for the containing <table> or <tr> tag. Their values can be either RGB color values or standard color names, both of which we describe fully in Appendix G.

10.2.4.10 The char and charoff attributes

Just as for the <tr> tag, you may use the char attribute with <th> or <td> to indicate which letter in the table cell should be the axis for alignment, such as for decimal numbers. You need not include a value with char in HTML. If you don't, the default character is language based: it's a period in English, for example, and a comma in French. Include the char attribute and a single letter as its value to specify a different alignment character.

Use the charoff attribute and an integer value to specify the offset to the first occurrence of the alignment character in the cell. If a cell doesn't include the alignment character, it should be shifted horizontally to end at the alignment position.

The char and charoff attributes are standard in HTML 4 and XHTML but are not yet supported by any of the popular browsers.

10.2.4.11 The headers and scope attributes

The headers attribute associates header cells with a data cell in the table. The value of this attribute is a quote-enclosed list of names that have been defined for various header cells using the id attribute. The headers attribute is especially useful for non-visual browsers, which might speak the contents of a header cell before presenting the associated data cell contents.

Use the scope attribute to associate data cells with a header cell. With a value of row, all cells in the header's row are associated with the header cell. Specifying col binds all the cells in the current column to the cell. Using rowgroup or colgroup binds all the cells in the cell's row group (defined by a <thead>, <tbody>, or <tfoot> tag) or column group (defined by a <col> or <colgroup> tag) with the header cell.

10.2.4.12 The abbr attribute

The value of this attribute should be an abbreviated description of the cell's contents. When short on space, browsers might choose to render the abbreviation instead, or they might use it in nonvisual contexts.

10.2.4.13 The axis attribute

Tables are usually chock-full of data, prompting the reader to ask questions. A tabular expense report, for example, naturally leads to queries like "How much did I spend on meals?" or "What did my cab fares total?" In the future, browsers may support such queries with the help of the axis attribute.

The value of this attribute is a quote-enclosed list of category names that might be used to form a query. As a result, if you used axis=meals on the cells containing meal purchases, the browser could locate those cells, extract their values, and produce a sum.

10.2.5 The <caption> Tag

A table commonly needs a caption to explain its contents, so the popular browsers provide a table-caption tag. Authors typically place the <caption> tag and its contents immediately after the <table> tag, but you can place it nearly anywhere inside the table and between the row tags. The caption may contain any body content, much like a cell within a table.

<caption>

Function	Defines a table caption
Attributes	align ⬚, class, dir, id, lang, onClick, onDblClick, onKeyDown, onKeyPress, onKeyUp, onMouseDown, onMouseMove, onMouseOut, onMouseOver, onMouseUp, style, title, valign ⬚
End tag	</caption>; never omitted
Contains	body_content
Used in	table_content

10.2.5.1 The align and valign attributes

By default, browsers place the caption's contents centered above the table. You may place it below the table with the align attribute set to the value bottom (the value top, of course, is equivalent to the default).

Also use the align attribute to control the horizontal position of the caption, but the interpretation of the alternative values varies with the popular browsers: with Internet Explorer and Opera, for example, setting the align attribute to left or right respectively left-justifies or right-justifies the caption text against the horizontal edge at the top of the table. With Netscape and Firefox, the caption text gets placed next to and at the top of the left or right side of the table, respectively.

Internet Explorer additionally supports the valign attribute with top or bottom values for <caption>. In combination with align, you place the caption text aligned at any of the four corners of the table, but not along either side. The other browsers ignore valign.

For example, Figure 10-4 demonstrates how Internet Explorer displays the following caption at the bottom of the table and left-justified, whereas Firefox, because it ignores valign and interprets left alignment differently, places the caption against the left side of the table (Figure 10-5):

```
<caption valign=bottom align=left>
    Kumquat versus a poked eye, by gender
</caption>
```

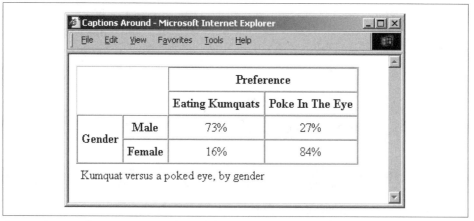

Figure 10-4. Combining Internet Explorer's align and valign <caption> attributes lets you place the text at any of the table's four corners as well as centered top or bottom

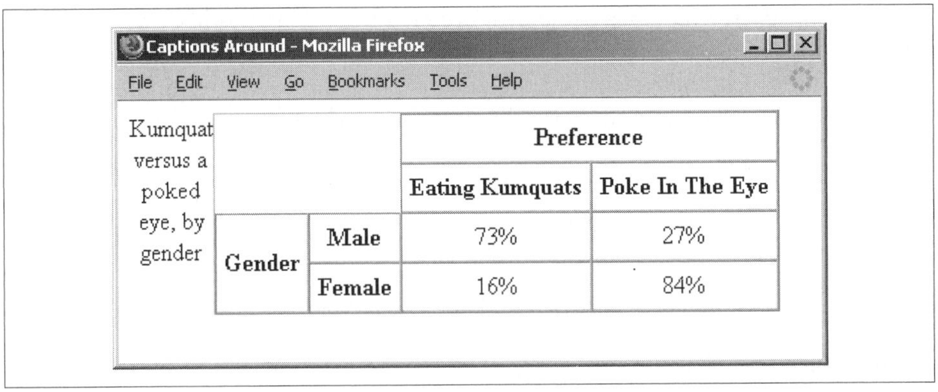

Figure 10-5. Firefox, like Netscape, ignores valign and places the left-aligned caption to the left of the table

10.2.5.2 The many other attributes

Like the other table tags, <caption> supports the many and various language-, event-, and styles-related attributes, which we described earlier in "Common Table Attributes." Use them in good health. Just be sure to use the contextual selector TABLE CAPTION when referring to caption styles at the document level or in external stylesheets.

10.3 Advanced Table Tags

While it is possible to build a simple table quickly, complex tables with varying border styles, running headers and footers, and column-based layout were not easily constructed from the old HTML 3.2 table model. Microsoft rectified this inadequacy somewhat by adding a number of table-layout controls to Internet Explorer version 3.0. These very useful extensions found their way into the HTML 4 standard and subsequently into XHTML. They provide row-based grouping and running headers and footers, along with column-based layout features.

10.3.1 Defining Table Sections

Within tables, all rows are created equal. In real tables, some rows are more equal than others. And most tables have header and footer rows that repeat from page to page. In large tables, adjacent rows are grouped and delineated with different rule lines to make the tables easier to read and understand. HTML 4 and XHTML support all of these features with the <thead>, <tfoot>, and <tbody> tags.

10.3.2 The <thead> Tag

Use the <thead> tag to define a set of table header rows. The <thead> tag may appear only once per table and is placed at the beginning, just after the <table> tag. Within the <thead> tag, you may place one or more <tr> tags, defining the rows within the table header. If given the opportunity, the HTML 4/XHTML-compliant browser replicates these heading rows when the table is printed or displayed in multiple sections. Thereafter, it repeats these headings on each printed page if the table appears on more than one page.

<thead>

Function	Defines a table header
Attributes	align, char, charoff, class, dir, id, lang, onClick, onDblClick, onKeyDown, onKeyPress, onKeyUp, onMouseDown, onMouseMove, onMouseOut, onMouseOver, onMouseUp, style, title, valign
End tag	</thead>; may be omitted in HTML
Contains	table_content
Used in	table_content

The ending </thead> tag is optional for HTML. Because the <thead> tag appears only in tables where, presumably, other rows are designated as the table body or footer, browsers automatically close the <thead> tag when they encounter a <tbody> or <tfoot> tag or when the table ends.

The many attributes of the <thead> tag operate identically, take the same values, and affect all the enclosed <tr> contents as though you had specified them individually for each <tr> entry. For example, the align attribute accepts values of left, right, or center, controlling the horizontal alignment of text in all of the heading's rows. Similarly, the valign attribute accepts values of top, middle, baseline (Internet Explorer only), or bottom, dictating the vertical alignment of text in all of the heading rows.

If you don't specify any alignments or styles, the browser centers the heading text vertically and horizontally within the respective cells, equivalent to specifying align=center and valign=middle for each. Of course, individual row and cell or stylesheet specifications may override these attributes.

10.3.3 The <tfoot> Tag

Use the <tfoot> tag to define a footer for a table. The <tfoot> tag may appear only once, just before the <tbody> tag. Like <thead>, it may contain one or more <tr> tags that let you define those rows that the currently popular browsers use as the table footer. Thereafter, the browser repeats these rows if the table is broken across multiple physical or virtual pages. Most often, the browser repeats the table footer at the bottom of each portion of a table printed on multiple pages.

	\<tfoot\>
Function	Defines a table footer
Attributes	align, char, charoff, class, dir, id, lang, onClick, onDblClick, onKeyDown, onKeyPress, onKeyUp, onMouseDown, onMouseMove, onMouseOut, onMouseOver, onMouseUp, style, title, valign
End tag	\</tfoot\>; may be omitted in HTML
Contains	*table_content*
Used in	*table_content*

The closing \</tfoot\> tag is optional in HTML because the footer ends at the following \<tbody\> tag or at the end of the table.

10.3.4 The \<tbody\> Tag

Use the \<tbody\> tag to divide your table into discrete sections. The \<tbody\> tag collects one or more rows into a group within a table. It is perfectly acceptable to have no \<tbody\> tags within a table, although where you might include one, you probably will have two or more \<tbody\> tags within a table. So identified, you can give each \<tbody\> group different rule line sizes above and below the section. Within a \<tbody\> tag, only table rows may be defined using the \<tr\> tag. And, by definition, a \<tbody\> section of a table stands alone. For example, you may not span from one \<tbody\> into another.

	\<tbody\>
Function	Defines a section within a table
Attributes	align, char, charoff, class, dir, id, lang, onClick, onDblClick, onKeyDown, onKeyPress, onKeyUp, onMouseDown, onMouseMove, onMouseOut, onMouseOver, onMouseUp, style, title, valign
End tag	\</tbody\>; may be omitted in HTML
Contains	*table_content*
Used in	*table_content*

The closing `</tbody>` tag is optional in HTML because the section ends at the next `<tbody>` tag, or when the table ends. Like `<tfoot>`, there are many attributes for the `<tbody>` tag, but none is supported by the popular browsers. If you have special alignment attributes for this section, you'll need to specify them for each row within the `<tbody>` tag.

10.3.5 Using Table Sections

From a presentation standpoint, the most important thing you can do with the `<thead>`, `<tfoot>`, and `<tbody>` tags is divide your table into logical sections that are delimited by different borders. By default, Internet Explorer does not do anything special with the borders around the headers, footers, and sections within your table. By adding the rules attribute to the `<table>` tag, however, you can draw thicker rule lines between your `<thead>`, one or more `<tbody>`, and `<tfoot>` table sections, helping readers better understand your table's organization. [The align attribute (deprecated), 10.2.1.1]

For example, here is the simple table you saw earlier in this chapter, augmented with a header and footer. Notice that we've omitted many of the closing tags for brevity and readability of the HTML but that the tags must appear in an XHTML-compliant document:

```
<table border cellspacing=0 cellpadding=5 rules=groups>
  <caption align=bottom>Kumquat versus a poked eye, by gender</caption>
  <thead>
    <tr>
      <td colspan=2 rowspan=2>
      <th colspan=2 align=center>Preference
    </tr>
    <tr>
      <th>Eating Kumquats
      <th>Poke In The Eye
    </tr>
  </thead>
  <tfoot>
    <tr>
      <td colspan=4 align=center>
        Note: eye pokes did not result in permanent injury
    </tr>
  </tfoot>
  <tbody>
    <tr align=center>
      <th rowspan=2>Gender
      <th>Male
      <td>73%
      <td>27%
    </tr>
    <tr align=center>
```

```
          <th>Female
          <td>16%
          <td>84%
        </tr>
      </tbody>
    </table>
```

· The table as rendered by Opera is shown in Figure 10-6. Notice that the rules after the table header and before the footer are thinner than the borders around the other table rows. This happened because we included the special rules=groups attribute to the <table> tag. You may obtain similar effects by specifying rules=rows or rules=all.

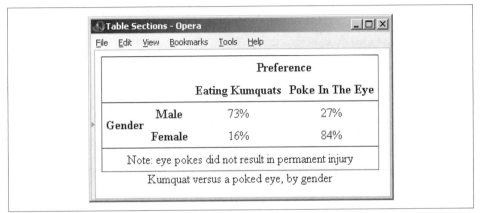

Figure 10-6. Use HTML 4/XHTML table tags to specially section your tables

Long tables often benefit from thicker rules every few rows, making it easier to read the tables. Do this by grouping the rules in your table with several <tbody> tags. Each set of rows contained in a single <tbody> tag will have thicker rules before and after it.

Here is an expanded version of our HTML table example, with additional sections set off as separate groups:

```
<table border cellspacing=0 cellpadding=5 rules=groups>
  <caption align=bottom>Kumquat versus a poked eye, by gender</caption>
  <thead>
    <tr>
      <td colspan=2 rowspan=2>
      <th colspan=2 align=center>Preference
    <tr>
      <th>Eating Kumquats
      <th>Poke In The Eye
  <tfoot>
    <tr>
      <td colspan=4 align=center>
        Note: eye pokes did not result in permanent injury
```

```
<tbody>
  <tr align=center>
    <th rowspan=4>Gender
    <th>Males under 18
    <td>94%
    <td>6%
  <tr align=center>
    <th>Males over 18
    <td>73%
    <td>27%
<tbody>
  <tr align=center>
    <th>Females under 18
    <td>34%
    <td>66%
  <tr align=center>
    <th>Females over 18
    <td>16%
    <td>84%
</table>
```

The result is shown in Figure 10-7. Notice the Gender column? Netscape versions 4 and earlier placed it to the left and centered between the Males and Females rows, as you might expect. However, the HTML 4 and XHTML standards explicitly disallow spanning <tbody> sections so that the compliant browsers all display the example with just up to four rows in the table, separated into two groups. You could create any number of groups within the table by adding more <tbody> tags.

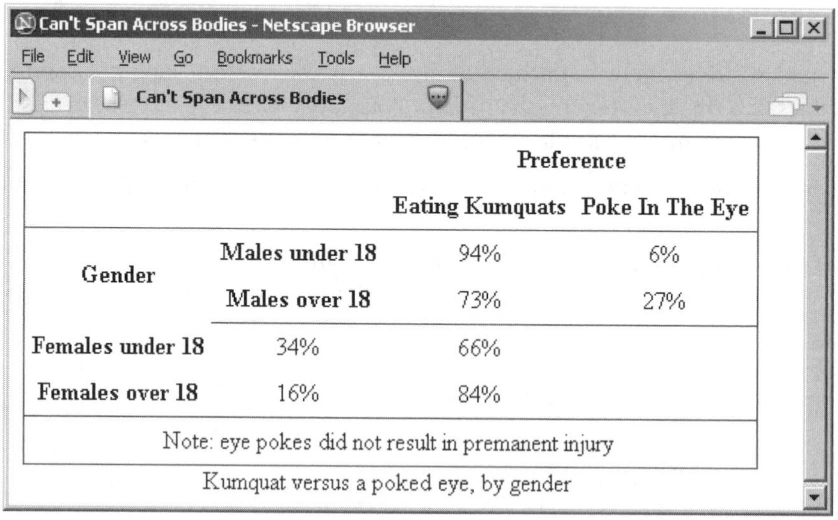

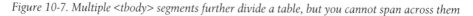

Figure 10-7. Multiple <tbody> segments further divide a table, but you cannot span across them

10.3.6 Defining Column Groups

The basic table model is row centric. Sometimes, though, it is easier to deal with your table as a collection of columns. Using the <colgroup> and <col> tags, HTML 4 and XHTML, as originally implemented by Internet Explorer through table extensions, help you turn the tables and think in columns.

Unlike the sectioning tags described in the previous sections, which are interspersed with the rows of a table to define headers, footers, and sections within the table, the column-related tags cannot be intermingled with the content of a table. You must place them at the very beginning of a table, before the content. They define the model by which HTML 4/XHTML-compliant browsers render the columns.

10.3.7 The <colgroup> Tag

The <colgroup> tag defines a column group. You can use the <colgroup> tag in two ways: as a single definition of several identical columns, or as a container for several dissimilar columns. You can put one or more <colgroup> tags within a <table> tag. The ending </colgroup> tag is rarely used in HTML but is required in XHTML. In HTML, the <colgroup> ends at the next <colgroup>, <thead>, <tbody>, <tfoot>, or <tr> tag.

All the currently popular browsers support <colgroup> and its attributes.

10.3.7.1 The span attribute

Use the span attribute with the <colgroup> tag to achieve the first type of column grouping. The value of the span attribute is the integer number of columns affected by the <colgroup> tag. For example, a table with six columns—four in the first group and two in the other—would appear in the source code as:

```
<colgroup span="4">
<colgroup span="2">
```

When the HTML 4/XHTML-compliant browser collects the table cells into columns by the example definition, it groups the first four cells in each row as the first column group and the next two cells into a second column group. Any other attributes of the individual <colgroup> tags then are applied to the columns contained within that group.

10.3.7.2 When to span and col

To use the <colgroup> tag as a container for dissimilar columns, leave out the span attribute, but include within each <colgroup> tag an individual <col> tag for each column within the group. For instance, in HTML:

```
<colgroup>
  <col>
  <col>
  <col>
  <col>
```

```
<colgroup>
  <col>
  <col>
```

This method creates the same number of columns in each group as we had with the span attribute, but it lets you specify column attributes individually. You can still supply attributes for all the columns via the <colgroup> tag, but the attributes in the <col> tags will override them, as appropriate.

<colgroup>

Function	Defines a column group within a table
Attributes	align, char, charoff, class, dir, id, lang, onClick, onDblClick, onKeyDown, onKeyPress, onKeyUp, onMouseDown, onMouseMove, onMouseOut, onMouseOver, onMouseUp, span, style, title, valign, width
End tag	</colgroup>; usually omitted in HTML
Contains	column_content
Used in	table_content

For instance, suppose we want our first example group of four columns to each occupy 20 percent of the table, and the remaining two columns to each take up 10 percent of the total table width. That's easy with the span attribute:

```
<colgroup span=4 width="20%">
<colgroup span=2 width="10%">
```

You can also create this structure with individually specified columns (in HTML):

```
<colgroup width="20%">
  <col>
  <col>
  <col>
  <col>
<colgroup width="10%">
  <col>
  <col>
```

You can use both methods in the same table. For instance, we could specify our example column groupings, complete with width attributes:

```
<colgroup span=4 width="20%" align=right>
<colgroup width="10%">
  <col align=left>
  <col align=right>
```

Notice that this lets us align the contents of the two columns of the second group individually (the default alignment is centered).

10.3.7.3 The other <colgroup> attributes

The many attributes common to tables control the familiar aspects of each column in the <colgroup>-encapsulated column group. These attributes accept the same values and behave exactly like the equivalent attributes for the <td> tag.

10.3.8 The <col> tag

Use the <col> tag to control the appearance of one or more columns within a column group.

<col>	
Function	Define a column within a column group
Attributes	align, char, charoff, class, dir, id, lang, onClick, onDblClick, onKeyDown, onKeyPress, onKeyUp, onMouseDown, onMouseMove, onMouseOut, onMouseOver, onMouseUp, span, style, title, valign, width
End tag	None in HTML; </col> or <col ... /> in XHTML
Contains	Nothing
Used in	*column_content*

The <col> tag may appear only within a <colgroup> tag within a table. It has no content and thus has no ending tag in HTML. Use </col> or a lone forward slash at the end of the tag (<col />) for the required XHTML end tag. The <col> tag represents one or more columns within a <colgroup> to which an HTML 4/XHTML-compliant browser applies the <col> tag's attributes.

All the currently popular browsers support the <col> tag and its attributes.

10.3.8.1 The span attribute

The span attribute for the <col> tag, like for the <colgroup> tag, lets you specify how many successive columns are affected by this <col> tag. By default, only one is affected. For example, let's create a <colgroup> that has five columns. We align the first and last columns to the left and right, respectively, and center the middle three:

```
<colgroup>
  <col align=left>
```

```
<col align=center span=3>
<col align=right>
```

You should use the <col> tag only within <colgroup> tags that do not themselves use the span attribute. Otherwise, the HTML 4/XHTML-compliant browsers ignore the individual <col> tags and their attributes.

10.3.8.2 The other <col> attributes

The many attributes common to tables control the familiar aspects of the column defined by the <col> tag. These attributes accept the same values and behave exactly like the equivalent attributes for the <td> tag.

10.3.9 Using Column Groups

Column groups are easier to use than they first appear. Think of them as a template for how to format your table columns. Their main purpose is to create groups that can be separated by thicker rules within your table and to streamline the process of applying formatting attributes to all the cells in one or more columns.

Returning to our original table example, we can place a thicker rule between the column labels and the data cells by placing the column labels in one column group and the data cells in another (in HTML):

```
<table border= cellspacing=0 cellpadding=5 rules=groups>
  <caption align=bottom>Kumquat versus a poked eye, by gender</caption>
  <colgroup span=2>
  <colgroup span=2>
  <thead>
    <tr>
      <td colspan=2 rowspan=2>
      <th colspan=2 align=center>Preference
    <tr>
      <th>Eating Kumquats
      <th>Poke In The Eye
  <tbody>
    <tr align=center>
      <th rowspan=4>Gender
      <th>Males under 18
      <td>94%
      <td>6%
    <tr align=center>
      <th>Males over 18
      <td>73%
      <td>27%
    <tr align=center>
      <th>Females under 18
      <td>34%</td>
      <td>66%</td>
    <tr align=center>
      <th>Females over 18
```

```
      <td>16%
      <td>84%
  <tfoot>
    <tr>
      <td colspan=4 align=center>
         Note: eye pokes did not result in permanent injury
  </table>
```

The results are shown in Figure 10-8. All we added were the two `<colgroup>` tags; the additional borders were drawn by the `rules=groups` attribute in the `<table>` tag. For borders between column groups to be drawn, the rules attribute must be set to groups, cols, or all. 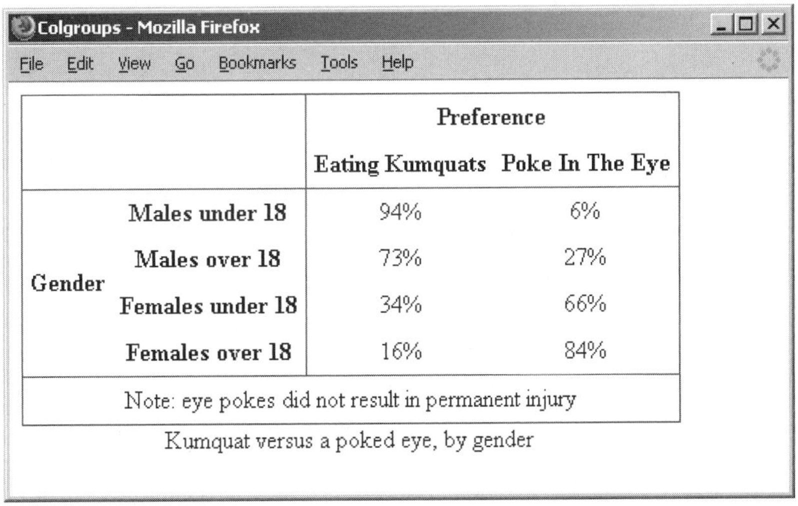

Figure 10-8. Example demonstrating the various HTML 4/XHTML table features

10.4 Beyond Ordinary Tables

On the face of it, tables are pretty ordinary: just a way for academics and other like-minded data crunchers to format items into columns and rows for easy comparison. Scratch below the surface, though, and you will see that tables are really extraordinary. Besides `<pre>`, the `<table>` tag and related attributes provide the only way for you to easily control the *layout* of your document. The content inside a `<pre>` tag, of course, is very limited. Tables, on the other hand, may contain nearly anything allowed in normal body content, including multimedia and forms. And the table structure lets you explicitly control where those elements appear in the user's browser window. With the right combinations of attributes, tables provide a way for you to create multicolumn text and side and straddle heads. They also enable you to make your forms easier to read, understand, and fill out. That's just for starters.

We don't know that we can recommend getting too caught up with page layout—tables or beyond. Remember, it ain't about looks, it's about content. But....

It's easy to argue that tables of information benefit from some controlled layout and that forms follow a close second. Tables provide the only way to create predictable, browser-independent layouts for your web pages. Used in moderation and filled with quality content, tables are a tool that every author should be able to wield.

And now that we've whetted your appetite for page layout with tables, don't despair that we've let you down by ending this chapter without examples—we have several in Chapter 17.

CHAPTER 11

Frames

You can divide the browser's main display window into independent window *frames*, each simultaneously displaying a different document—something like a wall of monitors in a TV control room. Netscape invented the feature in the mid-1990s. Instantly popular, frames now are standard features for HTML 4 and XHTML.

11.1 An Overview of Frames

Figure 11-1 is a simple example of a frame display. It shows how you can divide the document window into columns and rows of individual frames separated by rules and scroll bars. Although it is not immediately apparent in the example, each frame in the window contains an independent document. Frames may contain any valid content the browser is capable of displaying, including XHTML documents and multimedia. If the frame's contents include a hyperlink that the user selects, the new document's contents—even another frame document—may replace that same frame, another frame's content, or the entire browser window.

Frames are enabled with a special frame document. Its contents do not get displayed. Instead, the frame document contains tags that tell the browser how to divide its main display window into discrete frames and what documents go inside the frames.

The individual documents referenced and displayed in the frame document window act independently, to a degree; the frame document controls the entire window. You can, however, direct one frame's document to load new content into another frame. You do that by attaching a name to a frame and targeting the named frame with a special attribute for the hyperlink <a> tag.

11.2 Frame Tags

You need to know only two tags in order to create a frame document: `<frameset>` and `<frame>`. In addition, the HTML 4 and XHTML standards provide the `<iframe>` tag, which you may use to create inline, or *floating*, frames, and the `<noframes>` tag to handle browsers that cannot handle frames.

A *frameset* is simply the collection of frames that make up the browser's window. Column- and row-definition attributes for the `<frameset>` tag let you define the number of and initial sizes for the columns and rows of frames. The `<frame>` tag defines which document—HTML or otherwise—initially goes into the frame within those framesets and is where you may give the frame a name to use for document hyperlinks.

Here is the HTML source we used to generate Figure 11-1:

```
<html>
<head>
<title>Frames Layout</title>
</head>
<frameset rows="60%,*" cols="65%,20%,*">
  <frame src="frame1.html">
  <frame src="frame2.html">
  <frame src="frame3.html" name="fill_me">
  <frame scrolling=yes src="frame4.html">
  <frame src="frame5.html">
  <frame src="frame6.html" id="test">
  <noframes>
    Sorry, this document can be viewed only with a
    frames-capable browser.
    <a href = "frame1.html">Take this link</a>
    to the first HTML document in the set.
  </noframes>
</frameset>
</html>
```

Notice a few things in the simple frame example and its rendered image (Figure 11-1). First, like tables, the browser fills frames in a frameset row by row. Second, Frame 4 sports a scroll bar because we told it to, even though the contents may otherwise fit without scrolling. (Scroll bars automatically appear if the contents overflow the frame's dimensions, unless explicitly disabled with the `scrolling` attribute in the `<frame>` tag.)

Another item of interest is the `name` attribute in the example frame tags. Once named,[*] you can reference that particular frame as the target in which to display a hyperlinked document or perform some automated action. To do that, you add a special `target` attribute to the anchor (`<a>`) tag of the source link.

---

[*] But, interestingly, not id'd, even though the attribute exists for frames and can identify other HTML/XHTML elements as hyperlink targets.

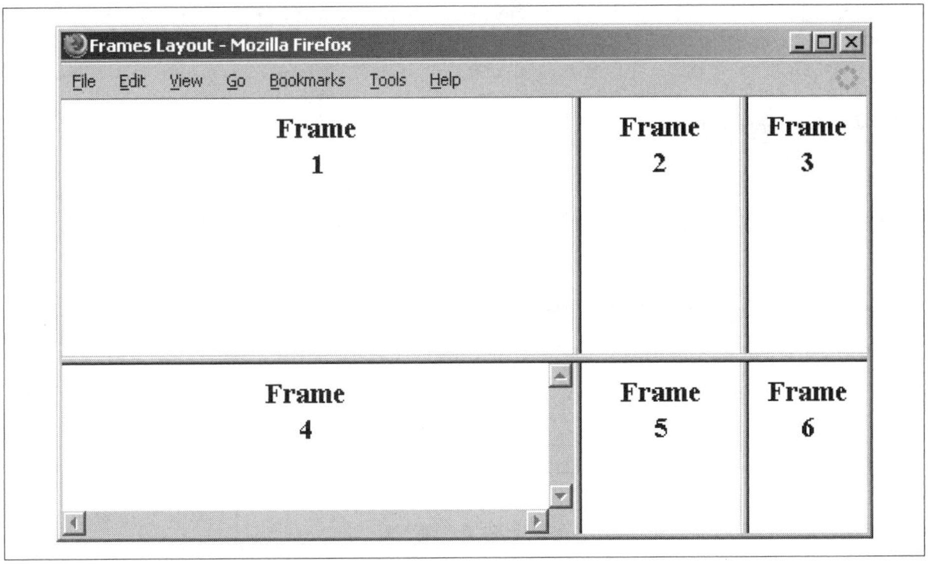

Figure 11-1. A simple six-panel frame layout

For instance, to link a document called *new.html* for display in Frame 3, which we've named fill_me, the anchor looks like this:

```
<a href="new.html" target="fill_me">
```

If the user chooses the hyperlink—say, in Frame 1—the *new.html* document replaces the original *frame3.html* contents in Frame 3. [The target Attribute for the <a> Tag, 11.7.1]

11.2.1 What's in a Frame?

Anyone who has opened more than one window on their desktop display to compare contents or operate interrelated applications knows instinctively the power of frames.

One simple use for frames is to put content that is common in a collection, such as copyright notices, introductory material, and navigational aids, into one frame, with all other document content in an adjacent frame. As the user visits new pages, each loads into the scrolling frame, while the fixed-frame content persists.

A richer frame document-enabled environment provides navigational tools for your document collections. For instance, assign one frame to hold a table of contents and various searching tools for the collection. Have another frame hold the user-selected document contents. As users visit your pages in the content frame, they never lose sight of the navigational aids in the other frame.

Another beneficial use of frame documents is to compare a returned form with its original to verify the content the user submitted. By placing the form in one frame and its submitted result in another, you let the user quickly verify that the result corresponds to the data entered in the form. If the results are incorrect, the form is readily available to be filled out again.

11.3 Frame Layout

Frame layout is similar to table layout. Using the <frameset> tag, you can arrange frames into rows and columns while defining their relative or absolute sizes.

11.3.1 The <frameset> Tag

Use the <frameset> tag to define a collection of frames and other framesets and to control their spacing and borders. You may also nest framesets, resulting in a richer set of layout capabilities.

<frameset>

Function	Defines a collection of frames
Attributes	border, bordercolor ⚑, class, cols, frameborder ⚑, framespacing ⚑, id, onLoad, onUnload, style, title
End tag	</frameset>; never omitted
Contains	*frameset_content*
Used in	*html_content*

Use the <frameset> tag in lieu of a <body> tag in the frame document. You may not include any other content except valid <head> and <frameset> content in a frame document. Combining frames with a conventional document containing a <body> section may result in unpredictable browser behavior.

11.3.1.1 The rows and cols attributes

The <frameset> tag has one required attribute: either cols or rows—your choice. They define the size and number of columns or rows of either frames or nested framesets for the document window. Both attributes accept a quote-enclosed, comma-separated list of values that specifies either the absolute (pixels) or relative (percentage or remaining space) width (for columns) or height (for rows) for the frames. The number of attribute values determines how many rows or columns of frames the browser displays in the document window.

As with tables, the browser matches the size you give a frameset as closely as possible. The browser does not, however, extend the boundaries of the main document window to accommodate framesets that would otherwise exceed those boundaries or fill the window with empty space if the specified frames don't fill the window. Rather, browsers allocate space to a particular frame relative to all other frames in the row and column and resolutely fill the entire document window. (Did you notice that the main frame window does not have scroll bars?)

For example:

```
<frameset rows="150,300,150">
```

creates three rows of frames, each extending across the entire document window. The first and last frames are set to 150 pixels tall, and the second is set to 300 pixels. In reality, unless the browser window is exactly 600 pixels tall, the browser automatically and proportionately stretches or compresses the first and last frames so that each occupies one-quarter of the window space. The center row occupies the remaining half of the window space.

Frame row- and column-size values expressed as percentages of the window dimensions are more sensible. For instance, the following example is effectively identical to the preceding one:

```
<frameset rows="25%,50%,25%">
```

Of course, if the percentages don't add up to 100 percent, the browser automatically and proportionally resizes each row to make up the difference.

If you are like us, making things add up is not a strength. Perhaps some of the frame designers suffer the same difficulty, which would explain why they included the very nifty asterisk option for <frameset> rows and cols values. It tells the browser to size the respective column or row to whatever space is left over after putting adjacent frames into the frameset.

For example, when the browser encounters the following frame tag:

```
<frameset cols="100,*">
```

it makes a fixed-size column 100 pixels wide and then creates another frame column that occupies all of the remaining space in the browser window.

Here's a fancier layout example:

```
<frameset cols="10,*,10">
```

This one creates two very thin columns down the edges of the window and gives the remaining center portion to the middle column.

You may also use the asterisk for more than one row- or column-attribute value. In that case, the corresponding rows or columns equally divide the available space. For example:

```
<frameset rows="*,100,*">
```

creates a 100-pixel-tall row in the middle of the browser display and equal-size rows above and below it.

If you precede the asterisk with an integer value, the corresponding row or column gets proportionally more of the available space. For example:

```
<frameset cols="10%,3*,*,*">
```

creates four columns: the first column occupies 10 percent of the overall width of the display. The browser then gives the second frame three-fifths of the remaining space, and the third and the fourth are each given one-fifth of the remaining space.

Using asterisks (especially with the numeric prefix) makes it easy to divide the remaining space in a frameset.

Be aware, too, that unless you explicitly tell it not to, the browser allows users to resize the individual frame document's columns and rows manually and, hence, change the relative proportions each frame occupies in the frame's display. To prevent this, use the noresize attribute for the <frame> tag, which we describe later. [<frame>, 11.4.1]

11.3.1.2 The border, frameborder, framespacing, and bordercolor attributes

The popular browsers provide attribute extensions that you may use to generally define and change the borders surrounding the frames in a frameset. The HTML 4 and XHTML standards prefer instead that you include these border-related display features via Cascading Style Sheet (CSS) styles.

By default, every frame in a frameset is surrounded by a thin 3D border (see Figure 11-1). Make these borders uniformly thicker or get rid of them altogether with the border attribute for the <frameset> tag. Set the value of border to 0 to turn off borders (see Figure 11-2). The value 1 is the same as the default. To uniformly increase the width of all the frame borders in the frameset, set the border attribute value to an integer greater than 1.

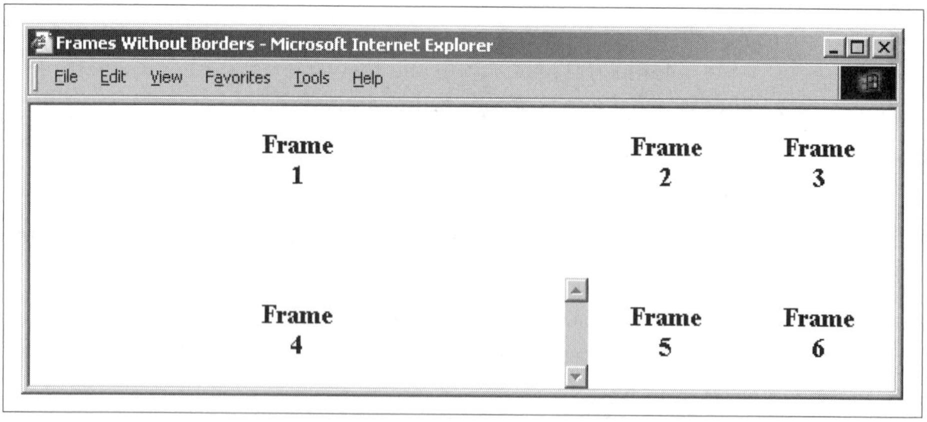

Figure 11-2. The border and frameborder attributes let you remove the borders between frames

Use the frameborder attribute with the value 1 or yes to enable, or with a value 0 or no to disable borders. Use the framespacing attribute with an integer value 1 or greater to thicken the border between frames. Why two separate attributes to achieve the same effect as the single border? Historical reasons, mostly. Suffice it to say here that some confusion still exists. All the popular browsers accept border for <frameset>, so please use it rather than the individual alternatives.

All the popular browsers, except Opera for some reason, also let you control the color of the frame borders with the bordercolor attribute (Figure 11-3). Use a color name or hexadecimal triple as its value. For example, although you can't see the color in this black-and-white book, the borders in Figure 11-3 are light green, corresponding to the red, green, and blue (RGB) value of "00CC00." (For clarity, we also increase the size of the border with the border attribute.) You can find a complete list of color names and values in Appendix G.

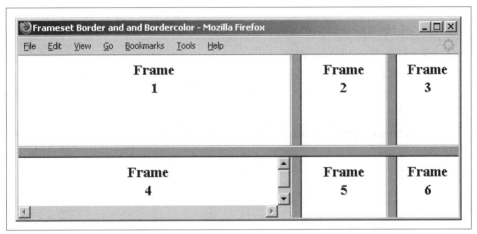

Figure 11-3. Use the bordercolor and border attributes to control the color and spacing between frames

11.3.1.3 Frames and JavaScript

All the popular browsers support JavaScript-related event handlers that let your frame documents react when they are first loaded and when the frame window gets resized (onLoad); when the user unloads them from the browser (onUnload); when the window containing the frameset loses focus, such as when the user selects another window (onBlur); or when the frameset becomes the active window (onFocus). Included as <frameset> attributes, these event handlers take quote-enclosed lists of JavaScript commands and function calls as their values.

For example, you might notify the user when all the contents have been loaded into their respective frames of a lengthy frameset:

```
<frameset onLoad="window.alert('Everything is loaded. You may now continue.')">
```

You also may use these four attributes with the <body> tag. We cover JavaScript event handlers in more detail in section 12.3.3.

11.3.1.4 Other <frameset> attributes

Like most of the other standard tags, the <frameset> tag honors four of the standard attributes: class, style, title, and id.

Use the class attribute to associate a predefined style class with this frame and, via style inheritance, its content. Alternatively, use the style attribute to define a style inline with the <frameset> tag. We cover styles more completely in Chapter 8.

The id attribute creates a unique identifier for the frame, and the title attribute creates a title for the frame that might be presented to the user or used by a nonvisual browser. [The id attribute, 4.1.1.4] [The title attribute, 4.1.1.5]

11.3.2 Nesting <frameset> Tags

You can create some elaborate browser displays with a single <frameset>, but the frame layout is unimaginative. Instead, create staggered frames and other, more complex, layouts with multiple <frameset> tags nested within a top-level <frameset> in the frame document.

For example, create a layout of two columns, the first with two rows and the second with three rows (as shown in Figure 11-4), by nesting two <frameset> tags with row specifications within a top-level <frameset> that specifies the columns:

```
<frameset cols="50%,*">
  <frameset rows="50%,*">
    <frame src="frame1.html">
    <frame src="frame2.html">
  </frameset>
  <frameset rows ="33%,33%,*">
    <frame src="frame3.html">
    <frame src="frame4.html">
    <frame src="frame5.html">
  </frameset>
</frameset>
```

11.4 Frame Contents

A frame document contains no displayable content, except perhaps a message for nonframes-enabled browsers. Instead, <frame> tags inside one or more <frameset> tags (which encapsulate the contents of a frame document) provide URL references to the individual documents that occupy each frame. [<noframes>, 11.5]

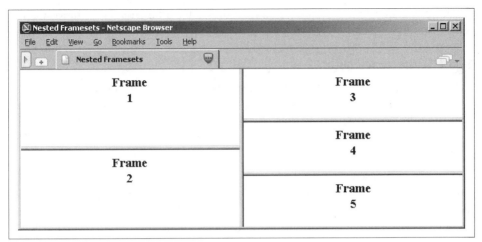

Figure 11-4. Staggered frame layouts use nested <frameset> tags

11.4.1 The <frame> Tag

The <frame> tag appears only within a <frameset>. Use it to set, via its associated src attribute, the URL of the document content that initially gets displayed inside the respective frame.

<table>
<tr><td colspan="2" align="center"><frame></td></tr>
<tr><td>Function</td><td>Defines a single frame in a <frameset></td></tr>
<tr><td>Attributes</td><td>bordercolor ⚑, class, frameborder ⚑, id, longdesc, marginheight, marginwidth, name, noresize, scrolling, src, style, title</td></tr>
<tr><td>End tag</td><td></frame>; rarely included in HTML</td></tr>
<tr><td>Contains</td><td>Nothing</td></tr>
<tr><td>Used in</td><td>frameset_content</td></tr>
</table>

Browsers place the frame contents into the frameset column by column, from left to right, and then row by row, from top to bottom. Accordingly, the sequence and number of <frame> tags inside the <frameset> tag are important.

The browser displays empty frames for <frame> tags that do not have src attributes. It also displays empty frames if the <frameset> tag calls for more frames than the corresponding <frame> tags define—if your frame document calls for three columns and you provide only two frames, for example. Orphan frames remain empty, and you cannot put content into them later, even if they have a target name or id for display redirection. [The name and id attributes, 6.3.1.3]

11.4.1.1 The src attribute

The value of the src attribute for the <frame> tag is the URL of the document that is to be displayed in the frame. There is no other way to provide content for a frame. You shouldn't, for instance, include any <body> content within the frame document; the browser ignores the frame tags and displays just the contents of a <body> tag if it comes first, or vice versa.

The document referenced by the src attribute may be any valid document or any displayable object, including images and multimedia. In particular, the referenced document may itself be composed of one or more frames. The frames are displayed within the referencing frame, providing yet another way of achieving complex layouts using nested frames.

Because the source may be a complete document, all the features of HTML/XHTML apply within a frame, including backgrounds and colors, tables, fonts, and the like. Unfortunately, this also means that multiple frames in a single browser window may conflict with each other. Specifically, if each nested frame document (not a regular HTML or XHTML document) has a different <title> tag, the title of the overall browser window is the title of the most recently loaded frame document. The easiest way to avoid this problem is to ensure that all related frame documents use the same title.

11.4.1.2 The name and id attributes

The optional name attribute for the <frame> tag labels that frame for later reference by a target attribute for the anchor (<a>) tag and the <form> tag. This way, you can alter the contents of a frame using a hyperlink in another frame. Otherwise, like normal browser windows, linked documents replace the contents of the source frame. We discuss names and targets at greater length later in this chapter. [The target Attribute for the <a> Tag, 11.7.1]

Similarly, the id attribute uniquely identifies a frame, but the browsers do not support its use for target redirection, even though they do support id's use as a hyperlink target in many other HTML and XHTML tags.

The value of the name or id attribute is a text string enclosed in quotation marks.

11.4.1.3 The noresize attribute

Even though you may explicitly set frame dimensions with attributes in the <frameset> tag, users can manually alter the size of a column or row of frames. To suppress this behavior, add the noresize attribute to the frame tags in the row or column whose relative dimensions you do not want users fiddling with. For example,

---

for a two-by-two frame document, a noresize attribute in any one of the four associated frame tags effectively freezes the relative proportions of all the frames.

The noresize attribute is especially useful for frames that contain fixed images serving as advertisements, a button bar, or a logo. By fixing the size of the frame to contain just the image and setting the noresize attribute, you guarantee that the image is displayed in the intended manner and that the remainder of the browser window is always given over to the other frames in the document.

11.4.1.4 The scrolling attribute

The browser displays vertical and horizontal scroll bars with frames whose contents are larger than the allotted window space. If there is sufficient room for the content, the scroll bars disappear. The scrolling attribute for the <frame> tag gives you explicit control over whether the scroll bars appear or disappear.

With scrolling="yes", all the popular browsers except Netscape add scroll bars to the designated frame even if there is nothing to scroll. If you set the scrolling attribute value to no, scroll bars are never added to the frame, even if the frame contents are larger than the frame itself. The value auto, the default, works as though you didn't include the scrolling attribute in the tag.

11.4.1.5 The marginheight and marginwidth attributes

The browser normally places a small amount of space between the edge of a frame and its contents. You can change those margins with the marginheight and marginwidth attributes, each including a value for the exact number of pixels to place around the frame's contents.

You cannot make a margin less than 1 pixel or make it so large that there is no room for the frame's contents. That's because, like most other HTML attributes, these advise; they do not dictate to the browser. If your desired margin values cannot be accommodated, the browser ignores them and renders the frame as best it can.

11.4.1.6 The frameborder and bordercolor attributes

With some earlier versions of Internet Explorer, you could add and remove borders from a single frame with the frameborder attribute. Values of yes or 1 and no or 0 respectively enable or disable borders for the frame and override the value of the frameborder attribute for any frameset containing the frame. Don't use it.

With all the popular browsers except Opera, you also can change the color of the individual frame's borders with the bordercolor attribute. Use a color name or hexadecimal triple as its value. If two adjacent frames have different bordercolor attributes, the resulting border color is undefined. You can find a complete list of color names and values in Appendix G.

11.4.1.7 The title and longdesc attributes

Like most other standard tags, you can provide a title for a frame with the `title` attribute. The value of the attribute is a quote-enclosed string that describes the contents of the frame. Browsers might display the title, for instance, when the mouse passes over the frame.

If the `title` attribute isn't quite enough for you, you can use the `longdesc` attribute. Its value is the URL of a document that describes the frame. Presumably, this long description might be in some alternative media, suitable for use by a nonvisual browser.

11.5 The <noframes> Tag

A frame document has no <body>. It must not because the browser ignores any frame tags if it finds any <body> content before it encounters the first <frameset> tag. A frame document, therefore, is all but invisible to any nonframes-capable browser. The <noframes> tag gives some relief to the frames-disabled.

<noframes>

Function	Supplies content for nonframes-capable browsers
Attributes	`class`, `dir`, `id`, `lang`, `onClick`, `onDblClick`, `onKeyDown`, `onKeyPress`, `onKeyUp`, `onMouseDown`, `onMouseMove`, `onMouseOut`, `onMouseOver`, `onMouseUp`, `style`, `title`
End tag	`</noframes>`; sometimes omitted in HTML
Contains	*body_content*
Used in	*frameset_content*

You should use the <noframes> tag only within the outermost <frameset> tag of a frame document. Content between the <noframes> tag and its required end tag (</noframes>) is not displayed by any frames-capable browser but is displayed in lieu of other contents in the frame document by browsers that do not handle frames. The content of the <noframes> tag can be any normal body content, including the <body> tag itself.

Although this tag is optional, experienced authors typically include the <noframes> tag in their frame documents with content that warns nonframes-capable browser users that they're missing the show. And smart authors give those users a way out, if not direct access to the individual documents that make up the frame document contents.

Remember our first frame example in this chapter? Figure 11-5 shows what happens when that frame document gets loaded into an old version of Mosaic.

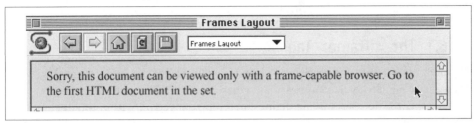

Figure 11-5. A <noframes> message in a nonframes-capable browser

The HTML to produce this message looks like this:

```
<noframes>
    Sorry, this document can be viewed only with a
    frame-capable browser. Go to the <a href="frame1.html">
    first HTML document</a> in the set.
</noframes>
```

<noframes> works because most browsers are extremely tolerant of erroneous tags and incorrect documents. A nonframes browser simply ignores the frame tags. What's left, then, is the content of the <noframes> tag, which the browser dutifully displays.

If your browser strictly enforces some version of HTML or XHTML that does not support frames, it may simply display an error message and refuse to display the document, even if it contains a <noframes> tag.

11.5.1 <noframes> Attributes

No attributes are specific to the <noframes> tag, but you can use any of the 16 standard attributes: class and style for style management, lang and dir for language type and display direction, title and id for titling and naming the enclosed content, and any of the event attributes for user-activated JavaScript processing within the <noframes> tag. [The dir attribute, 3.6.1.1] [The lang attribute, 3.6.1.2] [The id attribute, 4.1.1.4] [The title attribute, 4.1.1.5] [Inline Styles: The style Attribute, 8.1.1] [Style Classes, 8.3] [JavaScript Event Handlers, 12.3.3]

11.6 Inline Frames

To this point, our discussion has centered on frames that are defined as part of a frameset. A frameset, in turn, replaces the conventional <body> of a document and supplies content to the user via its contained frames.

The HTML 4 and XHTML standards let you do things a bit differently: you can also define a frame that exists within a conventional document, displayed as part of that document's text flow. These frames behave a lot like inline images, which is why they are known as *inline frames*.

All the popular browsers support inline frames.

11.6.1 The <iframe> Tag

Define an inline frame with the `<iframe>` tag. The `<iframe>` tag is *not* used within a `<frameset>` tag. Instead, it appears anywhere in your document that an `<img>` tag might appear. The `<iframe>` tag defines a rectangular region within the document in which the browser displays a separate document, including scroll bars and borders.

<iframe>	
Function	Defines an inline frame within a text flow
Attributes	align, class, frameborder, height, id, longdesc, marginheight, marginwidth, name, scrolling, src, style, title, width
End tag	</iframe>; never omitted
Contains	*body_content*
Used in	*text*

Use the `src` attribute with `<iframe>` to specify the URL of the document that occupies the inline frame. All of the other, optional attributes for the `<iframe>` tag, including name, class, frameborder, id, longdesc, marginheight, marginwidth, name, scrolling, style, and title, behave exactly like the corresponding attributes for the `<frame>` tag. [The <frame> Tag, 11.4.1]

Use the content of the `<iframe>` tag to provide information to users of browsers that do not support inline frames. Compliant browsers ignore these contents, whereas all other browsers ignore the `<iframe>` tag and therefore display its contents as though they were regular body content. For instance, use the `<iframe>` content to explain to users what they are missing:

```
...other document content...
<iframe src="sidebar.html" width=75 height=200 align=right>
Your browser does not support inline frames. To view this
<a href="sidebar.html">document</a> correctly, you need
to install a more recent browser on your computer.
</iframe>...subsequent document content...
```

In this example, we let the user know that she was accessing an unsupported feature and provided a link to the missing content.

11.6.1.1 The align attribute

Like the deprecated `align` attribute for the `<table>` and `<img>` tags, this inline frame attribute lets you control where the frame gets placed in line with the adjacent text or moved to the edge of the document, allowing text to flow around the frame.

For inline alignment, use `top`, `middle`, or `bottom` as the value of this attribute. The browser aligns the frame with the top, middle, or bottom of the adjacent text, respectively. To allow text to flow around the inline frame, use the `left` or `right` values for this attribute. The frame is moved to the left or right edge of the text flow, respectively, and the remaining content of the document is flowed around the frame. A value of `center` places the inline frame in the middle of the display, with text flowing above and below.

11.6.1.2 The height and width attributes

The popular browsers put the contents of an inline frame into a predefined, 150-pixel-tall, 300-pixel-wide box. Use the `height` and `width` attributes with values as the number of pixels to change those dimensions.

11.6.2 Using Inline Frames

Although you'll probably shy away from them for most of your web pages, inline frames can be useful, particularly for providing information related to the current document being viewed, similar to the sidebar articles you find in a conventional printed publication.

Except for their location within conventional document content, inline frames are treated exactly like regular frames. You can load other documents into the inline frame using its name (see the next section) and link to other documents from within the inline frame.

11.7 Named Frame or Window Targets

As we discussed earlier in section 11.4.1, you can label a frame by adding the `name` attribute to its `<frame>` tag.[*] Once named, the frame may become the destination display window for a hyperlinked document selected within a document displayed in some other frame. You accomplish this redirection by adding the special `target` attribute to the anchor that references the document.

---

[*] The `id` attribute provides the same unique labeling but you cannot use it for frame content redirection. Instead, the browser ignores the id-named target frame and displays the linked document in a new window.

11.7.1 The target Attribute for the <a> Tag

If you include a target attribute within an <a> tag, the browser loads and displays the document named in the tag's href attribute in a frame or window whose name matches the target. If the named frame or window doesn't exist, the browser opens a new window, gives it the specified label, and loads the new document into that window. Once this process has been completed, linked documents can target the new window.

Targeted hyperlinks make it easy to create effective navigational tools. A simple table of contents document, for example, might redirect documents into a separate window:

```
<h3>Table of Contents</h3>
<ul>
  <li><a href="pref.html" target="view_window">Preface</a>
  <li><a href="chap1.html" target="view_window">Chapter 1</a>
  <li><a href="chap2.html" target="view_window">Chapter 2</a>
  <li><a href="chap3.html" target="view_window">Chapter 3</a>
</ul>
```

The first time the user selects one of the table-of-contents hyperlinks the browser opens a new window, labels it view_window, and displays the desired document's contents inside it. If the user selects another hyperlink from the table of contents and the view_window is still open, the browser again loads the selected document into that window, replacing the previous document.

Throughout the whole process, the window containing the table of contents is accessible to the user. By clicking on a hyperlink in one window, the user causes the contents of the other window to change.

Instead of opening an entirely new browser window, a more common use of target is to direct hyperlink contents to one or more frames in a <frameset> display or to an inline <iframe> window. You might place the table of contents into one frame of a two-frame document and use the adjacent frame to display the selected documents:

```
<frameset cols="150,*">
  <frame src="toc.html">
  <frame src="pref.html" name="view_frame">
</frameset>
```

When the browser initially displays the two frames, the left frame contains the table of contents, and the right frame contains the Preface (see Figure 11-6).

When a user selects a hyperlink from the table of contents in the left frame (for example, Chapter 1), the browser loads and displays the associated document into the view_frame frame on the right side (Figure 11-7). As other links get selected, the right frame's contents change, while the left frame continuously makes the table of contents available to the user.

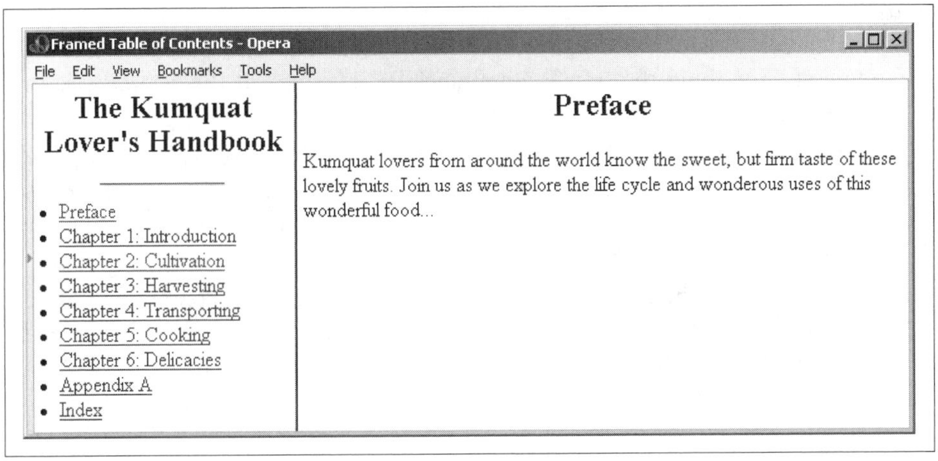

Figure 11-6. Table of contents frame controls content of adjacent frame

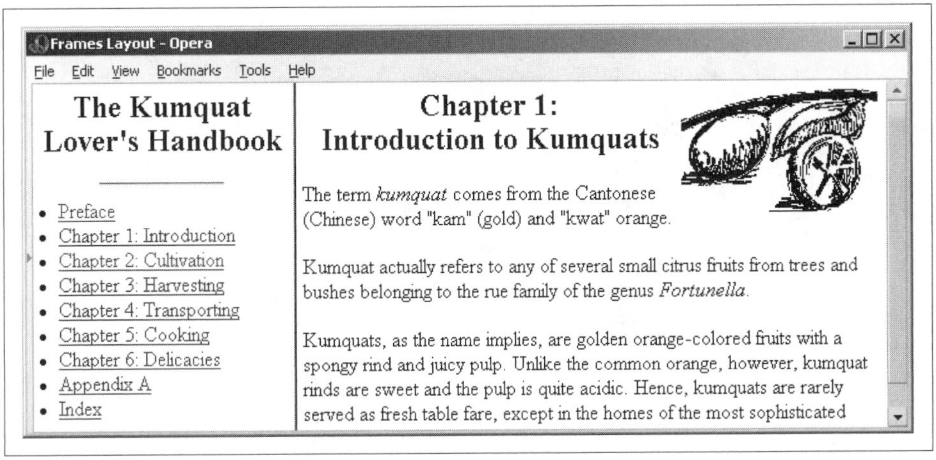

Figure 11-7. The contents of Chapter 1 are displayed in the adjacent frame

11.7.2 Special Targets

There are four reserved target names for special document-redirection actions:

_blank

> The browser always loads a target="_blank" linked document into a newly opened, unnamed window.

_self

> This target value is the default for all <a> tags that do not specify a target, causing the target document to be loaded and displayed in the same frame or window as the source document. This target is redundant and unnecessary unless used in combination with the target attribute in the <base> tag in a document's head (see the next section, 11.7.3).

_parent

> This target causes the document to be loaded into the parent window or frameset containing the frame containing the reference. If the reference is in a window or top-level frame, it is equivalent to the target _self.

> A brief example may help clarify how this hyperlink target works. Consider a link in a frame that is part of a three-column frameset. This frameset, in turn, is a row in the top-level frameset being displayed in the browser window. Figure 11-8 shows this arrangement.

> If no target is specified for the hyperlink, it is loaded into the containing frame. If a target of _parent is specified, the document is loaded into the area occupied by the three-column frameset containing the frame that contains the link.

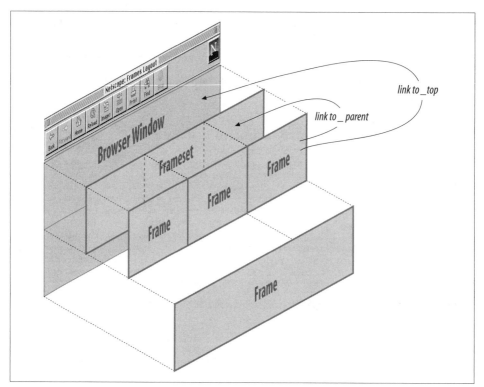

Figure 11-8. Using special targets in nested frames and framesets

_top

> This target causes the document to be loaded into the window containing the hyperlink, replacing any frames currently displayed in the window.

> Continuing with the frame hierarchy, as shown in Figure 11-8, using a target of _top would remove all the contained frames and load the document into the entire browser window.

All four of these target values begin with the underscore character. The browser ignores any other window or target beginning with an underscore, so don't use the underscore as the first character of any frame name or id you define in your documents.

11.7.3 The <base> Default Target

It can be tedious to specify a target for every hyperlink in your documents, especially when most are targeted at the same window or frame. To alleviate this problem, you can add a target attribute to the <base> tag. [<base>, 6.7.1]

The target attribute in the <base> tag sets the default target for every hyperlink in the current document that does not contain an explicit target attribute. For instance, in our example table of contents document, almost every link causes the document to be displayed in another window named view_frame. Instead of including that target in each hyperlink, you should place the common target in the table of contents' <base> tag within its <head>:

```
<head>
<title>Table of Contents</title>
<base target="view_frame">
</head>
<body>
<h3>Table of Contents</h3>
<ul>
  <li><a href="pref.html">Preface</a></li>
  <li><a href="chap1.html">Chapter 1</a></li>
  <li><a href="chap2.html" >Chapter 2</a></li>
  <li><a href="chap3.html">Chapter 3</a></li>
</ul>
</body>
```

Notice that we don't include any other target references in the list of hyperlinks, because the browser loads and displays all the respective documents in the base target view_frame.

11.7.4 Traditional Link Behavior

Before the onset of frames, each time you selected a hyperlink, the corresponding document replaced the contents of the browser window. With frames, this behavior is modified so that the corresponding document replaces the content of the referencing frame. This is often not the desired behavior, and it can be disconcerting to people browsing your documents.

For example, suppose you have arranged all of the documents on your site to present themselves in three frames: a navigational frame at the top of the browser window, a scrolling content frame in the middle, and a feedback form at the bottom. You named the content frame with the name attribute of the <frame> tag in the top-level document for your collection and used the `target` attribute of the `<base>` tag in every document on your site to ensure that all links are loaded into the center content frame.

This arrangement works perfectly for all the documents on your site, but what happens when a user selects a link that takes him to a different site? The referenced document is still loaded into the center content frame. Now the user is confronted by a document from some other site, surrounded by your navigation and feedback frames!* Very impolite.

The solution is to make sure that every hyperlink that references a remote document has a target of _top. This way, when the user selects a link that takes him away from your site, the remote document replaces the contents of the entire browser window, including your navigation and feedback frames. If the majority of the links in your documents are to other sites, you might consider adding `target="_top"` to a `<base>` tag in your document and using explicit `target` attributes in the links to your local documents.

11.8 XFrames

Frames are a rags-to-riches success story. From a nonstandard extension in the Netscape browser to a standard component of HTML and XHTML, frames have proven themselves as a core element of the HTML world. Nonetheless, there are problems with frames that have never been fully resolved:

- Navigation with a browser's Back button can be unpredictable.
- You cannot directly reference a document within a frameset.
- You cannot reference a particular collection of frames with a single URL.
- Search engines often do not follow framed content.

To correct these deficiencies while retaining the power of frames, the World Wide Web Consortium (W3C) has proposed a slightly different model for framed content. This model is still a working document, and has not yet been implemented in any browser. Still, we briefly describe it here to make authors aware of what they might expect from frames in the near future.

11.8.1 An XFrames Document

Within HTML and XHTML, frames replace the `<body>` of a document, leaving the `<html>` and `<head>` tags intact. In the XFrames model, an XFrames document replaces the entire `<html>` document, carrying with it its own `<head>` and framed content. Within the `<head>` tag, authors can provide a `<title>` and `<style>` tags; the framed

---

* Check out Chapter 17 for how to step out into the forefront when your pages happen to be on the other end of a targetless hyperlink.

content is then denoted within `<group>` and `<frame>` tags. A short XFrames document might look like this:

```
<frames xmlns="http://www.w3.org/2002/06/xframes/">
  <head>
    <title>Kumquat Lore</title>
    <style type="text/css">
      #header {height: 10em }
      #toc, #nav {width: 20%}
      #footer {height: 4em }
    </style>
  </head>
  <group compose="vertical">
    <frame xml:id="header" source="lore.xhtml"/>
    <group compose="horizontal">
      <frame xml:id="toc" source="toc.xhtml"/>
      <frame xml:id="main" source="intro.xhtml"/>
      <frame xml:id="nav" source="main-nav.xhtml"/>
    </group>
    <frame xml:id="footer" source="copyright.xhtml"/>
  </group>
</frames>
```

The `<head>` tag sets the title for the framed document and defines styles that will affect the display of the correspondingly named frames within the document set. The `<group>` tag, analogous to the `<frameset>` tag, defines a group of frames and other groups whose layout is controlled by the compose attribute. The `<frame>` tag defines a single document whose content is displayed within that frame in the document. In this document, five frames are arranged in three rows, with one frame at the top, one at the bottom, and three in the middle row. In that row, the left and right frames each occupy 20 percent of the available space, with the center frame taking up the remainder. Individual frames are named with the `xml:id` attribute; these names are referenced when loading new content in a frame, when associating styles with a frame, and when creating a URL to display a specific frameset, as described shortly.

The compose attribute in the `<group>` tag provides some additional layout capabilities that conventional frames do not allow. While the horizontal and vertical layout choices perform the appropriate action, the single and free choices are more interesting. Setting compose to single causes the browser to display only one of the frames in the group at a time, while providing some sort of mechanism to indicate the presence of other frames and a way to select them. One can imagine a pull-down menu that lets the user choose one frame at a time, for example.

The free value for the compose attribute displays the frames in a group as a set of freely movable windows within a display area. The user can move and rearrange the windows as desired, even overlapping them! Presumably, this would allow frames to be displayed in a sort of "desktop" within the browser, completely at the user's discretion.

11.8.2 XFrames URLs

To support explicit reference to frames within a framed document, the XFrames model extends the definition of a URL to include a special #frames keyword. This feature lets you specify the content for each frame in a document, something that is impossible with the current HTML and XHTML frames model.

To use this feature, add the special #frames keyword to the end of a URL referencing a frame document. Follow the keyword with a list of frame IDs and their desired content, all enclosed in parentheses. Sound difficult? It's not:

```
http://www.kumquat.com/lore.html#frames(toc=section7.xhtml,main=arctic-quats.xhtml)
```

This URL opens the framed document named *lore.html*, and loads the toc and main frames with the desired pages. The other frames named in the document are loaded with their default content because they are not mentioned in this URL. Frames without default content are left blank.

This powerful syntax has lots of benefits for authors and end users. Authors can now construct links that will open a complete set of framed documents in a specific, repeatable manner. And users can save a bookmark to a framed document, assured that when they return to the document, all the frames will be opened with the same content as when they saved the URL.

CHAPTER 12
Executable Content

One of the most useful web technologies is the ability to deliver applications directly to the browser. These typically small programs perform simple tasks on the client computer, from responding to user mouse or keyboard actions to spicing up your web page displays with multimedia-enabling software.

You can embed scripts in your documents using a language known as JavaScript. Or you can load and execute small, Java-based, platform-independent applications known as *applets*. During execution, these programs may generate dynamic content, interact with the user, validate form data, or even create windows and run entire applications independent of your pages. The possibilities are endless, and they go far beyond the simple document model originally envisioned for HTML.

In this chapter, we show you, with simple examples, how to include two kinds of executable content—scripts and applets—in your documents. We won't, however, teach you how to write and debug executable content. This is a book about HTML and XTHML, after all. Rather, get an expert opinion: turn to any of the many excellent texts from O'Reilly, especially the companion *JavaScript: The Definitive Guide*, by David Flanagan.

12.1 Applets and Objects

Applets represent a shift in the basic model of web communications. In most other web applications, servers perform most of the computational work, client browsers being not much more than glorified terminals. With applets, web technology shifts to the client, distributing some or all of the computational load from the server to the client computer and its browser.

Applets also represent a way of extending a browser's features without forcing users to acquire new browsers, as is the case when developers implement new tag and attribute extensions to HTML. Nor do users have to acquire and install a special application, as is required for helper or plug-in applications.* This means that once users have a browser that supports applets (all the currently popular ones do), you can deliver applets directly to the browser, including display and multimedia innovations.

12.1.1 The Object Model

Java-based applets—web page-referenced programs retrieved from a network server and executed on the user's client computer—are an example of what the HTML 4 and XHTML standards call *inclusions*. As with images, the browser first loads the HTML document, then examines it for inclusions—additional, separate, and discrete content that the client browser is to handle. A GIF image is one type of inclusion. A *.wav* sound file, an MPEG movie, and a Java-based clock program are other types.

The HTML 4 and XHTML standards generally call the inclusion contents *objects*. In fact, in your document you may identify and load nearly any object file over the network through a universal <object> tag, discussed in detail shortly in section 12.2.1.

Once the object has been downloaded, the standards dictate that the browser somehow render the object, by internal or external mechanisms. Otherwise, plug-ins and other helper applications may provide the necessary rendering mechanism. Internet Explorer, for example, has its internal resources play an AVI movie, whereas other browsers rely upon some third-party software, such as RealPlayer or QuickTime, to show the movie.

12.1.1.1 The applet model

With Java applets, the browser sets aside a portion of the document display space. You may control the size and position of this display area; the applet controls what is presented inside.

The applet is software, an executable program. Accordingly, besides providing a display space, the browser, in tandem with the client computer environment and resources, provides the applet with a runtime environment called a *virtual machine*.

During execution, Java applets have access to a restricted environment within the user's computer. For instance, applets have access to the mouse and keyboard so that they may receive input from the user. Depending on the security policy in place, applets also may initiate network connections and retrieve data from other servers on

---

* Actually, Internet Explorer 6 users must download and install Java support. Read on for details.

the Internet. In sum, applets are full-fledged programs, complete with a variety of input and output mechanisms, along with a full suite of network services.

You may place several applets in a single document; they all execute in parallel and may communicate with each other. While the browser may limit their access to its computer system, applets have complete control of their virtual environment within the browser.

12.1.1.2 The applet advantage

There are several advantages of applets, not the least of which is providing more compelling user interfaces within a web page. For instance, an applet might create a unique set of menus, choices, text fields, and similar user-input tools different from those available through the browser. When the user clicks a button within the applet's interaction/display region, the applet might respond by displaying results within the region, signaling another applet, or even loading a completely new page into the browser.

We don't mean to imply that the only use of applets is to enhance the user interface. An applet is a full-fledged program that can perform any number of computational and user-interactive tasks on the client computer. An applet might implement a real-time video display, perform circuit simulation, engage the user in a game, provide a chat interface, and so on.

12.1.1.3 Using applets correctly

An applet is nothing more than another tool you can use to produce compelling and useful web pages. Keep in mind that an applet uses computational resources on the client to run and therefore places a load on the user's computer. It can degrade system performance.

Similarly, if an applet uses a lot of network bandwidth to accomplish its task (a real-time video feed, for example), it may make other network communication unbearably slow. While such applications are fun, they do little more than annoy your target audience.

To use an applet correctly, balance the load between the browser and the server. For each page, decide which tasks are best left to the server (forms processing, index searches, and the like) and which tasks are better suited for local processing (user-interface enhancements, real-time data presentation, small animations, input validation, and so on). Divide the processing accordingly. Remember that many users have slower network connections and computers than you do, and design your applets to satisfy the majority of your audience.

Used the right way, applets seamlessly enhance your pages and provide a satisfying experience for your audience. Used improperly, applets are just another annoying bandwidth waster, alienating your users and hurting your pages.

12.1.1.4 Writing applets

Creating Java applets is a programming task, not usually a job for the HTML or XHTML author. For details, we recommend that you consult any of the many Java programming texts, including those from O'Reilly.

Developed by Sun Microsystems, Inc. of Mountain View, California, Java supports an object-oriented programming style wherein classes of applets can be used and reused to build complex applications. One would think that applets written in the same language should run in any browser that supports Java. As is so often the case, reality is more complex. Until Netscape 6 and Internet Explorer 6, browsers included their own Java Virtual Machines (JVMs), and their implementations, especially Microsoft's, could be quirky. Certain Microsoft implementation decisions in Internet Explorer 4 and earlier caused some valid Java applets to fail when running. Microsoft fixed these problems with Internet Explorer version 5 but, because of its lawsuit with Sun, chose not to include a JVM in Internet Explorer 6.* Although this may sound like bad news for applets, in fact, Internet Explorer 6 prompts you to download Microsoft's JVM. Sun's Java Plug-in is free over the Internet. Users of any browser can install the Java Plug-in to get state-of-the-art Java support.

We should take this opportunity also to mention ActiveX, an alternative executable content technology originally developed by Microsoft. ActiveX itself is proprietary, closely coupled with various versions of Microsoft Windows, and Microsoft's plug-in works only when used with Internet Explorer, though alternative plug-in implementations now exist for all the popular browsers.

ActiveX controls (as they are called) run on browser versions targeted to various versions of Windows, but a single ActiveX control will not run on these different versions without recompilation. This is in contrast with Java applets; a single Java applet can be written and compiled once and immediately run on a broad range of browsers and operating systems.

ActiveX also presents an unacceptably high security risk to any user whose browser supports ActiveX technology.† Though over the years security has gotten better, it is ridiculously easy to penetrate and damage a computer running a browser that allows ActiveX applets to be executed. In fact, all the popular browsers, Internet Explorer included, let users explicitly block ActiveX applets. For this reason, we cannot recommend ActiveX as a viable applet implementation technology and we go so far as to recommend that users disable ActiveX capability within their browsers.

---

* As we wrote this, even this situation may change, with Microsoft reversing itself and deciding to include a JVM in a service pack for Windows XP. There is still no sign of default inclusion of a JVM in Internet Explorer 6 downloads, however.

† You can find a good description of the risks at *http://www.digicrime.com/activex*.

12.2 Embedded Content

In this section, we cover three tags that support embedded content. The <object> tag is in the HTML 4 and XHTML standards. It is a generalized hybrid of the deprecated <applet> tag for embedding applets, particularly Java applets, and the <embed> tag extension that lets you include an object whose Multipurpose Internet Mail Extension (MIME) type references the plug-in needed to process and possibly display that object.

The latest standards strongly encourage you to use the <object> tag to incorporate applets and other discrete inclusions in your documents, including images (although the standards do not go so far as to deprecate the <img> tag). Use <object> with the classid attribute to insert Java and other applets into a document, along with their execution parameters as contents of the associated <param> tag. Use <object> with the data attribute to download and display non-HTML/XHTML content, such as multimedia, in the user's computing environment. Object data may be processed and rendered by an included applet, by utilities that come with your browser, or by a plug-in (helper) application that the user supplies.

For applets, the browser creates a display region in the containing text flow exactly like an inline image or an <iframe>: without line breaks and as a single large entity. The browser then downloads and executes the applet's program code, if specified, and downloads and renders any included data just after download and display of the document. Execution of the applet continues until the code terminates itself or when the user stops viewing the page containing the applet.

With data, the browser decodes the object's data type and either handles its rendering directly, such as with GIF, PNG, and JPEG images, or invokes an associated plug-in application for the job.

12.2.1 The <object> Tag

The <object> tag was originally implemented by Microsoft to support its ActiveX controls. Only later did Microsoft add Java support. In a similar manner, Netscape initially supported the alternative <embed> and <applet> tags for inclusion objects and later provided limited support for the <object> tag.

All that jostling for position by the browser giants* made us nervous, and we were hesitant in previous editions of this book to even suggest that you use <object> at all. We now heartily endorse it, based on the strength of the HTML 4 and (particularly) XHTML standards, especially because the currently popular browsers support <object>.

---

* Believe it or not, Netscape once dominated the browser market!

Nonetheless, be aware that the popular browsers interpret <object> and <embed> a bit differently. For example, Internet Explorer still treats <object> content as ActiveX controls and launches its helper program to display the data. By contrast, the browser displays <embed> content within the document display.

<object>

Function	Embeds an object or applet in a document
Attributes	align, archive, border, class, classid, codebase, codetype, data, declare, dir, height, hspace, id, lang, name, notab 🔅, onClick, onDblClick, onKeyDown, onKeyPress, onKeyUp, onLoad, onMouseDown, onMouseMove, onMouseOut, onMouseOver, onMouseUp, shapes, standby, style, tabindex, title, type, usemap, vspace, width
End tag	</object>; never omitted
Contains	*object_content*
Used in	*text*

The contents of the <object> tag may be any valid HTML or XHTML content, along with <param> tags that pass parameters to an applet. If the browser can retrieve the requested object and successfully process it, either by executing the applet or by processing the object's data with a plug-in application, the contents of the <object> tag, except for the <param> tags, are ignored. If any problem occurs during the retrieval and processing of the object, the browser won't insert the object into the document but instead will display the contents of the <object> tag, except for the <param> tags. In short, you should provide alternative content in case the browsers cannot handle the <object> tag or the object cannot be loaded successfully.

12.2.1.1 The classid attribute

Use the classid attribute to specify the location of the object, typically a Java class, which you want the browser to include. The value may be the absolute or relative URL of the desired object. Relative URLs are considered to be relative to the URL specified by the codebase attribute if it is provided; otherwise, they are relative to the current document's URL.

For example, to execute a clock Java applet contained in a file named *clock.class*, you might include the following code in your HTML document:

```
<object classid="java:clock.class">
</object>
```

The browser locates the code for the applet using the current document's base URL. Hence, if the current document's URL is:

```
http://www.kumquat.com/harvest_time.html
```

the browser retrieves the applet code for our *clock.class* example as:

```
http://www.kumquat.com/clock.class
```

12.2.1.2 The codebase attribute

Use the codebase attribute to provide an alternative base URL from which the browser should retrieve an object. The value of this attribute is a URL pointing to a directory containing the object referenced by the classid attribute. The codebase URL overrides, but does not permanently replace, the document's base URL, which is the default if you don't use codebase. [Referencing Documents: The URL, 6.2]

Continuing with our previous examples, suppose your document comes from *http://www.kumquat.com*, but the clock applet is kept in a separate directory named *classes*. You cannot retrieve the applet by specifying classid="classes/clock.class". Rather, include the codebase attribute and new base URL:

```
<object classid="clock.class" codebase="http://www.kumquat.com/classes/">
</object>
```

which resolves to the URL:

```
http://www.kumquat.com/classes/clock.class
```

Although we used an absolute URL in this example, you also can use a relative URL. For instance, applets typically are stored on the same server as the host documents, so we'd usually be better off, for relocation's sake, specifying a relative URL for the codebase, such as:

```
<object code="clock.class" codebase="/classes/">
</object>
```

The classid attribute is similar to the code attribute of the <applet> tag, providing the name of the file containing the object; it is used in conjunction with the codebase attribute to determine the full URL of the object to be retrieved and placed in the document.

12.2.1.3 The archive attribute

For performance reasons, you may choose to preload collections of objects contained in one or more archives. This is particularly true of Java-based applications, where one Java class relies on many other classes to get its work done. The value of the archive attribute is a quote-enclosed list of URLs, each pointing to an archive to be loaded by the browser before it renders or executes the object.

12.2.1.4 The codetype attribute

The codetype attribute is required only if the browser cannot determine an applet's MIME type from the classid attribute or if the server does not deliver the correct MIME type when downloading an object. This attribute is nearly identical to type (see section 6.7.2.4), except that it is used to identify program code type, whereas type should be used to identify datafile types.

The following example explicitly tells the browser that the object's code is Java:

```
<object code="clock.class" codetype="application/java">
</object>
```

12.2.1.5 The data attribute

Use the data attribute to specify the datafile, if any, that the object is to process. The data attribute's value is the URL of the file, either absolute or relative to the document's base URL or to that which you provide with the codebase attribute. The browser determines the data type by the type of object that is being inserted in the document.

This attribute is similar to the src attribute of the <img> tag, in that it downloads data to be processed by the included object. The difference, of course, is that the data attribute lets you include just about any file type, not just an image file. In fact, the <object> tag expects, but doesn't require, that you explicitly name an enabling application for the object with the classid attribute, or indicate the MIME type of the file via the type attribute to help the browser decide how to process and render the data.

For example, here is an image included as an object, rather than as an <img> file:

```
<object data="pics/kumquat.gif" type="image/gif">
</object>
```

12.2.1.6 The type attribute

The type attribute lets you explicitly define the MIME type of the data that appears in the file you declare with the data attribute. (Use codetype to indicate an applet's MIME type.) If you don't provide data, or if the MIME type of the data is apparent from the URL or is provided by the server, you may omit this attribute. We recommend that you include it anyway, to ensure that the browser handles your data correctly.

For examples of data MIME types, look in your browser preferences for applications. There you'll find a list of the many file data types your browser recognizes and the application, if not the browser itself, that processes and renders that file type.

12.2.1.7 The align, class, border, height, hspace, style, vspace, and width attributes

As with the corresponding attributes for the <img> tag, several attributes let you control the appearance of the <object> display region. The height and width attributes control the size of the viewing region. The hspace and vspace attributes define a margin around the viewing region. The value for each dimension attribute should be an actual number of pixels.

The align attribute determines how the browser aligns the region in context with the surrounding text.* Use top, texttop, middle, absmiddle, baseline, bottom, or absbottom to align the object display space with adjacent text, or left and right alignments for wraparound content.

The display region's dimensions often must match some other applet requirement, so be careful to check these values with the applet programmer. Sometimes the applet may scale its display output to match your specified region.

For instance, our example clock applet might grow or shrink to fit nearly any size display region. Instead, we might fix it to a square space, 100×100 pixels:

```
<object classid="clock.class" height="100" width="100">
</object>
```

As with <img>, use the border attribute to control the width of the frame that surrounds the object's display space when you include it as part of a hyperlink. The null value (border=0) removes the frame. [<img>, 5.2.6]

Use the class and style attributes to control the display style for the content enclosed by the tag and to format the content according to a predefined class of the <object> tag. [Inline Styles: The style Attribute, 8.1.1] [Style Classes, 8.3]

12.2.1.8 The declare attribute

The declare attribute lets you define an object but restrains the browser from downloading and processing it. Used in conjunction with the name attribute, this facility is similar to a forward declaration in a more conventional programming language that lets you defer download of an object until it actually gets used in the document.

12.2.1.9 The id, name, and title attributes

Use the id or name attribute to uniquely label an object. Use the title attribute to simply title the tag. Each attribute's value is a text string. The browser may choose to display a title to the user or may use it in some other manner while rendering the document. Use id or name to reference the object in other elements of your document, including hyperlinks and other objects.

For example, suppose you have two clock applets in your document, along with two applets the user operates to set those clocks. Provide unique labels for the clock

---

* The align attribute is deprecated in the HTML 4 and XHTML standards because of the CSS standard, but it is still popularly used and supported.

applets using the name or id attribute, then pass those labels to the setting applets using the <param> tag, which we discuss later in this chapter in section 12.2.2:

```
<object classid="clock.class" id="clock1">
</object>
<object classid="clock.class" id="clock2">
</object>
<object classid="setter.class">
  <param id="clockToSet" value="clock1">
</object>
<object classid="setter.class">
  <param id="clockToSet" value="clock2">
</object>
```

Because we have no need to distinguish between the setter applets, we choose not to identify their instances.

12.2.1.10 The shapes and usemap attributes

Recall from our detailed discussion of hyperlinks in Chapter 6 that you can divide a picture into geometric regions and attach a hyperlink to each, creating a so-called image map. The shapes and usemap attributes for the <object> tag generalize that feature to include other object types.

The standard shapes attribute informs the browser that the <object> tag's contents are a series of hyperlinks and shape definitions. The usemap attribute and required URL value point to a <map> where you define the shapes and associated hyperlinks, identical to the client-side image maps discussed in section 6.5.2.

For example, here is the image map we described in Chapter 6, rewritten in XHTML as a "shaped" object:

```
<object data="pics/map.gif" shapes="shapes">
  <a shape="rect" coords="0,0,49,49" href="main.html#link1"></a>
  <a shape="rect" coords="50,0,99,49" href="main.html#link2"></a>
  <a shape="rect" coords="0,50,49,99" href="main.html#link3"></a>
  <a shape="rect" coords="50,50,99,99" href="main.html#link4"></a>
</object>
```

and as the more familiar image map:

```
<object data="pics/map.gif" usemap="#map1">
</object>
...
<map name="map1">
  <area coords="0,0,49,49" href="main.html#link1" />
  <area coords="50,0,99,49" href="main.html#link2" />
  <area coords="0,50,49,99" href="main.html#link3" />
  <area coords="50,50,99,99" href="main.html#link4" />
</map>
```

You also may take advantage of all the attributes associated with the hyperlink, <map>, and <area> tags to define and arrange the image-map regions. For instance, we recommend that you include alternative (alt attribute) text descriptions for each sensitive region of the image map.

12.2.1.11 The standby attribute

The standby attribute lets you display a message—the attribute's value text string—during the time the browser is downloading the object data. If your objects are large or if you expect slow network responses add this attribute as a courtesy to your users.

12.2.1.12 The tabindex and notab attributes

For Internet Explorer with ActiveX objects only, the notab attribute excludes the object from the document tabbing order.

As an alternative to the mouse, users also may press the Tab key to select and the Return or Enter key to activate a hyperlink or to access a form control, and browsers may provide other mechanisms to select content. Normally, each time the user moves to the next object—by pressing the Tab key, for example—the browser steps to the next hyperlink or form control in the order in which they appear in the document. To change that order, use the HTML 4/XHTML standard tabindex attribute and an integer value to indicate the object's position in the sequence of selectable elements on the page.

12.2.1.13 The dir and lang attributes

Use the dir and lang attributes, like their counterparts for most other tags, to specify the language and dialect of the <object>-enclosed contents as well as the direction by which the browser adds text characters to the display. [The dir attribute, 3.6.1.1] [The lang attribute, 3.6.1.2]

12.2.1.14 Object event handling

As user-initiated mouse and keyboard events occur within the object, you may want to perform special actions. Accordingly, you can use the 10 standard event attributes to catch these events and execute JavaScript code. We describe JavaScript event handlers more fully shortly in section 12.3.3.

12.2.1.15 Supporting incompatible browsers

Because some browsers may not support applets or the <object> tag, sometimes you may need to tell readers what they are missing. You do this by including body content between the <object> and </object> tags.

Browsers that support the <object> tags ignore the extraneous content inside. Of course, browsers that don't support objects don't recognize the <object> tags. Being generally tolerant of apparent mistakes, browsers usually ignore the unrecognized tags and blithely go on to display whatever content appears inside. It's as simple as that. The following fragment tells object-incapable browser users that they won't see our clock example:

```
<object classid=clock.class>
  If your browser were capable of handling applets, you'd see
  a nifty clock right here!
</object>
```

More importantly, object-capable browsers display the contents of the <object> tag if they cannot load, execute, or render the object. If you have several objects of similar intent but with differing capabilities, you can nest their <object> tags. The browser tries each object in turn, stopping with the first one it can handle. Thus, the outer-most object might be a full-motion video. Within that <object> tag, you might include a simpler MPEG video, and within that <object> tag, a simple GIF image. If the browser can handle full-motion video, your users get the full effect. If that level of video isn't available, the browser can try the simpler MPEG video stream. If that fails, the browser can just display the image. If images aren't possible, the innermost <object> tag might contain a text description of the object.

12.2.2 The <param> Tag

The <param> tag supplies parameters for a containing <object> or <applet> tag. (We discuss the deprecated <applet> tag in the upcoming section, 12.2.3.)

<param>	
Function	Supplies a parameter to an embedded object
Attributes	id, name, type, value, valuetype
End tag	None in HTML; </param> or <param ... /> in XHTML
Contains	Nothing
Used in	*applet_content*

The <param> tag has no content and, with HTML, no end tag. It appears, perhaps with other <param> tags, only between an <object> or <applet> tag and its end tag. Use the <param> tag to pass parameters to the embedded object, such as a Java applet, as required for it to function correctly.

12.2.2.1 The id, name, and value attributes

The `<param>` tag has two required attributes: name or id, and value. You've seen these attributes before with forms. Together, they define a name/value pair that the browser passes to the applet.

For instance, our clock applet example might let users specify the time zone by which it sets its hour hand. To pass the parameter identified as "timezone" with the value "EST" to our example applet, specify the parameters as:

```
<object classid="clock.class">
  <param id="timezone" value="EST" />
</object>
```

The browser passes the name/value pairs to the applet, but that is no guarantee that the applet is expecting the parameters, that the names and values are correct, or that the applet will even use the parameters. Correct parameter names, including capitalization and acceptable values, are determined by the applet author. The wise HTML/XHTML author works closely with the applet programmer or has detailed documentation to ensure that the applet parameters are named correctly and are assigned valid values.

12.2.2.2 The type and valuetype attributes

Use the type and valuetype attributes to define the type of the parameter the browser passes to the embedded object and how that object is to interpret the value. The valuetype attribute can have one of three values: data, ref, or object. The value data indicates that the parameter value is a simple string. This is the default value. The ref value indicates that the value is a URL of some other resource on the Web. Finally, object indicates that the value is the name of another embedded object in the current document. This may be needed to support interobject communication within a document.

The value of the type attribute is the MIME media type of the value of the parameter. This usually is of no significance when the parameter value is a simple string, but it can be important when the value is actually a URL pointing to some other object on the Web. In those cases, the embedded object may need to know the MIME type of the object in order to use it correctly. For example, this parameter tells the embedded object that the parameter is actually the URL of a Microsoft Word document:

```
<param id="document" value="http://kumquats.com/quat.doc"
    type="application/msword" valuetype="ref" />
```

12.2.3 The <applet> Tag (Deprecated)

Use the `<applet>` tag within your documents to download and execute an applet. Also, use the tag to define a region within the document display for the applet's display area. You may supply alternative content within the `<applet>` tag for display by browsers that do not support applets.

`<applet>`

Function	Inserts an application into the current text flow
Attributes	align, alt, archive, class, code, codebase, height, hspace, id, mayscript, name, object, style, title, vspace, width
End tag	`</applet>`; never omitted
Contains	*applet_content*
Used in	*text*

Most applets require one or more parameters that you supply in the document to control their execution. Put these parameters between the `<applet>` tag and its corresponding `</applet>` end tag, using the `<param>` tag. The browser will pass the document-specific parameters to the applet at the time of execution. [<param>, 12.2.2]

The `<applet>` tag has been deprecated in the HTML 4 and XHTML standards in deference to the generalized `<object>` tag, which can do the same as `<applet>` and much more. Nonetheless, `<applet>` is a popular tag and remains supported by the popular browsers.

12.2.3.1 Applet rendering

The browser creates an applet's display region in the containing text flow exactly like an inline image: without line breaks and as a single large entity. The browser downloads and executes the applet just after download and display of the document and continues execution until the code terminates itself or the user stops viewing the page containing the applet.

12.2.3.2 The align attribute

As with an image or `<iframe>`, you can use the align attribute to control the applet's display region with respect to its surrounding text, although the standards prefer that you use respective Cascading Style Sheet (CSS) alignment properties. Set the align attribute's value to top, texttop, middle, absmiddle, baseline, bottom, or absbottom, or use the left and right alignments for wraparound content. For a detailed description, see section 5.2.6.

12.2.3.3 The alt attribute

The alt attribute gives you a way to tell users gracefully that something is missing if, for some reason, the applet cannot or will not execute on their computer. Its value is a quote-enclosed message string that, like the alt attribute for images, gets displayed in lieu of the applet itself. The alt message is only for browsers that support applets. See section 12.2.1.15 earlier in this chapter to find out how to inform users of applet-incapable browsers why they can't view an applet.

12.2.3.4 The archive attribute

The archive attribute collects common Java classes into a single library that is cached on the user's local disk. Once the data is cached, the browser doesn't need to use the network to access an applet; it retrieves the software from the local cache, thereby reducing the inherent delays of additional network activity to load the class.

The value of the archive attribute is a URL identifying the archive file. The suffix of the archive filename may be either *.zip* or *.jar*. Archived *.zip* files are in the familiar ZIP archive format. Archived *.jar* files are in the Java archive format. Archived *.jar* files support compression and advanced features such as digital signatures.

You can use the archive attribute with any <applet> tag, even if the class referenced by the tag's code attribute does not exist in the archive. If the class is not found in the archive, the browser simply attempts to retrieve the class relative to the document URL or the codebase URL, if specified.

12.2.3.5 The code and codebase attributes

The code attribute is required with <applet>. Use code to specify the filename, *not* the URL, of the Java class to be executed by the browser. Like <object>, make the search relative to another storage location by using the codebase attribute, described earlier in section 12.2.1.2, or an archive, as described earlier in section 12.2.1.3. The extension suffix of the filename should be *.class*. If you don't include the suffix, some browsers append *.class* automatically when searching for the applet.

Here is our clock example from earlier rewritten as an <applet>:

```
<applet code="clock.class" codebase="http://www.kumquat.com/classes/">
</applet>
```

which the browser retrieves and displays from:

```
http://www.kumquat.com/classes/clock.class
```

12.2.3.6 The name attribute

The name attribute lets you supply a unique name for this instance of the code class—the copy of the applet that runs on the individual user's computer. As with other named elements in your document, providing a name for the applet lets other parts of your document, including other applets, reference and interact with this one (e.g., for sharing computed results).

12.2.3.7 The height, hspace, vspace, and width attributes

Use the height and width attributes (identical to the counterparts for the <img> and <object> tags) to define the size of the applet's display region in the document. Use hspace and vspace to interpose some empty space around the applet region and thereby set it off from the text. They all accept values indicating the size of the region in pixels. [The height and width attributes, 5.2.6.10]

12.2.3.8 The mayscript attribute

The mayscript attribute indicates that the Java applet is accessing JavaScript features within the browser. Normally, Java applets attempting to access JavaScript cause a browser error. If your applets access JavaScript, you must specify mayscript in the <applet> tag.

12.2.3.9 The title attribute

The value of this attribute is a quoted string that provides a title, if necessary, for the applet.

12.2.3.10 The object attribute

This unfortunately named attribute and its string value reference the name of the resource that contains a serialized version of the applet. How and what it does is an enigma; none of the popular browsers supports it.

12.2.4 The <embed> Tag (Extension)

At one time, the <embed> tag was the only way you could include a reference in your document for the browser to handle some special plug-in application and perhaps data for that application. Today's standard is the <object> tag with the data attribute, and we recommend that you use it in lieu of <embed>. Nonetheless, <embed> currently remains well supported by all the popular browsers.

With <embed>, you reference the data object via the src attribute and URL value for download by the browser. The browser uses the MIME type of the src'd object to determine the plug-in that is required to process the object. Alternatively, you may also use the type attribute to specify a MIME type without an object and thereby initiate execution of a plug-in application, if it exists on the user's computer.

Like all other tags, the nonstandard <embed> tag extension has a set of predefined attributes that define parameters and modify the tag's behavior. Unlike most other

<embed>

Function	Embeds an object in a document
Attributes	align, border [⚑], height, hidden, hspace [⚑], name, palette [⚑], pluginspage [⚑], src, type, units, vspace [⚑], width
End tag	None
Contains	Nothing
Used in	*text*

tags, however, the browsers let you include plug-in-specific name/value attribute pairs in <embed> that, instead of altering the action of the tag itself, get passed to the plug-in application for further processing.

For example, this tag:

```
<embed src=movie.avi width=320 height=200 autostart=true loop=3>
```

has attributes that are processed by the <embed> tag (src, width, and height), and two that are not recognized, but rather are passed to the plug-in associated with AVI video clips: autostart and loop.[*]

It is not possible to document all the possible attributes that the many different plug-ins might need with their associated <embed> tags. Instead, you must turn to the plug-in developer to learn about all of their required and optional attributes for each plug-in that you plan to use in your pages.

12.2.4.1 The align, border, height, hspace, vspace, and width attributes

The browser displays embedded objects to the user in a region set aside within the document window. The <embed> tag's align, border, height, width, hspace, and vspace attributes let you control the appearance of that region exactly as they do for the <img> tag, so we won't belabor them. [<img>, 5.2.6]

Briefly, the height and width attributes control the size of the viewing region. Normally, you should specify the height and width in pixels, but you may use some other units of measure if you also specify the units attribute (see section 12.2.4.8, later in this chapter). The hspace and vspace attributes define a margin, in pixels, around the viewing region. The align attribute determines how the browser aligns

---

[*] Internet Explorer has built-in support for AVI movies; other browsers require that users download and install a plug-in that plays the AVI movie.

the region within surrounding text, and the border attribute determines the width of the border, if any, surrounding the viewing region.

All the popular browsers support the height, width, and align attributes, but unlike <applet> or <object>, Internet Explorer does not support border, hspace, or vspace for the <embed> tag.

12.2.4.2 The hidden attribute

The hidden attribute makes an object invisible to the user, forcing it to have a height and width of 0. Note that setting hidden does not cause the browser to display an empty region within the document, but rather completely removes the object from the containing text flow.

This attribute is useful for audio streams placed within documents. The HTML entry:

```
<embed src=music.wav hidden autostart=true loop=true>
```

embeds an audio object in the page. The browser does not show anything to the user, but rather plays background music for the page. By contrast, the plug-in associated with:

```
<embed src=music.wav>
```

might present an audio control panel to users so that they can start and stop the audio playback, adjust the volume, and so forth.

12.2.4.3 The name attribute

Like other name attributes, this one lets you label the embedded object for later reference by other elements in your document, including other objects. The value of the name attribute is a character string.

12.2.4.4 The palette attribute

Netscape and Internet Explorer support the palette attribute, but in completely different ways. With Netscape, the value of the palette attribute is either foreground or background, indicating which palette of window system colors the plug-in uses for its display.

With Internet Explorer, the value of palette is a pair of hexadecimal color values, separated by a vertical bar. The first value determines the foreground color used by the plug-in; the second sets the background color. Thus, specifying this palette:

```
palette=#ff0000|#00ff00
```

causes the plug-in to use red as its foreground color and green as its background color. For a complete description of hexadecimal color values, see Appendix G.

12.2.4.5 The pluginspage attribute

The pluginspage attribute, once supported only by Netscape, but no longer, specifies the URL of a web page that provides instruction on where to obtain and how to install the plug-in associated with the embedded object. Now all the popular browsers direct you to their supporting plug-in home pages for downloads.

12.2.4.6 The src attribute

Like its document-referencing counterparts for myriad other tags, the src attribute supplies the URL of the data object that you embed in the HTML document. The server providing the object must be configured so that it notifies the browser of the correct MIME type of the object. If not, the browser uses the suffix of the last element of the src value—the object's filename in the URL path—to determine the type of the object. The browser uses this MIME type to determine which plug-in it executes to process the object.

If you don't include an src attribute with the <embed> tag, you must include a type attribute to explicitly reference the MIME type and, as a result, the plug-in application.

12.2.4.7 The type attribute

Use the type attribute in addition to or in lieu of the src attribute. Its value explicitly indicates the MIME type of the embedded object, which in turn determines which plug-in the browser invokes to process the object. This attribute is not required if you include the src attribute and the browser can determine the object type from the object's URL or server. You must supply a type attribute if you don't include the src attribute.

It may seem odd to use an <embed> tag without an src attribute reference to some object, but this is common if the plug-in requires no data or retrieves its data dynamically after it is started. In these cases, the type attribute is required so that the browser knows which plug-in to invoke.

12.2.4.8 The units attribute

Pixels are the default unit of measure for the height and width attributes that control the <embed> display space. The units attribute lets you explicitly state that the absolute measure is pixels, or change it to the relative en, which is one-half the current point size of text in the document. With the en units, you tailor the object's viewing area (*viewport*) to be proportional to its immediately surrounding content, the size of which is varied by the user.

For example, this tag creates a viewport of 200×320 pixels:

```
<embed src=movie.avi height=200 width=320 units=pixels>
```

By changing units to en, that same viewport, when included within a flow of 12-point text, becomes 1200×1920 pixels.

12.2.5 The <noembed> Tag (Extension)

The <noembed> tag, although not part of the standards, is supported by the popular browsers; they consequently ignore the <noembed> enclosed text. On the other hand, browsers that do not recognize <embed> ignore <noembed>, too, consequently displaying the latter tag's enclosed text and thereby supplying alternative content to tell users what they are missing in the <embed> content.

<noembed>	
Function	Supplies content to <embed>-incompatible browsers
Attributes	None
End tag	</noembed>; never omitted
Contains	Nothing
Used in	*text*

Normally, you use the contents of the <noembed> tag to display some sort of message placating users of inadequate browsers:

```
<embed src=cool.mov autostart=true loop=true>
<noembed>To view the cool movie, you need to upgrade to a browser
that supports the &lt;embed&gt; tag!</noembed>
```

We recommend using a <noembed> message only in those cases where the object is crucial for the user to comprehend and use your document. And, in those cases, you should provide a link to a document that can stand alone without the embedded object, or nicely explain the difficulty.

12.3 JavaScript

All the executable content elements we've discussed so far have had one common trait: they are separate from the browser and the HTML/XHTML document—separate data, separate execution engine.

JavaScript is different. It is a scripting language that taps the native functionality of the browser. You may sprinkle JavaScript statements throughout your documents, either as blocks of code or as single statements attached to individual tags. JavaScript-enabled browsers, including all the currently popular ones, interpret and act upon the JavaScript statements you provide to do such things as alter the appearance of the document, control the display, validate and manipulate form elements, and perform general computational tasks.

As with Java, we do not pretend to teach JavaScript programming in this book. We'll show you how to embed and execute JavaScript within your documents, but we ask that you turn to books like the companion *JavaScript: The Definitive Guide* (O'Reilly) for a complete reference.

12.3.1 The <script> Tag

One way to place JavaScript code in your document is via the HTML and XHTML standard <script> tag.

The browser processes everything between <script> and </script> as executable JavaScript statements and data. You cannot place HTML or XHTML within this tag; the browser flags it as an error.

However, browsers that do not support <script> process its contents as regular HTML, to the confusion of the user. For this reason, we recommend that you include the contents of the <script> tag inside HTML comments, just like CSS <style> rules:

```
<script language="JavaScript">
<!--
     JavaScript statements go here
// -->
</script>
```

For browsers that ignore the <script> tag, the contents are masked by the comment delimiters <!-- and -->. JavaScript-enabled browsers, on the other hand, automatically recognize and interpret the JavaScript statements delimited by the comment tags. By using this skeleton for all your <script> tags, you can be sure that all browsers handle your document gracefully, if not completely.

Unfortunately, as we discuss in Chapter 16, script content for XHTML documents must be within a special CDATA declaration, rather than within comments. Hence, HTML browsers won't honor XHTML scripts, and vice versa. Our only recommendation at this point is to follow the popular browsers: write in HTML, but use as many of the features of XHTML as you can in preparation for the future.

You may include more than one <script> tag in a document, located in either the <head> or the <body>. The JavaScript-enabled browser executes the statements in order. Variables and functions defined within one <script> tag may be referenced by JavaScript statements in other <script> tags. In fact, one common JavaScript programming style is to use a single <script> in the document <head> to define common functions and global variables for the document and then to call those functions and reference their variables in other JavaScript statements sprinkled throughout the document.

<script>

Function	Defines an executable script within a document
Attributes	charset, defer, language, src, type
End tag	</script>; never omitted
Contains	*scripts*
Used in	*head_content, body_content*

12.3.1.1 The language and type attributes

Use the language or type attribute in the <script> tag to declare the scripting language that you used to compose the contents of the tag. The HTML 4 and XHTML standards deprecate the language attribute in favor of the type attribute. Regrettably, the value for each attribute is different.

If you are using JavaScript—by far the most common scripting language on the Web—use language=JavaScript or type="text/javascript". You may occasionally see the language value VBScript (text/vbscript for type), indicating that the enclosed code is written in Microsoft's Visual Basic script.

With JavaScript, you may also use the language value "JavaScript 1.2", indicating that the enclosed script is written for browsers that support version 1.2 of the language (most current browsers do). Versioning can be a problem, but it's not too severe. Netscape 2.0, for instance, supports JavaScript 1.0 but does not process scripts identified as "JavaScript 1.1". Then again, what proportion of your audience is still running Netscape 2.0?

12.3.1.2 The src and charset attributes

For particularly large JavaScript programs and ones you reuse often, you should store the code in a separate file. In these cases, have the browser load that separate file through the src attribute. The value of the src attribute is the URL of the file containing the JavaScript program. The stored file should have a MIME type of application/javascript, but it will be handled automatically by a properly configured server if the filename suffix is *.js*.

For example:

```
<script type="text/javascript" src="http://www.kumquat.com/quatscript.js">
</script>
```

tells the <script>-able browser to load a JavaScript program named *quatscript.js* from the server. Although there are no <script> contents, the ending </script> still is required.

Used in conjunction with the src attribute, the charset attribute tells the browser the character set used to encode the JavaScript program. Its value is the name of any International Organization for Standardization (ISO) standard character set encoding.

12.3.1.3 The defer attribute

Some JavaScript scripts create actual document content using the document.write method. If your scripts do not alter the contents of the document, add the defer attribute to the <script> tag to speed its processing. Because the browser knows that it can safely read the remainder of the document without executing your scripts, it defers interpretation of the script until after the document has been rendered for the user.

12.3.2 The <noscript> Tag

Use the <noscript> tag to tell users of browsers that do not support the <script> tag that they are missing something. You've already seen many examples of this type of tag. You know the drill....

<noscript>

Function	Supplies content to <script>-challenged browsers
Attributes	class, dir, id, lang, onClick, onDblClick, onKeyDown, onKeyPress, onKeyUp, onMouseDown, onMouseMove, onMouseOut, onMouseOver, onMouseUp, style, title
End tag	</noscript>; never omitted
Contains	*body_content*
Used in	*text*

Very old, albeit <script>-able, browsers like Netscape 2 and Internet Explorer 3 blithely display the contents of the <noscript> tag, to the confusion of their users. Given the paucity of users of these browsers, we question the need, but there are ways to detect and handle <script>-challenged browsers, detailed in any good Java-Script book.

The <noscript> tag supports the six standard HTML 4/XHTML attributes—class and style for style management, lang and dir for language type and display direction, title and id for titling and naming the enclosed content—and the event attributes for user-initiated processing. [The dir attribute, 3.6.1.1] [The lang attribute, 3.6.1.2] [The id attribute, 4.1.1.4] [The title attribute, 4.1.1.5] [Inline Styles: The style Attribute, 8.1.1] [Style Classes, 8.3] [JavaScript Event Handlers, 12.3.3]

12.3.3 JavaScript Event Handlers

One of the most important features JavaScript provides is the ability to detect and react to events that occur while a document is loading, rendering, and being browsed by the user. The JavaScript code that handles these events may be placed within the <script> tag, but more commonly, it is associated with a specific tag via one or more special tag attributes.

For example, you might want to invoke a JavaScript function when the user passes the mouse over a hyperlink in a document. The JavaScript-aware browsers support a special "mouse over" event-handler attribute for the <a> tag, called onMouseOver, to do just that:

```
<a href="doc.html" onMouseOver="status='Click me!';
return true">
```

When the mouse passes over this example link, the browser executes the JavaScript statements. (Notice that the two JavaScript statements are enclosed in quotes and separated by a semicolon, and that single quotes surround the text-message portion of the first statement.)

While a complete explanation of this code is beyond our scope, the net result is that the browser places the message "Click me!" in the status bar of the browser window. Commonly, authors use this simple JavaScript function to display a more descriptive explanation of a hyperlink, in place of the often cryptic URL that the browser traditionally displays in the status window.

HTML and XHTML both support a rich set of event handlers through related on-event tag attributes. The value of any of the JavaScript event-handler attributes is a quoted string containing one or more JavaScript statements separated by semicolons. If necessary, you can break extremely long statements across several lines. You also should take care to use entities for embedded double quotes in the statements, to avoid syntax errors when processing the attribute values.

12.3.3.1 Standard event handler attributes

Table 12-1 presents the current set of event handlers as tag attributes. Most are supported by the popular browsers, which also support a variety of nonstandard event handlers (tagged with asterisks in the table).

We put the event handlers into two categories: user related and document related. The user-related ones are the mouse and keyboard events that occur when the user handles either device on the computer. User-related events are quite ubiquitous, appearing as standard attributes in nearly all the standard tags (even though they may not yet be supported by any browser), so we don't list their associated tags in Table 12-1. Instead, we'll tell you which tags *do not* accept these event attributes: <applet>, <base>, <basefont>, <bdo>, <br>, <font>, <frame>, <frameset>, <head>, <html>, <iframe>, <isindex>, <meta>, <param>, <script>, <style>, and <title>.

Table 12-1. Event handlers

Event handler	HTML/XHTML tags
onAbort*	\<img\>
onBlur	\<a\>,\<area\>,\<body\>,\<button\>,\<frameset\>,\<input\>,\<label\>,\<select\>,\<textarea\>
onChange	\<input\>,\<select\>,\<textarea\>
onClick	Most tags
onDblClick	Most tags
onError*	\<img\>
onFocus	\<a\>,\<area\>,\<body\>,\<button\>,\<frameset\>,\<input\>,\<label\>,\<select\>,\<textarea\>
onKeyDown	Most tags
onKeyPress	Most tags
onKeyUp	Most tags
onLoad	\<body\>,\<frameset\>,\<img\>*
onMouseDown	Most tags
onMouseMove	Most tags
onMouseOut	Most tags
onMouseOver	Most tags
onMouseUp	Most tags
onReset	\<form\>
onSelect	\<input\>,\<textarea\>
onSubmit	\<form\>
onUnload	\<body\>,\<frameset\>

* Nonstandard handlers.

Some events, however, occur rarely and with special tags. These relate to the special events and states that occur during the display and management of a document and its elements by the browser.

12.3.3.2 The mouse-related events

The onClick, onDblClick, onMouseDown, and onMouseUp attributes refer to the mouse button. The onClick event happens when the user presses down and then quickly releases the mouse button. If the user then quickly clicks the mouse button for a second time, the onDblClick event gets triggered in the browser as well.

If you need to detect both halves of a mouse click as separate events, use onMouseDown and onMouseUp. When the user presses the mouse button, the onMouseDown event occurs. The onMouseUp event happens when the user releases the mouse button.

The onMouseMove, onMouseOut, and onMouseOver events happen when the user drags the mouse pointer. The onMouseOver event occurs when the mouse first enters the display region occupied by the associated HTML element. After entry, onMouseMove events are generated as the mouse moves about within the element. Finally, when the mouse exits the element, onMouseOut occurs.

For some elements, the onFocus event corresponds to onMouseOver, and onBlur corresponds to onMouseOut.

12.3.3.3 The keyboard events

The HTML 4 and XHTML standards currently support only three events relating to user keyboard actions: onKeyDown, onKeyUp, and onKeyPress. The onKeyDown event occurs when the user depresses a key on the keyboard; onKeyUp happens when the key is released. The onKeyPress event is triggered when a key is pressed and released. Usually, you'll have handlers for either the up and down events or the composite key-press event, but not for both.

12.3.3.4 Document events

Most of the document-related event handlers relate to the actions and states of form controls. For instance, onReset and onSubmit happen when the user activates the respective reset or submit button. Similarly, onSelect and onChange occur as users interact with certain form elements. See Chapter 9 for a detailed discussion of these forms-related events.

There also are some document-related event handlers that occur when various document elements get handled by the browser. For instance, the onLoad event may happen when a frameset is complete or when the body of an HTML or XHTML document gets loaded and displayed by the browser. Similarly, onUnload occurs when a document is removed from a frame or window.

12.3.4 javascript URLs

You can replace any conventional URL reference in a document with one or more JavaScript statements. The browser then executes the JavaScript code, instead of downloading another document, whenever the browser references the URL. The result of the last statement is taken to be the "document" referenced by the URL and is displayed by the browser accordingly. The result of the last statement is *not* the URL of a document; it is the actual content to be displayed by the browser.

To create a javascript URL, use javascript as the URL's protocol:

```
<a href="javascript:generate_document()">
```

In this example, the JavaScript function generate_document() gets executed whenever the user selects the hyperlink. The value returned by the function, presumably a valid HTML or XHTML document, is rendered and displayed by the browser.

It may be that the executed statement returns no value. In this case, the current document is left unchanged. For example, this javascript URL:

```
<a href="javascript:alert('Error!')">
```

pops up an alert dialog box and does nothing else. The document containing the hyperlink is still visible after the dialog box is displayed and dismissed by the user.

12.3.5 JavaScript Entities

Character entities in HTML and XHTML consist of an ampersand (&), an entity name or number, and a closing semicolon. For instance, to insert the ampersand character itself in a document text flow, use the character sequence &. Similarly, JavaScript entities consist of an ampersand, one or more JavaScript statements enclosed in curly braces, and a closing semicolon. For example:

```
&{document.fgColor};
```

You must separate multiple statements by semicolons within the curly braces. The value of the last (or only) statement is converted to a string and replaces the entity in the document.

Normally, entities can appear anywhere in a document. JavaScript entities, however, are restricted to values of tag attributes. This lets you write "dynamic tags" whose attributes are not known until the document is loaded and the JavaScript is executed. For example, this tag sets the text color of the document to the color value returned by the individual's favorite_color( ) function:

```
<body text=&{favorite_color( )};>
```

Support for JavaScript entities is inconsistent among the various browsers and for this reason we recommend against their use.

12.3.6 The <server> Tag

The <server> tag is a strange beast. The web server processes it and the browser never sees it, so what you can do with this tag depends on the server you are using, not on the reader's browser.

Netscape's web servers, for example (not to be confused with their browser), use the <server> tag to let you place JavaScript statements within a document that the server processes. The results of the executed JavaScript are then inserted into the document, replacing the <server> tag. A complete discussion of this so-called "server-side" JavaScript is completely beyond this book; we include this brief reference only to document the <server> tag.

Like the <script> tag, the <server> tag contains JavaScript code. However, the latter tag and content code must appear inside the document <head>. The server extracts it from the document and executes it when the document is requested for download.

<table>
<tr><td colspan="2" align="center"><server></td></tr>
<tr><td>Function</td><td>Defines server-side JavaScript</td></tr>
<tr><td>Attributes</td><td>None</td></tr>
<tr><td>End tag</td><td></server>; never omitted</td></tr>
<tr><td>Contains</td><td>JavaScript</td></tr>
<tr><td>Used in</td><td>head_content</td></tr>
</table>

Obviously, server-side JavaScript is tightly coupled to the server, not to the browser. To fully exploit this tag and the benefits of server-side JavaScript or other server-side programming languages, consult your web server's documentation.

12.4 JavaScript Stylesheets (Antiquated)

Much of a browser's work is manipulating the display, and much of its display code already has been exposed for JavaScripting. So it seemed only natural, perhaps even relatively easy, for the developers at Netscape to implement JavaScript Stylesheets (JSS). Based on the World Wide Web Consortium (W3C)-recommended CSS model, outlined in Chapter 8, this alternative document style technology lets you prescribe display properties for all the various HTML elements, either inline as tag attributes, at the document level, or for an entire document collection.

JSS is antiquated. Even the inventor eschews support for JSS entirely in favor of the standard CSS2. We are strong proponents of reasonable standards, and now that the CSS2 model is fully supported in HTML 4 and XHTML, we can't recommend that you use anything but CSS-standard stylesheets.

We thoroughly discuss the concepts and ideas behind stylesheets—specifically, Cascading Style Sheets—in Chapter 8, so we won't repeat ourselves here. Rather, we address only how to create and manipulate styles with JavaScript here purely for historical reasons. Before forging ahead in this section, we recommend that you first absorb the information in Chapter 8.

12.4.1 JavaScript Stylesheet Syntax

Netscape versions 4 and earlier implemented JSS by extending several existing HTML tags and defining a few objects that store your document's styles. Netscape no longer supports JSS, nor does any other browser.

12.4.1.1 External, document-level, and inline JSS

As with CSS, you can reference and load external JSS files with the `<link>` tag. For example:

```
<link href="styles.js" rel=stylesheet type=text/JavaScript>
```

The only real difference between this tag and the one for a CSS external stylesheet is that the type attribute of the `<link>` tag is set to `text/JavaScript` rather than `text/CSS`. The referenced file, *styles.js*, contains JavaScript statements that define styles and classes that Netscape then uses to control display of the current document.

Document-level JSS is defined within a `<style>` tag in the `<head>` of the document, just like with CSS. Again, there is only one real difference: the type attribute of the `<style>` tag is set to `text/JavaScript` rather than `text/CSS`.

The contents of the `<style>` tag for JSS are quite different from those for CSS, however. For example:

```
<style type=text/JavaScript>
<!--
    tags.BODY.marginLeft = "20px";
    tags.P.fontWeight = "bold";
  // -->
</style>
```

First, notice that we use the standard JavaScript and HTML comments to surround our JSS definitions, preventing noncompliant browsers from processing them as HTML content. Also notice that the syntax of the style definition is that of Java-Script, where letter case, among other things, *does* make a difference.

You associate inline JavaScript-based style rules with a specific tag using the style attribute, just like with CSS inline styles. The value of the attribute is a list of JSS assignments, separated by semicolons. For example:

```
<p style="color = 'green'; fontWeight = 'bold'">
```

creates a green, boldfaced text paragraph. Notice first that you need to enclose inline style values within single quotation marks, not double quotation marks, as you might use for document-level and external JSS styles. This is reasonable because the style attribute value itself must be enclosed in double quotation marks.

Also note that inline JSS definitions use only the property name, not the containing tag object that owns the property. This makes sense because inline JSS styles affect only the current tag, not all instances of the tag.

12.4.1.2 JSS values

In general, all of the values you may use for CSS you may also use in JSS definitions. For keyword, length, and percentage values, simply enclose the value in quotes and use it as you would any string value in JavaScript. Thus, the CSS value bold becomes "bold" or 'bold' for JSS document-level or inline styles, respectively; 12pt in CSS becomes '12pt' or "12pt" in JSS.

Specify color values as the color name or a hexadecimal color value, enclosed in single or double quotes. JSS does not support the CSS decimal red, green, and blue (RGB) notation.

JSS URL values are strings containing the desired URL. Thus, the CSS URL value url(http://www.kumquat.com) becomes 'http://www.kumquat.com' for a JSS inline style, or "http://www.kumquat.com" at the document level.

One unique power of JSS is that any value can be computed dynamically when the browser processes the document. Instead of statically specifying the font size, for example, you can compute it on the fly:

```
tags.P.fontSize = favorite_font_size( );
```

We assume that the JavaScript function favorite_font_size( ) somehow determines the desired font size and returns a string value containing that size. This, in turn, is assigned to the fontSize property for the <p> tag, defining the font size for all paragraphs in the document.

12.4.1.3 Defining styles for tags

JavaScript defines a document property called tags that contains the style properties for all HTML tags. To define a style for a tag, simply set the appropriate property of the desired style property within the tag property of the document object. For example:

```
document.tags.P.fontSize = '12pt';
document.tags.H2.color = 'blue';
```

These two JSS definitions set the font size for the <p> tag to 12 points and render all <h2> tags in blue. The equivalent CSS definitions are:

```
p {font-size : 12pt}
h2 {color : blue}
```

Because the tags property always refers to the current document, you may omit document from any JSS tag style definition. We could have written the preceding two styles as:

```
tags.P.fontSize = '12pt';
tags.H2.color = 'blue';
```

Moreover, as we mentioned previously, you may omit the tag name, as well as the document and tags properties for inline JSS, using the style attribute.

Capitalization and case are significant in JSS. The tag names within the tags property must always be fully capitalized. The embedded capital letters within the tag properties are significant: any deviation from the exact lettering produces an error, and Netscape won't honor your JSS declaration. All of the following JSS definitions are invalid, though the reasons are not overly apparent:

```
tags.p.fontsize = '12pt';
tags.Body.Color = 'blue';
tags.P.COLOR = 'red';
```

The correct versions are:

```
tags.P.fontSize = '12pt';
tags.BODY.color = 'blue';
tags.P.color = 'red';
```

It can be very tedious to specify a number of properties for a single tag, so you can take advantage of the JavaScript with statement to reduce your typing burden. These styles:

```
tags.P.fontSize = '14pt';
tags.P.color = 'blue';
tags.P.fontWeight = 'bold';
tags.P.leftMargin = '20%';
```

can more easily be written as:

```
with (tags.P) {
  fontSize = '14pt';
  color = 'blue';
  fontWeight = 'bold';
  leftMargin = '20%';
  }
```

You can apply similar styles to diverse tags just as easily:

```
with (tags.P, tags.LI, tags.H1) {
  fontSize = '14pt';
  color = 'blue';
  fontWeight = 'bold';
  leftMargin = '20%';
  }
```

12.4.1.4 Defining style classes

Like CSS, JSS lets you target styles for specific ways that a tag can be used in your document. JSS uses the classes property to define separate styles for the same tag. There are no predefined properties within the classes property; instead, any property you reference is defined as a class to be used by the current document. For example:

```
classes.bold.P.fontWeight = 'bold';
with (classes.abstract.P) {
  leftMargin = '20pt';
  rightMargin = '20pt';
  fontStyle = 'italic';
  textAlign = 'justify';
  }
```

The first style defines a class of the <p> tag named bold whose font weight is set to bold. The next style uses the with statement to create a class of the <p> tag named abstract with the specified properties. The equivalent CSS rules would be:

```
P.bold {font-weight : bold}
P.abstract {left-margin : 20pt;
   right-margin : 20pt;
   font-style : italic;
   text-align : justify
   }
```

Once defined, use a JSS class just like any CSS class: with the class attribute and the class name.

Like CSS, JSS also lets you define a class without defining the tag that uses the class. This lets you define generic classes that you can later apply to any tag. To create a generic style class in JSS, use the special tag property all:

```
classes.green.all.color = "green";
```

You can then add class="green" to any tag to have Netscape render its contents in green. The equivalent CSS is:

```
.green {color : green}
```

12.4.1.5 Using contextual styles

One of the most powerful aspects of CSS is its contextual style capability, wherein the browser applies a style to tags only if they appear in the document in a certain nesting. JSS supports contextual styles as well, through the special contextual( ) method within the tags property. The parameters to this method are the tags and classes that define the context in which Netscape applies the style. For example:

```
tags.contextual(tags.UL, tags.UL, tags.LI).listStyleType = 'disc';
```

defines a context wherein the elements (tags.LI) of an unordered list nested within another unordered list (tags.UL, tags.UL) use the disc as their bullet symbol. The CSS equivalent is:

```
ul ul li {list-style-type : disc}
```

You can mix tags and classes in the contextual( ) method. For instance:

```
tags.contextual(classes.abstract.P, tags.EM).color = 'red';
```

tells the browser to display in red <em> tags that appear within paragraphs that are of the abstract class. The CSS equivalent is:

```
p.abstract em {color : red}
```

Because the tags object is unambiguously included within the contextual( ) method, you may omit it from the definition. Hence, our nested list example may be rewritten as:

```
tags.contextual(UL, UL, LI).listStyleType = 'disc';
```

12.4.2 JavaScript Stylesheet Properties

A subset of the CSS style properties are supported in JSS. Table 12-2 shows the JSS style properties, their CSS equivalents, and the sections in which those properties are fully documented.

Table 12-2. JSS properties and CSS equivalents

JSS property	CSS property	See section
align	float	8.4.7.9
backgroundImage	background-image	8.4.5.2
backgroundColor	background-color	8.4.5.1
borderBottomWidth	border-bottom-width	8.4.7.4
borderLeftWidth	border-left-width	8.4.7.4
borderRightWidth	border-right-width	8.4.7.4
borderStyle	border-style	8.4.7.5
borderTopWidth	border-top-width	8.4.7.4
clear	clear	8.4.7.7
display	display	8.4.10.1
fontSize	font-size	8.4.3.2
fontStyle	font-style	8.4.3.5
height	height	8.4.7.10
lineHeight	line-height	8.4.6.2
listStyleType	list-style-type	8.4.8.3
marginBottom	margin-bottom	8.4.7.11
marginLeft	margin-left	8.4.7.11
marginRight	margin-right	8.4.7.11
marginTop	margin-top	8.4.7.11
paddingBottom	padding-bottom	8.4.7.12
paddingLeft	padding-left	8.4.7.12
paddingRight	padding-right	8.4.7.12
paddingTop	padding-top	8.4.7.12
textDecoration	text-decoration	8.4.6.4
textTransform	text-transform	8.4.6.7
textAlign	text-align	8.4.6.3
textIndent	text-indent	8.4.6.5
verticalAlign	vertical-align	8.4.6.7
whiteSpace	white-space	8.4.10.2
width	width	8.4.7.16

JSS also defines three methods that allow you to define margins, padding, and border widths within a single style property. The three methods, margins( ), paddings( ), and borderWidths( ), accept four parameters, corresponding to the top, right, bottom, and left margins, padding, and border width, respectively. Unlike their CSS counterparts (margin, discussed in section 8.4.7.11; padding, discussed in section 8.4.7.12; and border-width, discussed in section 8.4.7.4), these JSS methods require that you always specify all four parameters. There is no shorthand way in JSS to set multiple margins, paddings, or border widths with a single value.

## CHAPTER 13

Dynamic Documents

The standard HTML/XHTML document model is static. Once displayed on the browser, a document does not change until the user initiates some activity, such as selecting a hyperlink. The Netscape developers found that limitation unacceptable and built some special features into their browser that let you change HTML document content dynamically. In fact, they provide two different mechanisms for dynamic documents, which we describe in detail in this chapter. Internet Explorer supports some of these mechanisms, which we'll discuss as well.

We should mention that many of the features of dynamic documents have been displaced by plug-in browser accessories and, in particular, applets, as well as the new Asynchronous JavaScript and XML (Ajax) technologies. Nonetheless, Netscape and Internet Explorer continue to support dynamic documents, and we believe the technology has virtues you should be aware of, if not take advantage of, in your HTML documents. [Applets and Objects, 12.1]

13.1 An Overview of Dynamic Documents

Recall from our discussion in Chapter 1 that the client browser initiates data flow on the Web by contacting a server with a document request. The server honors the request by sending the document to the client. The client subsequently displays the document's contents to the user. For normal web documents, a single transaction initiated from the client side is all that is needed to collect and display the document. Once displayed, however, it does not change.

Dynamic documents, on the other hand, are the result of multiple transactions initiated from either or both the server side and the client side. A *client-pull* document is one that initiates multiple transactions from the client side. When the server is the instigator, the dynamic document is known as a *server-push* document.

In a client-pull document, special HTML codes tell the client to periodically request and download another document from one or more servers on the network, dynamically updating the display.

Server-push documents also advance the way servers communicate with clients. Normally, over the Web, the client stays connected with a server for only as long as it takes to retrieve a single document. With server-push documents, the connection remains open and the server continues to send data to the client periodically, adding to or replacing the previous contents.

Mozilla-based browsers, including Firefox and Netscape, currently are the only browsers able to handle HTTP server-push dynamic documents natively. And because server-push documents don't work without an HTTP server, you can't develop and test them unless you have a server running locally as well.

13.1.1 Another Word of Caution

As always, we tell you exactly how to use these exciting but nonstandard features, and we admonish you not to use them unless you have a compelling and overriding reason to do so. We are particularly strident with that admonition for dynamic documents, not only because they aren't part of the HTML standard, but also because dynamic documents can hog the network. They require larger, longer downloads than their static counterparts, and they require many more (in the case of client-pull) or longer-term (for server-push) client/server connections. Multiple connections on a single server are limited to a few of the millions of web users at a time. We'd hate to see your readers miss out because you've created a jiggling image in a dynamic document that would otherwise have been an effective and readily accessible static document that more people could enjoy.

13.2 Client-Pull Documents

Client-pull documents are relatively easy to prepare, and you can run them locally without requiring an HTTP server. That's because the client-pull document has the browser request and load another document, even if from local storage. All you need to do is embed a <meta> tag into the header of your HTML or XHTML document. The special tag tells the client browser to display the current document for a specified period of time and then load and display an entirely new one, just as though the user had selected the new document from a hyperlink. (Note that currently there isn't an easy way to change just a portion of a document dynamically using client-pull, though you could use frames if you wanted a split-screen effect.) [<meta>, 6.8.1]

13.2.1 Uniquely Refreshing

Client-pull dynamic documents work with all the popular browsers because they respond to a special HTTP header field called Refresh.

You may recall from previous discussions that whenever an HTTP server sends a document to the client browser, it precedes the document's data with one or more header fields. One header field, for instance, contains a description of the document's content type, used by the browser to decide how to display the document's contents. For example, the server precedes HTML documents with the header "Content-type: text/html," whose meaning should be fairly obvious.

As we discussed in Chapter 6, you can add your own special fields to an HTML document's HTTP header by inserting a <meta> tag into its <head>. [<meta>, 6.8.1]

The HTTP Refresh field implements client-pull dynamic HTML documents, enabled by the <meta> tag format:

```
<meta http-equiv="Refresh" content="field value">
```

The tag's http-equiv attribute tells the HTTP server to include the Refresh field, with a value specified by the content attribute (if any, carefully enclosed in quotation marks), in the string of headers it sends to the client browser just before it sends the rest of the document's content. The browser recognizes the Refresh header as the mark of a dynamic HTML document and responds accordingly, as we discuss in the next section.

13.2.2 The Refresh Header Contents

The value of the content attribute in the special Refresh <meta> tag determines when and how the browser updates the current document. Set it to an integer, and the browser delays that many seconds before automatically loading another document. You may set the content field value to 0, meaning no delay at all. In that case, the browser loads the next document immediately after it finishes rendering the current one, which allows you to achieve some very crude animation effects. [<meta>, 6.8.1]

13.2.2.1 Refreshing the same document

If the Refresh field's content value is just the number of seconds, the browser reloads that same document over and over again, delaying the specified time between each cycle, until the user goes to another document or shuts down the browser.

For example, the browser reloads the following client-pull document every 15 seconds:

```
<html>
<head>
  <meta http-equiv="Refresh" content="15">
  <title>Kumquat Market Prices</title>
</head>
<body>
```

```
<h3> Kumquat Market Prices</h3>
Kumquats are currently trading at $1.96 per pound.
</body>
</html>
```

The financial wizards among you may have noticed that, with some special software tricks on the server side, you can update the price of kumquats in the document so that it acts like a ticker-tape machine, with the latest kumquat commodity price updated every 15 seconds.

13.2.2.2 Refreshing with a different document

Instead of reloading the same document repeatedly, you can tell the browser to load a different document dynamically. You do so by adding that document's URL after the delay time and an intervening semicolon in the <meta> tag's content attribute. For example:

```
<meta http-equiv="Refresh"
   content="15; URL=http://www.kumquat.com/next.html">
```

causes the browser to retrieve the *next.html* document from the *www.kumquat.com* web server after having displayed the current document for 15 seconds.

13.2.2.3 Cycling between documents

Keep in mind that the effects of the Refresh <meta> tag apply only to the document in which it appears. Hence, to cycle between several documents, you must include a Refresh <meta> tag in each one. To achieve the effect, set the content value for each document in the cycle with a URL which points to the next document, and the last document pointing back to the first one to complete the cycle.

For example, the following are the <meta> tags for the headers of each in a three-HTML-document cycle.

The *first.html* document contains:

```
<meta http-equiv="Refresh"
   content="30; URL=second.html">
```

The *second.html* document contains:

```
<meta http-equiv="Refresh"
   content="30; URL=third.html">
```

And the *third.html* document has in its <head> (besides other crazy ideas):

```
<meta http-equiv="Refresh"
   content="30; URL=first.html">
```

If it is left alone, the browser endlessly loops between the three documents at 30-second intervals.

Cycling documents make excellent attractors, catching the attention of passers-by to a web-driven kiosk, for example. Users can navigate through the wider collection of kiosk documents by clicking hyperlinks in one of the kiosk's attractor pages and then by clicking subsequent ones.*

To complete the cycle, documents selected from an attractor page also should have their own Refresh fields that point back to the originating attractor document in the cycling set of attractors. You should specify a fairly long delay period for the nonat-tractor pages—120 to 300 seconds or more—so that the kiosk doesn't automatically reset while a user is reading the current document. However, the delay period should be short enough so that the kiosk resets to the attractor mode in a reasonable period of time after the user finishes.

13.2.3 Pulling Non-HTML Content

The client-pull feature is not restricted to HTML documents, although it is certainly easiest to create dynamic documents with HTML. With a bit of server-side program-ming, you can add a Refresh field to the HTTP header of any sort of document, from audio files to images to video clips.

For example, create a real-time video feed by adding a Refresh header field in each of a sequence of images grabbed and digitized from a camera. Include a delay of 0 with the URL that points to the next image so that as quickly as the browser displays one image, it retrieves the next. Assuming that the network keeps up, the result is a crude (really crude) TV.

Because the browser clears the window before presenting each subsequent image, the resulting flicker and flash make it almost impossible to present a coherent sequence of images. This technique is more effective when presenting a series of images designed to be viewed as a slide show, where the user expects some sort of display activity between each image.

Perhaps a better use of the client-pull feature is with long-playing multimedia docu-ments, which the popular browsers use special helper applications to display. On a multitasking computer, such as one running Linux or Windows, the browser down-loads one document, while a helper application plays another. Combine the client-pull capabilities with that multitasking to improve multimedia document perfor-mance. Instead of waiting for a single, large document such as a movie or audio file to download before playing, break it into smaller segments, each automatically downloaded by the previous segment via the Refresh header. The browser plays the first segment while downloading the second, then third, then fourth, and so on.

---

* This brings up a good point: the user may override the Refresh dynamic action at any time (for instance, by clicking a hyperlink before the client-pull timeout expires). The browser always ignores the Refresh action in lieu of user interaction.

13.2.4 Combining Refresh with Other HTTP Header Fields

You can have your client-pull dynamic documents perform some neat tricks by combining the effects of the Refresh field with other HTTP header fields. One combination that is particularly useful is Refresh with a Redirect field.

The Redirect field lets the server tell the browser to retrieve the requested document elsewhere at the field's accompanying URL value. The client browser automatically redirects its request to the new URL and gets the document from the new location, usually without telling the user. We retrieve redirected documents all the time and may never notice.

The most common cause for redirection is when someone moves an HTML document collection to a new directory or to a new server. As a courtesy, the webmaster programs the original host server to send an HTTP header field containing the Redirect field and new URL (without a document body) to any and all browsers that request the document from the original location. That way, the new document location is transparent to users, and they won't have to reset their browser bookmarks.

But sometimes you want the users to reset their bookmarks to the new location, because the old one won't be redirecting browsers forever (perhaps because it's being taken out of service). One way to notify users of the new location is to have the redirection URL point to some HTML document other than the home page of the new collection that contains a message about the new location. Once noted, users then take a "Continue" hyperlink to the new home page location and set their bookmarks accordingly.

By combining the Redirect and Refresh fields, you can make that notification screen automatically move to the new home page. If the browser receives an HTTP header with both fields, it honors both; it immediately fetches the redirected URL and displays it, and it sets the refresh timer and replacement URL, if specified. When the time expires, the browser automatically retrieves the next URL—your new home page location.

13.2.4.1 A random URL generator

Another application for the combination of Redirect and Refresh HTTP header fields is a perpetual, random URL generator. You'll need some programming skills to create a server-side application that selects a random URL from a prepared list and outputs a Redirect field that references that URL along with a Refresh field that reinvokes the random-URL application after some delay.

When the modern browser receives the complete header, it immediately loads and displays the randomly selected document specified in the Redirect field's URL. After the delay specified in the Refresh field, the browser reruns the random-URL generator on the server (as specified in the refresh URL), and the cycle starts over. The result is an endless cycle of random URLs displayed at regular intervals.

13.2.5 Performance Considerations

Client-pull documents consume extra network resources, especially when the refresh delay is small, because each refresh may involve a new connection to a server. It may take a browser several seconds to contact the server and begin retrieving the document. As a result, rapid updates generally are not feasible, especially over slow network connections.

Use client-pull dynamic documents for low-frequency updates of entire documents, or for cycling among documents without user intervention.

13.3 Server-Push Documents

Netscape invented server-push dynamic documents. With the technology, the client/server connection remains open after an initial transfer of data, and the server periodically sends new data to the client, updating the document's display. Server-push is made possible by some special programming on the server side and is enabled by the multipart/mixed-media type feature of Multipurpose Internet Mail Extensions (MIME), the computer industry's standard for multimedia document transmission over the Internet.

13.3.1 The Multipart/Mixed Media Type

As we mentioned earlier in this chapter in the discussion of client-pull dynamic documents, the HTTP server sends a two-part transmission to the client browser: a header describing the document, followed by the document itself. The document's MIME type is part of the HTTP header field. Normally, the server includes "Content-Type: text/html" in an HTML document's header before sending its actual contents. By changing that content type to "multipart/mixed," you can send an HTML document or several documents in several pieces, rather than in a single chunk. Only Mozilla-based browsers, such as Netscape and Firefox, though, understand and respond to the multipart header field; other browsers either ignore additional parts or refuse the document altogether.

The general form of the MIME multipart/mixed-media Content-Type header looks like this:

```
Content-type: multipart/mixed;boundary="SomeRandomString"
```

This HTTP header component tells the Mozilla client to expect the document to follow in several parts and to look for SomeRandomString, which separates the parts. That boundary string should be unique and should not appear anywhere, in any of the individual parts. The content of the server-to-client transmission looks like this:

```
--SomeRandomString
Content-type: text/plain
```

```
Data for the first part
--SomeRandomString
Content-type: text/plain

Data for the second part

--SomeRandomString--
```

The preceding example has two document parts, both composed of just plain text. The server sends each part, preceded by our `SomeRandomString` document-boundary delimiter (which itself is preceded by two dashes), followed by the `Content-Type` field and then the data for each part. The last transmission from server to client is a single reference to the boundary string, followed by two more dashes indicating that this was the last part of the document.

Upon receipt of each part, the Mozilla browser automatically adds the incoming data to the current document display.

You have to write a special HTTP server application to enable this type of server-push dynamic document—one that creates the special HTTP MIME multipart/mixed header and sends the various documents separated by the boundary delimiter.

13.3.2 The Multipart/X-Mixed-Replace Media Type

Server-push dynamic document authors may use an experimental variant of the MIME multipart/mixed media type known as *multipart/x-mixed-replace media*. The difference between this special content type and its predecessor is that, instead of simply adding content to the current display, the "replace" version has each subsequent part replace the preceding one.

The format of the mixed-replace HTTP header is very similar to its multipart/mixed counterpart; the only difference is in the `Content-Type`:

```
multipart/x-mixed-replace;boundary=SomeRandomString
```

All other rules regarding the format of the multipart content are the same, including the boundary string used to separate the parts and the individual `Content-Type` fields for each part of the content.

13.3.3 Exploiting Multipart Documents

It is easy to see how you can use the two special MIME multipart content types to create server-push dynamic documents. By delaying the time between parts, you might create an automatically scrolling message in the Mozilla browser window. Or by replacing portions of the document through the x-mixed-replace MIME type, you might include a dynamic billboard in your document, or perhaps even animation.

Note that server-push multipart documents need not apply only to HTML or other plain-text documents. Images, too, are a MIME-encoded content type, so you can have the HTTP server transmit several images in sequence as parts of a multipart transmission. Because you may also have each new image replace the previous one, the result is crude animation. Done correctly, over a network of sufficient bandwidth, the effect can be quite satisfying.

13.3.3.1 Efficiency considerations

Server-push documents maintain a connection between the client and server for the duration of the dynamic document's activity. For some servers, this may consume extra network resources and may also require that several processes remain active, servicing the open connection. Make sure the server-push process (and, hence, the client/server connection) expires upon completion or after some idle period. Otherwise, someone will inadvertently camp on an endlessly cycling server-push document and choke off other users' access to the server.

Before choosing to implement server-push documents, make sure that your server can support the added processing and networking load. Keep in mind that many simultaneous server-push documents may be active, multiplying the impact on the server and seriously affecting overall server performance.

13.3.4 Creating a Server-Push Document

Create a special application that runs with the HTTP server to enable server-push dynamic documents. The application must create the special MIME `Content-Type` header field that notifies the Mozilla browser that the following document comes in several parts—added to or replacing a portion of the current document. The application must create the appropriate boundary delimiter and send the `Content-Type` header and data for each part, perhaps also delaying transmission of each part by some period of time. Consult your server's documentation to learn how to create a server-side application that can be invoked by accessing a specific URL on the server. With some servers, this may be as simple as placing the application in a certain directory on the server. With others, you may have to bend over backward and howl at the moon on certain days.

13.3.4.1 Server-push example application for NCSA and Apache httpd

The National Center for Supercomputing Applications (NCSA) and Apache httpd servers run on most Unix and Linux systems. Administrators usually configure the servers to run server-side applications stored in a directory named *cgi-bin*.

The following is a simple shell script that illustrates how to send a multipart document to a Netscape or Firefox client via httpd:[*]

```
#!/bin/sh
#
```

---

[*] It is an idiosyncrasy of NCSA *httpd* that no spaces are allowed in the `Content-Type` field that precedes your multipart document. Some authors like to place a space after the semicolon and before the boundary keyword. Don't do this with NCSA *httpd*; run the whole `Content-Type` together without spaces to get the server to recognize the correct multipart content type.

```
# Let the client know we are sending a multipart document
# with a boundary string of "NEXT"
#
echo "HTTP/1.0 200"
echo "Content-type: multipart/x-mixed-replace;boundary=NEXT"
echo ""
echo "--NEXT"
while true
do
#
# Send the next part, followed by a boundary string
# Then sleep five seconds before repeating
#
 echo "Content-type: text/html"
 echo ""
 echo <html>
 echo <head>
 echo "<title>Processes On This Server</title>"
 echo "</head>"
 echo <body>
 echo "<h3> Processes On This Server</h3>"
 echo "Date:"
 date
 echo <p>
 echo <pre>
 ps -el
 echo "</pre>"
 echo "</body>"
 echo "</html>"
 echo "--NEXT"
 sleep 5
done
```

In a nutshell, this example script updates a list of the processes running on the server machine every five seconds. The update continues until the browser breaks the connection by moving on to another document.

We offer this shell script example to illustrate the basic logic behind any server-push document generator. In reality, you should try to create your server-side applications using a more conventional programming language, such as Perl or C. These applications will run more efficiently and can better detect when the client has severed the connection to the server.

CHAPTER 14

Mobile Devices

Just now, as most web developers have become very proficient at developing engaging content for the popular PC-based browsers, they are being confronted with the challenge of providing equally elegant pages for those ubiquitous, tiny mobile devices. But mobile web-enabled devices were not anticipated back in the early 1990s when HTML was first defined and refined, and the current standards don't help much, either. In this chapter, we look at the broad range of mobile web-enabled devices, the challenge they present to web designers, and a subset of XHTML that addresses those devices. We also offer some suggestions—and lots of sympathy—for creating effective content that works across many of these devices.

14.1 The Mobile Web

With the World Wide Web now firmly entrenched as a part of normal modern life, it is only natural that users want to access web content wherever they may be, at any time. Responding to this demand, vendors now offer an incredible array of devices and access methods to meet that need. Although the types of devices number in the hundreds, the overall market can be examined as a few key product categories.

14.1.1 Devices

Most of today's mobile devices—mobile phones and personal digital assistants (PDAs)—have digital displays, typically an LCD, and onboard processing. So why not a built-in browser?

14.1.1.1 Mobile phones

The browser software resides in the cell phone's core operating system and the end user cannot easily upgrade or extend it. And, as we discuss in more detail shortly, it has far fewer features than are normally associated with a typical desktop browser. Other features are available only to the persistent user willing to endure horrifically bad user interfaces to reach them.

The cell phone provider gives you access to the Internet by any one of several different technologies, and some restrict the available content, or make it difficult to access content outside of their proprietary web portal.

14.1.1.2 PDAs

PDAs arguably provide the best mobile web experience. The PDA marketplace is dominated by devices running the Palm OS operating system from PalmSource, Inc. (originally Palm Computing, Inc.) and those running the Windows Mobile operating system from Microsoft. Regardless of vendor, these devices provide a high-quality browser that may include many of the features you would normally find in a desktop browser. The end user can upgrade or extend the browser with relative ease. Other network applications, such as email and FTP, may be available as well.

PDAs typically rely on the Institute of Electrical and Electronics Engineers (IEEE) standard 802.11, commonly known as WiFi (pronounced "why fie"), for wireless Ethernet-based connectivity with a network and, ultimately, the Internet. Some PDAs use Bluetooth, an alternative wireless technology, to connect with another network device, such as a mobile phone, laptop computer, or Bluetooth network access point, in order to ultimately connect with the Web.

14.1.1.3 Convergence devices

Convergence devices attempt to marry the convenience of a mobile phone with the flexibility and power of a PDA. They use cellular network connectivity, but may also offer 802.11 networking, as well. They can run most applications available to PDA users and provide some integration between the PDA experience and conventional telephony features. Convergence products are currently offered by PalmSource (running Palm OS and Windows Mobile) and various cellular phone manufacturers (running Windows Mobile). Convergence devices offer distinct compromises between the PDA experience, with its larger screen and computing power, and mobile phones, with their small form factor and ease of use.

14.1.2 Cellular Access

In addition to the device type, users can choose from a number of access plans that allow their mobile device to connect with the Internet. As with mobile devices, hundreds of access plans are available, but they can generally be categorized into a few common groups.

14.1.2.1 Low speed

Often known as first- or second-generation data access, low-speed cellular access operates at rates similar to that of a 56-kilobaud dial-up modem. Providers typically charge by the byte (!), with packages offering blocks of bytes on a monthly basis. Because of its speed and relatively high cost, low-speed access is intended for intermittent, sparse use for specific small-volume tasks. Continuous access using these plans is not feasible, both from the cost perspective and from its arduously slow data rate. This kind of low-speed access is available exclusively on mobile phones and some convergence devices from many different vendors.

14.1.2.2 High-speed cellular access

Recent advances in cellular technology have enabled carriers to offer high-speed cellular access with speeds ranging up to 1.5 megabits per second. At these speeds, users can enjoy a high-quality web experience that includes video and audio content. Recognizing the market potential, most carriers offer high-speed access in a single-price, unlimited-usage plan. Marketed under a variety of monikers (such as EDGE and EVDO, among others), this kind of connectivity was originally deployed in mobile phones, but is fast showing up in PDAs, convergence devices, and some laptop computers.

14.1.2.3 WiFi

Many web-enabled PDAs and some convergence devices include 802.11 wireless networking and, consequently, can connect with compatible wireless LAN access points that have become ubiquitous in the last few years. Whole cities and campuses now provide pervasive wireless and consequent mobile access to the Internet. While most devices offer the "b" version of the technology (802.11b), which operates at a maximum of 11 megabits per second, some newer devices include the "g" version, which provides for rates up to 54 megabits per second. Access costs range from free (home networks, employer networks, and public access points) to tens of dollars per month for independent suppliers, such as Cingular and T-Mobile.

Based on this device and access taxonomy, the mobile web content designer has nine potential user environments to consider. Unfortunately, it gets much worse because each specific device and access plan may have its own restrictions and idiosyncrasies. As we'll see in the next section, dozens of variables can affect the overall mobile web user experience.

14.2 Device Considerations

When designing content for mobile devices, the developer needs to keep many design constraints in mind. If the developer neglects any one of them, the resulting web pages will be difficult if not impossible to use on the mobile web. We suggest that the successful mobile web designer always keep browser, input, network, and display constraints in mind to keep from getting in a bind.*

14.2.1 Browser Constraints

Browser variations present the biggest challenge to the mobile web content designer. Limited by the host device, mobile browsers cannot support the full range of tags available in a conventional desktop browser. For those tags that are supported, implementation is not consistent across a range of mobile devices. As a result, designers need to carefully consider which tags they will use in their content and often have to sacrifice more complicated page designs in favor of simpler pages that display correctly on a larger number of devices.

Beyond tag availability, mobile browsers may or may not support scripting, stylesheets, frames, embedded objects, layers, cookies, and other support structures within the page content. Even widely supported <meta> tags, such as refresh tags, may not be supported. In general, cautious designers will avoid any of these elements in their content. While the resulting content will certainly be simpler, it is guaranteed to be viewable on many devices. Unlike desktop browsers that try to muddle through when presented with unsupported tags, many mobile browsers just give up when confronted with complex content. More than anything else, mobile web designers do not want attempts to access their content to result in a "page not viewable" error within the browser.

Even when the content sticks to the "safe" tags, as described later in this chapter, the results are unpredictable among different browsers. There are no standard fonts, and some mobile browsers offer only one font, in one size, without bold or italic embellishment. Most devices allow the user to select different font sizes for the device to accommodate aging eyes and small displays; these size differences can dramatically affect the rendering of content on the device's small screen.

Some mobile browsers cannot handle any sort of images in their pages, although this is becoming less of a problem in more recent mobile devices. Almost all mobile browsers have a difficult time with large images and may ignore or alter such images as they see fit. There is no clear definition of what constitutes a "large" image; it is in the eye of the browser and may be determined by both image dimensions and overall size. Formatting and wrapping of text with images is inconsistent, and mobile browsers often ignore image alignment attributes altogether. Needless to say, the current generation of devices cannot handle any sort of embedded video, flash, or animated content in any form.

---

* The astute reader will note that "browser, input, network, and display" form the clever and helpful acronym BIND.

14.2.2 Input Constraints

Cellular phones lack the single most convenient input device that makes the desktop browser successful: a mouse. PDAs and convergence devices do not suffer this limitation, typically allowing the user to tap on the screen with a stylus, but the majority of your target audience for mobile content is using a cellular phone. Consequently, general page navigation is a chore on mobile devices. Moving the focus within a page to select a link can be tedious at best, especially when there are several links to navigate among.

Entering text on a cellular phone is tiresome, too. Most phones offer two text entry modes: a multitap mode where pressing a key cycles through the letters on that key, and a predictive mode where the user adds letters until the phone finds the desired word based on the letter pattern. The former is tedious but ultimately more accurate; the latter may be quicker, but usually fails because typing URLs is the most common mobile web activity and does not follow typical spelling patterns.

For both modes, typing punctuation is difficult because fewer common punctuation symbols are often available through a single key, which cycles through a dozen or more symbols.

14.2.3 Network Constraints

Most mobile content designers are keenly aware of the constraints imposed by the slow networking speeds of most mobile devices. What many fail to appreciate, however, is how much users have to pay for each byte of mobile web content. Ironically, today's mobile web designers need to return to a 1995-era design mindset, when advanced dial-up speeds were reaching just 56 kilobits per second and connection times were metered by the Internet service provider (ISP). Is your content so valuable that users are willing to pay every time they want to view your pages?

Beyond bandwidth concerns, mobile device users often operate within odd, carrier-imposed limitations that network PC users would never tolerate. Some URLs may be blocked by certain carriers, and others may be passed through proxy servers that alter or translate content for the mobile device. It is difficult to predict how a particular carrier will treat a particular page. The best defensive strategy is to keep your content as simple as possible to avoid odd translation and conversion of your pages.

Finally, network connectivity is not constant while viewing content on a mobile device. Users may reach your site, view a page or two, and suddenly lose their connection as they pass into a dead zone in their coverage. Content that requires lots of navigation among pages can be frustrating in marginal coverage areas.

14.2.4 Display Constraints

There is no denying one attribute of all mobile devices: the display is small, even tiny. Even convergence device displays, which manufacturers boast to be the largest within the mobile phone market, are miniscule when compared to a conventional desktop browser. Most devices provide vertical scrolling, allowing content to flow beyond the bottom of the display, but very few support horizontal scrolling. As a result, content must be consciously designed to work in a small display with tightly bounded horizontal space and a limited amount of vertical space.

To make matters worse, the actual display dimensions are different for almost every device that reaches the market. Unlike desktops, where designers typically assume 800×600 or 1024×768 displays, the dimensions of a mobile device can range from 128×128 on some cellular phones to 320×480 and higher on some PDAs. Cell phones often sport odd display sizes, such as 176×220 or 122×96. In general, you cannot make any assumptions about display size nor should you target a specific size with your content. This is good design advice for *any* web page in *any* environment!

14.3 XHTML Basic

Recognizing the inherent limitations in mobile browsing, and seeking to promote a standard content model for those devices, the World Wide Web Consortium (W3C) has defined a reduced version of XHTML that caters to these devices. Known as *XHTML Basic*, this version of XHTML defines a standard set of tags that are sufficient for creating effective content for mobile devices, yet are simple enough to ensure that they will be consistently adopted across a wide range of mobile browsers.

Be forewarned: just because a standard supports mobile devices doesn't mean that a browser will. Often hardware limitations prevent implementation.

14.3.1 Supported Tags

XHTML Basic is best addressed as several groups of tags that together define a minimal but useful version of XHTML.

14.3.1.1 Basic content

XHTML Basic wouldn't work if it didn't support the four core tags that define any document: <html>, <head>, <title>, and <body>. You should never write a document without these tags, of course, and you should use them to delimit your document accordingly.

More complicated document structure is not supported. XHTML Basic specifically excludes frames and layers from mobile web devices.

Within the document body, XHTML Basic supports a core set of text-structural tags, including the six heading tags (<h1> through <h6>), <br>, <p>, <pre>, and <blockquote>. These are sufficient to create flows of text that are organized into paragraphs and blocks of text and are identified by headings at various levels, which makes for a readable document in any browser.

Within a text flow, XHTML Basic also supports all of the content-based style tags, including `<abbr>`, `<acronym>`, `<address>`, `<cite>`, `<code>`, `<dfn>`, `<em>`, `<kbd>`, `<q>`, `<samp>`, `<strong>`, and `<var>`. But given the paucity of fonts on most mobile devices, especially mobile phones, a mobile browser may be hard-pressed to even have more than one way to represent all these tags. This warning also applies to the heading tags, as it is highly unlikely that most mobile phones can offer six font sizes to distinguish the six heading tags.

Device font limitations also force the XHTML Basic standard to rule out the physical style tags, such as bold and italic text. With no guarantee that those styles will be available, it would be misleading to support the equivalent tags. Bidirectional text also is not supported; many mobile devices have a hard enough time rendering conventional text flows.

XHTML Basic has a strong focus on using stylesheets to manage the presentation of your mobile content, but not within the context of the page itself: the `<style>` tag itself is not supported. Instead, XHTML Basic defers to external stylesheets and, to support them, includes the `<div>` and `<span>` tags so that you can delimit your content and apply styles to it as needed. Use the `class` attribute to associate a style with that text.

Of course, XHTML Basic also supports the `<a>` tag so that you can link your pages to other documents.

14.3.1.2 Images, objects, and scripting

Although you should use it very judiciously, XHTML Basic does include the `<img>` tag. You should never drop images into your documents without due consideration, and even more so for mobile browsing, because they can dramatically affect the time needed to download a document and even may break certain browsers if they are too large. We offer more advice on using images effectively in your documents later in this chapter.

XHTML Basic also supports more general object embedding in mobile content with the `<object>` and `<param>` tags. While the intent is noble, these tags pave the road to heck for mobile browsing. Support is highly browser and device specific, and the mobile market is not yet mature enough to let authors assume broad support for any sort of embedded content beyond simple images. Nonetheless, if you are able to target your content to a specific device that provides appropriate support, these tags are here for your use.

XHTML Basic does not support scripting or event handling. None of the event-handling attributes is supported, nor are the `<script>` and `<noscript>` tags. Given the limited memory and computing power of the typical mobile device, this is not unreasonable. Highly dynamic, script-driven pages are better left to a full desktop browser.

14.3.1.3 Lists

In order to provide additional structure to your content, XHTML Basic supports ordered (`<ol>`), unordered (`<ul>`), and definition (`<dfn>`) lists and their supporting

<li>, <dl>, <dd>, and <dt> tags. These lists can really help to organize and structure your content, especially navigation pages that offer multiple links to the user.

In particular, coupling a numbered list of links with the accesskey attribute in their associated <a> tags makes it very easy for a cell phone-based browser user to navigate your pages with a single press of a key.

14.3.1.4 Forms

Interactivity is another feature critical to web browsing, so XHTML Basic provides support for forms, including the basic structure and input elements <form>, <input>, <label>, <select>, <option>, and <textarea> tags. The XHTML Basic specification does not restrict the kinds of form elements that you might use, but keep in mind that some mobile devices may not support extremely large choice items or menus.

The only form elements specifically prohibited by the XHTML Basic standard are file and image uploading elements. Ironically, these would be attractive browser options for all those cell phones that sport built-in cameras by allowing users to upload pictures to a web server.

14.3.1.5 Tables

Web designers commonly use tables to structure content display. While you may achieve similar effects for the mobile browser, be judicious. Although not explicitly stated, the XHTML standard bearers frown on the practice and want you to use tables for tables of information, not layout.

XHTML Basic supports only the core table tags: <table>, <tr>, <td>, <th>, and <caption>. Fancier things, such as spanning columns and even nested tables, are specifically not supported by the XHTML Basic standard. Complex tables may not be rendered correctly, and the narrow display size can easily disrupt your intended table presentation. Subtle table effects, such as varying cell margins and rule widths, will almost certainly be handled inconsistently between mobile browsers and are best avoided to ensure broad compatibility of your content.

14.3.1.6 Document header

XHTML Basic supports a few of the common tags found in the document <head>; specifically, the <meta>, <link>, and <base> tags. The primary intent of the <link> and <base> tags is to allow you to link to your stylesheets from within your mobile documents. Be somewhat cautious with the <meta> tag, though: the mobile browsers do not support all variations of its attributes.

14.3.2 Design Versus Intent

While the XHTML Basic standard defines a specific set of tags that should work on any compliant mobile browser, do not be misled into thinking that you can push the elements of XHTML Basic to the limit in designing your content. The mobile device market is too young and the browsers too immature to provide consistent support for every possible tag variation within XHTML Basic. More, ahem, mature designers may think back to when they were designing pages in the mid-90s, when creating content that worked across Netscape Navigator and early versions of Internet Explorer was challenging at best and more likely infuriating. Both browsers attempted to implement the early HTML standards, but there were too many variations in the products to make anyone's life easy.

The intent of the mobile-web standard is to create a small set of tags that work reasonably well across a wide range of devices, from phones to PDAs to set-top boxes and other devices. The W3C even lists appliances such as smart refrigerators and washing machines as potential targets for human interactions through web pages. Good designers will stay within the intent of the design, using the tags in a reasonable manner and avoiding tricks and clever coding to implement a particular page. The resulting content will work well on lots of devices, and the designers will be calmer and happier people.

14.4 Effective Mobile Web Design

There is no secret to creating effective mobile content. In fact, the advice we've been giving throughout this book applies to mobile devices just like it does for their larger desktop cousins: know your audience, know their needs, and know their browsing environment. With that said, the mobile browsing experience is different enough from the desktop that we'd be remiss if we did not offer some specific hints to make your web content look and act great.

With the popularity of mobile web access mushrooming, there is an abundance of mobile web design advice, good and bad. In the following sections, we'll offer up our favorite bits of guidance, based upon personal experience and many visits to many bad mobile sites.

14.4.1 Understand Your User

People turn to a mobile browser for different reasons than when they access the Web from the desktop or laptop. Most users are not seeking an extended perusal of some deep, thought-provoking dissertation, nor are they looking to apply for their next home mortgage. Instead, they most often need small bits of data delivered quickly: news headlines, weather information, flight information, sports scores, and the like. Browsers have become the interface to many other networked devices, too, so a mobile browser can have commercial and industrial applications. They won't be looking to download large pictures or a feature-length movie. They may want to receive driving directions, to obtain a price check, to buy tickets to a movie in a real theater, to adjust the operating parameters of a smart machine, to....

Keep this in mind when designing your content. What are you making available to your users? Why would they want to view it in a mobile browser? Is your content so useful that users will want to see it on the run, in their hand, while they do other things? Don't try to shoehorn your site into a mobile format just to say you did it. Select and deliver content that matters to people when they are in a mobile setting. In almost all cases, judicious editing is the first step to creating an effective mobile experience.

Once you have determined who will see and use your content in their mobile browser, think about their environment during the browsing session. Most likely, they will be distracted while viewing your site; many will be driving, in a meeting, or talking with others. Your content needs to punch through the distraction, quickly deliver the needed data, and get out of the way. It needs to be easily understood, readily navigated, and quickly accessed. Bandwidth restrictions will most likely make your content arrive slowly; don't make things worse by making users work to get what they want. *Fast* and *mobile* are the catchwords.

14.4.2 Links and Navigation

Except for overly large pages, poorly designed content navigation models are the worst aspect of most mobile web pages. Many pages offer useful content, but they make it so difficult to navigate that most users give up and surf elsewhere. It seems that many designers, having built complex navigation structures for a conventional desktop browser, feel compelled to reuse that same structure in a tiny, little mobile browser. It also seems apparent that these designers never actually try to use their content in a mobile environment. If they did, surely they would make things simpler and more accessible.

Moving around within a page on a mobile browser is much more difficult than in a desktop browser. Scrolling is a pain in a mobile browser, requiring many clicks of tiny buttons. Shifting focus from link to link is similarly tedious, often requiring use of slightly different tiny buttons. Be kind to your users: design your page navigation to avoid scrolling and focus movement wherever possible. If you require traditional "home," "next," and "previous" links in your pages, put them at the very top, where users can see them and access them immediately. Don't force users to scroll through the entire page to find your navigation elements at the very bottom. Use just a few effective navigational elements that clearly indicate where they will lead the user.

Some browsers support the accesskey attribute, allowing you to associate a key on the keypad with a link or form element in your content. Pressing the key selects the link or switches the focus to an appropriate form element. If you arrange your links as a numbered list map, each with an accesskey number, users can quickly jump to a link with a single key press, instead of tediously tapping to get to the desired link. For example:

```
Kumquat Resources:
<ol>
```

```
<li><a accesskey="1" href="growers.html">Growers</li>
<li><a accesskey="2" href="vendors.html">Vendors</li>
<li><a accesskey="3" href="fanclubs.html">Fan Clubs</li>
</ol>
```

enables the user to press "1" on the device keypad in order to access the kumquat growers page, "2" to see vendors, and "3" to find a fan club. Enable these as simple hyperlinks, and the user has to make several key presses to access and select the embedded link. Small design decisions like this can make a big difference in the overall user experience.

In general, following a link in a mobile browser is costly, in both time and money. Clearly identify your links so that the user knows where they lead and what they will provide. Anonymous "click here" links are annoying. Users do not want to explore your site; they want to get to the desired content quickly. If a link might lead to a large amount of content, such as an image, let users know in the linking page so that they can choose to avoid it.

Especially avoid image-based links, except when the images are very small. Many mobile browsers allow the user to navigate the page and select a link before the full page is loaded. Remember that the page gets fully downloaded from the server before going back and downloading supporting files such as images. Accordingly, text-based links appear nearly immediately, whereas image-based ones make the user wait. In any case, avoid image-map navigation because the regions in the map may not be easily visible or selectable, as they would in a browser with a mouse.

Resist the urge to link to other windows with the target attribute. Many mobile browsers cannot handle multiple windows and will simply drop the linking window content. Users will be confused and your content will certainly not be presented as you intended.

14.4.3 Forms

Forms present a challenge to the mobile web designer. To make the mobile experience interactive, you need to include forms for users to input requests and parameters and for them to receive customized content from a site. Unfortunately, most forms do not translate well to the mobile browser, where text input and field selection is difficult and error-prone. Mobile users crave quick, customized information. Design your forms to be easy to use, and your users will return again and again to use them.

As always, good content begins with good editing and forms are no exception. Make sure that your forms are short and to the point. Clearly and succinctly label the various input fields and elements so that users know immediately what is expected of them. Whenever possible, set default values in the form so that users need not fumble through every element before they can submit the form. This is especially useful when a user must return to a form to correct an error. Forcing the user to reenter data each time he visits the form is especially punitive.

Text entry is a special problem, especially when entering passwords and other masked text. Not all mobile devices handle masked text input cleanly, and entering a masked password using multitap text entry is exquisitely painful. In some mobile browsers, the text entry is conducted in a separate pop-up window provided by the browser, forcing the user to go through several levels of selection and acknowledgment to place a single text value in a field.

Keep it simple. Forms with many input elements do not translate well to the small mobile screen. As users scroll through the form to fill it out, they are unable to see the previous elements already entered and cannot see the items to come. This disorientation makes it harder to get forms right in a mobile setting. You might consider breaking your large form into multiple smaller forms, letting users incrementally enter their information. If you take this approach, make sure you validate data as you receive it; don't collect six screens of information and then force the user to return to the first screen to fix an error.

14.4.4 Layout and Presentation

The mobile web is not the place for fancy layout and slick content presentation. The limited tags in XHTML Basic help ensure this, and the prudent mobile designer will not try to go beyond those limits. While the transition from the feature-rich desktop browser to the minimal mobile environment can be difficult, designers must remember that the point of content design is to inform the user, not to impress your designer peers.

14.4.4.1 Stylesheets

All is not lost for those wanting to create attractive mobile content. Good designers use stylesheets to separate their content from its presentation attributes. This also makes it easier to have a single content source whose appearance is controlled by different stylesheets depending on the user device. Because inline styles are not recommended or supported in the standard for mobile content, use external links to your mobile content stylesheets. For example:

```
<link rel="stylesheet" type="text/css" media="handheld" href="sheet.css">
```

In this link, the media attribute is key: it ensures that this stylesheet will be applied when your content is viewed on a mobile device, and will be ignored otherwise. You'll want to keep your stylesheets small because they contribute to the delay required to load your pages over a slower mobile connection.

Know, too, that not all mobile browsers support stylesheets. For those that do, connectivity issues may prevent the browser from loading the stylesheet. Test all your content without any stylesheet, and make sure that it presents well without styles.

14.4.4.2 Text fonts

Fonts present a particular problem to mobile content designers. Unlike desktop browsers with access to hundreds of fonts in many variations, mobile browsers often have just one available. It may come in only one or two sizes, and may not offer italic and bold characters. The reality is that the tiny displays on mobile devices are not equipped to show complex fonts, so the device vendors avoid them because they would be illegible.

To work around these font restrictions, use header tags to enable different font sizes, if they are available, instead of relative or absolute font sizing. Most mobile browsers try to make a distinction between the <h1>, <h2>, and <h3> tags, so use them as intended for page titles, section headers, and content delimiters in your pages. Keep in mind, too, that many mobile browsers represent all the various emphasis tags (bold, italic, emphasis, and the like) with bold text. If you try to use different emphasis tags in a single page, your users may see only one kind of emphasized text.

14.4.4.3 Margins and spacing

The narrow display on mobile devices constrains how you lay out your pages. Avoid any sort of margins; you'll just be giving up precious horizontal space. The same is true for nested lists: deep nesting will cause your content to creep to the right, forcing your text into a single river of words down the right edge of the display.

Absolute spacing and layout control is difficult on mobile devices. Common desktop tricks, such as 1×1 images and transparent GIFs, just don't work as you would expect on a mobile device. Standard HTML elements such as frames and layers are generally not supported, and limited table support makes table-based layout difficult as well. In general, view the mobile device as a simple vertical flow of content and allow the mobile browser to format your content as best it can without your interference.

Finally, be aware that *adaptation* may occur with your content. Adaptation is the automated conversion of your content to make it more suitable for a mobile client. It may occur at the server, when a mobile device is found to be requesting a page. It often occurs within the carrier networks, where pages are stripped of offending tags and images are dramatically reduced to make them more acceptable to the mobile device. It also occurs implicitly in the mobile browser, where unsupported tags and attributes are ignored during rendering.

You cannot prevent adaptation. Your best bet is to avoid it by creating simple content that will not be subjected to adaptation at any layer. In short, the simpler that your content is, the more likely it is going to appear as intended on the mobile device.

14.4.5 Images

In the early days of the Web, images made life difficult. Dial-up connections just weren't able to deliver large images in a timely fashion, leading to user frustration and unusable pages. Older web users may remember the days when links often had parenthetical sizes appended to them. When running on a 28.8 kilobit modem, selecting a link followed by "(132K)" gave you time to grab a coffee while the image made its way to your browser.

Fabulous advances in cheap bandwidth have made an image-rich web experience the norm. Designers are used to using large images to make their pages beautiful. Unfortunately, these kinds of designs fail on slow mobile devices, as well as fast mobile devices with limited memory. As a result, images, especially large images, are a luxury in a mobile environment.

That isn't to say that images are forbidden in your mobile content. Instead, use images sparingly. A small logo may work just fine in your pages, and tiny navigational icons will certainly make your pages easier to use. If you must deliver large images do it with a separate link, with a warning about the size of the object the user will be accessing. This way, users understand the cost before they select the link.

When you do deliver large images, use common file formats such as GIF89a and JPEG. We know of no mobile browser that cannot handle these well-established file formats. Keeping in mind the small display sizes of mobile devices, use images that are close to the display size. In any case, do not send an enormous image and expect the browser to scale it to the display size. It is downright mean to send a "gigantic" 1024×768 image over a slow mobile connection, swamping the mobile device's memory and forcing the device to shrink the image to fit its display. To further assist the browser, always use the height and width attributes in the <img> tag to let the browser know what to expect as the image trickles in.

14.4.6 General Advice

In closing, we offer one final bit of advice: less is more. The mobile web is not the place to show off your cutting-edge page-layout skills or fancy image library. Instead, it is about quick delivery of great content that meets a specific need at a specific point in time.

To stay focused on this minimalist approach, consider adopting the W3C's recommended mobile page design guidelines:

- Design all your pages to work within a display that is 120 pixels wide. While many newer devices are wider than this, targeting this smaller number will ensure reasonable presentation on a broad range of devices, old and new.

- Use GIF89a or JPEG images. As we noted before, this ensures that your images will render on almost any mobile device.

- Do not deviate from the XHTML Basic document type. Using tags not supported by XHTML Basic almost guarantees rendering errors on a large percentage of mobile devices.

- Use stylesheets to separate content from presentation. XHTML Basic defines the best way to integrate stylesheets with your mobile content.

- Keep your total page size under 20 kilobytes. This includes the base page content, any associated stylesheets, and all included images.

By adopting these guidelines, judiciously editing your content, and structuring your pages to be easily navigated, you'll be creating remarkable mobile content that will have your users cheering.

CHAPTER 15

XML

HTML is a maverick. It only loosely follows the rules of formal electronic document-markup design and implementation. The language was born out of the need to assemble text, graphics, and other digital content and send them over the global Internet. In the early days of the Web's boom, the demand for better browsers and document servers—driven by hordes of new users with insatiable appetites for more and cooler web pages—left little time for worrying about things like standards and practices.

Of course, without guiding standards, HTML would eventually have devolved into Babel. That almost happened, during the browser wars in the mid- to late 1990s. Chaos is not an acceptable foundation for an industry whose value is measured in the trillions of dollars. Although the standards people at the World Wide Web Consortium (W3C) managed to rein in the maverick HTML with standard version 4, it is still too wild for the royal herd of markup languages.

The HTML 4.01 standard is defined using the Standard Generalized Markup Language (SGML). While more than adequate for formalizing HTML, SGML is far too complex to use as a general tool for extending and enhancing HTML. Instead, the W3C has devised a standard known as the Extensible Markup Language, or XML. Based on the simpler features of SGML, XML is kinder, gentler, and more flexible, well suited to guiding the birth and orderly development of new markup languages. With XML, HTML is being reborn as XHTML.

In this chapter, we cover the basics of XML, including how to read it, how to create simple XML Document Type Definitions (DTDs), and the ways you might use XML to enhance your use of the Internet. In the next chapter, we explore the depths of XHTML.

You don't have to understand everything there is to know about XML to write XHTML. We think it's helpful, but if you want to cut to the chase, feel free to skip to the next chapter. Before you do, however, you may want to take a look at some of the uses of XML covered at the end of this chapter, starting with section 15.8.

This chapter provides only an overview of XML. Our goal is to whet your appetite and make you conversant in XML. For full fluency, consult *Learning XML* by Erik T. Ray or *XML in a Nutshell* by W. Scott Means and Elliotte Rusty Harold, both from O'Reilly.

15.1 Languages and Metalanguages

A language is composed of commonly accepted symbols that we assemble in a meaningful way in order to express ourselves and to pass along information that is intelligible to others. For example, English is a language with rules (grammar) that define how to put its symbols (words) together to form sentences, paragraphs, and, ultimately, books like the one you are holding. If you know the words and understand the grammar, you can read the book, even if you don't necessarily understand its contents.

An important difference between human and computer-based languages is that human languages are self-describing. We use English sentences and paragraphs to define how to create correct English sentences and paragraphs. Our brains are marvelous machines that have no problem understanding that you can use a language to describe itself. However, computer languages are not so rich and computers are not so bright that you could easily define a computer language with itself. Instead, we define one language—a *metalanguage*—that defines the rules and symbols for other computer languages.

Software developers create the metalanguage rules and then define one or more languages based on those rules.* The metalanguage also guides developers who create the automated agents that display or otherwise process the contents of documents that use its language(s).

XML is the metalanguage the W3C created and that developers use to define markup languages such as XHTML. Browser developers rely on XML's metalanguage rules to create automated processes that read the language definition of XHTML and implement the processes that ultimately display or otherwise process XHTML documents.

Why bother with a markup metalanguage? Because, as the familiar proverb goes, the W3C wants to teach us how to fish so that we can feed ourselves for a lifetime. With XML, there is a standardized way to define markup languages for different needs, instead of having to rely upon HTML extensions. Mathematicians need a way to express mathematical notations, for instance; composers need a way to present musical scores; businesses want their web sites to take sales orders from customers; physicians look to exchange medical records; plant managers want to run their factories

---

* The use of metalanguages has long been popular in the world of computer programming. The C programming language, for instance, has a set of rules and symbols defined by one of several metalanguages, including *yacc*. Developers use *yacc* to create compilers, which in turn process language source files into computer-intelligible programs (hence, its name: Yet Another Compiler Compiler). *yacc*'s only purpose is to help developers create new programming languages.

from web-based documents. All of these groups need an acceptable, resilient way to express these different kinds of information so that the software industry can develop the programs that process and display these diverse documents.

XML provides the answer. Each content sector—the business group, the factory-automation consortium, a trade association—may define a markup language that suits their particular need for information exchange and processing over the Web. Computer programmers then create XML-compliant processes—parsers—that read the new language definitions and allow the server to process the documents of those languages.

15.1.1 Creation Versus Display

While there is no limit to the kinds of markup languages that you can create with XML, displaying your documents may be more complicated. For instance, when you write HTML, a browser understands what to do with the <h1> tag because it is defined in the HTML DTD.

With XML, you create the DTD.* For example, wouldn't a recipe DTD be a great way to capture and standardize all those kumquat recipes you've been collecting in your kitchen drawers? With special <ingredient> and <portion> tags, the recipes are easy to define and understand. However, browsers won't know what to do with these new tags unless you attach a stylesheet that defines their handling. Without a stylesheet, XML-compliant browsers render these tags in a very generic way—certainly not the flourishing presentation your kumquat recipes deserve.

Even with stylesheets, there are limitations to presenting XML-based information. Let's say you want to create something more challenging, such as a DTD for musical notation or silicon chip design. While describing these data types in a DTD is possible, displaying this information graphically is certainly beyond the capabilities of any stylesheets we've seen yet; properly displaying this type of graphically rich information would require a specialized rendering tool.

Nonetheless, your recipe DTD is a great tool for capturing and sharing recipes. As we'll see later in this chapter, XML isn't simply about creating markup languages for displaying content in browsers. It has great promise for sharing and managing information so that those precious kumquat dishes will be preserved for many generations to come. Just bear in mind that, in addition to writing a DTD to describe your new XML-based markup language, in most cases you will want to supplement the DTD with a stylesheet.†

---

* An alternative to DTDs is XML Schemas. Schemas offer features related to data typing and are more programmatically oriented than document-oriented. For more information, check out *XML Schema* by Eric van der Vlist (O'Reilly).

† In fact, it is possible to write XML documents using only a stylesheet. DTDs are highly recommended but optional. See *http://www.w3c.org/TR/xml-stylesheet* for details.

15.1.2 A Little History

To complete your education into the whys and wherefores of markup languages, it helps to know how all these markup languages came to be.

In the beginning, there was SGML. SGML was intended to be the only metalanguage from which all markup languages would derive. With SGML, you can define everything from hieroglyphics to HTML, negating the need for any other metalanguage.

The problem with SGML is that it is so broad and all-encompassing that mere mortals cannot use it. Using SGML effectively requires very expensive and complex tools that are completely beyond the scope of regular people who just want to bang out an HTML document in their spare time. As a result, developers created other markup languages that are greatly reduced in scope and are much easier to use. The HTML standards themselves were initially defined using a subset of SGML that eliminated many of its more esoteric features. The DTD in Appendix D uses this subset of SGML to define the HTML 4.01 standard.

Recognizing that SGML was too unwieldy to describe HTML in a useful way and that there was a growing need to define other HTML-like markup languages, the W3C defined XML. XML is a formal markup metalanguage that uses select features of SGML to define markup languages in a style similar to that of HTML. It eliminates many SGML elements that aren't applicable to languages such as HTML, and simplifies other elements to make them easier to use and understand.

XML is a middle ground between SGML and HTML, a useful tool for defining a wide variety of markup languages. XML is becoming increasingly important as the Web extends beyond browsers and moves into the realm of direct data interchange among people, computers, and disparate systems. A small number of people wind up creating new markup languages with XML, and many more people want to be able to understand XML DTDs in order to use all of these new markup languages.

15.2 Documents and DTDs

To be perfectly correct, we must explain that "XML" has come to mean many subtly different things. An *XML document* is a document containing content that conforms to a markup language defined from the XML standard. An *XML Document Type Definition* (XML DTD) is a set of rules—more formally known as entity and element declarations—that define an XML markup language; i.e., how the tags are arranged in a correct (valid) XML document. To make things even more confusing, entity and element declarations may appear in an XML document itself, as well as within an XML DTD.

An XML document contains character data, which consists of plain content and markup in the form of tags and XML declarations. Thus:

```
<blah>harrumph</blah>
```

is a line in a *well-formed* XML document. Well-formed XML documents follow certain rules, such as the requirement for every tag to have a closing tag. These rules are presented in the context of XHTML in Chapter 16.

To be considered *valid*—a valid XML document conforms to a DTD—every XML document must have a corresponding set of XML declarations that define how the tags and content should be arranged within it. These declarations may be included directly in the XML document, or they may be stored separately in an XML DTD. If an XML DTD exists that defines the `<blah>` tag, our well-formed XML document is valid, provided you preface it with a `<!DOCTYPE>` tag that explains where to find the appropriate DTD:

```
<?xml version="1.0"?>
<!DOCTYPE blah SYSTEM "blah.dtd">
<blah>harrumph</blah>
```

The example document begins with the optional `<?xml>` directive declaring the version of XML it uses. It then uses the `<!DOCTYPE>` directive to identify the DTD that some automated system, such as a browser, uses to process and perhaps display the contents of the document. In this case, a DTD named `blah.dtd` should be accessible to the browser* so that the browser can determine whether the `<blah>` tag is valid within the document.

XML DTDs contain only XML entity and element declarations. XML documents, on the other hand, may contain both XML element declarations and conventional content that uses those elements to create a document. This intermingling of content and declarations is perfectly acceptable to a computer processing an XML document, but it can get confusing for humans trying to learn about XML. For this reason, we focus our attention in this chapter on the XML entity and element declaration features that you can use to define new tags and document types. In other words, we are addressing only the DTD features of XML; the content features mirror the rules and requirements you already know and use in order to create HTML documents.

15.3 Understanding XML DTDs

To use a markup language defined with XML, you should be able to read and understand the elements and entities found in its XML DTD. But don't be put off: while XML DTDs are verbose, filled with obscure punctuation, and designed primarily for computer consumption, they are actually easy to understand once you get past all the syntactic sugar. Remember, your brain is better at languages than any computer.

---

* We use the word *browser* here because that's what most people will use to process and view XML documents. The XML specification uses the more generic phrase "processing application" because, in some cases, the XML document will be processed not by a traditional browser, but by some other tool that knows how to interpret XML documents.

As we said previously, an XML DTD is a collection of XML entity and element declarations and comments. Entities are name/value pairs that make the DTD easier to read and understand, and elements are the actual markup tags defined by the DTD, such as HTML's <p> and <h1> tags. The DTD also describes the content and grammar for each tag in the language. Along with the element declarations, you'll also find attribute declarations that define the attributes authors may use with the tags defined by the element declarations.

There is no required order, although the careful DTD author arranges declarations in such a way that humans can easily find and understand them, computers notwithstanding. The beloved DTD author includes lots of comments, too, that explain the declarations and how they can be used to create a document. Throughout this chapter, we use examples taken from the XHTML 1.0 DTD, which you can find in its entirety at the W3C web site. Although it is lengthy, you'll find this DTD to be well written, complete, and, with a little practice, easy to understand.

XML also provides for conditional sections within a DTD, allowing groups of declarations to be optionally included or excluded by the DTD parser. This is useful when a DTD actually defines several versions of a markup language; the desired version can be derived by including or excluding appropriate sections. The XHTML 1.0 DTD, for example, defines both the "regular" version of HTML and a version that supports frames. By allowing the parser to include only the appropriate sections of the DTD, the rules for the <html> tag can change to support either a <body> tag or a <frameset> tag, as needed.

15.3.1 Comments

The syntax for comments within an XML DTD is exactly like that for HTML comments: comments begin with <!-- and end with -->. The XML processor ignores everything between these two elements. Comments may not be nested.

15.3.2 Entities

An *entity* is a fancy term for a constant. Entities are crucial to creating modular, easily understood DTDs. Although they may differ in many ways, all entities associate a name with a string of characters. When you use the entity name elsewhere within a DTD, or in an XML document, language parsers replace the name with the corresponding characters. Drawing an example from HTML, the < entity is replaced by the < character wherever it appears in an HTML document.

Entities come in two flavors: *parsed* and *unparsed*. An XML processor will handle parsed entities and ignore unparsed ones. The vast majority of entities are parsed. An unparsed entity is reserved for use within attribute lists of certain tags; it is nothing more than a replacement string used as a value for a tag attribute.

You can further divide the group of parsed entities into *general* entities and *parameter* entities. General entities are used in the XML document, and parameter entities are used in the XML DTD.

You may not realize that you've been using general entities within your HTML documents all along. They're the ones that have an ampersand (&) character preceding their name. For example, the entity for the copyright (©) symbol (©) is a general entity defined in the HTML DTD. Appendix F lists all of the other general entities you know and love.

To make life easier, XML predefines the five most common general entities, which you can use in any XML document. While it is still preferred that they be explicitly defined in any DTD that uses them, these five entities are always available to any XML author:

```
&amp;          &
&apos;         '
&gt;           >
&lt;           <
&quot;         "
```

You'll find parameter entities littered throughout any well-written DTD, including the HTML DTD. Parameter entities have a percent sign (%) preceding their names. The percent sign tells the XML processor to look up the entity name in the DTD's list of parameter entities, insert the value of the entity into the DTD in place of the entity reference, and process the value of the entity as part of the DTD.

That last bit is important. By processing the contents of the parameter entity as part of the DTD, the XML processor allows you to place any valid XML content in a parameter entity. Many parameter entities contain lengthy XML definitions and may even contain other entity definitions. Parameter entities are the workhorses of the XML DTD; creating DTDs without them would be extremely difficult.[*]

15.3.3 Entity Declarations

Let's define an entity with the `<!ENTITY>` tag in an XML DTD. Inside the tag, first supply the entity name and value, and then indicate whether it is a general or a parameter entity:

```
<!ENTITY name value>
<!ENTITY % name value>
```

The first version creates a general entity; the second, because of the percent sign, creates a parameter entity.

For both entity types, the name is simply a sequence of characters beginning with a letter, colon, or underscore and followed by any combination of letters, numbers,

---

[*] C and C++ programmers may recognize that the entity mechanism in XML is similar to the #define macro mechanism in C and C++. The XML entities provide only simple character-string substitution and do not employ C's more elaborate macro parameter mechanism.

periods, hyphens, underscores, or colons. The only restriction is that names may not begin with a symbol other than the colon or underscore, or the sequence "xml" (either upper- or lowercase).

The entity value is either a character string within quotes (unlike HTML markup, you must use quotes even if it is a string of contiguous letters) or a reference to another document containing the value of the entity. For these external entity values, you'll find either the keyword SYSTEM, followed by the URL of the document containing the entity value, or the keyword PUBLIC, followed by the formal name of the document and its URL.

A few examples will make this clear. Here is a simple general entity declaration:

```
<!ENTITY fruit "kumquat or other similar citrus fruit">
```

In this declaration, the entity "&fruit;" within the document is replaced with the phrase "kumquat or other similar citrus fruit" wherever it appears.

Similarly, here is a parameter entity declaration:

```
<!ENTITY % ContentType "CDATA">
```

Anywhere the reference %ContentType; appears in your DTD, it is replaced with the word CDATA. This is the typical way to use parameter entities: to create a more descriptive term for a generic parameter that will be used many times in a DTD.

Here is an external general entity declaration:

```
<!ENTITY boilerplate SYSTEM "http://server.com/boilerplate.txt">
```

It tells the XML processor to retrieve the contents of the file *boilerplate.txt* from *server.com* and use it as the value of the boilerplate entity. Anywhere you use &boilerplate; in your document, the contents of the file are inserted as part of your document content.

Here is an external parameter entity declaration, lifted from the HTML DTD, which references a public external document:

```
<!ENTITY % HTMLlat1 PUBLIC "-//W3C//ENTITIES Latin 1 for XHTML//EN"
     "xhtml-lat1.ent">
```

It defines an entity named HTMLlat1 whose contents are to be taken from the public document identified as *-//W3C//ENTITIES Latin 1 for XHTML//EN*. If the processor does not have a copy of this document available, it can use the URL *xhtml-lat1.ent* to find it. This particular public document is actually quite lengthy, containing all of the general entity declarations for the Latin 1 character encodings for HTML.[*] Accordingly, simply writing this in the HTML DTD:

```
%HTMLlat1;
```

causes all of those general entities to be defined as part of the language.

---

[*] You can enjoy this document for yourself at *http://www.w3.org/TR/xhtml1/DTD/xhtml-symbol.ent*.

A DTD author can use the PUBLIC and SYSTEM external values with general and parameter entity declarations. You should structure your external definitions to make your DTDs and documents easy to read and understand.

You'll recall that we began the section on entities with a mention of unparsed entities whose only purpose is to be used as values to certain attributes. You declare an unparsed entity by appending the keyword NDATA to an external general entity declaration, followed by the name of the unparsed entity. If we wanted to convert our general boilerplate entity to an unparsed general entity for use as an attribute value, we could say:

```
<!ENTITY boilerplate SYSTEM "http://server.com/boilerplate.txt" NDATA text>
```

With this declaration, attributes defined as type ENTITY (as described in section 15.5.1) could use boilerplate as one of their values.

15.3.4 Elements

Elements are definitions of the tags that you can use in documents based on your XML markup language. In some ways, element declarations are easier than entity declarations because all you need to do is specify the name of the tag and what sort of content that tag may contain:

```
<!ELEMENT name contents>
```

The *name* follows the same rules as names for entity definitions. The *contents* section may be one of four types described here:

- The keyword EMPTY defines a tag with no content, such as <hr> and <br> in HTML. Empty elements in XML get a bit of special handling, as described in section 15.4.5.

- The keyword ANY indicates that the tag can have any content, without restriction or further processing by the XML processor.

- The content may be a set of grammar rules that defines the order and nesting of tags within the defined element. You use this content type when the tag being defined contains only other tags, without conventional content allowed directly within the tag. In HTML, the <ul> tag is such a tag, as it can contain only <li> tags.

- Mixed content, denoted by a comma-separated list of element names and the keyword #PCDATA, is enclosed in parentheses. This content type allows tags to have user-defined content, along with other markup elements. The <li> tag, for example, may contain user-defined content as well as other tags.

The last two content types form the meat of most DTD element declarations. This is where the fun begins.

15.4 Element Grammar

The grammar of human language is rich with a variety of sentence structures, verb tenses, and all sorts of irregular constructs and exceptions to the rules. Nonetheless, you mastered most of it by the age of three. Computer language grammars typically are simple and regular, and have few exceptions. In fact, computer grammars use only four rules to define how elements of a language may be arranged: sequence, choice, grouping, and repetition.

15.4.1 Sequence, Choice, Grouping, and Repetition

Sequence rules define the exact order in which elements appear in a language. For instance, if a sequence grammar rule states that element A is followed by B and then by C, your document must provide elements A, B, and C in that exact order. A missing element (A and C, but no B, for example), an extra element (A, B, E, then C), or an element out of place (C, A, then B) violates the rule and does not match the grammar.

In many grammars, XML included, sequences are defined by simply listing the appropriate elements, in order and separated by commas. Accordingly, our example sequence in the DTD would appear simply as A, B, C.

Choice grammar rules provide flexibility by letting the DTD author choose one element from among a group of valid elements. For example, a choice rule might state that you may choose elements D, E, or F; any one of these three elements would satisfy the grammar. Like many other grammars, XML denotes choice rules by listing the appropriate choices separated by a pipe character (|). Thus, we could write our simple choice in the DTD as D | E | F. If you read the vertical bar as the word *or*, choice rules become easy to understand.

Grouping rules collect two or more rules into a single rule, building richer, more usable languages. For example, a grouping rule might allow a sequence of elements, followed by a choice, followed by a sequence. You can indicate groups within a rule by enclosing them in parentheses in the DTD. For example:

```
Document ::= A, B, C, (D | E | F), G
```

requires that a document begin with elements A, B, and C, followed by a choice of one element out of D, E, or F, followed by element G.

Repetition rules let you repeat one or more elements some number of times. With XML, as with many other languages, you denote repetition by appending a special character suffix to an element or group within a rule. Without the special character, that element or group must appear exactly once in the rule. Special characters include the plus sign (+), meaning that the element may appear one or more times in the document; the asterisk (*), meaning that the element may appear zero or more times; and the question mark (?), meaning that the element may appear either zero or one time.

For example, the rule:

```
Document ::= A, B?, C*, (D | E | F)+, G*
```

creates an unlimited number of correct documents with the elements A through F. According to the rule, each document must begin with A, optionally followed by B, followed by zero or more occurrences of C, followed by at least one, but perhaps more, of either D, E, or F, followed by zero or more Gs. All of the following examples (and many others) match this rule:

```
ABCDG
ACCCFFGGG
ACDFDFGG
```

You might want to work through these examples to prove to yourself that they are, in fact, correct with respect to the repetition rule.

15.4.2 Multiple Grammar Rules

By now, you can probably imagine that specifying an entire language grammar in a single rule is difficult, although possible. Unfortunately, the result would be an almost unreadable sequence of nearly unintelligible rules. To remedy this situation, the items in a rule may themselves be rules containing other elements and rules. In these cases, the items in a grammar that are themselves rules are known as *nonterminals*, and the items that are elements in the language are known as *terminals*. Eventually, all the nonterminals must reference rules that create sequences of terminals, or the grammar would never produce a valid document.

For example, we can express our sample grammar in two rules:

```
Document ::= A, B?, C*, Choices+, G*
Choices ::= D | E | F
```

In this example, Document and Choices are nonterminals, and A, B, C, D, E, F, and G are terminals.

There is no requirement in XML (or most other grammars) that dictates or limits the number of nonterminals in your grammar. Most grammars use nonterminals wherever it makes sense for clarity and ease of use.

15.4.3 XML Element Grammar

The rules for defining the contents of an element match the grammar rules we just discussed. You may use sequences, choices, groups, and repetition to define the allowable contents of an element. The nonterminals in rules must be names of other elements defined in your DTD.

A few examples show how this works. Consider the declaration of the <html> tag, taken from the HTML DTD:

```
<!ELEMENT html (head, body)>
```

This defines the element named `html` whose content is a head element followed by a body element. Notice you do not enclose the element names in angle brackets within the DTD; you use that notation only when the elements are actually used in a document.

Within the HTML DTD, you can find the declaration of the `<head>` tag:

```
<!ELEMENT head (%head.misc;,
    ((title, %head.misc;, (base, %head.misc;)?) |
    (base, %head.misc;, (title, %head.misc;))))>
```

Gulp. What on Earth does this mean? First, notice that a parameter entity named `head.misc` appears several times in this declaration. Let's go get it:

```
<!ENTITY % head.misc "(script|style|meta|link|object)*">
```

Now things are starting to make sense: `head.misc` defines a group of elements, from which you may choose one. However, the trailing asterisk indicates that you may include zero or more of these elements. The net result is that anywhere `%head.misc;` appears, you can include zero or more `script`, `style`, `meta`, `link`, or `object` elements, in any order. Sound familiar?

Returning to the head declaration, we see that we are allowed to begin with any number of the miscellaneous elements. We must then make a choice: either a group consisting of a `title` element, optional miscellaneous items, and an optional base element followed by miscellaneous items; or a group consisting of a `base` element, miscellaneous items, a `title` element, and some more miscellaneous items.

Why such a convoluted rule for the `<head>` tag? Why not just write:

```
<!ELEMENT head (script|style|meta|link|object|base|title)*>
```

which allows any number of head elements to appear, or none at all? The HTML standard requires that every `<head>` tag contain exactly one `<title>` tag. It also allows for only one `<base>` tag, if any. Otherwise, the standard does allow any number of the other head elements, in any order.

Put simply, the head element declaration, while initially confusing, forces the XML processor to ensure that exactly one `title` element appears in the head element and that, if specified, just one `base` element appears as well. It then allows for any of the other head elements, in any order.

This one example demonstrates a lot of the power of XML: the ability to define commonly used elements using parameter entities and the use of grammar rules to dictate document syntax. If you can work through the head element declaration and understand it, you are well on your way to reading any XML DTD.

15.4.4 Mixed Element Content

Mixed element content extends the element grammar rules to include the special `#PCDATA` keyword. PCDATA stands for "parsed character data" and signifies that the content of the element will be parsed by the XML processor for general entity references. After the entities are replaced, the character data is passed to the XML application for further processing.

What this boils down to is that parsed character data is the actual content of your XML document. Elements that accept parsed character data may contain plain old text, plus whatever other tags you allow, as defined in the DTD.

For instance:

```
<!ELEMENT title (#PCDATA)>
```

means that the title element may contain only text with entities. No other tags are allowed, just as in the HTML standard.

A more complex example is the <p> tag, whose element declaration is:

```
<!ELEMENT p %Inline;>
```

Another parameter entity, %Inline;, is defined in the HTML DTD as:

```
<!ENTITY % Inline "(#PCDATA | %inline; | %misc;)*">
```

which expands to these entities when you replace the parameters:

```
<!ENTITY % special "br | span | bdo | object | img | map">
<!ENTITY % fontstyle "tt | i | b | big | small">
<!ENTITY % phrase "em | strong | dfn | code | q | sub | sup | samp | kbd |
        var | cite | abbr | acronym">
<!ENTITY % inline.forms "input | select | textarea | label | button">
<!ENTITY % misc "ins | del | script | noscript">
<!ENTITY % inline "a | %special; | %fontstyle; | %phrase; | %inline.forms;">
```

What do we make of all this? The %Inline; entity defines the contents of the p element as parsed character data, plus any of the elements defined by %inline; and any defined by %misc;. Note that case does matter: %Inline; is different from %inline;.

The %inline; entity includes lots of stuff: special elements, font-style elements, phrase elements, and inline form elements. %misc includes the ins, del, script, and noscript elements. You can read the HTML DTD for the other entity declarations to see which elements are also allowed as the contents of a p element.

Why did the HTML DTD authors break up all these elements into separate groups? If they were simply defining elements to be included in the p element, they could have built a single long list. However, HTML has rules that govern where inline elements may appear in a document. The authors grouped elements that are treated similarly into separate entities that could be referenced several times in the DTD. This makes the DTD easier to read and understand, as well as easier to maintain when a change is needed.

15.4.5 Empty Elements

Elements whose content is defined to be empty deserve a special mention. XML introduced notational rules for empty elements, different from the traditional HTML rules that govern them.

HTML authors are used to specifying an empty element as a single tag, such as <br> or <img>. XML requires that every element have an opening and a closing tag, so an image tag would be written as <img></img>, with no embedded content. Other empty elements would be written in a similar manner.

Because this format works well for nonempty tags but is a bit of overkill for empty ones, you can use a special shorthand notation for empty tags. To write an empty tag in XML, just place a slash (/) immediately before the closing angle bracket of the tag. Thus, you can write a line break as <br/> and an image tag as <img src="myimage.gif"/>. Notice that the attributes of the empty element, if any, appear before the closing slash and bracket.

15.5 Element Attributes

The final piece of the DTD puzzle involves attributes. You know attributes: they are the name/value pairs included with tags in your documents that control the behavior and appearance of those tags. To define attributes and their allowed values within an XML DTD, use the <!ATTLIST> directive:

```
<!ATTLIST element attributes>
```

The *element* is the name of the element to which the attributes apply. The *attributes* are a list of attribute declarations for the element. Each attribute declaration in this list consists of an attribute name, its type, and its default value, if any.

15.5.1 Attribute Values

Attribute values can be of several types, each denoted in an attribute definition with one of the following keywords:

CDATA
> Indicates that the attribute value is a character or string of characters. This is the attribute type you would use to specify URLs or other arbitrary user data. For example, the src attribute of the <img> tag in HTML has a value of CDATA.

ID
> Indicates that the attribute value is a unique identifier within the scope of the document. This attribute type is used with an attribute, such as the HTML id attribute, whose value defines an ID within the document, as discussed in "Core Attributes" in Appendix B.

IDREF *or* IDREFS

> Indicate that the attribute accepts an ID defined elsewhere in the document via an attribute of type ID. You use the ID type when defining IDs; you use IDREF and IDREFS when referencing a single ID and a list of IDs, respectively.

ENTITY *or* ENTITIES

> Indicate that the attribute accepts the name or list of names of unparsed general entities defined elsewhere in the DTD. The definition and use of unparsed general entities is covered in section 15.3.2.

NMTOKEN *or* NMTOKENS

> Indicate that the attribute accepts a valid XML name or list of names. These names are given to the processing application as the value of the attribute. The application determines how they are used.

In addition to these keyword-based types, you can create an enumerated type by listing the specific values allowed with this attribute. To create an enumerated type, list the allowed values, separated by pipe characters and enclosed in parentheses, as the type of the attribute. For example, here is how the method attribute for the <form> tag is defined in the HTML DTD:

```
method      (get|post)    "get"
```

The method attribute accepts one of two values, either get or post; get is the default value if nothing is specified in the document tag.

15.5.2 Required and Default Attributes

After you define the name and type of an attribute, you must specify how the XML processor should handle default or required values for the attribute. You do this by supplying one of four values after the attribute type.

If you use the #REQUIRED keyword, the associated attribute must always be provided when the element is used in a document. Within the XHTML DTD, the src attribute of the <img> tag is required because an image tag makes no sense without an image to display.

The #IMPLIED keyword means that the attribute may be used but is not required and that no default value is associated with the attribute. If it is not supplied by the document author, the attribute has no value when the XML processor handles the element. For the <img> tag, the width and height attributes are implied because the browser derives sizing information from the image itself if these attributes are not specified.

If you specify a value, it then becomes the default value for that attribute. If the user does not specify a value for the attribute, the XML processor inserts the default value (the value specified in the DTD).

If you precede the default value with the keyword #FIXED, the value is not only the default value for the attribute, it is the *only* value that can be used with that attribute if it is specified.

For example, examine the attribute list for the form element, taken (and abridged) from the HTML DTD:

```
<!ATTLIST form
action              CDATA           #REQUIRED
method              (get|post)      "get"
enctype             CDATA           "application/x-www-form-urlencoded"
onsubmit            CDATA           #IMPLIED
onreset             CDATA           #IMPLIED
accept              CDATA           #IMPLIED
accept-charset      CDATA           #IMPLIED
>
```

This example associates seven attributes with the form element. The action attribute is required and accepts a character string value. The method attribute has one of two values, either get or post. get is the default, so if the document author doesn't include the method attribute in the form tag, the XML parser assumes method=get automatically.

The enctype attribute for the form element accepts a character string value and, if not specified, defaults to a value of application/x-www-form-urlencoded. The remaining attributes all accept character strings, are not required, and have no default values if they are not specified.

If you look at the attribute list for the form element in the HTML DTD, you'll see that it does not exactly match our example. That's because we've modified our example to show the types of the attributes after any parameter entities have been expanded. In the actual HTML DTD, the attribute types are provided as parameter entities whose names give a hint of the kinds of values the attribute expects. For example, the type of the action attribute appears as %URI;, not CDATA, but elsewhere in the DTD is defined to be CDATA. By using this style, the DTD author lets you know that the string value for this attribute should be a URL, not just any old string. Similarly, the type of the onsubmit and onreset attributes is given as %Script. This is a hint that the character string value should name a script to be executed when the form is submitted or reset.

15.6 Conditional Sections

As we mentioned earlier in this chapter, XML lets you include or ignore whole sections of your DTD, so you can tailor the language for alternative uses. The HTML DTD, for instance, defines transitional, strict, and frame-based versions of the language. DTD authors can select the portions of the DTD they plan to include or ignore by using XML conditional directives:

```
<![INCLUDE [
    ...any XML content...
]]>
```

or:

```
<![IGNORE [
   ...any XML content...
]]>
```

The XML processor either includes or ignores the contents, respectively. Conditional sections may be nested, with the caveat that all sections contained within an ignored section are ignored, even if they are set to be included.

You rarely see a DTD with the INCLUDE and IGNORE keywords spelled out. Instead, you see parameter entities that document why the section is being included or ignored. Suppose you are creating a DTD to exchange construction plans among builders. Because you have an international customer base, you build a DTD that can handle both English and metric units. You might define two parameter entities:

```
<!ENTITY % English "INCLUDE">
<!ENTITY % Metric "IGNORE">
```

You would then place all the English-specific declarations in a conditional section and isolate the metric declarations similarly:

```
<![%English [   ...English stuff here...
]]>
<![%Metric [   ...Metric stuff here...
]]>
```

To use the DTD for English construction jobs, define %English as INCLUDE and %Metric as IGNORE, which causes your DTD to use the English declarations. For metric construction, reverse the two settings, ignoring the English section and including the metric section.

15.7 Building an XML DTD

Now that we've emerged from the gory details of XML DTDs, let's see how they work by creating a simple example. You can create a DTD with any text editor and a clear idea of how you want to mark up your XML documents. You'll need an XML parser and processing application to actually interpret and use your DTD, as well as a stylesheet to permit XML-capable browsers to display your document.

15.7.1 An XML Address DTD

Let's create a simple XML DTD that defines a markup language for specifying documents containing names and addresses. We start with an address element, which contains other elements that tag the address contents. Our address element has a single attribute indicating whether it is a work or a home address:

```
<!ELEMENT address (name, street+, city, state, zip?)>
<!ATTLIST address type (home|business) #REQUIRED>
```

Voilà! The first declaration creates an element named address that contains a name element, one or more street elements, a city and state element, and an optional zip element. The address element has a single attribute, type, which must be specified and can have a value of either home or business.

Let's define the name elements first:

```
<!ELEMENT name (first, middle?, last)>
<!ELEMENT first (#PCDATA)>
<!ELEMENT middle (#PCDATA)>
<!ELEMENT last (#PCDATA)>
```

The name element also contains other elements—a first name, an optional middle name, and a last name—each defined in the subsequent DTD lines. These three elements have no nested tags and contain only parsed character data; i.e., the actual name of the person.

The remaining address elements are easy, too:

```
<!ELEMENT street (#PCDATA)>
<!ELEMENT city (#PCDATA)>
<!ELEMENT state (#PCDATA)>
<!ELEMENT zip (#PCDATA)>
<!ATTLIST zip length CDATA "5">
```

All these elements contain parsed character data. The zip element has an attribute named length that indicates the length of the zip code. If the length attribute is not specified, it is set to 5.

15.7.2 Using the Address DTD

Once we have defined our address DTD, we can use it to mark up address documents. For example:

```
<address type="home">
   <name>
      <first>Chuck</first>
      <last>Musciano</last>
   </name>
   <street>123 Kumquat Way</street>
   <city>Cary</city>
   <state>NC</state>
   <zip length="10">27513-1234</zip>
</address>
```

With an appropriate XML parser and an application to use this data, we can parse and store addresses, create addresses to share with other people and applications, and create display tools that would publish addresses in a wide range of styles and media. Although our DTD is simple, it has defined a standard way to capture address data that is easy to use and understand.

15.8 Using XML

Our address example is trivial. It hardly scratches the surface of the wide range of applications that XML is suited for. To whet your appetite, here are some common uses for XML that you will certainly be seeing now and in the future.

15.8.1 Creating Your Own Markup Language

We touched on this earlier when we mentioned that the latest versions of HTML are being reformulated as compliant XML DTDs. We cover the impact XML has on HTML in the next chapter.

But even more significantly, XML enables communities of users to create languages that best capture their unique data and ideas. Mathematicians, chemists, musicians, and professionals from hundreds of other disciplines can create special tags that represent unique concepts in a standardized way. Even if no browser exists that can accurately render these tags in a displayable form, the ability to capture and standardize information is tremendously important for future extraction and interpretation of these ideas.

For more mainstream XML applications with established audiences, it is easy to envision custom browsers being created to appropriately display the information. Smaller applications or markets may have more of a challenge creating markup languages that enjoy such wide acceptance. Creating the custom display tool for a markup language is difficult; delivering that tool for multiple platforms is expensive. As we've noted, you can mitigate some of these display concerns through appropriate use of stylesheets. Luckily, XML's capabilities extend beyond document display.

15.8.2 Document Exchange

Because XML grew out of the tremendous success of HTML, many people think of XML as yet another document-display tool. In fact, the real power of XML lies not in the document-display arena, but in the world of data capture and exchange.

Despite the billions of computers deployed worldwide, sharing data is as tedious and error-prone as ever. Competing applications do not operate from common document-storage formats, so sending a single document to a number of recipients is fraught with peril. Even when vendors attempt to create an interchange format, it still tends to be proprietary and often is viewed as a competitive advantage for participating vendors. There is little incentive for vendors to release application code for the purpose of creating easy document-exchange tools.

XML avoids these problems. It is platform neutral, is generic, and can perform almost any data-capture task. It is equally available to all vendors and can easily be integrated into most applications. The stabilization of the XML standard and the increasing availability of XML authoring and parsing tools is making it easier to create XML markup languages for document capture and exchange.

Most importantly, document exchange rarely requires document presentation, thus eliminating "display difficulties" from the equation. Often, an existing application uses XML to include data from another source and then uses its own internal display capabilities to present the data to the end user. The cost of adding XML-based data exchange to existing applications is relatively small.

15.8.3 Connecting Systems

A level below applications, there is also a need for systems to exchange data. As business-to-business communication increases, this need grows even faster. In the past, this meant that someone had to design a protocol to encode and exchange the data. With XML, exchanging data is as easy as defining a DTD and integrating the parser into your existing applications.

The data sets exchanged can be quite small. Imagine shopping for a new PC on the Web. If you could capture your system requirements as a small document using an XML DTD, you could send that specification to a hundred different vendors to quote you a system. If you extend that model to include almost anything you can shop for—from cars to hot tubs—XML provides an elegant base layer of communication among cooperating vendors on the Internet.

Almost any data that is captured and stored can more easily be shared using XML. For many systems, the XML DTDs may define a data-transfer protocol and nothing more. The data may never actually be stored using the XML-defined markup; it may exist in an XML-compatible form only long enough to pass on the wire between two systems.

One increasingly popular use of XML is web services, which make it possible for diverse applications to discover each other and exchange data seamlessly over the Internet, regardless of their programming language or architecture. For more information on web services, consult *Web Services Essentials* by Ethan Cerami (O'Reilly).

In conjunction with XML-based data exchange, the Extensible Stylesheet Language, or XSL, is increasingly being used to describe the appearance and definition of the data represented by these XML DTDs. Much like Cascading Style Sheets (CSS) and its ability to transform HTML documents, XSL supports the creation of stylesheets for any XML DTD. You can use CSS with XML documents as well, but it is not as programmatically rich as XSL. While CSS stops with stylesheets, XSL is a style language. XSL certainly addresses the need for data display, and it provides rich tools that allow data represented with one DTD to be transformed into another DTD in a controlled and deterministic fashion. A complete discussion of XSL is beyond the scope of this book; consult *XSLT* by Doug Tidwell (O'Reilly) for complete details.

The potential for XML goes well beyond that of traditional markup and presentation tools. What we now see and use in the XML world is only scratching the surface of the potential for this technology.

15.8.4 Standardizing HTML

Last, but certainly not least, the W3C uses XML to define a standard version of HTML known as XHTML. XHTML retains almost all of the features of HTML 4.01, but it also introduces a number of minor (and a few not-so-minor) differences. The next chapter compares and contrasts XHTML and HTML, mapping out the differences so that you can begin creating documents that comply with both the HTML and XHTML standards.

Despite its name, you don't use the Extensible Markup Language (XML) to directly create and mark up web documents. Instead, you use XML to define a new markup language, which you then use to mark up web documents. This should come as no surprise to anyone who has read the preceding chapter in this book. Nor, then, should it surprise you that one of the first languages defined using XML is an XML-ized version of HTML, the most popular markup language ever. HTML is being disciplined and cleaned up by XML, to bring it back into line with the larger family of markup languages. This standard is XHTML 1.0.[*]

Because of HTML's legacy features and oddities, using XML to describe HTML was not an easy job for the World Wide Web Consortium (W3C). In fact, certain HTML rules, as we'll discuss later, cannot be expressed with XML. Nonetheless, if the W3C has its way, XHTML will ultimately replace the HTML we currently know and love.

So much of XHTML is identical to HTML's current standard, version 4.01, that you can apply almost everything presented elsewhere in this book to both HTML and XHTML. We detail the differences, both good and bad, in this chapter. To become fluent in XHTML, you'll first need to absorb the rest of this book, and then adjust your thinking to embrace what we present in this chapter.

---

[*] Throughout this chapter, we use "XHTML" to mean the XHTML 1.0 standard. There is a nascent XHTML 1.1 standard that diverges from HTML 4.01 and is more restrictive than XHTML 1.0. We describe the salient features of XHTML 1.1 in section 16.4.

16.1 Why XHTML?

As we described in the preceding chapter, HTML began as a simple markup language similar in appearance and usage to other Standard Generalized Markup Language (SGML)-based markup languages. In its early years, little effort was put into making HTML perfectly SGML compliant. As a result, odd features and a lax attitude toward enforcing the rules became standard parts of both HTML and the browsers that processed HTML documents.

As the Web grew from an experiment into an industry, the desire for a standard version of HTML led to the creation of several official versions, culminating most recently with version 4.01. As HTML has stabilized into this latest version, browsers have become more alike in their support of various HTML features. In general, the world of HTML has settled into a familiar set of constructs and usage rules.

Unfortunately, HTML offers only a limited set of document-creation primitives, is incapable of handling nontraditional content such as chemical formulae, musical notation, or mathematical expressions, and fails to adequately support alternative display media such as handheld computers or intelligent cellular phones. We need new ways to deliver information that can be parsed, processed, displayed, sliced, and diced by the many different communication technologies that have emerged since the Web sparked the digital communication revolution a decade ago.

Instead of trying to rein in another herd of maverick, nonstandard markup languages, the W3C introduced XML as a standard way to create new markup languages. XML is the framework upon which organizations can develop their own markup languages to suit the needs of their users. XML is an updated version of SGML, streamlined and enhanced for today's dynamic systems. And while the W3C originally intended it as a tool to create document markup languages, XML is also becoming quite useful as a standard way to define small languages that different applications use as data-exchange protocols.

Of course, we don't want to abandon the plethora of documents already marked up with HTML, or the infrastructure of knowledge, tools, and technologies that currently support HTML and the Web. Yet, we do not want to miss the opportunities of XML, either. XHTML is the bridge. It uses the features of XML to define a markup language that is nearly identical to standard HTML 4.01 and gets us all started down the XML road.

16.1.1 XHTML Document Type Definitions

HTML 4.01 comes in three variants, each defined by a separate SGML Document Type Definition (DTD). XHTML also comes in three variants, with XML DTDs corresponding to the three SGML DTDs that define HTML 4.01. To create an XHTML document, you must choose one of these DTDs and then create a document that uses that DTD's elements and rules.

The first XHTML DTD corresponds to the "strict" HTML DTD. The strict definition excludes all deprecated elements (tags and attributes) in HTML 4.01 and forces authors to use only those features that are fully supported in HTML. Many of the HTML elements and attributes dealing with presentation and appearance, such as the <font> tag and the align attribute, are missing from the strict XHTML DTD and have been replaced by the equivalent properties in the Cascading Style Sheets (CSS) model.

Most HTML authors find the strict XHTML DTD too restrictive because many of the deprecated elements and attributes are still in widespread use throughout the Web. More importantly, lots of content out there on the Web uses the legacy elements and attributes, and the popular browsers still support most of the deprecated elements. The only real advantage of using the strict XHTML DTD is that compliant documents are guaranteed to be fully supported in future versions of XHTML.[*]

Most authors will probably choose to use the "transitional" XHTML DTD. It's closest to the current HTML standard and includes all those wonderful, but deprecated, features that make life as an HTML author easier. With the transitional XHTML DTD, you can ease into the XML family while staying current with the browser industry.

The third DTD is for frames. It is identical to the transitional DTD in all other respects; the only difference is the replacement of the document body with appropriate frame elements. You might think that, for completeness's sake, there would be strict and transitional frame DTDs, but the W3C decided that if you use frames, you might as well use all the deprecated elements as well.

16.2 Creating XHTML Documents

For the most part, creating an XHTML document is no different from creating an HTML document. Using your favorite text editor, simply add the markup elements to your document's contents in the right order, and display it using your favorite browser. To be strictly correct ("valid," as they say at the W3C), your XHTML document needs a boilerplate declaration upfront that specifies the DTD you used to create the document and defines a namespace for the document.

---

[*] If the W3C has its way, HTML won't change beyond version 4.01. No more HTML; all new developments will be in XHTML and many other XML-based languages.

16.2.1 Declaring Document Types

For an XHTML browser to correctly parse and display your XHTML document, you should tell it which version of XML is being used to create the document. You must also state which XHTML DTD defines the elements in your document.

The XML version declaration uses a special XML processing directive. In general, these XML directives begin with <? and end with ?>, but otherwise they look like typical tags in your document.* To declare that you are using XML version 1.0, place this directive in the first line in your document:

```
<?xml version="1.0" encoding="UTF-8"?>
```

This tells the browser that you are using XML 1.0 along with the 8-bit Unicode character set, the one most commonly used today. The encoding attribute's value should reflect the character set used in your document. Refer to the appropriate International Organization for Standardization (ISO) standards for other encoding names.

Once you've gotten the important issue of the XML version squared away, you should then declare the markup language's DTD:

```
<!DOCTYPE html
    PUBLIC "-//W3C//DTD XHTML 1.0 Strict//EN"
    "http://www.w3.org/TR/xhtml1/DTD/xhtml1-strict.dtd">
```

With this statement, you declare that your document's root element is html, as defined in the DTD whose public identifier is defined as "-//W3C//DTD XHTML 1.0 Strict//EN". The browser may know how to find the DTD matching this public identifier. If it does not, it can use the URL following the public identifier as an alternative location for the DTD.

As you may have noticed, the preceding <!DOCTYPE> directive told the browser to use the strict XHTML DTD. Here's the one you'll probably use for your transitional XHTML documents:

```
<!DOCTYPE html
    PUBLIC "-//W3C//DTD XHTML 1.0 Transitional//EN"
    "http://www.w3.org/TR/xhtml1/DTD/xhtml1-transitional.dtd">
```

And, as you might expect, the <!DOCTYPE> directive for the frame-based XHTML DTD is:

```
<!DOCTYPE html
    PUBLIC "-//W3C//DTD XHTML 1.0 Frameset//EN"
    "http://www.w3.org/TR/xhtml1/DTD/xhtml1-frameset.dtd">
```

---

* <! was already taken.

16.2.2 Understanding Namespaces

As described in the last chapter, an XML DTD defines any number of element and attribute names as part of the markup language. These elements and attributes are stored in a *namespace* that is unique to the DTD. As you reference elements and attributes in your document, the browser looks them up in the namespace to find out how they should be used.

For instance, the <a> tag's name (a) and attributes (e.g., href and style) are defined in the XHTML DTD, and their names are placed in the DTD's namespace. Any processing agent—usually a browser, but your eyes and brain can serve the same function—can look up the name in the appropriate DTD to figure out what the markup means and what it should do.

With XML, your document actually can use more than one DTD and therefore require more than one namespace. For example, you might create a transitional XHTML document but also include special markup for some math expressions according to an XML math language. What happens when both the XHTML DTD and the math DTD use the same name to define different elements, such as <a> for XHTML hypertext and <a> for an absolute value in math? How does the browser choose which namespace to use?

The answer is the xmlns* attribute. Use it to define one or more alternative namespaces within your document. You can place it within the start tag of any element within your document, and its URL-like† value defines the namespace that the browser should use for all content within that element.

With XHTML, according to XML conventions, you should at the very least include within your document's <html> tag an xmlns attribute that identifies the primary namespace used throughout the document:

```
<html xmlns="http://www.w3.org/TR/xhtml1">
```

If and when you need to include math markup, use the xmlns attribute again to define the math namespace. So, for instance, you could use the xmlns attribute within some math-specific tag of your otherwise common XHTML document (assuming the MATH element exists, of course):

```
<div xmlns="http://www.w3.org/1998/Math/MathML">x2/x</div>
```

---

* XML namespace—xmlns—get it? This is why XML doesn't let you begin any element or attribute with the three-letter prefix of "xml": it's reserved for special XML attributes and elements.

† It looks like a URL, and you might think that it references a document that contains the namespace, but alas, it doesn't. It is simply a unique name that identifies the namespace. Display agents use that placeholder to refer to their own resources for how to treat the named element or attribute.

In this case, the XML-compliant browser would use the *http://www.w3.org/1998/ Math/MathML* namespace to divine that this is the MATH, not the XHTML, version of the <div> tag, and should therefore be displayed as a division equation.

It would quickly become tedious if you had to embed the xmlns attribute into each and every <div> tag anytime you wanted to show a division equation in your document. A better way—particularly if you plan to apply it to many different elements in your document—is to identify and label the namespace at the beginning of your document, and then refer to it by that label as a prefix to the affected element in your document. For example:

```
<html xmlns="http://www.w3.org/TR/xhtml1"
      xmlns:math="http://www.w3.org/1998/Math/MathML">
```

The math namespace can now be abbreviated to "math" later in your document. So the streamlined:

```
</math:div>x2/x</div>
```

now has the same effect as the lengthy earlier example of the math <div> tag containing its own xmlns attribute.

The vast majority of XHTML authors will never need to define multiple namespaces and so will never have to use fully qualified names containing the namespace prefix. Even so, you should understand that multiple namespaces exist and that you will need to manage them if you choose to embed content based on one DTD within content defined by another DTD.

16.2.3 A Minimal XHTML Document

As a courtesy to all fledgling XHTML authors, we now present the minimal and correct XHTML document, including all the appropriate XML, XHTML, and namespace declarations. With this most difficult part out of the way, you need only supply content to create a complete XHTML document:

```
<?xml version="1.0" encoding="UTF-8"?>
<!DOCTYPE html
    PUBLIC "-//W3C//DTD XHTML 1.0 Transitional//EN"
    "http://www.w3.org/TR/xhtml1/DTD/xhtml1-transitional.dtd">
<html xmlns="http://www.w3.org/TR/xhtml1" xml:lang="en" lang="en">
  <head>
    <title>Every document must have a title</title>
  </head>
  <body>
    ...your content goes here...
  </body>
</html>
```

Working through the minimal document one element at a time, we begin by declaring that we are basing the document on the XML 1.0 standard and using 8-bit

Unicode characters to express its contents and markup. We then announce, in the familiar HTML-like `<!DOCTYPE>` statement, that we are following the markup rules defined in the transitional XHTML 1.0 DTD, which allow us free rein to use nearly any HTML 4.01 element in our document.

Our document content actually begins with the `<html>` tag, which has its `xmlns` attribute declare that the XHTML namespace is the default namespace for the entire document. Also note the `lang` attribute, in both the XML and XHTML namespaces, which declares that the document language is English.

Finally, we include the familiar document `<head>` and `<body>` tags, along with the required `<title>` tag.

16.3 HTML Versus XHTML

The majority of HTML is completely compatible with XHTML, and this book is devoted to that majority. In this chapter, however, we talk about the minority: where the HTML 4.01 standard and the XHTML DTD differs. If you truly desire to create documents that are both HTML and XHTML compliant, you must heed the various warnings and caveats we outline in the following sections.

The biggest difference—that's Difference with a capital D and that spells difficult—is that writing XHTML documents requires much more discipline and attention to detail than even the most fastidious HTML author ever dreamed necessary. In W3C parlance, that means your documents must be impeccably well formed. Throughout the history of HTML—and in this book—authors have been encouraged to create well-formed documents, but you have to break rank with the HTML standards for your documents to be considered well formed by XML standards.

Nonetheless, your efforts to master XHTML will be rewarded with documents that are well formed and a sense of satisfaction from playing by the new rules. You will truly benefit in the future, too: through XML, your documents will be able to appear in places you never dreamed would exist (mostly good places, we hope).

16.3.1 Correctly Nested Elements

One requirement of a well-formed XHTML document is that its elements are nested correctly. This isn't any different from the HTML standards: simply close the markup elements in the order in which you opened them. If one element is within another, the end tag of the inner element must appear before the end tag of the outer element.

Hence, in the following well-formed XHTML segment, we end the italics tag before we end the bold one, because we started italicizing after we started bolding the content:

```
<b>Close the italics tag <i>first</i></b>.
```

On the other hand, the following:

```
<b>Well formed, this is <i>not!</b></i>
```

is not well formed.

XHTML strictly enforces other nesting restrictions that have always been part of HTML but have not always been enforced. These restrictions are not formally part of the XHTML DTD; they are instead defined as part of the XHTML standard that is based on the DTD.[*]

Nesting restrictions include the following:

- The `<a>` tag cannot contain another `<a>` tag.
- The `<pre>` tag cannot contain `<img>`, `<object>`, `<big>`, `<small>`, `<sub>`, or `<sup>` tags.
- The `<button>` tag cannot contain `<input>`, `<select>`, `<textarea>`, `<label>`, `<button>`, `<form>`, `<fieldset>`, `<iframe>`, or `<isindex>` tags.
- The `<label>` tag cannot contain other `<label>` tags.
- The `<form>` tag cannot contain other `<form>` tags.

These restrictions apply to nesting at any level. For example, because an `<a>` tag cannot contain any other `<a>` tags, any tag contained within that `<a>` tag cannot itself contain an `<a>` tag, even though it might otherwise.

16.3.2 End Tags

As we've documented throughout this book, any HTML tag that contains other tags or content has a corresponding end tag. However, one of the hallmarks of HTML (codified in the 4.01 standard) is that you may leave out the end tags if the processing agent can infer their presence. This is why most of us HTML authors commonly leave out the `</p>` end tag between adjacent paragraphs. Also, lists and tables can be complicated to wade through, and not having to visually stumble over all the `</li>`, `</td>`, `</th>`, and `</tr>` end tags certainly makes HTML easier to read, albeit a bit more ambiguous.

This is not so for XHTML. Every tag that contains other tags or content must have a corresponding end tag present, correctly nested within the XHTML document. A missing end tag is an error and renders the document noncompliant. Although seemingly draconian, this and the nesting rules nonetheless remove any and all ambiguities as to where one tag starts and another tag ends.

---

[*] This is hair splitting within the XHTML standard. The XML standard has no mechanism to define which tags may not be placed within another tag. SGML, upon which XML is based, does have such a feature, but it was removed from XML to make the language easier to use and implement. As a result, these restrictions are simply listed in an appendix of the XHTML standard instead of being explicitly defined in the XHTML DTD.

16.3.3 Handling Empty Elements

In XML, and thus XHTML, every tag must have a corresponding end tag—even those that aren't allowed to contain other tags or content. Accordingly, XHTML expects the line break to appear as
</br> in your document. Ugh.

Fortunately, there is an acceptable alternative: include a slash before the closing bracket of the tag to indicate its ending (e.g., <br />). If the tag has attributes, the slash comes after all the attributes so that an image could be defined as:

```
<img src="kumquat.gif" />
```

While this notation may seem foreign and annoying to an HTML author, it actually serves a useful purpose. Any XHTML element that has no content can be written this way. Thus, an empty paragraph can be written as <p />, and an empty table cell can be written as <td />. This is a handy way to mark empty table cells.

Clever as it may seem, writing empty tags in this abbreviated way may confuse HTML browsers. To avoid compatibility problems, you can fool the HTML browsers by placing a space before the forward slash in an empty element using the XHTML version of its end tag. For example, use <br />, with a space between the br and /, instead of the XHTML equivalents <br/> and
</br>. Table 16-1 contains all of the empty HTML tags, expressed in their acceptable XHTML (transitional DTD) forms.

Table 16-1. HTML empty tags in XHTML format

<area />	<base />	<basefont />
 	<col />	<frame />
<hr />	<img />	<input />
<isindex />	<link />	<meta />
<param />		

16.3.4 Case Sensitivity

If you thought getting all those end tags in the right place and cleaning up the occasional nesting error would make writing XHTML documents difficult, hold on to your hat. XHTML is case-sensitive for *all* tag and attribute names. In an XHTML document, <a> and <A> are different tags; src and SRC are different attributes, and so are sRc and SrC! How forgiving HTML seems now.

The XHTML DTD defines all former HTML tags and attributes using lowercase letters. Uppercase tag or attribute names are not valid XHTML tags or attributes.

This can be a difficult situation for any author wishing to convert existing HTML documents into XHTML-compliant ones. Lots of web pages use uppercase tag and attribute names, to make them stand out from the surrounding lowercase content.

To become compliant, all those names must be converted to lowercase—even the ones you used in your CSS stylesheet definitions. Fortunately, it's easy to accomplish this kind of change with various editing tools, and XHTML authoring systems should perform the conversion for you.

16.3.5 Quoted Attribute Values

As if all those case-sensitive attribute names weren't aggravating enough, XHTML requires that you enclose every attribute value—even the numeric ones—in double quotes. In HTML, you could quote anything your heart desired, but quote marks are required only if the attribute value included whitespace or other special characters. To be XHTML compliant, every attribute must be enclosed in quotes.

For example:

```
<table rows=3>
```

is wrong in XHTML. It is correctly written as:

```
<table rows="3">
```

16.3.6 Explicit Attribute Values

Within HTML, there are a small number of attributes that have no value. Instead, their mere presence within a tag causes that tag to behave differently. In general, these attributes represent a sort of on/off switch for the tag, like the compact attribute for the various list tags or the ismap attribute for the <img> tag.

In XHTML, every attribute must have a value. Those without values must use their own names. Thus, compact in XHTML is correctly specified as compact="compact", and checked becomes checked="checked". Each must contain the required attribute value enclosed in quotes. Table 16-2 contains a list of attributes with the required XHTML values.

Table 16-2. XHTML values for valueless HTML attributes

checked="checked"	compact="compact"	declare="declare"
defer="defer"	disabled="disabled"	ismap="ismap"
multiple="multiple"	noresize="noresize"	noshade="noshade"
nowrap="nowrap"	readonly="readonly"	selected="selected"

Be aware that this attribute value requirement may cause some old HTML browsers to ignore the attribute altogether. All the modern browsers don't have that problem, so the vast majority of users won't notice any difference. There is no good solution to this problem, other than distributing HTML 4.0-compliant browsers to the needy.

16.3.7 Handling Special Characters

XHTML is more sensitive than HTML to the use of the < and & characters in Java-Script and CSS declarations within your documents. In HTML, you can avoid potential conflicts by enclosing your scripts and stylesheets in comments (`<!--` and `-->`). XML browsers, however, may simply remove all the contents of comments from your document, thereby deleting your hidden scripts and stylesheets.

To properly shield your special characters from XML browsers, enclose your styles or scripts in a CDATA section. This tells the XML browser that any characters contained within are plain old characters, without special meanings. For example:

```
<script language="JavaScript">
<![CDATA[
   ...JavaScript here...
 ]]>
</script>
```

This doesn't solve the problem, though. HTML browsers ignore the contents of the CDATA XML tag but honor the contents of comment-enclosed scripts and stylesheets, whereas XML browsers do just the opposite. We recommend that you put your scripts and styles in external files and reference them in your document with appropriate external links.

Special characters in attribute values are problematic in XHTML, too. In particular, you always should write an ampersand within an attribute value using & and not simply an & character. Similarly, play it safe and encode less-than and greater-than signs using their < and > entities. For example, while:

```
<img src=seasonings.gif alt="Salt & pepper">
```

is perfectly valid HTML, you must write it as:

```
<img src="seasonings.gif" alt="Salt &amp; pepper" />
```

for it to be compliant XHTML.

16.3.8 The id and name Attributes

Early versions of HTML used the name attribute with the <a> tag to create a fragment identifier in the document. This fragment could then be used in a URL to refer to a particular spot within a document. The name attribute was later added to other tags, such as <frame> and <img>, allowing those elements to be referenced by name from other spots in the document.

With HTML 4.0, the W3C added the id attribute to almost every tag. Like name, id lets you associate an identifier with nearly any element in a document for later reference and use, perhaps by a hyperlink or a script.

XHTML has a strong preference for the id attribute as the anchor of choice within a document. The name attribute is defined but formally deprecated for those elements that have historically used it. With widespread support of HTML 4.0 now in place, you should begin to avoid the name attribute where possible and instead use the id attribute to bind names to elements in your documents. If you must use the name attribute on certain tags, include an identical id attribute to ensure that the tag will behave similarly when processed by a strict XHTML browser.

16.4 XHTML 1.1

In May 2001, the W3C released an updated the XHTML standard, XHTML 1.1. While most standards expand upon their previous versions, XHTML 1.1 takes the unusual step of defining a more restrictive version of XHTML. If you think of XHTML 1.0 as unwieldy, picky, and time consuming, you'll find XHTML 1.1 even more so. In our opinion, XHTML 1.1 is an example of the standards process taken to absurd levels, defining a standard that may be academically pure but is essentially unusable.

16.4.1 Differences in XHTML 1.1

XHTML 1.1 begins with the XHTML 1.0 strict DTD and makes a few modifications. By supporting only the strict version of XHTML 1.0, version 1.1 eliminates all deprecated elements and all browser extensions still in common use on the Web. It also makes the following minor changes:

- The lang attribute has been removed from every element. Instead, authors should use the xml:lang attribute.

- The name attribute has been removed from the <a> and <map> elements. Authors should use the id attribute in its place.

Finally, the XHTML 1.1 standard defines a new set of elements that implement a typographic feature known as *ruby text*. Ruby text is short runs of text placed alongside the base text; it is often used to annotate the text or to indicate pronunciation. Ruby text has its roots in East Asian documents, particularly Chinese schoolbooks and Japanese books and magazines. Ruby text is typically displayed in a smaller font* than the base text and follows certain alignment rules to ensure that it appears adjacent to the appropriate base text element.

You define and manage ruby text with a set of elements that provides grouping and layout control. We'll be blunt: this new feature is so esoteric and of so little importance to the vast majority of HTML authors—even those who would subject themselves to the needless agony of XHTML 1.1 conformance—that it does not warrant

---

* The origin of the name "ruby" lies in the name that printers use for the 5.5-point font used by the British press to set this smaller adjacent text.

extensive coverage in this book. Those who are interested can find a complete discussion of ruby text at *http://www.w3.org/TR/ruby*.

For the rest of us, it is sufficient to know that there are a few new elements in XHTML 1.1 that you would be wise not to use in your own DTDs, if only to prevent confusion with the XHTML 1.1 DTD. These new elements are:

`<ruby>`
Defines a segment of ruby text

`<rb>`
Defines the ruby base text

`<rt>`
Defines the ruby text associated with the base text

`<rp>`
Is used as a "ruby parenthesis" to group related ruby elements

`<rbc>`
Serves as a ruby base text container to group several base text elements

`<rtc>`
Serves as a ruby text container to group several ruby elements

Should you encounter any of these elements in a document, refer to the aforementioned specification for details on how they are used. In general, you'll find a single outer `<ruby>` element with at least one `<rb>` and `<rt>` element within it. You can collect multiple `<rb>` and `<rt>` elements within an `<rp>` element or group them within the `<rbc>` or `<rtc>` container element.

16.5 Should You Use XHTML?

For a document author used to HTML, XHTML is clearly a more painful and certainly a less forgiving document markup language. Whereas at one time we prided ourselves on being able to crank out HTML with pencil and paper, it's much more tedious to write XHTML without special document-preparation applications. Why should any author want to take on that extra baggage?

16.5.1 The Dusty Deck Problem

Over just a few years, authors have generated billions upon billions of web pages. It is a safe bet that the majority of these pages are not compliant with any defined version of HTML. It is an even safer bet that the vast majority of these pages are not XHTML compliant.

The harsh reality is that these billions of pages will never be converted to XHTML. Who has the time to go back, root out these old pages, and tweak them to make them XHTML compliant—especially when the end result, as perceived by the user, will not change? Like the dusty decks of COBOL programs that lay unchanged for decades before Y2K forced programmers to bring them up to snuff, these dusty decks of web pages will also lie untouched until a similarly dramatic event forces us to update them.

However, the dusty-deck problem is no excuse for not writing compliant documents going forward. Leave those old documents alone, but don't create a new conversion problem every time you create a new document. A little effort now will help your documents work across a wider range of browsers in the future.

16.5.2 Automatic Conversion

If your sense of responsibility leads you to undertake the conversion of your existing HTML documents into XHTML, you'll find a utility named Tidy to be exceptionally useful. Written by Dave Raggett, one of the movers and shakers at the W3C, it automates a significant amount of the work required to convert HTML documents into XHTML.

While Tidy's capabilities are too varied and wonderful to be fully listed here, we can at least assure you that Tidy can detect and correct case conversion, quoted attributes, and proper element nesting. For the complete list of features and the latest version of Tidy for various computing platforms, visit *http://tidy.sourceforge.net*.

16.5.3 Lenient Browsers and Lazy Authors

There is a good rule of thumb regarding data sharing, especially on the Internet: be lenient in what you accept and strict in what you produce. This is a not a commentary on social policy, but rather a pragmatic admonition to tolerate ambiguity and errors in data you receive while making sure that anything you send is scrupulously correct.

Web browsers are good examples of lenient acceptors. Most current web pages have some sort of error in them, albeit often just an error of omission. Nonetheless, browsers accept the error and present a reasonable document to the user. This leniency lets authors get away with all sorts of things, often without even knowing they've made a mistake.

Most authors stop developing a page when it looks good and works the way they want it to. Very few take the time to run their pages through the various HTML-compliance tools to catch potential errors. Many of those who do try to test for compliance are so overwhelmed by the number of minor errors they have committed that they simply give up and continue to create bad pages that can be handled by good browsers.

Because the number of bad pages continues to grow, browsers cannot afford to start being strict. Any browser that tried to enforce even the most basic rules of the HTML standard would be abandoned by users who want to see web pages, not error messages. A vicious cycle ensues: bad pages force the use of lenient browsers, which encourage the creation of more bad pages. Break the cycle by vowing to create only XHTML-compliant content whenever you can.

16.5.4 Time, Money, and Standards

XHTML was developed as an XML representation of the HTML standard. It is intended, going forward, to become the single standard everyone should use to create content for the Web.

In a perfect world, standards are universally adopted and used. Full compliance is required of any document before it is placed on the Web. Conversion of legacy documents is done immediately.

In the real world, a shortage of time and money prevents the universal use of standards. Under pressure to quickly deliver something that works, developers turn out pages that work only well enough. Because browsers allow second-rate content to exist on the Web, the need to comply with a standard becomes a secondary issue—one that is too quickly ignored in the dizzying pace of web development.

16.5.5 Man Versus Machine

All is not lost, however. While XHTML is painful and tedious for humans to create, it is quite easy for machines to create. The number of web-authoring tools continues to increase, and the pages created by these machines should be completely XHTML compliant. While it doesn't make much economic sense for a web author to spend a lot of time getting all those end tags in the right spot, it does make sense for the programmer developing an authoring tool to ensure that the tool generates all those correct end tags. The effort the web author expends is leveraged exactly once for each page; the effort of the tool creator is leveraged over and over, each time the tool produces a new page.

It seems that the real future of XHTML lies in the realm of machine-generated content. XHTML is far too picky to be successfully used by the millions of casual web authors who create small sites. However, if those same authors use a tool to create their pages, they could be generating XHTML-compliant pages and never even know it.

If you are among that small community of developers who create tools that generate HTML output, you are doing a great disservice to your many potential customers if your tool does not generate excruciatingly correct XHTML-compliant output. There is no technical excuse for any tool not to generate XHTML-compliant output. If there are compatibility issues surrounding how the output might be used (with a nonXHTML browser, perhaps), the tool should provide a switch that lets the author select XHTML-compliant output as an option.

16.5.6 What to Do?

We recommend that all HTML authors take the time to absorb the differences between HTML and XHTML outlined in this chapter. Given the resources and opportunity, you should try to create XHTML-compliant pages wherever possible for the sites you are creating. Certainly you should choose authoring tools that support XHTML and give you the option of generating XHTML-compliant pages.

One day, XHTML may replace HTML as the official standard language of the Web. Even so, the number of noncompliant pages on the Web is overwhelming, forcing browsers to honor old HTML constructs and features for at least the next five years. For better or worse, HTML is here to stay as the de facto standard for web authors for years to come.

In this chapter:
- Top of the Tips
- Cleaning Up After Your HTML Editor
- Tricks with Tables
- Tricks with Windows and Frames

CHAPTER 17

Tips, Tricks, and Hacks

We've sprinkled a number of tips, tricks, and hacks throughout this book, along with style guidelines, examples, and instructions. So why have a special chapter on tips, tricks, and hacks? Because HTML and XHTML are the languages, albeit constrained, that make the Web the exciting place that it is, and interested readers want to know, "How do I do the cool stuff?"

17.1 Top of the Tips

The most important tip for even veteran authors is to surf the Web yourself. We can show and explain a few neat tricks to get you started, but hundreds of thousands of authors out there are combining and recombining HTML and XHTML tags and juggling content to create compelling and useful documents.

All the popular browsers provide a way to view the source for the web pages that you download. Examine (don't steal) them for how they create the eye-catching and effective features, and use them to guide your own creations. Get a feel for the more effective web collections. How are their documents organized? How large is each document?

We all learn from experience, so go get it!

17.1.1 Design for Your Audience

We repeatedly argue throughout this book that content matters most, not look. But that doesn't mean presentation doesn't matter.

Effective documents match your target audience's expectations, giving them a familiar environment in which to explore and gather information. Serious academicians, for instance, expect a journal-like appearance for a treatise on the physiology of the kumquat: long on meaningful words, figures, and diagrams and short on frivolous trappings like cute bullets and font abuse. Don't insult the reader's eye, except when exercising artistic license to jar or to attack your reader's sensibilities. By anticipating your audience and designing your documents to appeal to their tastes, you also subtly deflect unwanted surfers from your pages.

For instance, use subtle colors and muted text transitions between sections for a classical art museum's collection, to mimic the hushed environment of a real classical art museum. The typical rock 'n' roll-crazed web-surfer maniac probably won't take more than a glance at your site, but the millionaire arts patron might.

Also, use effective layout to gently guide your readers' eyes to areas of interest in your documents. Do that, by adhering to the basic rules of document layout and design, such as placing figures and diagrams near (if not inline with) their content references. Nothing's worse than having to scroll up and down the browser window in a desperate search for a picture that can explain everything.

We won't lie and suggest that we're design experts. We aren't, but they're not hard to find. So, another tip for the serious web page author is to seek professional help. The best situation is to have design experience yourself. Next best is to have a pro looking over your shoulder, or at least somewhere within earshot.

Make a trip to your local library and do some reading on your own, too. Better yet, browse the various online guides. Check out *Web Design in a Nutshell* by Jennifer Niederst Robbins (O'Reilly). Your readers will be glad you did. [Tools for the Web Designer, 1.6]

17.1.2 Consistent Documents

The next best tip we can give you is to reuse your documents. Don't start from scratch each time. Rather, develop a consistent framework, even to the point of a content outline into which you add the detail and character for each page. And endeavor to create CSS2-based stylesheets so that the look and feel of your documents remains consistent across your collection.

17.2 Cleaning Up After Your HTML Editor

Although you can create and edit HTML/XHTML documents with a text editor, such as vi or Notepad, most HTML authors use an application that is designed for creating web pages—several are free of charge, many offer a free evaluation period, and most are available for download over the Web. Be forewarned, though; in our experience, you will rarely (if ever) be able to create a web document from one of these editors without having to inspect, add to, edit, and sometimes even repair the source HTML that the editor generates. The following sections discuss a few things that you should know about and watch out for.

17.2.1 Where Did My Document Go?

One of the first things you will notice is that many of the HTML editors automatically introduce into your document markup that you did not explicitly select or write. Remember this very simple HTML document that we started with in Chapter 2?

```
<html>
<head>
<title>My first HTML document</title>
</head>
<body>
<h2>My first HTML document</h2>
Hello, <i>World Wide Web!</i>
 <!-- No "Hello, World" for us -->
<p>
Greetings from<br>
<a href="http://www.ora.com">O'Reilly Media</a>
<p>
Composed with care by:
<cite>(insert your name here)</cite>
<br>&copy;2000 and beyond
</body>
</html>
```

Here is what the source looks like after you load it into Microsoft Word from Office XP:

```
<html xmlns:o="urn:schemas-microsoft-com:office:office"
xmlns:w="urn:schemas-microsoft-com:office:word"
xmlns="http://www.w3.org/TR/REC-html40">

<head>
<meta http-equiv=Content-Type content="text/html; charset=windows-1252">
<meta name=ProgId content=Word.Document>
<meta name=Generator content="Microsoft Word 10">
<meta name=Originator content="Microsoft Word 10">
<link rel=File-List href="html_files/filelist.xml">
<title>&lt;html&gt;</title>
<!--[if gte mso 9]><xml>
 <w:WordDocument>
  <w:Compatibility>
   <w:BreakWrappedTables/>
   <w:SnapToGridInCell/>
   <w:WrapTextWithPunct/>
   <w:UseAsianBreakRules/>
  </w:Compatibility>
```

```
  <w:BrowserLevel>MicrosoftInternetExplorer4</w:BrowserLevel>
 </w:WordDocument>
</xml><![endif]-->
<style>
<!--
 /* Style Definitions */
 p.MsoNormal, li.MsoNormal, div.MsoNormal
    {mso-style-parent:"";
    margin:0in;
    margin-bottom:.0001pt;
    mso-pagination:widow-orphan;
    font-size:12.0pt;
    font-family:"Times New Roman";
    mso-fareast-font-family:"Times New Roman";}
p.MsoPlainText, li.MsoPlainText, div.MsoPlainText
    {margin:0in;
    margin-bottom:.0001pt;
    mso-pagination:widow-orphan;
    font-size:10.0pt;
    font-family:"Courier New";
    mso-fareast-font-family:"Times New Roman";}
@page Section1
    {size:8.5in 11.0in;
    margin:1.0in 65.95pt 1.0in 65.95pt;
    mso-header-margin:.5in;
    mso-footer-margin:.5in;
    mso-paper-source:0;}
div.Section1
    {page:Section1;}
-->
</style>
<!--[if gte mso 10]>
<style>
 /* Style Definitions */
 table.MsoNormalTable
    {mso-style-name:"Table Normal";
    mso-tstyle-rowband-size:0;
    mso-tstyle-colband-size:0;
    mso-style-noshow:yes;
    mso-style-parent:"";
    mso-padding-alt:0in 5.4pt 0in 5.4pt;
    mso-para-margin:0in;
    mso-para-margin-bottom:.0001pt;
    mso-pagination:widow-orphan;
    font-size:10.0pt;
    font-family:"Times New Roman";}
</style>
<![endif]-->
</head>

<body lang=EN-US style='tab-interval:.5in'>
```

```
<div class=Section1>

<p class=MsoPlainText>&lt;html&gt;<o:p></o:p></p>

<p class=MsoPlainText>&lt;head&gt;<o:p></o:p></p>

<p class=MsoPlainText>&lt;title&gt;My first HTML document&lt;/title&gt;<o:p></o:p></p>

<p class=MsoPlainText>&lt;/head&gt;<o:p></o:p></p>

<p class=MsoPlainText>&lt;body&gt;<o:p></o:p></p>

<p class=MsoPlainText>&lt;h2&gt;My first HTML document&lt;/h2&gt;<o:p></o:p></p>

<p class=MsoPlainText>Hello, &lt;i&gt;World Wide Web!&lt;/i&gt;<o:p></o:p></p>

<p class=MsoPlainText><span style='mso-spacerun:yes'> </span>&lt;!-- No
&quot;Hello, World&quot; for us --&gt;<o:p></o:p></p>

<p class=MsoPlainText>&lt;p&gt;<o:p></o:p></p>

<p class=MsoPlainText>Greetings from&lt;br&gt;<o:p></o:p></p>

<p class=MsoPlainText>&lt;a href=&quot;http://www.ora.com&quot;&gt;O'Reilly
Media&lt;/a&gt;<o:p></o:p></p>

<p class=MsoPlainText>&lt;p&gt;<o:p></o:p></p>

<p class=MsoPlainText>Composed with care by: <o:p></o:p></p>

<p class=MsoPlainText>&lt;cite&gt;(insert your name here)&lt;/cite&gt;<o:p></o:p></p>

<p class=MsoPlainText>&lt;br&gt;&amp;copy;2000 and beyond<o:p></o:p></p>

<p class=MsoPlainText>&lt;/body&gt;<o:p></o:p></p>

<p class=MsoPlainText>&lt;/html&gt;</p>

</div>

</body>

</html>
```

Yeow! Where did the document go? Excessive markup makes the source document almost humanly impossible to read. What infuriates document purists like us, beyond the fact that lots of stuff that we neither wanted nor asked for was added, is that Word automatically treats any text document containing HTML markup as fodder for its mill. You can remove the *.html* or *.htm* suffix from the filename or delete <html> and <head> from the document, to no avail—Word will still get you.

Microsoft isn't alone in cluttering the source. Most HTML editors add at least a <meta> tag that contains their product information. Many go through and "fix" your document to comply with current standards and practices, too—for example, by adding all those paragraph and list-item end tags that HTML allows you to omit. (From an XHTML standpoint, we admit that this meddling is probably valid.)

To its credit, Word runs well, unlike other tools that routinely crashed without warning as we fought with their treatment of the markup. Microsoft even offers a Word plug-in that removes the additional markup so that you can recover a reasonable facsimile of the original document.*

17.2.2 When and Why to Edit the Editor

No matter how good the HTML editor is, you'll inevitably have to edit the (albeit cluttered) source it generates. We've had to do it a lot ourselves, and so have all the web developers we've talked with over the last few years.

Not all HTML editors provide an easy means to add JavaScript to your documents, and many are not up-to-date with the HTML/XHTML and CSS2 standards. Remember, too, that the popular browsers don't always agree on how they render a tag, and even different versions of the same browser may differ. Furthermore, even the best HTML editors don't necessarily support extensions to the language.

So into the source you'll have to go, whether to include some HTML feature not yet supported by the editor (such as a new CSS2 property), to insert an attribute value or keyword, or to modify ones that the editor added.

The tip is this: compose first. Try to start with a clean, finished document. Concentrate on content from the outset, and add the special effects later. Use a good HTML editor from the start, or prepare your documents in two steps with two different tools—a good content editor followed by a good HTML editor—particularly if you plan to distribute the document in a format other than HTML.

17.2.3 Use the Best

If you compose web pages, we can't imagine you not using an HTML editor of some sort. The convenience is just too compelling. But choose carefully: some HTML editors are abysmal, and you'll spend more time hunting down misplaced tags and errant attributes than you'll spend actually creating the document. Top tip: you get what you pay for.

---

* You can find this plug-in at *http://office.microsoft.com/downloads/2000/Msohtmf2.aspx*.

It's no surprise that HTML editors vary greatly in their features. Many editors let you switch the display from source text to what may appear when rendered by a browser. Some simply let you add tags and modify attribute values through pull-down menus and hot-key options. Others are WYSIWYG layout tools that make it easy to include graphics and other multimedia content. Other advanced features include embedding and testing applets and scripts.

In general, HTML editors fall into one of two categories: either they are good layout tools, including advanced styling features and tools for dynamic content, or they excel at content creation and management. Obviously, if you are producing flashy, commercial web pages that rely on advanced layout techniques and include lots of different styles and dynamic content, use a good layout tool. If you are producing a content-rich document, use a tool that provides good editorial assistance.

No matter which type you use, there are some common considerations to keep in mind when selecting an HTML editor:

Is it up-to-date?
> No HTML editor is yet entirely up-to-date with the current standards, particularly CSS2. Read the product specifications and update often.

Does it include a source editor?
> Although you may load an HTML editor-generated document into a different text editor to change the source, it's much more convenient if the editor itself lets you view and edit the HTML source. Also, make sure that your HTML editor doesn't automatically "fix" your source edits.

Is it modifiable?
> Ideally, the HTML editor should let you customize its behavior to fit your specifications. For example, at a minimum you should be allowed to choose your own font colors, styles, and backgrounds, if those are automatically included in the editor's boilerplate document.

Is it affordable and reliable?
> We can't stress enough that you get what you pay for. If creating web pages is more than just a passing fancy, get the best editor you can find. Find one that is well supported and well reviewed by other HTML authors. Ask around, and perhaps join an HTML author's newsgroup to get the latest scoop on products.

17.3 Tricks with Tables

By design, tables let authors create appealing, accessible tables of information. But the table tags also can be exploited to create innovative, attractive page designs that are otherwise unattainable in standard HTML and XHTML.

17.3.1 Multicolumn Pages

One very common and popular page-layout element missing from HTML and XHTML is multiple columns of text. Here's a tip on how to use tables to achieve that effect.[*]

17.3.1.1 Basic multicolumn layout

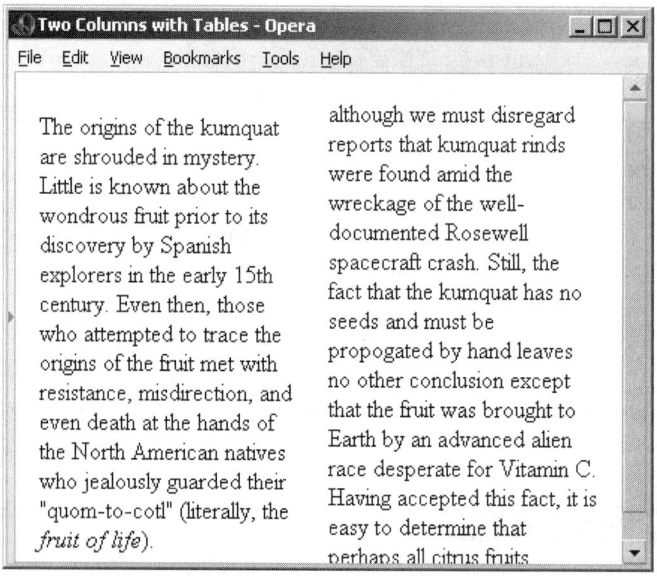

The basic two-column layout using <table> has a single table row with three data cells: one each for the columns of text and an intervening empty cell to more attractively separate the two columns. We've also added a large cellspacing attribute value to create additional intervening space between the columns.

The following example HTML table is an excellent template for a simple two-column text layout:

```
<table border=0 cellspacing=7>
  <tr>
    <td>Copy for column 1...
    <td><br>
    <td>Copy for column 2...
  </table>
```

See Figure 17-1 for the results.

Figure 17-1. A simple two-column layout

---

[*] Okay, it's true that earlier versions of Netscape supported the <multicol> extension. No longer. This is a more universal solution.

The one thing the browsers won't do is automatically balance the text in the columns, resulting in adjacent columns of approximately the same length. You'll have to experiment with your document, manually shifting text from one column to another until you achieve a nicely balanced page.

Keep in mind, though, that users may resize their display windows, and the columns' contents will shift accordingly. So don't spend a lot of time getting the last sentences of each column to line up exactly; they're bound to be skewed in other browser-window widths.

Of course, you can easily convert the example layout to three or more columns by dividing the text among more cells in the table. But keep in mind that pages with more than three columns may prove difficult to read on small displays, where the actual column width might be quite small.

17.3.1.2 Straddle heads

The basic multicolumn format is just the start. By adding cells that span across the columns, you create headlines. Similarly, you can make figures span across more than one column: simply add the colspan attribute to the cell containing the headline or figure. Figure 17-2 shows an attractive three-column layout with straddle heads and a spanning figure, created from the following HTML source with table tags:

```
<table border=0 cellspacing=7>
  <tr>
    <th colspan=5><h2>The History of the Kumquat</h2>
  <tr valign=top>
    <td rowspan=2>Copy for column 1...
    <td rowspan=2 width=24><br>
    <td>Copy for column 2...
    <td width=24><br>
    <td>Copy for column 3...
  <tr>
    <td colspan=3 align=center><img src="pics/fruit.gif">
    <p>
    <i>The Noble Fruit</i>
</table>
```

To achieve this nice layout, we used the colspan attribute on the cell in the first row to span all five table columns (three with copy and the two intercolumn spaces). We used the rowspan attribute on the first column and its adjacent column spacer to extend the columns down beside the figure. The figure's cell has a colspan attribute so that the contents span the other two columns and intervening spaces.

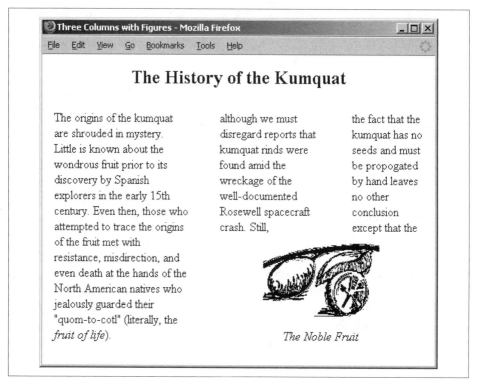

The History of the Kumquat

The origins of the kumquat are shrouded in mystery. Little is known about the wondrous fruit prior to its discovery by Spanish explorers in the early 15th century. Even then, those who attempted to trace the origins of the fruit met with resistance, misdirection, and even death at the hands of the North American natives who jealously guarded their "quom-to-cotl" (literally, the *fruit of life*).

although we must disregard reports that kumquat rinds were found amid the wreckage of the well-documented Rosewell spacecraft crash. Still,

the fact that the kumquat has no seeds and must be propogated by hand leaves no other conclusion except that the

The Noble Fruit

Figure 17-2. Fancy straddle heads and spanning figures with HTML table tags

17.3.2 Side Heads

The only text-heading features available in HTML and XHTML are the <h1> through <h6> tags. These tags are always embedded in the text flow, separating adjacent paragraphs of text. Through multiple columns, you can achieve an alternative style that places headings into a separate side column, running vertically alongside the document text.

Figure 17-3 shows you a fairly fancy pair of side heads, the result of the following bit of source XHTML table code:

```
<table>
  <tr>
    <th width="20%" align="right">
      <h3>Section 1</h3></th>
    <td></td>
    <td>
      Copy for section 1 goes on and on a bit
      so that it will take up more than one line in the
      table cell window... </td>
  </tr>
  <tr>
```

```
      <th align="right">
        <h3>Section 2</h3></th>
      <td></td>
      <td>
        Copy for section 2 goes on and on a bit
        so that it will take up more than one line in the
        table cell window...</td>
    </tr>
  </table>
```

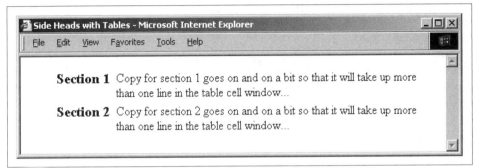

Figure 17-3. Table tags created these side heads

Notice how we created reasonably attractive side heads set off from the left margin of the browser window by adjusting the first header cell's width and right-justifying the cell contents.

Just as in our multicolumn layout, the example side-head layout uses an empty column to create a space between the narrow left column containing the heading and the wider right column containing the text associated with that heading. It's best to specify that column's width as a percentage of the table width instead of explicitly in numbers of pixels, to make sure that the heading column scales to fit both wide and narrow display windows.

17.3.3 Better Forms Layout

Of all the features in HTML and XHTML, forms cry out for better layout control. Unlike other structured elements, forms look best when rendered in a fixed layout with precise margins and vertical alignment of elements. However, except for carefully planned, <pre>-formatted form segments, the standards just don't give us any special tools to better control forms layout. You can accomplish a lot with stylesheets, but that gets complicated quickly. Instead, tables provide easy forms layout.

17.3.3.1 Basic forms layout

Your forms almost always look better and are easier for your readers to follow if you use a table to structure and align the elements. For example, you might use a vertical alignment to your forms, with field labels to the left and their respective form elements aligned to an adjacent vertical margin on the right. Don't try that with just standard HTML or XHTML. Rather, prepare a form that contains a two-column table. The following HTML source does just that, as shown in Figure 17-4:

```
<form method=post action="http:/cgi-bin/process">
  <table>
    <tr>
      <th align=right>Name:
      <td><input type=text size=32>
    <tr>
      <th align=right>Address:
      <td><input type=text size=32>
    <tr>
      <th align=right>Phone:
      <td><input type=text size=12>
    <tr>
      <td colspan=2 align=center>
      <input type=submit value="Register">
  </table>
</form>
```

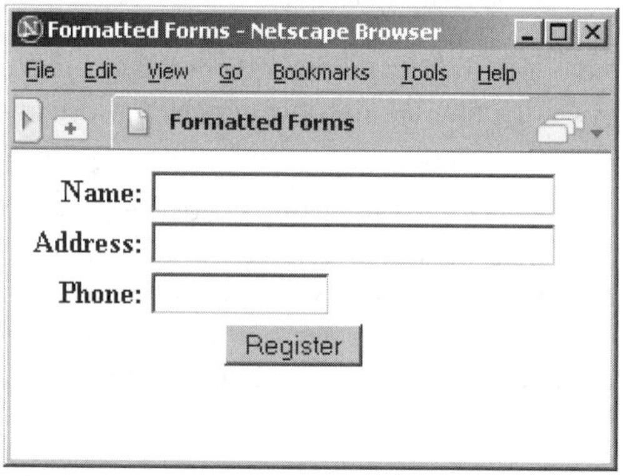

Figure 17-4. Align your forms nicely with tables

Of course, more complex form layouts can be managed with tables, too. We recommend that you first sketch the form layout on paper and plan how various combinations of table elements, including row- and column-straddled table cells, might be used to affect the layout.

17.3.3.2 Building forms with nested tables

As we mentioned earlier, you can place a table inside a cell in another table. While this alone can lead to some elaborate table designs, nested tables also are useful for managing a subset of form elements within the larger table containing the entire form. The best application for using a nested table in a form is for laying out check-boxes and radio buttons.

For example, insert the following row containing a table into the form table in the previous example. It creates a checkbox with four choices:

```
<tr>
  <th align=right valign=top>Preferences:
  <td>
  <table>
    <tr>
    <td><input type=checkbox name=pref>Lemons
    <td><input type=checkbox name=pref>Limes
    <tr>
    <td><input type=checkbox name=pref>Oranges
    <td><input type=checkbox name=pref>Kumquats
  </table>
```

Figure 17-5 shows you how this nested table attractively formats the checkboxes, which browsers would otherwise render on a single line and not well aligned.

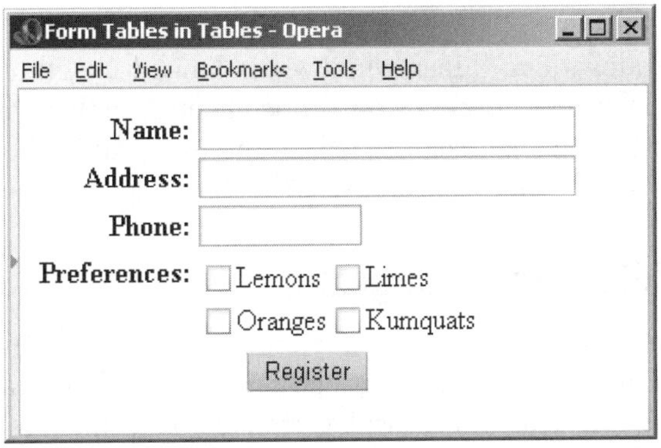

Figure 17-5. Nesting tables to format elements of a form

17.4 Tricks with Windows and Frames

For the vast majority of links in your documents, you'll want the newly loaded document displayed in the same window, replacing the previous one. That makes sense because your users usually follow a sequential path through your collection.

But sometimes it makes sense to open a document in a new window so that the new document and the old document are both directly accessible on the user's screen. If the new document is related to the original, for instance, it makes sense to have both in view. Other times, you might want to open more than one document in multiple windows in a frameset. More commonly, the new document starts the user down a new web of documents, and you want her to see and remember where she came from.

Regardless of the reason, it is easy to open a new browser window from your document. All you need to do is add the target attribute in the appropriate hyperlink (<a>) tag.

17.4.1 Targeting Windows

We normally use the target attribute to load a document into a specific frame that we've named in a frameset. It also serves to create a new window, by one of two methods:

Reference a new name

> If you use a name you haven't previously defined as the value for the target attribute of a hyperlink, the popular browsers automatically create a new window with that name and load the referenced document into that window. This is the preferred way to create new windows because you can subsequently use the name to load other documents into the same window. Using this technique, you can control which document gets loaded where.

Create an unnamed window

> All the popular browsers support a special target named _blank* that lets you create a new window. The _blank window has limited use, though, because it is nameless—you cannot direct any other documents into that window. (New documents loaded via hyperlinks selected by the user within the window get displayed in that same window, of course.)

17.4.2 Overriding Others' Targets

Ever visited a site whose home page is a frame document that never gives up? You know, the kind that leaves its great big logo on the top of the window and its site TOC running down the side of the display, staring you in the face long after you've hyperlinked away from the site? What if your site's frameset gets trapped into one of their window frames? What to do? (Apparently their webmasters haven't heard about the _blank target.)

The short answer is to use JavaScript to force open a new window for your documents. But that, too, is potentially confusing for users because they may already have a full window ready for your document. So, to embellish, let JavaScript discover whether your page is destined for a corner frame or for the whole window.

Here is an example script that loads a web page called *index2.html* into its own full window. Note that JavaScript-enabled browsers won't let you clear a previously loaded document display unless your document owns it. So, in the case where the target is not the whole window (i.e., self is not window.top), the example script

---

* Some browsers also accept the name _new. If you can't get _blank to work with your browser, try _new.

opens a new window that becomes the target for your pages. The user may choose to close your document window and return to the other one, or vice versa:

```
<html>
<head>
<title>I need a window of my own</title>
<script language="JavaScript">
<!--
  if (self != window.top)
      window.open("http://www.kumquats.com/index2.html");
  else
      self.location.href = "http://www.kumquats.com/index2.html";
//-->
</script>
</head>
<body>
Your browser apparently doesn't support JavaScript. Please
<a href="http://www.kumquats.com/index2.html"> hyperlink to our site manually.</a>
</body>
</html>
```

17.4.3 Multiple Frames in One Link

Loading a new document from a hyperlink is a snap, even if you put the new document into an alternative frame or window from its hyperlink parent. Occasionally, though, you'll want to load documents into two frames when the user clicks just one link. With a bit of trickery, you can load two or more frames at once, provided they are arranged a certain way in the browser window.

Consider this frame layout:

```
<frameset rows=2>
  <frameset cols=2>
    <frame name=A>
    <frame name=B>
  </frameset>
  <frameset>
    <frame name=C>
    <frame name=D>
  </frameset>
</frameset>
```

If someone clicks a link in frame A, the only thing you can do is update one of the four frames. Suppose you wanted to update frames B and D at the same time. The trick is to replace frames B and D with a single frame, like this:

```
<frameset cols=2>
  <frameset rows=2>
    <frame name=A>
    <frame name=C>
  </frameset>
  <frame name=BD>
</frameset>
```

Aha! Now you have a single target in which to load a single document, frame BD. The document you load should contain the original frames B and D in one column, like this:

```
<frameset cols=2>
  <frame name=B>
  <frame name=D>
</frameset>
```

The two frames fill frame BD. When you update frame BD, both frames are replaced, giving the appearance of two frames being updated at once.

The drawback to this is that the frames must be adjacent and able to be grouped into a single document. For most pages, though, this solution works fairly well.

We've only scratched the surface of HTML and XHTML tips and tricks here. Our advice: keep hacking!

HTML Grammar

For the most part, browsers do not rigidly enforce the exact syntax of an HTML or even an XHTML document. This gives authors wide latitude in creating documents and gives rise to documents that work on most browsers but actually are incompatible with the HTML and XHTML standards. Our advice is to stick to the standards, unless your documents are fly-by-night affairs.

The standards explicitly define the ordering and nesting of tags and document elements. This syntax is embedded within the appropriate Document Type Definition (DTD) and is not readily understood by those who are not versed in Standard Generalized Markup Language (SGML; for the HTML 4.01 DTD, see Appendix D) or Extensible Markup Language (XML; for the XHTML 1.0 DTD, see Appendix E). Accordingly, we provide an alternate definition of the allowable HTML and XHTML syntax, using a fairly common tool called a *grammar*.

Grammar, whether it defines English sentences or HTML documents, is just a set of rules that indicates the order of language elements. These language elements can be divided into two sets: *terminal* (the actual words of the language) and *nonterminal* (all other grammatical rules). In HTML and XHTML, the words correspond to the embedded markup tags and text in a document.

To use the grammar to create a valid document, follow the order of the rules to see where the tags and text may be placed to create a valid document.

Grammatical Conventions

We use a number of typographic and punctuation conventions to make our grammar easy to understand.

Typographic and Naming Conventions

For our grammar, we denote the terminals with a monospaced typeface. The nonterminals appear in italicized text.

We also use a simple naming convention for the majority of our nonterminals: if a nonterminal defines the syntax of a specific tag, its name is the tag name followed by _tag. If a nonterminal defines the various language elements that may be nested within a certain tag, its name is the tag name followed by _content.

For example, if you are wondering exactly which elements are allowed within an `<a>` tag, you can look for the a_content rule within the grammar. Similarly, to determine the correct syntax of a definition list created with the `<dl>` tag, look for the dl_tag rule.

Punctuation Conventions

Each rule in the grammar starts with the rule's name, followed by the replacement symbol (::=) and the rule's value. We've intentionally kept the grammar simple, but we do use three punctuation elements to denote alternation, repetition, and optional elements in the grammar.

Alternation

Alternation indicates a rule may actually have several different values, of which you must choose exactly one. Pipes (|) separate the alternatives for the rule.

For example, the heading rule is equivalent to any one of six HTML heading tags, so it appears in the table as:

heading	::=	*h1_tag*
	|	*h2_tag*
	|	*h3_tag*
	|	*h4_tag*
	|	*h5_tag*
	|	*h6_tag*

The heading rule tells us that wherever the heading nonterminal appears in a rule, you can replace it with exactly one of the actual heading tags.

Repetition

Repetition indicates that an element within a rule may be repeated some number of times. Repeated elements are enclosed in curly braces ({...}). The closing brace has a subscripted number other than 1 if the element must be repeated a minimum number of times.

For example, the `<ul>` tag may contain only `<li>` tags, or it may be empty. The rule, therefore, is:

ul_tag	::=	`<ul>`
		`{li_tag }`$_0$
		`</ul>`

This rule says that the syntax of the `<ul>` tag requires the `<ul>` tag and zero or more `<li>` tags, followed by a closing `</ul>` tag. We spread this rule across several lines and indented some of the elements to make it more readable; your documents need not actually be formatted this way.

Optional elements

Some elements may appear in a document but are not required. Optional elements are enclosed in square brackets ([. . .]). The `<table>` tag, for example, has an optional caption:

```
table_tag       ::=     <table>
                        [ caption_tag ]
                        {tr_tag }0
                        </table>
```

In addition, the rule says that a table begins with the `<table>` tag, followed by an optional caption and zero or more table-row tags, and ends with the `</table>` tag.

More Details

Our grammar stops at the tag level; it does not delve further to show the syntax of each tag, including tag attributes. For these details, refer to the quick-reference card included with this book.

Predefined Nonterminals

The HTML and XHTML standards define a few specific kinds of content that correspond to various types of text. We use these content types throughout the grammar. They are:

literal_text
> Text is interpreted exactly as specified; no character entities or style tags are recognized.

plain_text
> Regular characters in the document character encoding, along with character entities denoted by the ampersand character, are recognized.

style_text
> Like *plain_text*, with physical and content-based style tags allowed.

The Grammar

The grammar is a composite of the HTML 4.01 and XHTML 1.0 standard tags and special extensions to the language as currently supported by the popular browsers.

The rules are in alphabetical order. The starting rule for an entire document is named *html_document*.

a_content[a]	::=	*heading*
	|	*text*
a_tag	::=	`<a>`
		{a_content}0
		`</a>`
abbr_tag	::=	`<abbr>` *text* `</abbr>`
acronym_tag	::=	`<acronym>` *text* `</acronym>`
address_content	::=	*p_tag*
	|	*text*
address_tag	::=	`<address>`
		{address_content}0
		`</address>`
applet_content	::=	*{`<param>`}0*
		body_content
applet_tag	::=	`<applet>` *applet_content* `</applet>`
b_tag	::=	`<b>` *text* `</b>`
basefont_tag	::=	`<basefont>` *body_content* `</basefont>`
bdo_tag	::=	`<bdo>` *text* `</bdo>`
big_tag	::=	`<big>` *text* `</big>`
blink_tag	::=	`<blink>` *text* `</blink>`
block	::=	*{block_content}0*
block_content	::=	`<isindex>`
	|	*basefont_tag*
	|	*blockquote_tag*
	|	*center_tag*
	|	*dir_tag*
	|	*div_tag*
	|	*dl_tag*
	|	*form_tag*
	|	*listing_tag*
	|	*menu_tag*
	|	*multicol_tag*
	|	*nobr_tag*
	|	*ol_tag*
	|	*p_tag*

		pre_tag
		table_tag
		ul_tag
		xmp_tag
blockquote_tag	::=	`<blockquote>` *body_content* `</blockquote>`
body_content	::=	`<bgsound>`
		`<hr>`
		address_tag
		block
		del_tag
		heading
		ins_tag
		layer_tag
		map_tag
		marquee_tag
		text
body_tag	::=	`<body>`
		{*body_content*}0
		`</body>`
caption_tag	::=	`<caption>` *body_content* `</caption>`
center_tag	::=	`<center>` *body_content* `</center>`
cite_tag	::=	`<cite>` *text* `</cite>`
code_tag	::=	`<code>` *text* `</code>`
colgroup_content	::=	{`<col>`}0
colgroup_tag	::=	`<colgroup>`
		colgroup_content
content_style	::=	*abbr_tag*
		acronym_tag
		cite_tag
		code_tag
		dfn_tag
		em_tag
		kbd_tag
		q_tag
		strong_tag
		var_tag
dd_tag	::=	`<dd>` *flow* `</dd>`
del_tag	::=	`<del>` *flow* `</del>`

dfn_tag	::=	`<dfn>` *text* `</dfn>`
dir_tag[b]	::=	`<dir>`
		{li_tag}
		`</dir>`
div_tag	::=	`<div>` *body_content* `</div>`
dl_content	::=	*dt_tag dd_tag*
dl_tag	::=	`<dl>`
		{dl_content}
		`</dl>`
dt_tag	::=	`<dt>`
		text
		`</dt>`
em_tag	::=	`<em>` *text* `</em>`
fieldset_tag	::=	`<fieldset>`
		[legend_tag]
		{form_content}0
		`</fieldset>`
flow	::=	*{flow_content}0*
flow_content	::=	*block*
	|	*text*
font_tag	::=	`<font>` *style_text* `</font>`
form_content[c]	::=	`<input>`
	|	`<keygen>`
	|	*body_content*
	|	*fieldset_tag*
	|	*label_tag*
	|	*select_tag*
	|	*textarea_tag*
form_tag	::=	`<form>`
		{form_content}0
		`</form>`
frameset_content	::=	`<frame>`
	|	*noframes_tag*
frameset_tag	::=	`<frameset>`
		{frameset_content}0
		`</frameset>`
h1_tag	::=	`<h1>` *text* `</h1>`
h2_tag	::=	`<h2>` *text* `</h2>`

h3_tag	::=	`<h3>` *text* `</h3>`
h4_tag	::=	`<h4>` *text* `</h4>`
h5_tag	::=	`<h5>` *text* `</h5>`
h6_tag	::=	`<h6>` *text* `</h6>`
head_content	::=	`<base>`
	|	`<isindex>`
	|	`<link>`
	|	`<meta>`
	|	`<nextid>`
	|	*style_tag*
	|	*title_tag*
head_tag	::=	`<head>`
		{*head_content*}0
		`</head>`
heading	::=	*h1_tag*
	|	*h2_tag*
	|	*h3_tag*
	|	*h4_tag*
	|	*h5_tag*
	|	*h6_tag*
html_content	::=	*head_tag body_tag*
	|	*head_tag frameset_tag*
html_document	::=	*html_tag*
html_tag	::=	`<html>` *html_content* `</html>`
i_tag	::=	`<i>` *text* `</i>`
ilayer_tag	::=	`<ilayer>` *body_content* `</ilayer>`
ins_tag	::=	`<ins>` *flow* `</ins>`
kbd_tag	::=	`<kbd>` *text* `</kbd>`
label_content[d]	::=	`<input>`
	|	*body_content*
	|	*select_tag*
	|	*textarea_tag*
label_tag	::=	`<label>`
		{*label_content*}0
		`</label>`
layer_tag	::=	`<layer>` *body_content* `</layer>`
legend_tag	::=	`<legend>` *text* `</legend>`

li_tag	::=	`<li>` *flow* `</li>`
listing_tag	::=	`<listing>` *literal_text* `</listing>`
map_content	::=	`{<area>}0`
map_tag	::=	`<map>` *map_content* `</map>`
marquee_tag	::=	`<marquee>` *style_text* `</marquee>`
menu_tag[e]	::=	`<menu>`
		{li_tag}0
		`</menu>`
multicol_tag	::=	`<multicol>` *body_content* `</multicol>`
nobr_tag	::=	`<nobr>` *text* `</nobr>`
noembed_tag	::=	`<noembed>` *text* `</noembed>`
noframes_tag	::=	`<noframes>`
		{body_content}0
		`</noframes>`
noscript_tag	::=	`<noscript>` *text* `</noscript>`
object_content	::=	`{<param>}0`
		body_content
object_tag	::=	`<object>` *object_content* `</object>`
ol_tag	::=	`<ol>`
		{li_tag}
		`</ol>`
optgroup_tag	::=	`<optgroup>`
		{option_tag}0
		`</optgroup>`
option_tag	::=	`<option>` *plain_text* `</option>`
p_tag	::=	`<p>` *text* `</p>`
physical_style	::=	*b_tag*
	|	*bdo_tag*
	|	*big_tag*
	|	*blink_tag*
	|	*font_tag*
	|	*i_tag*
	|	*s_tag*
	|	*small_tag*
	|	*span_tag*
	|	*strike_tag*
	|	*sub_tag*
	|	*sup_tag*

	|	*tt_tag*
	|	*u_tag*
pre_content	::=	` `
	|	`<hr>`
	|	*a_tag*
	|	*style_text*
pre_tag	::=	`<pre>`
		{*pre_content*}0
		`</pre>`
q_tag	::=	`<q>` *text* `</q>`
s_tag	::=	`<s>` *text* `</s>`
samp_tag	::=	`<samp>` *text* `</samp>`
script_tag[f]	::=	`<script>` *plain_text* `</script>`
select_content	::=	*optgroup_tag*
	|	*option_tag*
select_tag	::=	`<select>`
		{*select_content*}0
		`</select>`
server_tag [g]	::=	`<server>` *plain_text* `</server>`
small_tag	::=	`<small>` *text* `</small>`
span_tag	::=	`<span>` *text* `</span>`
strike_tag	::=	`<strike>` *text* `</strike>`
strong_tag	::=	`<strong>` *text* `</strong>`
style_tag	::=	`<style>` *plain_text* `</style>`
sub_tag	::=	`<sub>` *text* `</sub>`
sup_tag	::=	`<sup>` *text* `</sup>`
table_cell	::=	*td_tag*
	|	*th_tag*
table_content	::=	`<tbody>`
	|	`<tfoot>`
	|	`<thead>`
	|	*tr_tag*
table_tag	::=	`<table>`
		[*caption_tag*]
		{*colgroup_tag*}0
		{*table_content*}0
		`</table>`
td_tag	::=	`<td>` *body_content* `</td>`

text	::=	{text_content}0
text_content	::=	
	|	<embed>
	|	<iframe>
	|	<img>
	|	<spacer>
	|	<wbr>
	|	a_tag
	|	applet_tag
	|	content_style
	|	ilayer_tag
	|	noembed_tag
	|	noscript_tag
	|	object_tag
	|	physical_style
	|	plain_text
textarea_tag	::=	<textarea> plain_text </textarea>
th_tag	::=	<th> body_content </th>
title_tag	::=	<title> plain_text </title>
tr_tag	::=	<tr>
		{table_cell}0
		</tr>
tt_tag	::=	<tt> text </tt>
u_tag	::=	<u> text </u>
ul_tag	::=	<ul>
		{li_tag}
		</ul>
var_tag	::=	<var> text </var>
xmp_tag	::=	<xmp> literal_text </xmp>

[a] *a_content* may not contain *a_tags*; you may not nest <a> tags within other <a> tags.

[b] The *li_tag* within the *dir_tag* may not contain any element found in a block.

[c] *form_content* may not contain *form_tags*; you may not nest one <form> within another <form>.

[d] As with the <form> tag, you cannot embed <form> or <label> tags within a <label> tag.

[e] The *li_tag* within the *menu_tag* may not contain any element found in a block.

[f] A *script_tag* may be placed anywhere within an HTML document, without regard to syntactic rules.

[g] A *server_tag* may be placed anywhere within an HTML document, without regard to syntactic rules.

HTML/XHTML Tag Quick Reference

In this appendix, we list in alphabetical order all the known (and some undocumented) HTML and XHTML tags and attributes currently supported by one or more of today's popular browsers.

Core Attributes

Prior to HTML 4.0, few attributes could be used consistently for all the HTML tags. HTML 4.0 changed this, defining a set of 16 core attributes that you can apply to almost all the elements in both HTML 4.01 and XHTML 1.0. For brevity, we list these core attributes in this section and spare you the redundancies in the table that follows:

`class=`*name*	Specify a style class controlling the appearance of the tag's contents.
`dir=`*dir*	Specify the rendering direction for text—either left to right (`ltr`) or right to left (`rtl`).
`id=`*name*	Define a reference name for the tag that is unique in the document.
`lang=`*language*	Specify the human language for the tag's contents with an International Organization for Standardization (ISO) 639 standard two-character name and optional dialect subcode.
`onclick=`*applet*	Specify an applet to be executed when the user clicks the mouse on the tag's content display area.
`ondblclick=`*applet*	Specify an applet to be executed when the user double-clicks the mouse button on the tag's content display area.
`onkeydown=`*applet*	Specify an applet to be executed when the user presses down on a key while the tag's contents have input focus.
`onkeypress=`*applet*	Specify an applet to be executed when the user presses and releases a key while the tag's contents have focus.
`onkeyup=`*applet*	Specify an applet to be executed when the user releases a pressed key while the tag's contents have focus.

onmousedown=*applet*	Specify an applet to be executed when the user presses down on the mouse button while pointing to the tag's content display area.
onmousemove=*applet*	Specify an applet to be executed when the user moves the mouse in the tag's content display area.
onmouseout=*applet*	Specify an applet to be executed when the user moves the mouse off the tag's content display area.
onmouseover=*applet*	Specify an applet to be executed when the user moves the mouse into the tag's content display area.
onmouseup=*applet*	Specify an applet to be executed when the user releases the mouse button while in the tag's content display area.
style=*style*	Specify an inline style for the tag.
title=*string*	Specify a title for the tag.

Only a small handful of tags accept none or only some, but not all, of these attributes. They are:

<applet>	<base>	<basefont>
<bdo>	 	<comment>
<embed>	<font>	<frame>
<frameset>	<head>	<hr>
<html>	<iframe>	<isindex>
<keygen>	<marquee>	<meta>
<nextid>	<nobr>	<noembed>
<param>	<script>	<server>
<spacer>	<style>	<title>
<wbr>		

For convenience, we've marked each of these tags with an asterisk (*) in the following table, and we list all of the attributes supported by these special tags, including the common ones. For all other tags (those without an asterisk), assume that the common attributes listed previously apply. Do note, however, that the popular browsers *do not* support all of the HTML 4.0 standard attributes, common or not. Please refer to the main text for details.

HTML Quick Reference

We use the alert icon to the far right of each item to indicate tags and attributes that are extensions to the HTML 4.01 and XHTML 1.0 standards. We use the Internet Explorer icon to identify those extension tags and attributes that are unique to Internet Explorer and are not well supported by the other popular browsers. Even though we include them in the main text, we have not included here any of the antiquated or obsolete elements or attributes that are explicitly not part of the standards and are no longer supported by any browser.

We include the possible attributes (some required) indented below their respective tags. In the description, we give possible attribute values as either a range of integer numbers or a definitive list of options, where possible.

`<a> ... </a>`	Create a hyperlink anchor (`href` attribute) or fragment identifier (`id` attribute).
`accesskey=char`	Define the hot-key character for this anchor.
`charset=encoding`	Specify the character set used to encode the target.
`coords=list`	Specify a list of shape-dependent coordinates.
`href=url`	Specify the URL of a hyperlink target.
`hreflang=language`	Specify the language encoding for the target.
`name=name`	Specify the name of a fragment identifier.
`rel=relationship`	Indicate the relationship of this document to the target.
`rev=relationship`	Indicate the reverse relationship of the target to this document.
`shape=shape`	Define the region's shape to be `circ`, `circle`, `poly`, `polygon`, `rect`, or `rectangle`.
`tabindex=value`	Define the position of this anchor in the document's tabbing order.
`target=name`	Define the name of the frame or window to receive the referenced document.
`type=type`	Specify the Multipurpose Internet Mail Extension (MIME) type of the target.
`<abbr> ... </abbr>`	The enclosed text is an abbreviation.
`<acronym> ... </acronym>`	The enclosed text is an acronym.
`<address> ... </address>`	The enclosed text is an address.
`<applet> ... </applet>`	Define an executable applet within a text flow.
`align=position`	Align the `<applet>` region to either the `top`, `middle`, `bottom` (default), `left`, `right`, `absmiddle`, `baseline`, or `absbottom` of the text in the line.
`alt=string`	Specify alternative text to replace the `<applet>` region within browsers that support the `<applet>` tag but cannot execute the application.
`archive=url`	Specify a class archive to be downloaded to the browser and then searched for code class.
`class=name`	Specify a style class controlling the appearance of this tag.
`code=class`	Specify the class name of the code to be executed (required).
`codebase=url`	Specify the URL from which the code is retrieved.
`height=n`	Specify the height, in pixels, of the `<applet>` region.
`hspace=n`	Specify additional space, in pixels, to allow to the left and right of the `<applet>` region.
`id=name`	Define a name for this applet that is unique to this document.
`mayscript`	Allow the applet to access JavaScript within the page.
`name=name`	Specify the name of this particular instance of the applet.

`object=data`	Specify a representation of the object's execution state.	
`style=style`	Specify an inline style for this tag.	
`title=string`	Provide a title for the applet.	
`vspace=n`	Specify additional space, in pixels, to allow above and below the `<applet>` region.	
`width=n`	Specify the width, in pixels, of the `<applet>` region.	
`<area>`	Define a mouse-sensitive area in a client-side image map.	
`accesskey=char`	Define the hot-key character for this area.	
`alt=string`	Provide alternative text to be displayed by nongraphical browsers.	
`coords=list`	Specify a comma-separated list of shape-dependent coordinates that define the edge of this area.	
`href=url`	Specify the URL of a hyperlink target associated with this area.	
`nohref`	Indicate that no document is associated with this area; clicking in the area has no effect.	
`notab`	Do not include this area in the tabbing order.	🛑
`onblur=applet`	Specify an applet to be run when the mouse leaves the area.	
`onfocus=applet`	Specify an applet to be run when the mouse enters the area.	
`shape=shape`	Define the region's shape to be `circ`, `circle`, `poly`, `polygon`, `rect`, or `rectangle`.	
`tabindex=value`	Define the position of this area in the document's tabbing order.	
`taborder=n`	Specify this area's position in the tabbing order.	🛑
`target=name`	Specify the frame or window to receive the document linked by this area.	🛑
`<b> ... </b>`	Format the enclosed text using a bold typeface.	
`<base>`	Specify the base URL for all relative URLs in this document.	*
`href=url`	Specify the base URL (required).	
`target=name`	Define the default target of all `<a>` links in the document.	🛑
`<basefont>`	Specify the font size for subsequent text (deprecated; do not use).	🔲 *
`color=color`	Specify the base font's color.	🔲
`face=name`	Specify the local font to be used for the base font.	🔲
`id=name`	Define a name for this tag that is unique to this document.	
`name=name`	Specify the local font to be used for the base font.	🔲
`size=value`	Set the base font size, from 1 to 7 (required; default is 3).	🔲
`<bdo> ... </bdo>`	Bidirectional override, changing the rendering direction of the enclosed text.	*
`class=name`	Specify a style class controlling the appearance of this tag.	
`dir=dir`	Specify the rendering direction for text—either left to right (`ltr`) or right to left (`rtl`).	
`id=name`	Define a name for this tag that is unique to this document.	

`lang=`*language*	Specify the language used for this tag's contents using a standard two-character ISO language name.	
`style=`*style*	Specify an inline style for this tag.	
`title=`*string*	Specify a title for this tag.	
`<bgsound>`	Define background audio for the document.	*
`loop=`*value*	Set the number of times to play the audio; *value* may be an integer or the value `infinite`.	
`src=`*url*	Provide the URL of the audio file to be played.	
`<big> ... </big>`	Format the enclosed text using a bigger typeface.	
`<blink> ... </blink>`	Cause the enclosed content to blink.	
`<blockquote> ... </blockquote>`	The enclosed text is a block quotation.	
`cite=`*url*	Specify the URL of the source of the quoted material.	
`<body> ... </body>`	Delimit the beginning and end of the document body.	
`alink=`*color*	Set the color of active hypertext links in the document.	
`background=`*url*	Specify the URL of an image to be tiled in the document background.	
`bgcolor=`*color*	Set the background color of the document.	
`bgproperties=`*value*	With *value* set to `fixed`, prevent the background image from scrolling with the document content.	
`leftmargin=`*value*	Set the size, in pixels, of the document's left margin.	
`link=`*color*	Set the color of unvisited hypertext links in the document.	
`onblur=`*applet*	Specify an applet to be run when the mouse leaves the document window.	
`onfocus=`*applet*	Specify an applet to be run when the mouse enters the document window.	
`onload=`*applet*	Specify an applet to be run when the document is loaded.	
`onunload=`*applet*	Specify an applet to be run when the document is unloaded.	
`text=`*color*	Set the color of regular text in the document.	
`topmargin=`*value*	Set the size, in pixels, of the document's top margin.	
`vlink=`*color*	Set the color of visited links in the document.	
` `	Break the current text flow, resuming at the beginning of the next line.	*
`class=`*name*	Specify a style class controlling the appearance of this tag.	
`clear=`*margin*	Break the flow and move downward until the desired *margin*, either `left`, `right`, `none`, or `all`, is clear.	
`id=`*name*	Define a name for this tag that is unique to this document.	
`style=`*style*	Specify an inline style for this tag.	
`title=`*string*	Specify a title for this tag.	
`<button>`	Create a push-button element within a `<form>`.	
`accesskey=`*char*	Define the hot-key character for this button.	
`disabled`	Disable the button, preventing the user from clicking it.	

name=*name*	Specify the name of the parameter to be passed to the forms-processing application if the input element is selected (required).
onblur=*applet*	Specify an applet to be run when the mouse moves out of the button.
onfocus=*applet*	Specify an applet to be run when the mouse moves into the button.
tabindex=*n*	Specify this element's position in the tabbing order.
type=*type*	Specify the button type—either `button`, `submit`, or `reset`.
value=*string*	Specify the value of the parameter sent to the forms-processing application if this form element is selected (required).
`<caption> ... </caption>`	Define a caption for a table.
align=*position*	Set the horizontal alignment of the caption to `left`, `center`, or `right`.
valign=*position*	Set the vertical position of the caption to either `top` or `bottom`.
`<center> ... </center>`	Center the enclosed text.
`<cite> ... </cite>`	The enclosed text is a citation.
`<code> ... </code>`	The enclosed text is a code sample.
`<col>`	Define a column within a `<colgroup>`.
align=*position*	Set the column alignment to `left`, `center`, or `right`.
char=*character*	Specify the alignment character for text in these cells.
charoff=*value*	Set the offset within the cell at which the alignment character is placed.
span=*n*	Define the number of columns affected by this `<col>` tag.
valign=*position*	Set the vertical alignment of text within the column to `top`, `middle`, or `bottom`.
width=*n*	Set the width, in pixels or as a percentage, of the column.
`<colgroup>`	Define a column group within a table.
align=*position*	Set the horizontal alignment of text within the columns to `left`, `center`, or `right`.
char=*character*	Specify the alignment character for text in these cells.
charoff=*value*	Set the offset within the cell at which the alignment character is placed.
span=*n*	Define the number of columns in the group.
valign=*position*	Set the vertical alignment of text within the columns to `top`, `middle`, or `bottom`.
width=*n*	Set the width, in pixels or as a percentage, of each column in the group.
`<comment> ... </comment>`	Place a comment in the document (comments are visible in all other browsers).
`<dd> ... </dd>`	Define the definition portion of an element in a definition list.
`<del> ... </del>`	Delineate a deleted section of a document.
cite=*url*	Cite a document justifying the deletion.
datetime=*date*	Specify the date and time of the deletion.

`<dfn>...</dfn>`	Format the enclosed text as a definition.	
`<dir>...</dir>`	Create a directory list containing `<li>` tags.	▣
type=*bullet*	Set the bullet style for this list to `circle`, `disc` (default), or `square`.	▣
`<div>...</div>`	Create a division within a document.	
align=*type*	Align the text within the division to `left`, `center`, or `right`.	▣
nowrap	Suppress word wrapping within this division.	▨
`<dl>...</dl>`	Create a definition list containing `<dt>` and `<dd>` tags.	
compact	Make the list more compact if possible.	▣
`<dt>...</dt>`	Define the definition term portion of an element in a definition list.	
`<em>...</em>`	Format the enclosed text with additional emphasis.	
`<embed>`	Embed an application in a document.	▣ *
align=*position*	Align the applet area to either the `top` or `bottom` of the adjacent text, or to the `left` or `right` margin of the page, with subsequent text flowing around the applet.	▣
border=*n*	Specify the size, in pixels, of the border around the applet.	▣
height=*n*	Specify the height, in pixels, of the applet.	
hidden	If present, hide the applet on the page.	
hspace=*n*	Define, in pixels, additional space to be placed to the left and right of the applet.	
name=*name*	Provide a name for the applet.	▣
palette=*value*	In Netscape and Opera, a value of `foreground` causes the applet to use the foreground palette (in Windows only), and `background` uses the background palette; with Internet Explorer and Firefox, provide the foreground and background colors for the applet, specified as two color values separated by a pipe (`|`).	▣
src=*url*	Supply the URL of the data to be fed to the applet.	
type=*type*	Specify the MIME type of the plug-in to be used.	
units=*type*	Set the units for the `height` and `width` attributes to either `pixels` (the default) or `en` (half the text point size).	
vspace=*n*	Define, in pixels, additional space to be placed above and below the applet.	
width=*n*	Specify the width, in pixels, of the applet.	▣
`<fieldset>...</fieldset>`	Create a group of elements in a form.	
`<font>...</font>`	Set the size or color of the enclosed text (deprecated; do not use).	▣ *
class=*name*	Specify a style class controlling the appearance of this tag.	
color=*color*	Set the color of the enclosed text to the desired color.	
dir=*dir*	Specify the rendering direction for text—either left to right (`ltr`) or right to left (`rtl`).	
face=*list*	Set the typeface of the enclosed text to the first available font in the comma-separated list of font names.	▣
id=*name*	Define a name for this tag that is unique to this document.	

lang=*language*	Specify the language used for this tag's contents using a standard two-character ISO language name.
size=*value*	Set the size to an absolute size, from 1 to 7, or relative to the `<basefont>` size, using +n or -n (required).
style=*style*	Specify an inline style for this tag.
title=*string*	Specify a title for this tag.
`<form>` ... `</form>`	Delimit a form.
accept-charset=*list*	Specify a list of character sets accepted by the server processing this form.
action=*url*	Specify the URL of the application that processes the form (required).
enctype=*encoding*	Specify how the form element values are encoded.
method=*style*	Specify the parameter-passing style—either get or post (required).
name=*name*	Supply a name for this form for use by JavaScript.
onreset=*applet*	Specify an applet to be run when the form is reset.
onsubmit=*applet*	Specify an applet to be run when the form is submitted.
target=*name*	Specify the name of the frame or window to receive the results of the form after submission.
`<frame>` ... `</frame>`	Define a frame within a frameset. *
bordercolor=*color*	Set the color of the frame's border.
class=*name*	Specify a style class controlling the appearance of this tag.
frameborder=*n*	If *value* is 1, enable frame borders; if *value* is 0, disable frame borders
id=*name*	Define a name for this tag that is unique to this document.
longdesc=*url*	Provide the URL of a document describing the contents of the frame.
marginheight=*n*	Place *n* pixels of space above and below the frame contents.
marginwidth=*n*	Place *n* pixels of space to the left and right of the frame contents.
name=*name*	Define the name of the frame.
noresize	Disable user resizing of the frame.
scrolling=*type*	Always add scroll bars (yes), never add scroll bars (no), or, for Netscape only, add scroll bars when needed (auto).
src=*url*	Define the URL of the source document for this frame.
style=*style*	Specify an inline style for this tag.
title=*string*	Specify a title for this tag.
`<frameset>` ... `</frameset>`	Define a collection of frames or other framesets. *
border=*n*	Set the thickness of the frame borders in this frameset.
bordercolor=*color*	Define the color of the borders in this frameset.
cols=*list*	Specify the number and width of frames within this frameset.
frameborder=*value*	If *value* is 1, enable frame borders; if *value* is 0, disable frame borders.
framespacing=*n*	Define the thickness of the frame borders in this frameset.
onblur=*applet*	Define an applet to be run when the mouse leaves this frameset.

onfocus=*applet*	Define an applet to be run when the mouse enters this frameset.
onload=*applet*	Define an applet to be run when this frameset is loaded.
onunload=*applet*	Define an applet to be run when this frameset is removed from the display.
rows=*list*	Specify the number and height of frames within a frameset.
<h*n*> ... </h*n*>	The enclosed text is a level-*n* header, for level *n* from 1 to 6.
align=*type*	Specify the heading alignment as left (default), center, or right. 🖹
<head> ... </head>	Delimit the beginning and end of the document head. *
dir=*dir*	Specify the rendering direction for text—either left to right (ltr) or right to left (rtl).
lang=*language*	Specify the language used for this tag's contents using a standard two-character ISO language name.
profile=*url*	Provide the URL of a profile for this document.
<hr>	Break the current text flow and insert a horizontal rule. *
align=*type*	Specify the rule alignment as left, center (default), or right. 🖹
class=*name*	Specify a style class controlling the appearance of the rule.
color=*color*	Define the color of the rule. 🖼
dir=*dir*	Specify the rendering direction for text—either left to right (ltr) or right to left (rtl).
id=*name*	Define a name for this tag that is unique to this document.
lang=*language*	Specify the language used for this tag's contents using a standard two-character ISO language name.
noshade	Do not use 3D shading to render the rule. 🖹
onclick=*applet*	Specify an applet to be executed when the mouse button is clicked on this tag.
ondblclick=*applet*	Specify an applet to be executed when the mouse button is double-clicked on this tag.
onkeydown=*applet*	Specify an applet to be executed when a key is pressed down while this tag has input focus.
onkeypress=*applet*	Specify an applet to be executed when a key is pressed and released while this tag has focus.
onkeyup=*applet*	Specify an applet to be executed when a key is released while this tag has focus.
onmousedown=*applet*	Specify an applet to be executed when a mouse button is pressed down on this tag.
onmousemove=*applet*	Specify an applet to be executed when the mouse is moved over this tag.
onmouseout=*applet*	Specify an applet to be executed when the mouse moves out of this tag's display area.
onmouseover=*applet*	Specify an applet to be executed when the mouse moves into this tag's display area.

onmouseup=*applet*	Specify an applet to be executed when a mouse button is released while over this tag.
size=*pixels*	Set the thickness of the rule to an integer number of pixels.
style=*style*	Specify an inline style for this tag.
title=*string*	Specify a title for this tag.
width=*value* or %	Set the width of the rule to either an integer number of pixels or a percentage of the page width.
<html> ... </html>	Delimit the beginning and end of the entire Hypertext Markup Language (HTML) document.
dir=*dir*	Specify the rendering direction for text—either left to right (ltr) or right to left (rtl).
lang=*language*	Specify the language used for this tag's contents using a standard two-character ISO language name.
version=*string*	Indicate the HTML version used to create this document.
<i> ... </i>	Format the enclosed text in an italic typeface.
<iframe> ... </iframe>	Define an inline frame.
align=*position*	Set the position of the frame aligned to the top, center, or bottom of the surrounding text, or flush against the left or right margins with subsequent text flowing around the frame.
class=*name*	Specify a style class controlling the appearance of the frame.
frameborder=*value*	If *value* is 1, enable frame borders; if *value* is 0, disable frame borders.
height=*n*	Set the height, in pixels, of the frame.
id=*name*	Define a name for this tag that is unique to this document.
longdesc=*url*	Provide the URL of a document describing the contents of the frame.
marginheight=*n*	Place *n* pixels of space above and below the frame contents.
marginwidth=*n*	Place *n* pixels of space to the left and right of the frame contents.
name=*name*	Define the name of the frame.
scrolling=*type*	Always add scroll bars (yes) or never add scroll bars (no).
src=*url*	Define the URL of the source document for this frame.
style=*style*	Specify an inline style for this tag.
title=*string*	Specify a title for this tag.
width=*n*	Set the width, in pixels, of the frame.
<img>	Insert an image into the current text flow.
align=*type*	Align the image to the top, middle, bottom (default), left, right, absmiddle, baseline, or absbottom of the text.
alt=*text*	Provide alternative text for nonimage-capable browsers.
border=*n*	Set the pixel thickness of the border around images contained within hyperlinks.
controls	Add playback controls for embedded video clips.
dynsrc=*url*	Specify the URL of a video clip to be displayed.

`height=`*n*	Specify the height of the image in scan lines.	
`hspace=`*n*	Specify the space, in pixels, to be added to the left and right of the image.	
`ismap`	Indicate that the image is mouse-selectable when used within an `<a>` tag.	
`longdesc=`*url*	Provide the URL of a document describing the image.	🛈
`loop=`*value*	Set the number of times to play the video; *value* may be an integer or the value `infinite`.	🖼
`lowsrc=`*url*	Specify a low-resolution image to be loaded by the browser first, followed by the image specified by the `src` attribute.	🛈
`name=`*name*	Provide a name for the image for use by JavaScript.	🛈
`onabort=`*applet*	Provide an applet to be run if image loading is aborted.	
`onerror=`*applet*	Provide an applet to be run if image loading is unsuccessful.	
`onload=`*applet*	Provide an applet to be run if image loading is successful.	
`src=`*url*	Specify the source URL of the image to be displayed (required).	
`start=`*start*	Specify when to play the video clip—either `fileopen` or `mouseover`.	🖼
`usemap=`*url*	Specify the map of coordinates and links that define the hypertext links within this image.	
`vspace=`*n*	Specify the vertical space, in pixels, added at the top and bottom of the image.	
`width=`*n*	Specify the width of the image in pixels.	🛈
`<input type=button>`	Create a push-button element within a `<form>`.	
`accesskey=`*char*	Define the hot-key character for this element.	
`disabled`	Disable this control, making it inactive.	
`name=`*name*	Specify the name of the parameter to be passed to the forms-processing application if the input element is selected (required).	
`notab`	Specify that this element is not part of the tabbing order.	🛈
`onblur=`*applet*	Specify an applet to be run when the mouse leaves this control.	
`onfocus=`*applet*	Specify an applet to be run when the mouse enters this control.	
`tabindex=`*n*	Specify this element's position in the tabbing order.	
`taborder=`*n*	Specify this element's position in the tabbing order.	🛈
`value=`*string*	Specify the value of the parameter sent to the forms-processing application if this form element is selected (required).	
`<input type=checkbox>`	Create a checkbox input element within a `<form>`.	
`accesskey=`*char*	Define the hot-key character for this element.	
`checked`	Mark the element as initially selected.	
`disabled`	Disable this control, making it inactive.	
`name=`*string*	Specify the name of the parameter to be passed to the forms-processing application if the input element is selected (required).	

notab	Specify that this element is not part of the tabbing order. 🛇
readonly	Prevent user modification of this element.
tabindex=*n*	Specify this element's position in the tabbing order.
taborder=*n*	Specify this element's position in the tabbing order. 🛇
value=*string*	Specify the value of the parameter sent to the forms-processing application if this form element is selected (required).
`<input type=file>`	Create a file-selection element within a `<form>`.
accept=*list*	Specify a list of MIME types that can be accepted by this element.
accesskey=*char*	Define the hot-key character for this element.
disabled	Disable this control, making it inactive.
maxlength=*n*	Specify the maximum number of characters to accept for this element.
name=*name*	Specify the name of the parameter that is passed to the forms-processing application for this input element (required).
notab	Specify that this element is not part of the tabbing order. 🛇
onblur=*applet*	Specify an applet to be run when the mouse leaves this control.
onchange=*applet*	Specify an applet to be run when the user changes the value of this element.
onfocus=*applet*	Specify an applet to be run when the mouse enters this control.
readonly	Prevent user modification of this element.
size=*n*	Specify the number of characters to display for this element.
tabindex=*n*	Specify this element's position in the tabbing order.
taborder=*n*	Specify this element's position in the tabbing order. 🛇
value=*string*	Specify the value of the parameter sent to the forms-processing application if this form element is selected (required).
`<input type=hidden>`	Create a hidden element within a `<form>`.
name=*name*	Specify the name of the parameter that is passed to the forms-processing application for this input element (required).
value=*string*	Specify the value of this element that is passed to the forms-processing application.
`<input type=image>`	Create an image input element within a `<form>`.
accesskey=*char*	Define the hot-key character for this element.
align=*type*	Align the image to the top, middle, or bottom of the form element's text. 🛇
alt=*string*	Provide an alternative description for the image.
border=*n*	Set the pixel thickness of the border of the image. 🛇
disabled	Disable this control, making it inactive.
name=*name*	Specify the name of the parameter to be passed to the forms-processing application for this input element (required).
notab	Specify that this element is not part of the tabbing order. 🛇
src=*url*	Specify the source URL of the image (required).

tabindex=*n*	Specify this element's position in the tabbing order.
taborder=*n*	Specify this element's position in the tabbing order. 📄
usemap=*url*	Specify the URL of a map to be used with this image.
`<input type=password>`	Create a content-protected text-input element within a `<form>`.
accesskey=*char*	Define the hot-key character for this element.
disabled	Disable this control, making it inactive.
maxlength=*n*	Specify the maximum number of characters to accept for this element.
name=*name*	Specify the name of the parameter to be passed to the forms-processing application for this input element (required).
notab	Specify that this element is not part of the tabbing order. 📄
onblur=*applet*	Specify an applet to be run when the mouse leaves this element.
onchange=*applet*	Specify an applet to be run when the user changes the value of this element.
onfocus=*applet*	Specify an applet to be run when the mouse enters this element.
onselect=*applet*	Specify an applet to be run if the user clicks this element.
readonly	Prevent user modification of this element.
size=*n*	Specify the number of characters to display for this element.
tabindex=*n*	Specify this element's position in the tabbing order.
taborder=*n*	Specify this element's position in the tabbing order. 📄
value=*string*	Specify the initial value for this element.
`<input type=radio>`	Create a radio-button input element within a `<form>`.
accesskey=*char*	Define the hot-key character for this element.
checked	Mark the element as initially selected.
disabled	Disable this control, making it inactive.
name=*string*	Specify the name of the parameter to be passed to the forms-processing application if the input element is selected (required).
notab	Specify that this element is not part of the tabbing order. 📄
readonly	Prevent user modification of this element.
tabindex=*n*	Specify this element's position in the tabbing order.
taborder=*n*	Specify this element's position in the tabbing order. 📄
value=*string*	Specify the value of the parameter sent to the forms-processing application if this form element is selected (required).
`<input type=reset>`	Create a reset button within a `<form>`.
accesskey=*char*	Define the hot-key character for this element.
disabled	Disable this control, making it inactive.
notab	Specify that this element is not part of the tabbing order. 📄
tabindex=*n*	Specify this element's position in the tabbing order.
taborder=*n*	Specify this element's position in the tabbing order. 📄
value=*string*	Specify an alternate label for the reset button (default is "Reset").

`<input type=submit>`	Create a submit button within a `<form>`.	
`accesskey=char`	Define the hot-key character for this element.	
`disabled`	Disable this control, making it inactive.	
`name=name`	Specify the name of the parameter that is passed to the forms-processing application for this input element (required).	
`notab`	Specify that this element is not part of the tabbing order.	⚠
`tabindex=n`	Specify this element's position in the tabbing order.	
`taborder=n`	Specify this element's position in the tabbing order.	⚠
`value=string`	Specify an alternate label for the submit button, as well as the value passed to the forms-processing application for this parameter if this button is clicked.	
`<input type=text>`	Create a text-input element within a `<form>`.	
`accesskey=char`	Define the hot-key character for this element.	
`disabled`	Disable this control, making it inactive.	
`maxlength=n`	Specify the maximum number of characters to accept for this element.	
`name=name`	Specify the name of the parameter that is passed to the forms-processing application for this input element (required).	
`notab`	Specify that this element is not part of the tabbing order.	⚠
`onblur=applet`	Specify an applet to be run when the mouse leaves this element.	
`onchange=applet`	Specify an applet to be run when the user changes the value of this element.	
`onfocus=applet`	Specify an applet to be run when the mouse enters this element.	
`onselect=applet`	Specify an applet to be run if the user clicks this element.	
`readonly`	Prevent user modification of this element.	
`size=n`	Specify the number of characters to display for this element.	
`tabindex=n`	Specify this element's position in the tabbing order.	
`taborder=n`	Specify this element's position in the tabbing order.	⚠
`value=string`	Specify the initial value for this element.	
`<ins> ... </ins>`	Delineate an inserted section of a document.	
`cite=url`	Cite a document dissatisfying the insertion.	
`datetime=date`	Specify the date and time of the insertion.	
`<isindex>`	Create a "searchable" HTML document (deprecated; do not use).	⚠ *
`action=url`	For Internet Explorer only, provide the URL of the program that performs the searching action.	⚠
`class=name`	Specify a style class controlling the appearance of this tag.	
`dir=dir`	Specify the rendering direction for text—either left to right (`ltr`) or right to left (`rtl`).	
`id=name`	Define a name for this tag that is unique to this document.	
`lang=language`	Specify the language used for this tag's contents using a standard two-character ISO language name.	

prompt=*string*	Provide an alternate prompt for the input field.	🛈
style=*style*	Specify an inline style for this tag.	
title=*string*	Specify a title for this tag.	
<kbd> ... </kbd>	The enclosed text is keyboard-like input.	
<keygen>	Generate key information in a form.	*
challenge=*string*	Provide a challenge string to be packaged with the key.	
name=*name*	Provide a name for the key.	
<label> ... </label>	Define a label for a form control.	
accesskey=*char*	Define the hot-key character for this label.	
for=*id*	Specify the form element associated with this label.	
onblur=*applet*	Specify an applet to be run when the mouse leaves this label.	
onfocus=*applet*	Specify an applet to be run when the mouse enters this label.	
<legend> ... </legend>	Define a legend for a form field set.	
accesskey=*char*	Define the hot-key character for this legend.	
align=*position*	Align the legend to the top, bottom, left, or right of the field set.	🛈
<li> ... </li>	Delimit a list item in an ordered (<ol>) or unordered (<ul>) list.	
type=*format*	Set the type of this list element to the desired *format*—for <li> within <ol>: A (capital letters), a (lowercase letters), I (capital Roman numerals), i (lowercase Roman numerals), or 1 (Arabic numerals; default); for <li> within <ul>: circle, disc (default), or square.	
value=*n*	Set the number for this list item to *n*.	
<link>	Define a link between this document and another document in the document <head>.	
charset=*charset*	Specify the character set used to encode the target of this link.	
href=*url*	Specify the hypertext reference URL of the target document.	
hreflang=*language*	Specify the language used for the target's contents using a standard two-character ISO language name.	
media=*list*	Specify a list of media types upon which this object can be rendered.	
rel=*relation*	Indicate the relationship from this document to the target.	
rev=*relation*	Indicate the reverse relationship from the target to this document.	
type=*string*	Specify the MIME type for the linked document. Usually used in conjunction with links to stylesheets, when the type is set to text/css.	
<map> ... </map>	Define a map containing hotspots in a client-side image map.	
name=*name*	Define the name of this map (required).	
<marquee> ... </marquee>	Create a scrolling-text marquee (Internet Explorer only).	🛈 *
align=*position*	Align the marquee to the top, middle, or bottom of the surrounding text.	🛈
behavior=*style*	Define the marquee style to be scroll, slide, or alternate.	🛈

bgcolor=*color*	Set the background color of the marquee.	☐
class=*name*	Specify a style class controlling the appearance of this tag.	
direction=*dir*	Define the direction, left or right, in which the text is to scroll.	☐
height=*n*	Define the height, in pixels, of the marquee area.	
hspace=*n*	Define the space, in pixels, to be inserted to the left and right of the marquee.	
loop=*value*	Set the number of times to animate the marquee; *value* is an integer or infinite.	☐
scrollamount=*value*	Set the number of pixels to move the text for each scroll movement.	☐
scrolldelay=*value*	Specify the delay, in milliseconds, between successive movements of the marquee text.	☐
style=*style*	Specify an inline style for this tag.	
vspace=*n*	Define the space, in pixels, to be inserted above and below the marquee.	
width=*n*	Define the width, in pixels, of the marquee area.	☐
<menu> ... </menu>	Define a menu list containing <li> tags.	☐
type=*bullet*	Set the bullet style for this list to circle, disc (default), or square.	☐
<meta>	Provide additional information about a document.	*
content=*string*	Specify the value for the meta-information (required).	
dir=*dir*	Specify the rendering direction for text—either left to right (ltr) or right to left (rtl).	
http-equiv=*string*	Specify the HTTP equivalent name for the meta-information and cause the server to include the name and content in the HTTP header for this document when it is transmitted to the client.	
lang=*language*	Specify the language used for this tag's contents using a standard two-character ISO language name.	
name=*string*	Specify the name of the meta-information.	
scheme=*scheme*	Specify the profile scheme used to interpret this property.	
<nextid>	Define the next valid document entity identifier (obsolete; do not use).	☐ *
n=*n*	Set the next ID number.	☐
<nobr> ... </nobr>	No breaks allowed in the enclosed text.	☐ *
<noembed> ... </noembed>	Define content to be presented by browsers that do not support the <embed> tag.	☐ *
<noframes> ... </noframes>	Define content to be presented by browsers that do not support frames.	
<noscript> ... </noscript>	Define content to be presented by browsers that do not support the <script> tag.	

`<object>`	Insert an object into a document.
`align=`*position*	Align the object with the surrounding text (`texttop`, `middle`, `textmiddle`, `baseline`, `textbottom`, or `center`) or against the margin with subsequent text flowing around the object (`left` or `right`).
`archive=`*list*	Specify a list of URLs of archives containing resources used by this object.
`border=`*n*	Define, in pixels, the object's border width.
`classid=`*url*	Supply the URL of the object.
`codebase=`*url*	Supply the URL of the object's code base.
`codetype=`*type*	Specify the MIME type of the code base.
`data=`*url*	Supply data for the object.
`declare`	Declare this object without instantiating it.
`height=`*n*	Define, in pixels, the height of the object.
`hspace=`*n*	Provide extra space, in pixels, to the right and left of the object.
`name=`*name*	Define the name of this object.
`notab`	Do not make this object part of the tabbing order.
`shapes`	Specify that this object has shaped hyperlinks.
`standby=`*string*	Define a message to display while the object loads.
`tabindex=`*n*	Specify this object's position in the document tab order.
`type=`*type*	Specify the MIME type for the object data.
`usemap=`*url*	Define an image map for use with this object.
`vspace=`*n*	Provide extra space, in pixels, above and below the object.
`width=`*n*	Define, in pixels, the width of the object.
`<ol>` ... `</ol>`	Define an ordered list containing numbered (ascending) `<li>` elements.
`compact`	Present the list in a more compact manner.
`start=`*n*	Start numbering the list at *n* rather than 1.
`type=`*format*	Set the numbering *format* for this list to `A` (capital letters), `a` (lowercase letters), `I` (capital Roman numerals), `i` (lowercase Roman numerals), or `1` (Arabic numerals; default).
`<optgroup>` ... `</optgroup>`	Define a group of options within a `<select>` element.
`disabled`	Disable this group, making it inactive.
`label=`*string*	Provide a label for this group.
`<option>` ... `</option>`	Define an option within a `<select>` item in a `<form>`.
`disabled`	Disable this option, making it inactive.
`label=`*string*	Provide a label for this option.
`selected`	Make this item initially selected.
`value=`*string*	Return the specified value to the forms-processing application instead of the `<option>` contents.

`<p> ... </p>`	Start and end a paragraph.	
`align=type`	Align the text within the paragraph to `left`, `center`, or `right`.	🗋
`<param> ... </param>`	Supply a parameter to a containing `<applet>`.	*
`id=name`	Define the unique identifier for this parameter.	
`name=name`	Define the name of the parameter.	🗋
`type=type`	Specify the MIME type of the parameter.	
`value=string`	Define the value of the parameter.	
`valuetype=type`	Define the type of the `value` attribute, either as `data`, `ref` (the value is a URL pointing to the data), or `object` (the value is the name of an object in this document).	
`<pre> ... </pre>`	Render the enclosed text in its original, preformatted style, honoring line breaks and spacing verbatim.	
`width=n`	Size the text, if possible, so that *n* characters fit across the display window.	🗋
`<q> ... </q>`	The enclosed text is an inline quotation (not supported by Internet Explorer).	
`cite=url`	Specify the URL of the source of the quoted material.	
`<s> ... </s>`	Same as `<strike>`; the enclosed text is struck through with a horizontal line.	🗋
`<samp> ... </samp>`	The enclosed text is a sample.	
`<script> ... </script>`	Define a script within a document.	*
`charset=encoding`	Specify the character set used to encode the script.	
`defer`	Defer execution of this script.	
`language=encoding`	Specify the language used to create the script.	
`src=url`	Provide the URL of the document containing the script.	
`type=encoding`	Specify the MIME type of the script.	
`<select> ... </select>`	Define a multiple-choice menu or scrolling list within a `<form>`, containing one or more `<option>` tags.	
`disabled`	Disable this control, making it inactive.	
`multiple`	Allow the user to select more than one `<option>` within the `<select>`.	
`name=name`	Define the name for the selected `<option>` values that, if selected, are passed to the forms-processing application (required).	🗋
`onblur=applet`	Specify an applet to be run when the mouse leaves this element.	
`onchange=applet`	Specify an applet to be run when the user changes the value of this element.	
`onfocus=applet`	Specify an applet to be run when the mouse enters this element.	
`size=n`	Display *n* items using a pull-down menu for `size=1` (without `multiple` specified) and a scrolling list of *n* items otherwise.	
`tabindex=n`	Specify this element's position in the tabbing order.	

`<small> ... </small>`	Format the enclosed text using a smaller typeface.	
`<span> ... </span>`	Define a span of text for style application.	
`<strike> ... </strike>`	Strike through the enclosed text with a horizontal line.	
`<strong> ... </strong>`	Strongly emphasize the enclosed text.	
`<style> ... </style>`	Define one or more document-level styles.	*
`dir=`*dir*	Specify the rendering direction for the title text—either left to right (`ltr`) or right to left (`rtl`).	
`lang=`*language*	Specify the language used for this tag's title using a standard two-character ISO language name.	
`media=`*list*	Specify a list of media types upon which this object can be rendered.	
`title=`*string*	Specify a title for this tag.	
`type=`*type*	Define the format of the styles (always `text/css`).	
`<sub> ... </sub>`	Format the enclosed text as subscript.	
`<sup> ... </sup>`	Format the enclosed text as superscript.	
`<table> ... </table>`	Define a table.	
`align=`*position*	Align the table in the center and flow the subsequent text around the table.	
`background=`*url*	Define a background image for the table.	
`bgcolor=`*color*	Define a background color for the entire table.	
`border=`*n*	Create a border that is *n* pixels wide.	
`bordercolor=`*color*	Define the border color for the entire table.	
`bordercolordark=`*color*	Define the dark border-highlighting color for the entire table.	
`bordercolorlight=`*color*	Define the light border-highlighting color for the entire table.	
`cellpadding=`*n*	Place *n* pixels of padding around each cell's contents.	
`cellspacing=`*n*	Place *n* pixels of spacing between cells.	
`cols=`*n*	Specify the number of columns in this table.	
`frame=`*type*	Define where table borders are displayed—`border` (default), `void`, `above`, `below`, `hsides`, `lhs`, `rhs`, `vsides`, or `box`.	
`height=`*n*	Define the height of the table in pixels.	
`hspace=`*n*	Specify the horizontal space, in pixels, added at the left and right of the table.	
`nowrap`	Suppress text wrapping in table cells.	
`rules=`*edges*	Determine where inner dividers are drawn—`all` (default), `groups` (only around row and column groups), `rows`, `cols`, or `none`.	
`summary=`*string*	Provide a summary description of this table.	
`valign=`*position*	Align text in the table to the `top`, `center`, `bottom`, or `baseline`.	
`vspace=`*n*	Specify the vertical space, in pixels, added at the top and bottom of the table.	
`width=`*n*	Set the width of the table to *n* pixels or a percentage of the window width.	

`<tbody>` ... `</tbody>`	Create a row group within a table.
`align=`*position*	Align the table body cells' contents to the `left`, `center`, or `right`.
`char=`*char*	Specify the body group cell alignment character.
`charoff=`*value*	Specify the offset within the cells of the alignment position.
`valign=`*position*	Vertically align the body group cells' contents to the `top`, `center`, `bottom`, or `baseline` of the cell.
`<td>` ... `</td>`	Define a table data cell.
`abbr=`*string*	Specify an abbreviation for the cell's contents.
`align=`*position*	Align the cell contents to the `left`, `center`, or `right`.
`axis=`*string*	Provide a name for a related group of cells.
`background=`*url*	Define a background image for this cell.
`bgcolor=`*color*	Define the background color for the cell.
`bordercolor=`*color*	Define the border color for the cell.
`bordercolordark=`*color*	Define the dark border-highlighting color for the cell.
`bordercolorlight=`*color*	Define the light border-highlighting color for the cell.
`char=`*char*	Specify the cell alignment character.
`charoff=`*value*	Specify the offset of the alignment position within the cell.
`colspan=`*n*	Have this cell straddle *n* adjacent columns.
`headers=`*list*	Provide a list of header cell IDs associated with this cell.
`height=`*n*	Define the height, in pixels, for this cell.
`nowrap`	Do not automatically wrap and fill text in this cell.
`rowspan=`*n*	Have this cell straddle *n* adjacent rows.
`scope=`*scope*	Define the scope of this header cell—`row`, `col`, `rowgroup`, or `colgroup`.
`valign=`*position*	Vertically align this cell's contents to the `top`, `center`, `bottom`, or `baseline` of the cell.
`width=`*n*	Set the width of this cell to *n* pixels or a percentage of the table width.
`<textarea>` ... `</textarea>`	Define a multiline text-input area within a `<form>`; the content of the `<textarea>` tag is the initial, default value.
`accesskey=`*char*	Define the hot-key character for this element.
`cols=`*n*	Display *n* columns (characters) of text within the text area.
`disabled`	Disable this control, making it inactive.
`name=`*string*	Define the name for the text-area value that is passed to the forms-processing application (required).
`onblur=`*applet*	Specify an applet to be run when the mouse leaves this element.
`onchange=`*applet*	Specify an applet to be run when the user changes the value of this element.
`onfocus=`*applet*	Specify an applet to be run when the mouse enters this element.

`onselect=`*applet*	Specify an applet to be run if the user clicks this element.	
`readonly`	Prevent user modification of this element.	
`rows=`*n*	Display *n* rows of text within the text area.	
`tabindex=`*n*	Specify this element's position in the tabbing order.	
`<tfoot>` ... `</tfoot>`	Define a table footer.	
`align=`*position*	Align the footer cells' contents to the `left`, `center`, or `right`.	🛈
`char=`*char*	Specify the cell alignment character.	
`charoff=`*value*	Specify the offset within the cell of the alignment position.	
`valign=`*position*	Vertically align the footer cells' contents to the `top`, `center`, `bottom`, or `baseline` of the cell.	🛈
`<th>` ... `</th>`	Define a table header cell.	
`abbr=`*string*	Specify an abbreviation for the cell's contents.	
`align=`*position*	Align the cell contents to the `left`, `center`, or `right`.	🛈
`axis=`*string*	Provide a name for a related group of cells.	
`background=`*url*	Define a background image for this cell.	🛈
`bgcolor=`*color*	Define the background color for the cell.	🛈
`bordercolor=`*color*	Define the border color for the cell.	🖼
`bordercolordark=`*color*	Define the dark border-highlighting color for the cell.	🖼
`bordercolorlight=`*color*	Define the light border-highlighting color for the cell.	🖼
`char=`*char*	Specify the cell alignment character.	
`charoff=`*value*	Specify the offset of the alignment position within the cell.	
`colspan=`*n*	Have this cell straddle *n* adjacent columns.	
`headers=`*list*	Provide a list of header cell IDs associated with this cell.	
`height=`*n*	Define the height, in pixels, for this cell.	
`nowrap`	Do not automatically wrap and fill text in this cell.	🖼
`rowspan=`*n*	Have this cell straddle *n* adjacent rows.	
`scope=`*scope*	Define the scope of this header cell—`row`, `col`, `rowgroup`, or `colgroup`.	
`valign=`*position*	Vertically align this cell's contents to the `top`, `center`, `bottom`, or `baseline` of the cell.	🛈
`width=`*n*	Set the width of this cell to *n* pixels or a percentage of the table width.	
`<thead>` ... `</thead>`	Define a table heading.	
`align=`*position*	Define the horizontal text alignment in the heading—`left`, `center`, `right`, or `justify`.	🛈
`char=`*char*	Specify the cell alignment character for heading cells.	
`charoff=`*value*	Specify the offset within the cells of the alignment position.	
`valign=`*position*	Define the vertical text alignment in the heading—`left`, `center`, `right`, or `justify`.	🛈

`<title>` ... `</title>`	Define the HTML document's title.	*
dir=*dir*	Specify the rendering direction for text—either left to right (ltr) or right to left (rtl).	
lang=*language*	Specify the language used for this tag's contents using a standard two-character ISO language name.	
`<tr>` ... `</tr>`	Define a row of cells within a table.	
align=*type*	Align the cell contents in this row to the left, center, or right.	🗋
background=*url*	Define a background image for this cell.	🗋
bgcolor=*color*	Define the background color for this row.	🗋
bordercolor=*color*	For Internet Explorer, define the border color for this row.	🗋
bordercolordark=*color*	For Internet Explorer, define the dark border-highlighting color for this row.	🖭
bordercolorlight=*color*	For Internet Explorer, define the light border-highlighting color for this row.	🖭
char=*char*	Specify the cell alignment character for this row.	
charoff=*value*	Specify the offset of the alignment position within the cells of this row.	
nowrap	Disable word wrap for all cells in this row.	🖭
valign=*position*	Vertically align the cell contents in this row to the top, center, bottom, or baseline of the cell.	🗋
`<tt>` ... `</tt>`	Format the enclosed text in teletype-style (monospaced) font.	
`<u>` ... `</u>`	Underline the enclosed text.	🗋
`<ul>` ... `</ul>`	Define an unordered list of bulleted `<li>` elements.	
compact	Display the list in a more compact manner, if possible.	🗋
type=*bullet*	Set the bullet style for this list to circle, disc (default), or square.	🗋
`<var>` ... `</var>`	The enclosed text is a variable's name.	
`<wbr>`	Indicate a potential word break point within a `<nobr>` section.	🗋 *

Cascading Style Sheet Properties
Quick Reference

In the following table, we list, in alphabetical order, all the properties defined in the World Wide Web Consortium's (W3C's) Recommended Specification for Cascading Style Sheets (CSS), Level 2 (*http://www.w3.org/pub/WWW/TR/REC-CSS2*). We include each property's possible values, defined as either an explicit keyword (shown in constant width) or as one of these values:

angle

A numeric value followed by deg, grad, or rad.

color

Either a color name or hexadecimal RGB value, as defined in Appendix G, or an RGB triple of the form:

    rgb(*red, green, blue*)

where *red*, *green*, and *blue* are either numbers in the range 0 to 255 or percentage values indicating the brightness of that color component. Values of 255 or 100% indicate that the corresponding color component is at its brightest; values of 0 or 0% indicate that the corresponding color component is turned off completely. For example:

    rgb(27, 119, 207)
    rgb(50%, 75%, 0%)

are both valid color specifications.

frequency

A numeric value followed by hz or khz, indicating hertz or kilohertz.

length

An optional sign (either + or –), immediately followed by a number (with or without a decimal point), immediately followed by a two-character unit identifier. For values of 0, the unit identifier may be omitted.

The unit identifiers em and ex refer to the overall height of the font and to the height of the letter "x," respectively. The unit identifier px is equal to a single pixel on the display device. The unit identifiers in, cm, mm, pt, and pc refer to inches, centimeters, millimeters, points, and picas, respectively. There are 72.27 points in an inch and 12 points in a pica.

number

An optional sign, immediately followed by a number (with or without a decimal point).

percent

An optional sign, immediately followed by a number (with or without a decimal point), immediately followed by a percent sign. The actual value is computed as a percentage of some other element property, usually the element's size.

shape

A shape keyword, followed by a parentheses-enclosed list of comma-separated, shape-specific parameters. Currently, the only supported shape keyword is rect, which expects four numeric parameters denoting the offsets of the top, right, bottom, and left edges of the rectangle.

time

A numeric value followed by s or ms, designating a time in seconds or in milliseconds.

url

The keyword url, immediately followed (no spaces) by a left parenthesis, followed by a URL optionally enclosed in single or double quotes, followed by a matching right parenthesis. For example:

```
url("http://www.oreilly.com/catalog")
```

is a valid URL value.

Finally, some values are lists of other values and are described as a "list of" some other value. In these cases, a list consists of one or more of the allowed values, separated by commas.

If several different values are allowed for a property, these alternative choices are separated by pipes (|).

If the standard defines a default value for the property, that value is underlined.

azimuth	*angle* | left-side | far-left | left | center-left | center | center-right | right | far-right | right-side	Determines the position around the listener at which a sound is played.	8.4.12.7
background		Composite property for the background-attachment, background-color, background-image, background-position, and background-repeat properties; value is any of these properties' values, in any order.	8.4.5.6
background-attachment	scroll | fixed	Determines whether the background image is fixed in the window or scrolls as the document scrolls.	8.4.5.3
background-color	*color* | transparent	Sets the background color of an element.	8.4.5.1
background-image	*url* | none	Sets the background image of an element.	8.4.5.2
background-position	*percent* | *length* | top | center | bottom | left | right	Sets the initial position of the element's background image, if specified; values normally are paired to provide X,Y positions; default position is 0% 0%.	8.4.5.4
background-repeat	repeat | repeat-x | repeat-y | no-repeat	Determines how the background image is repeated (tiled) across an element.	8.4.5.5
border		Sets all four of an element's borders; value is one or more of a *color*, a value for border-width, and a value for border-style.	8.4.7.6
border-bottom		Sets an element's bottom border; value is one or more of a *color*, a value for border-bottom-width, and a value for border-style.	8.4.7.6
border-bottom-width	*length* | thin | medium | thick	Sets the thickness of an element's bottom border.	8.4.7.4
border-collapse	collapse | separate	Sets the table border rendering algorithm.	8.4.9.1
border-color	*color*	Sets the color of all four of an element's borders; default is the color of the element.	8.4.7.3
border-left		Sets an element's left border; value is one or more of a *color*, a value for border-left-width, and a value for border-style.	8.4.7.6
border-left-width	*length* | thin | medium | thick	Sets the thickness of an element's left border	8.4.7.4
border-right		Sets an element's right border; value is one or more of a *color*, a value for border-right-width, and a value for border-style.	8.4.7.6
border-right-width	*length* | thin | medium | thick	Sets the thickness of an element's right border.	8.4.7.4

border-spacing		With separate borders, sets the spacing between borders—one value sets vertical and horizontal spacing; two values set horizontal and vertical spacing, respectively.	8.4.9.1
border-style	dashed|dotted|double| groove|inset|<u>none</u>|outset |ridge|solid	Sets the style of all four of an element's borders.	8.4.7.5
border-top		Sets an element's top border; value is one or more of a *color*, a value for border-top-width, and a value for border-style.	8.4.7.6
border-top-width	*length*|thin|<u>medium</u>|thick	Sets the thickness of an element's top border.	8.4.7.4
border-width	*length*|thin|<u>medium</u>|thick	Sets the thickness of all four of an element's borders.	8.4.7.4
bottom	*length*|*percent*	Used with the position property to place the bottom edge of an element.	8.4.7.14
caption-side	<u>top</u>|bottom|left|right	Sets the position for a table caption.	8.4.9.2
clear	both|left|<u>none</u>|right	Sets which margins of an element must not be adjacent to a floating element; the element is moved down until that margin is clear.	8.4.7.7
clip	*shape*	Sets the clipping mask for an element.	8.4.7.8
color	*color*	Sets the color of an element.	8.4.5.7
content		Inserts generated content around an element; see text for details.	8.4.11.2
counter-increment		Increments a counter by 1; value is a list of counter names, with each name optionally followed by a value by which it is incremented.	8.4.11.4
counter-reset		Resets a counter to zero; value is a list of counter names, with each name optionally followed by a value to which it is reset.	8.4.11.4
cue-after	*url*|<u>none</u>	Plays the designated sound after an element is spoken.	8.4.12.5
cue-before	*url*|<u>none</u>	Plays the designated sound before an element is spoken.	8.4.12.5
display	<u>block</u>|inline|list-item| marker|none	Controls how an element is displayed.	8.4.10.1
elevation	*angle*|below|level|above| higher|lower	Sets the height at which a sound is played.	8.4.12.7
empty-cells	hide|<u>show</u>	With separate borders, hides empty cells in a table.	8.4.9.1

float	left | none | right	Determines whether an element floats to the left or right, allowing text to wrap around it or be displayed inline (using none).	8.4.7.9
font		Sets all font attributes for an element; value is any of the values for font-style, font-variant, font-weight, font-size, line-height, and font-family, in that order.	8.4.3.8
font-family	List of font names	Defines the font for an element, either as a specific font or as one of the generic fonts serif, sans-serif, cursive, fantasy, and monospace.	8.4.3.1
font-size	xx-small | x-small | small | medium | large | x-large | xx-large | larger | smaller | *length* | *percent*	Defines the font size.	8.4.3.2
font-size-adjust	none | *ratio*	Adjusts the current font's aspect ratio.	8.4.3.4
font-stretch	wider | normal | narrower | ultra-condensed | extra-condensed | condensed | semi-condensed | semi-expanded | expanded | extra-expanded | ultra-expanded	Determines the amount to stretch the current font.	8.4.3.3
font-style	normal | italic | oblique	Defines the style of the face, either normal or some type of slanted style.	8.4.3.5
font-variant	normal | small-caps	Defines a font to be in small caps.	8.4.3.6
font-weight	normal | bold | bolder | lighter | *number*	Defines the font weight—if a *number* is used, it must be a multiple of 100 between 100 and 900; 400 is normal, 700 is the same as the keyword bold.	8.4.3.7
height	*length* | auto	Defines the height of an element.	8.4.7.10
left	*length* | *percent*	Used with the position property to place the left edge of an element.	8.4.7.14
letter-spacing	*length* | normal	Inserts additional space between text characters.	8.4.6.1
line-height	*length* | *number* | *percent* | normal	Sets the distance between adjacent text baselines.	8.4.6.2
list-style		Defines list-related styles using any of the values for list-style-image, list-style-position, and list-style-type.	8.4.8.4
list-style-image	*url* | none	Defines an image to be used as a list item's marker, in lieu of the value for list-style-type.	8.4.8.1

`list-style-position`	`inside` | <u>`outside`</u>	Indents or extends (default) a list item's marker with respect to the item's content.	8.4.8.2
`list-style-type`	`circle` | <u>`disc`</u> | `square` | `decimal` | `lower-alpha` | `lower-roman` | `none` | `upper-alpha` | `upper-roman`	Defines a list item's marker either for unordered lists (`circle`, `disc`, or `square`) or for ordered lists (`decimal`, `lower-alpha`, `lower-roman`, `none`, `upper-alpha`, or `upper-roman`).	8.4.8.3
`margin`	*length* | *percent* | `auto`	Defines all four of an element's margins.	8.4.7.11
`margin-bottom`	*length* | *percent* | `auto`	Defines the bottom margin of an element; default value is 0.	8.4.7.11
`margin-left`	*length* | *percent* | `auto`	Defines the left margin of an element; default value is 0.	8.4.7.11
`margin-right`	*length* | *percent* | `auto`	Defines the right margin of an element; default value is 0.	8.4.7.11
`margin-top`	*length* | *percent* | `auto`	Defines the top margin of an element; default value is 0.	8.4.7.11
`orphans`	*number*	Sets the minimum number of lines allowed in an orphaned paragraph fragment.	8.4.13.5
`overflow`	`auto` | `hidden` | `scroll` | <u>`visible`</u>	Determines how overflow content is rendered.	8.4.7.13
`padding`		Defines all four padding amounts around an element.	8.4.7.12
`padding-bottom`	*length* | *percent*	Defines the bottom padding of an element; default value is 0.	8.4.7.12
`padding-left`	*length* | *percent*	Defines the left padding of an element; default value is 0.	8.4.7.12
`padding-right`	*length* | *percent*	Defines the right padding of an element; default value is 0.	8.4.7.12
`padding-top`	*length* | *percent*	Defines the top padding of an element; default value is 0.	8.4.7.12
`page`	*name*	Associates a named page layout with an element.	8.4.13.3
`page-break-after`	<u>`auto`</u> | `always` | `avoid` | `left` | `right`	Forces or suppresses page breaks after an element.	8.4.13.4
`page-break-before`	<u>`auto`</u> | `always` | `avoid` | `left` | `right`	Forces or suppresses page breaks before an element.	8.4.13.4
`page-break-inside`	<u>`auto`</u> | `avoid`	Suppresses page breaks within an element.	8.4.13.4
`pause-after`	*percent* | *time*	Pauses after speaking an element.	8.4.12.4
`pause-before`	*percent* | *time*	Pauses before speaking an element.	8.4.12.4
`pitch`	*frequency* | `x-low` | `low` | `medium` | `high` | `x-high`	Sets the average pitch of an element's spoken content.	8.4.12.3

pitch-range	*number*	Sets the range of the pitch, from 0 (flat) to 100 (broad); default is 50.	8.4.12.3
play-during	*url*	mix	none	repeat	If a URL is provided, it is played during an element's spoken content—specifying repeat loops the audio; mix causes it to mix with, rather than replace, other background audio.	8.4.12.6
position	absolute	fixed	relative	static	Sets the positioning model for an element.	8.4.7.14
quotes	List of strings	Sets the quote symbols used to quote text.	8.4.11.3
richness	*number*	Sets the richness of the voice, from 0 (flat) to 100 (mellifluous); default is 50.	8.4.12.3
right	*length*	*percent*	Used with the position property to place the right edge of an element.	8.4.7.14
speak	normal	none	spell-out	Determines how an element's content is spoken.	8.4.12.2
speak-header	always	once	Determines whether table headers are spoken once for each row or column or each time a cell is spoken.	8.4.9.3
speak-numeral	continuous	digits	Determines how numerals are spoken.	8.4.12.2
speak-punctuation	code	none	Determines whether punctuation is spoken or used for inflection.	8.4.12.2
speech-rate	*number*	x-slow	slow	medium	fast	x-fast	faster	slower	Sets the rate of speech; a *number* sets the rate in words per minute.	8.4.12.3
stress	*number*	Sets the stress of the voice, from 0 (catatonic) to 100 (hyperactive); default is 50.	8.4.12.3
table-layout	auto	fixed	Determines the table-rendering algorithm.	8.4.9.4
text-align	center	justify	left	right	Sets the text alignment style for an element.	8.4.6.3
text-decoration	blink	line-through	none	overline	underline	Defines any decoration for the text; values may be combined.	8.4.6.4
text-indent	*length*	*percent*	Defines the indentation of the first line of text in an element; default is 0.	8.4.6.5
text-shadow	See text	Creates text drop shadows of varying colors and offsets.	8.4.6.6
text-transform	capitalize	lowercase	none	uppercase	Transforms the text in the element accordingly.	8.4.6.7
top	*length*	*percent*	Used with the position property to place the top edge of an element.	8.4.7.14

vertical-align	*percent* | baseline | bottom | middle | sub | super | text-bottom | text-top | top	Sets the vertical positioning of an element.	8.4.6.8
visibility	collapse | hidden | visible	Determines whether an element is visible in the document or table.	8.4.7.15
voice-family	List of voices	Selects a named voice family to speak an element's content.	8.4.12.3
volume	*number* | *percent* | silent | x-soft | soft | medium | loud | x-loud	Sets the volume of spoken content; numeric values range from 0 to 100.	8.4.12.1
white-space	normal | nowrap | pre	Defines how whitespace within an element is handled.	8.4.10.2
widows	*number*	Sets the minimum number of lines allowed in a widowed paragraph fragment.	8.4.13.5
width	*length* | *percent* | auto	Defines the width of an element.	8.4.7.16
word-spacing	*length* | normal	Inserts additional space between words.	8.4.6.9
z-index	*number*	Sets the rendering layer for the current element.	8.4.7.17

The HTML 4.01 DTD

The HTML 4.01 standard is formally defined as three Standard Generalized Markup Language (SGML) Document Type Definitions (DTDs): the Strict DTD, the Transitional DTD, and the Frameset DTD. The Strict DTD defines only those elements that are not deprecated in the 4.0 standard. Ideally, everyone would create HTML documents that conform to the Strict DTD. The Transitional DTD includes all those deprecated elements and more accurately reflects the HTML in use today, with many older elements still in common use. The Frameset DTD is identical to the Transitional DTD, with the exception that the document <body> is replaced by the <frameset> tag.

Since the Transitional DTD provides the broadest coverage of all HTML elements currently in use, it is the DTD upon which this book is based and the one we reproduce here. Note that we have reprinted this DTD verbatim and have not attempted to add extensions to it. Where our description and the DTD deviate, assume the DTD is correct:

```
<!--
    This is the HTML 4.01 Transitional DTD, which includes
    presentation attributes and elements that W3C expects to phase out
    as support for style sheets matures. Authors should use the Strict
    DTD when possible, but may use the Transitional DTD when support
    for presentation attributes and elements is required.
    HTML 4 includes mechanisms for style sheets, scripting,
    embedding objects, improved support for right to left and mixed
    direction text, and enhancements to forms for improved
    accessibility for people with disabilities.
        Draft: $Date: 2006/09/27 15:34:23 $
```

```
      Authors:
            Dave Raggett <dsr@w3.org>
            Arnaud Le Hors <lehors@w3.org>
            Ian Jacobs <ij@w3.org>
    Further information about HTML 4.01 is available at:
        http://www.w3.org/TR/1999/REC-html401-19991224
    The HTML 4.01 specification includes additional
    syntactic constraints that cannot be expressed within
    the DTDs.
-->
<!ENTITY % HTML.Version "-//W3C//DTD HTML 4.01 Transitional//EN"
  -- Typical usage:
    <!DOCTYPE HTML PUBLIC "-//W3C//DTD HTML 4.01 Transitional//EN"
          "http://www.w3.org/TR/html4/loose.dtd">
    <html>
    <head>
    ...
    </head>
    <body>
    ...
    </body>
    </html>
    The URI used as a system identifier with the public identifier allows
    the user agent to download the DTD and entity sets as needed.
    The FPI for the Strict HTML 4.01 DTD is:
        "-//W3C//DTD HTML 4.01//EN"
    This version of the strict DTD is:
        http://www.w3.org/TR/1999/REC-html401-19991224/strict.dtd
    Authors should use the Strict DTD unless they need the
    presentation control for user agents that don't (adequately)
    support style sheets.
    If you are writing a document that includes frames, use
    the following FPI:
        "-//W3C//DTD HTML 4.01 Frameset//EN"
    This version of the frameset DTD is:
        http://www.w3.org/TR/1999/REC-html401-19991224/frameset.dtd
    Use the following (relative) URIs to refer to
    the DTDs and entity definitions of this specification:
    "strict.dtd"
    "loose.dtd"
    "frameset.dtd"
    "HTMLlat1.ent"
    "HTMLsymbol.ent"
    "HTMLspecial.ent"
-->
<!--================== Imported Names =====================================-->
<!-- Feature Switch for frameset documents -->
<!ENTITY % HTML.Frameset "IGNORE">
<!ENTITY % ContentType "CDATA"
    -- media type, as per [RFC2045]
    -->
<!ENTITY % ContentTypes "CDATA"
    -- comma-separated list of media types, as per [RFC2045]
    -->
```

```
<!ENTITY % Charset "CDATA"
    -- a character encoding, as per [RFC2045]
    -->
<!ENTITY % Charsets "CDATA"
    -- a space-separated list of character encodings, as per [RFC2045]
    -->
<!ENTITY % LanguageCode "NAME"
    -- a language code, as per [RFC1766]
    -->
<!ENTITY % Character "CDATA"
    -- a single character from [ISO10646]
    -->
<!ENTITY % LinkTypes "CDATA"
    -- space-separated list of link types
    -->
<!ENTITY % MediaDesc "CDATA"
    -- single or comma-separated list of media descriptors
    -->
<!ENTITY % URI "CDATA"
    -- a Uniform Resource Identifier,
       see [URI]
    -->
<!ENTITY % Datetime "CDATA" -- date and time information. ISO date format -->
<!ENTITY % Script "CDATA" -- script expression -->
<!ENTITY % StyleSheet "CDATA" -- style sheet data -->
<!ENTITY % FrameTarget "CDATA" -- render in this frame -->
<!ENTITY % Text "CDATA">
<!-- Parameter Entities -->
<!ENTITY % head.misc "SCRIPT|STYLE|META|LINK|OBJECT" -- repeatable head elements -->
<!ENTITY % heading "H1|H2|H3|H4|H5|H6">
<!ENTITY % list "UL | OL |  DIR | MENU">
<!ENTITY % preformatted "PRE">
<!ENTITY % Color "CDATA" -- a color using sRGB: #RRGGBB as Hex values -->
<!-- There are also 16 widely known color names with their sRGB values:
    Black  = #000000    Green  = #008000
    Silver = #C0C0C0    Lime   = #00FF00
    Gray   = #808080    Olive  = #808000
    White  = #FFFFFF    Yellow = #FFFF00
    Maroon = #800000    Navy   = #000080
    Red    = #FF0000    Blue   = #0000FF
    Purple = #800080    Teal   = #008080
    Fuchsia= #FF00FF    Aqua   = #00FFFF
  -->
<!ENTITY % bodycolors "
  bgcolor     %Color;        #IMPLIED  -- document background color --
  text        %Color;        #IMPLIED  -- document text color --
  link        %Color;        #IMPLIED  -- color of links --
  vlink       %Color;        #IMPLIED  -- color of visited links --
  alink       %Color;        #IMPLIED  -- color of selected links --
  ">
<!--================== Character mnemonic entities ==========================-->
<!ENTITY % HTMLlat1 PUBLIC
   "-//W3C//ENTITIES Latin1//EN//HTML"
   "HTMLlat1.ent">
%HTMLlat1;
```

```
<!ENTITY % HTMLsymbol PUBLIC
   "-//W3C//ENTITIES Symbols//EN//HTML"
   "HTMLsymbol.ent">
%HTMLsymbol;
<!ENTITY % HTMLspecial PUBLIC
   "-//W3C//ENTITIES Special//EN//HTML"
   "HTMLspecial.ent">
%HTMLspecial;
<!--==================== Generic Attributes ============================-->
<!ENTITY % coreattrs
 "id          ID          #IMPLIED  -- document-wide unique id --
  class       CDATA       #IMPLIED  -- space-separated list of classes --
  style       %StyleSheet; #IMPLIED  -- associated style info --
  title       %Text;      #IMPLIED  -- advisory title --"
  >
<!ENTITY % i18n
 "lang        %LanguageCode; #IMPLIED  -- language code --
  dir         (ltr|rtl)   #IMPLIED  -- direction for weak/neutral text --"
  >
<!ENTITY % events
 "onclick     %Script;    #IMPLIED  -- a pointer button was clicked --
  ondblclick  %Script;    #IMPLIED  -- a pointer button was double clicked--
  onmousedown %Script;    #IMPLIED  -- a pointer button was pressed down --
  onmouseup   %Script;    #IMPLIED  -- a pointer button was released --
  onmouseover %Script;    #IMPLIED  -- a pointer was moved onto --
  onmousemove %Script;    #IMPLIED  -- a pointer was moved within --
  onmouseout  %Script;    #IMPLIED  -- a pointer was moved away --
  onkeypress  %Script;    #IMPLIED  -- a key was pressed and released --
  onkeydown   %Script;    #IMPLIED  -- a key was pressed down --
  onkeyup     %Script;    #IMPLIED  -- a key was released --"
  >
<!-- Reserved Feature Switch -->
<!ENTITY % HTML.Reserved "IGNORE">
<!-- The following attributes are reserved for possible future use -->
<![ %HTML.Reserved; [
<!ENTITY % reserved
 "datasrc     %URI;       #IMPLIED  -- a single or tabular Data Source --
  datafld     CDATA       #IMPLIED  -- the property or column name --
  dataformatas (plaintext|html) plaintext -- text or html --"
  >
]]>
<!ENTITY % reserved "">
<!ENTITY % attrs "%coreattrs; %i18n; %events;">
<!ENTITY % align "align (left|center|right|justify)  #IMPLIED"
                 -- default is left for ltr paragraphs, right for rtl --
  >
<!--==================== Text Markup =======================================-->
<!ENTITY % fontstyle
 "TT | I | B | U | S | STRIKE | BIG | SMALL">
<!ENTITY % phrase "EM | STRONG | DFN | CODE |
                   SAMP | KBD | VAR | CITE | ABBR | ACRONYM" >
<!ENTITY % special
   "A | IMG | APPLET | OBJECT | FONT | BASEFONT | BR | SCRIPT |
    MAP | Q | SUB | SUP | SPAN | BDO | IFRAME">
```

```
<!ENTITY % formctrl "INPUT | SELECT | TEXTAREA | LABEL | BUTTON">
<!-- %inline; covers inline or "text-level" elements -->
<!ENTITY % inline "#PCDATA | %fontstyle; | %phrase; | %special; | %formctrl;">
<!ELEMENT (%fontstyle;|%phrase;) - - (%inline;)*>
<!ATTLIST (%fontstyle;|%phrase;)
  %attrs;                           -- %coreattrs, %i18n, %events --
  >
<!ELEMENT (SUB|SUP) - - (%inline;)*   -- subscript, superscript -->
<!ATTLIST (SUB|SUP)
  %attrs;                           -- %coreattrs, %i18n, %events --
  >
<!ELEMENT SPAN - - (%inline;)*        -- generic language/style container -->
<!ATTLIST SPAN
  %attrs;                           -- %coreattrs, %i18n, %events --
  %reserved;                        -- reserved for possible future use --
  >
<!ELEMENT BDO - - (%inline;)*         -- I18N BiDi over-ride -->
<!ATTLIST BDO
  %coreattrs;                       -- id, class, style, title --
  lang        %LanguageCode; #IMPLIED -- language code --
  dir         (ltr|rtl)     #REQUIRED -- directionality --
  >
<!ELEMENT BASEFONT - O EMPTY          -- base font size -->
<!ATTLIST BASEFONT
  id          ID            #IMPLIED -- document-wide unique id --
  size        CDATA         #REQUIRED -- base font size for FONT elements --
  color       %Color;       #IMPLIED -- text color --
  face        CDATA         #IMPLIED -- comma-separated list of font names --
  >
<!ELEMENT FONT - - (%inline;)*        -- local change to font -->
<!ATTLIST FONT
  %coreattrs;                       -- id, class, style, title --
  %i18n;                            -- lang, dir --
  size        CDATA         #IMPLIED -- [+|-]nn e.g. size="+1", size="4" --
  color       %Color;       #IMPLIED -- text color --
  face        CDATA         #IMPLIED -- comma-separated list of font names --
  >
<!ELEMENT BR - O EMPTY                -- forced line break -->
<!ATTLIST BR
  %coreattrs;                       -- id, class, style, title --
  clear       (left|all|right|none) none -- control of text flow --
  >
<!--================== HTML content models ===================================-->
<!--
    HTML has two basic content models:
        %inline;    character level elements and text strings
        %block;     block-like elements e.g. paragraphs and lists
-->
<!ENTITY % block
     "P | %heading; | %list; | %preformatted; | DL | DIV | CENTER |
     NOSCRIPT | NOFRAMES | BLOCKQUOTE | FORM | ISINDEX | HR |
     TABLE | FIELDSET | ADDRESS">
<!ENTITY % flow "%block; | %inline;">
```

```
<!--==================== Document Body =====================================-->
<!ELEMENT BODY O O (%flow;)* +(INS|DEL) -- document body -->
<!ATTLIST BODY
  %attrs;                               -- %coreattrs, %i18n, %events --
  onload        %Script;   #IMPLIED    -- the document has been loaded --
  onunload      %Script;   #IMPLIED    -- the document has been removed --
  background    %URI;      #IMPLIED    -- texture tile for document background --
  %bodycolors;                         -- bgcolor, text, link, vlink, alink --
  >
<!ELEMENT ADDRESS - - ((%inline;)|P)* -- information on author -->
<!ATTLIST ADDRESS
  %attrs;                               -- %coreattrs, %i18n, %events --
  >
<!ELEMENT DIV - - (%flow;)*            -- generic language/style container -->
<!ATTLIST DIV
  %attrs;                               -- %coreattrs, %i18n, %events --
  %align;                               -- align, text alignment --
  %reserved;                            -- reserved for possible future use --
  >
<!ELEMENT CENTER - - (%flow;)*         -- shorthand for DIV align=center -->
<!ATTLIST CENTER
  %attrs;                               -- %coreattrs, %i18n, %events --
  >
<!--==================== The Anchor Element =================================-->
<!ENTITY % Shape "(rect|circle|poly|default)">
<!ENTITY % Coords "CDATA" -- comma-separated list of lengths -->
<!ELEMENT A - - (%inline;)* -(A)       -- anchor -->
<!ATTLIST A
  %attrs;                               -- %coreattrs, %i18n, %events --
  charset       %Charset;   #IMPLIED    -- char encoding of linked resource --
  type          %ContentType; #IMPLIED  -- advisory content type --
  name          CDATA       #IMPLIED    -- named link end --
  href          %URI;       #IMPLIED    -- URI for linked resource --
  hreflang      %LanguageCode; #IMPLIED -- language code --
  target        %FrameTarget; #IMPLIED  -- render in this frame --
  rel           %LinkTypes; #IMPLIED    -- forward link types --
  rev           %LinkTypes; #IMPLIED    -- reverse link types --
  accesskey     %Character; #IMPLIED    -- accessibility key character --
  shape         %Shape;     rect        -- for use with client-side image maps --
  coords        %Coords;    #IMPLIED    -- for use with client-side image maps --
  tabindex      NUMBER      #IMPLIED    -- position in tabbing order --
  onfocus       %Script;    #IMPLIED    -- the element got the focus --
  onblur        %Script;    #IMPLIED    -- the element lost the focus --
  >
<!--==================== Client-side image maps ============================-->
<!-- These can be placed in the same document or grouped in a
     separate document although this isn't yet widely supported -->
<!ELEMENT MAP - - ((%block;) | AREA)+ -- client-side image map -->
<!ATTLIST MAP
  %attrs;                               -- %coreattrs, %i18n, %events --
  name          CDATA       #REQUIRED   -- for reference by usemap --
  >
```

```
<!ELEMENT AREA - O EMPTY              -- client-side image map area -->
<!ATTLIST AREA
  %attrs;                             -- %coreattrs, %i18n, %events --
  shape        %Shape;      rect      -- controls interpretation of coords --
  coords       %Coords;     #IMPLIED  -- comma-separated list of lengths --
  href         %URI;        #IMPLIED  -- URI for linked resource --
  target       %FrameTarget; #IMPLIED -- render in this frame --
  nohref       (nohref)     #IMPLIED  -- this region has no action --
  alt          %Text;       #REQUIRED -- short description --
  tabindex     NUMBER       #IMPLIED  -- position in tabbing order --
  accesskey    %Character;  #IMPLIED  -- accessibility key character --
  onfocus      %Script;     #IMPLIED  -- the element got the focus --
  onblur       %Script;     #IMPLIED  -- the element lost the focus --
  >
<!--=================== The LINK Element ======================================-->
<!--
  Relationship values can be used in principle:
   a) for document specific toolbars/menus when used
      with the LINK element in document head e.g.
      start, contents, previous, next, index, end, help
   b) to link to a separate style sheet (rel=stylesheet)
   c) to make a link to a script (rel=script)
   d) by stylesheets to control how collections of
      html nodes are rendered into printed documents
   e) to make a link to a printable version of this document
      e.g. a postscript or pdf version (rel=alternate media=print)
-->
<!ELEMENT LINK - O EMPTY              -- a media-independent link -->
<!ATTLIST LINK
  %attrs;                             -- %coreattrs, %i18n, %events --
  charset      %Charset;    #IMPLIED  -- char encoding of linked resource --
  href         %URI;        #IMPLIED  -- URI for linked resource --
  hreflang     %LanguageCode; #IMPLIED -- language code --
  type         %ContentType; #IMPLIED -- advisory content type --
  rel          %LinkTypes;  #IMPLIED  -- forward link types --
  rev          %LinkTypes;  #IMPLIED  -- reverse link types --
  media        %MediaDesc;  #IMPLIED  -- for rendering on these media --
  target       %FrameTarget; #IMPLIED -- render in this frame --
  >
<!--=================== Images ======================================-->
<!-- Length defined in strict DTD for cellpadding/cellspacing -->
<!ENTITY % Length "CDATA" -- nn for pixels or nn% for percentage length -->
<!ENTITY % MultiLength "CDATA" -- pixel, percentage, or relative -->
<![ %HTML.Frameset; [
<!ENTITY % MultiLengths "CDATA" -- comma-separated list of MultiLength -->
]]>
<!ENTITY % Pixels "CDATA" -- integer representing length in pixels -->
<!ENTITY % IAlign "(top|middle|bottom|left|right)" -- center? -->
<!-- To avoid problems with text-only UAs as well as
   to make image content understandable and navigable
   to users of non-visual UAs, you need to provide
   a description with ALT, and avoid server-side image maps -->
```

```
<!ELEMENT IMG - O EMPTY                -- Embedded image -->
<!ATTLIST IMG
  %attrs;                              -- %coreattrs, %i18n, %events --
  src          %URI;         #REQUIRED -- URI of image to embed --
  alt          %Text;        #REQUIRED -- short description --
  longdesc     %URI;         #IMPLIED  -- link to long description
                                          (complements alt) --
  name         CDATA         #IMPLIED  -- name of image for scripting --
  height       %Length;      #IMPLIED  -- override height --
  width        %Length;      #IMPLIED  -- override width --
  usemap       %URI;         #IMPLIED  -- use client-side image map --
  ismap        (ismap)       #IMPLIED  -- use server-side image map --
  align        %IAlign;      #IMPLIED  -- vertical or horizontal alignment --
  border       %Pixels;      #IMPLIED  -- link border width --
  hspace       %Pixels;      #IMPLIED  -- horizontal gutter --
  vspace       %Pixels;      #IMPLIED  -- vertical gutter --
  >
<!-- USEMAP points to a MAP element which may be in this document
  or an external document, although the latter is not widely supported -->
<!--===================== OBJECT ========================================-->
<!--
  OBJECT is used to embed objects as part of HTML pages
  PARAM elements should precede other content. SGML mixed content
  model technicality precludes specifying this formally ...
-->
<!ELEMENT OBJECT - - (PARAM | %flow;)*
  -- generic embedded object -->
<!ATTLIST OBJECT
  %attrs;                              -- %coreattrs, %i18n, %events --
  declare      (declare)     #IMPLIED  -- declare but don't instantiate flag --
  classid      %URI;         #IMPLIED  -- identifies an implementation --
  codebase     %URI;         #IMPLIED  -- base URI for classid, data, archive--
  data         %URI;         #IMPLIED  -- reference to object's data --
  type         %ContentType; #IMPLIED  -- content type for data --
  codetype     %ContentType; #IMPLIED  -- content type for code --
  archive      CDATA         #IMPLIED  -- space-separated list of URIs --
  standby      %Text;        #IMPLIED  -- message to show while loading --
  height       %Length;      #IMPLIED  -- override height --
  width        %Length;      #IMPLIED  -- override width --
  usemap       %URI;         #IMPLIED  -- use client-side image map --
  name         CDATA         #IMPLIED  -- submit as part of form --
  tabindex     NUMBER        #IMPLIED  -- position in tabbing order --
  align        %IAlign;      #IMPLIED  -- vertical or horizontal alignment --
  border       %Pixels;      #IMPLIED  -- link border width --
  hspace       %Pixels;      #IMPLIED  -- horizontal gutter --
  vspace       %Pixels;      #IMPLIED  -- vertical gutter --
  %reserved;                           -- reserved for possible future use --
  >
<!ELEMENT PARAM - O EMPTY              -- named property value -->
<!ATTLIST PARAM
  id           ID            #IMPLIED  -- document-wide unique id --
  name         CDATA         #REQUIRED -- property name --
  value        CDATA         #IMPLIED  -- property value --
```

```
    valuetype    (DATA|REF|OBJECT) DATA    -- How to interpret value --
    type         %ContentType;  #IMPLIED  -- content type for value
                                             when valuetype=ref --
    >
<!--===================== Java APPLET ====================================-->
<!--
  One of code or object attributes must be present.
  Place PARAM elements before other content.
-->
<!ELEMENT APPLET - - (PARAM | %flow;)* -- Java applet -->
<!ATTLIST APPLET
    %coreattrs;                            -- id, class, style, title --
    codebase     %URI;         #IMPLIED  -- optional base URI for applet --
    archive      CDATA         #IMPLIED  -- comma-separated archive list --
    code         CDATA         #IMPLIED  -- applet class file --
    object       CDATA         #IMPLIED  -- serialized applet file --
    alt          %Text;        #IMPLIED  -- short description --
    name         CDATA         #IMPLIED  -- allows applets to find each other --
    width        %Length;      #REQUIRED -- initial width --
    height       %Length;      #REQUIRED -- initial height --
    align        %IAlign;      #IMPLIED  -- vertical or horizontal alignment --
    hspace       %Pixels;      #IMPLIED  -- horizontal gutter --
    vspace       %Pixels;      #IMPLIED  -- vertical gutter --
    >
<!--==================== Horizontal Rule =================================-->
<!ELEMENT HR - O EMPTY -- horizontal rule -->
<!ATTLIST HR
    %attrs;                                -- %coreattrs, %i18n, %events --
    align        (left|center|right) #IMPLIED
    noshade      (noshade)     #IMPLIED
    size         %Pixels;      #IMPLIED
    width        %Length;      #IMPLIED
    >
<!--==================== Paragraphs ======================================-->
<!ELEMENT P - O (%inline;)*              -- paragraph -->
<!ATTLIST P
    %attrs;                                -- %coreattrs, %i18n, %events --
    %align;                                -- align, text alignment --
    >
<!--==================== Headings ========================================-->
<!--
  There are six levels of headings from H1 (the most important)
  to H6 (the least important).
-->
<!ELEMENT (%heading;)  - - (%inline;)* -- heading -->
<!ATTLIST (%heading;)
    %attrs;                                -- %coreattrs, %i18n, %events --
    %align;                                -- align, text alignment --
    >
<!--==================== Preformatted Text ===============================-->
<!-- excludes markup for images and changes in font size -->
<!ENTITY % pre.exclusion "IMG|OBJECT|APPLET|BIG|SMALL|SUB|SUP|FONT|BASEFONT">
<!ELEMENT PRE - - (%inline;)* -(%pre.exclusion;) -- preformatted text -->
```

```
<!ATTLIST PRE
  %attrs;                                -- %coreattrs, %i18n, %events --
  width        NUMBER        #IMPLIED
  >
<!--====================== Inline Quotes ====================================-->
<!ELEMENT Q - - (%inline;)*             -- short inline quotation -->
<!ATTLIST Q
  %attrs;                                -- %coreattrs, %i18n, %events --
  cite         %URI;         #IMPLIED -- URI for source document or msg --
  >
<!--==================== Block-like Quotes ==================================-->
<!ELEMENT BLOCKQUOTE - - (%flow;)*      -- long quotation -->
<!ATTLIST BLOCKQUOTE
  %attrs;                                -- %coreattrs, %i18n, %events --
  cite         %URI;         #IMPLIED -- URI for source document or msg --
  >
<!--==================== Inserted/Deleted Text ==============================-->
<!-- INS/DEL are handled by inclusion on BODY -->
<!ELEMENT (INS|DEL) - - (%flow;)*       -- inserted text, deleted text -->
<!ATTLIST (INS|DEL)
  %attrs;                                -- %coreattrs, %i18n, %events --
  cite         %URI;         #IMPLIED -- info on reason for change --
  datetime     %Datetime;    #IMPLIED -- date and time of change --
  >
<!--==================== Lists ===============================================-->
<!-- definition lists - DT for term, DD for its definition -->
<!ELEMENT DL - - (DT|DD)+               -- definition list -->
<!ATTLIST DL
  %attrs;                                -- %coreattrs, %i18n, %events --
  compact     (compact)     #IMPLIED -- reduced interitem spacing --
  >
<!ELEMENT DT - O (%inline;)*            -- definition term -->
<!ELEMENT DD - O (%flow;)*              -- definition description -->
<!ATTLIST (DT|DD)
  %attrs;                                -- %coreattrs, %i18n, %events --
  >
<!-- Ordered lists (OL) numbering style
    1    arablic numbers    1, 2, 3, ...
    a    lower alpha        a, b, c, ...
    A    upper alpha        A, B, C, ...
    i    lower roman        i, ii, iii, ...
    I    upper roman        I, II, III, ...
    The style is applied to the sequence number which by default
    is reset to 1 for the first list item in an ordered list.
    This can't be expressed directly in SGML due to case folding.
  -->
<!ENTITY % OLStyle "CDATA"              -- constrained to: "(1|a|A|i|I)" -->
<!ELEMENT OL - - (LI)+                  -- ordered list -->
<!ATTLIST OL
  %attrs;                                -- %coreattrs, %i18n, %events --
  type         %OLStyle;     #IMPLIED -- numbering style --
  compact     (compact)     #IMPLIED -- reduced interitem spacing --
  start        NUMBER        #IMPLIED -- starting sequence number --
  >
```

```
<!-- Unordered Lists (UL) bullet styles -->
<!ENTITY % ULStyle "(disc|square|circle)">
<!ELEMENT UL - - (LI)+              -- unordered list -->
<!ATTLIST UL
  %attrs;                           -- %coreattrs, %i18n, %events --
  type        %ULStyle;   #IMPLIED  -- bullet style --
  compact     (compact)   #IMPLIED  -- reduced interitem spacing --
  >
<!ELEMENT (DIR|MENU) - - (LI)+ -(%block;) -- directory list, menu list -->
<!ATTLIST DIR
  %attrs;                           -- %coreattrs, %i18n, %events --
  compact     (compact)   #IMPLIED  -- reduced interitem spacing --
  >
<!ATTLIST MENU
  %attrs;                           -- %coreattrs, %i18n, %events --
  compact     (compact)   #IMPLIED  -- reduced interitem spacing --
  >
<!ENTITY % LIStyle "CDATA"          -- constrained to: "(%ULStyle;|%OLStyle;)" -->
<!ELEMENT LI - O (%flow;)*          -- list item -->
<!ATTLIST LI
  %attrs;                           -- %coreattrs, %i18n, %events --
  type        %LIStyle;   #IMPLIED  -- list item style --
  value       NUMBER      #IMPLIED  -- reset sequence number --
  >
<!--================= Forms ====================================-->
<!ELEMENT FORM - - (%flow;)* -(FORM)  -- interactive form -->
<!ATTLIST FORM
  %attrs;                           -- %coreattrs, %i18n, %events --
  action      %URI;       #REQUIRED -- server-side form handler --
  method     .(GET|POST)  GET       -- HTTP method used to submit the form--
  enctype     %ContentType; "application/x-www-form-urlencoded"
  accept      %ContentTypes; #IMPLIED -- list of MIME types for file upload --
  name        CDATA       #IMPLIED  -- name of form for scripting --
  onsubmit    %Script;    #IMPLIED  -- the form was submitted --
  onreset     %Script;    #IMPLIED  -- the form was reset --
  target      %FrameTarget; #IMPLIED -- render in this frame --
  accept-charset %Charsets; #IMPLIED -- list of supported charsets --
  >
<!-- Each label must not contain more than ONE field -->
<!ELEMENT LABEL - - (%inline;)* -(LABEL) -- form field label text -->
<!ATTLIST LABEL
  %attrs;                           -- %coreattrs, %i18n, %events --
  for         IDREF       #IMPLIED  -- matches field ID value --
  accesskey   %Character; #IMPLIED  -- accessibility key character --
  onfocus     %Script;    #IMPLIED  -- the element got the focus --
  onblur      %Script;    #IMPLIED  -- the element lost the focus --
  >
<!ENTITY % InputType
  "(TEXT | PASSWORD | CHECKBOX |
    RADIO | SUBMIT | RESET |
    FILE | HIDDEN | IMAGE | BUTTON)"
  >
```

```
<!-- attribute name required for all but submit and reset -->
<!ELEMENT INPUT - O EMPTY                    -- form control -->
<!ATTLIST INPUT
  %attrs;                                    -- %coreattrs, %i18n, %events --
  type        %InputType;    TEXT            -- what kind of widget is needed --
  name        CDATA          #IMPLIED        -- submit as part of form --
  value       CDATA          #IMPLIED        -- specify for radio buttons and checkboxes --
  checked     (checked)      #IMPLIED        -- for radio buttons and checkboxes --
  disabled    (disabled)     #IMPLIED        -- unavailable in this context --
  readonly    (readonly)     #IMPLIED        -- for text and passwd --
  size        CDATA          #IMPLIED        -- specific to each type of field --
  maxlength   NUMBER         #IMPLIED        -- max chars for text fields --
  src         %URI;          #IMPLIED        -- for fields with images --
  alt         CDATA          #IMPLIED        -- short description --
  usemap      %URI;          #IMPLIED        -- use client-side image map --
  ismap       (ismap)        #IMPLIED        -- use server-side image map --
  tabindex    NUMBER         #IMPLIED        -- position in tabbing order --
  accesskey   %Character;    #IMPLIED        -- accessibility key character --
  onfocus     %Script;       #IMPLIED        -- the element got the focus --
  onblur      %Script;       #IMPLIED        -- the element lost the focus --
  onselect    %Script;       #IMPLIED        -- some text was selected --
  onchange    %Script;       #IMPLIED        -- the element value was changed --
  accept      %ContentTypes; #IMPLIED        -- list of MIME types for file upload --
  align       %IAlign;       #IMPLIED        -- vertical or horizontal alignment --
  %reserved;                                 -- reserved for possible future use --
  >
<!ELEMENT SELECT - - (OPTGROUP|OPTION)+ -- option selector -->
<!ATTLIST SELECT
  %attrs;                                    -- %coreattrs, %i18n, %events --
  name        CDATA          #IMPLIED        -- field name --
  size        NUMBER         #IMPLIED        -- rows visible --
  multiple    (multiple)     #IMPLIED        -- default is single selection --
  disabled    (disabled)     #IMPLIED        -- unavailable in this context --
  tabindex    NUMBER         #IMPLIED        -- position in tabbing order --
  onfocus     %Script;       #IMPLIED        -- the element got the focus --
  onblur      %Script;       #IMPLIED        -- the element lost the focus --
  onchange    %Script;       #IMPLIED        -- the element value was changed --
  %reserved;                                 -- reserved for possible future use --
  >
<!ELEMENT OPTGROUP - - (OPTION)+ -- option group -->
<!ATTLIST OPTGROUP
  %attrs;                                    -- %coreattrs, %i18n, %events --
  disabled    (disabled)     #IMPLIED        -- unavailable in this context --
  label       %Text;         #REQUIRED       -- for use in hierarchical menus --
  >
<!ELEMENT OPTION - O (#PCDATA)            -- selectable choice -->
<!ATTLIST OPTION
  %attrs;                                    -- %coreattrs, %i18n, %events --
  selected    (selected)     #IMPLIED
  disabled    (disabled)     #IMPLIED        -- unavailable in this context --
  label       %Text;         #IMPLIED        -- for use in hierarchical menus --
  value       CDATA          #IMPLIED        -- defaults to element content --
  >
```

```
<!ELEMENT TEXTAREA - - (#PCDATA)        -- multi-line text field -->
<!ATTLIST TEXTAREA
  %attrs;                               -- %coreattrs, %i18n, %events --
  name        CDATA          #IMPLIED
  rows        NUMBER         #REQUIRED
  cols        NUMBER         #REQUIRED
  disabled    (disabled)     #IMPLIED   -- unavailable in this context --
  readonly    (readonly)     #IMPLIED
  tabindex    NUMBER         #IMPLIED   -- position in tabbing order --
  accesskey   %Character;    #IMPLIED   -- accessibility key character --
  onfocus     %Script;       #IMPLIED   -- the element got the focus --
  onblur      %Script;       #IMPLIED   -- the element lost the focus --
  onselect    %Script;       #IMPLIED   -- some text was selected --
  onchange    %Script;       #IMPLIED   -- the element value was changed --
  %reserved;                            -- reserved for possible future use --
  >
<!--
  #PCDATA is to solve the mixed content problem,
  per specification only whitespace is allowed there!
  -->
<!ELEMENT FIELDSET - - (#PCDATA,LEGEND,(%flow;)*) -- form control group -->
<!ATTLIST FIELDSET
  %attrs;                               -- %coreattrs, %i18n, %events --
  >
<!ELEMENT LEGEND - - (%inline;)*        -- fieldset legend -->
<!ENTITY % LAlign "(top|bottom|left|right)">
<!ATTLIST LEGEND
  %attrs;                               -- %coreattrs, %i18n, %events --
  accesskey   %Character;    #IMPLIED   -- accessibility key character --
  align       %LAlign;       #IMPLIED   -- relative to fieldset --
  >
<!ELEMENT BUTTON - -
     (%flow;)* -(A|%formctrl;|FORM|ISINDEX|FIELDSET|IFRAME)
     -- push button -->
<!ATTLIST BUTTON
  %attrs;                               -- %coreattrs, %i18n, %events --
  name        CDATA          #IMPLIED
  value       CDATA          #IMPLIED   -- sent to server when submitted --
  type        (button|submit|reset) submit -- for use as form button --
  disabled    (disabled)     #IMPLIED   -- unavailable in this context --
  tabindex    NUMBER         #IMPLIED   -- position in tabbing order --
  accesskey   %Character;    #IMPLIED   -- accessibility key character --
  onfocus     %Script;       #IMPLIED   -- the element got the focus --
  onblur      %Script;       #IMPLIED   -- the element lost the focus --
  %reserved;                            -- reserved for possible future use --
  >
<!--======================= Tables =========================================-->
<!-- IETF HTML table standard, see [RFC1942] -->
<!--
  The BORDER attribute sets the thickness of the frame around the
  table. The default units are screen pixels.
  The FRAME attribute specifies which parts of the frame around
```

```
the table should be rendered. The values are not the same as
CALS to avoid a name clash with the VALIGN attribute.
The value "border" is included for backwards compatibility with
<TABLE BORDER> which yields frame=border and border=implied
For <TABLE BORDER=1> you get border=1 and frame=implied. In this
case, it is appropriate to treat this as frame=border for backwards
compatibility with deployed browsers.
-->
<!ENTITY % TFrame "(void|above|below|hsides|lhs|rhs|vsides|box|border)">
<!--
The RULES attribute defines which rules to draw between cells:
If RULES is absent then assume:
    "none" if BORDER is absent or BORDER=0 otherwise "all"
-->
<!ENTITY % TRules "(none | groups | rows | cols | all)">

<!-- horizontal placement of table relative to document -->
<!ENTITY % TAlign "(left|center|right)">
<!-- horizontal alignment attributes for cell contents -->
<!ENTITY % cellhalign
   "align       (left|center|right|justify|char) #IMPLIED
    char        %Character;    #IMPLIED -- alignment char, e.g. char=':' --
    charoff     %Length;       #IMPLIED -- offset for alignment char --"
   >
<!-- vertical alignment attributes for cell contents -->
<!ENTITY % cellvalign
   "valign      (top|middle|bottom|baseline) #IMPLIED"
   >
<!ELEMENT TABLE - -
     (CAPTION?, (COL*|COLGROUP*), THEAD?, TFOOT?, TBODY+)>
<!ELEMENT CAPTION  - - (%inline;)*      -- table caption -->
<!ELEMENT THEAD    - O (TR)+            -- table header -->
<!ELEMENT TFOOT    - O (TR)+            -- table footer -->
<!ELEMENT TBODY    O O (TR)+            -- table body -->
<!ELEMENT COLGROUP - O (COL)*           -- table column group -->
<!ELEMENT COL      - O EMPTY            -- table column -->
<!ELEMENT TR       - O (TH|TD)+         -- table row -->
<!ELEMENT (TH|TD)  - O (%flow;)*        -- table header cell, table data cell-->
<!ATTLIST TABLE                         -- table element --
   %attrs;                              -- %coreattrs, %i18n, %events --
   summary     %Text;        #IMPLIED   -- purpose/structure for speech output--
   width       %Length;      #IMPLIED   -- table width --
   border      %Pixels;      #IMPLIED   -- controls frame width around table --
   frame       %TFrame;      #IMPLIED   -- which parts of frame to render --
   rules       %TRules;      #IMPLIED   -- rulings between rows and cols --
   cellspacing %Length;      #IMPLIED   -- spacing between cells --
   cellpadding %Length;      #IMPLIED   -- spacing within cells --
   align       %TAlign;      #IMPLIED   -- table position relative to window --
   bgcolor     %Color;       #IMPLIED   -- background color for cells --
   %reserved;                           -- reserved for possible future use --
   datapagesize CDATA        #IMPLIED   -- reserved for possible future use --
   >
```

```
<!ENTITY % CAlign "(top|bottom|left|right)">
<!ATTLIST CAPTION
  %attrs;                            -- %coreattrs, %i18n, %events --
  align       %CAlign;      #IMPLIED -- relative to table --
  >
<!--
COLGROUP groups a set of COL elements. It allows you to group
several semantically related columns together.
-->
<!ATTLIST COLGROUP
  %attrs;                            -- %coreattrs, %i18n, %events --
  span        NUMBER        1        -- default number of columns in group --
  width       %MultiLength; #IMPLIED -- default width for enclosed COLs --
  %cellhalign;                       -- horizontal alignment in cells --
  %cellvalign;                       -- vertical alignment in cells --
  >
<!--
COL elements define the alignment properties for cells in
one or more columns.
The WIDTH attribute specifies the width of the columns, e.g.
    width=64        width in screen pixels
    width=0.5*      relative width of 0.5
The SPAN attribute causes the attributes of one
COL element to apply to more than one column.
-->
<!ATTLIST COL                        -- column groups and properties --
  %attrs;                            -- %coreattrs, %i18n, %events --
  span        NUMBER        1        -- COL attributes affect N columns --
  width       %MultiLength; #IMPLIED -- column width specification --
  %cellhalign;                       -- horizontal alignment in cells --
  %cellvalign;                       -- vertical alignment in cells --
  >
<!--
    Use THEAD to duplicate headers when breaking table
    across page boundaries, or for static headers when
    TBODY sections are rendered in scrolling panel.
    Use TFOOT to duplicate footers when breaking table
    across page boundaries, or for static footers when
    TBODY sections are rendered in scrolling panel.
    Use multiple TBODY sections when rules are needed
    between groups of table rows.
-->
<!ATTLIST (THEAD|TBODY|TFOOT)        -- table section --
  %attrs;                            -- %coreattrs, %i18n, %events --
  %cellhalign;                       -- horizontal alignment in cells --
  %cellvalign;                       -- vertical alignment in cells --
  >
<!ATTLIST TR                         -- table row --
  %attrs;                            -- %coreattrs, %i18n, %events --
  %cellhalign;                       -- horizontal alignment in cells --
  %cellvalign;                       -- vertical alignment in cells --
  bgcolor     %Color;       #IMPLIED -- background color for row --
  >
```

```
<!-- Scope is simpler than headers attribute for common tables -->
<!ENTITY % Scope "(row|col|rowgroup|colgroup)">
<!-- TH is for headers, TD for data, but for cells acting as both use TD -->
<!ATTLIST (TH|TD)                            -- header or data cell --
  %attrs;                                    -- %coreattrs, %i18n, %events --
  abbr        %Text;        #IMPLIED -- abbreviation for header cell --
  axis        CDATA         #IMPLIED -- comma-separated list of related headers--
  headers     IDREFS        #IMPLIED -- list of id's for header cells --
  scope       %Scope;       #IMPLIED -- scope covered by header cells --
  rowspan     NUMBER        1        -- number of rows spanned by cell --
  colspan     NUMBER        1        -- number of cols spanned by cell --
  %cellhalign;                       -- horizontal alignment in cells --
  %cellvalign;                       -- vertical alignment in cells --
  nowrap      (nowrap)      #IMPLIED -- suppress word wrap --
  bgcolor     %Color;       #IMPLIED -- cell background color --
  width       %Length;      #IMPLIED -- width for cell --
  height      %Length;      #IMPLIED -- height for cell --
  >
<!--================== Document Frames ======================================-->
<!--
  The content model for HTML documents depends on whether the HEAD is
  followed by a FRAMESET or BODY element. The widespread omission of
  the BODY start tag makes it impractical to define the content model
  without the use of a marked section.
-->
<![ %HTML.Frameset; [
<!ELEMENT FRAMESET - - ((FRAMESET|FRAME)+ & NOFRAMES?) -- window subdivision-->
<!ATTLIST FRAMESET
  %coreattrs;                             -- id, class, style, title --
  rows       %MultiLengths; #IMPLIED -- list of lengths, default: 100% (1 row) --
  cols       %MultiLengths; #IMPLIED -- list of lengths, default: 100% (1 col) --
  onload     %Script;       #IMPLIED -- all the frames have been loaded   --
  onunload   %Script;       #IMPLIED -- all the frames have been removed --
  >
]]>
<![ %HTML.Frameset; [
<!-- reserved frame names start with "_" otherwise starts with letter -->
<!ELEMENT FRAME - O EMPTY              -- subwindow -->
<!ATTLIST FRAME
  %coreattrs;                             -- id, class, style, title --
  longdesc    %URI;         #IMPLIED -- link to long description
                                         (complements title) --
  name         CDATA        #IMPLIED -- name of frame for targetting --
  src          %URI;        #IMPLIED -- source of frame content --
  frameborder (1|0)         1        -- request frame borders? --
  marginwidth %Pixels;      #IMPLIED -- margin widths in pixels --
  marginheight %Pixels;     #IMPLIED -- margin height in pixels --
  noresize    (noresize)    #IMPLIED -- allow users to resize frames? --
  scrolling   (yes|no|auto) auto     -- scrollbar or none --
  >
]]>
```

```
<!ELEMENT IFRAME - - (%flow;)*         -- inline subwindow -->
<!ATTLIST IFRAME
  %coreattrs;                          -- id, class, style, title --
  longdesc     %URI;         #IMPLIED  -- link to long description
                                          (complements title) --
  name         CDATA         #IMPLIED  -- name of frame for targetting --
  src          %URI;         #IMPLIED  -- source of frame content --
  frameborder (1|0)          1         -- request frame borders? --
  marginwidth %Pixels;       #IMPLIED  -- margin widths in pixels --
  marginheight %Pixels;      #IMPLIED  -- margin height in pixels --
  scrolling   (yes|no|auto)  auto      -- scrollbar or none --
  align       %IAlign;       #IMPLIED  -- vertical or horizontal alignment --
  height      %Length;       #IMPLIED  -- frame height --
  width       %Length;       #IMPLIED  -- frame width --
  >
<![ %HTML.Frameset; [
<!ENTITY % noframes.content "(BODY) -(NOFRAMES)">
]]>
<!ENTITY % noframes.content "(%flow;)*">
<!ELEMENT NOFRAMES - - %noframes.content;
 -- alternate content container for non frame-based rendering -->
<!ATTLIST NOFRAMES
  %attrs;                              -- %coreattrs, %i18n, %events --
  >
<!--================= Document Head =========================================-->
<!-- %head.misc; defined earlier on as "SCRIPT|STYLE|META|LINK|OBJECT" -->
<!ENTITY % head.content "TITLE & ISINDEX? & BASE?">
<!ELEMENT HEAD O O (%head.content;) +(%head.misc;) -- document head -->
<!ATTLIST HEAD
  %i18n;                               -- lang, dir --
  profile      %URI;         #IMPLIED  -- named dictionary of meta info --
  >
<!-- The TITLE element is not considered part of the flow of text.
     It should be displayed, for example as the page header or
     window title. Exactly one title is required per document.
  -->
<!ELEMENT TITLE - - (#PCDATA) -(%head.misc;) -- document title -->
<!ATTLIST TITLE %i18n>
<!ELEMENT ISINDEX - O EMPTY            -- single line prompt -->
<!ATTLIST ISINDEX
  %coreattrs;                          -- id, class, style, title --
  %i18n;                               -- lang, dir --
  prompt      %Text;         #IMPLIED  -- prompt message -->  ·
<!ELEMENT BASE - O EMPTY               -- document base URI -->
<!ATTLIST BASE
  href        %URI;          #IMPLIED  -- URI that acts as base URI --
  target      %FrameTarget;  #IMPLIED  -- render in this frame --
  >
<!ELEMENT META - O EMPTY               -- generic metainformation -->
<!ATTLIST META
  %i18n;                               -- lang, dir, for use with content --
  http-equiv  NAME           #IMPLIED  -- HTTP response header name   --
  name        NAME           #IMPLIED  -- metainformation name --
```

```
    content     CDATA           #REQUIRED -- associated information --
    scheme      CDATA           #IMPLIED  -- select form of content --
    >
<!ELEMENT STYLE - - %StyleSheet        -- style info -->
<!ATTLIST STYLE
    %i18n;                                 -- lang, dir, for use with title --
    type        %ContentType;   #REQUIRED -- content type of style language --
    media       %MediaDesc;     #IMPLIED  -- designed for use with these media --
    title       %Text;          #IMPLIED  -- advisory title --
    >
<!ELEMENT SCRIPT - - %Script;          -- script statements -->
<!ATTLIST SCRIPT
    charset     %Charset;       #IMPLIED  -- char encoding of linked resource --
    type        %ContentType;   #REQUIRED -- content type of script language --
    language    CDATA           #IMPLIED  -- predefined script language name --
    src         %URI;           #IMPLIED  -- URI for an external script --
    defer       (defer)         #IMPLIED  -- UA may defer execution of script --
    event       CDATA           #IMPLIED  -- reserved for possible future use --
    for         %URI;           #IMPLIED  -- reserved for possible future use --
    >
<!ELEMENT NOSCRIPT - - (%flow;)*
    -- alternate content container for non script-based rendering -->
<!ATTLIST NOSCRIPT
    %attrs;                                -- %coreattrs, %i18n, %events --
    >
<!--================= Document Structure ===================================-->
<!ENTITY % version "version CDATA #FIXED '%HTML.Version;'">
<![ %HTML.Frameset; [
<!ENTITY % html.content "HEAD, FRAMESET">
]]>
<!ENTITY % html.content "HEAD, BODY">
<!ELEMENT HTML O O (%html.content;)    -- document root element -->
<!ATTLIST HTML
    %i18n;                                 -- lang, dir --
    %version;
    >
```

The XHTML 1.0 DTD

The XHTML 1.0 standard is formally defined as three Extensible Markup Language (XML) Document Type Definitions (DTDs): the Strict DTD, the Transitional DTD, and the Frameset DTD. These DTDs correspond to the respective HTML 4.01 DTDs, defining the same elements and attributes using XML rather than the Standard Generalized Markup Language (SGML) as the DTD authoring language.

The Strict DTD defines only those elements that are not deprecated in the HTML 4. 01 standard. Ideally, everyone would create XHTML documents that conform to the Strict DTD. The Transitional DTD includes all those deprecated elements and more accurately reflects the HTML in use today, with many older elements still in common use. The Frameset DTD is identical to the Transitional DTD, with the exception that the document <body> is replaced by the <frameset> element.

Since the HTML Transitional DTD is the one upon which this book is based, it is only appropriate that we include the corresponding XHTML DTD. Note that we have reprinted this DTD verbatim and have not attempted to add extensions to it. Where our description and the DTD deviate, assume the DTD is correct:

```
<!--
    Extensible HTML version 1.0 Transitional DTD
    This is the same as HTML 4.0 Transitional except for
    changes due to the differences between XML and SGML.
    Namespace = http://www.w3.org/1999/xhtml
    For further information, see: http://www.w3.org/TR/xhtml1
    Copyright (c) 1998-2000 W3C (MIT, INRIA, Keio),
    All Rights Reserved.
    This DTD module is identified by the PUBLIC and SYSTEM identifiers:
    PUBLIC "-//W3C//DTD XHTML 1.0 Transitional//EN"
    SYSTEM "http://www.w3.org/TR/xhtml1/DTD/xhtml1-transitional.dtd"
```

```
    $Revision: 1.17 $
    $Date: 2006/09/27 15:34:26 $
-->
<!--================= Character mnemonic entities =========================-->
<!ENTITY % HTMLlat1 PUBLIC
    "-//W3C//ENTITIES Latin 1 for XHTML//EN"
    "xhtml-lat1.ent">
%HTMLlat1;
<!ENTITY % HTMLsymbol PUBLIC
    "-//W3C//ENTITIES Symbols for XHTML//EN"
    "xhtml-symbol.ent">
%HTMLsymbol;
<!ENTITY % HTMLspecial PUBLIC
    "-//W3C//ENTITIES Special for XHTML//EN"
    "xhtml-special.ent">
%HTMLspecial;
<!--=================== Imported Names =====================================-->
<!ENTITY % ContentType "CDATA">
    <!-- media type, as per [RFC2045] -->
<!ENTITY % ContentTypes "CDATA">
    <!-- comma-separated list of media types, as per [RFC2045] -->
<!ENTITY % Charset "CDATA">
    <!-- a character encoding, as per [RFC2045] -->
<!ENTITY % Charsets "CDATA">
    <!-- a space separated list of character encodings, as per [RFC2045] -->
<!ENTITY % LanguageCode "NMTOKEN">
    <!-- a language code, as per [RFC1766] -->
<!ENTITY % Character "CDATA">
    <!-- a single character from [ISO10646] -->
<!ENTITY % Number "CDATA">
    <!-- one or more digits -->
<!ENTITY % LinkTypes "CDATA">
    <!-- space-separated list of link types -->
<!ENTITY % MediaDesc "CDATA">
    <!-- single or comma-separated list of media descriptors -->
<!ENTITY % URI "CDATA">
    <!-- a Uniform Resource Identifier, see [RFC2396] -->
<!ENTITY % UriList "CDATA">
    <!-- a space separated list of Uniform Resource Identifiers -->
<!ENTITY % Datetime "CDATA">
    <!-- date and time information. ISO date format -->
<!ENTITY % Script "CDATA">
    <!-- script expression -->
<!ENTITY % StyleSheet "CDATA">
    <!-- style sheet data -->
<!ENTITY % Text "CDATA">
    <!-- used for titles etc. -->
<!ENTITY % FrameTarget "NMTOKEN">
    <!-- render in this frame -->
<!ENTITY % Length "CDATA">
    <!-- nn for pixels or nn% for percentage length -->
<!ENTITY % MultiLength "CDATA">
    <!-- pixel, percentage, or relative -->
<!ENTITY % MultiLengths "CDATA">
    <!-- comma-separated list of MultiLength -->
```

```
<!ENTITY % Pixels "CDATA">
    <!-- integer representing length in pixels -->
<!-- these are used for image maps -->
<!ENTITY % Shape "(rect|circle|poly|default)">
<!ENTITY % Coords "CDATA">
    <!-- comma separated list of lengths -->
<!-- used for object, applet, img, input and iframe -->
<!ENTITY % ImgAlign "(top|middle|bottom|left|right)">
<!-- a color using sRGB: #RRGGBB as Hex values -->
<!ENTITY % Color "CDATA">
<!-- There are also 16 widely known color names with their sRGB values:
    Black  = #000000    Green  = #008000
    Silver = #C0C0C0    Lime   = #00FF00
    Gray   = #808080    Olive  = #808000
    White  = #FFFFFF    Yellow = #FFFF00
    Maroon = #800000    Navy   = #000080
    Red    = #FF0000    Blue   = #0000FF
    Purple = #800080    Teal   = #008080
    Fuchsia= #FF00FF    Aqua   = #00FFFF
-->
<!--==================== Generic Attributes ============================-->
<!-- core attributes common to most elements
  id        document-wide unique id
  class     space separated list of classes
  style     associated style info
  title     advisory title/amplification
-->
<!ENTITY % coreattrs
 "id         ID              #IMPLIED
  class      CDATA           #IMPLIED
  style      %StyleSheet;    #IMPLIED
  title      %Text;          #IMPLIED"
  >
<!-- internationalization attributes
  lang        language code (backwards compatible)
  xml:lang    language code (as per XML 1.0 spec)
  dir         direction for weak/neutral text
-->
<!ENTITY % i18n
 "lang        %LanguageCode; #IMPLIED
  xml:lang    %LanguageCode; #IMPLIED
  dir         (ltr|rtl)      #IMPLIED"
  >
<!-- attributes for common UI events
  onclick       a pointer button was clicked
  ondblclick    a pointer button was double clicked
  onmousedown   a pointer button was pressed down
  onmouseup     a pointer button was released
  onmousemove   a pointer was moved onto the element
  onmouseout    a pointer was moved away from the element
  onkeypress    a key was pressed and released
  onkeydown     a key was pressed down
  onkeyup       a key was released
-->
```

```
<!ENTITY % events
 "onclick      %Script;      #IMPLIED
  ondblclick   %Script;      #IMPLIED
  onmousedown  %Script;      #IMPLIED
  onmouseup    %Script;      #IMPLIED
  onmouseover  %Script;      #IMPLIED
  onmousemove  %Script;      #IMPLIED
  onmouseout   %Script;      #IMPLIED
  onkeypress   %Script;      #IMPLIED
  onkeydown    %Script;      #IMPLIED
  onkeyup      %Script;      #IMPLIED"
  >
<!-- attributes for elements that can get the focus
  accesskey    accessibility key character
  tabindex     position in tabbing order
  onfocus      the element got the focus
  onblur       the element lost the focus
-->
<!ENTITY % focus
 "accesskey    %Character;   #IMPLIED
  tabindex     %Number;      #IMPLIED
  onfocus      %Script;      #IMPLIED
  onblur       %Script;      #IMPLIED"
  >
<!ENTITY % attrs "%coreattrs; %i18n; %events;">
<!-- text alignment for p, div, h1-h6. The default is
     align="left" for ltr headings, "right" for rtl -->
<!ENTITY % TextAlign "align (left|center|right) #IMPLIED">
<!--==================== Text Elements ========================================-->
<!ENTITY % special
    "br | span | bdo | object | applet | img | map | iframe">
<!ENTITY % fontstyle "tt | i | b | big | small | u
                      | s | strike |font | basefont">
<!ENTITY % phrase "em | strong | dfn | code | q | sub | sup |
                   samp | kbd | var | cite | abbr | acronym">
<!ENTITY % inline.forms "input | select | textarea | label | button">
<!-- these can occur at block or inline level -->
<!ENTITY % misc "ins | del | script | noscript">
<!ENTITY % inline "a | %special; | %fontstyle; | %phrase; | %inline.forms;">
<!-- %Inline; covers inline or "text-level" elements -->
<!ENTITY % Inline "(#PCDATA | %inline; | %misc;)*">
<!--==================== Block level elements ==============================-->
<!ENTITY % heading "h1|h2|h3|h4|h5|h6">
<!ENTITY % lists "ul | ol | dl | menu | dir">
<!ENTITY % blocktext "pre | hr | blockquote | address | center | noframes">
<!ENTITY % block
    "p | %heading; | div | %lists; | %blocktext; | isindex |fieldset | table">
<!ENTITY % Block "(%block; | form | %misc;)*">
<!-- %Flow; mixes Block and Inline and is used for list items etc. -->
<!ENTITY % Flow "(#PCDATA | %block; | form | %inline; | %misc;)*">
<!--==================== Content models for exclusions =====================-->
<!-- a elements use %Inline; excluding a -->
```

```
<!ENTITY % a.content
    "(#PCDATA | %special; | %fontstyle; | %phrase; | %inline.forms; | %misc;)*">
<!-- pre uses %Inline excluding img, object, applet, big, small,
     sub, sup, font, or basefont -->
<!ENTITY % pre.content
    "(#PCDATA | a | br | span | bdo | map | tt | i | b | u | s |
     %phrase; | %inline.forms;)*">
<!-- form uses %Flow; excluding form -->
<!ENTITY % form.content "(#PCDATA | %block; | %inline; | %misc;)*">
<!-- button uses %Flow; but excludes a, form, form controls, iframe -->
<!ENTITY % button.content
    "(#PCDATA | p | %heading; | div | %lists; | %blocktext; |
     table | br | span | bdo | object | applet | img | map |
     %fontstyle; | %phrase; | %misc;)*">
<!--================= Document Structure ====================================-->
<!-- the namespace URI designates the document profile -->
<!ELEMENT html (head, body)>
<!ATTLIST html
  %i18n;
  xmlns       %URI;        #FIXED 'http://www.w3.org/1999/xhtml'
  >
<!--================= Document Head =========================================-->
<!ENTITY % head.misc "(script|style|meta|link|object|isindex)*">
<!-- content model is %head.misc; combined with a single
     title and an optional base element in any order -->
<!ELEMENT head (%head.misc;,
     ((title, %head.misc;, (base, %head.misc;)?) |
     (base, %head.misc;, (title, %head.misc;))))>
<!ATTLIST head
  %i18n;
  profile     %URI;        #IMPLIED
  >
<!-- The title element is not considered part of the flow of text.
       It should be displayed, for example as the page header or
       window title. Exactly one title is required per document.
    -->
<!ELEMENT title (#PCDATA)>
<!ATTLIST title %i18n;>
<!-- document base URI -->
<!ELEMENT base EMPTY>
<!ATTLIST base
  href        %URI;        #IMPLIED
  target      %FrameTarget; #IMPLIED
  >
<!-- generic metainformation -->
<!ELEMENT meta EMPTY>
<!ATTLIST meta
  %i18n;
  http-equiv  CDATA        #IMPLIED
  name        CDATA        #IMPLIED
  content     CDATA        #REQUIRED
  scheme      CDATA        #IMPLIED
  >
```

```
<!--
   Relationship values can be used in principle:

     a) for document specific toolbars/menus when used
        with the link element in document head e.g.
        start, contents, previous, next, index, end, help
     b) to link to a separate style sheet (rel="stylesheet")
     c) to make a link to a script (rel="script")
     d) by stylesheets to control how collections of
        html nodes are rendered into printed documents
     e) to make a link to a printable version of this document
        e.g. a PostScript or PDF version (rel="alternate" media="print")
-->
<!ELEMENT link EMPTY>
<!ATTLIST link
  %attrs;
  charset      %Charset;       #IMPLIED
  href         %URI;           #IMPLIED
  hreflang     %LanguageCode;  #IMPLIED
  type         %ContentType;   #IMPLIED
  rel          %LinkTypes;     #IMPLIED
  rev          %LinkTypes;     #IMPLIED
  media        %MediaDesc;     #IMPLIED
  target       %FrameTarget;   #IMPLIED
  >
<!-- style info, which may include CDATA sections -->
<!ELEMENT style (#PCDATA)>
<!ATTLIST style
  %i18n;
  type         %ContentType;   #REQUIRED
  media        %MediaDesc;     #IMPLIED
  title        %Text;          #IMPLIED
  xml:space    (preserve)      #FIXED 'preserve'
  >
<!-- script statements, which may include CDATA sections -->
<!ELEMENT script (#PCDATA)>
<!ATTLIST script
  charset      %Charset;       #IMPLIED
  type         %ContentType;   #REQUIRED
  language     CDATA           #IMPLIED
  src          %URI;           #IMPLIED
  defer        (defer)         #IMPLIED
  xml:space    (preserve)      #FIXED 'preserve'
  >
<!-- alternate content container for non script-based rendering -->
<!ELEMENT noscript %Flow;>
<!ATTLIST noscript
  %attrs;
  >
<!--======================= Frames =========================================-->
<!-- inline subwindow -->
<!ELEMENT iframe %Flow;>
<!ATTLIST iframe
  %coreattrs;
  longdesc     %URI;           #IMPLIED
```

```
  name         NMTOKEN        #IMPLIED
  src          %URI;          #IMPLIED
  frameborder (1|0)           "1"
  marginwidth %Pixels;        #IMPLIED
  marginheight %Pixels;       #IMPLIED
  scrolling    (yes|no|auto)  "auto"
  align        %ImgAlign;     #IMPLIED
  height       %Length;       #IMPLIED
  width        %Length;       #IMPLIED
  >
<!-- alternate content container for non frame-based rendering -->
<!ELEMENT noframes %Flow;>
<!ATTLIST noframes
  %attrs;
  >
<!--==================== Document Body =====================================-->
<!ELEMENT body %Flow;>
<!ATTLIST body
  %attrs;
  onload       %Script;       #IMPLIED
  onunload     %Script;       #IMPLIED
  background   %URI;          #IMPLIED
  bgcolor      %Color;        #IMPLIED
  text         %Color;        #IMPLIED
  link         %Color;        #IMPLIED
  vlink        %Color;        #IMPLIED
  alink        %Color;        #IMPLIED
  >
<!ELEMENT div %Flow;>  <!-- generic language/style container -->
<!ATTLIST div
  %attrs;
  %TextAlign;
  >
<!--==================== Paragraphs =======================================-->
<!ELEMENT p %Inline;>
<!ATTLIST p
  %attrs;
  %TextAlign;
  >
<!--==================== Headings =========================================-->
<!--
  There are six levels of headings from h1 (the most important)
  to h6 (the least important).
-->
<!ELEMENT h1  %Inline;>
<!ATTLIST h1
  %attrs;
  %TextAlign;
  >
<!ELEMENT h2 %Inline;>
<!ATTLIST h2
  %attrs;
  %TextAlign;
  >
```

```
<!ELEMENT h3 %Inline;>
<!ATTLIST h3
  %attrs;
  %TextAlign;
  >
<!ELEMENT h4 %Inline;>
<!ATTLIST h4
  %attrs;
  %TextAlign;
  >
<!ELEMENT h5 %Inline;>
<!ATTLIST h5
  %attrs;
  %TextAlign;
  >
<!ELEMENT h6 %Inline;>
<!ATTLIST h6
  %attrs;
  %TextAlign;
  >
<!--==================== Lists ========================================-->
<!-- Unordered list bullet styles -->
<!ENTITY % ULStyle "(disc|square|circle)">
<!-- Unordered list -->
<!ELEMENT ul (li)+>
<!ATTLIST ul
  %attrs;
  type        %ULStyle;     #IMPLIED
  compact     (compact)     #IMPLIED
  >
<!-- Ordered list numbering style
    1    arabic numbers     1, 2, 3, ...
    a    lower alpha        a, b, c, ...
    A    upper alpha        A, B, C, ...
    i    lower roman        i, ii, iii, ...
    I    upper roman        I, II, III, ...
    The style is applied to the sequence number which by default
    is reset to 1 for the first list item in an ordered list.
-->
<!ENTITY % OLStyle "CDATA">
<!-- Ordered (numbered) list -->
<!ELEMENT ol (li)+>
<!ATTLIST ol
  %attrs;
  type        %OLStyle;     #IMPLIED
  compact     (compact)     #IMPLIED
  start       %Number;      #IMPLIED
  >
<!-- single column list (DEPRECATED) -->
<!ELEMENT menu (li)+>
<!ATTLIST menu
  %attrs;
  compact     (compact)     #IMPLIED
  >
```

```
<!-- multiple column list (DEPRECATED) -->
<!ELEMENT dir (li)+>
<!ATTLIST dir
  %attrs;
  compact     (compact)     #IMPLIED
  >
<!-- LIStyle is constrained to: "(%ULStyle;|%OLStyle;)" -->
<!ENTITY % LIStyle "CDATA">
<!-- list item -->
<!ELEMENT li %Flow;>
<!ATTLIST li
  %attrs;
  type        %LIStyle;     #IMPLIED
  value       %Number;      #IMPLIED
  >
<!-- definition lists - dt for term, dd for its definition -->
<!ELEMENT dl (dt|dd)+>
<!ATTLIST dl
  %attrs;
  compact     (compact)     #IMPLIED
  >
<!ELEMENT dt %Inline;>
<!ATTLIST dt
  %attrs;
  >
<!ELEMENT dd %Flow;>
<!ATTLIST dd
  %attrs;
  >
<!--==================== Address ====================================-->
<!-- information on author -->
<!ELEMENT address %Inline;>
<!ATTLIST address
  %attrs;
  >
<!--==================== Horizontal Rule ===========================-->
<!ELEMENT hr EMPTY>
<!ATTLIST hr
  %attrs;
  align       (left|center|right) #IMPLIED
  noshade     (noshade)     #IMPLIED
  size        %Pixels;      #IMPLIED
  width       %Length;      #IMPLIED
  >
<!--==================== Preformatted Text =========================-->
<!-- content is %Inline; excluding
       "img|object|applet|big|small|sub|sup|font|basefont" -->
<!ELEMENT pre %pre.content;>
<!ATTLIST pre
  %attrs;
  width       %Number;      #IMPLIED
  xml:space   (preserve)    #FIXED 'preserve'
  >
```

```
<!--==================== Block-like Quotes ==================================-->
<!ELEMENT blockquote %Flow;>
<!ATTLIST blockquote
  %attrs;
  cite        %URI;         #IMPLIED
  >
<!--==================== Text alignment ====================================-->
<!-- center content -->
<!ELEMENT center %Flow;>
<!ATTLIST center
  %attrs;
  >
<!--==================== Inserted/Deleted Text ==============================-->
<!--
    ins/del are allowed in block and inline content, but its
    inappropriate to include block content within an ins element
    occurring in inline content.
-->
<!ELEMENT ins %Flow;>
<!ATTLIST ins
  %attrs;
  cite        %URI;         #IMPLIED
  datetime    %Datetime;    #IMPLIED
  >
<!ELEMENT del %Flow;>
<!ATTLIST del
  %attrs;
  cite        %URI;         #IMPLIED
  datetime    %Datetime;    #IMPLIED
  >
<!--==================== The Anchor Element =================================-->
<!-- content is %Inline; except that anchors shouldn't be nested -->
<!ELEMENT a %a.content;>
<!ATTLIST a
  %attrs;
  charset     %Charset;     #IMPLIED
  type        %ContentType; #IMPLIED
  name        NMTOKEN       #IMPLIED
  href        %URI;         #IMPLIED
  hreflang    %LanguageCode; #IMPLIED
  rel         %LinkTypes;   #IMPLIED
  rev         %LinkTypes;   #IMPLIED
  accesskey   %Character;   #IMPLIED
  shape       %Shape;       "rect"
  coords      %Coords;      #IMPLIED
  tabindex    %Number;      #IMPLIED
  onfocus     %Script;      #IMPLIED
  onblur      %Script;      #IMPLIED
  target      %FrameTarget; #IMPLIED
  >
<!--==================== Inline Elements ====================================-->
<!ELEMENT span %Inline;> <!-- generic language/style container -->
<!ATTLIST span
  %attrs;
  >
```

```
<!ELEMENT bdo %Inline;>  <!-- I18N BiDi over-ride -->
<!ATTLIST bdo
  %coreattrs;
  %events;
  lang        %LanguageCode; #IMPLIED
  xml:lang    %LanguageCode; #IMPLIED
  dir         (ltr|rtl)      #REQUIRED
  >
<!ELEMENT br EMPTY>   <!-- forced line break -->
<!ATTLIST br
  %coreattrs;
  clear       (left|all|right|none) "none"
  >
<!ELEMENT em %Inline;>   <!-- emphasis -->
<!ATTLIST em %attrs;>
<!ELEMENT strong %Inline;>   <!-- strong emphasis -->
<!ATTLIST strong %attrs;>
<!ELEMENT dfn %Inline;>   <!-- definitional -->
<!ATTLIST dfn %attrs;>
<!ELEMENT code %Inline;>   <!-- program code -->
<!ATTLIST code %attrs;>
<!ELEMENT samp %Inline;>   <!-- sample -->
<!ATTLIST samp %attrs;>
<!ELEMENT kbd %Inline;>  <!-- something user would type -->
<!ATTLIST kbd %attrs;>
<!ELEMENT var %Inline;>   <!-- variable -->
<!ATTLIST var %attrs;>
<!ELEMENT cite %Inline;>   <!-- citation -->
<!ATTLIST cite %attrs;>
<!ELEMENT abbr %Inline;>   <!-- abbreviation -->
<!ATTLIST abbr %attrs;>
<!ELEMENT acronym %Inline;>   <!-- acronym -->
<!ATTLIST acronym %attrs;>
<!ELEMENT q %Inline;>   <!-- inlined quote -->
<!ATTLIST q
  %attrs;
  cite        %URI;          #IMPLIED
  >
<!ELEMENT sub %Inline;> <!-- subscript -->
<!ATTLIST sub %attrs;>
<!ELEMENT sup %Inline;> <!-- superscript -->
<!ATTLIST sup %attrs;>
<!ELEMENT tt %Inline;>   <!-- fixed pitch font -->
<!ATTLIST tt %attrs;>
<!ELEMENT i %Inline;>   <!-- italic font -->
<!ATTLIST i %attrs;>
<!ELEMENT b %Inline;>   <!-- bold font -->
<!ATTLIST b %attrs;>
<!ELEMENT big %Inline;>   <!-- bigger font -->
<!ATTLIST big %attrs;>
<!ELEMENT small %Inline;>   <!-- smaller font -->
<!ATTLIST small %attrs;>
<!ELEMENT u %Inline;>   <!-- underline -->
<!ATTLIST u %attrs;>
```

```
<!ELEMENT s %Inline;>   <!-- strike-through -->
<!ATTLIST s %attrs;>
<!ELEMENT strike %Inline;>   <!-- strike-through -->
<!ATTLIST strike %attrs;>
<!ELEMENT basefont EMPTY>  <!-- base font size -->
<!ATTLIST basefont
  id            ID              #IMPLIED
  size          CDATA           #REQUIRED
  color         %Color;         #IMPLIED
  face          CDATA           #IMPLIED
  >
<!ELEMENT font %Inline;> <!-- local change to font -->
<!ATTLIST font
  %coreattrs;
  %i18n;
  size          CDATA           #IMPLIED
  color         %Color;         #IMPLIED
  face          CDATA           #IMPLIED
  >
<!--===================== Object =========================================-->
<!--
  object is used to embed objects as part of HTML pages.
  param elements should precede other content. Parameters
  can also be expressed as attribute/value pairs on the
  object element itself when brevity is desired.
-->
<!ELEMENT object (#PCDATA | param | %block; | form | %inline; | %misc;)*>
<!ATTLIST object
  %attrs;
  declare       (declare)       #IMPLIED
  classid       %URI;           #IMPLIED
  codebase      %URI;           #IMPLIED
  data          %URI;           #IMPLIED
  type          %ContentType;   #IMPLIED
  codetype      %ContentType;   #IMPLIED
  archive       %UriList;       #IMPLIED
  standby       %Text;          #IMPLIED
  height        %Length;        #IMPLIED
  width         %Length;        #IMPLIED
  usemap        %URI;           #IMPLIED
  name          NMTOKEN         #IMPLIED
  tabindex      %Number;        #IMPLIED
  align         %ImgAlign;      #IMPLIED
  border        %Pixels;        #IMPLIED
  hspace        %Pixels;        #IMPLIED
  vspace        %Pixels;        #IMPLIED
  >
<!--
  param is used to supply a named property value.
  In XML it would seem natural to follow RDF and support an
  abbreviated syntax where the param elements are replaced
  by attribute value pairs on the object start tag.
-->
```

```
<!ELEMENT param EMPTY>
<!ATTLIST param
  id          ID              #IMPLIED
  name        CDATA           #REQUIRED
  value       CDATA           #IMPLIED
  valuetype   (data|ref|object) "data"
  type        %ContentType;   #IMPLIED
  >
<!--==================== Java applet ===================================-->
<!--
  One of code or object attributes must be present.
  Place param elements before other content.
-->
<!ELEMENT applet (#PCDATA | param | %block; | form | %inline; | %misc;)*>
<!ATTLIST applet
  %coreattrs;
  codebase    %URI;           #IMPLIED
  archive     CDATA           #IMPLIED
  code        CDATA           #IMPLIED
  object      CDATA           #IMPLIED
  alt         %Text;          #IMPLIED
  name        NMTOKEN         #IMPLIED
  width       %Length;        #REQUIRED
  height      %Length;        #REQUIRED
  align       %ImgAlign;      #IMPLIED
  hspace      %Pixels;        #IMPLIED
  vspace      %Pixels;        #IMPLIED
  >
<!--==================== Images =============================================-->
<!--
  To avoid accessibility problems for people who aren't
  able to see the image, you should provide a text
  description using the alt and longdesc attributes.
  In addition, avoid the use of server-side image maps.
-->
<!ELEMENT img EMPTY>
<!ATTLIST img
  %attrs;
  src         %URI;           #REQUIRED
  alt         %Text;          #REQUIRED
  name        NMTOKEN         #IMPLIED
  longdesc    %URI;           #IMPLIED
  height      %Length;        #IMPLIED
  width       %Length;        #IMPLIED
  usemap      %URI;           #IMPLIED
  ismap       (ismap)         #IMPLIED
  align       %ImgAlign;      #IMPLIED
  border      %Length;        #IMPLIED
  hspace      %Pixels;        #IMPLIED
  vspace      %Pixels;        #IMPLIED
  >
<!-- usemap points to a map element which may be in this document
  or an external document, although the latter is not widely supported -->
```

```
<!--==================== Client-side image maps =========================-->
<!-- These can be placed in the same document or grouped in a
     separate document although this isn't yet widely supported -->
<!ELEMENT map ((%block; | form | %misc;)+ | area+)>
<!ATTLIST map
  %i18n;
  %events;
  id          ID              #REQUIRED
  class       CDATA           #IMPLIED
  style       %StyleSheet;    #IMPLIED
  title       %Text;          #IMPLIED
  name        CDATA           #IMPLIED
  >
<!ELEMENT area EMPTY>
<!ATTLIST area
  %attrs;
  shape       %Shape;         "rect"
  coords      %Coords;        #IMPLIED
  href        %URI;           #IMPLIED
  nohref      (nohref)        #IMPLIED
  alt         %Text;          #REQUIRED
  tabindex    %Number;        #IMPLIED
  accesskey   %Character;     #IMPLIED
  onfocus     %Script;        #IMPLIED
  onblur      %Script;        #IMPLIED
  target      %FrameTarget;   #IMPLIED
  >
<!--================ Forms ===================================================-->
<!ELEMENT form %form.content;>   <!-- forms shouldn't be nested -->
<!ATTLIST form
  %attrs;
  action      %URI;           #REQUIRED
  method      (get|post)      "get"
  name        NMTOKEN         #IMPLIED
  enctype     %ContentType;   "application/x-www-form-urlencoded"
  onsubmit    %Script;        #IMPLIED
  onreset     %Script;        #IMPLIED
  accept      %ContentTypes;  #IMPLIED
  accept-charset %Charsets;   #IMPLIED
  target      %FrameTarget;   #IMPLIED
  >
<!--
  Each label must not contain more than ONE field
  Label elements shouldn't be nested.
-->
<!ELEMENT label %Inline;>
<!ATTLIST label
  %attrs;
  for         IDREF           #IMPLIED
  accesskey   %Character;     #IMPLIED
  onfocus     %Script;        #IMPLIED
  onblur      %Script;        #IMPLIED
  >
```

```
<!ENTITY % InputType
  "(text | password | checkbox |
    radio | submit | reset |
    file | hidden | image | button)"
  >
<!-- the name attribute is required for all but submit & reset -->
<!ELEMENT input EMPTY>     <!-- form control -->
<!ATTLIST input
  %attrs;
  type         %InputType;     "text"
  name         CDATA           #IMPLIED
  value        CDATA           #IMPLIED
  checked      (checked)       #IMPLIED
  disabled     (disabled)      #IMPLIED
  readonly     (readonly)      #IMPLIED
  size         CDATA           #IMPLIED
  maxlength    %Number;        #IMPLIED
  src          %URI;           #IMPLIED
  alt          CDATA           #IMPLIED
  usemap       %URI;           #IMPLIED
  tabindex     %Number;        #IMPLIED
  accesskey    %Character;     #IMPLIED
  onfocus      %Script;        #IMPLIED
  onblur       %Script;        #IMPLIED
  onselect     %Script;        #IMPLIED
  onchange     %Script;        #IMPLIED
  accept       %ContentTypes;  #IMPLIED
  align        %ImgAlign;      #IMPLIED
  >
<!ELEMENT select (optgroup|option)+>  <!-- option selector -->
<!ATTLIST select
  %attrs;
  name         CDATA           #IMPLIED
  size         %Number;        #IMPLIED
  multiple     (multiple)      #IMPLIED
  disabled     (disabled)      #IMPLIED
  tabindex     %Number;        #IMPLIED
  onfocus      %Script;        #IMPLIED
  onblur       %Script;        #IMPLIED
  onchange     %Script;        #IMPLIED
  >
<!ELEMENT optgroup (option)+>   <!-- option group -->
<!ATTLIST optgroup
  %attrs;
  disabled     (disabled)      #IMPLIED
  label        %Text;          #REQUIRED
  >
<!ELEMENT option (#PCDATA)>      <!-- selectable choice -->
<!ATTLIST option
  %attrs;
  selected     (selected)      #IMPLIED
  disabled     (disabled)      #IMPLIED
  label        %Text;          #IMPLIED
  value        CDATA           #IMPLIED
  >
```

```
<!ELEMENT textarea (#PCDATA)>      <!-- multi-line text field -->
<!ATTLIST textarea
  %attrs;
  name         CDATA          #IMPLIED
  rows         %Number;       #REQUIRED
  cols         %Number;       #REQUIRED
  disabled     (disabled)     #IMPLIED
  readonly     (readonly)     #IMPLIED
  tabindex     %Number;       #IMPLIED
  accesskey    %Character;    #IMPLIED
  onfocus      %Script;       #IMPLIED
  onblur       %Script;       #IMPLIED
  onselect     %Script;       #IMPLIED
  onchange     %Script;       #IMPLIED
  >
<!--
  The fieldset element is used to group form fields.
  Only one legend element should occur in the content
  and if present should only be preceded by whitespace.
-->
<!ELEMENT fieldset (#PCDATA | legend | %block; | form | %inline; | %misc;)*>
<!ATTLIST fieldset
  %attrs;
  >
<!ENTITY % LAlign "(top|bottom|left|right)">
<!ELEMENT legend %Inline;>      <!-- fieldset label -->
<!ATTLIST legend
  %attrs;
  accesskey    %Character;    #IMPLIED
  align        %LAlign;       #IMPLIED
  >
<!--
 Content is %Flow; excluding a, form, form controls, iframe
-->
<!ELEMENT button %button.content;>  <!-- push button -->
<!ATTLIST button
  %attrs;
  name         CDATA          #IMPLIED
  value        CDATA          #IMPLIED
  type         (button|submit|reset) "submit"
  disabled     (disabled)     #IMPLIED
  tabindex     %Number;       #IMPLIED
  accesskey    %Character;    #IMPLIED
  onfocus      %Script;       #IMPLIED
  onblur       %Script;       #IMPLIED
  >
<!-- single-line text input control (DEPRECATED) -->
<!ELEMENT isindex EMPTY>
<!ATTLIST isindex
  %coreattrs;
  %i18n;
  prompt       %Text;         #IMPLIED
  >
```

```
<!--======================= Tables =========================================-->
<!-- Derived from IETF HTML table standard, see [RFC1942] -->
<!--
The border attribute sets the thickness of the frame around the
table. The default units are screen pixels.
The frame attribute specifies which parts of the frame around
the table should be rendered. The values are not the same as
CALS to avoid a name clash with the valign attribute.
-->
<!ENTITY % TFrame "(void|above|below|hsides|lhs|rhs|vsides|box|border)">
<!--
The rules attribute defines which rules to draw between cells:
If rules is absent then assume:
    "none" if border is absent or border="0" otherwise "all"
-->
<!ENTITY % TRules "(none | groups | rows | cols | all)">

<!-- horizontal placement of table relative to document -->
<!ENTITY % TAlign "(left|center|right)">
<!-- horizontal alignment attributes for cell contents
  char         alignment char, e.g. char=':'
  charoff      offset for alignment char
-->
<!ENTITY % cellhalign
  "align       (left|center|right|justify|char) #IMPLIED
   char        %Character;     #IMPLIED
   charoff     %Length;        #IMPLIED"
  >
<!-- vertical alignment attributes for cell contents -->
<!ENTITY % cellvalign
  "valign      (top|middle|bottom|baseline) #IMPLIED"
  >
<!ELEMENT table
     (caption?, (col*|colgroup*), thead?, tfoot?, (tbody+|tr+))>
<!ELEMENT caption  %Inline;>
<!ELEMENT thead     (tr)+>
<!ELEMENT tfoot     (tr)+>
<!ELEMENT tbody     (tr)+>
<!ELEMENT colgroup (col)*>
<!ELEMENT col       EMPTY>
<!ELEMENT tr        (th|td)+>
<!ELEMENT th        %Flow;>
<!ELEMENT td        %Flow;>
<!ATTLIST table
  %attrs;
  summary      %Text;          #IMPLIED
  width        %Length;        #IMPLIED
  border       %Pixels;        #IMPLIED
  frame        %TFrame;        #IMPLIED
  rules        %TRules;        #IMPLIED
  cellspacing  %Length;        #IMPLIED
  cellpadding  %Length;        #IMPLIED
  align        %TAlign;        #IMPLIED
  bgcolor      %Color;         #IMPLIED
  >
```

```
<!ENTITY % CAlign "(top|bottom|left|right)">
<!ATTLIST caption
  %attrs;
  align         %CAlign;        #IMPLIED
  >
<!--
colgroup groups a set of col elements. It allows you to group
several semantically related columns together.
-->
<!ATTLIST colgroup
  %attrs;
  span          %Number;        "1"
  width         %MultiLength;   #IMPLIED
  %cellhalign;
  %cellvalign;
  >
<!--
 col elements define the alignment properties for cells in
 one or more columns.
 The width attribute specifies the width of the columns, e.g.
     width=64        width in screen pixels
     width=0.5*      relative width of 0.5
 The span attribute causes the attributes of one
 col element to apply to more than one column.
-->
<!ATTLIST col
  %attrs;
  span          %Number;        "1"
  width         %MultiLength;   #IMPLIED
  %cellhalign;
  %cellvalign;
  >
<!--
    Use thead to duplicate headers when breaking table
    across page boundaries, or for static headers when
    tbody sections are rendered in scrolling panel.
    Use tfoot to duplicate footers when breaking table
    across page boundaries, or for static footers when
    tbody sections are rendered in scrolling panel.
    Use multiple tbody sections when rules are needed
    between groups of table rows.
-->
<!ATTLIST thead
  %attrs;
  %cellhalign;
  %cellvalign;
  >
<!ATTLIST tfoot
  %attrs;
  %cellhalign;
  %cellvalign;
  >
```

```
<!ATTLIST tbody
  %attrs;
  %cellhalign;
  %cellvalign;
  >
<!ATTLIST tr
  %attrs;
  %cellhalign;
  %cellvalign;
  bgcolor      %Color;          #IMPLIED
  >
<!-- Scope is simpler than headers attribute for common tables -->
<!ENTITY % Scope "(row|col|rowgroup|colgroup)">
<!-- th is for headers, td for data and for cells acting as both -->
<!ATTLIST th
  %attrs;
  abbr         %Text;           #IMPLIED
  axis         CDATA            #IMPLIED
  headers      IDREFS           #IMPLIED
  scope        %Scope;          #IMPLIED
  rowspan      %Number;         "1"
  colspan      %Number;         "1"
  %cellhalign;
  %cellvalign;
  nowrap       (nowrap)         #IMPLIED
  bgcolor      %Color;          #IMPLIED
  width        %Pixels;         #IMPLIED
  height       %Pixels;         #IMPLIED
  >
<!ATTLIST td
  %attrs;
  abbr         %Text;           #IMPLIED
  axis         CDATA            #IMPLIED
  headers      IDREFS           #IMPLIED
  scope        %Scope;          #IMPLIED
  rowspan      %Number;         "1"
  colspan      %Number;         "1"
  %cellhalign;
  %cellvalign;
  nowrap       (nowrap)         #IMPLIED
  bgcolor      %Color;          #IMPLIED
  width        %Pixels;         #IMPLIED
  height       %Pixels;         #IMPLIED
  >
```

Character Entities

The following table lists the defined standard and proposed character entities for HTML and XHTML, as well as several that are nonstandard but generally supported.

Entity names, if defined, appear for their respective characters and can be used in the character-entity sequence &name; to define any character for display by the browser. Otherwise, or alternatively for named characters, use the character's three-digit numeral value in the sequence &#nnn; to specially define a character entity. Actual characters, however, may or may not be displayed by the browser, depending on the computer platform and user-selected font for display.

Not all 256 characters in the International Organization for Standardization (ISO) character set appear in the table. Missing ones are not recognized by the browser as either named or numeric entities.

To be sure that your documents are fully compliant with the HTML 4.0 and XHTML 1.0 standards, use only those named character entities with no entries in the Conformance column. Characters with a value of "!!!" in the Conformance column are not formally defined by the standards; use them at your own risk.

Numeric entity	Named entity	Symbol	Description	Conformance
&#009;			Horizontal tab	
&#010;			Line feed	
&#013;			Carriage return	
&#032;			Space	
&#033;		!	Exclamation point	
&#034;	&quot;	"	Quotation mark	
&#035;		#	Hash mark	
&#036;		$	Dollar sign	
&#037;		%	Percent sign	
&#038;	&amp;	&	Ampersand	
&#039;		'	Apostrophe	
&#040;		(	Left parenthesis	

Numeric entity	Named entity	Symbol	Description	Conformance
&#041;		)	Right parenthesis	
&#042;		*	Asterisk	
&#043;		+	Plus sign	
&#044;		,	Comma	
&#045;		-	Hyphen	
&#046;		.	Period	
&#047;		/	Slash	
0–9		0–9	Digits 0–9	
&#058;		:	Colon	
&#059;		;	Semicolon	
&#060;	&lt;	<	Less than sign	
&#061;		=	Equals sign	
&#062;	&gt;	>	Greater than sign	
&#063;		?	Question mark	
&#064;		@	Commercial at sign	
A–Z		A–Z	Letters A–Z	
&#091;		[	Left square bracket	
&#092;		\	Backslash	
&#093;		]	Right square bracket	
&#094;		^	Caret	
&#095;		_	Underscore	
&#096;		`	Grave accent	
a–z		a–z	Letters a–z	
&#123;		{	Left curly brace	
|				Vertical bar	
&#125;		}	Right curly brace	
&#126;		~	Tilde	
&#130;		‚	Low left single quote	!!!
&#131;		ƒ	Florin	!!!
&#132;		„	Low left double quote	!!!
&#133;		…	Ellipsis	!!!
&#134;		†	Dagger	!!!
&#135;		‡	Double dagger	!!!
&#136;		^	Circumflex	!!!
&#137;		‰	Permil	!!!
&#138;		Š	Capital S, caron	!!!
&#139;		‹	Less than sign	!!!
&#140;		Œ	Capital OE ligature	!!!

Numeric entity	Named entity	Symbol	Description	Conformance
&#142;		Ž	Capital Z, caron	!!!
&#145;		`	Left single quote	!!!
&#146;		'	Right single quote	!!!
&#147;		"	Left double quote	!!!
&#148;		"	Right double quote	!!!
&#149;		•	Bullet	!!!
&#150;		-	En dash	!!!
&#151;		—	Em dash	!!!
&#152;		~	Tilde	!!!
&#153;		™	Trademark	!!!
&#154;		š	Small s, caron	!!!
&#155;		>	Greater than sign	!!!
&#156;		œ	Small oe ligature	!!!
&#158;		ž	Small z, caron	!!!
&#159;		Ÿ	Capital Y, umlaut	!!!
			Nonbreaking space	
&#161;	&iexcl;	¡	Inverted exclamation point	
&#162;	&cent;	¢	Cent sign	
&#163;	&pound;	£	Pound sign	
&#164;	&curren;	¤	General currency sign	
&#165;	&yen;	¥	Yen sign	
&#166;	&brvbar;	¦	Broken vertical bar	
&#167;	&sect;	§	Section sign	
&#168;	&uml;	¨	Umlaut	
&#169;	&copy;	©	Copyright	
&#170;	&ordf;	ª	Feminine ordinal	
&#171;	&laquo;	«	Left angle quote	
&#172;	&not;	¬	Not sign	
&#173;	&shy;	-	Soft hyphen	
&#174;	&reg;	®	Registered trademark	
&#175;	&macr;	¯	Macron accent	
&#176;	&deg;	°	Degree sign	
&#177;	&plusmn;	±	Plus or minus	
&#178;	&sup2;	^{2}	Superscript 2	
&#179;	&sup3;	^{3}	Superscript 3	
&#180;	&acute;	´	Acute accent	

Numeric entity	Named entity	Symbol	Description	Conformance
&#181;	&micro;	μ	Micro sign (Greek mu)	
&#182;	&para;	¶	Paragraph sign	
&#183;	&middot;	·	Middle dot	
&#184;	&cedil;	¸	Cedilla	
&#185;	&sup1;	1	Superscript 1	
&#186;	&ordm;	º	Masculine ordinal	
&#187;	&raquo;	»	Right angle quote	
&#188;	&frac14;	¼	Fraction one-fourth	
&#189;	&frac12;	½	Fraction one-half	
&#190;	&frac34;	¾	Fraction three-fourths	
&#191;	&iquest;	¿	Inverted question mark	
&#192;	&Agrave;	À	Capital A, grave accent	
&#193;	&Aacute;	Á	Capital A, acute accent	
&#194;	&Acirc;	Â	Capital A, circumflex accent	
&#195;	&Atilde;	Ã	Capital A, tilde	
&#196;	&Auml;	Ä	Capital A, umlaut	
&#197;	&Aring;	Å	Capital A, ring	
&#198;	&AElig;	Æ	Capital AE ligature	
&#199;	&Ccedil;	Ç	Capital C, cedilla	
&#200;	&Egrave;	È	Capital E, grave accent	
&#201;	&Eacute;	É	Capital E, acute accent	
&#202;	&Ecirc;	Ê	Capital E, circumflex accent	
&#203;	&Euml;	Ë	Capital E, umlaut	
&#204;	&Igrave;	Ì	Capital I, grave accent	
&#205;	&Iacute;	Í	Capital I, acute accent	
&#206;	&Icirc;	Î	Capital I, circumflex accent	
&#207;	&Iuml;	Ï	Capital I, umlaut	
&#208;	&ETH;	Œ	Capital eth, Icelandic	
&#209;	&Ntilde;	Ñ	Capital N, tilde	
&#210;	&Ograve;	Ò	Capital O, grave accent	
&#211;	&Oacute;	Ó	Capital O, acute accent	
&#212;	&Ocirc;	Ô	Capital O, circumflex accent	
&#213;	&Otilde;	Õ	Capital O, tilde	
&#214;	&Ouml;	Ö	Capital O, umlaut	
&#215;	&times;	×	Multiply sign	
&#216;	&Oslash;	Ø	Capital O, slash	
&#217;	&Ugrave;	Ù	Capital U, grave accent	
&#218;	&Uacute;	Ú	Capital U, acute accent	

Numeric entity	Named entity	Symbol	Description	Conformance
&#219;	&Ucirc;	Û	Capital U, circumflex accent	
&#220;	&Uuml;	Ü	Capital U, umlaut	
&#221;	&Yacute;	Ý	Capital Y, acute accent	
&#222;	&THORN;	Þ	Capital thorn, Icelandic	
&#223;	&szlig;	ß	Small sz ligature, German	
&#224;	&agrave;	à	Small a, grave accent	
&#225;	&aacute;	á	Small a, acute accent	
&#226;	&acirc;	â	Small a, circumflex accent	
&#227;	&atilde;	ã	Small a, tilde	
&#228;	&auml;	ä	Small a, umlaut	
&#229;	&aring;	å	Small a, ring	
&#230;	&aelig;	æ	Small ae ligature	
&#231;	&ccedil;	ç	Small c, cedilla	
&#232;	&egrave;	è	Small e, grave accent	
&#233;	&eacute;	é	Small e, acute accent	
&#234;	&ecirc;	ê	Small e, circumflex accent	
&#235;	&euml;	ë	Small e, umlaut	
&#236;	&igrave;	ì	Small i, grave accent	
&#237;	&iacute;	í	Small i, acute accent	
&#238;	&icirc;	î	Small i, circumflex accent	
&#239;	&iuml;	î	Small i, umlaut	
&#240;	&eth;	ð	Small eth, Icelandic	
&#241;	&ntilde;	ñ	Small n, tilde	
&#242;	&ograve;	ò	Small o, grave accent	
&#243;	&oacute;	ó	Small o, acute accent	
&#244;	&ocirc;	ô	Small o, circumflex accent	
&#245;	&otilde;	õ	Small o, tilde	
&#246;	&ouml;	ö	Small o, umlaut	
&#247;	&divide;	÷	Division sign	
&#248;	&oslash;	ø	Small o, slash	
&#249;	&ugrave;	ù	Small u, grave accent	
&#250;	&uacute;	ú	Small u, acute accent	
&#251;	&ucirc;	û	Small u, circumflex accent	
&#252;	&uuml;	ü	Small u, umlaut	
&#253;	&yacute;	y	Small y, acute accent	
&#254;	&thorn;	þ	Small thorn, Icelandic	
&#255;	&yuml;	ÿ	Small y, umlaut	

Color Names and Values

With the popular browsers, and according to the Cascading Style Sheets (CSS) standard, you may prescribe the display color for various elements in your documents. You do so by specifying a color value or a standard name. The user may override these color specifications through her browser preferences.

Color Values

In all cases, you may set the color value for an HTML element, such as <body> text, <table> background, and so on, as a six-digit hexadecimal number that represents the red, green, and blue (RGB) components of the color. The first two digits correspond to the red component of the color, the next two are the green component, and the last two are the blue component. A value of 00 corresponds to a component being completely off; the hexadecimal value of FF (decimal 255) corresponds to the component being completely on. Thus, bright red is FF0000, bright green is 00FF00, and bright blue is 0000FF. Other primary colors are mixtures of the components, such as yellow (FFFF00), magenta (FF00FF), and cyan (00FFFF). White (FFFFFF) and black (000000) also are easy to figure out.

You use these values in a tag by replacing the color with the RGB triple, preceded by a pound sign (#). Thus, to make all visited links display as magenta, use this body tag:

```
<body vlink="#FF00FF">
```

Color Names

Determining the RGB-triple value for anything other than the simplest colors (you try figuring out esoteric colors like "papaya whip" or "navajo white") is not easy. You can go crazy trying to adjust the RGB triple for a color to get the shade just right, especially when each adjustment requires loading a document into your browser to view the result.

To make life easier, the standards define 16 standard color names that you can use anywhere you can use a numeric color value. For example, you can make all visited links in the display magenta with the following attribute and value for the body tag:

```
<body vlink="magenta">
```

The color names and RGB values defined in the HTML/XHTML standards are:

aqua (#00FFFF)	gray (#808080)	navy (#000080)	silver (#C0C0C0)
black (#000000)	green (#008000)	olive (#808000)	teal (#008080)
blue (#0000FF)	lime (#00FF00)	purple (#800080)	yellow (#FFFF00)
fuchsia (#FF00FF)	maroon (#800000)	red (#FF0000)	white (#FFFFFF)

The popular browsers go well beyond the standard and support the several hundred color names defined for use in the X Window System. Note that these color names may contain no spaces; also, the word *gray* may be spelled *grey* in any color name.

Those colors marked with an asterisk (*) actually represent a family of colors numbered one through four. Thus, there are actually four variants of blue, named "blue1," "blue2," "blue3," and "blue4," along with plain old "blue." Blue1 is the lightest of the four; blue4 is the darkest. The unnumbered color name is the same color as the first; thus, blue and blue1 are identical.

Finally, if all that isn't enough, there are 100 variants of gray (and grey), numbered 1 through 100. "Gray1" is the darkest, "gray100" is the lightest, and "gray" is very close to "gray75."

The extended color names are:

aliceblue	darkturquoise	lightseagreen	palevioletred*
antiquewhite*	darkviolet	lightskyblue*	papayawhip
aquamarine*	deeppink*	lightslateblue	peachpuff*
azure*	deepskyblue*	lightslategray	peru
beige	dimgray	lightsteelblue*	pink*
bisque*	dodgerblue*	lightyellow*	plum*
black	firebrick*	limegreen	powderblue
blanchedalmond	floralwhite	linen	purple*
blue*	forestgreen	magenta*	red*

blueviolet	gainsboro	maroon*	rosybrown*
brown*	ghostwhite	mediumaquamarine	royalblue*
burlywood*	gold*	mediumblue	saddlebrown
cadetblue*	goldenrod*	mediumorchid*	salmon*
chartreuse*	gray	mediumpurple*	sandybrown
chocolate*	green*	mediumseagreen	seagreen*
coral*	greenyellow	mediumslateblue	seashell*
cornflowerblue	honeydew*	mediumspringgreen	sienna*
cornsilk*	hotpink*	mediumturquoise	skyblue*
cyan*	indianred*	mediumvioletred	slateblue*
darkblue	ivory*	midnightblue	slategray*
darkcyan	khaki*	mintcream	snow*
darkgoldenrod*	lavender	mistyrose*	springgreen*
darkgray	lavenderblush*	moccasin	steelblue*
darkgreen	lawngreen	navajowhite*	tan*
darkkhaki	lemonchiffon*	navy	thistle*
darkmagenta	lightblue*	navyblue	tomato*
darkolivegreen*	lightcoral	oldlace	turquoise*
darkorange*	lightcyan*	olivedrab*	violet
darkorchid*	lightgoldenrod*	orange*	violetred*
darkred	lightgoldenrodyellow	orangered*	wheat*
darksalmon	lightgray	orchid*	white
darkseagreen*	lightgreen	palegoldenrod	whitesmoke
darkslateblue	lightpink*	palegreen*	yellow*
darkslategray*	lightsalmon*	paleturquoise*	yellowgreen

The Standard Color Map

Supporting hundreds of color names and millions of RGB triples is nice, but the reality is that a large (albeit shrinking) population of users can display only 256 colors on their systems. When confronted with a color not defined in this set of 256, the browser has two choices: convert the color to one of the existing colors, or dither the color using the available colors in the color map.

Conversion is easy; the color is compared to all the other colors in the color map and is replaced by the closest color found. Dithering is more difficult. Using two or more colors in the color map, the errant color is approximated by mixing different ratios of the available colors. When you view them up close, you'll see a pattern of alternating pixels using the available colors. At a distance, the pixels blend to form a color close to the original color.

In general, your images will look best if you can avoid both conversion and dithering. Conversion will make your colors appear "off"; dithering makes them look fuzzy. How to avoid these problems? Easy: use colors in the standard color map when creating your images.

The standard color map actually has 216 values in it. There are six variants of red, six of green, and six of blue that are combined in all possible ways to create these 216 (6×6×6) colors. These variants have decimal brightness values of 0, 51, 102, 153, 204, and 255, corresponding to hexadecimal values of 00, 33, 66, 99, CC, and FF. Colors such as 003333 (dark cyan) and 999999 (medium gray) exist directly in the color map and won't be converted or dithered.

Keep in mind that many of the extended color names are not in the standard color map and will be converted or dithered to a (hopefully) similar color. Using color names, while convenient, does not guarantee that the browser will use the desired color.

When creating images, try to use colors in the standard color map. When selecting colors for text, links, or backgrounds, make sure you select colors in the standard color map. Your pages will look better and will be more consistent when viewed with different browsers.

Netscape Layout Extensions

From the start of their enterprise before the turn of the century, the developers at Netscape were at the forefront of browser design that addressed the needs of commercial interests. During those heady years, Netscape extended HTML to provide authors with far more sophisticated page-layout capabilities than otherwise available in any other browser. And they were very successful in that enterprise. Netscape Navigator was the dominant browser by far until the early 2000s with the advent of Cascading Style Sheets (CSS) and other standards. Microsoft finally caught on, too.

In this appendix, we document for historical purposes three features that were unique to Netscape versions 4 and earlier and no other browsers since then: spacers, multiple columns, and layers. These tags lure the designer with exciting page-layout capabilities. Play with them as you will, but we warn you: they won't ever become part of HTML/XHTML standards. They aren't even supported by the latest version of Netscape Navigator.

Creating Whitespace

One of the simplest elements in any page design is the empty space surrounding content. Empty space is often just as important to the look and feel of a page as the areas filled with text and images. Commonly known as *whitespace*, these empty areas shape and contain the content of your page.

Native HTML has no way to create empty space on your page, short of using a <pre> tag filled with blank lines or an empty image. In fact, browsers—acting according to the HTML/XHTML standards—remove leading, trailing, and any other extra spaces in text and ignore extra linefeeds. Netscape 4 fills this void with the <spacer> tag. [The
 Tag, 4.6.1]

The <spacer> Tag (Antiquated)

Use the <spacer> tag to create horizontal, vertical, and rectangular whitespace in documents rendered by Netscape 4.

<spacer>

Function	Defines a blank area in a document
Attributes	align, height, size, type, width
End tag	None in HTML
Contains	Nothing
Used in	*text*

Creating horizontal space

The most common use of the <spacer> tag is to indent a line of text. To achieve this effect, set the value of the type attribute to horizontal, and use the size attribute to define the width, in pixels (not text characters), of the horizontal area. For example:

```
<spacer type=horizontal size=100>
```

inserts 100 pixels of space in line with the current line of text. Netscape 4 appends subsequent content at the end of the spacer if sufficient space remains on the current line. Otherwise, it places the next element onto the next line, following its normal word-wrap behavior.

If there is not enough room to place the entire <spacer> tag's whitespace on the current line, the browser shortens the space to fit on the current line. In a sense, the size of the spacer is soft, telling the browser to insert up to the specified number of pixels until the end of the current line is reached.

For example, if a spacer is 100 pixels wide, and only 75 pixels of space remain on the current line within the browser's display window, Netscape 4 inserts 75 pixels of space into the line and places the next element at the beginning of the next line in the display. Accordingly, a horizontal spacer is never broken across a line, creating space at the end of one line and the beginning of the next.

By far, the most common application of the horizontal spacer is to indent the first line of a paragraph. Simply place a horizontal spacer at the start of a paragraph to get the desired result:

```
<spacer type=horizontal size=50>
The effects of cooler weather on the kumquat's ripening process
vary based upon the temperature. Temperatures above 28&deg;
sweeten the fruit, while four or more hours below 28&deg; will
damage the tree.
```

Figure H-1 shows the results.

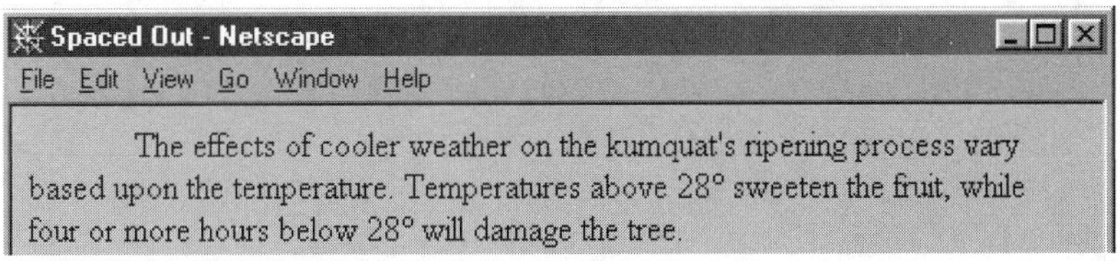

Figure H-1. Indenting a paragraph with a horizontal spacer (Netscape 4 only)

Of course, you also can use horizontal spacers to insert additional space between let-ters or words in a line of text. This might be useful for displaying poetry or special-ized ad copy. But don't use a spacer to create an indented block of text—you cannot predict the size of the user's browser window, font sizes, and so forth, and, hence, where it will break a particular line of text. Instead, use the <blockquote> tag or adjust the paragraph's left margin with an appropriate style.

Creating vertical space

You may insert extra whitespace between lines of text and paragraphs in your docu-ments by setting the type attribute in the <spacer> tag to vertical. You also must include the size attribute. Make its value a positive integer equal to the amount of whitespace, in pixels.

The vertical spacer acts just like the <br> tag. Both tags cause an immediate line break. The difference is that with the vertical spacer, you control how far below the current line of text Netscape 4 should start the subsequent line. The whitespace is added to—and therefore is never less than—the normal amount of space that would appear below the current line of text as a result of the paragraph's line spacing.

Because HTML pages are infinitely tall, the vertical space may be any number of pix-els high. Of course, it'd be sophomoric to be excessive (oh, OK, try size=100000000). Most of today's monitors have a vertical scan of no more than 1,024 lines, so a verti-cal pixel size value of 1,025 ensures that the next line of text is placed off the user's screen, if that is the effect you desire.

Vertical spacers aren't quite as common as horizontal spacers, but they can still be useful. In the following text, we've used a vertical spacer to provide a bit more sepa-ration between the document's header and the regular text:

```
<h1 align=right>Temperature Effects</h1>
<spacer type=vertical size=50>
The effects of cooler weather on the kumquat's ripening process
vary based upon the temperature. Temperatures above 28&deg;
sweeten the fruit, while four or more hours below 28&deg; will
damage the tree.
```

Figure H-2 shows the results.

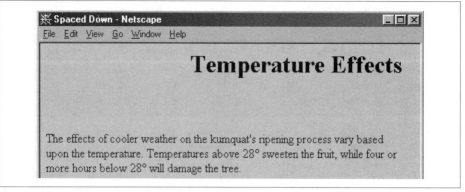

Figure H-2. Using a vertical spacer to separate a header from the text (Netscape 4 only)

Creating blocks of space

The third spacer type creates a rectangular block of blank space, much like a blank image. Set the type attribute to block and include three other attributes to fully define the space: width, height, and align.

The width and height attributes specify the size of the spacer in pixels or as a percentage of the element containing the spacer. These attributes are used only when the type attribute is set to block and otherwise are ignored. Similarly, the size attribute is ignored when the <spacer> type is block. If specifying a size in pixels, you must give a positive integer value to both the width and height attributes; their default value is 0.

The third required block spacer attribute, align, controls how Netscape 4 places the empty block relative to the surrounding text. The values for this attribute are identical to those for the align attribute in the <img> tag. Use the top, texttop, middle, absmiddle, baseline, bottom, and absbottom values to obtain the desired vertical alignment of the block spacer. Use the left and right values to force the block spacer to the indicated margin and cause the following text to flow up and around the spacer. The default value is bottom. For a complete description of the align attribute and its values, see section 4.1.1.1.

This HTML fragment places the compass points around an empty area:

```
<center>
North
<br>
West
<spacer type=block width=50 height=50 align=absmiddle>
East
<br>
South
</center>
```

Figure H-3 shows the resulting document.

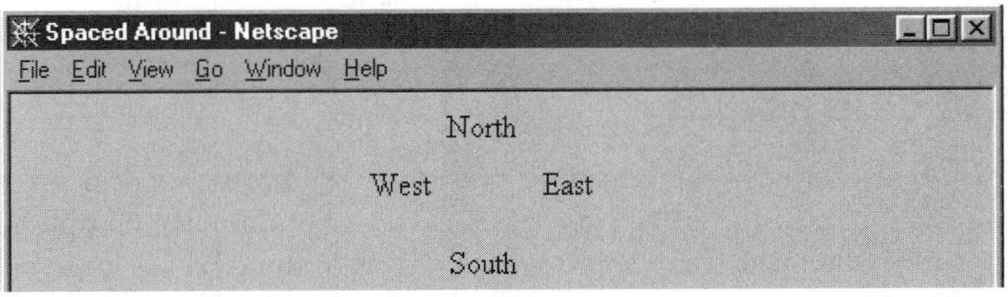

Figure H-3. Using a block spacer to create space in a document (Netscape 4 only)

Mimicking the <spacer> Tag

Because only Netscape versions 4 and earlier support the <spacer> tag, other browsers ignore it, ruining your carefully contrived layout. We strongly suggest that you instead use the CSS standard text-indent property for identical results.

You might also emulate the <spacer> tag with the <img> tag and a special, small image. This way, you can achieve <spacer>-like effects even with browsers that don't support CSS. For an image to emulate <spacer>, you'll need a GIF that is completely transparent. Because no part of the image is ever seen, you can make it as small as you want; we recommend a 1 × 1-pixel GIF image. In the following examples, our tiny 1 × 1-pixel transparent image is named *small.gif*.

To emulate a horizontal spacer of the form:

```
<spacer type=horizontal size=n>
```

use this <img> tag:

```
<img src=small.gif width=n height=1>
```

Replace *n* with the desired pixel width. Keep in mind, however, that the width of the <img> tag is fixed and may not integrate into the text flow exactly like the <spacer> tag would, especially if the <img> tag falls at or near the end of a line of text.

To emulate a vertical spacer of the form:

```
<spacer type=vertical size=n>
```

use this HTML fragment:

```
<br>
<img src=small.gif width=1 height=n>
<br>
```

The <br> tags are needed in the example to emulate the line-breaking behavior of the vertical spacer. Again, replace *n* with the desired height.

To emulate a block spacer of the form:

```
<spacer type=block width=w height=h align=a>
```

use this <img> tag:

```
<img src=small.gif width=w height=h align=a>
```

Replace *w*, *h*, and *a* with the desired width, height, and alignment values.

Multicolumn Layout

Multicolumn text formatting is one of the most common features of desktop publishing. In addition to creating attractive pages in a variety of formats, multiple columns let you present your text using shorter, easier-to-read lines. HTML page designers have longed for the ability to easily create multiple text columns in a single page, but they have been forced to use various tricks, such as multicolumn tables (see Chapter 17).

Netscape 4 neatly solved this problem with the unique <multicol> tag. While fancy unbalanced columns and straddling are not possible with this tag, as they are with tables, conventionally balanced text columns are easy to create with <multicol>. And while this capability is available only with Netscape 4, the <multicol> tag degrades nicely in other browsers.

The <multicol> Tag (Antiquated)

The <multicol> tag creates multiple columns of text and lets you control the size and number of columns.

<multicol> (Antiquated)

Function	Formats text with multiple columns
Attributes	class, cols, gutter, style, width
End tag	</multicol>; never omitted
Contains	*body_content*
Used in	*block*

The <multicol> tag can contain any other HTML content, much like the <div> tag. All of the content within the <multicol> tag is displayed just like conventional content, except that Netscape 4 places the contents into multiple columns rather than just one.

The <multicol> tag creates a break in the text flow and inserts a blank line before rendering its content into multiple columns. After the tag, another blank line is added and the text flow resumes using the previous layout and formatting.

Netscape 4 automatically balances the columns, making each approximately the same length. Where possible, the browser moves text between columns to accomplish the balancing. In some cases, the columns cannot be balanced perfectly because of embedded images, tables, or other large elements.

You can nest <multicol> tags, embedding one set of columns within another set of columns. While infinite nesting is supported, more than two levels of nesting are generally impractical and results in unattractive text flows.

The cols attribute

The cols attribute is required by the <multicol> tag to define the number of columns. If this attribute is omitted, Netscape 4 creates just one column, as though the <multicol> tag isn't there at all. You may create any number of columns, but in practice, more than three or four columns make text unreadable on most displays.

The following example creates a three-column layout:

```
<h1 align=right>Temperature Effects</h1>
<multicol cols=3>
The effects of cooler weather on the kumquat's ripening process
vary based upon the temperature. Temperatures above 28&deg;
sweeten the fruit, while four or more hours below 28&deg; will
damage the tree. The savvy quat farmer will carefully monitor
the temperature, especially in the predawn hours when the mercury
dips to its lowest point. Smudge pots and grove heaters may be
required to keep the trees warm; many growers will spray the trees
with water to create an insulating layer of ice over the fruit and
leaves.
<p>
If a disastrous frost is predicted, below 20&deg;, the only recourse
may be to harvest the fruit early to save it from an assured disaster.
Kumquats may subsequently be ripened using any of the popular methane
and cyanoacrylate injection systems used for other citrus fruits.
Used correctly, these systems will produce fruit whose taste is
indistinguishable from tree-ripened kumquats.
</multicol>
```

Figure H-4 shows the results.

You can see in Figure H-4 how Netscape 4 has balanced the columns to approximately equal lengths. You also can see how several lines within the columns appear shorter because longer words were wrapped to the next line of text. These overly ragged right margins within the columns are unavoidable and serve to emphasize that you shouldn't create more than four or five columns in a flow. Our example is still barely readable if displayed as five columns; it breaks down completely and even induces rendering errors if cols is set to 7, as shown in Figure H-5.

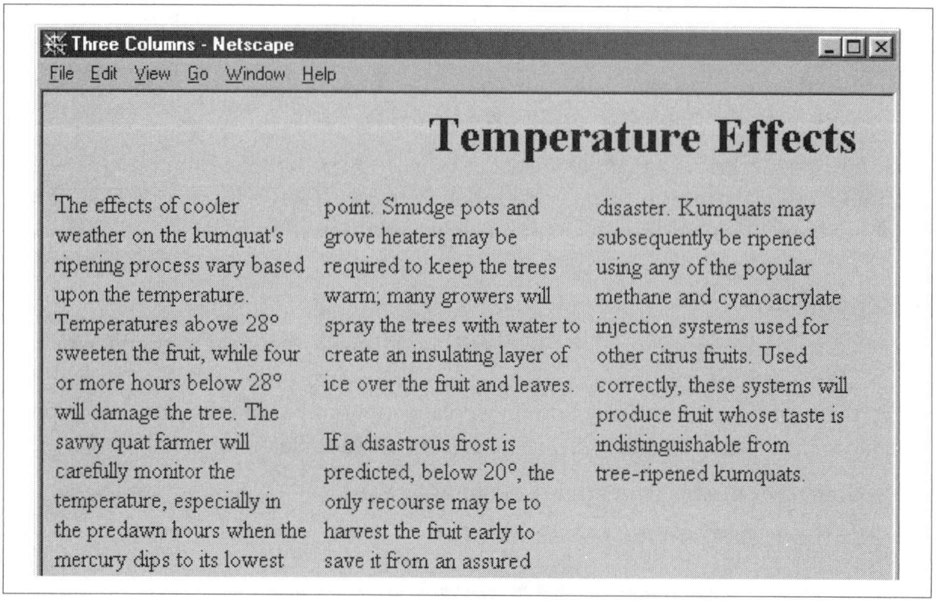

Temperature Effects

(Three Columns — Netscape)

The effects of cooler weather on the kumquat's ripening process vary based upon the temperature. Temperatures above 28° sweeten the fruit, while four or more hours below 28° will damage the tree. The savvy quat farmer will carefully monitor the temperature, especially in the predawn hours when the mercury dips to its lowest point. Smudge pots and grove heaters may be required to keep the trees warm; many growers will spray the trees with water to create an insulating layer of ice over the fruit and leaves.

If a disastrous frost is predicted, below 20°, the only recourse may be to harvest the fruit early to save it from an assured disaster. Kumquats may subsequently be ripened using any of the popular methane and cyanoacrylate injection systems used for other citrus fruits. Used correctly, these systems will produce fruit whose taste is indistinguishable from tree-ripened kumquats.

Figure H-4. A three-column <multicol> document segment (Netscape 4 only)

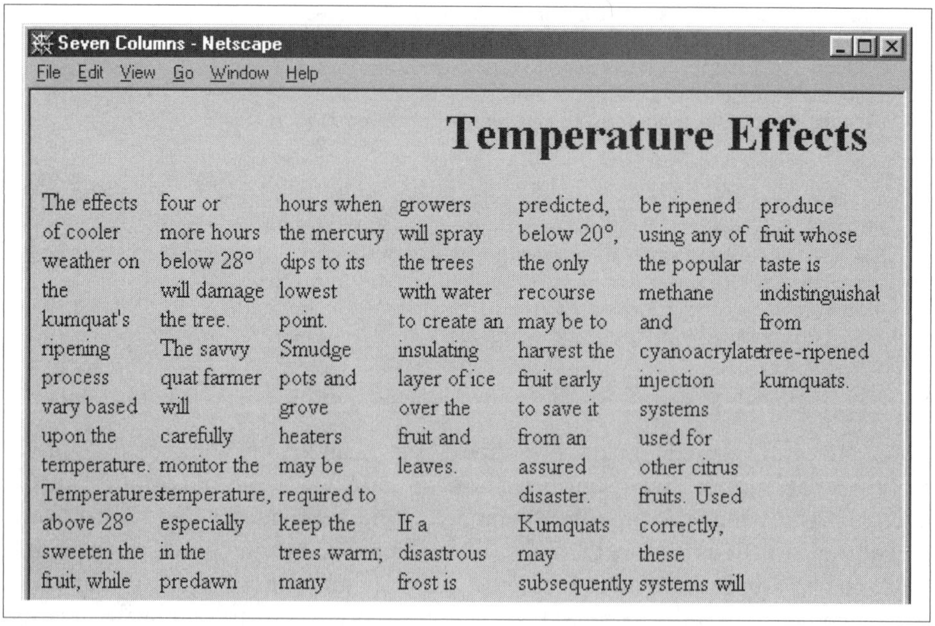

Temperature Effects

(Seven Columns — Netscape)

The effects of cooler weather on the kumquat's ripening process vary based upon the temperature. Temperatures above 28° sweeten the fruit, while four or more hours below 28° will damage the tree. The savvy quat farmer will carefully monitor the temperature, especially in the predawn hours when the mercury dips to its lowest point. Smudge pots and grove heaters may be required to keep the trees warm; many growers will spray the trees with water to create an insulating layer of ice over the fruit and leaves. If a disastrous frost is predicted, below 20°, the only recourse may be to harvest the fruit early to save it from an assured disaster. Kumquats may subsequently be ripened using any of the popular methane and cyanoacrylate injection systems used for other citrus fruits. Used correctly, these systems will produce fruit whose taste is indistinguishable from tree-ripened kumquats.

Figure H-5. Too many columns create unreadable pages (Netscape 4 only)

The gutter attribute

The space between columns is known as the *gutter*. By default, Netscape creates a gutter that is 10 pixels wide between each of your columns. To change this, set the gutter attribute's value to the desired width in pixels. Netscape 4 reserves this much space between your columns; the remaining space is used for the columns themselves.

Figure H-6 shows the effect this can have on your columns. In this figure, we've reformatted our sample text using <multicol cols=3 gutter=50>. Contrast this with Figure H-4, which uses the default 10-pixel gutters.

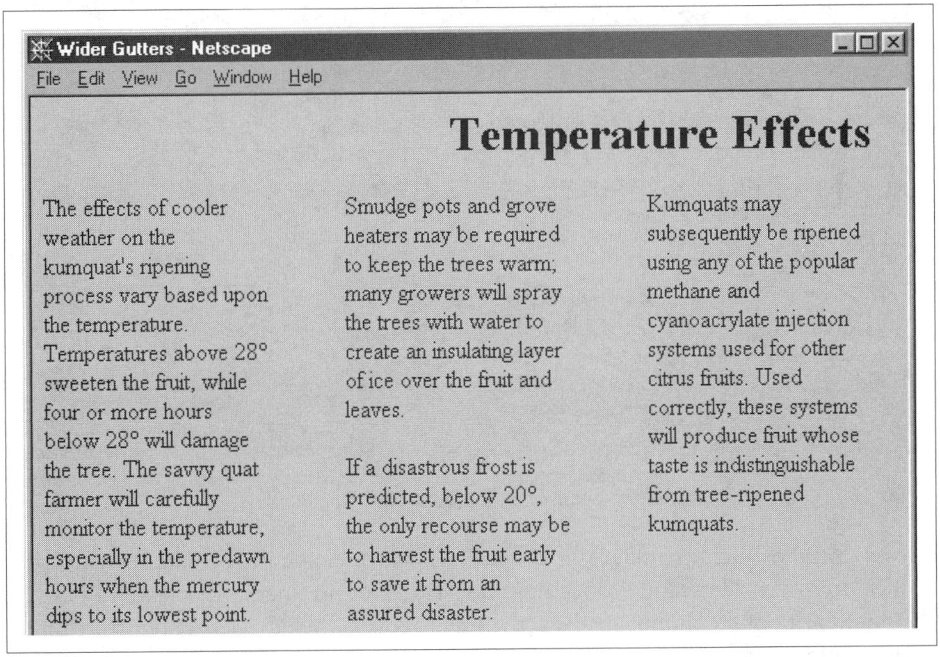

Figure H-6. Change gutter widths with the <multicol> gutter attribute (Netscape 4 only)

The width attribute

Normally, the <multicol> tag fills the current width of the current text flow. To have your multiple columns occupy a thinner space, or to extend them beyond the visible window, use the width attribute to specify the overall width of the <multicol> tag. The columns are resized so that the columns plus the gutters fill the width you've specified.* The width may be specified as an absolute number of pixels or as a percentage of the width of the current text flow.

---

* To be exact, each column is $(w - g(n - 1))/n$ pixels wide, where w is the width of the <multicol> tag, g is the width of a gutter, and n is the number of columns. Thus, using <multicol cols=3 gutter=10 width=500> creates columns that are 160 pixels wide.

Figure H-7 shows the effects of adding width="75%" to our column example, retaining the default gutter width of 10 pixels.

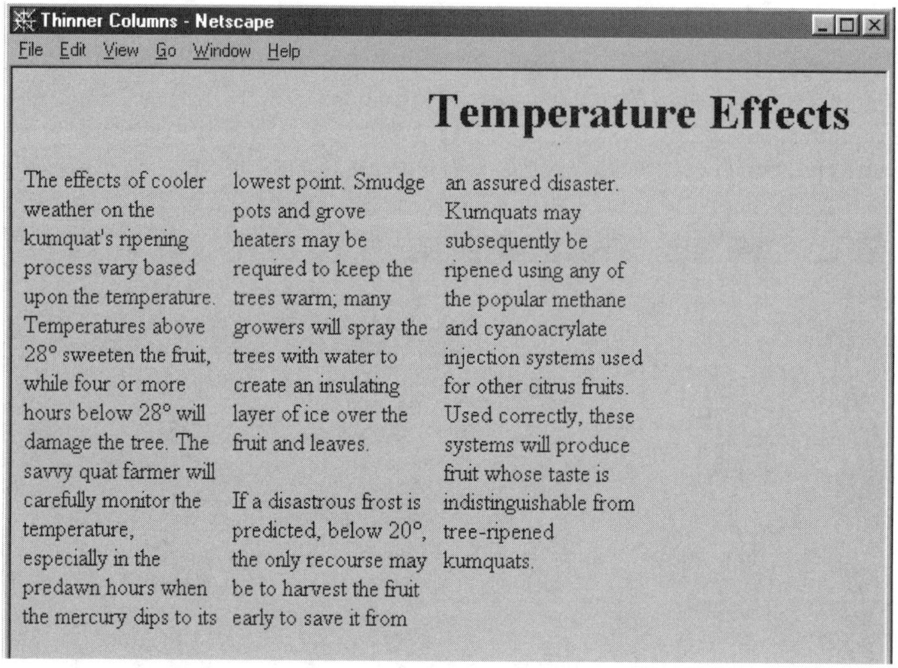

Figure H-7. Changing the width of <multicol> columns (Netscape 4 only)

If your columns include images or other fixed-width elements, be careful when you reduce their size. Netscape 4 does not wrap text around images that extend beyond the boundaries of a column. Instead, the image covers the adjacent columns, ruining your document.

Always make sure that embedded elements in columns are small enough to fit within your columns, even on fairly small browser displays.

The style and class attributes

Use the style attribute with the <multicol> tag to create an inline style for all the content inside the tag. The class attribute lets you label the section with a name that refers to a predefined class of the <multicol> tag declared in some document-level or externally defined stylesheet. [Inline Styles: The style Attribute, 8.1.1] [Style Classes, 8.3]

Multiple Columns and Other Browsers

As we've noted, the <multicol> tag is supported only by Netscape versions 4 and earlier. Fortunately, when other browsers encounter the <multicol> tag, they ignore it and render the enclosed text as part of the normal text flow, usually with little consequent disruption to the document.

The only problem is that the contents of the <multicol> tag flow up into the previous flow, without an intervening break. Thus, you might consider preceding every <multicol> tag with a <p> tag. Netscape 4 won't mind, and other browsers at least perform a paragraph break before rendering your multicolumn text in a single column.

It is possible to emulate the <multicol> tag using tables, but the results are crude and difficult to manage across multiple browsers. To do so, create a single-row table with a cell for each column. Place an appropriate amount of the text flow in each cell to achieve balanced columns. The difficulty, of course, is that the "appropriate amount" varies wildly between browsers, making it almost impossible to create multiple columns that are attractive on several different browsers.

If you must have multiple columns and can tolerate your columns reverting to a single column on incompatible browsers, we recommend that you use <multicol>.

Effective Multicolumn Layouts

We've offered advice on columns throughout these sections. Here is a quick recap of our tips for creating effective column layouts:

- Use a small number of columns.
- Don't use excessively wide gutters.
- Ensure that embedded elements such as images and tables fit in your columns on most displays.
- Precede each <multicol> tag with a <p> tag to improve your document's appearance on other browsers.
- Avoid nesting <multicol> tags more than two deep.

Layers

Spacers and multiple columns are natural extensions to conventional HTML, existing within a document's normal flow. With version 4, Netscape took HTML into an entirely new dimension with layers. It transforms the single-element document model into one containing many layered elements that are combined to form the final document. Regrettably, layers are not supported by Netscape 6 or any version of Internet Explorer.

Layers supply the layout artist with a critical element missing in standard HTML: absolute positioning of content within the browser window. Layers let you define a self-contained unit of HTML content that can be positioned anywhere in the browser window, placed above or below other layers, and made to appear and disappear as you desire. Document layouts that were impossible with conventional HTML are trivial with layers.

If you think of your document as a sheet of paper, layers are like sheets of clear plastic placed on top of your document. For each layer, you define the content of the layer, its position relative to the base document, and the order in which it is placed on the document. Layers can be transparent or opaque, visible or hidden, providing an endless combination of layout options.

The <layer> Tag (Antiquated)

Each HTML document content layer is defined with the <layer> tag. A layer can be thought of as a miniature HTML document whose content is defined between the <layer> and </layer> tags. Alternatively, the content of the layer can be retrieved from another HTML document by using the src attribute with the <layer> tag.

<layer> (Antiquated)

Function	Defines a layer of content within a document
Attributes	above, background, below, bgcolor, class, clip, left, name, src, style, top, visibility, width, z-index
End tag	</layer>; never omitted
Contains	body_content
Used in	block

Regardless of its origin, Netscape 4 formats a layer's content exactly like a conventional document, except that the result is contained within that separate layer, apart from the rest of your document. You control the position and visibility of this layer using the attributes of the <layer> tag.

Layers can be nested, too. Nested layers move with the containing layer and are visible only if the containing layer itself is visible.

The name attribute

If you plan on creating a layer and never referring to it, you needn't give it a name. However, if you plan to stack other layers relative to the current layer, as we demonstrate later in this appendix, or to modify your layer using JavaScript, you'll need to name your layers using the name attribute. The value you give name is a text string, whose first character must be a letter, not a number or symbol.

Once you name the layer, you can refer to it elsewhere in the document and change it while the user interacts with your page. For example, this bit of HTML:

```
<layer name="warning" visibility=hide>
Warning! Your input parameters were not valid!
</layer>
```

---

creates a layer named warning that is initially hidden. If in the course of validating a form using a JavaScript routine, you find an error and want to display the warning, you would use this command:

```
warning.visibility = "show";
```

Netscape 4 then makes the layer visible to the user.

The left and top attributes

Without attributes, a layer gets placed in the document window as though it were part of the normal document flow. Layers at the very beginning of a document get put at the top of the Netscape 4 window; layers that are between conventional document content get placed in line with that content.

The power of layers, however, is that you can place them anywhere in the document. Use the top and left attributes for the <layer> tag to specify its absolute position in the document display.

Both attributes accept an integer value equal to the number of pixels offset from the top-left (0,0) edge of the document's display space or, if nested inside another layer, the containing layer's display space. As with other document elements whose size or position extends past the edge of the browser's window, Netscape gives the user scroll bars to access layered elements outside the current viewing area.

The following is a simple layer example that staggers three words diagonally down the display—not something you can do easily, and certainly not with the same precision, in conventional HTML:

```
<layer left=10 top=10>
  Upper left!
</layer>
<layer left=50 top=50>
  Middle!
</layer>
<layer left=90 top=90>
  Lower right!
</layer>
```

Figure H-8 shows the result.

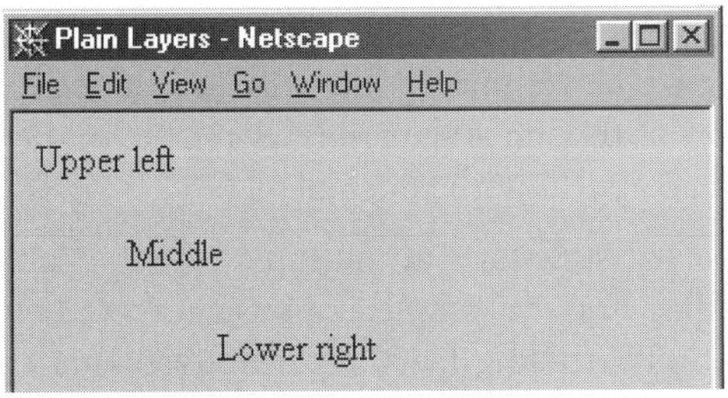

Figure H-8. Simple text positioning with the <layer> tag

Admittedly, this example is a bit dull. Here's a better one that creates a drop shadow behind a heading:

```
<layer>
  <layer left=2 top=2>
    <h1><font color=gray>Introduction to Kumquat Lore</font></h1>
  </layer>
  <layer left=0 top=0>
    <h1>Introduction to Kumquat Lore</h1>
  </layer>
</layer>
<h1> </h1>
Early in the history of man, the kumquat played a vital role in the
formation of religious beliefs. Central to annual harvest celebrations
was the day upon which kumquats ripened. Likened to the sun (<i>
sol</i>), the golden fruit was taken (<i>stisus</i>) from the trees on
the day the sun stood highest in the sky. We carry this day forward
even today, as our summer <i>solstice</i>.
```

Figure H-9 shows the result. Figure H-10 demonstrates what happens with layers when viewed with a browser other than Netscape 4.

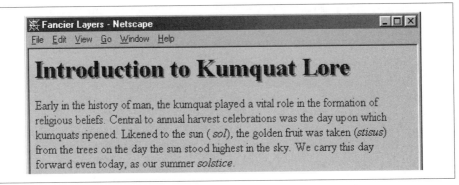

Figure H-9. Creating drop-shadow effects with multiple layers (Netscape 4 only)

We used a few tricks to create the drop-shadow effect for the example header. Netscape 4 covers layers created earlier in the document with later layers. Hence, we create the gray shadow first, followed by the actual heading, so that it appears on top, above the shadow. We also enclosed these two layers in a separate containing layer. This way, the shadow and header positions are relative to the containing layer, not the document itself. The containing layer, lacking an explicit position, is placed into the document flow as though it were normal content and winds up where a conventional heading would appear in the document.

Normal content, however, still starts at the top of the document and could end up behind the fancy heading in our example. To push content below our layered heading, we include an empty heading (save for a nonbreaking space—) before including our conventional document text.

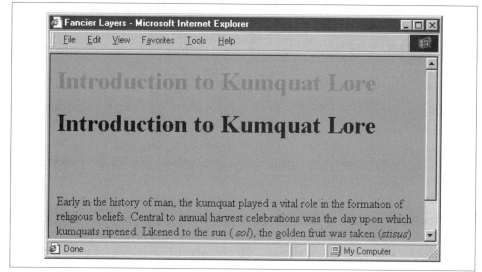

Figure H-10. Internet Explorer doesn't support multiple layers

This is important enough to repeat: normal document content following a `<layer>` tag is positioned directly under the layer it follows. You can circumvent this effect using an inline layer, described in "The <ilayer> Tag (Antiquated)" section later in this chapter.

The above, below, and z-index attributes

Layers exist in three dimensions, occupying space on the page and stacked on top of one another as well as on top of conventional document content. As we mentioned earlier, layers normally are stacked in order of their appearance in the document: layers at the beginning get covered by later layers in the same display area.

You can control the stacking order of the layers with the above, below, and z-index attributes for the `<layer>` tag. These attributes are mutually exclusive; use only one per layer.

The value for the above or below attribute is the name of another layer in the current document. Of course, that referenced layer must have a name attribute whose value is the same name you use with the above or below attribute in the referring `<layer>` tag. You also must have created the referenced layer earlier in the document; you cannot refer to a layer that comes later.

In direct contradiction with what you might expect, Netscape 4 puts the current layer below the above-named layer and above the below-named layer.[*] Oh, well. Note that the layers must occupy the same display space for you to see any effects.

---

[*] One cannot help but imagine that the above and below attributes were implemented in the wee hours.

Let's use our drop-shadow layer example again to illustrate the above attribute:

```
<layer>
  <layer name=text left=0 top=0>
    <h1>Introduction to Kumquat Lore</h1>
  </layer>
  <layer name=shadow above=text left=2 top=2>
    <h1><font color=gray>Introduction to Kumquat Lore</font></h1>
  </layer>
</layer>
```

The above attribute in the layer named shadow tells Netscape 4 to position the shadow layer so that the layer named text is above it. The effect is identical to Figure H-9.

The above and below attributes can get confusing when you stack several layers. We find it somewhat easier to use the z-index attribute for keeping track of which layers go over which. With z-index, you specify the order in which Netscape stacks the layers: higher z-index value layers are put on top of lower z-index value layers.

For example, to create our drop shadow using the z-index attribute, we would use the following:

```
<layer>
  <layer left=0 top=0 z-index=2>
    <h1>Introduction to Kumquat Lore</h1>
  </layer>
  <layer left=2 top=2 z-index=1>
    <h1><font color=gray>Introduction to Kumquat Lore</font></h1>
  </layer>
</layer>
```

Again, the effect is identical to Figure H-9. Normally, Netscape 4 would display the second layer—the gray one in this case—on top of the first layer. But because we've given the gray layer a lower z-index value, it is placed behind the first layer.

The z-index values need not be sequential, although they must be integers, so we could have used the values 99 and 2, respectively, and gotten the same result in the previous example. And you need not specify a z-index for all the layers that occupy the same display space—you need specify it only for those that you want to raise or lower in relation to other layers. However, be aware that the order of precedence may get confusing if you don't z-index all related layers.

For instance, what order of precedence by color would you predict when Netscape 4 renders the following sequence of layers?

```
<layer left=0 top=0 z-index=3>
  <h1><font color=red>Introduction to Kumquat Lore</font></h1>
</layer>
<layer left=4 top=4>
  <h1><font color=green>Introduction to Kumquat Lore</font></h1>
</layer>
```

```
<layer left=8 top=8 z-index=2>
  <h1><font color=blue>Introduction to Kumquat Lore</font></h1>
</layer>
```

Give yourself a star if you said that the green header goes on top of the red header, which goes on top of the blue header. Why? Because the red header is of lower priority than the green header based on order of appearance, and we forced the blue layer below the red one by giving it a lower z-index value. Netscape 4 displays z-indexed layers according to their given order and non-z-indexed layers according to their order of appearance in the document. Precedence based on order of appearance also applies for layers that have the same z-index value. If you nest layers, all the layers at the same nesting level are ordered according to their z-index attributes. This group is then ordered as a single layer among all the layers at the containing level. In short, layers nested within a layer cannot be interleaved among layers at a different level.

For example, consider these nested layers with their content and end tags omitted for clarity (indentation indicates nest level):

```
<layer name=a z-index=20>
  <layer name=a1 z-index=5>
  <layer name=a2 z-index=15>
<layer name=b z-index=30>
  <layer name=b1 z-index=10>
  <layer name=b2 z-index=25>
  <layer name=b3 z-index=20>
<layer name=c z-index=10>
```

Layers a, b, and c are at the same level, with layers a1 and a2 nested within a and b1, b2, and b3 nested within b. Although the z-index numbers might, at first glance, appear to cause Netscape 4 to interleave the various nested layers, the actual ordering of the layers, from bottom to top, is c, a, a1, a2, b, b1, b3, and b2.

If two layers are nested within the same layer and they have the same z-index value, the layer defined later in the document is placed on top of the previously defined layer.[*]

The background and bgcolor attributes

As with the corresponding attributes for the <body> tag, you can define the background color and an image for a Netscape 4 layer with the bgcolor and background attributes, respectively.[†] By default, the background of a layer is transparent, allowing lower layers to show through.

The bgcolor attribute accepts a color name or RGB triple as its value, as defined in Appendix G. If specified, Netscape sets the entire background of the layer to this

---

[*] This, of course, applies to layers inside the same containing nest only.

[†] Note that you can control the background color (as well as many other display features) of not just a single tag but all <DEFANGED_layer> tags within your document using stylesheets. See section 5.3.1.8, "The style and class attributes."

color, rendering the layer opaque. This attribute is handy for creating a colored box behind text, as a highlighting or attention-getting mechanism. It does, however, hide any layers below it, including conventional HTML content.

The background attribute accepts the URL of an image as its value. The image is tiled to fill the area occupied by the layer. If portions of the image are transparent, those portions of the layer are transparent, and underlying layers show through.

If you include both attributes, the background color shows through the transparent spots in the background image. The whole layer is opaque.

The background attribute is useful for placing a texture behind text, but it fails miserably when the goal is to render text in front of a fixed image. Because the size of a layer is dictated by its contents, not the background image, using the image as the background causes it to be clipped or tiled, depending on the size of the text.

To place text reliably on top of an image, use one layer nested within another:

```
<layer>
  <img src="sunset.gif">
  <p>
  <layer top=75>
    <h2 align=center>And they lived happily ever after...</h2>
  </layer>
</layer>
```

Netscape 4 sets aside space for the entire image in the outer layer. The inner layer occupies the same space, except that we shift it down 75 pixels to align the text better over the image. Figure H-11 shows the result.

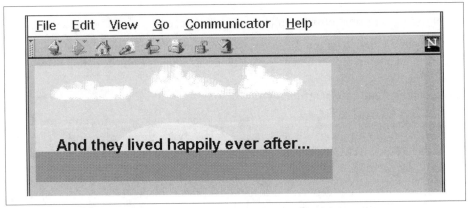

Figure H-11. Placing text over an image using layers (Netscape 4 only)

The visibility attribute

By default, layers usually are visible. You can change that by setting the visibility attribute to show, hide, or inherit. As expected, show forces the layer to be seen, hide hides it from view, and inherit explicitly declares that you want the layer to inherit its parent's visibility. The default value for this attribute is `inherit`. Layers that are not nested are considered to be children of the main document, which is always visible. Thus, non-nested layers lacking the `visibility` attribute are initially visible.

It makes little sense to hide layers unless you plan to reveal them later. In general, you should use this attribute only when you include some JavaScript routines with your document that reveal the hidden layers as a result of some user interaction. [JavaScript Event Handlers, 12.3.3]

Layers that are hidden do not block layers below them from view. Instead, a hidden layer can best be thought of as being transparent. One way to hide content in the main document is to place an opaque layer over the content. To display the hidden context, hide the opaque layer, revealing the content underneath.

The width attribute

Layers are only as big as necessary to contain their content. The initial width of a layer is defined to be the distance from the point at which the layer is created in the current text flow to the right margin. Netscape 4 then formats the layer's contents to that width and makes the height of the layer tall enough to contain all of the layer's contents. If the contents of the layer wind up smaller than the initial width, the layer's width is reduced to this smaller amount.

You can explicitly set the width of a layer using the `width` attribute. The value of this attribute defines the width of the layer in pixels or as a percentage of the containing layer. As expected, Netscape 4 then sets the height based upon the size of the layer's contents, wrapped to the specified width. If elements in the layer—such as images—cannot be wrapped and instead extend past the right margin of the layer, only a portion of the element is shown. The remainder is clipped by the edge of the layer and is not shown. This is similar to the behavior of an image in the main document window. If the image extends beyond the edge of the browser window, only a portion of the image is displayed. Unlike the browser window, however, layers cannot sport scroll bars allowing the user to scroll around in the layer's contents.

The src attribute

The contents of a layer are not restricted to what you type between its `<layer>` and `</layer>` tags; you can also refer to and automatically load the contents of another document into the layer with the `src` attribute. The value of the `src` attribute is the URL of the document containing the layer's content.

Note that the `layer` src'd document should *not* be a full-fledged HTML document. In particular, it should not contain `<body>` or `<head>` tags, although other HTML content is allowed.

You can combine conventional layer content with content taken from another file by using the `src` attribute and placing content within the `<layer>` tag. In this case, the content from the file is placed in the layer first, followed by any inline content within the tag itself. If you choose to use the src attribute without supplying additional inline content, you still must supply the closing </layer> tag to end the definition of the layer.

The src attribute provides, for the first time, a source inclusion capability in HTML. Previously, to insert content from one HTML document into another, you had to rely on a server-based capability to read the other file and insert it into your document at the correct location. Because layers are positioned, by default, at their defining point within the current flow, including another file in your document is simple:

```
...other content...
<layer src="boilerplate"></layer>...more content...
```

Because a layer is rendered as a separate HTML entity, the content of the included file is not flowed into the containing text. Instead, it is as though the inserted text were contained within a <div> tag or other block-level HTML element.

The clip attribute

Normally, users see the entire layer unless it is obscured by a covering layer. With the clip attribute, you can mask off portions of a layer, revealing only a rectangular portion within the layer. The area of the layer outside the visible area is made transparent, allowing whatever is under the layer to show through.

The value of the clip attribute is two or four integer values, separated by commas, defining pixel offsets into the layer corresponding to the left, top, right, and bottom edges of the clip area. If only two values are supplied, they correspond to the right and bottom edges of the visible area, and Netscape assumes the top and left values are 0. Therefore, clip="75,100" is equivalent to clip="0,0,75,100".

The clip attribute is handy for hiding portions of a layer, or for creating fade and wipe effects using JavaScript functions to change the clipping window over time.

The style and class attributes

Use the style attribute with the <layer> tag to create an inline style for all the content inside a layer. The class attribute lets you label the layer with a name that refers to a predefined class of the <layer> tag declared in some document-level or externally defined stylesheet. Accordingly, you may choose to use a stylesheet rather than individual and redundant bgcolor tag attributes to define a background color for all your document layers or for a particular class of layers. [Inline Styles: The style Attribute, 8.1.1] [Style Classes, 8.3]

The <ilayer> Tag (Antiquated)

While you control the position of a <layer> using top and left attribute coordinates relative to the document's entire display space, Netscape 4 provides a separate tag,

`<ilayer>`, that lets you position individual layers with respect to the current flow of content, much like an inline image.

<ilayer> (Antiquated)

Function	Defines an inline layer of content within a text flow
Attributes	above, background, below, bgcolor, class, clip, left, name, src, style, top, visibility, width, z-index
End tag	`</ilayer>`; never omitted
Contains	*body_content*
Used in	*text*

An `<ilayer>` tag creates a layer that occupies space in the containing text flow. Subsequent content is placed after the space occupied by `<ilayer>`. This is in contrast to the `<layer>` tag, which creates a layer above the containing text flow, allowing subsequent content to be placed under the layer just created.

The `<ilayer>` tag removes the need for an enclosing, attribute-free `<layer>` that serves to put a nest of specially positioned layers inline with the content flow, much like we did in most of the examples in the previous sections of this appendix. The attributes of `<ilayer>` are the same as those for the `<layer>` tag.

The top and left attributes

The only attributes that distinguish the actions of the `<ilayer>` tag from its `<layer>` sibling are top and left: Netscape 4 renders `<ilayer>` content directly in the containing text flow, offset by the top and left attribute values from the upper-left corner of that inline position—not the document's upper-left display corner, as with `<layer>`. Netscape 4 also accepts negative values for the top and left attributes of the `<ilayer>` tag, letting you shift the contents above and to the left of the current flow.

For example, to subscript, superscript, or shift words within the current line, you could use:

```
This <ilayer top=4>word</ilayer> is shifted down, while
this <ilayer left=10>one</ilayer> is shifted over. With a negative
value, words can be moved <ilayer top=-4>up</ilayer> and to
the <ilayer left=-10>left</ilayer>.
```

Figure H-12 shows the resulting effects. Notice how the shifted words overlap and obscure the surrounding text. Netscape 4 makes no effort to make room for the shifted elements; they are simply placed in a different spot on the page.

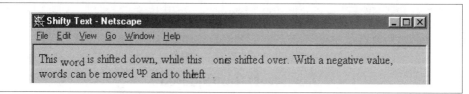

Figure H-12. Moving inline layers with respect to the adjacent text (Netscape 4 only)

Combining <layer> and <ilayer>

Anything you can create with a regular layer you can use within an inline layer. However, bear in mind that the top and left attribute offsets are indeed from the <ilayer> content's allotted position, not from the document display space. Accordingly, use <ilayer> to position content inline with the conventional HTML document flow, and use <layer> to position elements and content precisely in the document display space.

Also (and fortunately), Netscape 4 does not distinguish between <ilayer> and <layer> tags when it comes to order of appearance. You may declare that an <ilayer> appear below some <layer> by using the name and above attributes:

```
<layer name=me>I'm on top</layer>
<ilayer above=me>I'm on the bottom</ilayer>
```

Similarly, you can reorder the appearance of both absolute and inline layers where they overlap by assigning z-index attribute values to the various elements. Nesting rules apply, too.

Index

We'd like to hear your suggestions for improving our indexes. Send email to *index@oreilly.com*.

to external content, 158
image maps, clickable, 29, 138, 139, 189,
    192, 193, 199
images and, 189
linking within documents, 184
to multiple frames, 523
navigating with Tab and hot keys, 183
relationships between, 180
states of, 248
targets for, 182, 197, 205, 318, 405, 522
Hypertext Markup Language, 6
Hypertext Transfer Protocol, 6

I

id attribute, 140, 535
    <a>, 179
    <address>, 101
    <basefont>, 104
    <blockquote>, 97
    <center>, 93
    <div>, 58, 59
    <dl>, <dt>, and <dd>, 225
    <form>, 319
    <frameset>, 398
    <isindex>, 203
    <label>, 347
    <map>, 193
    <object>, 421
    <p>, 64, 67
    <q>, 99
    <ul>, <ol>, and <li>, 214
    form controls, 342
    for hyperlink targets, 184
    for style classes, 247
    table tags, 367
    XHTML documents, 503
identifiers (IDs)
    articles in newsgroups, 174
    messages on news servers, 174
IE, 14
IETF (Internet Engineering Task Force), 8
ignored HTML tags, 41
image maps, 610
    areas, 194, 196
    clickable, 29, 138, 189, 192, 193, 199
    client-side, 29, 139, 191, 198
    coordinates, 190
    HTML documents and, 199
    performance, 191
    server-side, 29, 190

images, 27, 116, 157
    alignment, 128, 133
    background, 144, 148, 149, 262, 263,
        264, 265, 363, 376, 627
    borders, 134, 178
    clickable, 189
    combining attributes for, 141
    custom image buttons (forms), 332
    download performance, 121
    flowing text around, 84
    graphics formats, 117, 124
    in headings, 69
    hyperlinks and, 189
    as list item signifiers, 286
    margins around, 137
    preventing from scrolling, 145, 263
    resizing, 136
    reusing, 123
    rules, 109
    size, 135
    text flow around, 84
    text in place of, 126
    when to use, 121
    wrapping text around, 131
implicit label associations (forms), 347
imported external style sheets, 235, 308
    linked vs., 237
inclusions, 414
indentation, 36
    abusing <dt> for, 225
    block quotes, 96
    nested unordered lists, using for, 213
    paragraphs, with <spacer>, 612
    text-indent property for, 269
infinite value (marquee looping), 155
inherit value (layer visibility), 628
inheritance, styles and, 251, 254
inline
    frames, 403
    images, 28
    items, 291
    layers, 630
    references, 187
    styles, 231, 309, 441
input constraints, mobile devices, 461
inset borders, 277
interaction pseudoclasses, 248
interlacing, 118
internationalization
    dir and lang attributes, 47
    dir attribute, overriding with <bdo>, 55

O

object attribute (<applet>), 428
object model (HTML v4.0), 414
obsolete tags, 80
offset, 623
omitting HTML tags, 40
onAbort attribute, 140, 437
onBlur attribute, 437
onChange attribute, 437, 438
onClick attribute, 437, 535
onDblClick attribute, 437, 535
onError attribute, 140
onFocus attribute, 437
onKeyDown attribute, 438, 535
onKeyPress attribute, 438, 535
onKeyRelease attribute, 438
onKeyUp attribute, 535
onLoad attribute, 141, 437, 438
onMouseDown attribute, 437, 536
onMouseMove attribute, 437, 536
onMouseOut attribute, 196, 437, 536
onMouseOver attribute, 180, 196, 436, 437, 536
onMouseUp attribute, 437, 536
onReset attribute, 320, 437, 438
onSelect attribute, 437, 438
onSubmit attribute, 320, 437, 438
onUnload attribute, 437, 438
ordered (numbered) lists, 30, 214
    list marker style properties, 286
    nesting, 222
    numbering style, 218
    using appropriately, 227
orphans, 306
outset borders, 277
overflow property, 282
overlining, 269
overriding hyperlink targets, 522

P

padding, 364
padding properties, 282
page boxes, 303
    size property, 303
page layout, 20, 351
    alignment, 351
    columns, 616
    designing for your audience, 509
    forms, 351, 519
    frames, 394
    HTML tags for, 83

layers, 621
    multiple columns, 516
    style sheets, 33
    tables, 31
    wrapping text, 131
page-break properties, 305
palette attribute (<embed>), 430
panose-1 descriptor, 261
paragraphs, 23, 61
    indenting with <spacer>, 612
parameter entities, XML, 478
parameters, form, 318, 355
parsed and unparsed entities, XML, 477
password input fields, 326
pathnames, 25, 166
pause properties, 301
PCDATA, XML tags, 480, 483
PDAs, 458
percent sign (%)
    for character encoding, 161
    in URL encoding, 314
percentage property values, 252
performance
    applets, 415
    background images, 149
    client-pull documents, 453
    colors, 150
    flood-filling, 136
    image maps, 191
    images and, 121
    lowsrc attribute (<img>) for, 126
    marquee movement, 156
    server-push documents, 455
    text, 122
physical style tags, 21, 71
    summary of, 81
    table of, 81
physical text wrapping, 337
pitch property, 300
pitch-range property, 300
play-during property, 301
plug-in accessories, 6, 27, 141, 158
pluginspage attribute (<embed>), 431
plus sign (+) in URL encoding, 314
polygonal image map area, 194
ports
    ftp servers, 172
    gopher servers, 176
    nntp, 174
    telnet, 175
    web servers, 165
position properties, 283

title attribute (*continued*)
    <img>, 140
    <isindex>, 203
    <link>, 206
    <map>, 193
    <object>, 421
    <p>, 64, 67
    <ul>, <ol>, and <li>, 214
    form controls, 342
    table tags, 367
titles
    bibliographic, 72
    choosing, 49
    document, 19, 48, 67
    forms, 319
    frames, 402
    hyperlinked documents, 182, 206
    image map area, 197
    sections, 60
    table captions, 377
top attribute
    <ilayer>, 631
    <layer>, 623
top value, 28
topline descriptor, 261
topmargin attribute (<body>), 147
Transitional DTD, 565, 583
transparent GIFs, 119
troubleshooting background
        images/colors, 149
tty value (style media), 233
tv value (style media), 233
type attribute
    <a>, 183
    <button>, 335
    <embed>, 431
    <input>, 314
    <li>, 218, 287
    <link>, 207
    <object>, 420
    <ol>, 216
    <param>, 425
    <script>, 434
    <spacer>, 612, 613, 614
    <style>, 233
    <ul>, 213
type in gopher URLs, 176
typecodes in ftp URLs, 172
typographic conventions for HTML, 526

U

underscoring, 81, 269
unicode-range descriptor, 260
uniform resource locators, 260
unique identifiers (IDs)
    articles in newsgroups, 174
    messages on news servers, 174
units attribute (<embed>), 431
units-per-em descriptor, 260
universal child selectors, 242
unnamed form parameters, 356
unordered lists, 30
    bulleted, 211, 218, 220, 226, 286
    directory lists, 227
unsafe characters in URLs, 161
URLs (uniform resource locators), 25, 160
    absolute vs. relative, 163, 203
    as style property values, 253
    character encodings in, 161
    file URLs, 169
    form parameters in, 318, 355
    ftp URLs, 171
    generating randomly, 452
    gopher URLs, 175
    http URLs, 164
    JavaScript pseudoprotocol, 172
    javascript URLs, 438
    mailto URLs, 170, 314, 321
    news and nntp URLs, 173
    query URLs, 202
    telnet URLs, 175
    XFrames, 412
usemap attribute
    <img>, 29, 138, 191
    <object>, 422
Usenet news system, 173
user and password, telnet URLs, 175
user-interface design, 350
user-related event handlers, 436

V

valid XML documents, 476
valign attribute
    <caption>, 378
    <table>, 366
    <th> and <td>, 373
value attribute
    <li>, 219
    <option>, 340
    <param>, 425

valuetype attribute (<param>), 425
version attribute (<html>), 46
vertical, 612
   margins, 137
   whitespace, 613
vertical-align property, 271
video, 141, 157
   <img> extensions, 141
   client-pull feature for, 451
   inline, 141
virtual text wrapping, 337
visibility attribute (<layer>), 628
visibility property, 284
vlink attribute (<body>), 146
voice-family property, 300
volume property, 298
vspace attribute
   <embed>, 429
   <img>, 137
   <marquee>, 156

W

W3C (World Wide Web Consortium), 7
Web, 3
   information on, 6
   navigating with hyperlinks, 26
web browsers, 5
   <link> tags and, 207
   applet rendering, 426
   character entities, rendering, 43
   client-pull documents, 448
   client-side image maps and, 199
   executable content, 413
   form limitations, 349
   HTML documents, use in editing, 16
   HTML tags, 40, 41
   image borders, 134
   image presentation, 125
   images, rendering, 178
   incompatible with embedded objects, 432
   incompatible with executable
      content, 423
   incompatible with frames, 402
   JavaScript, 432
   leniency in data acceptance, 506
   Mosaic browser, 3
   Netscape Navigator, 4
   obtaining, 13
   styles, 33
   text-only, 5, 127

web servers, 164
   <server> tags, 439
   server-push documents, 453
webs, private, 7
weight, font, 257
well-formed documents
   XHTML and, 41
   XML, 476, 499
whitespace, 611
   <img> tags for, 615
   <nobr> tags, 86
   <spacer> tags, 612
   around horizontal rules, 110
   around table cells, 364
   between columns (gutters), 619
   blocks of, 612
   frames and, 396
   handling in block tags, 291
   hanging indents, 269
   HTML tags for, 83
   indentation, 96
   letter spacing, 267
   line breaks, 36
   line height, 268
   margins, 137, 147, 156
   paragraphs, 36
   readability and, 38
   tabs in preformatted text, 90
   word spacing, 274
white-space property, 291
widows, 306
width attribute
   <applet>, 428
   <embed>, 429
   <hr>, 113
   <iframe>, 405
   <img>, 135
   <layer>, 629
   <marquee>, 155
   <multicol>, 619
   <pre>, 91
   <spacer>, 614
   <table>, 366
   <th> and <td>, 373
width property, 284
widths descriptor, 261
WiFi, 459
windows, 32, 393
   as hyperlink targets, 182, 197, 205, 318,
      405, 522
   tips and tricks, 521

About the Authors

Chuck Musciano (*cmusciano@aol.com*) acquired a B.S. in computer science from Georgia Tech in 1982. He spent 15 years in the employ of Harris Corporation, in Melbourne, Florida, first as a compiler writer and crafter of tools and later as a member of Harris's Advanced Technology Group. His focus on Unix- and Internet-based technology enabled him to support early web initiatives within Harris. After various positions of increasing responsibility in the IT industry, he currently serves as the Vice President of Information Services for Martin Marietta Materials in Raleigh, North Carolina. Throughout his career he has written for various trade publications, both in print and as an online columnist, including the "Webmaster" column for *SunWorld* and the "Tag of the Week" column for *WebReview*. In his spare time, he enjoys life in North Carolina with his wife Cindy, daughter Courtney, and son Cole.

Bill Kennedy (*bkennedy@mobilerobots.com*) is currently Chief Technology Officer for MobileRobots, Inc., a developer and manufacturer of intelligent mobile robots and other smart machines. How he came to chasing AI robots around is not surprising, given his many roundabout careers. Bill has a Ph.D. in biochemistry and biophysics from Loyola University of Chicago and did over 12 years of biomedical research through the 1970s and early '80s. Infected by the PC bug (32K Apple II; really!), he created a software company that developed computer games and educational programs. Needing a real job with benefits, Bill also served as technical editor, senior editor, and editor-in-chief for various International Data Group magazines, including *inCider, Sun Technology Journal, SunWorld,* and *A+ Publishing/Mac Computing,* among others, in the '80s and '90s. An avid user of the Internet since the mid '80s, Bill, with his wife Jeanne Dietsch, founded ActivMedia Research, the first market-research firm ever to formally study businesses on the Web. Their first report, published in 1995, contained data gathered by actually visiting each and every business web site in existence back then, if you can imagine. Always ready to embrace emerging technologies, Bill and his partners formed ActivMedia Robotics in 1996, which now, as MobileRobots Inc. (*http://www.mobilerobots.com*), sells more intelligent mobile platforms to more artificial and machine-intelligent researchers around the world than anyone else. And the company's mobile-robotics navigation technologies are quickly being adopted for commercial and industrial applications. So, what's next?

Colophon

The animal on the cover of *HTML & XHTML: The Definitive Guide* is a koala. The koala is an Australian marsupial, the only member of the *Phascolarctidae* family.

When they are born, koalas are tiny, weighing approximately 0.5 grams. A young koala stays in its mother's pouch for approximately seven months. Unlike most marsupials, the koala's pouch opens near the rear, not near the head. Koalas have a high mortality rate and face extinction in Australia due to epidemics in 1887–1889 and 1900–1903, and unrestrained hunting throughout the 20th century. They are a protected species. Populations are rebuilding, but at present, they survive only in eastern Australia.

The cover image is a 19th-century engraving from the Dover Pictorial Archive. The cover font is Adobe ITC Garamond. The text font is Linotype Birka; the heading font is Adobe Myriad Condensed; and the code font is LucasFont's TheSans Mono Condensed.

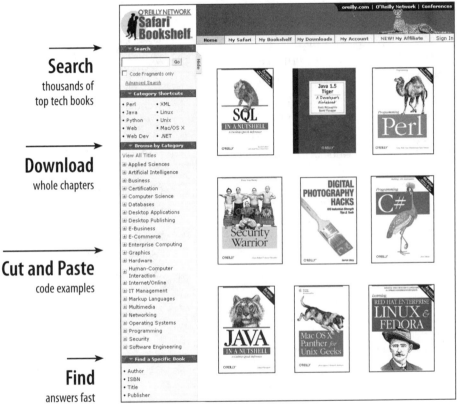

Related Titles from O'Reilly

Web Programming

ActionScript 3 Cookbook

ActionScript for Flash MX: The Definitive Guide, *2nd Edition*

Ajax Design Patterns

Ajax Hacks

Building Scalable Web Sites

Dynamic HTML: The Definitive Reference, *2nd Edition*

Flash Hacks

Essential PHP Security

Google Advertising Tools

Google Hacks, *2nd Edition*

Google Map Hacks

Google Pocket Guide

Google: The Missing Manual, *2nd Edition*

Head First HTML with CSS & XHTML

Head Rush Ajax

HTTP: The Definitive Guide

JavaScript & DHTML Cookbook

JavaScript Pocket Reference, *2nd Edition*

JavaScript: The Definitive Guide, *4th Edition*

Learning PHP 5

Learning PHP and MySQL

PHP Cookbook

PHP Hacks

PHP in a Nutshell

PHP Pocket Reference, *2nd Edition*

PHPUnit Pocket Guide

Programming ColdFusion MX, *2nd Edition*

Programming PHP, *2nd Edition*

Upgrading to PHP 5

Web Database Applications with PHP and MySQL, *2nd Edition*

Web Site Cookbook

Webmaster in a Nutshell, *3rd Edition*

Web Administration

Apache Cookbook

Apache Pocket Reference

Apache: The Definitive Guide, *3rd Edition*

Perl for Web Site Management

Squid: The Definitive Guide

Web Performance Tuning, *2nd Edition*

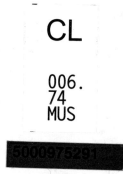